The Strategies of Informing Technology in the 21st Century

Andrew Targowski
Independent Researcher, USA

A volume in the Advances in IT Standards and
Standardization Research (AITSSR) Book Series

Published in the United States of America by
  IGI Global
  Engineering Science Reference (an imprint of IGI Global)
  701 E. Chocolate Avenue
  Hershey PA, USA 17033
  Tel: 717-533-8845
  Fax: 717-533-8661
  E-mail: cust@igi-global.com
  Web site: http://www.igi-global.com

Library of Congress Cataloging-in-Publication Data

Names: Targowski, Andrew, 1937- author.
Title: The strategies of informing technology in the 21st century / by
  Andrew S. Targowski.
Description: Hershey, PA : Engineering Science Reference, [2021] | Includes
  bibliographical references and index. | Summary: "With digital
  technology changing rapidly, this book digs into the developmental
  trends of IT (infrastructure, information systems, automation,
  robotization, artificial intelligence, and terminology), the
  digitalization of enterprise, agriculture, health care, education
  (schools and colleges), home, friendly state, cities, humanities, and
  civilization within the boundaries of ethics and law"-- Provided by
  publisher.
Identifiers: LCCN 2021021803 (print) | LCCN 2021021804 (ebook) | ISBN
  9781799880363 (h/c) | ISBN 9781799880370 (s/c) | ISBN 9781799880387
  (eISBN)
Subjects: LCSH: Information society. | Information superhighway.
Classification: LCC HM851 .T37525 2021 (print) | LCC HM851 (ebook) | DDC
  303.48/33--dc23
LC record available at https://lccn.loc.gov/2021021803
LC ebook record available at https://lccn.loc.gov/2021021804

This book is published in the IGI Global book series Advances in IT Standards and Standardization Research (AITSSR) (ISSN: 1935-3391; eISSN: 1935-3405)

British Cataloguing in Publication Data
A Cataloguing in Publication record for this book is available from the British Library.

For electronic access to this publication, please contact: eresources@igi-global.com.

Advances in IT Standards and Standardization Research (AITSSR) Book Series

Kai Jakobs
RWTH Aachen University, Germany

ISSN:1935-3391
EISSN:1935-3405

MISSION

IT standards and standardization are a necessary part of effectively delivering IT and IT services to organizations and individuals, as well as streamlining IT processes and minimizing organizational cost. In implementing IT standards, it is necessary to take into account not only the technical aspects, but also the characteristics of the specific environment where these standards will have to function.

The **Advances in IT Standards and Standardization Research (AITSSR) Book Series** seeks to advance the available literature on the use and value of IT standards and standardization. This research provides insight into the use of standards for the improvement of organizational processes and development in both private and public sectors.

COVERAGE

- Standards for information infrastructures
- Descriptive Theory of Standardization
- Managing Standardization Implementation
- Standardization and regulation
- Open source and standardization
- Standardization and Public Policy Formation
- Standardization for Organizational Development
- Standards in the Private Sector
- Standards in the Public Sector
- Standardization and economic development

IGI Global is currently accepting manuscripts for publication within this series. To submit a proposal for a volume in this series, please contact our Acquisition Editors at acquisitions@igi-global.com or visit: https://www.igi-global.com/publish/.

Titles in this Series

IGI Global
PUBLISHER of TIMELY KNOWLEDGE

701 East Chocolate Avenue, Hershey, PA 17033, USA
Tel: 717-533-8845 x100 • Fax: 717-533-8661
E-Mail: cust@igi-global.com • www.igi-global.com

Table of Contents

Foreword

This book is a unique monograph in the world so extensively concerning the field of knowledge and human activity of informing technology, which has been transforming civilization from the Industrial Revolution of the 19th century into a civilization that undermines the achievements of industrialization. Specifically, industrialization gave rise to engines and machines. This led to the creation of thousands of different kinds of work, giving permanent employment to millions of people who have also achieved good living conditions and even prosperity in many countries through compulsory education.

However, we are now facing an Informing Revolution that involves universal digitization with the support of artificial intelligence. This is leading to automation and robotization, which are in the course to eliminate human work. Big tech companies perpetuate the claim that IT progress cannot be inhibited because it is the essential value of civilization. However, these companies do not say what the unemployed are supposed to do, for they want machines to work, decide, and think for them.

The problem of the acceptable range of applications of informing technology is solved in this book, which analyzes and defines wise development strategies for IT applications. Author Andrew Targowski is one of the unique IT specialists in the world, who has been involved in this field since the 1950s and has passed through all levels of the profession, including executing IT development at the government level in Poland. He offered the National Information System connected by the INFOSTRADA network (1972), which was the forerunner of the later civil Internet (1983) and the information highway paradigm in the U.S.

As a result of the chicanery of the Communist authorities, he left for the United States in 1980, where he obtained political asylum. In the early 1990s, he launched TeleCity in Kalamazoo, Michigan, one of the first U.S. digital cities. As an IT professor, he specialized in business applications within the enterprise-wide framework. He conducts research in the fields of enterprise computing, societal computing, wisdom theory, and theory of civilization. Thanks to such extensive knowledge and practice, documented in more than 50 books, this monograph could be created.

Andrzej Dyżewski
Former Editor-in-Chief of Computerworld, *Poland*

Introduction

Strategic information technology is a specialization in the field of informiation technology. It is a tool-oriented field that has assisted the cognitive development of human beings since 1951, when the commercial American UNIVAC I computer (and soon others, such as the IBM 1400 family of machines) was used in election analyses and business processes. Thus, computer-based information technology is only 70 years old. However, machine computing of mass data is associated with the use of punch-card machines, beginning with the American census of 1890.

What is most important in these considerations is the fact that, in less than 100 years (IBM, which in its pioneering period dominated IT, was organized in 1924), the field of information technology has become omnipresent in civilization, co-existing with other ubiquitous sectors such as construction, transportation, and health care, which have been developing for over 6,000 years from the times when the Mesopotamia civilization (the Sumerian tribe) organized itself in the valley between the Tigris and Euphrates rivers.[1]

In this 6,000-year history of civilization, there have been nearly 30 varieties, organized in different geographic areas and climates. For example, Western civilization has existed for approximately 1,200+ years, while Chinese civilization has existed for about 5,000 years (Targowski, 2014a). By comparison, in just one generation, IT has caused the development of Global Civilization and Virtual Civilization (Targowski, 2014b, 2015).

The role of information technology in these rapid cultural and civilizational transformations has come as a shock (Toffler, 1971) to people who are not able to adapt quickly to these sudden civilizational transformations. Up until now, biological transformations have taken millennia. The main drivers of these changes were tools for manipulating materials and the natural environment. Now, this tool is computer-aided artificial intelligence and control, which develops our intellect, that is, cognizing, thinking, and deciding.

Today, in the 21st century, the number of applications of information processing in the networking environment is in the millions and is used by half of the world's population. It is a development that motivates and fascinates people. Still, it is also chaotic and sometimes dangerous because it is driven by the substantial wealth of Big Tech and Big Business, which break the law and the code of professional ethics in the name of profit with the help of lobbyists (discussed in this book). Worse, it destroys the achievements of the Industrial Revolution, which created cyclical work, and the Digital Revolution (explained in this book) minimizes these achievements and even wants to abolish them. Unfortunately, this would lead to the dehumanization of humankind, although some predict the transformation of self-thinking humans into machine-thinking cyborgs would somehow be for the better.

Meanwhile, despite the almost universal use of computers, only 5% of people in Western civilization know how to search for and understand information correctly. Worse yet, in the same civilization, there is a threefold difference between the inhabitants of its different countries concerning their ability to solve problems with the help of IT tools. These matters are discussed in this book. As this data shows, most people are excluded from the prudent use of computers. Poor people even increase their poverty because of information exclusion.

To prevent this as well as digital crime, one must use IT wisely, that is, have a specific goal and strategy for its implementation. This monograph is intended to serve this purpose. It deals comprehensively with this strategic specialization in information technology.

The book consists of four sections:

1. **The Essence of Strategic Informing Technology:** The essence of the Digital Revolution and the structure of the field of IT are discussed. They are broken down into disciplines and specializations since terminological issues hinders trans-domain and trans-specialization cooperation and prevents a deepening of humanizing knowledge and the development of skills in computer applications.
2. **Challenges of Technological Progress in the 21st Century:** This is a typical topic of popular publications. The advancement of information technology is categorized and cautiously and strategically analyzed.
3. **Applications of Strategic Informing Technology:** The strategies of strategic information technology are characterized in essential areas of civilization, such as business, agriculture, healthcare, education, and widespread domestic use.
4. **Challenges of Strategic Informing Technology:** Strategies for solving the challenges of strategic information technology are characterized in terms of the computerization of humanity, the state, and civilization. Also, the strategic aspects of digital security, ethics, and IT law are analyzed.

The book is critical in some of its chapters about the IT community and journalism's enthusiasm in applying digitalization to all forms of human work, based on the belief that the work thus released will lead to new innovative tasks for human activities. The practice of a very computerized American civilization does not confirm this enthusiasm. For example, the removal of 70,000 factories to Asia at the end of the 20th century "liberated" Americans from that work and offered them pizza delivery instead. This almost led to the collapse of the middle class and the development of a creeping social revolution in 2020 in the United States.

There is a concept of Nikolai Kondratiev (1892-1938)—*Kondratiev waves*—which have these properties; however, the idea that the next wave of technical progress will impact the freed workers from the previous wave does not work with regard to the digitalization wave. Granted, after modernizing the agricultural wave, the industrialization wave transformed the laid-off farmers into factory workers. The current wave of digitalization, however, has created a demand for only several million IT professionals worldwide and is therefore unable to manage the tens of millions of laid-off workers in manufacturing (in developed countries) as well as redundant workers in IT services.

Since *information technology* has evolved from relying on static information sources to network-based interactive information sources, it is now more apt to refer to this pheneomon as *informing technology*. The book also discusses the most common use terms of this field, such as *computer science, information technology, informatics, IT, ICT, digital,* and *informing*, which to a certain degree are synonyms.

This book should be in the hands of not only technology leaders but also of daily users of computer applications, who should be aware of what such applications lead to. Most importantly, do they lead to a sustainable civilization and humanized living?

Andrew Targowski
Los Angeles, USA, 2021

REFERENCES

Targowski, A. (2014a). *Chinese civilization in the 21st century*. NOVA Science Publishers.

Targowski, A. (2014b). *Global civilization in the 21st century*. NOVA Science Publishers.

Targowski, A. (2015). *Virtual civilization in the 21st century*. NOVA Science Publishers.

Toffler, A. (1971). *Future shock*. Bantam Books.

ENDNOTE

[1] People first settled in Mesopotamia in the Paleolithic era. Up to 14,000 B.C., the inhabitants of the region lived in small settlements with round houses. Five thousand years later, these homes formed farming communities following the domestication of animals and the development of agriculture, particularly irrigation techniques that took advantage of the proximity of the Tigris and Euphrates rivers. Its history is marked by many important inventions that changed the world, including the concepts of time, math, wheels, boats, maps, and writing. The region is now home to modern day Iraq, Kuwait, Turkey, and Syria.

Section 1
The Essence of Strategic Informing Technology

Chapter 1
Waves of Civilization Development and the Digital Revolution

ABSTRACT

This chapter analyzes the evolution of civilization via the concept of civilizational waves. Seven waves are identified: (1) the agricultural wave, (2) the industrialization wave, (3) the information wave, (4) the globalization wave, (5) the virtualization wave, (6) the bio-material wave, and (7) the artificial intelligence wave. After discussing the key characteristics of each wave as well as their impacts upon civilization, the chapter then analyzes and discusses the two most important revolutions in the last 220 years: the Industrial Revolution and the IT Revolution. The chapter also develops a model showing the relationship between the civilizational waves and revolutions.

THE EVOLUTION OF WAVES OF CIVILIZATION DEVELOPMENT

By analyzing the history of civilization's development, one can distinguish essential characteristics that dominated in each period. Such periods can be referred to as "waves" since the importance of each epoch waxes and wanes over time, with the force of each generally subsiding as another comes to dominate. Seven such waves can be distinguished, and the role of ICT in the formation of some can be identified.

The Agriculture Wave

Civilization began about 6,000 years ago when people settled and began to develop agriculture using tools and with the help of irrigation systems, which resulted in an increase in agricultural productivity and an increase in the wealth of the best farmers and owners of irrigation systems. This consequently led to the creation of organized cities, bureaucratic administrations, and the military as well as the governing bodies. Over time, city-states began to merge, and the strongest states began to forge empires. Competitive empires waged wars, resulting in a demand for armaments and tool development. This, in

DOI: 10.4018/978-1-7998-8036-3.ch001

turn, resulted in improved techniques for the manual (artisan) production of goods, including everyday items. This period, lasting several millennia, is a period of civilization development based on the Agriculture Wave, which continues to this day because people need food to live.

The Industrialization Wave

The invention of printing in Europe by Johann Gutenberg in 1454 led to the rapid development and dissemination of knowledge, which soon gave rise to modern science in the 17th century (Isaac Newton 1642-1726). One effect of this development of knowledge and science was the invention of the steam engine by James Watt in 1776. This gave rise to the Industrialization Wave, where machines in mechanized factories replaced manual labor. As a result, artisan manufacturing was replaced by high efficiency industrialized production. These products were distributed by railways, which have become the driving force behind human mobility. What is essential is that the Industrialization Wave continues to this day because people still need these products. This wave is also called the Industrial Revolution. Its beginnings are marked by the changes in English society due the development of the factory system around the year 1840, which was supported by the development of railways.

The Information Wave

After World War II, computers (starting with ENIAC in 1946), telecommunications networks, and the Internet began to be used, automating the production of services and decision-making and revolutionizing communication between people and organizations on a global scale. This gave rise to the Information Wave, which could not have come into existence without the previous civilizational waves. This wave has radically improved the functioning of both the Agricultural Wave and the Industrialization Wave. Its beginnings are marked by the silent and creeping revolution of personal computers in the year 1980.

The Globalization Wave

The development of hypertext, the World-Wide-Web, and search engines like Netscape, Explorer, Firefox, Safari, and Chrome have resulted in ubiquitous Internet use in every country of the world. This has contributed to the removal of manufacturing from Western civilization to third world countries, where there is cheap labor. Because of high-speed Internet and accessible email communication, the world has seemed to have shrunk. Distance has ceased to be a restriction on communication for companies, which has led to the development of the global labor market and consumers. This process is accompanied by strong support for the free movement of capital without border control. As a result, the global transportation of people and goods in the form of airline industries and transoceanic shipping has developed. This created the Globalization Wave around 2000. An important feature of this wave is the unification of solutions (a la McDonald's) as well as the gradual integration of different civilizations.

The Virtualization Wave

The global use of the Internet has resulted in the emergence of virtual social networks such as Facebook, Instagram, Twitter and others, which has led to the development of virtual communities that operate parallel to real communities and have a strong influence on the them. Gradually, this "virtuality" is integrated into previous waves, such as the Agriculture, Industrialization, and Information Wave. Thus, this wave does not just replace the others. Its beginnings are marked by the appearance of the mass social network Facebook, which began to operate in the year 2004.

The Bio-Material Wave

This wave involves information and spatial communication (GPS) between people (Internet of People) and things (Internet of Things) using artificial intelligence, robotics, e-assistants (e.g., Apple Siri), quantum computers, genetic engineering, and the 3D printing of products and biomaterials. This is leading to the realization of hybrid minds, which consist of electronics implanted into the human brain to support human thinking with the help of online supercomputers. The need for such advancements arises from the developments of existing waves as well as innovations instigated by the achievements of inventors. This wave consequently results in further reductions in the operating costs of the current waves, which will continue up to point of the development of a mindless, post-scarcity economy, probably to the misfortune of people. This will cause consumers to disappear, and investments developing this type of economy will collapse. The beginnings of this wave are marked by the 3D printing of biomaterials such as skin tissues and bones in 2015, although 3D printing technology was developed much earlier in the 1980s.

The Artificial Intelligence Wave

This wave involves the use of artificial intelligence (AI) to solve the enormous challenges associated with the analysis of big data. The idea is to utilize advanced computer algorithms to help enable people to do what they do best: creatively solve problems. Eminent developers have produced platforms such as IBM Watson, Microsoft Cognitive Services, and Google TensorFlow, which provide users with vast amounts of valuable information and data from a variety of sources. Although AI has existed as a concept since the 1950s, it seemed for a long time that it would never be able to support mainstream businesses and technologies. Over the past few years, however, the potential of AI has increased in many areas, including its ability to help the development of many companies. One area where AI is of undoubted importance is innovation and idea management. Using machine learning capabilities, creative implementations of corporate ideas are supported, constantly leading to important innovations.

FROM THE INDUSTRIAL REVOLUTION TO THE INFORMING REVOLUTION

A model showing the relationships between these developmental waves of civilization is illustrated in Figure 1. These seven waves are additive because the tools and technologies of civilization complement each other (modernize) over time and do not exclude the influence of one another (unless something is harmful to human health and/or the environment). However, progression through these waves is not the only developmental trajectory of civilization. Another trajectory is the Revolution (Industrial Revolution) path, in which civilization veers into denial of the existing situation.

The model of civilizational waves and revolutionary development can be understood in the context of the development trends of strategic informatics, the essence of which will be explained in the next section.

The latter civilizational waves—i.e., the information, globalization, virtual, bio-material, and artificial intelligence waves—function simultaneously and are interdependent. All in all, they form the Informing,

Figure 1. A model of the relation between waves and revolutions in civilization's development in 2020

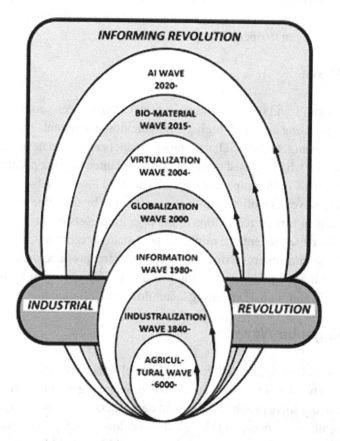

or Information Revolution, which opposes the development of the Industrial Revolution, ongoing since the 19th century. To briefly sketch this dialectic, the Industrial Revolution introduced a new quality to the Agricultural Wave by replacing the merchant economy with a capitalist economy, which was based on the power of large capital investments. These large investments were able to finance the development of the factory system, which is based on the work of machines and machine operators. This revolution introduced the concepts of regular work, occupations, and training and education in various professions. Furthermore, in these professions, it is necessary to distinguish between workers, specialists, managers, and owners.

For the next 200 years up to the present, these social classes involved in the capitalist economy have been in constant conflict over the right to decent work, fair distributions of wealth, and lower costs of living. Managers and owners, for their part, have monitored and supported the manufacturing processes. As is apparent from the waves and development trends associated with computerization, the economy is now incredibly sophisticated, and it is developing into a workerless society. Furthermore, the *human species (homo sapiens)* that we have known for several million years is transforming into a new species of *human-machine (homo machine)*. This entails unfamiliar lifestyles and governance, for this process of conversion is taking place right before our very eyes and will, in fact, be even more "tangible" in a few decades, unless this process is adjusted to maintain the status quo.

Strategic thought has led this author to conclude that we are dealing with a new revolution that is the antithesis of the previous revolution. The latest wave of technology-oriented developments will transform society and usher in this new revolution. This will be similar to how the Bolshevik Revolution of 1917, by preaching collectivization, was the antithesis of the liberation of citizens from the "property" of the king, proclaimed by the French Revolution of 1789. This raises the question of how the Polish Solidarity Revolution of 1989 negated the collectivization paradigm of the Bolshevik Revolution after 72 years and returned to the 200 year-old paradigm of the French Revolution.

This revolutionary dialectic was also examined by Francis Fukuyama (1992), who published the bestselling book *the End of History and the Last Man*, in which he argued that the liberal democracy that French philosophers and revolutionaries came up with is the final form of government. However, Fukuyama's judgement was hasty and was countered by Samuel Huntington (1996) four years later in 1996, who argued that *the New World Order* would lead to a *Clash of Civilizations* in which there would be a war of Western and Eastern Civilization against Islamic Civilization based on terrorism on the part of the weaker side. A few years later, in 2005, Thomas Friedman (2005), in his bestselling book *The World is Flat,* excitedly discussed the outsourcing of American jobs. Friedman argued that the inhabitants of Western civilization should stop working because, thanks to online communication, they can sub-contract with *Asia,* where for a fraction of the cost, the work can be done and sent "over the wire" to their places of residence. His book reinforced the "scientifically-oriented" Globalization Wave, which collapsed during the Coronavirus pandemic in 2020.

Next, this cockeyed optimist and promoter of *la dolce vita* published another book, *That Used to Be US,* in which he claims that employment is only guaranteed in higher education (Friedman & Mandelbaum, 2011). In this thesis, he is also wrong, because artificial intelligence can and will eliminate jobs in higher education—at least jobs whose work can be completed by machine learning—which will result in layoffs, for we, the people, are too expensive.

In the 21st century, such facts are evident, although unfavorable, in world civilization and in political spaces; however, these developments may go unnoticed because the Information Wave began a silent "creeping" revolution of microcomputers (commonly called "personal computers" or "PCs") in the early

Table 1. Characteristics of the Information Revolution

Development Waves Of Civilization	Strategic Technology	Strategic Impact	Sustainable Strategic Outcome
Information	Microcomputers	Mass of use	Handheld computer in various forms
Globalization	Internet	Communicating across the world	Death of distance
Virtual	Cyberspace – Social Networks	Broad communication of people from afar and isolation for those in close proximity	Smartphone addiction and collective intelligence
Bio-Material	Printing biological elements	Development of cyborgs	Longer life?
Artificial Intelligence	Algorithmizing decision-deciding	Unemployment	*Homo Machina*
Time	The power of information technology	Consumerism at the expense of resource depletion and nature	The extraordinary activity of the small elite and passivity of the rest of society

1980s. In the same way, the IT Revolution has been developing silently and slyly like a venomous snake over the last 30 years. This revolution is more dangerous for humanity and civilization than the clash of civilizations, pandemics, and political instability because it degrades a person to a passive resident of social welfare homes, who can only look on as AI-driven machines work for him and make key life decisions. Table 1 shows the characteristics of the Information Revolution.

Table 2 compares the characteristics of the two most important revolutions in the last 220 years.

Table 2. Comparing the paradigms of the Industrial and Information Revolution

Criteria	Paradigms		
	Industrial Revolution 1820 to 2020	**IT Revolution from 1980-2020+**	**Solution 2020+**
Producing goods and services	Constant work of machines and people	Human work gradually eliminated by robots, automation, and computerization	A healthy state capable of regulating technological progress
Preferred mode of communicating	Face-to-face	Online and via SMSs	Vital universal and higher education capable of intensifying direct communication
Preferred development of human behavior	In reality	In virtuality	A strong culture grounded in the real world, limiting virtuality
Governance and administration	Hierarchical, representative	Direct, flattened	Representative but passive and flattened
Preferred education	Specialized in the small-term	Application of computational thinking, effective at any price	Universally specialized in computational, informational, and ethical thinking
Infrastructure development	Continuation of millennia of actions that have pushed the limits of environmental sustainability	Disregard of traditional infrastructure for digital, including cloud computing	Develop sustainable eco-infrastructure in sustainable formats
Development of public culture	Participating in physically-oriented events	Participate in virtually oriented events	Develop a sustainable eco-culture in sustainable formats

Based on the comparison between the Industrial Revolution and the IT revolution, it appears that the former developed humanity at the expense of nature. In contrast, the latter is developing technology at the cost of humanity. So far, the counter-reaction of society to this state of development of civilization has not been sufficient and has been devoid of the instinct for self-preservation.

SUMMARY

1. The Information Waves do not displace either the Agricultural Wave or the Industrialization Wave; rather, the former penetrate and change the latter.
2. The sum of post-industrial waves, i.e., the information, globalization, virtual, bio-material, and artificial intelligence waves, has created the Informing Revolution. This revolution is negating the

legacy of the Industrial Revolution, which for 200 years has been developing a model of sustainable employment. The IT Revolution is attacking this model in that it is trying to minimize work.

3. Computerization has dramatically increased the amount of information people have access to. However, people use this information badly, for, in the name of technical progress, they want to replace themselves with thinking machines.

4. To exploit the intellectual possibilities of the Information Revolution, people must legally regulate it to prevent self-harm.

5. Matters of legally regulating the Information Revolution are not the foremost interest of politicians. When (if ever) this does happen, will it be too late?

REFERENCES

Friedman, T. (2005). *The world is flat*. Farrar, Straus and Giroux.

Friedman, T. L., & Mandelbaum, M. (2012). *That used to be us: How America fell behind in the world it invented and how we can come back*. Macmillan.

Fukuyama, F. (1992). *The end of history and the last man*. Free Press.

Huntington, H. (1996). *The clash of civilizations and remaking the world order*. Simon and Schuster.

KEY TERMS AND DEFINITIONS

Agriculture Wave: The first civilizational wave, which began some 6,000 years ago with the advent of agriculture.

Artificial Intelligence Wave: The most recent civilizational wave (2020), which aims to use artificial intelligence (AI) to solve problems associated with using big data.

Bio-Material Wave: The civilizational wave that involves the communication of information between people and things using the Internet.

Globalization Wave: The civilizational wave characterized by the integration of solutions and the merging of civilizations.

Industrialization Wave: The second civilizational wave, characterized by the mechanization of production.

Information Wave: The civilizational wave characterized by the widespread use of computers for communicating and storing information.

Virtualization Wave: The civilizational wave characterized by the widespread use of the Internet and the widespread growth of virtual social communities.

Chapter 2
Informing Science:
The Ubiquitous Field of Knowledge and Action

ABSTRACT

This chapter defines the scope of informing science. The chapter begins by examining whether informing science is a discipline or field of knowledge. Next, the development of software engineering and informing science are discussed. The chapter then analyzes four key periods in the history of information processing models: (1) machine-centric computing, (2) application-oriented data processing, (3) service-oriented utility environments, and (4) interactive approaches. Next, the concept of informing science is analyzed, and a matrix model of informing science is presented. The chapter concludes by considering some of the contemporary issues with informing science, including (1) the relationship between ICT as it is applied in businesses and ICT as it is developed as a science in higher education (2) as well as the strategies used by universities for educating students in this field.

INTRODUCTION: IS INFORMING SCIENCE A DISCIPLINE OR A FIELD OF KNOWLEDGE AND ACTION?[1]

Informing science characterizes the progress of information technology (IT) in the 21st century as well as, by extension, information-communication technology (ICT), which makes IT more active and interactive among users and applications due to world-wide telecommunications networks. The term "informing science" was proposed for the first time by Eli Cohen (1999), who founded the Institute of Informing Science[2] and the Informing Science Press.[3] An important first question to ask in regard to informing science is whether it is best understood as a discipline or field of knowledge.

Research activities generally focus on selected areas of interest, where new knowledge and new ways of using IT are sought. If such areas of interest relate to a wide range of recurring research, they are then referred to as scientific fields. Fields of science include, for example, the social sciences, mathematical sciences, medical sciences, humanities, natural sciences, and technical sciences. Each field generally includes several disciplines. Technical or engineering sciences, for instance, include electronics, telecom-

DOI: 10.4018/978-1-7998-8036-3.ch002

munications, automation, and robotics. Disciplines are, therefore, distinguished by the subject matter and purpose of the research. They can also be divided into specializations, e.g., computer science, computer architecture, or software engineering. Specializations are introduced to focus attention on selected aspects of a broader research area and to mark specific methodologies. The classification of research into fields and disciplines makes it possible to manage science and assess researchers and research teams more efficiently. It also facilitates prioritizing funding amongst the disciplines and distinguishing between the scope of titles and degrees awarded by the relevant scientific committees.

The classification of fields, disciplines, and scientific specializations is the result of both tradition and the progress of research. According to the *panta rhei principle,* however, such classifications should only be viewed as indicative: It is essential to leave some flexibility of interpretation, especially in borderline cases. Therefore, interdisciplinary or even transdisciplinary research should be appreciated, that is, research at borders of related areas of inquiry or even more remote areas.

For our purposes, we will only deal with ICT, which generally concerns the processing of information from various sources. Such information may take numerous forms and have different meanings depending on the research perspective. So, should informing science be treated broadly as a field of knowledge or narrowly as just one of the disciplines? On the one hand, informing science methods are so versatile (e.g., algorithms or applications) that they are widely used in different fields and disciplines. On the other hand, attractive ICT solutions are born in specific fields and disciplines (e.g., in medicine, photo analysis contributes to the development of new algorithms for their recognition, and in robotics, autonomous systems are being built, which require a new perspective also in computer science). So, taking into account this specificity, should informing science be classified in a particular discipline or as an independent field?

We will assume that informing science is not a technical specialization, but something that encompasses the whole of society: health care, transportation, education, automotive technology, etc. ICT includes the design, construction, and operation of ICT products in both organizations and by individual users. Not only does ICT support human civilization, it also converts prior forms into global and virtual civilization, which is already happening before our eyes. An abbreviated historiosophy of the worldwide development of ICT will be presented from the beginning of ICT's inception to give a sense of its meanings and complexity (Targowski, 2014, 2015).

Informing science and machine processing of information dates back to the first census, recorded on analytical machines (on punch cards) in 1890 in the US. This means that ICT has been developing on substantial social grounds for almost 130 years. This is a brief period in which to define this pervasive and complex area of social life. For example, the field of construction has been developing for more than 6,000 years and is now well-formed. Therefore, our reflections on this subject are neither too late nor too early.

Informing science is associated with advanced professions (obtained via postsecondary education), skilled crafts (requiring excellent qualifications, although not necessarily supported by higher education), as well as various tools supporting activities and new knowledge for ordinary people. While such areas are supported by informing science, the field as a whole is not a science in the same way that health care is not a science *per se*, but is based on medical science.

TECHNICAL PROGRESS ENSURES THE BROAD APPLICATION OF INFORMING SCIENCE

As a result of progress in the development of digital technologies enabling the construction of increasingly complex devices and computer systems, there was a need to describe their practical uses, which in turn led to the emergence of a whole range of programming languages, enabling the presentation of different operating procedures of systems using sequential or concurrent programs (on supercomputers with parallel processors). To facilitate the use of available applications, methods of cooperation between systems and users have developed in the form of graphical interfaces and visualization systems. This type of progress has enabled the widespread use of informing science, which has mainly been concerned with computer games and applications related to online purchases and banking operations. As a result, software engineering was born to develop rules, methods, and platforms for software development in the shortest possible time, at the lowest cost, and with the highest quality possible. As a result, proprietary software (such as the operating system) and application software have become increasingly efficient and useful to users. Over time, there has been a proliferation of mobile services and applications running on smartphones, which deal with many administrative matters (e.g., remote registration for a doctor appointment or for different offices) and support individual life decisions (e.g., a change of place of work or place of residence).

Analyzing technological advances in information technology, it is easy to see that the pace of development is substantial, even unimaginable. For example, from the invention of the transistor to programmable digital devices and mobile microcomputer systems that allow for the creation of various types of digital spaces such as the *Internet of Things* (IoT), it has only been 70 years! Similarly, we have gone from developing assembler languages specialized for different types of programmable devices (such as thermostats or process optical recorders) to universal high-order programming languages that can be used on various types of computers and control devices. Database and internet languages have also evolved to describe different kinds of scenarios (often defined by colloquial or spoken language expressions) in complex cyberspaces. In the case of computer graphics, progress is also enormous, from simple algorithms for presenting static objects, to dynamic objects, and finally to various types of digital videos and interactive computer games, which are now a lucrative form of business.

THE DEVELOPMENT OF SOFTWARE ENGINEERING

All of these solutions are made possible by the substantial advances in software engineering, which has developed effective methods of developing applications and information systems based on teams of both IT specialists (system scientists, programmers, coders, testers) as well as field experts and specialists in marketing and business. Especially impressive is the development of the Internet, including a whole range of tools, services, and platforms supporting the work of both software development teams and systems supporting specific areas of professional and personal activities. In addition to the real world, a virtual world is constantly being created and developed, in which it is easy to get lost without realizing the consequences. An example is the loss of the ability to communicate in reality (F2F, Face-to-Face), which has become the bane of modern young people.

Despite such apparent progress, humankind is continually looking for new and more sophisticated solutions related to its inherent possibilities. An example of such achievements is artificial intelligence.

This is the area of computer science involved in creating models of intelligent behavior and computer programs that simulate human behavior. In general, intelligent systems correctly interpret data provided from the outside. On this basis, ICT creates the right kind of knowledge to perform necessary and adequate actions. In other words, AI often acts like a human being.

The greatest successes are currently being achieved in the analysis and synthesis of natural languages, including the translation of texts from different languages and the simultaneous transcription of speech. Artificial intelligence is also used in customer service (e.g., help centers), claims processing (e.g., insurance claims), diagnostic systems (e.g., disease recognition), knowledge management (e.g., credit ratings), transportation (e.g., autonomous vehicles), and management of everyday tasks (e.g., homework). Compared to human performance, autonomous systems have an advantage in speed, allowing them to analyze much larger data sets. In various types of games, for example, AI can provide fast analyses about enemy movements and redefine their strategy accordingly. Artificial intelligence can also be used on the macroscale to build smart cities (such as Dubai) or even so-called "smart metropolises". The use of AI ensures adequate monitoring, which protects the safety of residents as well as police robots responding to looming threats. However, there are also negative effects, such as the censorship of opinions on social networks, the development of cultures of hate, cybercrimes and cyber wars, and disruptions in the traditional economy, leading to unemployment and social discontent.

Artificial intelligence is still far from being on par with human capabilities, for the human brain and human mind have not been thoroughly studied. Further progress depends on the development of informing science, including cognitive science—which deals with the observation and analysis of cognitive activities and which builds models of these processes—as well as neuroinformatics, which is designed to transfer minds between objects (i.e., copying and transferring human consciousness to a computer by accurately mapping all neural connections and faithfully reproducing their actions). It is also essential to highlight the successes of neurosurgery, which allows implants to be inserted into the brain to take over certain functions of the body (e.g., an artificial hand) or to influence behavioral dispositions (e.g., improving one's social mood).

THE DEVELOPMENT OF INFORMING SCIENCE

It can, therefore, be concluded that informing science lives in symbiosis with practical solutions, which makes it much more visible and spectacular for society. Figure 1 presents the range of informing (ICT) science in regard to the theoretical frameworks, methodologies, and tools developed through ICT-oriented research. By clarifying many terms, proposing appropriate definitions, and developing adequate processing models and operating principles, we achieve significant improvements in practical proposals in a qualitative sense. Thus, for example, clearly defining the scope of interest for software engineering or artificial intelligence has contributed to the rapid development of many applications for general use (e.g., product price comparison, choices for holiday destinations, choices for airlines, and hotel selections).

PERIODS IN THE EVOLUTION OF INFORMATION PROCESSING MODELS

The impact of informing science can be seen through the evolution of information processing models. The following development periods can be discerned:

Figure 1. Typology of informing technology and science. Although some methods and techniques were first introduced by business, over time, science has taken them "under the magnifying glass" and is now developing a scientific approach in these areas

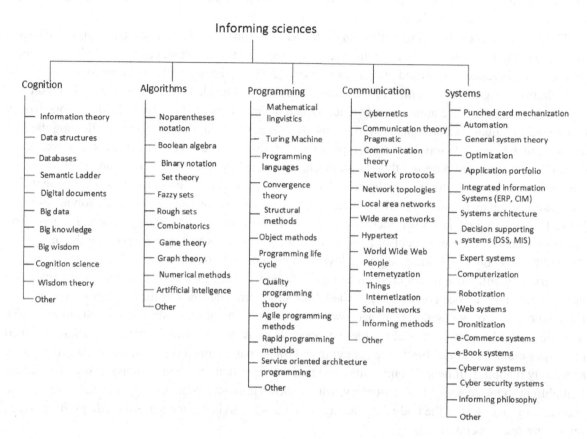

- **Period of machine-centric computing (1890–1960):** In the first period of computational development, the theory of computation, numerical and combinatorial algorithms, and methods for modeling and simulating various events and physical phenomena were advanced. In general, ICT was able to deliver results that provided the basis for verifying assumptions that had been made, which was further supported by a common-sense approach.

- **Application-oriented data processing period (1960-2000):** During this second period of computational development, the focus was on integrating telecommunications and information processing methods to build distributed computer systems that could offer various types of *application-centric* services for businesses and administration. The concept of component-oriented programming and enterprise-wide applications was developed. Formal research has since validated the correctness of such solutions and has contributed to the improvement of methods for managing both a system's resources and its users' needs.

- **Service-oriented utility environment period (2000+):** This means not only improving existing and developing new programming languages and methods for creating web applications, but it also means developing integrated computing environments (*service-centric computing*), including cloud computing and data service centers. Such platforms are maintained outside the user's area of interest and are made available to the user through market-based services. This means that ICT is growing into new areas without burdening users with problems involved in maintaining the services and applications used. This also moves ICT in the direction of *green computing*.

- **A period of interactive approach (2010+):** In this period, human decisions are integrated directly into how a system functions. This approach involves the use of various types of interactive algorithms, effective communication, and a whole range of internet services. It requires arranging the available ICT systems into cyberspaces that are partially integrated and controlled by proper action scenarios and that are assisted by human decisions. One of the main problems is ensuring credibility and cybersecurity.

It is clear that these four development periods initially occurred in the order outlined above. Today, although they are all continually being dynamically developed, the latter approach is increasingly beginning to dominate, mainly due to the development of efficient mobile systems. The large-scale use of smartphone applications opens up new possibilities for the use of ICT according to current needs. Services and applications are run and supervised in such environments, not only by qualified administrators, but also by the users, such as engineers, doctors, writers, journalists, teachers, professors, artists, nurses, students, and all kinds of employees. Furthermore, the almost unlimited amount of cyberspace enables cooperation between professionals from different fields at great distances.

In conclusion, it should be emphasized that the applications of ICT have contributed to the following developmental trends in humanity:

1. The development of new ICT services, cloud computing, big data sets, and the Internet of Things has led to the creation of many online services and applications for desktop and mobile devices, which are directly accessible for millions of users. However, the lack of digital skills in society as a whole can increasing lead to so-called "digital exclusion" and, consequently, financial exclusion, which in turn gives rise to populism and social disturbances.

2. The development of the Internet and digital data has led to a flood of information that is growing day by day. On the one hand, ICT makes people more informed (e.g., through the use of Wikipedia or other electronic news sources); however, on the other hand, they become more confused because of the difficulty of assessing the quality of the data and its consequences. This leads to easier manipulation of human behavior, which in turn can lead (and probably will lead) to bad decisions, which consequently means a deterioration of human flourishing.

3. The development of artificial intelligence for replacing human decision-making discourages people from putting in more effort to solve problems, thereby causing humanity to lose its ability to reason. Consequently, this means reducing the role of humans in life and giving initiative to machines, called "cyborgs".

4. Life in cyberspace has begun to dominate real life, leading to the disappearance of direct communication, causing people to become isolated and very dependent on e-communication. This is especially true for the teenage generation, for who being in virtuality has become an addiction, often requiring hospital treatment.

This raises the first question about the importance of informing science: will it contribute to the elimination of the threats mentioned above? The second question is related to the development of cyborgs: Will IT be able to develop complex cyberspaces or virtual characters that can think as wisely as the best of humankind? The third question concerns eliminating the overarching role of humankind in increasingly complex and intelligent cyberspaces: Will cyborgs take over key roles played by humans in cyberspace? In other words, will we see *a period of cyborg-centric computing*, and on what scale? These are not just questions for ICT scientists. There seems to be somewhere a limit to what human needs can be suitably addressed by human cognition. If ICT creates complex cyberspaces that outstrip the cognitive capabilities of humans, this could lead to its collapse and, consequently, to a catastrophe for the human race. Are we in danger? Yes, even back in the 20th century, this seemed to be the case if we consider the simultaneous degradation of the environment and the depletion of strategic resources.

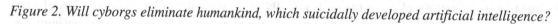

Figure 2. Will cyborgs eliminate humankind, which suicidally developed artificial intelligence?

THE CONCEPT OF INFORMING SCIENCE

After these historical considerations, it is worth explaining how to understand ICT in a broad sense and how to treat ICT as a scientific field. Let's first present a list of critical scientific fields:

1. Humanities deal with humans as social beings and domains such as language, literature, art, history, philosophy, and culture.
2. Social sciences explore social phenomena and the structure and functions of societies and civilizations, which includes the history of civilization, culture, law, economics, geography, sociology, pedagogy, politics, and so forth.
3. Natural sciences are involved in the study of various aspects of the material, living, and inanimate world (biology, chemistry, physics, astronomy, geography, environmental protection, ecology, etc.).
4. Medical sciences deal with health and general medical care, including medicine, pharmacy, dentistry, nursing, and physiotherapy.
5. Technical sciences are involved in the design, construction, and operation of tools, equipment, vending machines, and technological systems as well as the production of goods, materials, and

related services, which includes construction, architecture, urban planning, electronics, energy, and transportation.

6. Mathematical sciences deal with abstract, formal models, which are described via principles as well as inferences about their properties; in addition to mathematics, this includes logic, the theory of graphs, etc.

7. ICT science deals with intangible goods, including data, information, knowledge, wisdom, and various virtual entities. It is characterized by multiple types of activities, such as data collection, messaging, transformation, analysis of digital documents, and the computer-assisted development of knowledge, learning, inferencing, and predicting.

Figure 3. The wide range of ICT sciences and their integration with other sciences (with examples of hybrid informing sciences)

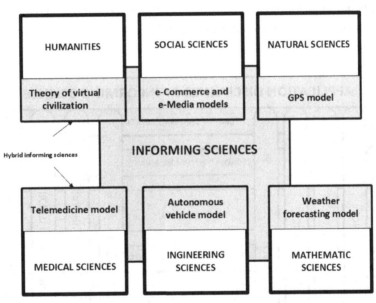

The different fields of science differ primarily in their subject matter and in the methodologies they apply to specific factors. Figure 3 provides examples of research areas common to informing science and other fields called "hybrid sciences". Informing science, together with the humanities, is creating Virtual Civilization, and with the social sciences, it has formed the foundations of e-commerce and e-business. Cooperation between ICT and the life sciences enabled the construction of popular GPS systems, and its symbiosis with the medical sciences resulted in remote advisory systems and the online monitoring of patient conditions. In addition, the joining of informing science with the technical sciences has led to the construction of autonomous vehicles and home robots, and combined with the mathematical sciences, it has contributed to the development of very complex weather models, where achievements of the natural sciences were also used.

It is also worth noting that researchers strongly associated with different research fields than informing science generally see their field as central, and they point out that other fields (including informing science) also include hybrid sciences related to their own. This proves how difficult it is to define the boundary of each field; however, it also confirms that informing science should be treated as a field of science.

THE MATRIX MODEL OF INFORMING SCIENCE

Figure 4 shows the Matrix Model of Informing Science (MMIS) with disciplines and specializations. The specializations corresponding to the disciplines of informing science are marked horizontally, and they relate to specific areas and stages of applying computer-assisted activities and processes for humans and machines.

Figure 4. The Matrix Model of Informing Science (MMIS 2020), including disciplines and specializations that penetrate society, religion, culture, and infrastructure. Of particular importance are the philosophy of computer science and strategic informatics because they determine the success of informing science applications in society

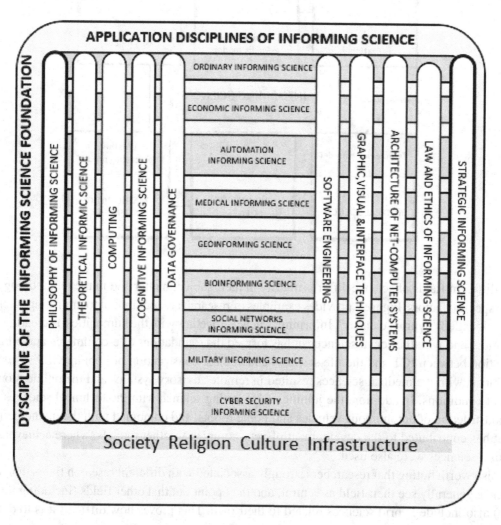

One can distinguish the following categories of application-oriented disciplines of informing science:

- **Ordinary informing science** provides methods of access to computers and the Internet and aids in the use of basic applications available on smartphones for the implementation of essential info-communication functions related to communicating with people, searching for necessary information, and dealing with simple life matters by electronic means.

- **Economic informing science** is oriented toward various types of business and public organizations, and it helps to enable modeling and analysis of management, administration, production, and service processes that are supported by appropriate digital tools and systems. It also enhances the effectiveness of the functioning of various types of human collaboration, and it expands the possibilities of computer-aided decision-making.

- **Automation informing science** is concerned with processes occurring within organizations responsible for the production of material and information goods. It enables the construction of automated control systems for real-time operations as well as supervision systems, which ensures the functioning of such systems.

- **Medical informing science** covers health and medical procedures. On the one hand, ICT improves access to medical services and systems, and on the other hand, it offers devices to help diagnose patients. It also has the task of relieving medical professionals from administrative work.

- **Geoinforming science** focuses on automating the acquisition and analysis of geospatial data, including digital maps necessary for satellite navigation as well as the real-time location of various objects in a given geographical space (GPS location systems).

- **Bioinforming science** uses ICT methods and tools to solve selected problems within the biological sciences, including the structure and evolution of genes, genomes, and proteins as well as the principles of structure formation and interaction with other proteins. It enables the construction of bioinformatics databases containing DNA/RNA sequences, and it offers services for searching, comparing, and analyzing these sequences.

- **Social networks informing science** takes into account info-communication and legal phenomena in social networks. It confronts virtual life with real-life and analyzes the issues of democracy, freedom, totalitarianism, censorship, and quality of life, including work and interpersonal relations.

- **Military informing science** deals with a variety of computerized military systems as well as computer-aided command systems. It enables the virtual generation of different types of situations, analysis, and selection of the most appropriate action scenarios.

- **Cybersecurity informing science** deals with the methods of protecting computer systems and networks against theft and damage to hardware, software, or electronic data as well as disruption or misrouting of services. This discipline is becoming increasingly important due to (a) increased reliance on computer systems, the Internet, and wireless network standards, such as Bluetooth and Wi-Fi, as well as (b) the development of "smart devices", including smartphones, TVs, and various devices that make up the so-called "Internet of Things." Due to its complexity, both politically and technologically, digital security is one of the main challenges in the modern world, which is always looking for peace.

- **Other disciplines** may arise as a result of the development of computerization.

The rows marked vertically correspond to the specializations of informing science related to universal solutions, whose results can be used in all or any other specializations, disciplines, or fields (Figure 3). One can discern the following specializations of informing science:

- **The philosophy of informing science** is a cognITive-ethical-logical assessment of the applications of computers and networks as well as the development of this field to determine whether IT is good for humanism and the environment. For example, will the unregulated development of automation and robotization lead to an economy with limited employment, where people will live equally on unemployment benefits as in communism?

- **Theoretical informing science** is related to automata theory, calculation theory, algorithm theory, systems theory, and their analysis. This specialization develops models and solutions for different ICT systems and facilitates the research and evaluation of the models and solutions.

- **Computing** deals with methods for scientific, economic, engineering, social, meteorological, and even cosmological calculations, including simulation and modeling. Computing of this type uses professional program packages and is generally carried out on supercomputers.

- **Cognitive informing science** (Targowski, 2011) supports thinking and decision-making processes and is based on the evolution of reason (mind versus brain) and the theory of wisdom. It aims at understanding intelligent behavior and developing computer programs that can simulate these behaviors. It is concerned with the analysis and synthesis of natural languages, claims processing (in insurance), the recognition of diseases, and the construction of autonomous vehicles and other robots. In a nutshell, it is concerned with modeling correct behavior for such domains based on the available data, concepts, knowledge, and wisdom.

- **Data governance** deals with data sources, transfer, and transformation methods of various types of data, such as characters, texts, digital documents, photos, audio, and multimedia. It assumes the use of unified standards for description and interpretation and effective procedures for storage and processing.

- **Software engineering** deals with the entire software lifecycle of applications, from specifications to design, programming, testing, deployment, and operation. It takes into account the different developmental methodologies and support tools available, and it focuses on organizing project teams and providing high-quality applications and services.

- **Graphic, visual, and interface techniques** are the subjects of development and operations that take into account various types of human communication with devices and computer systems as well as communication between systems. They develop input/output standards, tools, devices, and interfaces that use computer graphics, video, and streaming signals.

- **The architecture of net-computer systems** investigates and is related to the design and organization of centralized and distributed devices, networks, and application systems, including service platforms and web applications. It also includes private and public cloud computing and methods of administering and managing ICT. In addition, this specialization stimulates the development of new technologies necessary for the production of a whole range of new architectures.

- **Law and ethics of informing science** (also known as "cyberlaw") address the societal issues of automation, computerization, robotization, and Internet applications. It regulates the digital dissemination of information, including information disseminated in media, video/film, software, e-commerce, and other forms of handling information. This specialization considers specific issues regarding intellectual property in the field of computers, networks, the Internet, contract law, privacy, freedom of expression, and others.

- **Strategic IT** specializes in the most critical issues, challenges, and problems of informing science that impact various areas of life. It covers all levels of society, such as provinces, regions, countries, as well as continents and the world, including enterprises, institutions, and NGOs. It also addresses the problems of ICT education, which is the foundation of the wise application of modern information technologies.
- Others.

The number of ICT disciplines and specialties may expand due to technological advances, the development of new technical solutions and products, and the emergence of new possibilities for their applications. It should be noted that some of the listed specialties could grow into disciplines and that development in such areas would be the largest and fastest. As a consequence, the field of informing science will increase while enriching other scientific fields. In conclusion, it should be stated that:

1. The presented realm of intersecting disciplines and specialties of informing science indicates difficulties in defining all possible disciplines and specialties of the field and, in particular, difficulties in including them in education and training programs. It is essential to be open to innovative interdisciplinary and transdisciplinary approaches because, in this way, there is the possibility of progress and prosperity for our society.
2. Treating all of the ICT disciplines (foundational and application-based) in an integrated, unified way is a challenge. Assuming that there is one discipline—say, for example, economic informing science—IT management in a given company should be additionally proficient in the other foundational specializations of informing science. As a result, each organizer or ICT executive, such as CIOs (Chief Information Officer), must be familiar with a total of 10 types of informing science specializations. It is an enormous challenge for both theorists and practitioners of that kind of technology. There is a lack of such versatile ICT professionals. This area is, therefore, currently in a constant crisis of personnel and conceptual development.
3. Treating informing science (or informing technology) as an integrated field of knowledge enables great opportunities to ensure the well-being of society while highlighting new categories of risks to be taken into account in the strategies being developed. This means seeking wise compromises, which, however, are often ignored due to the desire to achieve short-term success, both prestigious and financial (including business).

THE DILEMMAS OF INFORMING SCIENCE

The need for a broad look at informing science stems from the presentation of the resulting ICT products over the last eight decades. During this period, incredible developments were brought about, which revolutionized our lives and opened new possibilities of the human mind. One must realize that it makes no sense to treat informing science as a narrow specialty in technical or mathematical sciences. Information and knowledge related to ICT occur in all fields of science, giving them new developmental impulses. Of course, there are problems of ambiguity across scientific fields, which is natural and confirms the importance of interdisciplinary research (when the areas share similar problems) and intradisciplinary (when there are significant thematic differences). Attention should also be drawn to new approaches to training ICT professionals that allow them to be educated in four levels of ICT skills.

One can also note an existing ICT paradox regarding the cooperation of ICT professionals and other professionals. Other professionals are more open to solving IT problems encountered in their fields than indigenous ICT professionals. There is also a contradiction between the ICT business and ICT science. The development of information techniques is carried out primarily by businesses, and universities barely keep up with this development because information systems are expensive and rapidly aging. In business, new solutions appear almost every day.

This is not to disregard the fact that some universities are pioneers of innovation, but this is much more difficult than in other fields or disciplines, such as electrical engineering and electronics or the study of Wi-Fi networks, where science (mainly physics) has developed the foundation for business development in these industries. Moreover, the growth of ICT science is mostly limited to university faculty, and they publish their achievements in nearly 750 ICT scientific journals that are anonymously reviewed (blind refereed).

While the average computer/informing scientist has access to a few of these writings, ICT practitioners do not read them at all. This is because, while they work in wealthy companies, they use research studies from consulting firms, which, although they report on important findings and use rigorous scientific methods and relevant empirical data, charge from a few to tens of thousands of dollars. In general, professionals and doctoral students do not have access to these studies. ICT researchers and IT practitioners, therefore, operate in two non-communicating areas of knowledge development.

Worse still, many professors and Ph.D. students have never worked in the computer/informing science profession in business or administration, and it is doubtful whether, after giving up their job at a university, they would be able to work as a computer/informing science professional. Another problem is whether a university professor who has never worked outside universities knows the challenges of practice and whether he/she will formulate research tasks and solve them to the benefit of their practice.[4]

Another dilemma of applying science in the development of computer/informing science is the strategy of universities in the educating of computer/informing scientists so that immediately after graduation, they have "market" professional qualifications. It is a business-friendly strategy, but it is nevertheless short-sighted, as the graduate has specific skills (which, moreover, needs to be updated very quickly), but has minimal universal theoretical knowledge, especially from the humanities, sciences, and natural sciences. After all, when you computerize the work of a director or doctor, you need to know it better, sometimes better than the practicing director or doctor knows it! It is challenging to learn in college; it is necessary to work in interdisciplinary teams.

SUMMARY

1. The field of informing science is as all-encompassing as medicine. It has a similar role in improving people's lives as medicine has had for millennia; however, informing science has been developing for only several decades. Nevertheless, informing science is already transforming the founding of civilization into a global and virtual society, where people will have to learn how to live "a new life."

2. The field of informing science is based on the integration of many other fields, disciplines, and specializations, and it is both general and specialized. Furthermore, above all, it requires thorough

and broad knowledge, wisdom, and qualifications to use it effectively, which is not yet adequately mastered by ICT promoters and users.

3. Informing science introduces a specific information order and allows people to access a great deal of information. Nonetheless, it is also dangerous because ICT enables a culture of hate, cybercrimes, and even cyberwar, and it also produces other adverse effects like IT exclusion. ICT requires its leaders to use wisdom in ICT applications, otherwise ICT will become one of the greatest threats to civilization.

REFERENCES

Cohen, E. (1999). Reconceptualizing information systems as a field of the transdiscipline informing science: From ugly duckling to swan. *CIT. Journal of Computing and Information Technology*, 7(3), 213–219.

Targowski, A. (2011). *Cognitive informatics and wisdom development*. IGI Global. doi:10.4018/978-1-60960-168-3

Targowski, A. (2014). *Global civilization in the 21st century*. Nova Science Publishers.

Targowski, A. (2015). *Virtual civilization in the 21st century*. Nova Science Publishers.

KEY TERMS AND DEFINITIONS

Artificial Intelligence: Computer programs and functions designed to mimic human cognitive abilities.

Cyberspace: The online, virtual environment created by computers and digital technologies, in contrast with the physical reality that lies outside of digital spaces.

Cyborg: A cybernetic organism, constructed from biological and machine parts.

Discipline: A division of knowledge researched in higher education institutes, such as history, computer science, biology, and chemistry.

Field of Knowledge: Groups of related disciplines within higher education, such as the social sciences, natural sciences, medical sciences, and humanities.

Neuroinformatics: A specialization aimed at successfully transferring minds between objects (e.g., between a computer and a human).

Software Engineering: A specialization aimed at developing rules, methods, and platforms for software.

ENDNOTES

[1]   This chapter is developed based on the article by Targowski, A. and Krawczyk, H. (2020). Informatics as a field of knowledge supporting implementation of human undertakings. *Filozofia i Nauka*, *8*(1), 97-136.

[2]   Informing Science Institute. Accessed September 12, 2020. https://www.informingscience.org/

[3]   Informing Science Press. Accessed September 12, 2020. https://informingsciencepress.com/index.php?route=product/manufacturer/info&manufacturer_id=11

[4]   Reviewing doctorate papers on this subject (by the author), it is evident that American Ph.D. students tend to do well in surveying practitioners in a correlation of factors, but they do worse with inferring the results of studies for practice. Their studies are primarily inductive, while implication-based studies are uncommon.

Chapter 3
Strategic Digital Informing and Its Challenges in the 21st Century

ABSTRACT

This chapter examines the challenges faced by digital informing technologies and civilization in the 21st century. The chapter begins by analyzing (1) the stages of development of strategic information technologies from the early 20th century up to the present as well as (2) the strategies adopted by informing science specializations (such as cognitive science, software engineering, etc.). Next, the chapter surveys major innovations in the history of strategic information technologies. This is followed by an analysis and evaluation of the concept of a laborless economy. The chapter concludes by positing a set of rules for workers in the digital economy that will ensure the wise development of civilization.

INTRODUCTION

Modern informing technologies have created challenges that have not been encountered in the history of human development regarding the scale of the problems they have created as well as the interruptions they have caused to the ways people and organizations operate. The developments of modern informing technologies have also occurred in a relatively short period of time. The Agricultural Wave, for example, has been going on for several millennia, and the Industrialization Wave has been going on for 200 years. Furthermore, its impact on civilization has been, overall, positive since it improves productivity and creates better living conditions. By contrast, the current Waves—the Information, Globalization, Virtualization, Bio-Material, and Artificial Intelligence Waves—have approximately occurred in the last 25 years (1995-2020) [1], and the latter of the bunch have an even shorter history. Despite such a short duration, the technological systems involved in computerization, robotization, and automation threaten people with structural unemployment and war carried out via intelligent robots who are able to succeed thanks to the help of shortsighted hackers and global businessmen who own robot "populations". However, their lives also hang in the balance, as evidenced by the social riots in the United States in 2020.

DOI: 10.4018/978-1-7998-8036-3.ch003

This threat to civilization and technological systems will be strategically examined in this chapter, and remedies and an assessment of their feasibility will be proposed. This analysis can be contrasted with the picture of a highly intelligent civilization designed by deceptive ICT enthusiasts and naïve business people who aim to gain power over the world, like the SuperMind[2] Ernst Stavro Blofeld in James Bond, whose only friend was a white cat basking on his lap (Figure 1).

Figure 1. SuperMind Ernst Stavro Blofeld (played by Donald Pleasence) in the James Bond film You Only Live Twice (1967) (Photo: Wikipedia)

THE CONCEPT OF STRATEGIC DIGITAL INFORMING

In the 21st century, the science of informing technology is in a state that science fiction imagined in the 1960s and 1970s. Now self-driving vehicles and self-thinking robots have begun to appear. In the face of almighty and ubiquitous computerization, have humans become unnecessary? This may sound like science fiction, but the 2020 pandemic has helped in increasing the power of digitalization. The Internet has made physical visits to places such as banks, post offices, and cinemas mostly unnecessary, and the stay-at-home orders have caused a tendency to stay there permanently.

As our physical worlds shrink to avoid Covid-19 contact, our virtual platforms attempt to make up for it. In the foreseeable future, many of us, sitting at home and waiting for the vaccine, will attend virtual schools, pray in virtual churches, and socialize at virtual events. Furthermore, the history of the Internet suggests that when things move to the web, they rarely come back—just ask department stores and CD manufacturers. In the initial months of the lockdown and stay-at-home orders, there was a sharp division between people who work with information (e.g., images, words, numbers, video) and people who work with objects (e.g., groceries, packages, those who require medical attention). The former can take refuge and communicate through screens, but the latter must go out into the physical world, exposing themselves to infection (Kirsch, 2020).

Because ICT technology avoids the more significant burdens and dangers of physical existence, this class and division of work can persist with a virtual elite supported by a working-class that is physically active. Of course, risky forms of work have always been part of our society. For instance, during the American Civil War, Americans could pay for someone to take place in the military. Soon, turbo-capitalism will make it possible for someone to pay another to take their place in the physical world full of diseases and dangers so that they can stay safe behind a computer monitor.

The coronavirus crisis of 2020 will cause some governments to turn inward for at least the next decade and focus on what is happening within their borders rather than on what is happening abroad. A strategy of self-sufficiency is to be expected, and opposition to immigration is likely to increase. The commitment to tackling regional and global problems (including climate change) will be reduced given the need to allocate resources to ameliorate the consequences of the pandemic and economic crisis. Many countries will find it difficult to get out of this crisis in the face of weakness on the part of the state apparatus and leadership.

Informing technologies of the 21st century are global not only in terms of their commercial distribution and universal application, but also in terms of their global consequences, which are similar to the effects of the 2020 pandemic. Pathogens (bio-infections), artificial intelligence systems, computer viruses, and radiation that others might release incidentally can become just as much of a problem for us as for those it originates from. Standardized information systems (for reporting), joint controls, joint contingency plans, ethical principles, standards, and treaties must be urgently used as a means of reducing our numerous mutual dangers.

Strategic informing technology changes over time, requiring it to be updated and adapted to our needs and functional capabilities. Table 1. illustrates the changes in strategic informing technology from the 19th century up to the 2020s. It also shows the global strategy of the whole field of computer science for the modern era (2020s). This strategy should be the overarching strategy for the disciplines and specializations of informing technology (Figure 2).

Table 2 illustrates the strategies of informing science disciplines that are known in the 2020s. These strategies, alongside the strategies of scientific fields, are paramount for the specializations of IT.

As a result, we come to the strategies of specializations of informing science, which are characterized in Table 3.

The presented wise strategies of informing science's disciplines and specializations are not popular at present among business-oriented IT projects and firms.

DEVELOPMENT OF MAJOR STRATEGIC INFORMING SYSTEMS

An overview of the development of effective computerization strategies from its initial mechanization phase of data processing in the 19th century to the present (2020s) is given in Table 4. This table contains

Figure 2. The structure of ICT strategy

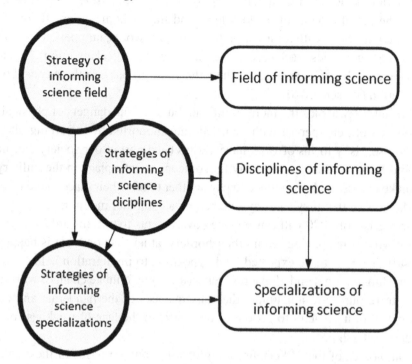

only the most essential computerization strategies that have made it practical to develop information technology and its applications. This is not a complete list of computational innovations and applications.[3]

Table 4 provides 21 of the most important computerization strategies applied in the world; however, some of them must be recognized as very dangerous for human well-being:

- The murder of some 4 million people occurred thanks to mechanized racial-oriented records by Germany between 1939 and 1945. This event indicates how computerization can threaten the good of humankind. It would seem that this type of system should no longer be used in modern times. However, Facebook's practice (based on the sale of personal data) indicates that this drama of mass murder may be repeated.

- The maintenance of IBM's computer centers in Nazi Germany contributed to this tragedy, and it was caused by a desire to have American intelligence inside Germany during World War II. IBM had a similar strategy during the Cold War when, in the 1960s and 1970s, it quietly collaborated on turning the IBM 360/370 computers into the Soviet Ryad system. In this way, American intelligence knew what was going on in the field of advanced technology behind the Iron Curtain. Furthermore, since IBM executive Thomas Watson Jr. was a personal pilot of Major General Follett Bradley during WWII (who oversaw the Lend-Lease program in regard to the Soviet Union), he knew the Soviet system well from so-called "first-hand experience".

- The development of AI is very fashionable and spectacular, but is a laborless economy a wise strategy for its application?

- The development of 5G based on Huawei's Chinese technology could lead to e-spying at almost every level of society. Hence, the United States is promoting the use of 5G technologies from

Table 1. Stages of development of strategic information technology (IT) in Western civilization

District	Tasks of Strategic IT	Examples
1890-1950	Mechanize standard data	Census, records, stocks, employees, accountants
1950-1960	Produce computers for business and administration	IBM 1400
1960-1970	Support business management and administration	IBM 360/370, Gamma 10, and MIS
1970-1980	Develop databases and networks	INFOSTRADA, Minitel
1980-2000	Develop the Internet via web and search engines	e-mail, e-commerce, e-press, e-book, Explorer, Safari, Chrome
2000-2010	Develop networks for communication and applications	Facebook, Twitter, digital platforms
2010-2020	Develop digital security	Firewalls, Industrial Control Systems (ICS)
2020-2030	Virtualize life to support human labor (not to eliminate it), including work, meetings, online religion, and the safe use of 5G	5G

Table 2. The strategies of informing science-oriented disciplines for 2020-2030

Informing Science Disciplines	Strategy	Examples
Ordinary	Create the ability to educate and work online	Virtual class
Economic	Support management (not the elimination of human labor); apply the recommendations for the digitization of the EU and other international countries; convert information systems into informing systems	Data interchangeability and standard access to European platforms; interactive information systems
Process Automation	Computerize the control of production and service processes	Control panels that take into account operator intervention; human (not robot) customer service
Medical	Universalize prescriptions and universalize patient data by EU standards	Easily accessible systems in EU countries
Geoinforming	Design top-down environmental control systems, including climate control systems	Establishment of the World Civilisation Organisation (WCO) and its branches in various continents and countries
Bioinforming	Develop genetic engineering	Unique genetic-oriented treatment for patients
Social networking	Support of social networking that is hate- and surveillance-free	Elimination of hate, surveillance, and marketing of personal data
Military	Protect against cyber-wars and conflicts	Impenetrable digital shields for informing systems in each country
Digital security	Create security against hacking, surveillance, and cyber-crimes	NORTON, Bitdefender, Acunetix

Table 3. The strategies of informing science-oriented specializations for 2020-2030

Informing Science Specializations	Strategy	Examples
Strategic informing science	Update and develop new computerization strategies	Post-pandemic strategy of 2020
Philosophy of informing science	Define the morality and ethics of computerization	Can the law regulate the progress of computerization?
Theoretical informing science	Develop an integrated information and computing approach	STEM-STEAM Semantic Ladder
Computing	Develop supercomputer applications that humanistically oriented	Climate control
Cognitive informing science	Develop AI according to laws and wisdom	Should cyborgs be developed?
Data governance	Develop Big Data as the foundation of Big Knowledge and Big Wisdom	Big Wisdom in medicine
Software engineering	Develop reliability and software that is easily updated	What to do if a software company goes bankrupt?
Graphic, visual, interface techniques	Develop 5G applications with secure personal data	The gap between Ericsson and Nokia and Huawei
The architecture of net-computer systems	Develop and operate reliable and secure architecture for computer systems	Is cloud computing secure and dependable?
Law and ethics of informing science	Develop lawful and ethical informing technology	Is personal data marketing by Big Tech legal?

Ericsson and Nokia. This is a strategic solution with significant consequences for the economy and culture.

- The development of the Internet of Things (IoT) (Figure 3) is launching a great wave of new business, much larger than the wave created by the Internet of People. It is, therefore, very motivating for entrepreneurs; however, the digitalization of cities, provinces, and states will make these places very unreliable and difficult to live in, not only for older generations but for younger as well. This kind of computerization is a significant strategic choice for thousands of towns and villages.

LABORLESS ECONOMY

The development of science and technology accelerated in Western civilization about 250 years ago when the following inventions were created: James Watt's commercial internal combustion engine in England (1774), Joseph Jacquard's mechanized weaving workshop in France (1804), and computers in the United States (commercial Univac I in 1951). Ever since, people have worried that machines will replace human labor. For example, during the Industrial Revolution (about 1820-40), English citizens became aware that a "social revolution" was taking place with the launch of "machines" and the factory system. However, these machines did not replace human labor; rather, there was created a need for their service.

With the development of the Industrial Revolution, the age of day jobs began, without which the factory system could not function. From this point on, there developed the concepts of jobs, specializations, and training programs. Regular work, say, from 8 a.m. to 4 p.m., provided economic stability for

Table 4. Major strategic IT innovations in the world

Year	Place	System	Importance	Consequences
1000	Arab University in occupied Spain	Future pope Sylvester II as a disguised student at an Arab university, discovers the concept "0."	Enabled the mechanization of Arabic numbers in place of Roman numbers	Commissioning of future computers
1495	Venice	Bookkeeping - debit-credit Luca Pacioli	Allowed for calculations of business transactions	Development of a universal accounting system
1844	USA	Morse Code in telegraphs	Ability to encode information	Development of punched cards and tapes by data coding
1890	USA	Mechanized Population Census (IBM)	Enabled the development of sociology and population policies in the United States	IBM's growth as a big IT company, which dominated the market and world standards in the data processing
1916	Poland	A controlled technique for producing quartz monocrystals by Jan Czochralski	Enabled the development of digital transistors based on an old patent (which is still valid)	Development of second generation computers and smartphones
1924	Poland	Polish arithmetic notation by Jan Łukasiewicz	Facilitated the design and use of handheld calculators	Used in mass-produced arithmetic calculators and notation applied in designing the logic circuitry of computers
1935	USA	Social security numbers F.D. Roosevelt In Poland, PESEL (1970), by Andrew Targowski	Became the foundation for computerizing the state	Residents of states get a social security number, which is foundational for the information systems of the administration and business
1937	USA	Electrification of binary code by Claude Shannon	Enabled the construction of computers in binary code	The most import factor in the manufacture of computers
1940-45	Germany	Murder of 4 million people (Targowski, 2014).	Mechanized genocide via IBM population data	Criticisms of IT as a source of espionage and crime
1951	USA	UNIVAC I Computer	Ushered in the commercial use of computers	Mass computerization of civilization
1956	USA	Artificial intelligence John McCarthy	Enabled the programming of decision-making	Robotization and the removal of human labor
1961-65	USA	IBM 1400 and IBM 360	Extensive computerization of business and administration	Opened the path to millions of computers applications
1970	USA	Relational databases E. F. Codd (IBM)	Eliminated data redundancy and random access to stored data records	Mass use of databases in information systems
1972	Poland	Infostrada by Andrew Targowski	Enabled the potential development of an informed society in totalitarian Poland	Information superhighway-paradigm a "new economy" in the US
1973	USA	GPS	Facilitated travel and spatial management	Mass use in cars and geoinformatics
1975	USA	Super-computer Cray I	Allowed for computing at the edge of knowledge	The development of cosmology physics
1978	USA	Apple II Steve Wozniak, Steve Jobs	Ushered in the silent revolution of minicomputers	Information wave
1983	USA	Internet of People (IoP) Paul Baran	Enabled worldwide communication among people and businesses	Global e-economy, virtualization, cybercrime, and cyberwar
1999	USA	Internet of Things (IoT)	Enabled communication between people and things	Digital cities and their unreliableness
2004	USA	Facebook Mark Zuckerberg	Enabled communication among the world's population	Monitoring people and the sale of personal data
2013	South Korea	5G (Samsung)	Allowed instant communication by video and IoT	Instant communication, surveillance, and human control

Figure 3. The concept of the Internet of Things (IoT)

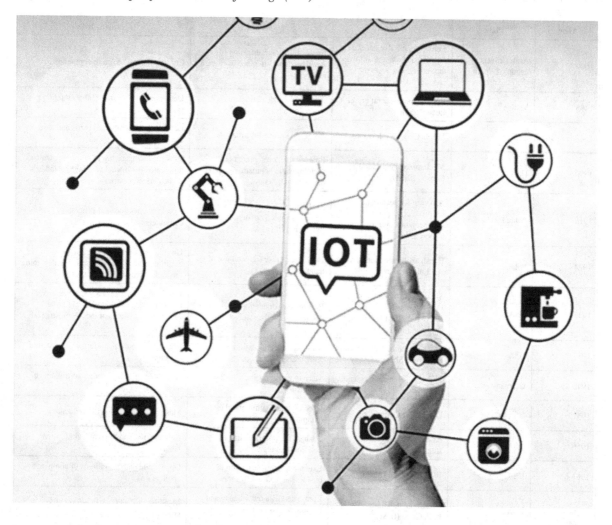

workers who, as they increased their knowledge, skills, and experience, could count on professional advancements and higher pay. However, one who thinks that work is only of productive and economic importance is wrong, for work is vital in the overall development of humanism, which makes us better members of society and sensitive to many aspects of human fate. This fate is a continuous struggle with problems and involves people of both good and ill will; it also involves playing politics with authorities of different political perspectives (Susskind, 2020).

In the 21st century, informing technology, which developed networking computer systems and automated the handling and processing of information, is attempting to replicate human thinking and decision-making. Robotics and automation not only reduce the need for workers in the schematic handling of machine tools, but they can also, thanks to artificial intelligence, replace workers in occupations that require higher intellectual qualifications. This makes the current situation in the economy reminiscent of the times when the Wave of Mechanization in Agriculture caused the number of agricultural workers to fall from 50% of the population (in the 19th century in the US and Western Europe) to about 2% in 2020. In this case, the Information Wave reduced employment from the Industrialization Wave, and "idle" employees needed to be retrained from being mechanical engineers to IT professionals. However, this did not apply to all workers who were made redundant. Those who failed to retrain went to work in fast-food restaurants and pizza delivery. This is why now we are dealing with structural unemployment, which should rather be called "persistent unemployment". Although statistics may show low unemployment, the question is whether workers are being paid in the service industry as they were before in manufacturing. The unemployment statistics do not display this kind of change in the nature of work. Nevertheless, some economists optimistically say there is always a job for them; however, they fail to mention that the jobs are often degrading and low paying.

The solution to this issue is a policy of improving the qualifications of redundant workers through training provided by employers and governments. However, the fact of the matter is a machine tool operator will not make as much a robot designer or medical doctor. Furthermore, a more extreme line of argumentation—one advanced by a young English economist, Daniel Susskind—is that human work will end (due to informing technology), just as horse work ended, despite lasting for many millennia (Susskind, 2020). He also claims, even with optimism, that people will happily live without work. For him, the problem of a laborless economy lies in the considerable wealth inequalities between workers and owners; however, he does not provide a solution to this problem. In addition, he predicts employees will be laid off by the AI Wave. His solution for this problem is Universal Basic Income (UBI), which is similar to a kind of unemployment insurance (Susskind, 2020, p. 120-121). He should be aware that this idea is like communism, where everybody receives equal pay.

Susskind probably thinks that people who lack permanent work but receive benefits will partake in entertainment and prayers and concentrate on raising children. He is wrong. These people will sooner or later organize and start a social revolution. The first inklings of such a strategy are visible in the election platforms of presidential candidates from the American Democratic Party in 2020. It should be recalled that the United States has not yet experienced any large-scale social revolution in its almost 250-year history. The often-mentioned American Revolution of the 18th century was a struggle for independence from British dominion. The Civil Rights Movement of the 1960s, on the other hand, was not a revolution but active civic insubordination in favor of these rights.

Are advances in technology an inevitable driving force behind our lives, just as one might say that a lack of electricity inevitably would cause houses to go dark? However, in such a case, we would not allow ourselves to remain in the dark, but would repair the power supply system. Similarly, with the AI Wave, we should not view it as an inevitability that it will eliminate human work. After all, in medicine, it has been determined that cloning humans is prohibited, despite the fact that it is likely possible to give birth to and raise humans with high intelligence by manipulating genetic engineering. We do not do this because, in such attempts to create a superior human, one could make a mistake and generate a monster that would exterminate us in the likeness of our *Cro-Magnon* ancestors, who put an end to *Neanderthals*. After all, we communicated better than they did and were better organized. Thus, we were smarter.

If we allow human labor to be eliminated, we must also accept humanistic degradation, but in the name of what? What good does a laborless economy bring to civilization? As it would seem, it will permit boundless free time, which most people will "kill" with fun and alcoholism or narcotics. It will resemble the narcotized Chinese in the 19th century when the British used Indians to sell opium in China because it made the Chinese easier to rule. The Soviets used similar policies on their citizens by promoting the sale of alcohol because intoxicated citizens were more tractable to govern.

Therefore, it is necessary to break the strategy of Big Tech companies, which see the progress of informing technology as imminent, and instead, to legally prevent such progress so as to assure human labor will not be replaced by artificial intelligence. Too see this, one simply has to ask the question: what is to be done with 150 million American workers or 18 million Polish workers? What are they supposed to do if business replaces them with robots and machines powered by AI? The boilerplate answer today is that these people need to be better educated and take over highly skilled jobs. While this is true, in large societies, everyone cannot be doctors, lawyers, surgeons, or professors. On the other hand, everyone cannot be waiters or caretakers of the elderly either. The balance between employment groups must be maintained, for a happy person is not one for whom the machine works, but one that creates the work process itself.

Therefore, the policies put forth by several countries as solutions to the deindustrialization crisis are questionable. Innovation in the service economy amounts to the further elimination of jobs. For example, the ICT-based automation of customer service is almost complete now in the U.S. This has resulted in destroying the human contact between customers and service agents (often after-sales) and replacing that contact with automated expert systems.

The push by IT companies to develop a laborless economy is likely to have the following effects:

1.   People living on social benefits will not be good consumers, causing the economy to decline. This will lead to the "suicide" of business through short-sighted policies aimed at reducing production costs through robotization and automation.
2.   People who are out of work will degenerate as a result of not needing to solve problems and isolating themselves from other people since they do not go to work.
3.   Most universities will be closed because the education of unemployed and idle people has no purpose. There will also be no resources available for universities since the owners of the robot society will not see the purpose in educating the unemployed (this will prevent the unemployed from sometimes knowing too much and from creating trouble for the owners).
4.   Robots will likely take care of their own training, functioning, and development, especially robot builders.
5.   The number of crimes committed by desperate people as well as sizeable social unrest—including "correcting" society in revolutionary ways—is likely to increase. The unemployed are perhaps leading to the defeat of robots.

The following laws should guide IT professionals in their ethics-driven work:[4]

The Universal Laws of Asimov-Targowski-Krawczyk

1.   The most important value and the primary decision-maker in any civilization is humankind.
2.   Smart objects can perform an overarching role, but they must obey every human order, except for orders contrary to Law I.
3.   AI agents should take care of their existence as long as this is not contrary to Laws I and II.

NEW ROLES FOR WORKERS IN THE DIGITAL ECONOMY

Are these laws respected at present in the 21st century? Probably not. Few IT professionals know about them. State standardization committees and professional associations are too weak to force their members to apply them. Global companies, including many IT companies, do not use them and do not intend to apply them. Finally, politicians have "more important" issues on their minds.

As a result of the new requirements of employers, the following roles for workers have emerged, each of which should be unquestionably committed to ethical practices in digitalizing one's social milieu (Susskind & Susskind, 2015):

- *The role of experts* is to look after the development of their knowledge, wisdom, and contacts in order to be able to solve complex problems and to be relied upon by employers and other recipients seeking advice and solutions.
- *The role of professionals* is to perform their work at the expected level following the techniques typical of the given profession. For example, they may have degrees in medicine, engineering, or law (such as judge, attorney, or prosecutor).
- *The role of assistants* is to know their profession well even though they are not experts. Still, they are capable of cooperation with experts in their field. For example, this role is played by assistants of lawyers and prosecutors, staff in patient registration in clinics and hospitals, specialists in the calculation of taxes, auditors of financial statements, and others. Unfortunately, as a result of computerization, the workforce of this group is shrinking.
- *The role of paraprofessionals* is to provide expert knowledge using information systems involved with this type of expertise, but at low costs. For example, this could include a young university lecturer who applies an online world-class computerized expert lecture, or it could include a good blogger who knows how to learn from social networks and provides information in professional formats to readers who subscribe to his/her blog. There are also many para-professionals who speak out on fashion issues, based on over-the-top knowledge from experts and celebrities.
- *The role of life coaches* is to help people in need of emotional support in their struggles with the difficulties of their fate. Unfortunately, many experts cannot emotionally support their clients. These include, for instance, surgeons, who may lack manners in dealing with patients, lawyers, who may treat their clients heartlessly, and teachers, who may act harshly toward weaker students. The use of life coaches is wildly popular among outstanding athletes, who can afford to hire such specialists. These specialist help athletes succeed and accept defeat.
- *The role of researchers* is to study the problems of one's discipline and their societal implications. This is especially true for the consumer electronics and drug manufacturing industries, as they have a strategy of continuous innovation to regularly sell "new" devices, such as smartphones and medications for weight loss, sleep, and depression.
- *The role of knowledge promoters* is a new function: It is a role for experts who have decided to step out of their ivory towers and offer their services via social networking systems. Knowledge promoters might provide e-bulletins for a fee or free of charge, or they might provide newsletters in an attempt to increase web traffic to their site so that they can sell marketing ads. One such social networking system for sharing knowledge is *Quora*, which is a platform for asking questions and receiving answers that are provided by interested members of the platform.[5] The business model of this network is still in development.
- *The role of process analyzers* is to streamline or define requirements for computerization, robotization, and/or automation. This role requires an excellent working knowledge of a given process, and it is difficult to transfer to countries with cheap labor because the authenticity of the analysis would not be ensured.

- *The role of moderators* is to referee the online content of debates in social networks.
- *The role of informing systems designers* is to develop informatization, automation, and robotization.
- *The role of organizers and supervisors* is to develop operational information, robotization, and automation systems.

Other roles include that of *ICT executives and managers*; *ICT staffers*; *ICT systems service providers*; *data specialists* (especially those involved with Big Data in information systems, robotization, and automation); and *local and long-range network administrators*.

The way these roles are carried out is changing the way the current waves are modernizing civilization (Susskind & Susskind, 2015):

- Contact between professionals and users in informing technology systems are currently taking place *online,* while *face-to-face* (F2F) contact had previously been dominant in business. The use of online contact has encountered resistance from many non-working users who were accustomed to F2F.
- Regarding the costs of communication, continuing F2F is much more expensive than communicating online.
- The user should have a certain degree of tolerance for expertise provided *online* and expertise provided primarily by artificial intelligence. This expertise (such as the "Help" function) cannot be expected to be 100% accurate when, say, diagnosing a technological system failure. In this respect, AI is only as good as the knowledge and practice of the robot designer.

SUMMARY

So what is the future of informing technology? The following points are worth emphasizing:

1. Until countries develop computerization strategies based on strategic and ethical designs, solutions will be chaotic, costly, and harmful to humanism.
2. ICT companies will strive to develop increasingly "modern" IT systems and equipment that will expand the E-Global Village and bring civilization closer to the Death Triangle of Civilization.[6]
3. Governments currently do not regulate the development of global Big Tech companies in the name of "not constraining" technological progress.
4. Paradoxically, globalization will seek to maintain nation-states, which are now beginning to form ICT services to fight crime at their borders. For example, hackers shut down the Estonian Government and its banking system in 2007, and daily attacks on Internet news in the US are now taking place. Because of this, the UK and Swedish governments have a special law that allows them to control content entering the country via the Internet (Demchak & Dombrowski, 2011). In China, the information transmissions from abroad have been checked via the addresses of each computer. In this way, nation-states are forced to set up digital borders, even though in the European Union, interstate borders have been abolished. This is creating a real *New World Order.*
5. Informing technology is evolving from a tool that supports civilization to a tool that finishes civilization with a human face. Physics has developed similarly due to the development of nuclear weapons. The same individuals who invented this weapon were later opposed to it in the Pugwash

Movement (founded by Polish physicist Joseph Rotblat and English philosopher Bertrand Russell in 1957), for which they even received the Nobel Peace Prize in 1995. This author has undergone a similar transformation of attitude towards digitalization.

6.   Is ICT capable of being influenced by a similar initiative? In any case, ICT should first of all support the evolution of reason, because in reason's wise application lies the future of civilization. If the worst case scenario for the future development of civilization plays out in the next few years (the population continues to grow uncontrollably, ecology is destroyed, and strategic raw materials become depleted), then authoritarian governments will most likely come to the fore, and they will distribute vouchers /cards to regulate the consumption and use of raw materials (water, gasoline, uranium, food, and others). In this case, ICT systems will have to be adapted accordingly at the level of citizens, businesses, and the Government, the last of which will be in control of distributing the limited resources. Whether one likes it or not, democracy will not have a path forward, and the governments will resemble modern communist China, which has a strong central government and places many limitations on the freedom of citizens.

In the sense of a universal strategy, computerization should support and not eliminate the role of humans in work processes—of course, except for work that involves severe risks to human health and safety. Informing technology will be successful as long as it improves production and services and makes them more well-organized, effective, and environmentally friendly, otherwise, informing technology will be harmful. Finally, ICT must not enslave humans politically: above all, it must serve humankind in developing humanism and a sustainable civilization.

REFERENCES

Demchak, C. C., & Dombrowski, P. (2011). Rise of a cybered Westphalian age. *Strategic Studies Quarterly*, *5*(1), 32–61.

Kirsch, A. (2020, June 20). Looking forward to the end of humanity. *Wall Street Journal*. https://www.wsj.com/articles/looking-forward-to-the-end-of-humanity-11592625661

Susskind, D. (2020). *A world without work*. Metropolitan Books.

Susskind, R. E., & Susskind, D. (2015). *The future of the professions: How technology will transform the work of human experts*. Oxford University Press. doi:10.1093/oso/9780198713395.001.0001

Targowski, A. (2014). *The deadly effect of informatics on the Holocaust*. Tate Publishing.

KEY TERMS AND DEFINITIONS

Automation: The use of robots and automated processes to complete jobs, particularly in manufacturing and service industries.

Humanism: A worldview that places the well-being of humans and human flourishing as being centrally important. This contrasts with views that prioritize other strategic objectives, such as technological progress (as an end in itself).

Informing Science Disciplines: Disciplines that rely on informing science to solve key problems in their area of study. Examples include economics, biology, and medicine.

Informing Science Specializations: Specializations that rely on informing science to solve key problems in their area of study. Examples include software engineering and data governance.

Internet of Things: An interlinked network of physical devices and objects that exchange information with other objects via the Internet.

Laborless Economy: An economy that has been fully automated and no longer requires human labor.

Laws of IT: Laws that should regulate robots and AI to assure human flourishing.

ENDNOTES

[1] This date relates to the development of the World-Wide-Web, which enabled the development of web crawlers.

[2] This is a paraphrase of the word "smart" in English, indicating the use of artificial intelligence.

[3] For example, there is no mention of the French achievement of creating Gamma 60, the first big computer, which did not play the same kind of role in the development of supercomputers as did American Cray computers. Furthermore, the achievements of so-called "Turing Machines" of the English, which is a great intellectual "puzzle", have no practical applications. Similarly, there are a number of successful computer structures that have been displaced on the British market by American licenses and equipment.

[4] For more discussion on these issues, see the chapter *Digital Security Strategy*.

[5] This author currently (2020) has about 1.5 million readers on this network.

[6] This is discussed in the chapter *Digital Strategy for a Sustainable Civilization*.

Chapter 4
The History and Repercussions of Strategic Informing Technology

ABSTRACT

This chapter outlines the history of strategic informing technology as well as its implications and impacts. The chapter begins by examining major developments that occurred in the United States, including the use of punch card machines and the creation of the internet. Next, the chapter turns to Germany and documents how strategic informing technology was employed by the Nazi state to develop advanced weapons such as the V-1 and V-2 rockets and to record demographic data used in concentration and death camps. The chapter then considers major figures and developments that occurred in Britain, such as Alan Turing's development of the Turing Machine. Next is France, with an emphasis on the role played by the company Bull. Japan is then briefly examined followed by the USSR and Poland. The chapter then examines the first attempt at a national computer development program, which took place in Poland from 1971-1975. It concludes with an examination of the Polish national information system (INFOSTRADA) and a critical evaluation the Lange economic model.

UNITED STATES

The concept of informing technology, or informatics (automated information), was developed by the French in the mid-1960s; however, the machine "processing" of information (a term borrowed from engineering, which describes metalworking) is 130 years old. The development of counting machines is also long, going back several hundred years, but their strategic application began in the United States in the 19th century when the 1890 census was recorded on punch cards. The exigence for the use of these machines was created by a massive migratory wave from Europe to the eastern and midwestern US and from China to the western US (the latter were expanding the American railway infrastructure over a large country).

DOI: 10.4018/978-1-7998-8036-3.ch004

Then, in the wake of the Great Depression, President F. D. Roosevelt introduced a number for every citizen in 1935 in connection with the Social Security Fund. Because of this, punch card machines were further developed, as so-called "collator matching transaction cards" were added to citizens' files to update them and to print social security checks. This represented a significant strategic application of the mechanization of data processing for the national welfare system, and this system continues to be used up to the present in its same basic form.

During World War II, the strategic weapon was the atomic bomb, which was developed at a research facility in Los Alamos, New Mexico. What would come to be known as the "Manhattan Project" was overseen by Vannevar Bush (1890–1974), who at the time headed the Office of Scientific Research and Development (OSRD). Before joining the Government, he was vice president of MIT's famous polytechnic school and dean of the University's Faculty of Engineering. He is most famously known for his engineering work on analog computers beginning in 1927. Bush constructed a differential analyzer, an analog computer with some digital components that could solve differential equations with up to 18 independent variables. The rise of Bush and others at MIT was the beginning of digital circuit design theory. Memex, which began to be developed in the 1930s, was a hypothetical microfilm browser with a structure analogous to hypertext. Memex and Bush's 1945 essay, "As We May Think," influenced generations of computer scientists, who drew inspiration from his vision of the future. He had a significant influence on the thesis (1937) and doctoral dissertation (1941) of Claude Shannon (Figure 1). Shannon, in his first work, developed the basics of making electrical computations in the binary code of Boolean algebra, which replaced the counting systems on electromagnetic relays (which also gave rise to the development of computers). It should also be mentioned that Bush supervised the construction of the ENIAC electronic computer, which was used to calculate artillery firing tables after its completion in 1946. Its development, however, was not a strategic solution for Americans; instead, its creation is owed to Bush's scientific interest.

Figure 1. Left - Vannevar Bush (1890–1974), the first American advanced technology strategist; right - his student Claude Shannon (1916-2001), inventor of the 1937 electrical circuit system for calculations in binary code, which makes modern computers work (Photo: Wikipedia)

Moreover, US intelligence likely informed Bush that the German engineer Konrad Zuse was working on a digital computer at the Berlin University of Technology. At that time, the Germans did fully grasp the potential of computers, but nevertheless, they released Zuse from military service and allowed him to work creatively on his projects. In any case, the Americans undertook developmental work on the ENIAC during this time in WWII.

Strategic applications of computers in the US gained momentum after the launch of Sputnik in 1957 by the USSR. The Soviets aimed at getting out of the cordon around their country that had been created by military pacts between US and surrounding countries. The Americans responded by launching Apollo 1, which resulted in two astronauts landing on the moon in 1969. Apollo stimulated many areas of technology, resulting in more than 1,800 byproducts. The on-board computer used in both lunar and command modules was, in addition to the *Polaris and* Minuteman missile systems, the driving force behind early chip research. Until 1963, Apollo used 60 percent of the production of integrated circuits in the United States. The main difference between Apollo's requirements and those of missile programs was the much greater need for reliability in the Apollo program. While the Navy and Air Force were able to get around reliability problems by deploying more missiles, the political and financial costs of mission failures by the Apollo program were unacceptable. The Apollo project was made possible by the National Aeronautics and Space Administration's (NASA) adoption of new developments in semiconductor electronic technology, including field transistors with metal oxide and semiconductors (MOSFETs) in the interplanetary monitoring platform (IMP) and silicon integrated circuits in the Apollo Guidance Computer (AGC).

Since Apollo 1, IT has become strategic technology in the United States, resulting in the development of the Internet. The internet was developed in response to the Cuban Crisis of 1962. At the time, the US RAND Corporation, a US Air Force think-tank in Santa Monica, California, received an order from the Pentagon to develop a telecommunications system for a "day after" scenario (i.e., a nuclear attack from 100 tactical atomic bombs installed by the Soviet Union in Cuba). Because the current system was centralized and built like a star (see Figure 2), and the destruction of the center of the "star" destroyed communication. The task was entrusted to Paul Baran, born in Poland, who in 1962 invented a packet switching network. In this network the packet, that is, the electronic envelope, has the addressee's address, and packets are passed onto whatever telecommunication links are free. This led to the creation

Figure 2. Left - Paul Baran (1926-2011), inventor of the Internet, born in Grodno, Poland; right - topologies of centralized, decentralized, and distributed networks (Photo: Wikipedia)

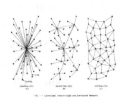

of the Advance Research Project Agency Network (ARPANET), which, at Paul Baran's request, was divided into the Milinet and the Internet in 1983.

Since then, computer networks have become a strategic system in both the US government and business. As part of this strategy, a system of geographical placement (GPS) for objects was developed, thanks to which (in addition to artificial intelligence) American aircraft can destroy someone in a bedroom while leaving the rest of the apartment untouched. This system is called "precision targeting", and it uses cruise missiles, a type of guided missile that stays in the atmosphere and flies for most of its flight path at a roughly constant speed. These missiles are designed to deliver a large warhead over long distances with high precision. Modern cruise missiles can travel at supersonic or high subsonic speeds, are self-adjusting, and can fly on a ballistic trajectory at a very low altitude. They are very dangerous because they are precise and effective. Recently, cheap but effective drones (remotely piloted) have become fashionable digital weapons (Figure 3).

Figure 3. An American computerized spy drone can provide accurate distance parameters for a rocket attack or kill the commander of enemy troops

Figure 4 provides the architecture of the US Department of Defense's Core Data Centers, which is characterized by advanced computerization and presentation.

The basis of the ICT strategy in the US is the proper development of ICT infrastructure, based on computer servers. Unfortunately, due to the relocation of manufacturing and production to Asia between 2000 and 2016, the United States has limited its research and development in servers. In fact, they have got rid of a large extent of their production. For example, IBM, which introduced the PC microcomputer standard, sold their research and production to Lenovo, which manufactures them in China and its US branches. Similarly, Apple has outsourced production to a company in Singapore that, in turn, produces Apple Mac Pro at its US branches!

In the early 1980s, there were about 200 companies producing microcomputers in the United States. In the 2020s, there are a few niche companies like Puget Systems and Lotus that produce PCs alongside large corporations such as Dell, which assembles computers from imported components. Similarly, HP is fighting the market, with 90% of its revenue coming from selling printers and ink. In the mainframe range, IBM and Unisys continue to manufacture and develop mainframes alongside a few specialized companies.

In a self-described way, social networks like Twitter and Facebook have become strategic ICT networks and systems. Because President Donald Trump communicates with the world via Twitter, there

Figure 4. The architecture of the US Department of Defense's Core Data Centers (CDC) demonstrates the complexity of computerization and the sophistication of its presentation (public version)

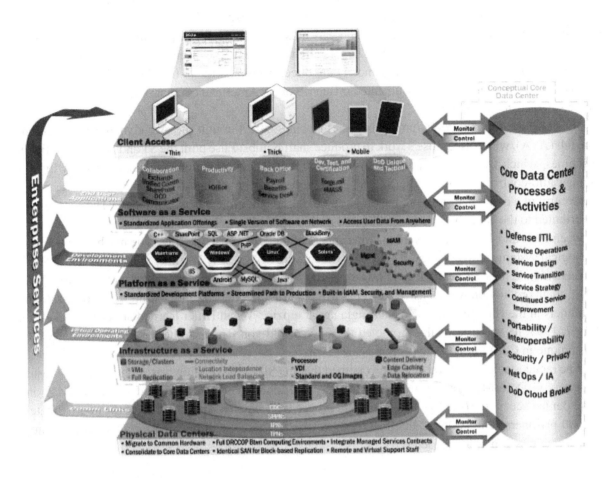

are many controversies. Furthermore, Facebook has become a censored platform for political marketing, and Big Tech companies have become strategic companies of American business, which are making money from the development of surveillance capitalism at the expense of the general good.

The 2020 pandemic has shown that, out of the ten essential medical products used by doctors and nurses in the US to treat infected patients, all are imported. This shock will probably cause the United States to produce essential goods in its own country, including PCs and servers. As it turns out, what is good for business is not good for society.

GERMANY

Nazi Germany was ruled by Adolf Hitler (1889-1945) for more than a decade, a man who did not graduate from high school and had an aversion to studying; however, he did show a passion for art and music.

Moreover, being a pathological anti-Semite, he did not like physics because he considered it "Jewish science." He gave the physicists six months to construct an atomic bomb that could not be built.

The Nazi authorities had an impassionate attitude towards the engineer Konrad Zuse (1910-1995), who was involved in constructing electric counting machines. In any case, he was not sent to the frontlines and was allowed to develop his machines at the Berlin University of Technology. Over time, he took on a strategic role in Germany's war machine. His most outstanding achievement was the world's first programmable computer. Because of this, Zuse is often considered the inventor of the modern computer. Due to World War II, Zuse's work was mostly unnoticed by the public in the United Kingdom and the United States. Perhaps his first documented influence on an American company was IBM's decision to purchase his patents in 1946.

In 1940, the German Government began financing Zuse through the Aerodynamische Versuch-sanstalt (AVA), which used Zuse's work to produce shaft bombs. Zuse built the S1 and S2 computational machines, which were special-purpose systems that calculated aerodynamic patches on the wings of flying radio-controlled bombs. The S2 had an integrated analog-to-digital converter, which was under the control of a computer program, making it the first computer to control the process. These machines contributed to the Henschel Werke Hs 293 and Hs 294 guided missiles, developed by the German army between 1941 and 1945. These were the forerunners of modern cruise missiles. The machines were also the logical systems for the V1 and V2 rockets, which were designed by Wernher von Braun (1912-1977) in Peenemünde near Szczecin at first; however, after the British bombed the factory on August 17-18, 1943, their production was transferred to the Mittelbau-Dora concentration camp in Nordhausen and to tunnels in the Harz mountains in Thuringia near Leipzig.[1] When Hitler learned about V2 rockets on July 7, 1943, he enthusiastically promoted the 31-year-old von Braun to the rank of professor, which was unique in Germany at such a young age.

The racial ideology of Nazi Germany claimed that the Slavic population was subhuman. As a result, prisoners in Dora-Mittelbau were treated brutally and inhumanely: they worked 14 hours a day and were denied access to basic hygiene, beds, and proper food rations. About a third of the approximately 60,000 prisoners sent to Dora-Mittelbau died because of these conditions or were murdered because they participated in acts of sabotage.[2]

Figure 5. Left - 31-year-old Konrad Zuse (1910-1995); right - 29-year-old Major SS Wernher Von Braun (1912-1977). They were the magic "youth" of German technology. Von Braun would later head of the American space program Apollo 1. K. Zuse, on the other hand, had a monument at his birthplace erected after the war (Photo: Wikipedia)

The V-weapons, known in its original German as *Vergeltungswaffen* ("retribution weapons"), were a unique set of long-range artillery weapons designed to strategically bomb cities. The weapons consisted of a V-1 "cruise-missile," a V-2 ballistic missile that used liquid fuel, and a V-3 gun. All of these weapons were intended for use in the military campaign against Britain. However, only the V-1 and V-2 were used in the 1944-45 campaign. After the Allied invasion of Europe on June 6, 1944, these weapons were also used against targets on the European continent, mainly in France and Belgium. The V-gun was used to terrorize and kill about 18,000 people, mostly civilians. The main targets were the cities of London, Antwerp, and Liège. The V-1 and V-2 rockets belonged to the *Wunderwaffen* ("miraculous weapons") of Nazi Germany. Germany was losing the war in 1944 and hoped that these missiles would turn the tide in their favor. The V-2 rocket contained the digital-logic system (which gave the rockets their accuracy) constructed by Konrad Zuse, who became, together with Wernher von Braun, strategic innovators of these "miraculous" German weapons.

In terms of the strategic application of digitalization in armaments, the Germans came to understand its potential at the end of the war and attempted to implement these weapons. On the other hand, regarding the implementation of *lebensraum*—that is, the policy aimed at creating "living space" in the East, which was a criminal ethnic policy from the very beginning of the Nazi regime—the Nazis used the mechanization of data processing to record information about ethnic and non-desirable groups. To this end, they supported the development of IBM under the German name "Dehomag" as early as the 1930s, which had American management. After the outbreak of the war with the US on December 11, 1941, the Germans nationalized IBM's business. At the head of the company and its branches were put German Nazis, but all the IBM specialists were retained, for they knew it would not be easy to train as efficient professionals as Americans. Interestingly, IBM moved its European headquarters from occupied Paris to Geneva in neutral Switzerland to be close to its branches in Germany. The idea was to keep IBM machines moving through the supply of spare parts, punch cards, etc.

Is it incredible that an American company was doing business with a country with which the United States was waging an openly bloody war at the time? Professor Thomas Carey claims that in this way, the Americans had their spies in the middle of the German Empire.[3]

The German strategy was to use punch card machines to record information about Jews, Gypsies, and other categories of people that need to be "addressed" and possibly eliminated. That is why Hollerith machines became a fundamental technology of the German administration, which for IBM meant significant profits from renting them, provided that they were well maintained and quickly repaired in the event of a failure. The German administration achieved its high-efficiency thanks to IBM machines, e.g., state railways were able to book tickets for 140 million passengers. Demand for IBM machines grew every day, requiring an increase of 1,000 jobs at the Dahomag plant in Lichterfelde. IBM machines contributed to the flourishing of scientific racism in Germany, which resulted in the racial conceptions of Jews and Aryans as well as, as a consequence, who has the right to live and who does not. This occurred when so-called "eugenics" was a prominent pseudoscience in the world. The IBM data machines allowed the Nazis to classify the ratio of "Jewishness" into levels of 100%, 50%, 25%, 12%, and even 5% thanks to analyses of genealogy records as well as records of marriages and divorces. Hitler used such data when granting citizenship and the status of being "Aryan". In fact, during the Battle of Stalingrad in 1942, he spent more time analyzing this ethnic data for potential Aryans than information about the course of the battle. Thus, IBM machines helped define who was "German": It could only be an Aryan, a person of the pure Nordic race who gave rise to a pure Germanic race whose representatives came from the mythical Atlantis.

Information on this subject, derived from mechanized censuses and population records in the Reich Statistical Offices, gave rise to the expansion of government offices that conducted further research on the racial backgrounds of German inhabitants. These offices included the Office of Racial Policy in the

Figure 6. The architecture of the German Information System for the Management of Concentration Camps. Source: Targowski, 2014, p. 97.

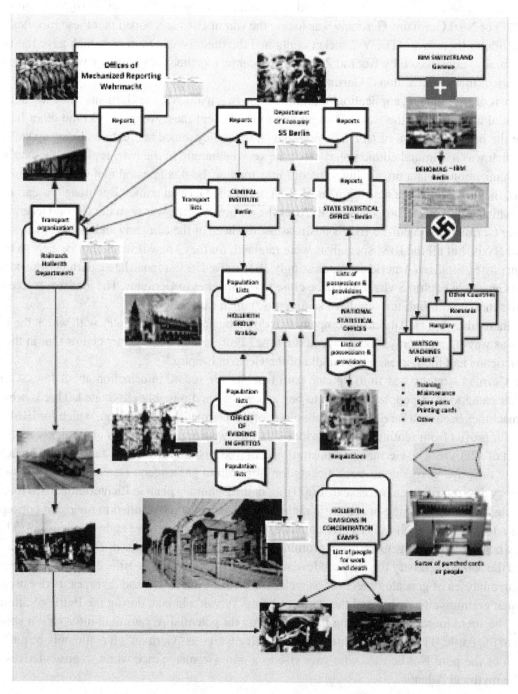

Führer's Office, the Ministry of Propaganda, the Reich Committee for the Protection of German Blood, the Health Care Office of the Ministry of the Interior, the Department of Justice and Home Affairs, and Genetics and Racial Hygiene.

The Nazi Party maintained racial policies via organizational units. The SS offices used information about the race of the German population to run death factories in concentration camps. The Reich Family Office, on the other hand, was the highest-ranking office that decided who was Jewish and who was Aryan. The obsession of the Germans with race was not limited to determining who was Jewish but had the goal of making the "real" German a tall blonde with blue eyes and physically and intellectually dominant.

As Germans died in the war, the Nazis held meetings with potential mothers and fathers (strangers to each other) to encourage procreation of such "perfect" Germans. For this purpose, women from Norway and Denmark were used, and, among the men, it was possible to meet "beautiful" Poles, whom the Germans selected from concentration camps or street roundups. The statistical and demographic information (including health) recorded by IBM machines was also used to decide who was productive and useful to the Reich and who needed to be sterilized and/or eliminated from society.

The corresponding codes on punch cards were used to sort and count how many people should be eliminated. For example, the code "1" meant socially harmful; the code "2" meant mental illness; the code "3" meant crippled; "4" meant blind; and "5" meant deaf. Professions and diseases were recorded via codes. If the relevant offices could not rent machines for their needs, they sent data forms to Dahomag branches for processing.

In 1934, based on information developed via IBM machines, the Court of Genetic Health issued forced sterilization sentences for 62,400 people and, a year later, 71,700 people. Each year between 1934 and 1939, Dehomag increased the number of customers who rented Hollerith machines or used data processing centers owned by IBM companies. The scope of these services consisted primarily of calculations concerning the Jewish population and their bank accounts, which, over time, were requisitioned by the German authorities.

The seizure of Poland by Germany on September 1, 1939 increased the demand for Hollerith analytical machines (IBM). Hitler's plan included the murder of 3 million Polish Jews, 2 million Poles, 100,000 Gypsies, and citizens of France, Italy, Greece, Hungary, Czechoslovakia, and other countries. These people were arrested and put in concentration camps, which required the systematic supply of all kinds of materials and food as well as the scheduling required for the mass killing of temporary residents of these camps. These types of logistics were well organized with the help of IBM machines.

The Germans were making censuses via punch card machines in occupied European countries. Gradually, such information was further developed through an integrated complex of information systems. Its architecture is shown in Figure 6. The basis of this system was the prisoner's punch card, which had the following codes:

- Prisoner number - XXXXXX (six or five digits punched in columns from 22 to 27).
- Date of birth: column 5.
- Arrested by special police: 1 in column 2.
- Date of arrest (e.g., October 5, 1942): 2 in section 3.
- Spanish Communist: 6 in column 4.
- Male: 1 in column 6.
- Bachelor: 1 in column 7.

- Child: a hole in column 8.
- Others.

The prisoners were coded in the following 16 categories: 1. Political prisoner. 2. Bible Researcher. 3. Homosexual. 4. Expelled from the army. 5. Priest, religious. 6. Spanish Communist. 7. Foreign civilian employee. 8. Jew. 9. Antisocial. 10. Common criminal. 11. Significant criminal. 12. Gypsy. 13. Prisoner of War. 14. Hidden prisoner. 15. Hard work prisoner. 16. Diplomat.

Each new prisoner received a 5-digit number upon arrival, along with a symbol sewn to the chest for easy identification by the camp service. For example, political prisoners had a red symbol, and homosexuals a pink one. Criminals were given a green symbol. The Jews, on the other hand, wore a double white triangle in the form of the Star of David. The *Zentral Institute* in Berlin recorded the type of death with the following codes:

- Natural Death - C-3.
- Execution - D-4.
- Suicide - E-5.
- Special treatment by SS - F-6.

Thus, these punch card machines and their codes helped to develop this mechanized political-ethnic system. One of the punch cards is shown in Figure 7.

Figure 7. IBM punch card (Photo: public domain)

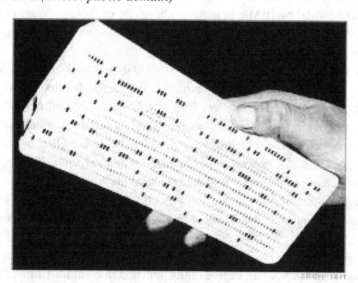

Millions of such cards had to be printed, and this was an excellent business for Dahomag. Also, card punching machines and verifying machines had to be provided that could repeat the punching processes without damaging the cards. For verifying machines, if a code matched a certain set criterion, the card went for further processing, e.g., sorting, matching, tapping, and printing.

In each concentration camp, there was a Hollerith Department (*Abteilung Hollerith*) that kept records of the camp, reports, and punch cards for each prisoner. The running of such a detailed bureaucracy was usually carried out by the prisoners themselves, who realized what kind of data they were processing but could do nothing about it. Reports and punched cards were sent to the Hollerith Group, which employed 500 people in Krakow. From there, they were sent to the Central Institute (*Zentral Institut*) in Berlin (at Friedrichstrasse 129 Block F) and then further to the State Statistics Office and the Department of Economy in the SS agency. This department conducted an assessment of the capacity of the camps as well as the number of people waiting for transportation and extermination (Jews). Within an hour of leaving the train, the prisoners were already dead.

As part of the capacity analysis, the Berlin Department organized new transports, sending lists to the railways (to prepare trains) and to the camps to speed up executions or to supplement groups for work. The starting point was usually the census of the region concerned. In Krakow, there was a National Bureau of Statistics, employing 600 people. Here, records of belongings and food were drawn up, followed by lists of items the Germans requisitioned among the population. At the head of the SS apparatus of violence stood the notorious Heinrich Himmler, second after Hitler, who was the central, most hardened administrator of ethnic cleansing and destruction, with help from the extensive Gestapo apparatus, police, and SS.[4]

Himmler, aware of the richness of information and documentation confirming the facts of the mass genocide, ordered that the files, transactions, and printouts documenting the operations of the death factories be destroyed before the expected seizure of the camps by the Allies in the spring of 1945. He reframed concentration camps as "labor camps" and advanced the propaganda that if someone died in them, it was due to illness or an epidemic. Himmler delivered this opinion to the Delegate of American Jews from New York, Norbert Masur (1901-1971), in a letter in March 1945 that attempted to negotiate the purchase of 10,000 Jewish women from concentration camps. The deal was opposed by Hitler but ended up saving several thousand prisoners of Scandinavian, Polish, and other ethnic backgrounds, who were deported to Sweden by so-called white buses.[5]

Without Hollerith's machines, the German machinery of genocide would not have been so efficient, and the Department of Economy of the SS in Oranienburg had great "discernment" in the placement of specialists using the machines. Furthermore, on each punch card that recorded prisoner data was the proudly printed symbol of the card manufacturer, Dahomag, once owned by IBM. Beginning in 1942, Jews began to be systematically murdered, according to these prisoner cards. The entire Jewish population was dismantled as part of the *Final Solution* planned by Adolf Eichmann. This Holocaust program was led by Reinhard Heydrich (who was overzealous to get rid of the suspicion that he is of Jewish origin), the head of the SS, and Heinrich Müller, head of the Gestapo. Their right hands were Roderich Plate, an expert on the ethnic census, and Richard Kerher, a specialist in Hollerith machines. This group had different census variants in the conquered areas compared to England and Ireland, where there was no German occupation.

The flow of information between IBM customers made completing tasks more efficient, which in this case meant the systematic extermination of the Jewish people. Lists of Jews were supplied by the Hollerith machines. They showed 11 million Jews in Europe, including England and Ireland, and 5 million in Russia, all of whom would have to be "liquidated." It was planned that two-thirds of this population would be killed in the camps by debilitating work or death in gas chambers. However, it is believed that the total number of Jews destined for the Holocaust was at that time overstated. Furthermore, the Final Solution was not 100% completed: Six million Jews were murdered. It is a considerable number, and a human tragedy unparalleled due to its bestial nature. Indeed, as the motion to implement this plan accelerated, individual Jewish prisoners no longer received Prisoner Cards because their names did not matter: They were simply a crowd to kill. They were dead within an hour of leaving the train, and in Auschwitz, groups of up to 2,000 people were killed at the same time. The total number of dead was sent to the Central Institute in Berlin.

Mass exterminations of Jews in mechanized records were reduced to the numbers in the transports, as all were sent to be killed. In this mass murder experiment, the Germans only had the "scientific" problem of how to get rid of hundreds of thousands of corpses. Today, after more than 75 years, it is clear that the information system architecture of the SS coincides with the logic of modern enterprise information systems. These systems can be analyzed and compared as follows:

- **The Bill of Material Processor (BOMP)**: The BOMB is a list of parts for product components. This is equivalent to the "censuses" compiled at the Ghetto statistical centers and aggregated in the Hollerith Group in Krakow, which were then detailed for each wave of arrests at the SS Central Institute in Berlin.
- **The Material Requirements Planning I (MRP I)**: Also known as planned material needs, this is equivalent to the lists of requirements needed for the transport of prisoners to concentration camps.
- **MRP II**: This is equivalent to planning the capacity of rail transports at a particular time in order to assure the transportation of the scheduled number of arrested people during the scheduled phase of arrest.
- **Shop-Floor Operations**: This is the planning and operational control of production, which is equivalent to the lists of the dead, that is, "freed" places in the concentration camp, to which new "resident" could be brought.

Based on these experiences, or unaware that such events took place, IBM developed two *comprehensive production information control systems* (PICS) in the 1960s and an upgraded version, the *communication-oriented production control system* (COPICS), in the 1970s.

A certain piquancy is added by the fact that at the end of the 20th century IBM withdrew from the development and sales of the aforementioned software systems and resold its solutions to the German company SAP, which is now the largest provider of this kind of software in the world. It turns out that Germans feel better about comprehensive management in large-scale systems than Americans. Is this due to war experiences and an emphasis on order, as is apparent from the proverb *Ordnung muss sein* (*there must be order*)?

Undoubtedly, in this computerized genocide, there were two similar systems of work, which were based on workers being thorough and diligent in the performance of their duties. Such were the Americans in the industrial revolution in the early and mid-20th century. Both systems, supported by analytical machines, improved work efficiency, and for Americans, working with the Third Reich (since 1933) was good for business. In this blinding modern work, aided by the mechanization of data processing, these people did not delve into the ethical consequences of their work, even though it was morally deplorable.

As a result of the mechanization of the data in the conquered nations of Germany, some 4 million people were murdered, including 2.5 million Jews, 0.9 million Poles, 0.4 million Western Europeans (French, Italians, Greeks, Belgians, Dutch, and others), and 0.2 million Roma (Gypsies). This represents

13% of all civilians murdered in the German crimes against humanity in Europe during World War II (Targowski, 2014; World War II casualties, n.d.).

After World War II, Germany began to rebuild its country, which had been divided into four zones: a US zone, British zone, French zone, and Soviet zone. This lasted from 1945 to 1949, when there was created the Federal Republic of Germany and the German Democratic Republic. During the Allied occupation, IBM regained its Dehomag-nationalized branches and, with its vast experience, began to mechanize and automate the processing of Dehomag's data. In this way IBM helped to implement the Marshal Plan in 1948, which provided capital to American and German companies for development. In the French sector, Bull sold its punch card machines, and in the UK sector, companies such as Ferranti and Elliott sold digital cameras.

In this situation, Konrad Zuse began to develop his computers with the foundation of Zuse KG in 1949. The Z4 was completed and delivered to the ETH Technical University in Zurich, Switzerland, in September 1950. It was the only working computer in continental Europe and the second computer to be sold. Other computers, all marked with the letter Z (up to Z43), were built by Zuse and his company. Notable are the Z11, which was sold to the optical industry and universities, and the Z22, the first computer with magnetic memory. By 1967, Zuse KG had built a total of 251 computers. Due to financial problems, however, the company was eventually sold to Siemens.

While the French IT industry is, to some extent, a wasted opportunity industry, the West German IT industry is an industry of "missed" opportunities.

Although Siemens & Halske (founded in 1848) was great at producing multiple electrical products at the time, it was not well-known in computer construction. In 1958, the company made a specialized computer for booking seats at events and on railways. In the late 1960s, the company purchased a license for the American RCA Spectra 70 (a copy of IBM 360), sold under the name Siemens 4004. Using this computer, the company computerized IT support for the 1972 Munich Olympic games. To meet its needs, Siemens developed the GOLEM and PRISMA software for remote (online) processing.[6]

After RCA faded from computer production and IBM 370 machines were introduced, Siemens computers became obsolete. To save its reputation, the company, together with the French company CII, created the Unidata project. The European market was divided into sales zones, and the company planned to produce the Unidata 7000, which was compatible with IBM 370 subsystems. It was a long-awaited undertaking as a response to the "American challenge."

Between 1974 and 1975, it became clear in Europe that the market expected smaller computers to facilitate *distributed computing*. Success in this direction was to be achieved by the American PDP mini-computers and the IBM machine concept under the name "Future System". The IBM series never came into use; however, the announcement of this concept showed that the planned Unidata machines were not a viable solution. Unidata broke up in 1975. Honeywell-Bull merged with CII because the French trusted American technology more than they did Unidata. The Dutch company Philips, which joined Unidata, abandoned the production of main-frame computers in favor of minicomputers.

Siemens, on the other hand, was looking for a connection with the Japanese company Fujitsu, which had a close relationship with the American company Amhdal (whose founder was at one time the primary builder of IBM 360/370 machines). As a result, Siemens formed a joint computer division with Fujitsu, but only in 1999. Before this, in 1990 Siemens had absorbed the fourth largest computer company in Europe, Nixdorf, which was founded in 1952. The company specialized in the production of BNC 886 (*Branch Network Computers*)—minicomputers for banking purposes—as well as cash registers that operated online with computers. In total, Nixdorf made 200,000 minicomputers of this type. Also established in 1999, the Siemens-Fujitsu-Nixdorf division was a well-conceived merger; however, it did not survive the invasion of American and then Asian microcomputers, and it disintegrated in 2009. Siemens ceased to be a computer company, although it has become one of the most advanced companies globally, specializing in the automation of production and transport processes. Nixdorf, on the other hand, has merged with Wincor and still operates today in the field of small computing for business needs.

The reason for the weak development of west Germany's IT industry was its strong economy, which was able to afford to import the best American and, more recently, Asian equipment. Thus, despite its significant industrialization, Germany is not a leader in the construction and production of computers. Only in end-to-end systems do companies use software from SAP *(Systemanalyse und Programmentwicklung* — System Analysis and Program Development), which has 40 percent of the world market in this software category. The company was founded in 1972 by former IBM employees (Dietmar Hopp, Klaus Tschira, Hans-Werner Hector, Hasso Plattner, and Claus Wellenreuther). They were acquainted with the US IBM PICS and IBM COPICS. These systems offered comprehensive software for many enterprise functions. When IBM withdrew from developing and selling such systems, these employees left the company and founded their own SAP company, and the R/1, R/2, and R/3 systems (subsequent versions of SAP) were based on an improved design of the US system. This was a mistake by IBM, which in the 1990s returned to selling and installing enterprise service systems (called *Enterprise Resources Planning* or *ERP)*. However, IBM has focused on SAP delivery in the absence of having up-to-date solutions.

In conclusion, Germany is currently basing its computerization on imported equipment and is subject to the strategic development of state-owned information technology in the European Union.

UNITED KINGDOM

In the 19th century, Britain was the most substantial empire globally, dominating the world from the beginning of Queen Victoria's reign (1837) until the beginning of World War I (1914). The British Empire initiated the Industrial Revolution in the 19th century, which radically changed the world in the following centuries. In addition, the Englishman Charles Babbage (1791–1871) made outstanding achievements in computers with his work on differential and analytical "engines" (i.e., machines). Although these projects did not contribute to the rapid evolutionary development of computational technology, it was only after 100 years that civilization began to work on similar machines (Randell, 1973).

Regarding to the history of Babbage's invention, his idea was far ahead of the needs of users and, therefore, could not be adequately appreciated. It would seem that many computer builders found themselves in a similar situation in the 1950s and 1960s. It is also necessary to pay attention to the significant role of the state as a mecenate, which in this case as well as many others did not rise to the occasion.

In the United Kingdom, the further development of computers would wait until the Second World War (1939 – 45). Progress in this area is linked to Alan Turing (1912–1954), a mathematician who, while studying in America, published the work "on computable numbers"[7] in 1937. In describing this process, he came to the concept of a universal automatic machine, later called the "Universal Turing Machine". The hypothetical machine is composed of a tape scroller with registered binary digits. The machine's head reads the numbers and then moves the tape. It is a logical machine, the simplicity of which has served as a measure of the ability of other machines. This machine can calculate everything that is computable.

Turing came to the concept of the Universal Turing machine during his doctoral studies at Princeton University at the Institute of Advanced Studies (where Albert Einstein and John von Neumann worked) between 1936 to 1938. He did not accept an offer from John von Neumann to become his assistant and instead returned to England.

Turing would benefit from creating his universal counting machine when breaking German ciphers while working for English intelligence before and during World War II. After returning from the United States in September 1938, he took a part-time job at the British Ministry of Foreign Affairs, and then, after the start of the war in September 1939, he moved to work at Bletchley Park, a famous British intelligence center. When first returning, he was sent with a Colonel of British Intelligence to Warsaw to get acquainted with the work of Polish mathematicians on deciphering the German Enigma Code (Polish intelligence had gotten ahold of a copy of the German encryption machine). At Bletchley Park, Turing worked closely with Polish mathematicians Marian Rejewski, Jerzy Różycki, and Henryk Zygelski on decoding German ciphers from German-conquered Poland (with the help of British intelligence).[8] At that time, he also met Claude Shannon, an American military encryption specialist who was in Bletchley Park for several months during time and who defended his doctoral thesis on binary code at MIT in 1937, which was the basis for the design of modern computers.

These essential and extensive contacts with who were then the most outstanding American and Polish mathematicians prepared Turing to propose the construction of an "electronic brain", later called an *Automatic Computing Engine* (ACE), which was also a reference to the Babbage engine. This machine was built in 1950 based on Turing's specifications but was initially developed at the National Physics Laboratory in Hampton back in 1946. The English consider ACE to be the first computer that they used for calculations and the world's first service computer.

Maurice Wilkes (1913–2010) was the second pioneer in developing computers in England. He built the modestly configured electronic delay storage automatic calculator (EDSAC) in 1949 at the University of Cambridge. He was familiar with the American electronic discrete variable automatic computer (EDVAC), which used a *stored program* concept developed by John von Neumann. He participated in the 1946 Symposium on Computers at Moore School at the University of Pennsylvania in Philadelphia, where the first American electronic computer, ENIAC (1946), was created. Since Turning was on sabbatical at Cambridge University in 1947, Wilkes often met with him and discussed the development of computing machines. Hence Wilkes was well acquainted with the development and design of early computers, and he decided to build one that would be reliable in operation and useful in applications at his university. This computer was made of proven components, such as memory on mercury pipes (which was also used later by the Polish XYZ computer in 1954).

The further advancement of computers in the United Kingdom was taken over by an industrial infrastructure that was well developed in the country, for this development had begun in the last century with the Industrial Revolution. Their well-developed industry helped the United Kingdom to win World War II (along with the Allies) in 1945. The fact that the industry took the initiative from universities in developing computer designs was a sensible move. It was considered an engineering rather than a scientific task, for only business could meet the enormous demand for these machines. This demand was created by the awareness of the potential applications of computers in the realm of analytical machine applications, which were widely used in the British capitalist economy.

Soon, J. Lyons & Co. and Elliott Brothers started to work on computers. Already in 1949, the former began work on the LEO I (Lyons electronic office I). This model was developed continuously so that in 1956 the LEO III had an ultra-fast photocopy printer that could print order cards for goods. In 1964, Lyons' computer division merged with English Electric and Marconi.

Elliott Brothers, on the other hand, was famous in Europe for producing the Elliott 803B, which had 2nd generation transistors (in collaboration with the American company Fairchild) for engineering calculations. Around 250 copies of this computer were made. This is a large number taking into account the early period of applying this type of computer in practice. The computer was programmed in the Mark II autocade and had storage on reels with magnetized tapes. In 1967, English Electric absorbed Elliott Brothers.

Until 1949, the British Tabulating Machine Company was involved in the sale and installation of IBM punch card machines. In 1959, this company merged with Powers Samas Accounting Machine Company (which manufactured Powers equipment, notable for a round hole in the card that was mechanically read). The newly formed company adopted the name International Computers and Tabulators (ICT). In the name was the announcement of the production of computers, but the term "tabulating," which was characteristic of punch card machines, was preserved. In the late 1950s, the company worked with the British General Electric Company on the ICT 1300. In the years that followed, the UK computer industry was consolidated, and engineers searched for the optimal computer for business and administration applications.

In England, during this pioneering period, computer production was geared towards users from engineering companies, as engineers were doing well with the complex electronic computing technology of the time. All the attention of computer builders was focused on the design of the central unit to the almost complete neglect of utility software. In particular, software for applications in business data processing and administration was not prioritized in development.

In the face of financial difficulties, ICT acquired an American license to manufacture the GE 400 (the French company BULL purchased the same license, and this computer was called "Gamma 30"). In England, this computer was called "ICT 1500". It was a mainframe computer. For smaller companies, ICT purchased a license for the UNIVAC 1004 minicomputer for data processing, calling it "ICT 1004". ICT, on the other hand, redesigned the ICT 1300 model in ICT 1301, hoping to find many users.

ICT's financial perils were temporarily relieved by subsidies from the Labour government and a government policy of preferring to buy English computers. The subsidies helped ICT to survive on the market and enabled them to produce 1,000 computers per year. ICT computers were also exported to France, Scandinavia, Italy, socialist countries, and commonwealth countries. ICT was similar to a half state-owned company (through constant grants and supervision), and many politicians were also placed in management positions. Hence, the company was rather poorly directed. As a result, under public pressure, ICT was merged with Plessey (data transmission) and English Electric and in 1968 became International Computers Limited (ICL). The co-shareholder of this new company was also the UK Government.

In 2002, ICL was acquired by the Japanese and was transformed into Fujitsu Services, based on IBM technologies and configurations. Fujitsu also bought Siemens Nixdorf Computers in 1999.

In the 21st century, the English economy transformed from an industrial economy into a service economy, which included a good deal of tourism and spectacular royal events put on by members of the royal family. As a result, the internal industrial development of computers completely froze. On the other hand, the country began to rely on computer imports from Asia. Great initial adventures and dedication to the development of computers by English computer pioneers have, to some extent, been wasted in England. However, two English men, Edgar F. Codd and Christopher Date, came up with the concept of relational databases, which are now widely used. When they invented this idea, they worked for IBM.

Today, after the pioneering work of the English, the splendor of the Turing Prize and the elite *British Computer Society* remain. In this way, the early English pioneers of computer technology have almost been given the status of the British royal family, which attracts tourists from abroad and maintains the service character of this country.

Since the rule of the "Iron Lady" Margaret Thatcher (1979-1990), Conservative Party governments have minimized the scope of public administration by using online services. The computerization strategy was subject to the EU strategy (discussed in Part IV); however, after Brexit and the Pandemic in 2020, there is probably no (for now) state-level computerization strategy. Business, on the other hand, is based on imported digital equipment (including critical software) and low-cost IT professionals from Poland and India who live in the country.

FRANCE

While the British industry began its development with medium-sized computers, the French industry started by producing large computers. Perturbations in the French information industry over computer needs were caused by the premature creation of a large computer, the Gamma 60 (1960). Later in 1966, conversely, perturbations arose because they did not have a supercomputer for atomic research for the so-called French *Force de Frappe*.

The French company Compagnie des Machines Bull was founded in 1931 and was based on a patent for 45-column cards, invented by the Norwegian Fredrik R. Bull (1882-1925). After World War II (1945), Bull produced distinguished punch card machines that competed effectively with IBM machines. In the early 1960s, Bull built and made a few Gamma 60 computers. The price of the machine at that time was a dizzying amount: 3 million dollars ($18 million by the standards of 2020). Not surprisingly, it was only ordered by entities such as the French Railways (SNCF), the Energy Board (*Electricite de France*), and wealthy insurance companies. This machine was created when it was thought that several computers of this type would meet all the needs of Europe. It was felt at that time that punch card machines would continue to be produced, while computers would be used only for particular applications. Based on this assumption, another original Bull construction was created: The Series 300 MCT (*Memoir Central Transit*). This was a hybrid of a punch card machine and a computer (MCT) programmed internally. Simultaneously, input and output devices with collators/sorters were programmed from external program tables.

Both the Gamma 60 and the Series 300 MCT were considerable contributions of the French to the development of computer science. However, the Gamma 60 was made too early, and the Series 300 MCT was too late. In the early 1960s, the market had already accepted IBM's information processing concepts in the form of IBM 1400 machines. In this situation, Bull purchased a license for the RCA 301 (together with the English company ICT/ICL) and produced it under the name "Gamma 30". The Series 300 MCT was used in such a way that the machine eventually was simplified into the world's first minicomputer for data processing, the Gamma 10. The production of this machine reached several thousand units, and over the next few years, the revenues from its sale were the basis for Bull's existence.

In the 1960s, Bull competed with the invasion of American computers, which were better programmed than its own machines. It had to expand its software and service center, which required a substantial investment. In 1963, Bull (51%) merged with the American company General Electric (GE) (49%), which produced GE 200, GE 400, and GE 600 computers. The merger led Bull to make the GE 400 in 1965 under the name "Gamma 40". This was the second American computer produced by BULL.[9]

In 1966, the US government imposed an embargo on selling the US supercomputer CDC 6600 for French atomic research. This led to efforts to revive the development of French computer production. Under the personal supervision of President Charles de Gaulle, the *Plan Calcul* was created to finance the creation of the French IT industry in the late 1960s. As a result of this plan, the company CII *(Compagnie International pour Informatique)* was established, composed of the computer divisions CITEC *(Compagnie Europeenne d'Automatisme Electronique)* and Jeumont-Schneider *(SAE-Societe d'Automatisme Electronique)*. There was also *Delegue pour l'Informatique,* which aimed to coordinate and supervise the implementation of the Plan Calcul. It is worth noting that the cradle and backbone of the French IT industry, Bull, did not participate with CII because it was linked to the American company GE.

The paradox of the Calcul Plan lies in two facts. First, CII based its designs on the American SDS Sigma machine patterns, producing the CII 10070 and CII 10010 (a computer later made in Hungary under the name "R10"). Second, after ten years, CII merged with BULL, which in the meantime had been bought from GE by another American company, Honeywell. Both GE and SDS withdrew from the IT industry at that time. The resources remained French, while the management fell into American hands (as in the English company ICL). The French IT industry can thus be called a wasted opportunity industry. As a consequence, the leading suppliers of computers on the French market became two American companies: IBM and Honeywell.[10]

This "missed opportunity" was a crossroads between the interests of private capital, government, and US companies looking for a way into the market in Europe. In the literature, this period of computer science development in France is referred to as the "l'affaire Bull" and the "attack on *Plan Calcul.*" (Jublin & Quatrepoint, 1976).

- The first "Bull affair" took place in 1964. The Government tried to finance the company's shortages on the initiative of the Minister of Scientific, Nuclear, and Space Research, Gaston Palewski. The aid proved insufficient, and the Minister of Industry and Trade, Maurice Bokanowski, and Michale Poniatowski, Director of the Cabinet of the Minister of Finance (at that time, headed by Valery Giscard d'Estaing, who would later be President), gave the green light to the merger of Bull with the American company GE. Simultaneously, the French Government was forced to spend a much more considerable amount than its aid to Bull because it took about 200 million dollars to finance the creation of the domestic industry in creating CII.

- The second "Bull affair" took place in 1970, when GE completely withdrew from the computer business in the US and France. It was then possible to correct a previous error and connect CII with Bull. Since Honeywell bought the US computer manufacturing division from GE (making the computers GE 200, 400, and 600), it automatically took over Bull's market in France, which was supplied by GE. The French President George Pompidou did not refuse the head of GE (F. Borch) this sale, whom he visited with for breakfast in Paris. Since the French President had once refused Westinghouse Electric's bid at a large merger, he feared that a second refusal would curb foreign investments in France. Against this backdrop, the Delegate of the Government for Information Technology, Maurice Allegre, managed to negotiate a paragraph in the agreement guaranteeing the right of pre-redemption to the French Government if the new owner (Honeywell) intended to "trade" Bull, which was a French diamond in the beautiful crown of the impressive tradition of French mathematics and computer science.

- The third "Bull affair" involved the dissolution of the Office of the Delegate for Information Technology in late 1974. President Valery Giscard d'Estaing came to power in May 1974, and he was a great opponent of the Plan Calcul. Because of this, the French administration did not prevent the liquidation of CII and even contributed to it. In the 1984 election campaign, the Socialists (supporters of future president Francois Mitterand) proclaimed the need to nationalize Honeywell-Bull, while the Communists talked about taking over only 51% of the shares. Republicans, on the other hand, preached the sale of the company, which they did after winning the election.

Bull endured significant perturbations in the French electronics and information technology industry between 1960 and 1990. In the meantime, the US IT industry has begun to dismantle itself by moving the production of some computers to Asia.

Today, Bull is an independent, long-standing European manufacturer of a full IT hardware program in Europe that includes large, medium, and small servers, personal computers and smartphones, memory, and software.[11]

The computerization situation in France is similar to that in the UK and Germany, where IT hardware companies have developed great application systems in business. On one hand, well-developed online services dominate at the level of public administration. On the other hand, the overall computerization strategy is to implement the EU's computerization strategy, discussed in the chapter *Digital State Strategy*.

JAPAN

The Japanese IT industry was created from foreign licenses within multi-branch corporations. The core of Japan's IT industry in the 1970s was made up of six companies, two of which were independent computer companies (Fujitsu and Oki) and four of which were part of multibillion-dollar corporations: Hitachi, Mitsubishi, NEC, and Toshiba. The largest of these was Fujitsu (16 percent of the market). The development strategy of the Japanese IT industry in the 1970s was based on the following:

1. Develop ultra-modern technological solutions that would challenge American technology.
2. Coordinate the specialization of the six production companies by MITI (Ministry of Foreign Trade and Industry).
3. Increase exports in this domain substantially, which in 1975 accounted for only 5 percent.

Japan treats the IT industry as a socially suitable industry. Its manufacturing techniques are clean and do not endanger the environment. Hence, in Japan, the first Information Society Development Plan, formulated by Yoneji Masuda, was established in 1972. According to Masuda (1980), the purpose of this society was the following:

The development of a society in which intellectual creativity will dominate activities leading to a prosperous consumption of material goods.

One significant project was the conceptualization of *Cosmopolis*, a computerized city that included *computer-controlled vehicle systems* (CVS), purchases carried out in automated supermarkets, and health controlled by a regional computerized system with an automated hospital. This also included local heating and cooling systems and schools based on computer-aided learning. Finally, it included environmental protection based on a monitoring and regulation system, assisted by a computer.

The Japanese expected that such a developed information society should bring the following benefits:

- Increases in free time
- Liberation from cumbersome work
- Increases in value in the human life cycle
- Satisfaction with the updates
- Creation of an information service infrastructure
- Implementation of participatory democracy
- The emergence of voluntary environments
- Others

The Japanese Information Society's plan is being gradually implemented. However, the structural economic crisis that has been going on in Japan since the 1990s (negative economic growth) has resulted in less enthusiasm than expected.

As for the further development of the Japanese IT industry, the strategy is mainly to improve the foreign design of computers and sell them under the banner of Japanese companies. Of the remaining companies on the market in the 21st century, Hitachi manufactures American microcomputers, disk drives, and mobile phones; Fujitsu manufactures monitors (on liquid crystals — LCD); NEC manufactures integrated circuits, peripherals, and network circuits; Toshiba manufactures microcomputers, monitors, and memory; and Canon manufactures microcomputers and peripherals such as printers. Active companies in this industry include Matsushita, Oki, Ricoh, and others.

Japan's IT industry has grown thanks to the knowledge it has gained from the US IT industry; however, Japan's IT industry has a higher quality of manufactured products than the US. In terms of software, native production covers only 20 percent of the needs. The Japanese youth do not go into the IT development profession, especially when there is a cheap workforce of Indian developers, which creates a competitive market for hiring Japanese.

Japan seems to have succumbed to international competition in the IT industry, except for the development of robots, in which it is an indisputable leader in the world. Japan uses robots for cumbersome and challenging work, but it does not completely eliminate the jobs of people whose functions are taken over by robots; rather, these people become the "guardians" of the robots.

USSR

In the Soviet Union, about 100 models of various computers were built by 1976, and almost all were used in practice. More than a dozen models were launched in production series. This achievement is only comparable to work in the US. The development of the Japanese IT industry was highly dynamic, but its products were created as followers of American and French products. Nonetheless, the development and application of information technology in the USSR lacked the business motivation present in the United States. Therefore, achievements in the construction of computers were considered to be of greater scientific than practical importance, which had consequences for the dissemination of solutions in society.

Many of the Soviet achievements in computer science stemmed from the excellent foreign intelligence that the Soviets had in the US. For example, regarding the construction of the atomic bomb, the secrets of the American design were transmitted to the USSR by successive spies. Two of them were even executed on the electric chair (i.e., Julius and Ethel Rosenberg). The tradition of Soviet foreign intelligence continues in Russia up to the present.

Soviet information technology had a significant impact on the development of computer science in socialist countries. By comparison, when the first computer designs were created in Poland and Czechoslovakia, there were already about 20 computer designs in the Soviet Union and the US. In the field of applications, the Soviet computers Minsk 22 and Minsk 23a were breakthroughs that increased the quantitative scope of IT applications in socialist countries. These computers were installed in Poland and Czechoslovakia in the 1960s. In the absence of domestic machines, Minsk computers played a significant role in popularizing computer science in these countries.

Data processing automation came second in the USSR compared to the development of scientific and engineering calculation machines. The USSR competed with the United States in the conquest of space, starting with the launch of Sputnik in 1957. This competition took place primarily at the scientific and engineering level at the border of basic sciences, where scientific calculations play a significant role.

The fundamental development of computer construction in the USSR began after Stalin's death in 1953. The political conditions became more predictable, whereas before there were "purges" in which no one was spared, and everyone was potentially suspected of a crime. The mostly favorable atmosphere for computer development began after the 20th Party Congress, when Nikita Khrushchev condemned Stalinism and announced the Soviet economy would surpass the American economy. The launch of Sputnik in 1957 marked the Soviet Union's exit from containment by various Western military pacts (NATO, SEATO, and others), for it now had long-range missiles that could also attack US territory. For good reason, Admiral A. I. Berg was appointed head of Soviet computer science. He played a very positive role in the state's support of the development of computer science. He criticized Stalin's assessment of cybernetics during this period. Indeed, in Stalin's time, the idea of cybernetics (formulated by Norbert Wiener in the US in 1948), which involved the transfer of functions of living systems to non-living systems, was considered a deliberate limitation on the intellectual development of humankind, who capitalists wanted to enslave.

This is why A. I. Berg's role was incredibly tricky. Without being a computer scientist (the term was not used at the time), he became chairman of the Cybernetics Committee at the Presidium of the Academy of Sciences in the USSR. Thanks to Admiral Berg's high military rank, the further development of computer technology in the USSR was subordinated to military purposes. On his initiative, the Ural family of computers was created in 1954, which the following year (1955) entered mass production. In the second half of the 1950s, the BESM-1, STRELA, and LEM-1 computers entered service. Research and development that began in this decade yielded results in the 1960s when dozens of computer models were created.[12]

In addition to the Moscow and Miński centers, another significant research and development center of Soviet computer science was the Institute of Cybernetics at the Ukrainian Academy of Sciences in Kyiv. In 1956, when Ukrainian Nikita Khrushchev came to power, this branch was transformed into an independent computing center. Its director was the academician Viktor M. Głuszkow (1923–1982). He was awarded the Lenin Prize in 1964 and the IEEE Computer Pioneer Award in 1966. He took over the role of Admiral Berg in formulating policy in the USSR. Academician Głuszkow was a specialist in computer science applications, but he did not promote the development of computer construction in his center.

When one looks at the development of technical information technology in the Western market economy, one can see that after a period of dispersal, there was a period of consolidation in the industry.

On the one hand, when some companies pulled out of the market, such as RCA and GE, others took over these companies' resources, which usually contained the best solutions and customers. On the other hand, there was a steady development of "families" or series of different computer configurations, as was the case with the IBM 1400, IBM 360, IBM 370, and IBM 390, as well as PDP 8, PDP 10, and PDP VAX.

In the political East, the authorities came to the same conclusions. Each country, a member of the Council for Mutual Economic Assistance (CMEA), developed its own licensed computer designs. This was especially the case in the USSR, where there were about 25 different computer models; however, similar processes took place in Poland, Czechoslovakia, Hungary, Bulgaria, and Romania. In these countries, numerous computer development centers were established, and there were many outstanding designers. Their activities were not supported by an effective sales service, after-sales service, user training service, or application software supply service. For this reason, these countries were unable to develop cost-effective IT equipment on their own and without conflict.[13]

In this situation, the International Commission on Electronic Computing Technology (ECA) was set up in 1968. This agreement laid the foundations for one of the largest joint projects in the 25-year history of the CMEA. It was decided that a Unified System (US) of Electronic Digital Machines would be constructed, commonly referred to as Ryad. The Board of Major Designers led the work on the Unified System. In each country, a Chief Designer was selected, subordinated to the Main Designer in the USSR. Specific tasks were developed within councils of specialists and working groups.

The first version of the US-Ryad family of machines included five central units: US-1010, US-1020, US-1030, US-1040, US-1050. Colloquially, they were abbreviated as R-10, R-20, R-30, R-40, and R-50. The models were to be developed and produced in specific countries, but all models were to be made in the USSR. For example, Poland specialized in making the R-30; however, it is clear that the Russians did not trust the Poles, for the "Polish" Ryad was also developed and produced in Yerevan, Armenia.

The Ryad family of machines was a copy of IBM 360/370 machines. IBM knew this, and unofficially even helped by sharing documentation and necessary information. For this reason, the IBM standard prevailed in the world.

US-Ryad primary strategy was to build machines for different applications with software and peripherals that were interchangeable. The specializations were R-10 (Hungary), R-20 (Bulgaria), R-20A (Czechoslovakia), R-30 (Poland), and R-40 (GDR). The USSR duplicated all models, not being confident in the feasibility of these machines as developed in these countries.[14]

The USSR proceeded methodically in computerization. First, it wanted to develop a good range of universal computers, and then it wanted to apply them in the economy, first at the level of the companies, of which there were a few million. The use of computerization at the level of the centrally planned economy in Gosplan was not talked about: it was a taboo subject. Only econometric models of the economy, such as the Lange model, were applied, but they were not rushed into practice because the authorities were afraid that these models could demolish the relatively well-functioning input-output system balancing products and materials in interbranch flows. This concept was based on the first 5-Year Plan, which was formulated by the then very young Vasyli Leontief (1906-1999). Leontief would then go to the United States in 1926, where he eventually received the Nobel Prize in 1973 for his econometric model (and raised 4 Nobel Prize winners among his doctoral students).[15,16]

In the USSR, there were many great mathematicians such as Vasily Niemczynov (1912-1964) and Leonid Kantorowicz (1912-1986), the latter of whom won the Nobel Prize in 1975 for formulating a linear programming method. In the decades after the Bolshevik Revolution, the economy was, at best, in "scientific stagnation". There was a joke that the best economists were candidates for "Stalin's special awards": first prize was execution; second, a semester as a prisoner in an exchange camp; and third, exile. That is why Soviet economists addressed abstract mathematical models for which they could not be accused of betraying the ideals of the 1917 Revolution.[17]

In this situation, the Gosplan and its backers in the 17 republics "centrally planned" the economy, in a sense. In reality, they bid for priorities among the most critical administrators, each wanting to secure the most resources in their sphere of activity. There was no room for so-called "optimization", which was written about by Soviet econometrists in the wake of Oskar Lange, who led the economy astray.

In this context, the computerization strategy of the Soviet Bloc in more recent years was to imitate the United States in the production of the Ryad family of computers and their use at the company level, leaving the top level in the hands of uncomputerized political and economic activists. Shortages of goods, especially food, were quickly replenished from countries such as Poland, Czechoslovakia, Hungary, and Bulgaria.[18]

POLAND

The development of the applications of information technology in Poland began as early as 1923 with the installation of Hollerith punch card machines at the Polish Post Office. In addition, in 1934, IBM began operating under the name Polski Hollerith, which adapted to provide services to its German occupier during World War II.

In 1945, after World War II, the mechanization of economic data processing developed well in Poland in several central clearing houses. These included the following:

- The Central Statistical Office (GUS), directed and developed by Z. Wojcieszak, A. Pietrasiński, and T. Walczak,
- The coal industry, led and developed by A. Golinowski,
- The construction industry, led and developed by J. Zagalski,
- Polish State Railways, directed and developed by J. Wyrzykowski, and then by A. Cape,
- The National Bank of Poland, directed and developed by J. Lipinski.

Polish IT professionals who worked on Western computers and received training in the West understood that computers were a very important, if not strategic, element of an economy with widespread automation and consumption. In Warsaw at that time, four western computers were operating: the English ICT 1300 at the Central Centre for Personnel Improvement (CODKK); American NCR 315 running at NBP; the French MCT Serie 300 (PKP); and the American IBM 1440. The leaders of the first three centers showed no willingness to promote the ECA in large scale in the economy. This specific "duty" rested on the director of ZETO-ZOWAR, Dr. Andrzej (Andrew) Targowski, who underwent IT internships in France (1962 and 1964) and the United Kingdom (1966), and had IBM training in Austria, France, Belgium, and the US in 1970.

Targowski's activities did come to the attention of the real center of power, the Ministry of Internal Affairs and its deputy-boss, Franciszek Szlachcic, who was preparing a coup (replacing Wladyslaw Gomulka by Edward Gierek). This coup was carried out in December 1970. He invited Targowski to a series of training courses on IT applications. He believed that the Polish People's Republic (de facto a Soviet totalitarian regime) would effectively develop if it focused on rejuvenation and the development of a professional staff assisted by computerization, which was making a commotion in the West at the time. At these meetings, Targowski informed Szlachcic[19] about the directions of development of IT in the West as well as how it could be used in the Polish economy. Targowski also talked about the *social security system* in the US and a similar approach in France, which he studied while in France in 1964.[20]

THE FIRST NATIONAL COMPUTER DEVELOPMENT PROGRAM FROM 1971-1975

On March 1, 1971, the National Bureau for Informatics in Poland (in Polish, the Krajowe Biuro Informatyki or KBI) was established. Dr. Zbigniew Gackowski was appointed as Director-General and Dr. Andrzej Targowski was appointed as his deputy.

KBI then proceeded to create a plan, which would be implemented expeditiously. The following strategic assumptions were made for this plan:

- Should fewer computers be made with the same systems as in the West or more? Targowski reached the conclusion that there should be fewer during a visit to IPCo (International Paper Company) in the US in 1970. About 60 computers had been installed in headquarters and branches; however, on average, only 30% were in use. In other words, Americans had installed too many computers.
- It was deemed necessary to computerize the centrally planned economy from above. If it were to be carried out from below at the level of enterprises (at that time, there were about 40,000 organized in 200 corporations), it would take 400 years to computerize these companies given the actual level of computer supplies.
- The Lange model, which combined all companies into a single input-output system to balance supply and demand, was rejected. This was because, as the author of the model himself claimed, there was no computer that could calculate these balances in real-time or even once a day. Simply put, this model was not feasible. The Western model was that any large economic organization should be internally computerized. Only then can it systematically provide real and up-to-date data to overarching systems, such as the ministry, the Planning Commission, etc.
- The goal of computerizing the economy was deemed to be the following:
  ○ Reduce the inventory of companies and states from around 12 percent to a few percent. In the market economy, inventory was below 1%, dramatically improving the efficiency of economic activity.
  ○ Reduce the bureaucracy in which 51% of all employees in the country worked.
  ○ Make rational (optimal) economic decisions.
- Transfer attention from the design of equipment to its applications, which involved the replacement of the term Electronic Computing Technology (ECT) by informatics.
- Significantly increase investment for the development of computerization in Poland.
- Activate research and research centers focused on the subject of computerization.

The plan targeted more than a dozen strategic National Information Systems (NISs): PESEL (social security numbers), CENSUS (national statistics), VECTOR (control of critical investment projects), TERRAIN (space governance), MAGMA (supply-chain management), TRAKT (railroads and highways), ŚWIATOWID (libraries), SOCRATES (scientific records), and other national information processing networks, such as INFOSTRADA, based on the ZETO National Computing Network. The following were also targeted:

- 18 production process automation systems,
- 3 time-sharing systems: CYFRONET, WASC and POLRAX,
- More than a dozen IT systems for key enterprises,
- Several IT systems for economic areas.

The computerization strategy gave rise to the following:

- The development of Departmental Information Centres: These were responsible for the development of information technology in dozens of ministries along the lines of the Central Ministerial Information Processing Center (CROPI), which was organized in the late 1960s by Dr. Wojciech Jaworski (who immigrated to Canada) in the Ministry of Machinery Industry.
- The State Council for Informatics: This organization brought together dozens of experts and IT leaders.
- The monthly Mathematical Machines journal being renamed *Informatyka*: This emphasized applications.
- The training of selected specialists in Western computing centers.
- The formation of expert interdepartmental teams for the development of NIS-type systems.
- The development of social security and VECTOR systems: This was delegated to Targowski, who substantively managed their development in parallel with his executive functions in the KBI.[21]
- Special attention to the organization of the KBI following the principle that 'structure follows strategy', as in Figure 8: This figure is modeled after the organization of the Pentagon, introduced by US Secretary of Defense Robert McNamara in the 1960s when the Vietnam War was underway.[22]

The organization of the KBI, in accordance with the arrangement of the US Pentagon, required the organization of working methods. This model was based on a concept developed at the famous RAND research facility (which is the "brain" of American Aviation), called PPBS from "Planning, Programming, Budgeting System". This method was implemented in 1962 at the Pentagon and in 1965 was promoted in the civilian offices of the United States government. Six years later, it was implemented in KBI in totalitarian Poland, but in a slightly modified form. The Polish variety of PPBS was called the 3P method from "Forecasting, Programming, and Planning." The entire plan for 1972-75 was developed using this method.

At KBI, the executives immediately broke with the course of development, which was to be applied by the central planning system. It was assumed that the main task of KBI (then conceived of as a research staff unit of the government) should be to steer, not command, the development of information technology. "Steering" meant indirect management by providing forecasts and developing programs, plans, and analyses for all participants involved in the computerization of the country. Based on KBI studies, each enterprise and agency were to make decisions independently, without the administrative coercion of the KBI. There was hope that "KBI scenarios" would lead to more profound reflections of these decisions, which is why, after its adaptation to Polish realities, the intermediate management style (congruent with American practice) was adapted. Thus, the 3P method adopted the following timetables for action:

- IT development forecasts - 30 years
- IT development programs - 5 to 10 years
- Allocation plans - 1 to 5 years

Figure 8. The management apparatus of the National Bureau of Informatics 1971-1974

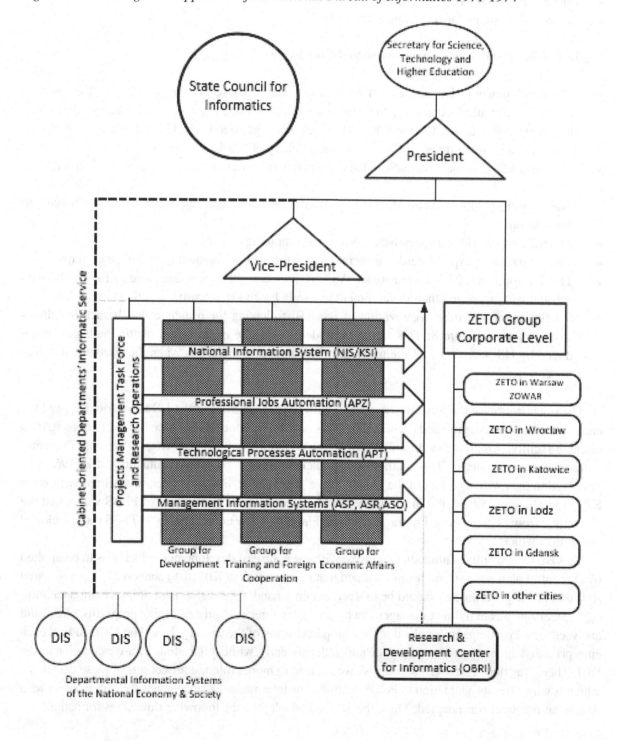

The planning system was based on the 3P method (Planning-Programming-Forecast) (Figure 9):[23]

Figure 9. The 3P system used in KBI in 1971-74

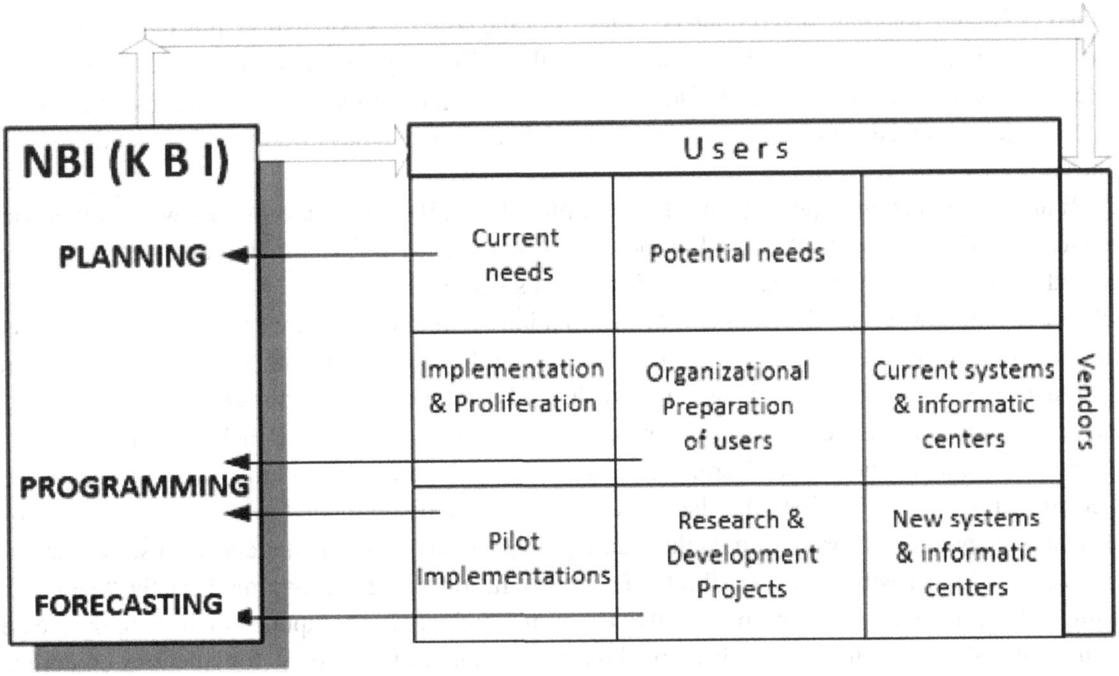

Unlike the US PPBS technique, Method 3P had formulated software questions for each phase:

- The forecast phase was considered in terms of the formulated objectives of computer development, the needs for IT systems, and the means of implementation;
- The program phase was considered in regard to the options for programs that would lead to the achievement of the goals, strategies, and priorities set out in the forecast;
- The planning phase consisted of the designation and allocation of tasks and resources.

Software questions were referred, among others, to teams designing state systems, such as the system for navigating issues in science and technology (called SOCRATES), the material supply system (called MAGMA), the system for steering natural resources (in the fields of surveying and cartography), and the transport steering system (called TRAKT).

As work began in designing the National Information System (KSI) in 1972, software questions such as the following were raised:

1. How many IT professionals will it take to build the KSI?
2. Will the KSI's need for IT professionals require additional expenses that are not in the existing plans?

3.   From 1972 – 74, what should the tasks of higher education be in IT-oriented education to ensure that the next Computer Development Program (for the period 1975 -2000) has a good starting point?

At the end of 1971, 78 data processing computers and 167 numerical computing computers were installed in Poland, totaling 245 computers. In terms of the country's population, this meant there were about 7.5 computers per 1 million inhabitants or roughly 133,000 people per computer. KBI's analysis showed that the use of computers in Poland was several times lower than in the leading western European countries, several dozen times lower than in the US, and three times lower than in other democratic countries.

KBI also calculated that the delay in implementing IT into the national economy was 4 years compared to the USSR, 8 years to Western Europe, and 14 years to the US. About the same degree of delay occurred at the technical level regarding hardware and software.

Poland's situation in the development of information technology required a specific development strategy to prevent further increases in delay. There was already at that time a model for the general dissemination of computers in the economy, which had been formulated and tested by other countries. This model followed statistics and was therefore considered valid for use in Polish conditions.

Forecasting the development of computer installations was based on demographic forecasts and projected national incomes. However, the way computers were disseminated was likened to the growth of a smallpox epidemic. It was assumed that gaining possession of a computer could, in some ways, be thought of as a disease without the possibility of recovery. In addition, it was assumed that the "feeling" of needing to have a computer was proportional to the number of existing computers in the country, treated as "outbreaks of contagion." The mathematical models of Harris and Huskey (for smallpox epidemics) and Stormer (for the spread of phones) were used for these calculations. A detailed description of these methods of forecasting is presented in Targowski (1980).

KBI research showed that the intensity of the "infection" of computer science in France and West Germany in the 1960s was much higher than in the US, UK, and Japan. Perhaps this resulted from the deliberate action of these countries, which aimed at economic recovery through computer science. For example, in France, there was the Office of Government Delegate for Information Technology. This created the animus that KBI could perhaps contribute in the same way in Poland.

KBI formulated three strategies to facilitate the development of IT in Poland:

- *The conservative strategy* was to maintain the current pace of development according to the development program of the period (1971-75), which required the complete (100%) implementation of this plan. According to this strategy, about 15,000 computers would be installed in Poland by 1990, an increase of 57 times the number of computers compared to 1971.
- *The natural development strategy* was characteristic of the US, UK, and Japan and would require an approximately 100% increase in the program. According to this strategy, about 30,000 computers would be installed in Poland by 1990, an increase of 114 times the number of computers compared to 1971.
- *The accelerated development strategy*, characteristic of France and Germany, required a further increase in the program. According to this strategy, about 40,000 computers would be installed in Poland by 1990, an increase of 163 times the number of computers compared to 1971.

Figure 10. One example of a KBI prediction (Bramski, Rybak, & Targowski, 1972)

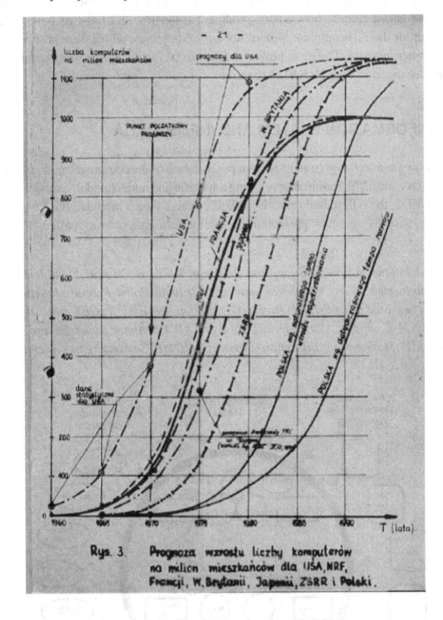

When KBI forecasts were reported, the forecasters were ridiculed. Questions were asked such as "how many thousands of computers in Poland and why?". From today's perspective in 2020, the development of ICT has surpassed everyone's imagination. There are now about 15 million personal computers in Poland in 2020. At any rate, the size of computers has changed. KBI's calculations involved *main-frames,* whereas personal computers now appear alongside main-frames, and they are often faster than the main-frames of the 1970s. It should be noted that the speed of the central unit's calculations alone does not determine the time required to execute a processing task: This is also determined by the printer speed, capacity, and disk speed.

Time showed that KBI forecasts were generally accurate, even though there was no microcomputer revolution in these calculations, which no one predicted at the time. KBI always believed that the core of Polish installations should be minicomputers, not large computers, which were pushed by the national and Soviet computer industry. The most powerful PCs are de facto servers, that is, minicomputers according to the classification used by KBI at the time.

NATIONAL INFORMATION SYSTEM AND INFOSTRADA

Andrew Targowski was asked to give an important presentation of the computerization plan to the highest state authorities. Of course, this required developing a specific and understandable model of computerization systems. In 1972, the NIS model (Figure 11) was created, which included the systems listed in the program back in 1970 but were now presented in a legible form in a network called "INFOSTRADA".

Figure 11. A model of the National Information System in 1972 (the Targowski model). INFOSTRADA would lead to an informed society, which was unacceptable to the Polish People's Republic, where information was often censored and falsified (Targowski, 1980, p. 198). [24,25,26] (CEN-central; SEC-sectorial; REG-regional; CAM-Computer Aided Manufacturing; CAD-Computer Aided Design; CAS-Computer Aided Services; MIS-Management Information Systems; COMP-Computing in professional work)

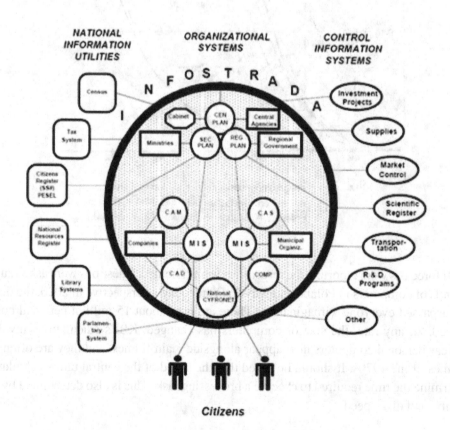

Citizens

However, the computerization strategy presented in the INFOSTRADA model made some party authorities aware that it would lead to an informed society, for the flow of information develops in a horizontal plane and does not solely travel from "top to bottom". Eventually, the NIS project was stopped by the Political Bureau of the Party.

PRESIDENT NIXON IN WARSAW AND CYFRONET

In June 1972, on his way to Moscow, President Richard Nixon and Secretary of State Henry Kissinger flew to Warsaw to propose a policy of *détente* and to discuss the purchase of a supercomputer for Polish science in connection with the looming 500-year anniversary (1473) of the birth of Nicholas Copernicus. The Americans did not want war and bought peace. The latest CDC Cyber 72 model was installed as the CYFRONET, a generation higher than the CDC 6600. The Americans also imposed an embargo on the French nuclear program *Force de Frappe*.[27]

CHILE

At the time when NIS was created in Poland, in Chile the left-wing (Marxist) President Salvador Allende (1971-73) commissioned the British cyberneticist Stafford Beer (1926-2002) to design and apply *Project Cybersyn*, which aimed to gradually integrate the materials and service transactions of every company into one super enterprise, i.e., the economy of the entire country. This was comparable to argument outlined by Oskar Lange (1967). However, Beer did not know the practices of a centrally planned economy and therefore, naively applied this model. On the other hand, NIS's author knew this type of economy well in addition to Western solutions (from numerous internships and contacts) and concluded that, first, the most important institutions of the country must be computerized, and only then should there be transactions between them; otherwise, there will be problems with the data and its reliability as well as the bandwidth of available, free computers.

The Polish NIS model has proven itself in concept, while the Lange model is today considered a naïve curiosity. Oskar Lange was a great cyberneticist, but by education, he was a lawyer and lecturer in statistics in the US. Today we know that he was also, while an American citizen, an adviser to Stalin in his dealings with Roosevelt and Churchill in Yalta. Stalin then brought Lange to the Polish People's Republic (through Wanda Wasilewska), and Lange repaid him with a model that would support a centrally planned economy, but only on paper (Lange, 1962).

As for Salvador Allende, he paid with his life during a right-wing coup and committed suicide with an AK-47 donated to him by Fidel Castro. NIS developers, on the other hand, can be proud that, in the practice of central planning, they were not deceived by Lange's utopian model and designed NIS in a Western way, as it is today and not 50 years ago! Derivatives of this model for the 3P method are given in Part IV.

LANGE'S MODEL

When writing about Lange's model, it must be stated that his politically conditioned theories of central planning served the economic system poorly. Professor Oskar Lange (1904-1965) was head of the department at the University of Warsaw and rector of the Main School of Planning and Statistics (SGPiS). Still, he felt best as Deputy Chairman of the Council of State (i.e., titular "vice-president") with minimal official tasks. While at the university of Warsaw, he wrote several econometric books with Dr. Antoni Banasiński (1908-1993), a statistician who refined the mathematics of the lawyer by education. Lange's models have never been tested in practice, even though he would have had no difficulty doing so. Lange tried to prove that an economic calculus in a collectivist system is possible. He believed a method of trial and error could achieve the same supply-demand equilibrium in collectivism (especially with the help of a supercomputer) that in capitalism is determined by the mechanism of the market. He also believed that the socialist economy should pursue the same equilibrium as is achieved under conditions of excellent competition.

Professor Jan Drewnowski (1908-2000) took a fundamentally different position, holding that it was clear that the equilibriums in each system in question must be different. He considered this inevitable because, in each of these systems, preferences – which exist at different levels – are specific to each system. Even in "individualistic" systems, equilibriums must differ from the equilibrium of perfect competition. In "collectivist" systems, this is even more inevitable. Did Lange, an American citizen with a dozen years of experience as a professor, not know that the preferences of a socialist economy are different from those of a capitalist economy? Why did he not test this assumption in his home country, where for 20 years he sat at the apex of science and power with the support of Stalin?

The answer is that Lange simply did not want to know the uncomfortable truth that would disprove his theories. Therefore he mathematicised them more and more to make them look like some kind of "super science". Moreover, his science of economics led to a kind of *carte blanche* in practice, for it took practitioners time to "fully grasp" his mathematically legitimate theory. In the meantime, he enjoyed the privileges of the ruling class to the maximum extent. Unfortunately, most Polish academic economists fled under the wing of his scientific school, which guaranteed success in moving up the literary and publishing ladder. And here is his greatest failure: He inhibited the intellectual development of Polish economists for years by giving a free hand to those in power to develop "real" socialism (rather than "scientific" socialism). Still, Lange was for some reason given intellectual freedom by the governing class to investigate the stagnant economy without improving it.

Oskar Lange comforted his political peers by alleging his theory of central market planning was superior to the capitalistic market economy. As a result, this centrally planned system was hardened, dogmatized, and unable to develop in the right direction. Due to these decisions, the computerization development program for 1971-75 was closed.

Let us be honest: a reasonable solution is a hybrid system[28] used by countries such as France and South Korea. This system goes by the name "indicative planning", and it provides recommendations but does not oblige business to follow these guidelines. This solution is visible after the 2020 pandemic. Of course, the art of mixed planning is finding the right balance between planning and the market.

SUMMARY

Table 1 provides a summary of the ICT strategies used for the selected countries.

Table 1. Summary of the ICT strategies used in selected states

State	Technology Strategy	Result
USA 1890-1945 1951-2000 · 2000+	Census, citizen's numbers Business data mechanization (IBM) Apollo program and business computerization (IBM) ARPANET, the Internet Cyberwar, cybersecurity, Big Tech abandonment of regulation, online services Computerization of knowledge Internet of Things	Success Success Success Success Outsourcing to Asia Business on surveillance At the level of data processing Lack of strategy and effort
Germany 1941-1945 1946-2020	Digital technology in V1 and V2 The mechanization of ethnic data Import of American computers SAP Export Online services	18,000 killed 4 million murdered "Missed" opportunity to make their own equipment Based on an EU strategy
The U. Kingdom 1945-1950 1950-2002 1971-2020	Digitization of war cryptography and computer development in university centers Developing native equipment production (ICL) Imports of US, Japanese, and Chinese ECA equipment	Enigma code breakage, Colossus ACE and EDSAC Displaced by imported hardware Based on an EU strategy
France 1945-1965 1966-1974 1975-2020	French Bull supercomputers, medium, and mini *Plan Calcul* – independence from American computers Independence of the French company Bull	Serie 300, MCT, Gamma 60, 30, 10 The Government's Delegate for Informatics, US Licenses and the Liquidation of the Delegate Full equipment production program Based on an EU strategy
USRR 1945-1967 1968-1991	Preferred development of computers mimicking the development of American computers Development of the Unified Ryad System (IBM) Business computerization	Sputnik 1 in 1957 R10, R20, R32, R40, R50
Chile 1971-1973	*Cybersyn system*, according to the Lange model: the combination of telexes of several hundred enterprises to manage the supply-demand cycle	Ceased after a right-wing coup
Poland 1945-1970 1971-1974 1975-1989 1990-2020	Mechanization of mass data processing in sector-oriented data centers in construction and pilot production of computers NIS/INFOSTRADA; development of an informed society ICT development was stopped ICT development based on the market in the supply of services to administrations	UMC 1, 10, Odra 1004, ZAM KBI, PESEL, VECTOR, TRAKT, CYFRONET, ŚWIATOWID, import of western computers Stagnation Based on an EU strategy
The world after the 2020 Pandemic	Strengthening of *online* public administration and teleworking services	Online coordination in crisis, working from home

The following conclusions can be drawn from the summary of the ICT strategies used over the last 100 years:

A.   General conclusions

1. The production of ICT equipment in the 21st century has been consolidated (along the lines of car production[29]) and has been mainly taken over by China and Taiwan. ICT equipment has become "invisible" similar to server farms. ICT applications, on the other hand, are now attracting the attention of a wide range of users.

2. Thanks to the networked digitization of publications and e-communications of almost all global researchers, computerization can aim at providing information for the development of knowledge and wisdom for humanity. However, it should not serve the purpose of surveillance; instead, it should help advance humanism, otherwise it will contribute to e-slavery.

3. A priority is to regulate the use of artificial intelligence worldwide to prevent the development of a laborless economy. This would lead to a digital pandemic destroying humanism, which has been fought for by social revolutions and just wars over long centuries, if not millennia.

4. The pioneering fascination with constructing an increasingly innovative ICT has been displaced by the enormous business success of certain IT professionals who have become the wealthiest people in the world. Many very talented IT professionals have abandoned their research and profession for IT business, supplementing their knowledge with MBA studies.

5. As ICT becomes a strategic technology, countries cannot merely rely on its cost-effective imports; rather, they must return to production, even at higher costs. This is what safety requires, which costs money.

6. ICT has proven to be a powerful weapon in dehumanizing societies, as it has favored the various ambitions of financial and political elites. Tackling this problem requires strong legal regulations, which will have to overcome lobbyists boycotting them.

7. The 2020 pandemic has shown that each state should have an ICT strategy to support residents during times of crisis. The strategy should focus on information, voting, medical and social assistance, online education, online provisions of food and medicine, and remote work in certain professions.

B. Conclusions about the countries of Atlantic (Western-Western) civilization:

1. While the United States wants to be "great again"[30] and support the "American dream" of social advancement, they need to develop and apply a broad computerization strategy that will ensure the self-sufficiency of ICT equipment. IT business will have to adjust according to the principle that "what is right for society is good for business", not vice versa, which currently dominates.

2. France, Germany, perhaps the UK after Brexit, and other countries of Europe should apply an EU computerization strategy reinforced by the self-sufficiency of ICT equipment and by the principle of prioritizing the welfare of IT business.

References

Bramski, S., Rybak, M., & Targowski, A. (1972). Forecast of an increase in the demand for computers in Poland by 2000. *Informatyka, 7-8*, 3–9.

Jublin, J., & Quatrepoint, J. M. (1976). *French ordinateurs: From the Bull case to the assassination of the computing plan*. Alain Moreau.

Lange, O. (1962). *Whole and development in the light of cybernetics.* PWE.

Lange, O. (1967). The computer and the market. In C. H. Feinstein (Ed.), *Socialism, capitalism and economic growth: Essays Presented to Maurice Dobb* (pp. 158–161). Cambridge University Press.

Masuda, Y. (1980). *The information society as post-industrial society.* World Future Society.

Randell, B. (1973). *The origins of digital computers: Selected papers.* Springler-Verlag. doi:10.1007/978-3-642-96145-8

Targowski, A. (1980). *Informatics: Models of systems and development.* State Economic Publishing House.

Targowski, A. (2001). *Computer science without illusions.* Adam Marshall.

Targowski, A. (2014). *The deadly effect of informatics on the Holocaust.* Tate Publishing.

Targowski, A. (2016). *The history, present-state and future information technology.* Informing Science Press.

World War II casualties. (n.d.). In *Wikipedia.* Retrieved from https://en.wikipedia.org/wiki/World_War_II_casualties

Key terms and definitions

Alan Turing: An English computer scientist (1912-1954) famous for developing the concept of a Turing machine and for working with the Polish mathematicians on breaking German ciphers during WWII.

Compagnie des Machines Bull: A French-owned computer company founded in 1931. Bull played an important role in French IT during the second half of the 20th century.

Dehomag: A German subsidiary of IBM during WWII.

Konrad Zuse: A German computer scientist (1910-1995) who played an important role in inventing the modern computer.

Lange Model: An economic model for socialist economies developed by Oskar Lange.

National Bureau for Informatics (KBI): An organization in Poland established in 1971 and charged with overseeing the development of computerization in the country.

Paul Baran: A Polish-American computer scientist (1926-2011) the inventor of packet switching networking technology, which gave the foundation for the Internet.

Punch Card Machine: A machine that processes cards containing digital data in the form of punched holes.

Ryad Computers: Copies of IBM computers created in the Soviet Union and Eastern Europe during the 1970s.

Wernher Von Braun: A German - American aerospace engineer (1912-1977) known for his role in developing rockets for Nazi Germany during WWII and for his role in NASA in the United States.

endnotes

[1]   Zuse believed after the war that his digital systems had been taken over by the Soviets during their occupation in 1945, which he believed helped launch Sputnik 1 into space in 1957.

[2]   Of the 7,500 V2 missiles launched into London and Amsterdam, 2,500 did not reach their target because of sabotage—the prisoners acted disobediently. Stanislaw Targowski (father of the author) was publicly hanged in this camp in March 1945 (three weeks before the liberation of the camp by the American military), along with other sabotaging prisoners. After the war, many German engineers from Mittelwerk were able to continue their professional careers in the US, the USSR, and Germany. Very few have been charged in connection with their role in the Nazi slave labor program.

[3]   Professor Thomas Carey's father was Edgar Hoover's associate, head of the FBI operation in South America during World War II, and his son was well informed about the arcana of American intelligence. He himself, moreover, was in a leadership role in this service in Europe during the Cold War.

[4]   Ironically, fate would have it that Heinrich Himmler was married to Margaret Concerzowo (Margaret Koncerzowa), who was of Polish origin. They had a daughter, Gudrun, who, with Polish blood, could not be a member of the SS, as determined by her father. Back in the 1990s, Gudrun Himmler supported her father's former colleagues.

[5]   Further negotiations on these transports were conducted by the Swedish diplomat Folke Bernadotte (1895-1948).

[6]   A prototype of the PESEL system under the name "MAGISTER" was made in Poland between 1972–76 on this computer using the PRISMA system.

[7]   Turing states that computable numbers are those that can be computed in a finite amount of time. His justification is that human minds are limited and a number that takes infinitely long to compute isn't very useful. He based his computational machine on the model of a person solving a problem.

[8]   Another notable "Pole", John Good (1916-2009), was born in London as Isidore Jacob Gudakwhose to parents of Polish-Jewish origin. On May 27, 1941, fresh from earning his Doctorate in Cambridge, he went to work at Bletchley Park, where German ciphers were broken. It was the same day the Royal Navy captured and destroyed the battleship Bismarck after the sinking of HMS *Hood*, the flagship of the British fleet. One night, Good dreamed a solution to decrypt the German messages. The technique involved reversing key enciphering processes: first apply a normal cipher and second a special cipher. When he woke up, he tried his theory on a decoded message and immediately broke it. He also worked closely with Turing and others on the pioneering computer *Colossus*, which was used to crack other German ciphers. He was the main statistician in the group. Turing had respect for him, but initially did not like him.

[9]   The author of this book received training on this machine in 1964.

[10]   Then the US-French model was replaced by the Hungarian MITRA 15 solution.

[11]   Most of the shares are owned by the French IT company Atos.

[12]   A detailed analysis of the development of the Soviet computing is contained in Targowski (2016), pp. 114-134.

[13]   The division of states into Western and Eastern was the result of the Cold War between capitalism and Soviet socialism.

[14]   The characteristics of Ryad machines are given in Targowski (2016), pp. 133-134.

15   Leontief Received a Master's degree in Economics from St. Petersburg University at the age of 19, where he started his studies at the age of 15.

16   The Soviet security service WAITS allowed him to leave the country because he was thought to have cancer and would not live long. He actually lived to 93.

17   Nikolai Kondriatev (1892-1938), author of the wave theory of technological development, was executed at the age of 42.

18   The Solidarity Revolution began in 1980 after railwaymen discovered that there were ham cans in petrol barrels on a train to the USSR.

19   Szlachcic brought Edward Gierek from house arrest in Katowice to Warsaw, where on December 20, 1970 he was elected First Secretary of the Polish United Workers' Party (PZPR).

20   The French 13-digit social security number (the Registration Number to the National Directory of Identification of Physical People—the NIRPP or NIR for short) was created by René Carmille, who died in the Dachau concentration camp in 1944. He created this system from April to August 1941 for the Vichy government, which was part of the preparations made for the secret mobilization of the French army. General Marie, who was in Algeria, was instructed to conduct a census of Jews, Muslims, and other groups of people. The aim was to create a log of the entire French population and to discriminate according to ethnic and/or statutory criteria, in accordance with Vichy's racial policy. The first digit, which is now used to distinguish between men and women, then had other purposes: 3 or 4 were used for Algerian non-Jewish indigenous peoples; 5 or 6 for indigenous Jews; 7 or 8 for foreigners; and 9 or 0 for undetermined status. This discriminatory categorization in Algeria was abolished in 1944 and was never applied in metropolitan France, where only '1' and '2' (for men and women) were used during the war. The administration of this system was allocated in 1946 to the new Statistical Institute (INSEE). This institute was also responsible for the RNIPP (National Repertory of Identification of Physical Persons), which for each person includes the following information: the NIR, surname, first name, gender, date and place of birth, and birth registration.

21   In the PESEL (Social Security) system, Targowski ranked second to the Deputy of the Representative of the Minister. He also was the Director of the Office of Studies and Projects, and in the VECTOR system, he was chairman of the Committee of Experts on the Modernisation of the Investment Control System. Finally, of particular importance, he was subordinate to the Deputy Prime Minister for Investment. These functions were performed in parallel with his function in the KBI, from which he received his only remuneration.

22   System McNamara is characterized in Targowski (2001), p. 209

23   The 3P system is described in Targowski (2000), p. 221

24   U.S. Vice President Al Gore translated INFOSTRADA as *information superhighway*, which became a paradigm of the American "New Economy" during the presidency of Bill Clinton (1993-2001) and in the following years.

25   Poland's INFOSTRADA was a precursor to the Internet, which was put into operation in 1983, 11 years after the start of the Polish network project, when the military ARPANET network was divided into the MILINET and the Internet. Censorship in the press has been imposed on the INFOSTRADA project.

26   Currently in China 2 million computer scientists are professionally censoring and controlling information on the Internet.

27   Targowski signed a clause allowing Americans to control calculations at any time (24/7) because the embargo was only lifted for peaceful purposes. This was signed without the consent of the Polish authorities, who could not agree to this politically uncomfortable condition.

28   A similar mixed system under the name of "market socialism" is used by China, which based on prices has become the world's foremost economic powerhouse in the 2020s. However, this system is overseen by the party's totalitarian policies that dehumanize society. Therefore, it cannot be a model solution for the rest of the world.

29   At the time of Henry Ford (1910) there were 2,400 manufacturers of passenger cars, each of whom produced only a few dozen vehicles per year usually at the price of a few thousand dollars. There are currently 3 American manufacturers: GM, Ford, and Chrysler (Fiat). Similarly, in the 1980s there were about 200 manufacturers of microcomputers. In 2020, there are two: DELL and HP and a few other niche companies. The same is true of main frame manufacturers: IBM and Unisys.

30   "Make America great again" was President Donald Trump's election slogan.

Chapter 5
Big Tech and Society in the 21st Century

ABSTRACT

This chapter examines the socio-political impacts of big tech in the 21ˢᵗ century. The chapter begins by examining the rise of big tech, and it compares the power and reach of big tech with the auto industry. The chapter next turns its attention to the concept of surveillance capitalism and reviews arguments developed by Shoshana Zuboff. Specifically, this section examines how capitalism has undergone fundamental changes in the digital age that require new responses to protect fundamental human rights. The chapter concludes by examining some of the key developments of surveillance capitalism, including facial recognition as well as government responses.

THE RISE OF BIG TECH COMPANIES

Hitherto, the intellectual powers of the world have owned outstanding newspapers; however, Big Tech companies, collectively known as FAAMG (Facebook, Amazon, Apple, Microsoft, Google), care little about the content of information and discussion. Their main goal is to increase the number of readers and revenue from advertising and sales based on behavior profiles delivered by marketing companies and unique services. Of course, these information technology giants (Table 1) censor unfavorable opinions and promote chaos and information disorientation as part of their "intellectual" wisdom. The current challenges of civilization mentioned in this section have no chance of overcoming the culture of hate on social networks and solving the problems of humanity.

Table 1 shows that Big Tech has almost ten times more productivity per employee than the most extensive global automotive companies and Big Tech's market value is 18 times larger. The FAAGM companies can afford the best lobbyists, who aim to maintain the *status quo*.[1] These companies are indeed working on improving information processes, that is, they contribute to developing ever-better knowledge about the world. They provide many software tools and digital platforms to support humanism; however, these companies are also destroying the humanistic tradition, as shown by the case of journalism and the deprivation of an active and wise information society that could control the quality

DOI: 10.4018/978-1-7998-8036-3.ch005

Table 1. Comparison of Big Tech (FAAMG) business with automotive companies in 2018

Company	Annual Sales (in Billions of US Dollars)	Market Value of the Company (in Billions of US Dollars)	Number of Employees	Productivity per 1 Employee (in US dollars)
Facebook	55	188	44,000	
Amazon	233	920	648,000	
Apple	266	268	123,000	
Microsoft	110	160	148,000	
Google	137	1,303	100,000	
Total	**801**	**2,839**	**1,063,000**	2,671,000
Volkswagen	11,8	74	656,000	
Renault-Nissan	10,3	43	183,000	
Toyota	9,7	186	369,000	
General Motors	7,7	144	173,000	
Ford	4,9	46	199,000	
Total	**44.4**	**490**	**1,580,000**	28,101

Market value of the company = number of shares sold (including as bonuses) x share price

of civilizational processes. It should be mentioned that Amazon fights against the publication of printed books because it promotes digital e-books and e-readings, which can be accessed via Kindle. Its fight against printed books (even though it sells them as well) is going very well. It blackmails large, competing book publishers into selling their works on Amazon's platform, provided they offer e-books and sell them for under $10 adapted to an Amazon's e-reader platform.

Thanks to the Internet, globalization has accelerated, including a global economics based on turbo-capitalism. This is possible thanks to outsourcing to countries with cheap labor, which has helped corporations make huge profits and has helped stateless capital to grow. In the 2020s, IT companies like FAAMG use the Internet to profile people and market to them, which brings the companies multibillion-dollar revenues. For example, these 5 IT companies have a total revenue that is 60% higher than the GDP of Poland, which consists of 18 million working people, much less than the 1 million IT professionals employed in these companies.

BIRTH OF SURVEILLANCE CAPITALISM

According to Shoshana Zuboff (2019), Big Tech companies introduced *surveillance capitalism* as a form of information capitalism, displacing the weaker turbo-capitalism (which controls modern globalization) with its dynamism and productivity.

Zuboff (2019) claims that throughout one's life, almost everyone holds a phone in their hand and has Google, Facebook, and other apps constantly collecting information to create a profile of who one is and what one likes. Google, for its part, keeps a record of all one's searches, reads one's email address (if one is using Gmail), and tracks where one is going via Google Maps and Android. Facebook has an unparalleled network of trackers installed on the Internet, constantly collecting information on what one is looking at online. Zuboff distinguishes between "surveillance resources" (human behavior data), "surveillance capital" (the value of human behavior data that is sold), and "surveillance capitalism". She also notes that dependence on the global computer mediation architecture, which she calls the "Great Other," has largely become an unquestionable new expression of power, which is a hidden mechanism of extraction, socialization, and control and one which threatens fundamental values such as freedom, democracy, and privacy.

According to Zuboff (2019), surveillance capitalism was initiated by Google and later Facebook, just as mass production and managerial capitalism were introduced at Ford and General Motors a century earlier. Now surveillance has become the dominant commodity of information capitalism. In her 2016 Oxford lecture, Zuboff identified the mechanisms and practices of surveillance capitalism, including the production of "predictive products" for sale in new "behavioral futures markets".[2] She also introduced the concept of "expropriation by surveillance" (that is, depriving citizens of fundamental human rights) and has argued that this undermines the psychological and political basis of self-regulation, for it concentrates rights in the surveillance system. She has described this as a "coup d'état" (Zuboff, 2016).

Zuboff is a student of B. F. Skinner's, and she follows his belief that humans can be conditioned like any other animal and that behavioral psychology can and should be used to build a technological utopia where citizens should be taught from birth to be altruistic and community - oriented. This idea is fleshed out in Skinner's 1948 novel *Walden Two*, which depicted what such a society would look like—a kind of "Brave New World" not gone awry. Zuboff says in a version of Skinner's future is possible thanks largely to Google, Facebook, and their peers who are invested in the "attention economy." According to her, Silicon Valley has invented, but has not yet refined, the technology that complements Skinner's vision. Thus, in her opinion, human behavioral engineering is now at hand.

There are two important arguments developed in Zuboff's works. The first is that she helps inform us about the relationship between capitalism and totalitarian control systems. The second is that she gives us a better and deeper understanding of what the protection of human freedom will mean in the future. It turns out that capitalism, in pursuit of business, is willing to use totalitarian techniques of human control. This is although a common Western belief is that the free market is a mainstay against the emergence of authoritarian systems, which was used as an argument against the practices of surveillance and spying on citizens used by the Soviet bloc. Based on this previous version of capitalism, privacy was revered and protected from surveillance, and property was embraced as an all-important value. People enjoyed privacy not only in their own homes with thick walls and separate bedrooms but also in semi-private spaces, such as bars and motels.

Today, however, the concept of privacy has changed: It is now based on ubiquitous digitalization. While homes are still built with cheap walls, digital surveillance industries are among the most important parts of the economy. Surveillance is at the heart of the business models of companies like Google and Facebook and is also part of Amazon, Uber, Lyft, and others. Surveillance capitalism is expanding to other industries: Admiral, a British insurance company, uses Facebook data to price its products differently for different potential customers. It seems that people who write in short, specific sentences and use lists are safer drivers. Excessive use of exclamation points, on the other hand, suggests recklessness behind the wheel. Furthermore, life insurance companies such as John Hancock offer discounts if a customer agrees to monitor their health on a Fitbit watch.[3]

Zuboff (2019) rightly argues that at the beginning of the 21st century, something transformative happened in the relationship between capitalism, privacy, and, consequently, human autonomy. She argues that a new form of power has emerged, which she calls "instrumentalism." According to her, this form of control does not depend on coercion or terror, as in the dictatorial system, but on "ownership of the means of behavioral modification". In other words, she thinks the future belongs to whoever controls Skinner's boxes.[4]

According to Tim Wu (2020):

We learned how Skinner and the secret police realize that knowing everything about someone creates the power to control that person. We may not be there yet, but there is a theoretical point - call it Skinnerlarity - where enough data about humanity will be collected to predict with some reasonable certainty what everyone on earth will do at any time. This achievement would change the very structure of human experience. As lawyer Jonathan Zittrain said, this would make life "a highly realistic but completely adapted video game in which nothing happens by accident." Therefore, we must dare to say what, at another age, would sound like blasphemy. Perhaps a little less knowledge will give us freedom.

The latest "achievement" of surveillance technology is facial recognition, made possible by AI systems that collect images from Facebook, Twitter, and even Venmo (with 3 billion photos). So far, 600 judicial agencies have purchased facial recognition systems, including the London Police. Apparently, facial identification will be as easy as looking for a quote on Google even if one only has a partial image

Figure 1. A model of surveillance capitalism (Big Brother) in the 2020s

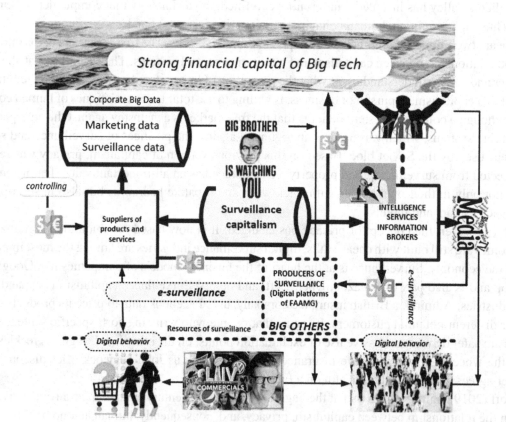

of someone's face (even with only 40% of the photo available). All this is done without our knowledge and consent in the name of profits.

Figure 1 presents a model of the surveillance capitalism in the 2020s. In addition to business surveillance, this system also includes government surveillance as a form of counterterrorism. This is indirectly used in one way or another for political purposes. An example of such a system is the very efficient Israeli software Pegasus, which infiltrates citizens' Wi-Fi communications.

Government interference in the disastrous role of the Internet is already in place. For example, since August 5, 2019, the Indian government has disrupted Internet services in Kashmir after giving the province autonomy because of counter-protests put on by activists dissatisfied with the policy. In China, citizens receive a social credit index under observation, along the lines of the Loan Index of Western Civilization, which is used by banks to decide when to lend to citizens. This measures the solvency of the borrower.

SUMMARY

1.   The power of Big Tech companies comes from trading data from unwitting users for marketing purposes, data which they acquire illegally in principle on their digital platforms. They can function like this because their lobbyists are well connected and know how to protect them.
2.   Dozens of countries are interested in the digital surveillance of their citizens. In democratic systems, this happens with the permission of the courts, and in non-democratic, with the consent of the dictator. Therefore, surveillance capitalism is not yet under threat.
3.   In the United States, President Trump began trying to regulate social networks in 2020.

REFERENCES

Wu, T. (2020, April 9). Bigger brother. *The New York Review of Books*. https://www.nybooks.com/articles/2020/04/09/bigger-brother-surveillance-capitalism/

Zuboff, S. (2016, March 5). Google as a fortune teller: The secrets of surveillance capitalism. *Frankfurter Allgemeine Zeitung*. https://www.faz.net/aktuell/feuilleton/debatten/the-digital-debate/shoshana-zuboff-secrets-of-surveillance-capitalism-14103616.html

Zuboff, S. (2019). *The age of surveillance capitalism: The fight for a human future at the new frontier of power*. Profile Books.

KEY TERMS AND DEFINITIONS

B. F. Skinner: An American psychologist, well renowned for his works in behaviorism.

FAAMG: An abbreviation standing for Facebook, Amazon, Apple, Microsoft, and Google, originally formulated by Goldman Sachs to indicate the top tech stocks.

Facial Recognition: A technology that can identify a human based on a digital image.

Globalization: The process by which people, companies, and governments increasing interact and become integrated across the globe. This process has been accelerated by ICT technologies.

Shoshana Zuboff: An American professor at Harvard Business School whose works have analyzed surveillance capitalism.

Surveillance Capitalism: An economic system in which the sale of personal data is a central activity.

ENDNOTES

[1] It should be mentioned that in 2019, the Department of Justice and the Federal Trade Commission (US) opened an investigation into Big Tech's practices. In Congress, Senator Josh Hawley developed several laws under the name *Dashboard Act*, which requires companies to show the value of the data they collect and sell about people. In addition, Senators Richard Blumenthal and Ed Markey have developed a law prohibiting the payment of cash prizes to participants in computer games, as this promotes hidden gambling. These laws, however, are not yet approved, and when they will be is not known. The University of Chicago School of Business has produced a report on the establishment of a "digital authority" (a "digital body"), which would oversee competitiveness in online business. It also organized a project of responsibility for content published on the Internet (the Internet Accountability Project), which aims to counter digital censorship of right-wing content.

[2] "The behavior of the (behaviorist)" like "futures" is an analogy of the Chicago Commodity Exchange, where stocks are sold for upcoming deliveries, some still offshore on ships.

[3] Fitbit, Inc. is a company based in San Francisco, California. Its products include activity trackers, smartwatches, and other wireless wearable technologies that measure data such as steps, heart rate, sleep quality, and other fitness-related acts.

[4] Skinner's box, also known as the *operant conditioning chamber*, is a closed device that contains a rod or key that an animal can press or manipulate to obtain food or water as a kind of reinforcement. Skinner himself did not call this device a "Skinner box", instead preferring the term "box of levers".

Chapter 6
Socio–Political Considerations of Informing Technology in the 21st Century

ABSTRACT

This chapter addresses socio-political issues surrounding informing technology in the 21st century. The chapter begins by considering the role that computers and informing technology have played in US elections. The chapter then critically examines what prosperity informing technology and turbo-capitalism has brought society. Next, global indexes that measure human well-being are considered within the broader context of growing economic equalities. The role that trade unions play in such measures is also considered. The chapter next considers the relationship between informing technology and the deep web and dark webs as well as its relation to corruption. Attention is then paid to the relation between informing technology and democracy as well as the socio-political impacts of hackers. The chapter concludes by considering the role informing technology has played in dictatorships and its role in the 2020 coronavirus pandemic as well as the positive impacts of hackers.

INTRODUCTION

Informing technology in the 21st century must listen to the voice of the people to use its remarkable ability to process and manipulate information for the good of humanity. The development of informing technology is dependent on politics, which shapes the behavior of society and determines policies that will directly impact ethics, IT law, and the design of application systems (implemented by around 20 million IT professionals worldwide). Bad policies can be perpetuated, or they can be counteracted. This chapter will address the problems of the modern world, which at first glance will appear far from, say, database programming. However, this is an illusion, and is an escape from dealing with problems that a computer strategist needs to understand so that he/she can develop important and meaningful applications of strategic informing technology.

DOI: 10.4018/978-1-7998-8036-3.ch006

Informing technology is a technology that is supposed to support various, if not all, socio-economic processes through which humankind develops and thrives. This includes supporting the use of information, the generation of data, communication with others, etc. Through informing technology, we learn about new information, evaluate it, and use it for ourselves, being a member in a family, group, institution, company, organization, and so forth. Nowadays, one has access to an incredible amount of information that can address a multitude of issues. Such quantities would have been unheard of in the times of Nicholas Copernicus, who, despite holding only a relatively "small" amount of information, was afraid of what he possessed. It was only on his deathbed that he agreed to hand over his manuscript about *the Rotation of Heavenly Bodies* for publication. This was not merely scientific information about the rotation of the Earth around the Sun, but it was, above all, political information that undermined the modern knowledge of the Church. Giordano Bruno, for putting forth similar information, was burned at the stake, and Galileo, following the Church's orders, had to abstain from advancing such ideas.

In the past, a lack of information was commonplace, even for state leaders who made key decisions. It is now expected that by 2050 all the information we possess about physical objects and people will be available *online*. Currently, people are involved in collecting data about everything. In the past, politicians had better access to certain domains of information; however, now, many people know how to get such domain-specific information better than politicians, and they can generate sound conclusions on that basis. This means many will be better versed than politicians, and they will be able to easily demonstrate the ignorance and poor decisions of political leaders; thus, such people are a significant threat to politicians.

Thanks to the Industrial Revolution of the 19th century, we understand the role of the atom in the construction of matter, which for the average person is understood as comprising tables, houses, cars, etc. In the Information Revolution of the 21st century, a similar role to the atom is being played by bits of information (basically the number 1 or 0), which comprises digital documents, newspapers, books, etc. The difference is that the universal digitization of information threatens to "end" civilization and all kinds of institutions, such as newspapers, publishing houses, universities, political parties, and even states. Why do we need politicians, if we live in one global village (McLuhan & Powers, 1989), informed and happy?

THE SIMULATION AND ALGORITHMIZATION OF DEMOCRACY[1]

In the 1950s, the first commercial computer in the world, produced by Remington Rand for the Census Bureau, was UNIVAC I. CBS News used it for election night, and the show's host, renowned journalist Walter Cronkite, called it the "miracle of the modern age, the electronic brain." This computer was supposed to predict the results before the final results were even known: "This is not a joke or a trick," said CBS journalist Charles Collingwood: "it's an experiment. We don't know. We think it'll work. We hope it will work." UNIVAC developers were able to predict early on in the evening that Eisenhower would win. Still, they were not brave enough to trust their computer and announce the expected result, for they sought to avoid being disgraced in the event of an error.

The pioneers of computer science also dreamed of a machine capable of performing fast calculations on large amounts of weather forecasting data. Atmospheric actions just boil down to physics, and the relevant equations were well known. John von Neumann claimed that computers would soon allow people not only to predict the weather but also control it. He believed there could be a degree of perfection that we now know is unattainable because weather is a chaotic system. Still, the methods he invented (such as game theory) are used in supercomputers that operate non-stop in all the world's meteorological centers. Computers predict the weather by simulating it, that is, by creating models and allowing them to play out.

In 1959, Edward Greenfield, an advertiser from Madison Avenue in New York, wanted to try the same approach to anticipate human behavior. He founded the company "Simulmatics", a combination of the words "simulation" and "automatic," which he saw as new territory for scientifically minded advertising in business and politics.

For the first time, large amounts of data were collected by dynamically growing political business surveys. When Greenfield and his team formed Simulmatics before the 1960 election, they bought Gallup Poll results from the last four national elections, which amounted to 100,000 polls on punched out ballots. They sorted the poll questions into fifty "problem attitudes" and sorted people into demographic fields.

At first, Simulmatics tried to sell its services to potential Democratic candidates. "Should the candidate speak on civil rights issues in the South? From our model, we will be able to predict what such a speech would mean for each of the 1,000 subgroups of the population...and consequently to indicate a state in which this may affect the electoral vote," Greenfield wrote. This is what every savvy political consultant offers today.

When the Democratic presidential nomination went to Kennedy, Simulmatics sent a proposal to his campaign. They argued like this: "With speed, accuracy, precision, and performance, Simulmatics provides a unique test tube for a political strategist. Before he acts, it tells him what the impact of his handling of certain issues would be on voters' behavior."

After John Kennedy won the election, all hell broke loose.

- *The New York Herald Tribune* disclosed Kennedy's "secret weapon" as a "large, bulky monster called "Simulmatics." "Voters, you, myself, Ms. Smith next door, and Professor Jones at the university," have been reduced "to small punching cards, and the devices that our new Lord uses." Kennedy's staff panicked and tried to deny the entire affair.
- Kennedy himself warned on the campaign trail of "a growing crisis of automation - replacing people with machines."

Around the same time, science fiction writer Isaac Asimov began his *Foundation series*, which were based on psychohistory. The wise who mastered this science could foresee the rise and fall of empires. Psychohistory was the essence of sociology: it was the science of human behavior reduced to mathematical equations. Asimov's fictional future was not based on computers used to predict the future; rather, it was the work of geniuses who create magic with their recipes. The difference between Asimov and Simulmatics was that Asimov knew he was dreaming and fantasizing (Asimov, 1953, p. 1). People do not behave as predictably as pool balls or water molecules. Atmospheric simulation is based on variables such as temperature, pressure, and humidity, while the science of psychology has discovered no such mental or social variables that can be described as fundamental or measured accurately. No matter how fast our computers are able to calculate, we do not possess the scientific laws of behavior they would need to process their data. Perhaps this is not an unwelcomed state of affairs.

Simulmatics specialists predicted minor events within larger, more significant events, appearing at critical moments in the 1960s. After racial unrest in Detroit, Los Angeles, and other cities, Simulmatics conducted a study for the Kerner Commission, set up by Lyndon Johnson, to investigate the riots and their causes. One sociologist told the committee: "Until we can forecast riots with such correctness as the weather forecast predicts shower or snow, it will be challenging to develop a control policy rationally." This was the company's last breath. In 1968, Simulmatics went bankrupt and closed. One of her consultants was future Senator Daniel Patrick Moynihan, a well-known intellectual.

Everyone knows about Facebook; however, few heard of Cambridge Analytica in 2016, which helped Donald Trump get elected President. Founded in London by two wealthy conservatives, Robert Mercer and Steve Bannon, Cambridge Analytica conducted behavioral research and provided political advice on "psychography." The company secretly collected personal information from Facebook from more than 50 million Americans, allegedly violating Facebook's policies.

Thanks to Cambridge Analytica and Trump's separate digital operation, led by Brad Parscale, users of Facebook, Google, Twitter, Snapchat, and others were the target of thousands of messages, many of which were fake, regularly updated, and improved. Brittany Kaiser, a former business development director at Cambridge Analytica, was quoted saying, "we bombarded them through blogs, websites, articles, videos, ads, any platform you can imagine." Trump's campaign designed negative ads to affect at least three categories of voters: African-Americans, former supporters of Bernie Sanders, and young women who may have affections for Bill Clinton.

That was 2016, but in 2020, Cambridge Analytica disappeared; nevertheless, Facebook has only become more influential. In September 2020, its founder and chief executive, young Mark Zuckerberg, announced that the company would reject new political ads in the final week before the election – a symbolic gesture that served primarily to highlight the extraordinary control that one person has over an essential communication platform informing people in the United States and most of the world. Officially, Facebook prohibits "misinformation," but the rules do not apply to political advertising.

Jaron Lanier, a virtual reality pioneer who has become a strong critic of social media, describes Facebook's features as a "machine to modify mass behavior." Facebook's goal is to make everyone dependent on Facebook, but the company also sells its manipulation services to companies with different purposes. For example, Lanier (2018, p. 33) says:

If you're reading on a computer, your reading behavior will be correlated with other people's behavior. If somebody who has a reading form like yours and bought something after it was recognized in a certain way, then the chances get higher that you will get the same ad. You may be a target before an election that wants to bring out internal cynicism in people who are like you, to reduce the chances that you will vote differently.

Previously, radio and television broadcasters were subject to federal regulations. The Federal Communications Commission (FCC) had a tricky job balancing the freedom of speech, justice, and truth in advertising. However, when personal computers gained the ability to communicate with each other across networks around the world, few wanted the government to put a heavy hand on this free, decentralized, individualistic phenomenon. Few also wanted to pay for the information, even if it came from newspapers or books, which meant that corporate entrepreneurs instead turned to advertising and collecting personal data as sources of revenue. After all, must not the majority of content be free since (apparently) the media now solve all problems and acts in the name of the common good? Governments in democratic countries have not yet established effective rules and standards to protect the ownership, collection, and marketing of personal data. Facebook, Google, and Amazon are lobbying hard to prevent it.

ARE HUMANS JUST OPEN BOXES OF INFORMATION?

Thanks to informing science, human logic has been replaced with information logic. According to Bill Gates, a computer is a "passport" to use the digital world. Presumably, what the second richest man in the world (in 2020) is referring to is "reservoirs" of information, where the library is nothing more than a wholesaler of information, while universities simply supply students with information because learning is nothing more than absorbing information. Organizations, on the other hand, coordinate information; conferences are information exchanges; business meetings are about consolidating information; and markets are a game of stimulators and responses measured by money, which is value-defining information. Describing a person in these terms leads to their degradation as does the use of their personal data by Big Tech and other "smart traffickers" of information.

IS THE DIGITAL PROSPERITY OF THE INFORMATION ELITE SUSTAINABLE, AND WHAT DOES IT MEAN FOR IT PROFESSIONALS?

For the above reasons, people who are well informed and liberated from the hierarchical systems that were in force in feudalism and industrial capitalism are more aware of their life condition, which they want to improve. Therefore, they ask themselves questions such as, "after the collapse of the USSR, is Western capitalism the ultimate political solution, or is there an alternative?". Francis Fukuyama (1992) rushed to respond when, in 1992, he wrote that we are facing the *End of History* and are returning to the ideals of the French Revolution. He was wrong. These ideals have been lost in the conflicts between civilizations, which involve terrorist attacks, cyberwarfare, and tricks of the global economy. These conflicts do not apply official rules of war. On the other hand, there are those who are enthusiastic (albeit naïve) and who glorify the global economy (as a liberal economy), which resulted in a considerable increase in the assets of the financial elite. This was assisted by electronic systems, which allow for the rapid transfer of money where it can be multiplied the fastest; however, it has resulted in the progressive impoverishment of people who work for this elite (including low-level IT professionals).

A good but sad example of this is a number of IT professionals employed by Apple and Google. Some cannot afford to buy or rent an apartment and instead live in recreational vehicles on the streets of the cities where they work (see Figure 1). In a similar condition are the teachers who live in these cities and who teach the children of these IT professionals. On the other hand, several CEOs earn tens of millions of dollars a year and get several hundred million in bonuses in the form of company shares.

Figure 2 shows that workers need to stand for their entire shift. They are only given a short break. They then go back to their working-class hotel and change beds with a "roommate", who will start their production shift. Is this the success of globalization?

The "wonderful" digital world is very confusing. It works on the imagination very strongly, and it is hard not to be lured into this rat race since, of the 10 wealthiest people in the world, 6 are IT professionals, including the two at the very top.

1. Jeff Bezos – informatician (Amazon)
2. Bill Gates – informatician (Microsoft)
3. Warren Buffett
4. Bernard Arnault & family

Figure 1. This is how some of Google's employees live in Mountain View, California (Photo: Bloomberg. com)

Figure 2. The production of Apple smartphones in the Chinese factory Foxconn (Photo: Bloomberg.com)

5. Carlos Slim Helú & family (a large part of the estate is in telecommunications)
6. Amancio Ortega
7. Larry Ellison – informatician (Oracle-database)
8. Mark Zuckerberg – informatician (Facebook)
9. Michael Blumberg – informatician (Blumberg e-Press)
10. Larry Page – informatician (Google)

Among the next wealthiest people, 8 billionaires are only 21 to 29 years of age.

IS IT NECESSARY TO ADMIRE THE EFFECTIVENESS OF INFORMING TECHNOLOGY AS THE ENGINE OF TURBO-CAPITALISM?

In most countries of the world, IT professionals are among the highest earners. Why? The answer is that IT systems take advantage of opportunities for establishing high-speed information links across regional and national borders. This is also a consequence of integrating many business factors into a single integrated business system, which allows for rapid market domination and spectacular financial success. Hence, these businesses are referred to as being part of "turbo-capitalism".

Examples include Apple's smartphone and Google's marketing machinery. These companies only need to have headquarters for management and developers as well as rooms for servers, because their product is digital information and patents (which are also a form of information) that they trade, on which they make unimaginable profits. Another even more profitable e-business is the success achieved by Uber, which serves as an intermediary between a passenger and the owner of a car that uses the transport service. Other examples are Airbnb Inc., which is used to organize and offer housing accommodations, and Turo, which is used to rent vehicles from private owners. The former does not own any real estate listings or organize any events itself: it simply acts as an intermediary, receiving commissions for each booking. In total, the company has the largest number of rooms for rent in the world. These types of business are part of what is called the *sharing economy.*

Designing and implementing this type of e-business requires IT professionals, who not only develop such systems for others but sometimes organize similar businesses for themselves, only on a smaller scale.

All in all, "nuclear capitalism", as it should be called, has led to the development of enormous economic inequality between the financial elite and the rest of the world. This is shown by the fact that the 26 wealthiest people in the world have more wealth than the bottom 50% of the world's population (Luhby, 2019). In the United States, an employee at a Fortune 100 company would have to work 300 years to earn as much as their CEO in 2010 (Epping, 2020). However, countries such as China, Brazil, and India have been able to get millions of people out of poverty in the 21st century, thanks to Western outsourcing.

INCOME INEQUALITY IS A SOURCE OF GROWING DISCONTENT

A measure of economic progress is provided by the *Intergenerational Income Elasticity* (IGE) indicator, which measures the probability that children will earn more than their parents, i.e., it measures whether children will have upward mobility in the social ladder. If IGE = 1, it means that the child will make the same as their parents. In the United States, unfortunately, the rate has almost doubled in the last 50 years, as it has increased from 0.3 to 0.5. A comparative analysis with other countries indicates that, where income inequality is low, social advancement (measured by income) is more likely. Such countries include, for example, Denmark and Norway. In countries such as Brazil and the US, however, advancement a la the Great Gatsby is less and less likely.[2]

A popular indicator of economic inequality is the Gini index, which assigns 0 for countries with perfect equality (utopian) and 100 for maximum inequality. According to the World Bank (2019), selected countries have the following Gini values[3]:

- (1) South Africa: 63.0
- (2) Lesotho: 54.2
- (8) Brazil: 53.3
- (26) Chile: 46.6
- (51) United States: 41.5
- (53) Argentina: 41.2
- (68) China: 38.6
- (77) Russia: 37.7
- (95) India: 35.7
- (98) Italy: 35.4
- (107) Canada: 34.0
- (116) The United Kingdom: 33.2
- (121) France: 32.7
- (129) Poland: 31.8
- (125) Switzerland: 32.3
- (133) Germany: 31.7
- (141) Sweden: 29.2
- (144) Denmark: 28.2
- (146) Iceland: 27.8
- (149) Norway: 27.5
- (157) Belarus: 25.4
- (159) Ukraine: 25.0

To improve the Gini ranking, governments should invest in the distribution of knowledge in society, reflected in the UN Human Development Index in Table 1 (United Nations Development Programme, 2019).

Norway is the best caring country for the development of its citizens, where the education period of the inhabitants is about 2 years greater than for Poland.

Referring to these computerization indicators in the categories concerned, we come to the following conclusions about the best countries in the world:[4]

- The country that best uses online applications *is* South Korea.
- The country that best uses *e-government* is France.
- The country with the most extensive access to ICT tools is Luxembourg.

Table 1. UN Human Development Index for Selected Countries in 2019 (United Nations Development Programme, 2019)

Rank-ing	State	Gross Domestic Product Per Capita Basket Prices (International Monetary Fund, 2020) in Us Dollars	Index	Average Length of Life	Expected Number of Years of Education
1	Norway	76.638	0.954	82.3	18.1
2	Switzerland	67.558	0.946	83.6	16.2
3	Ireland	86.988	0.942	82.1	18.8
4	Germany	55.306	0.939	81.2	17.1
12	Finland	49.548	0.925	81.7	19.3
15	USA	67.426	0.925	78.9	16.3
19	Japan	46.827	0.915	84.5	15.2
22	South Korea	46.452	0.906	82.8	16.4
25	Spain	43.007	0.893	83.4	17.9
26	France	48.640	0.891	82.5	15.5
26	Czech Republic	40.585	0.891	79.2	16.8
30	Estonia	37.606	0.882	78.6	16.1
31	Cyprus	42.956	0.873	80.8	14.7
32	Greece	31.616	0.872	82.1	17.3
33	Poland	35.657	0.872	78.5	16.4

One measure of human capital is the Global Innovation Index, shown in Table 2. Innovation is not only determined by the invention of a new solution, but also by the conditions for its implementation, which are relevant before and after the application of the innovative concept. The following conditions are taken into account:

- Before implementation:
  - **Institutions** – political environment, legal environment, business environment
  - **Human Capital and Research** – education, higher education, research, and development
  - **Infrastructure** – IT, general infrastructure, sustainable development
  - **Market Development** – lending, investment, foreign trade
  - **Business Advancement** – knowledge of workers, innovation-based, knowledge assimilation
- After implementation:
  - **New Knowledge and Technology** – creating new knowledge, the realization of new knowledge, the dissemination of new knowledge
  - **Creative Solutions** – intangible creativity, material creativity, online-oriented creativity, and services

It is worth noting that one of the most outstanding innovators in the history of the world, Thomas Edison (1841-1931), did not have a formal higher education. Similarly, Frank Lloyd Wright (1867–1959),

Table 2. Global Innovation Index 2019 (World Intellectual Property Organization, 2019)

Country/Economy	Score (0-100)	Rank
Switzerland	67.24	1
Sweden	63.65	2
United States of America	61.73	3
Netherlands	61.44	4
United Kingdom	61.30	5
Finland	59.83	6
Denmark	58.44	7
Singapore	58.37	8
Germany	58.19	9
Israel	57.43	10
Republic of Korea	56.55	11
Ireland	56.10	12
Hong Kong	55.54	13
China	54.82	14
Japan	54.68	15
France	54.25	16
Canada	53.88	17
Luxembourg	53.47	18
Norway	51.87	19
Iceland	51.53	20
Austria	50.94	21
Australia	50.34	22
Belgium	50.18	23
Estonia	49.97	24
New Zealand	49.55	25
Czech Republic	49.43	26
Malta	49.01	27
Cyprus	48.34	28
Spain	47.85	29
Italy	46.30	30
Slovenia	45.25	31
Portugal	44.65	32
Hungary	44.51	33
Latvia	43.23	34
Malaysia	42.68	35
United Arab Emirates	42.17	36
Slovakia	42.05	37
Lithuania	41.46	38
Poland	41.31	39
Bulgaria	40.35	40
Greece	38.90	41
Viet Nam	38.84	42
Thailand	38.63	43
Croatia	37.82	44

a highly innovative American architect, also had no formal higher education. In America, one can even distinguish a period of innovation known as *Yankee ingenuity*.[5] Yankee ingenuity is a stereotype of creativity, technical solutions to practical problems, "know-how," self-reliance, and individual enterprise. The Yankees originated in New England (in the northeastern region of the United States) and developed much of the Industrial Revolution in the United States after the 1800s. The Yankees' ingenuity involved solving problems with materials at hand. Ingenious improvisation, adaptation, and the overcoming of material shortages were also commonplace after World War II. The American army used engineering solutions to military problems. For example, the American military *jeep* is spartan and cramped, but functional. It has become the ubiquitous symbolic vehicle of World War II, Yankee ingenuity, conceited determination, and meritocratic *Yankee* effectiveness. Today, "jeep" refers essentially to a characteristic American pragmatic approach to problem-solving.

For the sake of fairness, one should recall that the Russians, forced by a lack of materials, also showed an ingenuity that was not inferior to that of the Yankees. Their T34 tank is considered the best WWII tank, and the *Kalashnikov* AK-47 machine gun is regarded as the best rifle in the world.[6] The Russian technique is captured in the dictum "*it can bend but not break*."

CAN TRADE UNIONS INFLUENCE SUSTAINABLE SOCIAL DEVELOPMENT?

In theory, trade unions can influence sustainable social development, but in practice, they fight for survival. It is often believed that they inhibit technical progress, which increases labor productivity (and reduces employment). High prices, on the other hand, increase the costs and expenses of products for consumers. Such views are also applied by IT professionals so that their systems reduce labor requirements. One consequence of this is that American companies are not competitive with Chinese companies. How can an American worker compete with a Chinese worker who earns one dollar an hour and has no other extra money? With this business philosophy, 70,000 American factories have been relocated to Asia, minimizing the middle class and growing the US service economy to the maximum extent. This type of economy is based on low paying jobs, and thus workers do not have money available for additional consumption (after paying fixed bills). Such addition consumption is what develops business and supports the growth of the economy to absorb new hands to work.

It has been forgotten that fair wages mean a high level of consumption. This rule was invented by Henry Ford 100 years ago, when he put the famous Model T car on sale for below $300 for the mass consumer, including his employees, who got raises to $5 a day so they could buy the car. It has also been forgotten that America's economic boom in the 1960s occurred when trade unions were strong and cared about fair wages for their members.

Today, the digital business of Uber exploits drivers by treating them as "entrepreneurs," even taking away the tips that passengers provide in digital bills that charge a previously provided credit card. Uber drivers struggle to cover the costs of their "business," while the company's 40-year-old owner, Travis Kalanick, owns about $6 billion in stocks. He was removed in 2017 from the management of the company by the shareholders' board for scandals involving women. At any rate, Uber already operates in 600 cities around the world and is worth $70 billion. The operational success of the company is due to the excellent IT system and the exploitation of drivers, de facto their employees, and not independent "entrepreneurs."

Table 3. Percent of affiliated workers in trade unions and quality of life

State	Percentage of Employees in Trade Unions	Rank in the Quality of Life Index	Quality of Life Index	Gini Index
Iceland	90.4	7	180.74	27.8
Sweden	66.1	13	172.18	29.2
Belgium	54.2	29	149.75	27.7
Italy	34.3	36	138.97	35.4
Canada	25.9	21	158.88	34.0
Ireland	24.2	27	150.16	31.8
U. Kingdom	23.2	19	161.20	33.2
Japan	17.1	17	163.23	32.1
Germany	16.7	9	177.25	31.7
Poland	15.2	46	125.20	31.8
Mexico	12.0	50	120.65	48.3
USA	10.1	15	169.78	41.5
Turkey	8.6	45	126.40	41.9
France	7.9	26	150.68	32.7

Source: (McCarthy, 2019; Numbeo, 2020; World Bank, 2019)

As shown in Table 3, countries with higher percentages of trade unions tend to have higher quality of life indices and the lowest rates of financial inequality (Gini). For example, Mexico, which has a low percentage of unionized workers, has a poor quality of life index and the highest rate of financial inequality. Similarly, the United States and Turkey have low trade union membership and high levels of inequality in wealth. This is due to the fact that the financial elite is doing everything in its power in these countries to make trade unions weak. Unfortunately, this elite is acting against its own interests, for through automation, robotics, and computerization, it is reducing labor costs while maintaining low wages; however, this simultaneously reduces consumerism and, consequently, its business.

IT professionals do not have a trade union. Still, they have their professional and scientific associations, so they should develop trends that are not only aimed at "modern" ICT, but are also human-friendly.

Is it not a paradox that IT professionals want to "rule the world" (via Big Tech), yet they cannot govern themselves?

HOW BIG IS THE "BLACK ECONOMY" AND WHAT IS THE ROLE OF DIGITAL INFORMING IN IT?

The ubiquitous and almighty Internet has opened up opportunities for illegal activities in business. Beneath official sites such as YouTube, Facebook, and Google, one finds the *deep web* and the *dark web*. It should be noted that deep web sites are not illegal. They are somewhat hidden because many companies do not want their operations to be visible to the general public. The deep web is, for example, where banking operations are carried out and where medical records are archived.

The terms "deep web" and "dark web" are sometimes used interchangeably, but their meanings are not synonymous. "Deep web" refers to everything that is not indexed on the Internet and is therefore not accessible through search engines such as Google. The deep web content includes everything behind a firewall and everything that requires login credentials. This includes any content that owners have blocked from indexing by online robots. Medical records, paid content, member sites, and confidential corporate pages are just a few examples of what makes up the deep web.

The dark web is a subset of the deep web. The dark web is intentionally hidden and requires access through specific browsers, such as Tor. No one knows the size of the dark web, but by most estimates, it is about 5% of the content of the entire Internet. On the other hand, it is estimated that the size of the deep web is about 95% of the Internet. Thus, only a small part of the Internet is accessible through a standard web browser, which is generally known as a "clean network."

In addition to legitimate functions, the dark web also includes illegal drug trafficking, spying, the sale of falsified human identities, and the trade of stolen credit cards, smartphones, weapons, and so forth. Networks such as Tor and the Invisible Internet Project (I2P) allow access to such sites while also guaranteeing the anonymity to the user. These networks use "deep browsers" and "deep search engines" to search for anything *a la* Google. The Tor browser directs a user to a website through a series of proxies supported by thousands of volunteers worldwide, making the IP address of the original recipient impossible to identify and undetectable.

The following categories are types of cyber-attacks and targeted data types:

- Infection or attacks, including malware, distributed denial-of-service (DDoS) attacks, and botnets
- Access, including remote access Trojans, keyloggers, and exploits
- Espionage, including services, customization, and targeting
- Support services such as tutorials
- Phishing attacks
- Customer data
- Operational data
- Financial data
- Intellectual property / trade secrets
- Other emerging threats

There are three risk variables for each attack category:

1. The devaluation of the company, which may include undervaluation of brand confidence, reputational damage, or loss of position as a competitor,
2. The disruption of business, which may include digital attacks or other malware affecting business operations,
3. The robbing of a business, which may include intellectual property theft or espionage that undermines the company's ability to compete or causes direct financial losses.

In 2013, the FBI dismantled the largest online black market, the *Silk Road* (a reference to the old trade route that ran from Europe to China), where various goods were traded. The operators and owners of this forum were arrested and sentenced to life in prison without the possibility of parole. However, drug trafficking continues, and the illicit drug market is estimated at half a trillion dollars per year. Combating this trade usually leads to the development of new gangs, the members of whom, in the name of fast and high wages, accept the risk of arrest. On the other hand, when the sale of marijuana was booming in Colorado in 2017, the state received a "boost" of $200 million in taxes from the sale of this substance.

One has to guard against hackers who gain access to codes that allow them to enter into the bank accounts of customers and make unauthorized online purchases. In addition, there are currently many illegal digital operations are being carried out by governments and political parties. Hence the question is, who can supervise these supervisors? The ethical and legal responsibility falls on IT professionals, who are absent in this process and can carry out such illegal operations.

IS CORRUPTION COMPUTERIZED?

Generally speaking, corruption involves the abuse of power by individuals in positions of authority for private gain. Corruption can be classified in different ways depending on the money lost and the sector in which it takes place. "Grand corruption" consists of acts committed at a high level of government that distort the central functioning of the state, enabling leaders to reap the benefits at the expense of the public good. "Petty corruption" refers to the daily abuse of the power conferred by low- and middle-level government officials when dealing with ordinary citizens, who often try to access essential goods or services in places such as hospitals, schools, police departments, and other agencies. "Systemic corruption" is corruption that results due to poor organizational processes established by policymakers at institutions. Overall, it can be said that politicians abuse their position to maintain their power, status, and wealth. Corrupt decisions affect societies in many ways. In the worst-case scenarios, it costs lives. Regardless, it concerns human freedom, health, and money. The cost of corruption can be divided into four main categories: political, economic, social, and environmental.

Globally, corruption is estimated to amount to about 3% of the gross world product (GWP). The least corrupt countries in the world are New Zealand and Denmark, with an index of 87/100. The most corrupt countries are Somalia – 9/100, South Sudan – 12/100, and Syria – 13/100, where civil wars and corruption are expected in everyday life (Transparency International, 2019). Table 4 shows the Corruption Index for selected countries.

Table 4. Corruption Index 2019 for selected countries

#	Country	Region	2019	2018	2017	2016	2015
41	Poland	Western Europe & European Union	58	60	60	62	63
41	Cyprus	Western Europe & European Union	58	59	57	55	61
41	Cabo Verde	Sub-Saharan Africa	58	57	55	59	55
44	Costa Rica	Americas	56	56	59	58	55
44	Latvia	Western Europe & European Union	56	58	58	57	56
44	Czech Republic	Western Europe & European Union	56	59	57	55	56

Source: (Transparency International, 2019)

The role of computer science in corruption is fundamental. Typical corruption activities include the following examples:

- Someone places money in a bank that believes the money comes from legitimate business, thanks to gradual payments of small sums, which increase overtime building to avoid suspicion. Of course, this "trust" can be bought from a banker. The IT system should be designed to detect this technique of corruption. In Caribbean banks, such techniques are generally not taken into account. Such a bank transfers corrupt money to New York, Paris, or Warsaw in small amounts, and it is challenging to detect such transactions.
- "Money laundering" consists of dispersing money in different banks in multiple transfers under various transaction names and then gathering them in one bank via a layering technique. In some cases, to make tracing the transactions difficult, transfers occur via digital currency like Bitcoin, which are usually anonymous with unclear places of origin. Often these transfers are gift cards like those from Amazon or iTunes. The scope of money laundering includes "winnings" from casinos and lotteries. A "customer" buys a yacht or Ferrari and claims that they were lucky enough to win money in the casino. In Peru, the authorities have concluded that if the mafia cannot be eliminated, it should be motivated to invest its capital in Peru and not abroad. For this reason, they were officially allowed to "launder" money in casinos. IT specialists supervising the IT system in banks should be well versed in "what" they are dealing with.
- Offshore (i.e., foreign) bank companies, such as in Cyprus where there is a so-called "tax haven", receive transfers from clients in another country who make fictitious purchases or sales at very high prices so that over time the origin of this money has a semblance of legality. An example is the Operação Lava Jato (Operation Car Wash), a corruption scandal in Brazil detected in 2019. The investigation into money laundering then expanded to allegations of corruption at Petrobras, where executives allegedly accepted bribes in exchange for awarding contracts to construction companies at inflated prices. The investigation is called "Operation Car Wash " because it was first discovered at a car wash in Brazil. It concerns members of the state administration of the oil company Petrobras, politicians from Brazil's largest parties (including Republican presidents), presidents of the Chamber of Deputies and the Federal Senate, state governors, and employees from large Brazilian companies who received money from "happy" contractors who inflated costs to assure there was money to pay out to politicians and their parties. Brazil's federal police consider the investigation to be the largest in the country's history. After the publication of the so-called "Panama Papers", it turned out that many famous people use this strategy, ranging from Queen Elizabeth II (who probably wasn't aware of what her stockbroker was doing) to Madonna, Bono, and others.

    Embezzlement involves misappropriating funds. For example, this could involve misappropriating money from large accounts in private medical practices for chemotherapy treatments, who receive large donations for the sick. The misappropriated money is usually invested in luxury apartments, shopping malls, or luxury golf courses. For example, in new luxury skyscrapers in New York City, 60% of apartments, priced at several hundred thousand dollars each, are bought by foreigners who do not live in them and do not rent them to others. In one of these skyscrapers, the owner can park his car on the same floor as his apartment. These skyscrapers are being built in some cities for "investors" such as the former President of Liberia, who was convicted of misappropriating USD 3 billion, its annual GDP.

Corruption on such a large scale introduces a lot of money into the economy for "legitimate" investments done via information systems. However, investing in large IT infrastructures may signal corruption. These are usually colossal outlays of millions of dollars. The main trick is to purchase the equipment inconspicuously and to install it quickly. Such equipment is installed in hundreds of rooms, and it looks quite impressive, but it is not used as it should be.

DOES COMPUTERIZATION HELP DEMOCRACY?

The problems of the 21st century can be compounded by powerful tools such as information technology, for whoever controls this information has power. However, citizens, thanks to informing technology, are better informed and do not always accept this state of affairs. This is especially the case in the United States, which, although it did not undergo a social revolution like France (1789) or Russia (1917), has recently seen large social movements. One such movement of the young generation in 2015-2020 was led by the well-seasoned politician Bernie Sanders, who spent his honeymoon in the USSR. This movement aimed to change the regime from capitalist to socialist, with a color similar to the real socialism that prevailed for 72 years in Eastern Europe. The answer to this movement was the populism of President Donald Trump, which has been undermining the foundations of liberal capitalism. A certain irony is added by the fact that President Trump is a billionaire.

In Europe, populist movements are also occurring in Hungary and Poland. To avoid the complicated definitions of political movements that are popular at present, it can be said that there are two clearly distinct political directions: one towards democracy and the other towards authoritarianism. The current state of politics is characterized by the Democracy Index, developed by the Economist Intelligence Unit. The index measures the conditions of democracy in 167 countries. It is based on 60 groups of indicators in five categories: electoral process and pluralism, government functioning, political participation, political culture, and civil liberties. Each country was awarded points from 0 to 10 in each of the five categories, which were then averaged for an overall score. Overall scores from 8.01 to 10 are considered full democracies, of which there are 20 in the world. There are ten countries with scores of 9.0 or higher. They are the most democratic nations in the world (Economist Intelligence Unit, 2019).[7]

Established authoritarian regimes strengthened their power in 2019, as exemplified by China. In addition, new authoritarian regimes are on the rise, such as in Hungary, Turkey, and the Philippines. Freedom House has titled its 2020 annual report on freedom worldwide "Democracy under Lockdown," noting that conditions for democracy and human rights have worsened in 80 countries (Repucci & Slipowitz, 2020). This means that liberal democracy based on turbo-capitalism and surveillance (see the chapter *the History and Repercussions of Strategic Informing Technology*) is under attack from influential leaders who believe that they represent the voices of many citizens.

In such a situation, IT workers may feel confused about what strategies are appropriate to adopt when developing informing technologies. Unfortunately, their fate in part depends on whether they work under democratic or authoritarian conditions. At any rate, computerization has the power to strengthen authoritarianism with the result that that it may be difficult to stop. For example, most dictatorships use the *Pegasus system*[8], which tracks every citizen in the country who uses digital equipment. In addition, computerization can cause chaos in democracy, gradually destroying it; however, it can also strengthen democracy.

IT professionals who are environmentally conscious know that both capitalism and socialism (as well as communism) are systems based on constant economic growth, which leads to population growth and increased depletion of the strategic resources of the small and exploited planet Earth. What responses do we expect from IT professionals? First of all, they should prioritize the development of ICT, which will lead to a sustainable civilization. Contrary to the idea that IT professionals merely stare at a computer, that they do not see the world they create, and that they do not realize the size of their own ego, they are actually increasingly involved in repairing the world.

THE ROLES OF HACKERS

One can distinguish between positive and negative roles played by hackers. They may be for or against an enemy state, may favor or oppose a certain political party, and may endorse or reject a political principle. Hackers who are IT professionals can stand up for democracy in their country and in the world; however, they can also serve authoritarian power. In other words, they can either perform their duties (whether they be deemed ethical or not) or enter into various types of agreements that do not comply with their obligations.

The globalization of the economy is intended to promote peace through international trade. However, "appetite comes with eating," and some countries want to dominate the economy and geopolitics. These countries include China, the United States, Russia, Israel, Iran, and others, all of which use computer science to help with espionage, counterintelligence, strategic sabotage, targeted attacks, enslavement, demonstrations, theft, blackmail, ransom, manipulation, and the widespread disruption of peace. As can be seen, the range of potential employment for IT professionals is wide.

One obstacle digital hackers attempt to overcome is the barrier of coded information, similar to the codes created by the German Enigma machine and the American SIGABA[9]. Currently, Apple allows any user of its smartphones to encode information that even the FBI cannot crack. The company goes so far as to deny the FBI access to coded information used by terrorists. Hence, the US National Security Agency (NSA) has developed many information code-breaking systems. These include NOBUS ("Nobody But US"), BULLRUN, Dual_EC_DRBG, ScreenOS, and so forth.

Below are examples of different types of hacking that have occurred (Buchanan, 2020):

- *Strategic spying* – Chinese hackers specialize in this regard, which involves penetrating the computer systems of American leaders in politics, business, engineering, and other strategic areas. Their goal is to gain advanced knowledge about American leaders and firms, without which China could not compete globally. As a result of such attacks, China has been able to develop the production of their weapons systems. One specific project was an attack called "Operation Aurora", which took place in 2010. The attack targeted the e-communications of 34 American companies, including Microsoft and Google. The aim was, among other things, to find Gmail messages of Chinese dissidents who used American informing technology. In addition, they wanted to find out what American hackers target in China. They also sought to take possession of secrets American leaders have about strategy. Another digital spying attack came in 2012. The hacking attempt was carried out by Su Bin, who worked for a small aerospace company in Canada. Bin would watch for trends in aviation worldwide and then give Chinese hackers the names and addresses of leaders in the field. The hackers would then specifically target these leaders in spying operations.

- *Counterintelligence* – This consists of protecting one's own intelligence agency against spying attempts by enemy intelligence agencies. To this end, the NSA initiated a project to track and destroy Chinese hackers on US networks, setting up a *Threat Operation Center*. Counterintelligence officers in the Tailored Access Operations (TAO) unit worked with computers hacked by the Chinese and on servers the Chinese used in other countries (e.g., Taiwan) to wipe their tracks. It turned out that Chinese hackers were not very careful and were easy to recognize. The TAO unit also penetrated the networks of the People's Liberation Army (PLA) and uncovered the intentions of their hackers before they even started their operations. Furthermore, the agency has developed the TUTELAGE system, which can block Chinese hackers—of course, until the Chinese improve their hacking. Americans can also indirectly spy on North Koreans by exploiting South Koreans, who know better how to spy their Northern compatriots.
- *Strategic sabotage* – The Americans developed *Stuxnet* (2007 and 2009) to sabotage nuclear installations (centrifuges) in Iran.
- *Destroying the target* – In 2012, Iranian hackers infiltrated computers connected with Aramco's oil facilities in Saudi Arabia in retaliation for its good relations with the United States. First, they got into Aramco via email and then into the company network to install a destructive viral program called "Shamoon" on its servers and PCs. This program began to gradually destroy the company data sets. The program then corrupted the codes of the master boot record, which is used when starting the computer. On the screens of the destroyed computers, the Iranians displayed a message: "Cutting Sword of Justice," which indicated who attacked Aramco. Repairing the installation took the company five months and millions of dollars. Another example from 2012 involved the North Koreans, who destroyed the digital assets of Sony Pictures Entertainment after gaining access to the email of company employee Nathan Gonsalez. This attack damaged 70% of Sony's IT infrastructure. Digital collections of films and documents were lost, and new videos prepared for distribution were made available to millions of people for free. However, the primary purpose of the attack was to stop Sony Pictures from showing the film the Interview, which involved a fictional plot to kill North Korean leader Kim Jong-un. Sony Pictures initially withdrew the film after the cyberattack and threats; however, upon President Barack Obama's suggestion, it later released the movie on screens and achieved great financial success thanks to this cyber scandal.
- *Political destabilization* – In the 2016 US presidential election, Russian hackers penetrated the Democratic National Committee's network and took possession of thousands of emails from the party's top activists, including presidential candidate Hillary Clinton. Gradually, these emails were released, along with documents from WikiLeaks. The documents contained compromising information that contributed to the defeat of Clinton. To this day, she cannot put the loss behind her, believing that Donald Trump, the winner of the election, was behind this leaked information. However, an almost two-year Special Counsel investigation with a large budget, culminating in a 500-page report, did not confirm Clinton's accusations.
- An example concerning Poland occurred in August 2018. Onet.pl revealed an online trolling campaign in the Ministry of Justice that sought to discredit judges critical of PiS (the ruling Law and Justice party). As a result of the publication, the then Deputy Minister who oversaw the running of the group resigned. In addition, certain lawyers for the troll network are on extended leave to "improve their health."

DICTATORSHIPS LIKE INFORMING TECHNOLOGY

Dictatorships need IT specialists who are dedicated to them because they treat ICT as a weapon. The following approaches in this area can be distinguished:

- **USSR and Russia**: In the USSR, IT involved in scientific computing was appreciated because it helped the USSR in the arms race with the United States from 1950 to 1991. On the other hand, IT was not appreciated as an information tool in the bureaucracy of the centrally planned economy. Even cybernetics, with its feedback loop necessary in automated systems, was seen as involved with services of capitalists who enslave the working class. IT applications were accepted at the company level because authorities did not want to improve information systems at the headquarters of the economy, which would publicize the truth about the economy and well-being of the citizens. Since the fall of the USSR in 1992, Internet access in the Russian Federation has been controlled by many rules and regulations. Since 2012 the Russian Federal Communications, Information Technology, and Media Surveillance Service *(Roskomnadzor)* has maintained a centralized blacklist (known as a "single register"). This list traces and censors individual URLs, domain names, and IP addresses. Initially, this service was used to block sites containing materials promoting drug abuse and production, descriptions of suicidal methods, and child pornography. Subsequently, however, its scope was expanded to include material classified as "inappropriate" in the Federal List of Extremist Material. According to Freedom House, these rules have often been used to block criticism of the federal government or local administrations. A law prohibiting the "abuse of freedom of the mass media" allows online media to be shut down. In March 2018, a law was passed that introduces fines for people who (according to the government) spread "fake news" and show a "gross disrespect" towards state authorities.
- **Poland**: In the Polish People's Republic after the fall of the Gomułka regime, a team of IT professionals oversaw a computer development program from 1971-75 based on the public INFOSTRADA network. This would have resulted in the horizontal spread of socio-economic information, which until that time was only possible from "top to bottom." Thanks to certain "scholars," mostly educated in the USSR, the computer development program was abolished.[10]
- **China**: Internet censorship is more extensive and advanced in China than any other country in the world. The Chinese government blocks the content of websites and monitors the access of individuals to the Internet. As required by the Chinese government, major online platforms and messaging services have to have extensive self-censorship mechanisms. Some employ thousands of employees to oversee content, and they invest in advanced AI algorithms. Many controversial events are prohibited from being present in the news, preventing Chinese citizens from knowing their government's actions. Such measures inspired the following nickname for this policy: "China's Great Firewall." Methods for blocking websites are widely used, including DNS blocking, blocking access to IP addresses, analyzing and filtering URLs, inspecting packets, and resetting connections. Back in 2006, Amnesty International (2006) noted that China has "the largest number of imprisoned journalists and cyber-dissidents in the world," and more recently Paris's Reporters Without Borders (2017) sharply rebuked China's Internet surveillance model. Common alleged crimes against Internet users include communicating with groups abroad, signing online petitions, and calling for government reform. The government stepped up efforts to repair relations and neutralize comments critical of the regime after a series of massive protests against pol-

lution and anti-corruption. Many of these protests and ethnic riots were organized or publicized via instant messaging, chat, and SMS. China's state Internet police employed around 2 million IT professionals in 2013.

- **Saudi Arabia**: As far as the information society is concerned, there are various contradictions. Although the Saudi government spends significant amounts on the ICT sector, this country, like China, is widely regarded as one of the most restrictive regarding Internet access. Before granting public Internet access in 1999, the Saudi government spent two years building infrastructure to control all Internet traffic through government-managed servers. Furthermore, the massive development of public networks and wireless access is now changing to allow for new technologies that maintain security and control over the use of the media, which is part of the socio-political culture of Saudi Arabia. The Internet Services Unit runs the national filtering system at King Abdulaziz City for Science and Technology (KACST)[11] and is regulated by the Communications and Information Technology Commission (CITC). This unit investigates clear violations of regulations (such as criminal activity, pornography, and gambling) by assessing all Internet traffic coming into the Kingdom of Saudi Arabia. It goes through a proxy farm system with content filtering software, a system commonly used by many governments to ensure that web content is compliant with national law. The system filters the list of addresses with prohibited pages. This unpublished list is updated daily by the security team based on content filtering policies. A list of sites considered "pornographic" is also periodically provided by the filter software provider.
- **North Korea**: Access to the Internet in North Korea is available but severely limited. It is allowed only with special permission and is used mainly for government purposes and by foreigners. The country has some broadband infrastructure, including fiber-optic connections between the central institutions; however, online services for most individuals and institutions are provided through a free national-only network, known as Kwangmyong. Access to the global Internet is limited to a much smaller group. The North Korean government is training computer hackers at the Kim Chaek University of Technology and Kim Il-sung University to make money abroad. For example, a group of hackers from North Korea based in Shenyang, China has developed and sold auto-programs (programs that allow players to gain experience and currency in a game).

THE 2020 CORONAVIRUS PANDEMIC

The coronavirus pandemic has demonstrated the invaluable advantages of ICT. Thanks to computerization, it was possible to buy food and medicine online and have these goods directly delivery to one's home. It was also possible to work remotely online for employers that accepted this change. Finally, it was possible for state and regional authorities to communicate with local authorities online. Other such advantages could also be noted; however, despite the many benefits of e-communication, Nobel laureate Olga Tokarczuk presented a rather sad picture of civilization amidst this pandemic:

I also fear that the virus will alert us to another old truth: how very much we aren't equal. While some of us fly off on private planes to homes on islands or in woodland isolation, others will remain in cities, operating power plants and waterworks. Still others will risk their lives working in shops and hospitals. Some will make money off the pandemic while others will lose everything they have. The coming crisis will undermine all of the principles that seemed to us so sound; many countries won't be able to handle it, and in the face of their downfalls, new orders will awaken, as is often the case after crises. We believe we are staying home, reading books and watching television, but, in fact, we are readying ourselves for a battle over a new reality that we cannot even imagine, slowly coming to understand that nothing will ever be the same. The condition of mandatory quarantine, of billeting the family at home, may make us aware of things we have no desire to admit: that our family depletes us, that the bonds of our marriage have long since slackened. Our children will come out of quarantine addicted to the Internet, and many of us will be aware of the senselessness and futility of circumstances in which we mechanically, by the power of inertia, remain. And what if the number of murders, suicides, and sufferers of mental illnesses grows? (Tokarczuk, 2020)

Tokarczuk (2020) concludes that "[b]efore our eyes, the smoke is dispersing from the civilizational paradigm that has shaped us over the past two hundred years: that we are the masters of creation, that we can do anything, that the world belongs to us. A new time draws near."

POSITIVE HACKERS

It is worth pointing out that hackers, as IT professionals, can play positive roles, such as defending democracy in their own country or in the world. In general, hackers have a bad reputation, being accused of destroying information technology infrastructure. However, some are creative individuals who disagree with the established social order in the name of the common good. Hence, some versions of hacking are expressions activism for democracy in the age of digitalization (Webb, 2020). Hackers are well aware of the risks posed by the concentration of financial power and digital surveillance by Big Tech and the State. This is why they are trying to preserve democracies, at least in cyberspace. Here are some examples of this type of activism:

- **The Chaos Computer Club** of the 1950s was founded at MIT (Massachusetts Institute of Technology). It developed an e-Code (principles) for programmers: access to computers should be equal for everyone; information from computers should be free; no one should have confidence in bureaucrats.
- **The People's Computer Company** (founded in the 1970s in Silicon Valley, California) provided programming courses for everyone and offered computers for 50 cents per hour of use, competing with IT business centers.
- **The Polish Committee for Automatic Information Processing (PKAPI) at the National Technical Organization** in Warsaw selected a group of volunteers under the direction of Andrew Targowski[12] and developed the Program for the Development of Informatics in 1970, which aimed to activate the Polish economy and society. This took place at the time of the fall of the communistic regime of Władysław Gomułka.
- **The Homebrew Computer Club** (founded in 1975 in Menlo Park, Silicon Valley and lasting until 1986) provided help to enthusiasts building digital cameras. It was as a member of this club that Steve Wozniak, inventor of Apple I, learned ICT. The Homebrew Computer Club newsletter was one of the most influential forces in connecting Silicon Valley culture. It was created and edited by its members, and it initiated the idea of the personal computer and helped its members

build original computers, such as Altair. One of the notable influences on current events was Bill Gates's 1976 "Open Letter to Hobbyists", which accused the first hackers of breaking the law.

- **The Chaos Computer Club** was created in Hamburg in 1982 by Wau Holland, who called for the formulation of data rights, software copyrights, and the right to encode information. In 1984 Holland and Steffen Wernery hacked the official telex channel Bildschmirmtext (Btx). The Club also fought the Federal Post (Deutsche Bundespost-DBP) because it monopolized the telex system.
- **Cypherpunks** are activists advocating the widespread use of strong cryptography and privacy-enhancing technologies as a path to social and political change. Initially communicating via an electronic mailing list, these supporters and their informal groups aim to achieve a high level of privacy and security through the proactive use of cryptography. They have been active since the late 1980s.
- **The Electronic Frontier Foundation (EFF)** is an international digital rights nonprofit group based in San Francisco, California. The Foundation was set up in July 1990 by John Gilmore, John Perry Barlow, and Mitch Kapor to promote civil liberties online. EFF provides funds for legal defense in court and sets out *amicus curiae* guidelines that underpin their activities. They also aim to protect individuals and new technologies against legal abuse. The organization works to expose government fraud, provides guidance in court, recommends and organizes political action and mass protests, supports certain new technologies (if they believe the technologies protect personal freedoms and civil liberties on the Internet), and runs databases and websites with relevant news and information. They also monitor and challenge laws they believe would violate personal freedoms and fair use.
- **Linux** is a free operating system designed in 1992 and put into public use by the Finn Linus Torvalds. It became competitive with OS Windows (Microsoft) and has been accepted by academic computing centers for minicomputers.
- **The Occupy movement** is an international progressive socio-political movement that opposes social and economic inequalities and the lack of "true democracy" around the world. The movement originated from the *Occupy Wall Street* movement in 2011. Its aim is primarily to promote social and economic justice and new forms of democracy. The movement had many different aims because local groups often had their own goals. Still, its main concern was how large corporations (and the global financial system) controlled the world in a way that disproportionately benefited a small minority, weakened democracy, and caused instability. Part of the Occupy movement is what Manfred Steger calls the "global justice movement." This movement was organized very quickly, thanks to the Internet, and focuses on digital capitalism.
- **WikiLeaks** is an international nonprofit organization that publishes leaked information and discloses media provided by anonymous sources. The website launched in 2006 in Iceland by the Sunshine Press. In the first ten years, WikiLeaks published 10 million documents online. Julian Assange, an Australian online activist, is generally described as its founder and director.
- **Edward Joseph Snowden** (born June 21st, 1983) is an American informant who copied and disclosed highly classified information from the National Security Agency (NSA) in 2013 when he was an employee and subcontractor of the Central Intelligence Agency (CIA). These disclosures revealed many global surveillance programs run by the NSA and the Five Eyes Intelligence Alliance in collaboration with telecommunications companies and European governments. This initiated a cultural discussion about national security and individual privacy.

- **"Privacy for the weak and transparency for the powerful"** was a slogan created due to the actions of WikiLeaks and Snowden. It was popularized among members of the Chaos Computer Club in the US and Europe and became a leading idea of hackers supporting democracy.
- **The Internet** has been the subject of many discussions and publications, including critical evaluations. Harry Halpin, for example, published the book *the Future of the Internet – and How to Stop It.*
- **Hacking Team** (a Milan-based company) produced software for the police and authoritarian regimes, which was met with fierce criticism. This ultimately led to the destruction of their digital resources in 2015 and the acquisition of the company in 2019 by Momento Labs.
- **Digital platforms** were created between 2010 and 2020 in Spain, Italy, and Canada to ameliorate the failing democratic processes in these countries.
- **LibrePlanet** is a community project that holds an annual conference hosted by the Free Software Foundation in Boston. LibrePlanet is a social platform for activists, domain experts, and concerned citizens to discuss current problems regarding technology and ethics. LibrePlanet participants and speakers discuss controversial issues, such as the free software movement, how to fight Facebook, how to make software-driven cars safe, how to stop algorithms from making terrible decisions, how to enjoy the convenience of mobile phones and digital home assistants without constant supervision, what the future of digital currency is, and whether we can have an Internet that facilitates respectful dialogue.
- **The Berkman Klein Center for Internet & Society** (Harvard University) is engaged in global issues and has been trying to understand how the development of Internet-related technologies is inspired by the social context in which they are embedded and how the use of these technologies affects society. It aims to help develop Internet-related laws, and it examines the impact of the Internet on democratic norms and modes, including its effects on civil society and the media. The center's research aims are to promote citizens' rights to access, develop, and share independent sources of information, to strengthen Internet networks, and to debate ideas freely with civil society and government.
- **The Panoptykon Foundation** was established in 2009 due to complaints that we live in an increasingly supervised society that lacks not only concrete guarantees protecting citizens from a loss of freedom but also substantive public debate on the subject. The foundation wants to fill this gap because our world faces the growing danger that each of our activities is monitored and recorded thanks to thousands of databases, surveillance cameras, mobile phones, and digital traces left on the Internet. Modern tools intersect with various manifestations of technological surveillance. Step by step, we are tamed with further control over our lives, and we often accept these measures of control as a civilizational necessity, from which there is no escape. The constant increase in surveillance is intended to help protect us from ourselves; however, little by little, we are giving up basic liberties, hoping that this will provide us with greater security (often in vain). "Either freedom or security" is a false dichotomy. Surveillance can improve safety, but just as often, there are entirely different objectives behind it, political or financial. At the very least, it is worth being aware of these issues.
- **The Digital Poland Foundation** (established in 2017) aims to create opportunities for the Polish economy by responding to digital challenges, and it wants to teach politicians and citizens about digital technologies. Issues such as 5G, blockchain, and PEM are utterly alien to most Poles, and artificial intelligence is associated with the bloodthirsty machines of the Terminator. It is no dif-

ferent among politicians. The Digital Poland Foundation wants to change this by initiating discussion about the digital future of Poland and by implementing educational actions aimed at both the government and voters. According to the foundation, information on new technologies is at a superficial level in Poland. Moreover, the foundation also holds that technological topics are not of great interest to Poles and, in the mainstream media, one would be hard-pressed to find them.

Table 5. Summary of the main global and local challenges for ICT-strategist in the 21st century.

Source	Effect	The Role of ICT	Feasibility
Big Tech	Surveillance capitalism	Counteract	Limited by lobbyists
Humanity as a source of information	Dehumanization	Support computerization with a human face	Hampered by the enthusiasm of young IT professionals
The prosperity of the digital elite who control corporations	Disproportionate distribution of earnings and bonuses to subordinate employees	Seek help from IT professionals	Hampered by the attitude of elite lobbyists
Concentration and monopolization; strategies of consumerism and unsustainable business growth	Nuclear capitalism	Develop legal systems and monitor business anomalies to create a dignified life	Hampered, but possible by grassroots movements; also possible through social revolution
Enormous income inequalities	Destabilization of trust in the state and the development of populism	Use ICT to be aware of reality and find ethical options	Hindered by lobbyists, unless they find a social revolution expedient or are seeking new social systems
The role of trade unions	A fight for existence as they increase business costs	Organize a trade union of ICT professionals	It is possible if there are suitable leaders
Black economy	The development of digital crime to the detriment of legal businesses and citizens' health	Avoid participation in such schemes and provide information about the services	Depends on the ethics of ICT professionals
Political destabilization of the world	Crises of established institutions and contentious relations between states	Cultivate a sharp awareness of the state of affairs and implement smart systems	ICT strategist may be confused about what ICT strategy to choose to support more overarching socio-political agendas; one should seek advice
Corruption	Social costs	Expose corruption	Computer scientists must take risks, but they should know how to expose corruption while also caring for their security
Hackers against other countries	Cyberwar and cyberwarfare	Create services in which digitalization is a weapon	If ICT strategists participate in it, they must make sure they are following international law
Hackers in defense of democracy	Publications about actions that destroy democracy	Organize clubs for democratic computing	Depends on the awareness and ethical commitment of ICT professionals
Hackers that serve dictatorships	Dictatorships are reinforced by computerization	Avoid participation	A high risk for ICT professionals who are employed in these types of systems
Pandemic and similar crises	Unexpectedly high mortality rates and the retreat of civilization	Develop reliable and wise systems that serve humankind	A very respectable role for IT professionals

SUMMARY

Table 5 provides a summary of global and local challenges that must be taken into account by ICT professionals in developing and implementing computerization strategies.

These 13 socio-political challenges show the wildly complex picture of the situation in which computerization strategies are being developed for particular objects and processes. Any computerization strategy should be situated within this broader context. Indeed, the strategy developed today may prove obsolete tomorrow. IT strategists must be sensitive and informed of these challenges.

To sum up the socio-political questions surrounding computerization in the 21st century, one can offer the following conclusions, which follow from the initial experiences of the 2020 coronavirus pandemic:

1. The glorification of the triumph of the self-sufficient person in every walk of life has been shattered by the still significant role of the state in defending weak citizens in times of crises, disasters, and wars.
2. The glorification of the youth as "eternally" young, healthy, and indestructible was shattered when it turned out that a large percentage of those infected were young people, many of whom disregarded the rules of social distancing.
3. The restoration of the importance of the values of empathy, solidarity, and enlightenment will help in saving the lives of others and will relieve those who are isolated in homes, shelters, hospitals, and nursing facilities.
4. Computerization is a human tool that, when wisely used, can lead to prosperity (Targowski, 1971); however, it can also lead to digital totalitarianism (Vestergaard, 2019) if it falls into the hands of cunning dictators or clever Big Tech CEOs who, thanks to the excesses of capitalistic freedom, have the power to turn people into passive and jobless "containers of information"

The world's democracies must defend and uphold their Enlightenment values and the ideological achievements of the 20th century. A global withdrawal from balancing power with legal legitimacy, such as democratic free elections, will result in the breakdown of social order both at home and internationally. However, this question of the legality of power cannot be resolved simultaneously with the efforts to overcome the scourge of coronavirus. Restraint is necessary from all sides, both internally and internationally. Priorities must be set. At the same time, we must move ahead with our efforts to eliminate the significant growing inequalities associated with these "prosperous" times, which come at the expense of human dignity. Now the historical challenge for leaders is to deal with many crises and, at the same time, build a sustainable future that every generation dreams of. Failure could set the world on fire and encourage revolution, and this could come through computerization! However, computerization can measure, monitor, conceptualize options, develop knowledge, forecast, and optimize information in life. In other words, it is about solving problems and doing the right thing.

REFERENCES

Amnesty International. (2006). *Undermining freedom of expression in China: The role of Yahoo! Microsoft and Google*. https://www.amnesty.org/download/Documents/80000/pol300262006en.pdf

Asimov, I. (1953). *Second foundation*. Gnome Press, Inc.

Buchanan, B. (2020). *The hacker and the state*. Oxford University Press. doi:10.4159/9780674246010

Economist Intelligence Unit. (2019). *Democracy Index 2019: A year of democratic setbacks and popular protests*. https://www.eiu.com/topic/democracy-index

Epping, R. C. (2020). *The new world economy*. Vintage Books.

Fukuyama, F. (1992). *The end of history and the last man*. Free Press.

Gleick, J. (2020, October 8). Simulating democracy. *The New York Review of Books*. https://www.nybooks.com/articles/2020/10/08/simulating-democracy/

International Monetary Fund. (2020, October). *World economic outlook – GDP per capita*. https://www.imf.org/en/Publications/WEO/weo-database/2020/October/weo-report

Lanier, J. (2018). *Ten arguments for deleting your social media accounts right now*. Henry Holt.

Lepore, J. (2020). *If then: How the Simulmatics Corporation invented the future*. Liveright Publishing Corporation.

Luhby, T. (2019, January 21). The top 26 billionaires own $1.4 trillion — as much as 3.8 billion other people. *CNN*. https://www.cnn.com/2019/01/20/business/oxfam-billionaires-davos/index.html

McCarthy, N. (2019, May 7). Labor unions: The state of global trade union membership. *Statista*. https://www.statista.com/chart/9919/the-state-of-the-unions/

McLuhan, M., & Powers, B. R. (1989). *The global village: Transformations in world life and media in the 21st century*. Oxford University Press.

Numbeo. (2020). *Quality of Life Index by country 2020 mid-year*. https://www.numbeo.com/quality-of-life/rankings_by_country.jsp

Reporters Without Boarders. (2017, December 9). *RSF opposes spread of China's Internet surveillance model*. https://rsf.org/en/news/rsf-opposes-spread-chinas-internet-surveillance-model

Repucci, S., & Slipowitz, A. (2020). Democracy under lockdown. *Freedom House*. https://freedomhouse.org/report/special-report/2020/democracy-under-lockdown

Targowski, A. (1971). *Informatyka klucz do dobrobytu* [Informatics a key to prosperity]. PiW.

Targowski, A. (2018). *Rozwój KSI I PESEL* [Development of KSI and PESEL]. Oficyna Publishing Kucharski.

Tokarczuk, O. (2020, April 8). A new world through my window. *The New Yorker*. https://www.newyorker.com/books/page-turner/a-new-world-through-my-window

Transparency International. (2019). *Corruption perceptions index 2019.* https://www.transparency.org/en/cpi/2019

United Nations Development Programme. (2019). *Human development report 2019.* http://report2019.archive.s3-website-us-east-1.amazonaws.com/

Vestergaard, M. (2019). *Digital totalitarianism.* Informations Forlag.

Webb, M. (2020). *Coding democracy.* MIT Press. doi:10.7551/mitpress/11669.001.0001

World Bank. (2019, December 28). *GINI index (World Bank estimate) – Country ranking.* Index Mundi. https://www.indexmundi.com/facts/indicators/SI.POV.GINI/rankings

World Intellectual Property Organization. (2019). *Global Innovation Index 2019 rankings.* https://www.wipo.int/edocs/pubdocs/en/wipo_pub_gii_2019-intro4.pdf

KEY TERMS AND DEFINITIONS

Algorithm: A sequence of computer instructions (mathematics-based) used to solve a well-defined problem.

Black Economy: The part of the economy whose activities fall outside of official rules and regulations.

Cambridge Analytica: A British political consulting firm notable for its role in the 2016 US presidential election in connection with Facebook.

Dark Web: A part of deep web that is intentionally hidden and that requires specific software and authorization to access.

Deep Web: The part of the Internet not searchable by traditional search engines such as Google.

Gini Index: An index used to measure a country's wealth inequality.

Simulmatics: An early US data firm that used informing technologies to provide information about voters.

Turbo Capitalism: A highly unregulated form of capitalism, associated with some of the early financial successes of large technology companies.

ENDNOTES

[1]   This section is developed on the basis of Lepore (2020) and Gleick (2020).

[2]   The Great Gatsby was novel written by F. Scott Fitzgerald about a fictitious millionaire, Jay Gatsby, who made a great fortune and lived exquisitely at the height of the 1920s on Long Island.

[3]   The most recent year for the selected countries varies. For instance, for South Africa, the most recent year is 2014 while for Chile, it is 2017.

[4]   Assessments of country ranks relative to the best country in each category are given in the tables quoted.

[5]   The term "Yankee ingenuity" comes from the construction of the Erie Canal through rural New York State. Work began in 1817. The canal opened on 26 October 1825.

6   This is the case even after seven decades (production started in 1947). The model and its variants remain the most popular and widely used rifles in the world due to its reliability in difficult conditions, low production costs compared to modern Western weapons, availability in virtually every geographical region, and ease of use. The AK-47 was manufactured in many countries and witnessed service in the armed forces as well as irregular forces and uprisings around the world. It was also the basis for the development of many other types of individual weapons. In 2004, of the approximately 500 million firearms worldwide, around 100 million belong to the Kalashnikov family, three quarters of which are AK-47s.

7   The most democratic states are Norway (9.87), Iceland (9.58), Sweden (9.39), New Zealand (9.26), Finland (9.25), Ireland (9.24), Denmark (9.22), Canada (9.22), Australia (9.09), Switzerland (9.03). The United States has an index of 7.96 (Economist Intelligence Unit, 2019).

8   The Israeli Pegasus spyware system is a very useful and effective tool for tracking terrorists and serious criminals. On many occasions, however, it has been used for completely different purposes, including the surveillance of people who question the status quo. Pegasus falls into the category of spyware. Its characteristic course of action is reminiscent of Trojan malware. For example, when installed on your smartphone, Pegasus takes control of it. From that point on, the software operator can do whatever he wants with the smartphone. Pegasus was created by NSO Group Technologies (an Israeli cyber-arms firm) probably for Mossad, the national intelligence agency of Israel. Today, any government can purchase a license to use the software. "We provide authorized authorities with technology to fight terrorism and crime" - this is how the Israeli company defines its mission.

9   The computer Mark II was a cipher machine used by the United States for message encryption from World War II until the 1950s. The machine was also known as the "SIGABA" or "Converter M-134" by the Army, or "CSP-888/889" by the Navy. A modified Navy version was termed "CSP-2900".

10   This case is presented by Targowski (2018). Also see the chapter *the History and Repercussions of Strategic Informing Technology*.

11   KACST is a scientific institution under the authority of the King of Saudi Arabia and the Prime Minister. It includes both Saudi Arabia's national science agency and its national laboratories.

12   In addition to Andrew Targowski, the group included Stefan Bratkowski and engineers Ryszard Dabrówka, Ryszard Farfał, Antoni Bossowski and Marek Wajcen.

Section 2
Technological Progress in the 21st Century

Chapter 7
Development Trends of Digital Infrastructure

ABSTRACT

The goal of this chapter is to analyze the main trends in the development of information communication technology (ICT) infrastructure and to discuss ICT strategies for decision-making in the 21st century. The chapter begins with a discussion of the development of the internet and its impact on civilization and human society. Next, the chapter considers the development of smartphone applications as well as other technologies used for personal communication. After this, developments in hardware and machine software platforms are considered. The chapter concludes by analyzing three trends: developments in computer architecture, developments in computer design, and developments in IT design.

INTRODUCTION

Modern civilization, hitherto based on the infrastructure of roads and bridges, telephones, energy systems, waterworks, and others, has been enriched with digital infrastructure. This infrastructure is driving the development of many industries and education. It is ubiquitous, but malfunctions can cause it to crash, immobilizing companies, agencies, and people.

This chapter will discuss the main trends in the development of ICT infrastructure and strategies for operational decision-making in the 21st century. The essential elements of this infrastructure and the design trends include the following:

- The Internet of People and the Internet of Things,
- Smartphones and other personal communication devices,
- Hardware and machine software,
- Computer design,
- Digital infrastructure design.

This summary will also highlight problems of ICT infrastructure related to unreliability and security.

DOI: 10.4018/978-1-7998-8036-3.ch007

THE DEVELOPMENT OF THE INTERNET

The widespread occurrence of internetization in the 21st century has been spectacular and has been, in principle, revered as a remedy for all socio-economic ills. Indeed, internetization has the following advantages (Figure 1):

- Strengthens users,
- Strengthens global business,
- Strengthens organizations,
- Strengthens society (but so far, only in the sense of responding to distortions).

It can, therefore, be concluded that ICT solutions live in symbiosis with other practical solutions; they are perhaps even more visible and spectacular for society.

The main network connecting people is the *Internet*. The development of the Internet has been particularly impressive, a development which includes a range of tools, services, and platforms that support both the work of software development teams and systems assisting specific areas of professional and private life. Next to the real world, a virtual world is consistently created, in which it is easier to get lost without realizing the consequences. An example is the loss of real-life communication (F2F, Face-to-Face), which has become the bane of modern young people. It can be said that the Internet has created a new direction of development, which can be called *internetization*. This concept covers both the development of the Internet itself as well as its users and their activities.

On one hand, internetization is a sensitive matter, for a significant failure in its development would disable many companies, agencies, and people. On the other hand, internetization supports the development of organizations and improves their activities. Figure 1 indicates both the advantages and disadvantages of the internetization process. Negative trends must be minimized. The trends in the development of this online community are as follows:

- **The intensification of Internet communication and the use of ICT services** will affect the majority of people on Earth, or about 5 billion (out of 7,6 billion) people, resulting in a high demand for all kinds of mobile devices, services, and applications. This guarantees trade and a great amount business for manufacturers of mobile devices (both hardware and software) and networks providing high-speed access to Internet services.
- **Growth in human-to-human and hybrid (human-robot) cooperation in different areas of human life** will occur as a result of personal and professional needs. This will occur regardless of existing distances and often at the expense of direct communication.
- **Creating different online communities through the ease of constructing different environments and online platforms that support the activities of communities with similar interests and missions** will ensure that they find their place in an unknown virtual world. The backdrop for this situation is that many cannot find a place for themselves in the *real world*. Unfortunately, many criminal e-communities are also being created.
- **The growth of a vast number of different types of data** will make it possible to discover and explore new forms of knowledge and to apply them anywhere and at any time for both research and novel practical applications, including day-to-day work, hobbies, and entertainment. Unfortunately, this will lead to *dataism (datamania)* and the sickness of internet addiction.

- **The development of innovative directions in research** will occur due to the creation of new interdisciplinary and transdisciplinary facts (data), changes (information), knowledge (principle, rules, laws), and wisdom (correct decision choices).
- **Creating collective intelligence**, mainly on social networking platforms, will enable us to analyze human needs, solve complex problems, counteract inappropriate trends, and develop innovation in different fields. As a result, this will lead to the creation of crucial and perhaps wise social relationships.
- **Various types of manipulation** will be attempted, not only as a protest of the disgruntled but also as a means of fighting for power, strengthening interests, and increasing advantages.
- **The gradual transformation of Western Civilization towards Global Civilization** will occur, which could result in Big Business' control over human activities; however, it could also influence the development of new culture and new arts.

Figure 1. Advantages and disadvantages of internetization in the 21st century (Targowski, 2016)

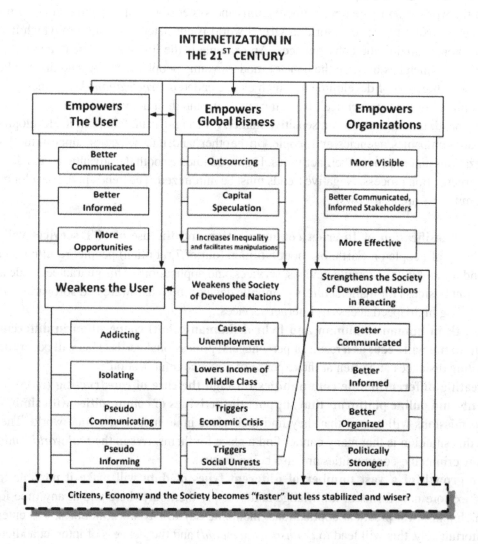

Internetization, however, also has disadvantages because it has weakened society by accelerating the disintegration of citizens and communities in developed countries due to increases global business, which has caused the following critical problems in the 21st century:

- unemployment,
- a reduction in the middle-class and in developed countries,
- local and global economic crises,
- political crises in developed countries,
- social unrest in developed countries (e.g., "Occupy Wall Street" and civil unrest in 2020).

Figure 2. Time is worried about how the Internet might be used to spread a culture of hate

There is good reason to think that internetization led Western Civilization to collapse and transformed it into Global Civilization, which is beneficial for developing countries but disadvantageous to developed countries. Nevertheless, the societies of developed countries will not accept this state of affairs. It will lead to riots and probably social revolution, and as a result, democracy and capitalism as we now know and practice them will be significantly changed. We will soon see whether these changes are positive, and therefore whether its main perpetrator—the Internet—is positive in terms of ushering in a macro-scale technopolis for humanity (Postman, 1992).

Unfortunately, the Internet is a very able tool for developing a culture of hate (Figure 2). Today, in the 21st century, anyone can be a commentator; anyone, anywhere and anyplace, can have an opinion on any topic. Unfortunately, almost all Internet users are willing to respond to the sometimes deranged posts of other anonymous debaters. The latter post their views and end up on the front pages of the discussion as if out of nowhere. The digital culture of hatred goes beyond offending; it uses dangerous discursive and cultural practices on the Internet to radicalize the public sphere and build support for radical left-wing and right-wing populist parties. Unfortunately, the digital culture of hatred is unmanageable because, ostensibly, it is protected under the right of freedom of speech. There is growing consensus, however, that a digital culture of hate is fueling hate crimes and, in some cases, motivating terrorist attacks. Furthermore, the culture of hate is shifting from social media to a vibrant policy in which no one can agree with anyone on almost any matter. Such disagreement will lead to a societal crisis and, potentially, collapse. For example, the once proud American nation of the 21st century has evolved into a political community made up of enclaves of citizens of different ethnic origins, whose affairs and interests have narrowed to that of their group.

As for the upcoming trends of internet application development, these can be characterized as follows:

- **Human communication** will intensify and cover most people on Earth, or about 6-7 billion people. By 2050, there will likely be a total of 10 billion, guaranteeing good business for hardware and software manufacturers as well as Internet access providers.
- **Socialization** will expand and intensify thanks to the ease of functioning online in virtual environments with various interests and missions. Most people will be able to find their place in the crowd.
- **Social research** will focus on new facts (data), change (information), knowledge (principle, rules, laws), and wisdom (correct decision choices).
- **Sharing information will intensify** discoveries and correlations of data, concepts, knowledge, and wisdom. This will occur mainly on social networking platforms, leading to the development of a **collective intelligence** that can be used by anyone who is actively involved in the exchange of information on these social platforms.
- **Cooperation** will increase because digital communication will be accessible and people will be happy to use it to get out of isolation. Thanks to the Internet, people will be able develop virtual connections with others from far away. At the same time, however, they will lose touch with people from their neighborhood, where they will be in isolation.
- **Trade** will increase with companies such as Alibaba, Allegro, Amazon, eBay, and others.
- **A culture of hate** will develop under the pseudo-name of "democracy" unless wise societies defend themselves with appropriate regulations.

The Internet does not provide essential information automatically. Among internet users, the following groups of citizens can be distinguished (Figure 3):

- **Internet illiterate (I)** are those who use traditional means of information (weak users). They are misinformed and only have reason; however, if they raise their knowledge/skills, they can become migrants and move (via the horizontal path to the right) to the category of information elite, who are working to adapt to the new conditions of communication. They could also just improve their

Figure 3. Exclusion of information among Internet users (Targowski, 2016)

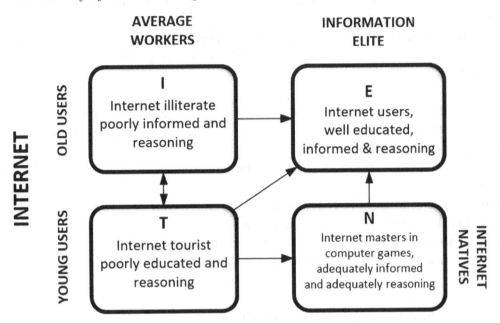

ability to use the Internet and its resources, thereby becoming internet tourists (via the downward path).

- **Internet elite** (**E**) are those with excellent professional knowledge/skills and the know-how to use the Internet. They can reason very well.
- **Internet tourists** (**T**) are those poorly educated who are good internet users (mainly the young generation) and who spend hours using the Internet. Still, their knowledge/ability to use and understand the data they collect is shallow, as is their ability to read. They sometimes collect too much data and become "data maniacs". Their reasoning is pseudo-reasoning: sometimes it is sound but mostly it is questionable. If they expand their professional knowledge/skills, they can become internet natives (via horizontal path to the right).

Internet natives (**N**) are those who are excellent users of the Internet. Often, they are masters of computer games. They are adequately informed. Along with age and professional experience, they can advance and become part of the internet elite (E).

Among the four categories of Internet users, the largest group are Internet tourists, who have "populated" the Internet and are developing a culture of hate because their knowledge of what they discuss is questionable. The way out of this situation is for this category of users to educate themselves in institutions of higher education. However, this is not guaranteed to raise them to a higher level of training than what they received in primary schools, gymnasiums, and high schools. The climate surrounding information in public media and state politics is significant in contributing to their education. A bad climate affects this category of Internet users the most and also worsens their already pseudo-reasoning.

The *Internet of Things* (IoT) is another universal connectivity platform, which followed the first *Internet of People* (IoP) platform. The Internet of Things refers to the interconnection of devices, systems, and services with digital interfaces for machine-to-machine communication (M2M) through different platforms, protocols, domains, and applications. Almost every object with a digital interface can be connected to another object to be supervised by people.

Today the Internet of Things is at an early stage of conceptual development, just as the Internet of People was in the 1960s (under the name ARPANET). Among the potential applications of IoT, the following can be distinguished:

- Monitoring the environment to ensure the sustainability of life on the planet,
- Supervising the infrastructure of civilization to guard against the event of a breakdown and to provide preventive maintenance,
- Monitoring production operations with industrial applications, especially in complex chemical processes,
- Controlling energy to optimize consumption,
- Ensuring health systems are accessible and reliable,
- Ensuring cars, trucks, buses, and transport systems are reliable.
- Preventing roads and bridges from breaking down and providing maintenance.
- Others

The Internet of Things will connect billions of new devices for monitoring and surveillance purposes. As these "things" add to possibilities such as context awareness, increased processing power, and energy independence and as the number of people and new types of information increases, civilization will quickly enter the Internet of Everything (IoE), where even inanimate objects will have a voice. Because billions or even trillions of sensors will be distributed around the world and in the atmosphere of our planet, humans will gain the ability to hear the heartbeat of the world. No doubt, we will know when the climate and environment of our planet are healthy or sick. With such a close monitoring, perhaps people will be able to start eliminating some of our greatest shortages, including the problem of hunger and the problem of ensuring the availability of fresh drinking water.

The general architecture of the Internet of Things is illustrated in Figure 4. It is mainly a structure of event-driven and machine-focused protocols. The Internet of Things ensures business development in the following areas:

- Application software,
- Devices for easy deployment,
- Monitoring and troubleshooting services,
- Service industries,
- Advertising on users' digital devices (similar to Google's practices),
- Selling all kinds of goods and services (similar to e-commerce on the Internet of People).

This new wave of business triggered by the Internet of Everything will affect civilization even more than the Industrial Revolution of the 19th century because big business will easily recognize the great potential for massive profits and has competent and skillful computer scientists and sufficient capital. From a business perspective, the development and establishment of the Internet of Everything seem unstoppable.

The question, however, is whether this new Internet of Things will sustain civilization. Will it make it more or less sensitive to crises, conflicts, and war? The answer is that it can cause both. From a purely

Figure 4. The general topology of the Internet of Things (IoT)

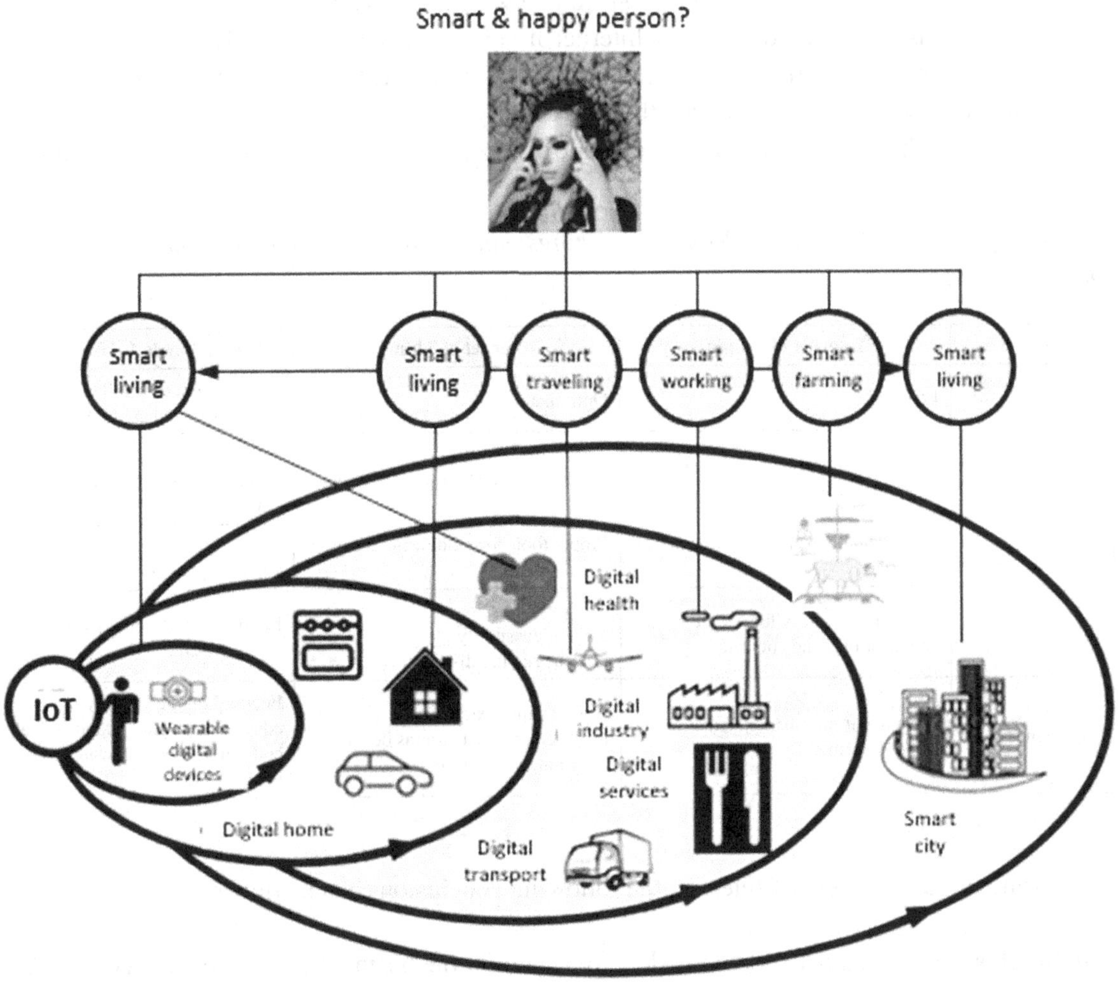

theoretical point of view, the new Internet of Things can generally optimize civilization's infrastructure, ensuring the best possible use of energy and materials. Its role and development are, therefore, decisive and should be promoted. On the other hand, human life might not become more comfortable because a person could find themselves surrounded by 3,000-5,000 e-compressed things, which, although perhaps making experience "optimal", would probably cause unhappiness. After all, excessive information and reduced human mobility can lead us into a so-called "frenzy" or at least frustration because of the flood of information and living in virtuality.

Furthermore, current experience with cybercrime and cyberwarfare indicates that these phenomena are almost unstoppable. It is possible for a cybercriminal to simulate a password in seconds and go through the firewall of an institution or company. This is why hackers can take over any advanced infrastructure in the Internet of Things. They can attack any electric car, pacemaker, e-hospital, e-school, e-college, e-office, e-home, and so on. Thus, both e-crime and "optimizing" infrastructure can pose a threat to civilization. Such risks will be inevitable if people choose to live only online. Maybe a safe life can only be achieved offline, but if so, why spend billions to live with such high risk?

Unfortunately, businesses will develop the Internet of Things and the Internet of Everything regardless of the human danger and misfortune. As long as a profit can be made, the percept that "what is good for business is good for society" will dominate the 21st century.

Table 1 provides the requirements of a sustainable civilization which should work safely for humans.

Table 1. Comparing the Internet of People and Things with the demands of a sustainable civilization (Targowski, 2016)

Criteria	Internet of People	Internet of Things	Sustainable Civilization
Short-term perspective	Low cost	Optimization	Business ethics legally established and applied
Long-term perspective	Super-consumerism and a worker-deprived economy	Limited use of strategic resources	Use of oil-based sand, reduced automation, robotization, and computerization
Balance	Accelerated depletion of strategic resources	Proper tools for monitoring resource consumption	Legal regulations for education and occupations
Security	Inadequate security for people, organizations, and countries	Minimum safety and the possibility of e-infrastructure disasters	Environmental and infrastructure safety ensured
User experience	A deluge of information, isolation, and cybercrime	A high complexity of use; insufficient qualifications beyond the younger generation	Focused on the ecology of education; education and ethical codes are respected around the world

Comparing of the two types of Internet, the following conclusions can be drawn:

1. In the short term, both networks provide good value for the business: IoP lowers the cost of business operations, and IoT optimizes the use of strategic resources.
2. In the long run, both types of Internet cause severe structural problems: the first (humans) leads to super-consumption and the rapid exhaustion of strategic resources, and the second (things) leads to infrastructure disasters caused by cybercrime and cyberwar.
3. To assure wise applications of both types of Internet and to protect the well-being of society, business ethics and informing science must be vigorously applied around the world and supported by appropriate political and legal regulations.

DEVELOPMENT OF APPLICATIONS FOR SMARTPHONES AND OTHER PERSONAL INFORMATION COMMUNICATORS

The mobile phone is one of the most successful products in consumer electronics, but this has come at the expense of many other products. The convergence of various phone features has caused mobile phones and, more recently, smartphones, to almost completely capture entire areas of the personal electronics market between 2005 and 2020. The evolving areas of audio/video and imaging have been particularly affected. In 2007, this type of product was targeted, and just three years later, demand for smartphones more than doubled. Both digital cameras and MP3 players have lost their importance. In just a single year, these two popular categories of personal electronics rapidly began to lose buyers.

At present, new products and alternative technologies for phones are emerging, which could reduce consumers' dependence on smartphones. These technologies offer new ways of using the internet and potentially more convenient and secure ways to communicate. E-sim, flexible displays, voice interface, and devices that are wearable via one's clothing (*wearables*) are all beginning to show that they can influence and even overturn the dominance of smartphones. Some smartphone features are already transferred to other personal "devices." One example is virtual personal assistants used at home and in vehicles. The early popularity of these devices suggests that smartphones are not the only way consumers want to access and control digital cloud services and hardware.

Flexible information manipulation technology is also suitable for head-mounted displays of entertainment programs. Virtual space is already a promising segment and catalyst for the growing personal entertainment market, which currently relies on devices such as smartphones, tablets, and computers. While the smartwatch market has stalled, there are still long-term prospects for wrist devices with a range of smartphone features. There are already clear benefits to some smart features. For example, there is greater security when using a payment device attached to the body rather than one loosely stored in a pocket or handbag.

The eSim design is set to eliminate the need for a physical SIM card and enable multiple devices to be enrolled in a single network identity. In a short time, our connected world could manifest itself in a series of more convenient application-specific devices and "connected accessories." The market for glasses, watches, wearables, and other independent screens or devices could take the place of smartphones, ushering in a more diverse and standalone personal electronics market, such as was the case 20 years ago. As the Consumer Internet of Things and the Smart Home Market progresses, we will rely less and less on our smartphones.

The smartphone will most likely remain the essential personal electronic device for consumers in the foreseeable future. Still, with advances in info-communication technology, we will not rely on or limit ourselves to the smartphone forever. The future smartphone market will eventually fall. New standalone devices will appear on the market, and inevitably another product will come into vogue.

DEVELOPMENT OF HARDWARE AND MACHINE SOFTWARE PLATFORMS

Changes in IT infrastructure, i.e., hardware, software, smartphones, and tele-networks, are caused by the following factors (UkEssays, 2018):

- Computing and software costs are rising due to competition in the market and a shortage of advanced IT professionals.
- Customer expectations about the efficiency of IT systems has increased, forcing manufacturers to develop increasingly advanced solutions.
- There is a need for cross-platform data integration, caused by the need to maintain Big Data.

The development of IT equipment and software as IT infrastructure has entered a similar phase as the production of electricity: Its users do not wonder how it is produced. They simply use the so-called "utility". Nevertheless, trends in public interest regarding informing technology will be analyzed in the following sections of the chapter.

IT Equipment Platforms

The current development trends are as follows:

- The integration of computing and telecommunications platforms,
- The development of high-speed information processing tasks by distributing processing and computing tasks on a network, available in so-called "server farms",
- The integration of phones with the Internet has resulted in the smartphone, a miniaturized computer with a built-in memory.
- Monetary savings for large infrastructures through the concentration of equipment and services,
- The increased efficiency of IT services, which are dominated by large IT companies employing high-end specialists.
- The development of cloud computing as an online service that relieves companies from developing their own expensive IT infrastructure (this does not mean that the securities of such services are risk-free for companies).
- The development of virtualization, which allows access to resources in many ways, regardless of geographical location and the physical configuration of the hardware.

Software Platforms

The current development trends are as follows:

- The Linux operating system is one of the most widely used open-source programs.
- Linux is supported by almost all platforms, such as HP, IBM, Intel, Dell, Sun etc.
- Linux is open-source software that can be customized to meet business needs.
- Python is an interactive programming language independent of the operating system and hardware processor (it is compatible with any hardware).
- Java VM has already been precisely defined.
- There has been an increased use of comprehensive software systems for businesses.
- AJAX *(Asynchronous JavaScript and XML)* are development tools used to create interactive web applications.
- Mashup is a web application that combines data and features from more than one source.
- Software outsourcing is becoming more popular.

Mobile Platforms

The current development trends are as follows:

- Service providers have upgraded mobile networks with next-generation services, such as 3G, 4G, and 5G, WAP, and GPRS. Banks are trying to capitalize on this growth in the telecommunications sector and provide services to customers via mobile phones. The main advantage of mobile banking over online banking is that it offers "anywhere, anytime" banking. The limitations of online banking have been overcome in mobile banking because it only requires a mobile phone, which is also accessible by people from developing countries.

- ○ The various services and information offered by banks via mobile devices include the following:
  - Account information,
  - Balance statements and account histories,
  - Insurance policy management,
  - The terms of fixed deposits,
  - Minimum balance alerts,
  - Management of pension plans,
  - Payments and transfers,
  - National and international transfers of funds,
  - Payments for various products acquired by e-Bay, Amazon, and other trading platforms.
  - Alerts and notifications about various exchange investment portfolios.
  - Assistance in exchange investments and investment funds.
- Interactive Voice Response (IVR), such as *Talkdesk*:
  - ○ In an IVR, the bank assigns a unique number to customers. When the client makes the call, they can choose options from the menu specified in the electronic message according to their requirements.
  - ○ IVR is expensive compared to data transmission via SMS or WAP. It can only be used for query-based services.
- Short Messaging Service (SMS)
  - ○ The most common technology used in mobile banking to provide services is short messaging service (SMS) technology. Using an SMS to respond to service orders, banks can provide customers with needed information by sending it to a predetermined number. The advantages of SMS are as follows:
    - Cheaper compared to IVR,
    - Banking "anytime, anywhere",
    - They allow standalone mobile client applications that handle e-bank transactions, such as stock market trading, securities investments, etc. The advantages of this technique are...
      It can easily be personalized according to the aim(s) of the user,
      It provides good security,
      It provides a reliable communication channel.
  - ○ The disadvantages of SMS are as follows:
    - Several different combinations of use may prevent a user from operating different devices and operating systems,
    - There may be inconsistencies in performance due to the different capabilities of the devices.
- Mobile banking is expected to grow. Some online banking users may switch to mobile banking. The leading cause of concern is the security of mobile banking. If this problem is persuasively resolved, mobile banking will be entirely accepted by most customers in the future.
- Advantages of mobile banking:

- ○ Reduces banking costs,
- ○ Helps both banks and service providers achieve growth,
- ○ Allows banks to provide customers with useful services, such as reminders about insurance terms, loan repayment dates, etc.,
- ○ Can be used in a large geographical area,
- ○ Requires fewer employees to provide services to consumers.
- General notifications can be sent, such as weather, messages, email, etc.
- Blockchain records reduce costs and eliminate the need for paper and manual systems (which are often unreliable) for tracking goods shipped long distances often unreliable. For example, the transoceanic container operator Maersk and IBM have introduced TradeLens, a blockchain-based system for tracking shipping containers and processing documents. This platform covers more than half of the world's ocean container cargo. A blockchain is a kind of distributed ledger, developed chronologically. It is a cryptographically signed persistent record in a database of transactions common to all participants in the network. It allows the parties to cooperate without the need for a centralized body. A complete *blockchain* can be characterized by five characteristics: distribution, immutability, decentralization, cipherability, and tokenization.

Platforms in Grid Computing

The current development trends are as follows:

Figure 5. The topology of grid computing

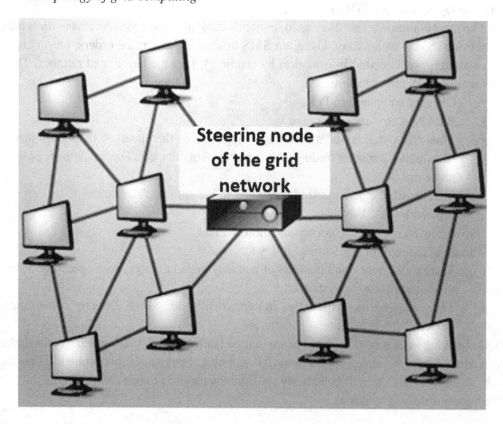

- The basic idea behind lattice network processing (grid computing) (Figure 5) is that software running on the network gives higher priority to local users. That said, when such computers become idle, they are used all over the web. In grid computing, computers are connected using middleware, which allows them to act as a virtual whole. Grid calculations use a distributed set of data centers instead of a single centralized source. If a company has a large number of computers, then such a cluster can be created by connecting all the computers. One central computer, named the *front-end*, is highlighted on the network. The other computers in the set are called *back-end* computers, which are only connected to the *front-end* computer. Companies such as AutoGrid Systems, Darktrace, and GridGain Systems are considered to be the leaders in grid computing. Their IBM grid data entry system is compatible with operating systems such as Unix, Linux, and Windows.

- The essential characteristics of grid computing are as follows:
  ○ An immense amount of power for information processing,
  ○ Remote access to IT resources,
  ○ Scalability of processing,
  ○ Flexibility (if a greater network information capacity is required, more computers are added to the network),
  ○ Cost-effective services from the network center.

- The advantages of grid computing are as follows:
  ○ The price of the task and the information are based on the time of use of IT resources,
  ○ Network calculations enable an efficient use of resources,
  ○ Redundancy and recovery are feasible,
  ○ Network environments are much more modular and do not contain single points of failure. If a fault occurs, there are a large number of backup IT resources to complete the task,
  ○ Network processing allows large tasks to be performed by dividing them into small elements and implementing them in parallel on different computers in the network.

- The disadvantages of grid computing are as follows:
  ○ There is network dependency on the Internet,
  ○ It requires a fast Internet connection,
  ○ Network security is put at risk,
  ○ Storing data in grid calculations is vulnerable to attack by intruders and hackers.
  ○ It is difficult to manage so many computers on the network,
  ○ Licensing on many different servers may prevent users from using specific applications.

- Processing in a grid network is not a new concept. This type of processing has been used by many institutions to perform complex calculations. Grid processing offers efficient, fast, reliable, and standards-based solutions to problems faced by banks. Network calculations will help banks quickly provide services to customers. If the security of processing is ensured in such networks, computing in a grid network can be widely used in the banking sector.

- A grid network is used to integrate hundreds of networks in the United States Department of Defense (Figure 6).

Figure 6. A grid network is supporting the operation of the U.S. Department of Defense's Core Data Centers (Department of Defense, 2012)

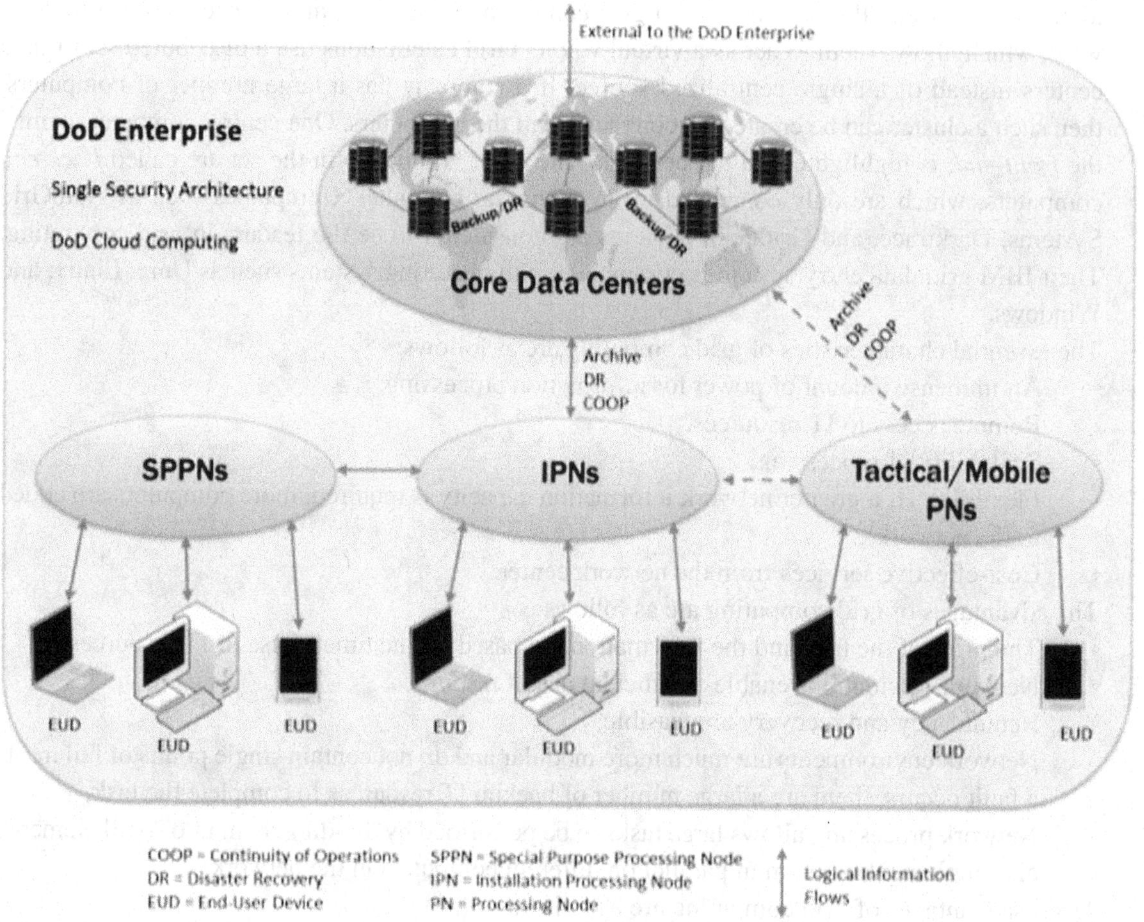

Digital Cloud Platforms

The development trends are as follows:

- Cloud computing (Figure 7) is one of the most popular technologies available in business. Cloud computing provides a range of services, such as bank account keeping, insurance services, and loans. Cloud computing is a flexible, customer-centric business model that will help banks make additional profits. The concept of cloud computing is that company data is stored in data centers owned by a service company, such as Amazon, Microsoft, Google, and others. The following Cloud computing services are available:
  - **Infrastructure as a Service** (IaaS): This service leases infrastructure such as servers, operating systems, virtual machines, networks, and storage (e.g., Amazon Web Service, Microsoft Azure).

Figure 7. The digital cloud (Harvey, 2017)

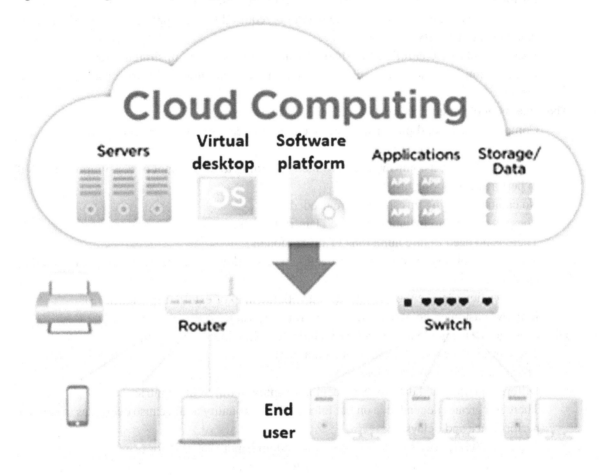

- ◦ **Platform as a Service** (PaaS): This service is used to develop, test, and maintain software. PaaS is just like IaaS, but it provides additional tools such as database management systems (DBMS) for business intelligence (e.g., Apprenda, Red Hat, OpenShift).
- ◦ **Database as a Service** (DaaS): In this service, third-party data is stored in a database located in the service company's cloud.
- ◦ **Software as a Service** (SaaS): This service allows users to connect to applications over the Internet on a subscription basis (e.g., Google Apps, Salesforce).
- The leading digital cloud service providers in 2020 include Adobe, Amazon Web Services, Dropbox, Egnyte, Google Cloud Platform, IBM Cloud, Kamatera, Microsoft Azure, Navisite, Oracle Cloud, phoenixNAP, Rackspace, Red Hat, Salesforce, SAP, ScienceSoft, Verizon Cloud, and VMware.
- There are four ownership-oriented types of digital clouds:
  - ◦ **Private clouds** are built into a company's data center, and the computing resources are distributed exclusively to internal business users via network services such as VAN (Value Added Network*)*.

- **Public clouds** are when companies share computing resources with other organizations outside of the business. The servers and networks required for the application to work are provided by a third party.
- **Social clouds** are controlled and shared by many companies with similar interests.
- **Hybrid clouds** are a combination of an internal private cloud with external public cloud features.
- The benefits of cloud computing services include the following:
  - Computing tasks and platform capacity can be increased or reduced depending on a company's computing power needs.
  - The cost of IT for a company is determined according to the amount of consumption needed to perform computing tasks.
  - No capital requiring investments are needed.
  - There is no need to maintain internal IT infrastructure.
  - There is no need to hire numerous IT professionals.
  - There is flexibility in business strategies, which allows responding quickly to a market challenge.
  - IT innovations can be rapidly introduced with the help of external specialists.
  - It allows customers to access the system from anywhere.
- Disadvantages of using cloud computing include the following:
  - There is a higher risk of hacking and data theft.
  - Maintaining data privacy is less secure.
  - Different privacy and data management laws apply in different countries.
  - There is a greater dependence on the Internet, whose quality could cause decreases in service performance and delays.
  - There could be periods of downtime if the system is not available for use.
  - Existing company applications (so-called *legacy*) cannot always be effortlessly migrated to the cloud.
  - It can be difficult to change the existing IT infrastructure layout to cloud computing.

Digital cloud computing is an evolving concept and has many advantages and disadvantages. Cloud services will help businesses deliver services quickly and at lower rates. They also help them provide customers with access to services at any time, all year around. However, companies that use digital clouds should have strategies for dealing with cases when the cloud is closed (for various reasons, such as weather disasters, social unrest, war, or even terrorist attacks). Is it the case that without a functioning digital cloud, the company's business will cease? Then, the company should consider drawing on the resources of two independent clouds in locations that are reasonably remote from each other.

The further development of the digital cloud will lead to distributed clouds, i.e., the distribution of public cloud services located outside the physical site of the provider. In a distributed cloud, the service provider is responsible for all aspects of the cloud service, such as the architecture, delivery, operations, management, and updates. In other words, this evolution will proceed from a centralized public cloud to a distributed public cloud. One could also organize a *hybrid cloud*, a system connecting external cloud providers and internal company services. The problem is that hybrid clouds are incredibly challenging to deploy in cost-effective and reasonable ways.

Nowadays, cloud computing is at an early stage of development, so most providers only offer a small subset of services in a distributed way, with plans to ultimately offer a full range of services. Another trend, *edge computing*, is developing, in which the information processing is done close to sources of information in order to maintain local traffic and reduce delays in the transmission of data. This approach will use the Internet of Things (IoT), and it will increase the number of *smart devices* and lay the foundations for *smart spaces*. In the 2020s, there will be a steady increase in the development of sensors, memory capacity, computational speed, and advanced AI capabilities in such devices. One can also anticipate an increase in hacking attempts and a number of failures for this type of intelligent information processing.

Computer architecture development trends

In recent years, memory, processors, and network technologies have made significant breakthroughs. As shown in Figure 8, a growing set of new hardware, architecture, and features are becoming the foundation of future computing platforms. Current trends indicate that these techniques are significantly changing the environment of traditional application management systems and databases, including high-performance processors and hardware accelerators, non-volatile memory (NVM), networks, and remote direct memory

Figure 8. Computer architecture in the 2020s (Pan et al., 2018). (RDMA = Remote Direct Memory Access; NIC = Network Interface Controller; OS = Operating System; Cache = buffer memory; app = application)

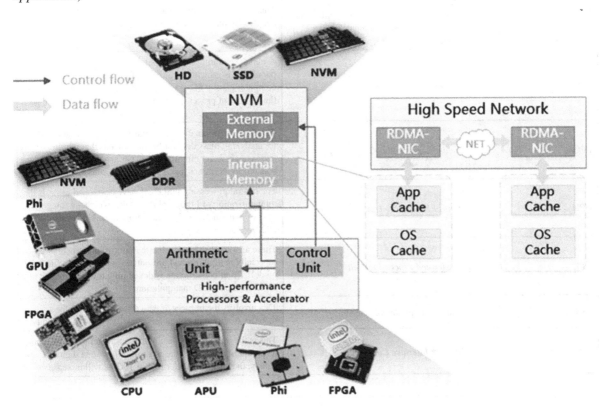

access. Importantly, existing environments with heterogeneous multicore architectures and hybrid memory hierarchies make the growing complexity of software design space a significant challenge for experts.

Development of the Central Processing Unit (CPU)

The development of processor technology has been going on for more than 40 years. Under Moore's law, the continuous increases in CPU speed are one of the most important ways of improving computer performance. At the same time, many optimization techniques are used, such as….

Table 2. Explanations and trends of crucial computer technologies

Abbreviation of The Name	Full Name	Applications and Trends
NVM	*Non-Volatile-Memory*	As memory capacity increases, the density of information is increased, and energy consumption for its operation decreases.
DDR	*Double Data Rate*	The most common type of internal memory used, it has developed in a series from DRAM memory (*Dynamic Random Access Memory*), including HMC (*Hybrid Memory Cube*). This has increases memory efficiency 15-folds and has reduced costs by as much as 70%. It consists of several layers, each with different memory cycles
Xeon Phi	The name comes from Phi CORE, where CORE=Community, Opportunity, Resources, and Edge. Phi chips are found in large quantities in computers with parallel architecture.	This is a multicore processor (x86) for supercomputers, adapted for high-speed memory
GPU	*Graphic Processing Unit*	A unit accelerating the manipulation of graphics, its popularity is growing as a result of the development of computer games, 3D graphics, and video. This has increased the number of processor cores from 4-8 to 5000+ in one pc set.
FPGA	*Field-Programmable Gate Array*	This is a programmable, user-coded electronic system for analyzing mass data for business needs that require increasingly faster circuits; this is not used in automotive, consumer electronics, or telecommunications.
CPU	*Central Processing Unit*	The central processing unit chips have developed towards the miniaturization of lithographic circuits, which are integrated below 7 nanometers ("The Incredible Shrinking Machine", 2020).[1]
APU	*Accelerated Processing Unit*	These are circuits that accelerate multitasking processing, especially in graphics and presentations of complex financial models. Their construction is developing towards greater sophistication in 3D manipulation.
RDMA	*Remote Direct Memory Access*	This involves the transfer of data directly between the memory of different computers; it will grow to 100+ Gbits.
NIC	*Network Interface Controller*	This is the interface connecting the computer to the network; its popularity is growing as a result of its use in digital clouds; the current transfer rate of 10Gb/s will increase.

- instruction-level parallelism,
- pipelines, prefetch, anticipate branching, execute out-of-order instructions,
- multi-level caches and automatic identification and use by software compiler processors.

Shortcuts for memory names and logical controls in Figure 8 are characterized in Table 2.

After 2005, high-performance processor technology entered the multicore era, and multicore parallel processing technology has become a mainstream development. Although data processing capabilities have been greatly improved in multicore configurations, the software cannot as of yet automatically benefit from this. Instead, developers must transform traditional serial programs into parallel programs and optimize algorithm performance for last-level cache through so-called niche LLC (Last Level Cache) multicore processors. However, general-purpose multicore processors are also unable to meet the demands of highly concurrent applications. CPU development can be optimized explicitly for applications as long as a computer has specialized hardware accelerators.

Storage Technology

As high-performance processors and hardware accelerator technologies increase their applications, the performance gap between processors and storage is growing year by year. The limitations called the "memory wall" make accessing data a real bottleneck for processing performance. Faced with the possibility of slow input/output (I/O) operations on traditional external storage devices, *Business Analytics* had to adopt specific software strategies, such as cache pools, concurrency control, and data-to-disk-oriented algorithms.

Although the characteristics and production processes of memory are different, they generally have some standard features, including durability, high storage density, random reading/low-latency reading, and fine-grained byte addressing. From a performance point of view, NVM (non-volatile memory) is similar to DDR (double data rate) memory, but it also has a non-volatile function. Therefore, it can gradually become the main memory device, with DDR being used as a temporary data cache. Today, *flash* memory technology has already matured, as can be seen in the single flash memories of many personal computers. Its capacity can reach up to 12.8 TB, and its read/write performance is also high. Based on this, it can serve a cache between the RAM and the hard disk drive, and it can also be an alternative to a hard disk drive as a permanent storage device.

Network Technology

In addition to the I/O bottleneck and computer storage, the network I/O bottleneck is also a significant concern for computing performance. The overall bandwidth of a distributed database system is significantly reduced due to a high percentage of distributed transactions that lead to a potentially high network load. Because of this, existing database management systems (DBMS) must resort to specific strategies, such as coordinated task portioning, loose data consistency, or reduced distributed transaction rates. However, most of these remedies do not produce the expected results due to unreasonable assumptions as well as the current conditions and capacity of the network topology for applications. In particular, system scalability is still very limited, especially when the load on computing tasks does not have characteristics that can be objectively divided and dispersed into different processors on the network. Data management and the analysis of modern distributed equipment will, therefore, soon become a new field of research.

COMPUTER DESIGN TRENDS

The great amount of space they occupied could characterize the first computers (Figure 9). Lamp computers, such as the ENIAC (1946) or Russian URAL, occupied spaces roughly the size of basketball courts with benches for the public. Transistor computers, on the other hand, already occupied less space, roughly the size of volleyball courts with seats for the public. Regardless, they were called *mainframes* for a reason, and they required large crews of designers, programmers, and administrators. With the IBM 360/50 (Figure 9), however, the requirements for space decreased significantly.

Figure 9. Central unit URAL II (left) in the Polish Academy of Sciences (PAN) Computing Center (1970s) and the IBM 360/50 computer (right) installed in ZETO-ZOWAR in 1971

Figure 10. Supercomputer IBM Blue Gene/P Intrepid,[2] installed at the Argonne National Laboratory University of Chicago, built with 164,000 parallel processors. (Photo: Wikipedia)

Figure 11. IBM Q quantum computer—nothing like a classic computer (Photo: Wikipedia)

In contrast, supercomputers, built from several thousand parallel processors, occupy an impressive area (Figure 10).

At the beginning of the 1980s, we were flooded with a wave of microcomputers, colloquially called *PCs* from the name *IBM PC*. Over the years, these microcomputers have started to be organized into server farms with a power equal to or even higher than that of supercomputers.

The following generations of computers are distinguished (Polish computers are in square brackets[3]):

- Generation 0 (1935-1940): on magnetic relays, laboratory computers,
- Generation 1 (1941-1956): on electron lamps, Z3 – 1941, Mark I, Manchester Mark I, ENIAC, IBM 701, [XYZ – 1958, UMC-1 and ZAM 2 – 1962],
- Generation 2 (1957-1963): on transistors, IBM 7070, RCA 501, IBM 1400, [ZAM 21 i ODRA 1204 - 1967],
- Generation 3 (1964-1971): on integrated circuits, IBM 360/370, [K-202 - 1971, ODRA1305-1974],
- Generation 4 (1972-2010): on large-scale integrated circuits, CDCCyber 72, Macintosh, IBM PC,
- Generation 5 (2011-present): large-scale integration, artificial intelligence, multicore, IBM Watson, Apple Siri, Microsoft Cortana
- Generation 6 (2017-present): Quantum Computers, IBM Q System One (Figure 11): computers of this type have not replaced classical computers; rather, they are used to solve very complex mathematical problems. They can design security codes that are very difficult to break. In particular, they are useful for predicting many interactions between chemical elements and other similar projects, typical in the sciences.

ICT DESIGN TRENDS

The goals and strategies of ICT infrastructure design are the result of business strategies and could lead to the development of the following types of designs:

1. For large companies, it is recommended that they develop internal IT infrastructure led by their private IT service.
2. For medium-sized companies, it is recommended that they develop a mixed IT infrastructure, with an internal IT service and cloud information services, provided that this cloud is legally and financially responsible for its failures and data thefts. Such companies must have strategies for how to operate if the cloud ceases to provide services.
3. For small businesses, it is recommended that they hire a head of IT and possibly use the cloud while ensuring the conditions listed in point 2 above.

The objectives and strategies for designing infrastructure for public administration, schools, and universities will be analyzed in Part II of this book.

SUMMARY

1. The development trends of information infrastructure continue to determine the level of modern computing technology, as evidenced by the plans for the production of quantum computers. However, their application is not intended to dislodge the computers of previous generations; rather, it is to facilitate the solving of very complex mathematical, chemical, or physical problems, typical of processes that must be simulated by not just digital modes, but by hybrid (analog-to-digital) modes.
2. The development of computers for typical ICT tasks of companies and agencies does not lead towards increases in speed but to the enrichment of computational processes using artificial intelligence and to a very friendly graphical user interface (GUI).
3. Significant innovations are to be expected in the development of personal information assistants (wearable devices such as *smartwatches* and *smartglasses),* whose mass use will increase the business of telecommunications networks as well as marketing to expand the service to mobile consumers.
4. The digital cloud business now drives the development of ICT infrastructure; however, errors in reliability and security contracts can lead to catastrophes for the company or agency.
5. The development of the Internet of Things is very inspiring and profitable for the sensor and interface industries; however, its naive use will lead to the malfunction of companies, agencies, and entire cities due to problems with digital codes, remote devices, and/or servers. In addition, IoT hacking will always be present.

REFERENCES

Department of Defense. (2012, July). *Information enterprise architecture (DoD IEA): Version 2.0.* https://chess.army.mil/content/PullFile?id=c9637495-83b4-4447-a7c4-15fd3d8c84e7

Harvey, C. (2017). Cloud computing. *Datamation.* https://www.datamation.com/cloud/what-is-cloud-computing/

Pan, W., Li, Z., Zhang, Y., & Weng, C. (2018). The new hardware development trend and the challenges in data management and analysis. *Data Science and Engineering, 3*(3), 263–276. doi:10.100741019-018-0072-6

Postman, N. (1992). *Technopoly: The surrender of culture to technology.* Knopf.

Targowski, A. (2016). *The history, present state, and future of information technology.* Informing Science Institute.

The incredible shrinking machine. (July 18th, 2020). *The Economist.* https://www.economist.com/science-and-technology/2020/07/18/a-new-material-helps-transistors-become-vanishingly-small

UkEssays. (2018). *Current trends in hardware platforms information technology.* https://www.ukessays.com/essays/information-technology/current-trends-in-hardware-platforms-information-technology-essay.php?vref=1

KEY TERMS AND DEFINITIONS

Cloud Computing: The use of data centers via the Internet by computer users for computer processes and data storage.

Edge Computing: A form of distributed computing where computations and data storage are close to the locations where they are needed.

Internet of Everything: An interrelated system of connections between people, things, and data processors over the internet.

Internet of People: The process by which relationships between people and the collection their data becomes digitized and connected over the internet.

Internet of Things: A network of physical objects that are connected to one another via computer technologies over the internet.

Quantum Computers: The application of quantum phenomenon to computer computations.

Short Messaging Service: A text messaging service of a computer device, such as a cell phone.

Supercomputers: A computer with a high level of computational power in comparison to general purpose computers.

ENDNOTES

1   In other words, it is a thousandth of the diameter of a red blood cell.

2   The name "Intrepid" was borrowed from a large aircraft carrier, which was launched in 1943 and survived 5 suicide kamikaze attacks.

3   According to the data, Polish computers produced in the Polish People's Republic (behind of the Iron Curtain) were one generation behind Western computers.

Chapter 8
Development Trends of Information Systems

ABSTRACT

The goal of this chapter is to discuss development trends of information systems. The chapter begins by discussing a framework known as the semantic ladder. This framework provides an overview and shows relations between data, information, concepts, knowledge, and wisdom. The chapter then discusses three domains of scientific activity: data science, knowledge science, and wisdom science. Next, the chapter considers how we can move from a science of information to a science focused on informing. Ways of measuring the quality of information is then considered. The chapter concludes by examining the latest trends in designing information system during the past century.

INTRODUCTION

Since the golden age of science fiction books, the development of computerization has increasingly brought the *fictional* ideas closer to reality. The initial dominance of computer science *syntax* has given way to the *semantics* of these applications, i.e., applications are now designed to use ICT with increasing amounts of cognitive content about the situation to make wise decisions based on knowledge and wisdom. It has led to a *pragmatism* about these applications, that is, an effort to answer why these systems are implemented. It is a question about the *wisdom* of the system being undertaken.

Over the last 100 years of mechanization, automation, and computerization, the design of ICT applications has evolved (a) from partial systems to enterprise-wide systems and (b) from internal ICT services to outsourced services, either to those domestic or abroad (where it is cheaper) or to a digital cloud service with an unknown location to reduce the cost of the service. These are at present urgent digitalization-oriented dilemmas, which will be discussed in this chapter.

DOI: 10.4018/978-1-7998-8036-3.ch008

FROM DATA TO WISDOM IN A COMPLETE CYCLE OF COGNITION

Presently in the 2020s, there is a great interest in data science, which is often treated as the first of two phases of cognition. It is followed by the conversion of data into knowledge based on techniques of data mining, categorizing, and grouping and, subsequently, correlating, calculating, and presenting of proposals for decision-making. Unfortunately, data and knowledge are only two phases of the process of thinking, problem-solving, and deciding. In modern data engineering, there is no room for other units of cognition, like information, concepts, and wisdom.

What is information? The term is mostly used in formal and popular publications and discussions when it comes to concrete matters. For example, there is talk of the Information Wave that dynamizes civilization. So why is "information" not defined?

Information is a product of human thinking that expresses our insights, opinions, suggestions, communication, decisions, relationships, and reporting. Information is a "bullet" (message) that we send through a communication channel, such as personal conversation, phones, letters, the press, radios, televisions, books, and others. So, information is a description of the material world and is the product of our brain/mind. Without information about the world and the environment, we would be blind and deaf. Communicating with information makes us active and conscious.

For a long time, information as knowledge, culture, and infrastructure (e.g., education, power, communication, etc.) has helped develop civilization. This has occurred through papyrus, books, inscriptions on buildings, libraries, school and university textbooks, constitutional documents, the Bible, the Koran, the Talmud, songs, music, scientific ideas, social and political ideas, and in other formats. This was already the case about 100 years ago, for in 1928, the information theorist Ralph V. R. Hartley published an article in which he proved that "the total amount of information that can be transmitted is proportional to the transmission frequency range and transmission time." Hartley's law eventually became one of the elements of *white noise*. Claude Shannon's (1948) theory of communication, formulated 20 years later in 1948, provided the following formula: (however the formula is about the size of information, not about its meaning):

$$I = - \log_2 p\,(a)$$

where I –information; the negative sign indicates a reduction in entropy (chaos); p – the probability of event a

It follows from this information formula that if it is Monday today, the statement that tomorrow is Tuesday is not information because the probability of this statement p=1 means that...

$$I = - \log_2 1 = 0 \text{ because } 2^0 = 1$$

In other words, that after Monday is Tuesday is not information because everyone knows it. In this way, we assume that information is one of the units of cognition that indicates a change in the situation, e.g., that the stock exchange has gone down by 10%.

To distinguish all the units of cognition, the Semantic Ladder will be used as a model that organizes cognition units from data to wisdom. This explanation of what information is (as a carrier of cognition) deals with the semantics of the science of cognition (Figure 1). This takes place in the applications of Management Information Systems (MIS). The semantics of information deals, for example, with the answer to the question of *what* information is needed to monitor the implementation of a production plan. Semantics in cognitive science, of course, requires knowledge of syntax, just as speaking in a foreign language requires knowledge of its grammar to be well understood.

Figure 1. Interdependent cognition processing platforms

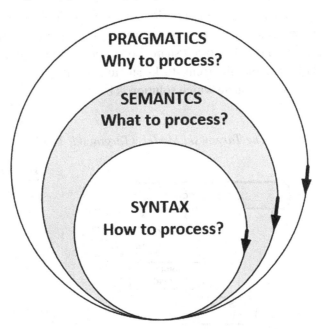

In the United States, there are about 600,000 English teachers who know *how to* apply grammar well, and that is what they are all about. Less know *what to* write in English. Such specialists are writers, columnists, and journalists. They know what to write about, and that is why they are being read. How many are there who know what to write about? Not more than a few thousand. The number of writers who persistently publish best-selling books ranges from a few dozen to several hundred, depending on the period and wave of creativity.

The same is true for digital informants. Consultants of complex ICT systems for enterprises earn several times more than programmers because they know *what* information to process and *why* to do it (here we are already dealing with the pragmatism of digital informing). They also know how to handle this information digitally.

Just as there are several simple molecules in the construction of an atom, such as the electron and proton, so too in digital informing, "information" is a general term that includes elementary particles of cognition, processed by the human brain/mind and computers. These particles include data, information, concepts, knowledge, and wisdom, as illustrated by the Model of the Semantic Ladder in Figure 2.

The definition of these terms will be fleshed out via an example of a decision-making situation: investing in stocks for a portfolio, which are being traded on the New York Stock Exchange:

- **Data:** Say the Dow Jones index is 10,000 points on a given Monday of some month and year.
- **Information:** Say that on Tuesday, the news reports that the Dow Jones is 8,000 points, which is 20% less than the day before. This is quite unpleasant information, which is characterized by a change in the indicator by minus 20%. The information, therefore, defines a change that requires the investor to conceptualize a new solution.
- **Concept:** The concept could consist of choosing one of 3 options. Since the shares have fallen in price and are cheap, one could buy a new share package (K_1). However, the shares may continue to fall; so, the second option (K_2) is to sell shares so as not to incur further loses. Finally, the third solution (K_3) is to hold onto one's current stocks and to not sell or buy new ones. With three concepts/options, one needs to evaluate which solution is best.

Figure 2. The Semantic Ladder (The Targowski Model) (Targowski, 1990)

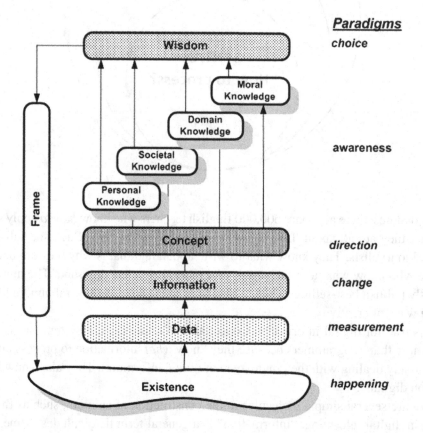

- **Knowledge:** Knowledge is scientific data and principles/rules/laws that the investor will use to evaluate each option. Basic knowledge indicates that one should buy stocks when they are cheap and sell when they are expensive. Theoretical knowledge may suggest that the fall in prices is due to the economy entering a recession. Global knowledge indicates that a war with some state is approaching and that this will increase the need for weapons. Universal knowledge, on the other hand, shows that when the economy enters a recession, the share profit decreases and increases from the trading of bonds.

- **Wisdom:** After the investor has assessed the situation for each of the four options based on knowledge, they now must choose the wisest option. Perhaps they decide that selling shares would result in a loss, and so reject K_2. Perhaps a war approaches, which would cause the share prices to go down; thus, they do not buy new shares (K_1), but keep the old and wait, that is, option K_3. Time will tell whether this was the right choice, and therefore wise.
- **Frame:** The frame implements the choice of the investment solution in practice.

Figure 3. Model of various IT systems supporting knowledge (Targowski, 2006). TPS-Transactions Processing Systems, EIS-Executive Information Systems, ERP-Enterprise Resources Planning, SCM-Supply Chain Management, CRN-Customer Relations Management

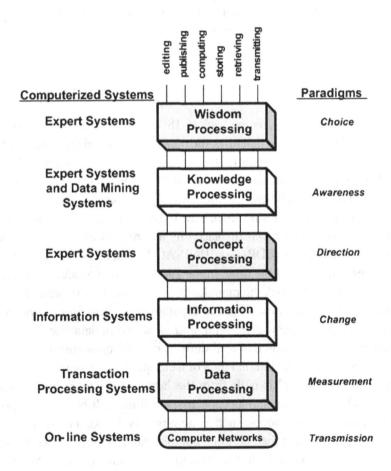

The Semantic Ladder explains that wisdom is not knowledge, information (in the sense of change), or data; rather, it is sound judgment and the choice of a concept for thinking and acting. To properly formulate a concept, one needs to be not only well informed but also have reliable and trusted data. To make a wise judgment, one needs to have the necessary sources of knowledge, including basic, theoretical, global, universal, digital, virtual, and others. Not everyone has such knowledge. Are their judgments leading to wise choices? This does not mean that a wider range of knowledge is a guarantor of wise judgments. Even possessing the full range of all categories of knowledge does not guarantee a wise assessment. There are many other factors at stake, such as emotion, intuition, luck in choosing, and the willpower to perform wise actions, among others. All this takes place within the scope of the art of living. The word "art" here is used to mean (a) an intuitional and innovative approach to principles of assessment that are known and sound as well as (b) the ability to create new rules and break those for a given case that are out of date.

The Semantic Ladder theory is a contemporary approach. Wisdom is clearly distinguished from the other units of cognition. Previously, wisdom was viewed as the holistic wisdom of humanity, which a single person was unable to possess. Hence no one could be wise. In modern psychology, wisdom is an expert attitude, that is, not accessible to an ordinary person. In cognitive informing (Targowski, 2011), wisdom is potentially reachable for every mentally healthy person (Targowski, 2013).

Thanks to the Semantic Ladder, one can distinguish different types of informing systems correctly, according to the units of cognition illustrated by the Model in Figure 3.

DATA SCIENCE[1]

Data processing has had a long history, dating back to 1890 when the first census in the United States took place on punched card machines. At that time, the punch cards contained business data, which led to the mechanization of data processing systems first on so-called "Hollerith machines" (i.e., on 80 column cards that were read electrically), then, since 1924, on IBM machines (in Europe on BULL machines) as well as on so-called "Powers machines" (on 90 column cards read mechanically), i.e., Remington/ UNIVAC machines (in Europe-Czechoslovakian, ARITMA). The mechanization of data processing lasted roughly until the 1960s, when it was displaced by automation of data processing (ADP)—also known as electronic data processing (EDP)—on UNIVAC I computers (1951) and then later on the popular IBM 1400 series computers of the time. In the 1960s, the first academic programs of so-called *computer science* were created, in which the main lectures were on *data structures*.

At first, the data sets in the files were stored in separate sequential *files* on magnetic tapes. Since 1971, they have been stored on magnetic disks with *random access* in databases (network, hierarchical, and relational). The data sets are composed of well-defined *records*, consisting of data *fields* with names such as "part number", etc. This is the internal data of a company or agency.

Since so-called "external storage" is built from the large-scale integration of electronic circuits, this kind of memory has been cheaper, and its capacity is unlimited. It has become possible to collect unstructured data from all kinds of sources, such as newspapers, books, newsletters, radio, television, etc. Not only can they be preserved in their entirety, but they can also be searched for via search engine techniques such as those used by Google. In this way, the development of *Big Data* with external data has enabled processes to assess impacts on internal data contexts, thereby enriching the quality of judgments and decisions made by users.

Big Data has enabled the development of artificial intelligence through *machine learning* and *deep learning* on massive data sets (examples are mentioned in Part III). However, Big Data processing technology is more complicated than well-defined database technology. Hence, there is a vital need for the development of data engineering as a science.

Data engineering is an interdisciplinary set of algorithms, methods, and programming techniques for recording, collecting, searching, and mining data to share it with other units of cognition. Data engineering enables the implementation of solutions, *business analytics,* the modeling of future trends, and the generation of advanced statistics about a market or business. So far, the following processes of processing and manipulating data have been developed:

- Collecting and cleaning data, which takes the most time: This includes processes such as
  - Completing raw data
  - Naming and categorizing data
  - Cleaning data with exceptional errors
  - Deleting inadequate data with unnecessary patterns
  - Others
- Data mining, based on understanding data via the following processes.:
  - Classifying data
  - Analyzing data sequencing
  - Analyzing situation paths
  - Grouping data
  - Sorting by categorizing criteria
  - Generating situation patterns in terms of…
    - Consumer behavior
    - Market dynamics
    - Economic Trends
    - Geographic information
    - Others
- Analyzing numerical and graphical data correlations
  - Logistic regression
  - Linear regression
  - Factor analysis
  - Heat analysis
  - Time series analysis
  - Others
- Modeling machine-based solutions and deep learning
- Detecting patterns typical of hacking and cybercrime
- Visualizing data in different forms, such as prints, graphs, tables, charts, maps, management panels, infographics, videos, and others.
- Sorting data into collections; updating and sharing accurate data in terms objectives and strategies.

Data engineering processes Big Data using the programming language Python, which is a high-level language of generalization for declarations and instructions. It is used in an open-source system for all interested parties. It is available on most commercial platforms such as UNIX, Android, MS-DOS, Windows, Mac, etc. Its AI programs operate well in, for example, the field of deep machine learning. It is used by big tech companies such as Google, YouTube, Drobox, Reddit, Pinterest, and others.

The data engineering model is depicted in Figure 4.

Figure 4. The decision-making model of data engineering

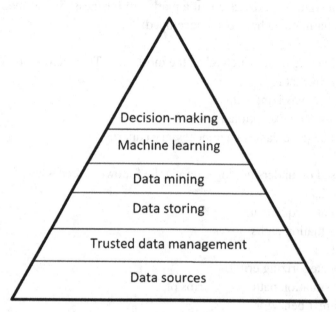

KNOWLEDGE SCIENCE

Knowledge means dealing with scientific data, principles, rules, trends, and laws, defined at different qualitative levels: at the level of common sense and the level of theoretical knowledge.

Many people usually think, decide, and communicate based on collective knowledge of the past and present. People with higher education enrich their intellectual capabilities with theoretical knowledge, which can be hundreds of years old, as in the case of the Copernican astronomical theory. Others develop their knowledge of experience by traveling abroad. Hence, there is a need to analyze the most important human organ—the brain. This organ is the most complex and has continuously been a "black box", even for educated people. However, the body stores our knowledge of the world, ultimately determining whether we know something and whether we are wise or stupid. The content of knowledge is determined by the information capacity of the brain, which appears to be unlimited since there are billions of neurons that record information from our thinking and sensory perceptions. These neurons and, de *facto,* their network of countless connections and nodes form the mind, or brain software, which by analogy is human "hardware."

Figure 5. A model of human minds (the Targowski Model) (Krawczyk & Targowski, 2017; Targowski, 2011, 2017)

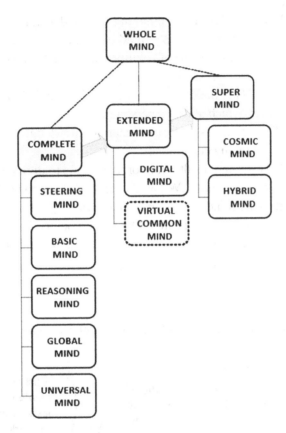

As civilization progresses, our mind makes our brain "swell" from remembering more and more information. Our mind also specializes (like computer software), just as our knowledge about the world is specialized. Indeed, no one can grasp the knowledge contained in 128 million different books and in several hundred thousand other publications that have been published since the invention of the print, that is, for nearly 600 years. Perhaps one can afford to be wrong because the computer engine (the "brain") of Google and the AI Watson can at present almost complete the task of grasping this knowledge.

Based on different types of knowledge, the following types of minds (Figure 5) can be distinguished:

- **COMPLETE mind:** The holder of this mind can function independently in complex situations because he/she has sufficient knowledge:
    - **CONTROL mind:** This is an analog-informational interface between the biological brain and the informational mind.
    - **BASIC mind:** This mind contains common knowledge based on so-called "common sense", obtained either from life practices or enriched by high school graduation. It is a dependent mind because it is unable to explain many theoretically complex cases.
    - **THEORETICAL mind:** This mind contains theoretical knowledge gained through the completion of higher education. The holder of this mind can think independently because

he/she has a basic theoretical understanding of life and the world and can sometimes understand complex matters.

- ○ **GLOBAL mind:** The holder of this mind has knowledge gained from traveling abroad and
knowledge of foreign languages. It is a mind that embraces issues occurring in other countries, which allows for comparisons of solutions and possible adaptations to improve a given
civilization in each place of residence.
- ○ **UNIVERSAL mind:** This mind knows human rights, civil rights, international rights, and
the values of religions, which allows a person to be tolerant and minimize conflicts.
- **EXTENDED mind:** This mind has expanded external knowledge thanks to the ability of computer science. It has the following constituents:
- ○ **DIGITAL mind**: This mind results from online access to digital libraries spread around the
world, including Goggle e-books, Wikipedia, and other e-knowledge centers.
- ○ **VIRTUAL mind:** This mind results from participating in discussions in blogs and social
networks (Facebook, Instagram, Twitter, Quora, and others).
- **SUPER mind:** This is a mind with unique knowledge at the present stage of civilizational development due to the following minds:

Figure 6. The architecture of a company's Knowledge Management System (KMS)

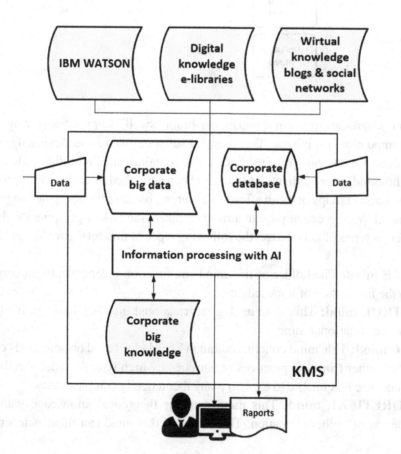

     ◦   **SPACE mind:** This mind has knowledge possessed by cosmonauts traveling to other planets and to/from the international space station as well as soldiers and officers of the US Space Force, which was established in December 2019.

     ◦   **HYBRID mind:** This is an improvement of the human mind/brain through digital implants in the biological brain, which is an interface between the steering mind and an external online computer that complements human thoughts with the knowledge of the digital mind (including Watson) in feedback.

Data and information processing systems provide insight into the current situations faced by companies and agencies, which usually lack the broader context of a given job. To this end, these systems should be enriched to provide a more comprehensive view of the company and its situation in regard to local, national, and global environments. An illustration of this knowledge at the company level is given in Figure 6, the architecture of the Knowledge Management System.

For example, Walmart, the world's largest company, owns 11,500 large department stores in 27 countries, employing 2.2 million employees and selling \$515 billion[2] of goods and services in 2019. Its KMS would have the following to say about the regularity of sales in the United States:

Diapers and beer are most sold on Mondays because during the weekend, diapers wear. So, wives instruct their husbands to go to Walmart after work and buy diapers. The husbands buy diapers, but they have also finished their beer stocks over the weekend, so they replenish them while purchasing diapers.

With this knowledge, the store manager can make *a wise* decision:

1. Stock up shop for Monday with more diapers and beer.
2. If the manager wants to satisfy the customers, he/she should place diapers and beer in the same isle of goods, so that the customer does not need to look for these goods all over the store.
3. However, if the manager wants to increase the store's business and get a bonus, he/she will put these two goods in two isles far apart, so that while looking for them, the customers are likely to buy other products, guided by momentary impulses.

Choosing one strategy or the other depends on the manager's judicious knowledge and awareness of the objective he/she intends to achieve, which will be an expression of his/her business wisdom. Every business, as well as every person, can implement their WMS to increase the quality of their knowledge in their decision-mking.

WISDOM SCIENCE

As the name suggests, "data" is not wisdom, nor is it knowledge; rather it is a record of facts. Wisdom, on the other hand, is the final phase of the cycle of cognition. The definition of wisdom is as follows:

Wisdom is right judgment and right choice supported by knowledge and practical actions. It is defined by skills and inspirations in the context of the art of living. The quality of wisdom depends on the art of

Figure 7. The cycle of Wisdom (Targowski Model) (Targowski, 2017)

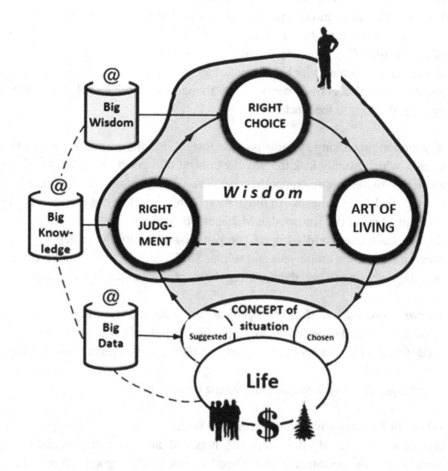

a living that results from one's genetics, character, morality, education, practices, relationships, environment, and ability to draw on the wisdom of one's family, profession, civilization, and other factors. In particular, the wisdom of a person or organization is based on a sense of responsibility for the future fate of the surrounding civilization. The effects of wisdom are survival, health, flourishing, goal fulfillment, cognition, the resolution of problems, action, suggestions, advice, opinions, decisions, and others.

In short, the definition of wisdom is:

Wisdom is right judgment based on knowledge and right choice based on practical actions defined by skills and inspirations in the context of the art of living.

The cycle of wisdom is shown in Figure 7.

However, the main factors affecting the quality of wisdom are given in the model in Figure 8, grouped in terms of knowledge, inspiration, and qualifications.

If Big Data and Big Knowledge are developed, Big Wisdom must be also. This results in the development of the Big Reservoir of Cognition, as illustrated by the model in Figure 9. Big wisdom is a

Figure 8. Model of the leading factors of wisdom (Krawczyk & Targowski, 2019)

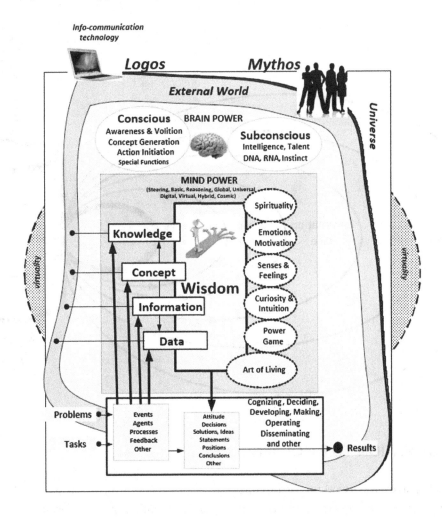

collection of so-called "wisdom seeds", which are stored in an unstructured computer recording in the external memory of the computer.

Figure 10 lists the architecture of the Wisdom Management System. It is the last phase of the cycle of cognition, which uses the Big Reservoir of cognition, composed of the Big Data, Big Information, Big Knowledge, and Big Wisdom of the company. An example of a company's wisdom is the decision of the Walmart department store manager who either scatters the diapers and beer around the store to motivate customers to buy other goods or puts them in one isle to please the customers. Walmart can check thousands of similar decisions made by two million employees every day, creating Big Wisdom that interested parties can use.

Figure 9. Seeds of wisdom in the Big Reservoir of Cognition (Krawczyk & Targowski, 2019)

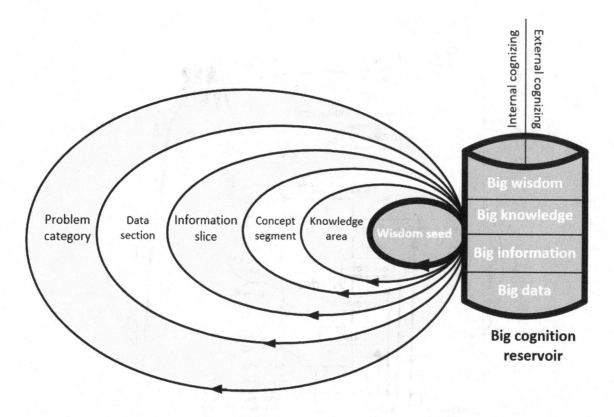

FROM INFORMATION TO INFORMING

In the comprehensive IT networking of organizations and people around the world, the focus is on moving from passive data processing to interactive, real-time online information for end-users. These end-users look not only at the endless pages of columns and rows of data but above all, they want to look for critical information that supports management by exception and management by purpose (MBO-*Management by Objectives)* and other management techniques. Large amounts of data are needed to run a company or public administration agency, but they are not particularly relevant to management, except for accounting and inventory management. Currently, management is looking for resonant IT systems, as noted by Gordon Gill (2009). Gil wants the system to inform and resonate, which implies its strengthening as it passes through an information channel. One is reminded of a sound produced by a string and then amplified by the instrument in a concert hall, which increases even more (acoustically) before it reaches the listeners (clients) (Gill, 2009).

Eli Cohen (2009b) goes even further, saying that the discipline of Management Information Systems (MIS) is looking for more rigor in the adequacy of information. The rigor of only adequate data leads to the bureaucratic implementation of IT systems that are less efficient, less effective, and less important. The response to this situation was an increase in the trend of redesigning information systems at the end of the 20th-century, which until now had been designed as "information islands." Systems such as *Enterprise Resource Planning* (ERP) had to address this problem from bottom-up, data-driven projects

Figure 10. The architecture of the company's Wisdom Management System

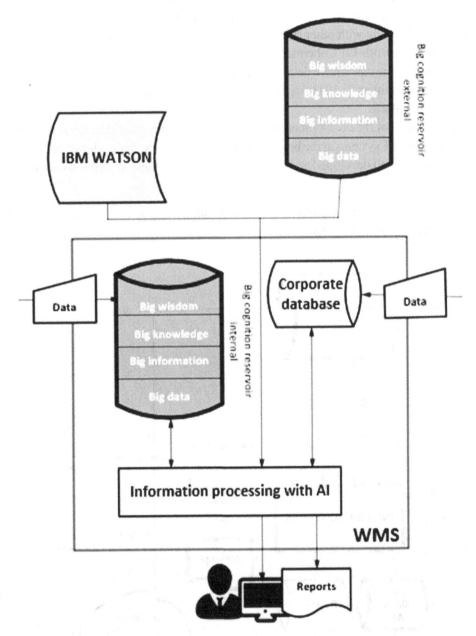

to top-down projects based on a comprehensive system. An exemplar of the ERP concept was implemented by the German company SAP, covering almost 40% of the global market. Unfortunately, this system is overflowing with the famous German rigor, which is very difficult to learn and apply. It is also costly and is not useful in informing management, especially in small and medium-size businesses that count every dollar/euro.

In search of the materiality of information, Grandon Gill (2009: 239) called for the resonance to be informed, which the customer should experience to help make the right decision on time, because, as

Gill states, "otherwise the customer is likely to remain misinformed." Gill (2009: 245-250) also noted that resonance information depends on customer information bias, cognitive biases, risk biases, and uncertainty biases, which, along with other filters and factors, he introduced into the Customer Resonance Model (Gill 2009: 249). Both Eli Cohen and Grandon Gill raised significant issues about the quality information, which in some cases have determined the fate of the world, such as the Japanese air strike on Pearl Harbor on December 7, 1941, in Hawaii, when the military base command disregarded the signal of an imminent attack.

The concept and trend of the development of information systems should be regarded as an improved layer to existing and new IT systems at the beginning of the 21ˢᵗ century. In developed countries, computer information systems are well developed and widely used, and all of these systems should not be expected

Figure 11. The architecture of the information and informing systems (Targowski model) (Targowski, 2016). Darkened symbols are elements of the informing system. AGI = Artificial General Intelligence, ANI = Artificial Narrow Intelligence

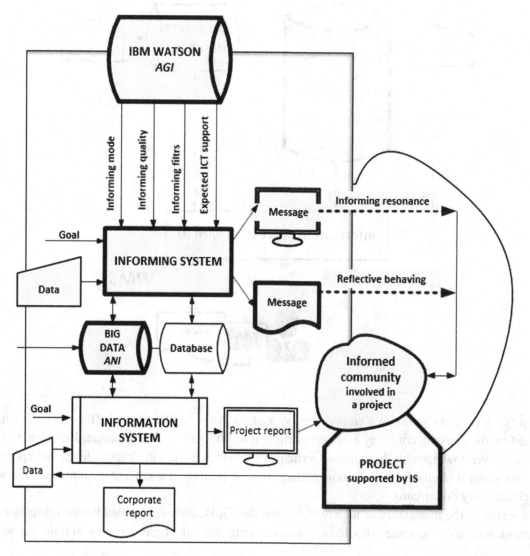

to be replaced by information systems. This situation is like the case of software programmed in COBOL between 1960 and 1980. This language was useful in data processing but was not suitable for interacting with the graphical user interface (GUI). Instead of rewriting all the software programmed in COBOL, one could add a new layer of interactive routines called GUIs, written in more modern languages (such as C++, Java, JavaScript, HTML, PHP, Python, Ruby, and others). Adding such a layer of interaction to COBOL-oriented software was an excellent business for service software companies from 1980 to 1990.

Furthermore, no information system needs to be informational (abbreviated). Many AI systems cover the entire enterprise, combining other systems. For example, the Bill of Material Processor combines a list of product elements with *Material Requirements Planning* (MRP I)- the latter being linked to MRP II-*Manufacturing Requirements Planning*. On the other hand, it is recommended that the final MRP I and MRP II reports include an informant function for the management of the company.

A classic example of an information system is a management dashboard designed for each director, mainly for CEOs and functional deputy directors. Therefore, the architecture of the informing system (presented in Figure 11) adopts the information system as the basis of the architecture. This architecture is illustrated for an informed environment composed of employees and executives, customers, suppliers, the market, and others. To ensure the adequacy of the information system, such as the management dashboard, the following attributes of the management dashboard must be provided about the situation:

- The informing modes: command-control, motivation, conflict management, exchange of information.
- The quality of information, i.e., the suitability for the user in which it is located, categorized via the following ways (Fig 2.2.6): transinforming, pseudoinforming, misinforming, parainforming, disinforming, data-informing, and meta-informing (Targowski & Bowman, 1988).
- The bias and filters of perception of information.
- Expected IT support for the user and the environment.

To attain these attributes of the information system, one must use artificial general intelligence (AGI), which can be purchased from IBM Watson, which is so far the only such system in the world that provides services in sharing their intelligence.

QUALITY OF INFORMATION

In social environments, the following levels of information quality are possible (Figure 12) (Targowski, 2016):

1. **Transinforming** occurs when the purpose of information (P), message (M), and resonance change (reflecting information) (C) are the same for the informant and the listener. This means that the message frame (F) for both is the same. The informant informed the listener without misunderstanding. The original message was not improved or distorted while being communicating and filtered through two communication channels (Chapter 3, Figure 8). This can be represented by the following formula (where j = 1, 2, 3, n):

$$F_{rj} = F_{sj} \text{ i } P_{rj} = P_{sj}; \text{ Mrj} = M_{sj}; C_{rj} = C_{sj}$$

Two people who know each other well can get high quality information in communication. The standard message and the consistent assessment of the resonant change are virtually identical. For example, such a message-forwarding session can take place in a command system where both sides use well-formatted elements of the communication process on a well-known or ongoing investigation.

2. **Pseudoinforming** occurs when the listener adds additional information to the informant's message. This situation is reflected in the following formula (assuming $P_{rj} = P_{sj):):}$

$$F_{rj} \neq F_{sj} \text{ i } M_{sj} + \Delta M_{rj},$$

For example, one politician could deliberately send an ambiguous message to which the receiver (or the media) would add additional layers of meaning, most of which were unintended by the politician. However, the receiver may insist that it understands the "true intentions" of the policy. If later events show that the concept of the receiver is incorrect, the receiver may conclude that the politician intended something else. Pseudoinformation can also occur when $P_{rj} \neq P_{sj}$.

3. **Misinforming** occurs when the informant and receiver exchange only part of a message and change the resonance; however, a compulsory part was lost in the communication channel. The following formula presents these situations:

   a) Assuming that $P_{rj} = P_{sj} F_{rj} \neq F_{sj}$ and $M_{sj} \subset M_{rj}$ and $C_{sj} \subset C_{rj}$ or
   b) Assuming that $Prj \neq P_{sj} F_{rj} \neq F_{sj}$ and $M_{sj} \subset M_{rj}$ and $C_{sj} \subset C_{rj}$

   Misinforming (a) could occur, for example, if a professor provided only a partial explanation of a subject and if the students read the rest of the description in their textbooks. Later, students may show that they are ill-informed, passing only a partial message and a partial resonance change in their exams. Misinforming (b) could occur, for example, if a dealer of used cars has different purposes than the buyer: namely, suppose the former does not have to tell the full truth about the condition of the vehicle, and the buyer has incomplete information about the car. This is a case of asymmetric information with a specific purpose.

4. **Parainforming** occurs when the listener's resonance change distorts the purpose of the informant. Unlike pseudoinformation, in which the resonance change adds additional layers of meaning, the original layers are distorted in parainformation. General semantics calls this "bypassing". This is the case, for example, in politics, when the informing party allegedly calls for elections, pretending to follow the constitution, but the elections will be fabricated. The following formula can illustrate parainforming:

   a) Assuming that $P_{rj} \neq P_{sj} F_{rj} \neq F_{sj}$ i $C_{sj} \neq C_{rj}$ ale $M_{rj} = M_{sj}$

   At the simplest level, parainformation occurs when two people use the same words to have different meanings. For example, in dictatorial political regimes, the word "freedom" means something other than in real democratic countries. Even in democratic states, when the president evaluates his accomplishments, citizens may disagree, because their resonant change is different from the president's feelings about the resonance change that has taken place in this country. Parainformation occurs when the informant's target is distorted by a resonance change in the listener (meaning a lack of trust). Parainformation very often involves deliberate manipulation of the hearing. The informative quality of parainformation can even be worse than misinformation. While disinformation may not be intentional and is usually due to the condition of the communication channel and the skills of the parties communicating, parainformation is the deliberately planned transmission

Figure 12. Quality of information (Targowski Model) (Targowski, 2016).

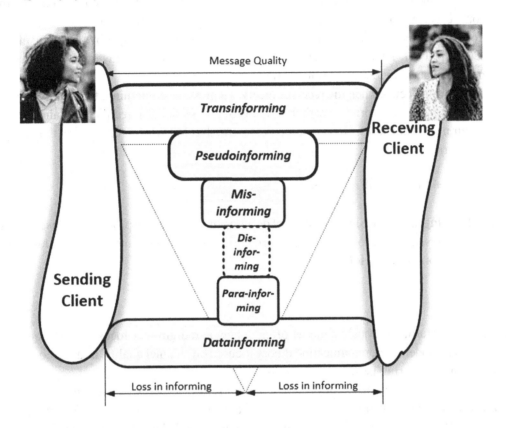

Table 1. Comparison of attributes in information and informing systems

Attributes	Information System	Informing System	Result
Customer support	Report	The message, resonances of the situation, reflective information influencing the user's behavior	Informed decision-makers and customers
Designed in terms of	Rigor	Rigor and adequacy	Dobry system
The main objective of the system	The report, report monitoring, the implementation of a task	Communication supporting the implementation of the organization's vision	Long and short-term synchronized goals
Information assistance	Data structures, Manipulating data, Search databases	Ensuring mode, quality, bias, and information filters; Application of Big Data and ANI	A system more semantically than syntactically oriented system that improves user cognition
Information, including bias and filters	Limited IT qualifications	Applications; IBM Watson and AGI	Information tailored to the nature of the user
Knowledge and qualifications of system implementers	Based on education by vertical specialization curriculum	New knowledge and skills require interdisciplinary knowledge	It is challenging to implement these attributes due to the long tradition of this way of training computer scientists
Needs for information systems	Not yet seen opportunities and ways to modernize traditional IT systems	For now, only the pioneers of information systems recognize such needs	The success of information systems depends on management, which should formulate the requirements for such systems

of a wrong framework of communication motivated by various objectives of the parties. In social situations, especially in politics, this is called "brainwashing" or "foaming."

5. **Disinforming** reflects the intention to deceive the customer-receiver by providing false information (Gill, 2015, p. 174). This means that $P_{rj} \neq P_{sj}$; however, the receiver may eventually find out later that the informant provided false information.

6. **Data informing** occurs when the receiver receives a message containing, for example, an address, telephone number, share price, weather conditions, and so on. The recipient obtains data according to their needs (purpose). Data creation is presented as follows (assuming that the goals of both parties are irrelevant):

$$F_{rj} = F_{sj} \text{ gdzie } M_{rj} = M_{sj}; C_{sj} = 0, \text{ ale } C_{rj} \neq 0$$

7. **Metainforming** takes place in the process of defining the information process, because the informant invents, designs, and controls the act of information. Because metainformation is done entirely in the mind, its formula is as follows:

$$F_{rj} = F_{sj} \text{ or } F_{rj} \neq F_{sj}$$

The presented information quality model offers a new paradigm that focuses on the quality of the message. Previous models of communication theory focused on channel quality, treating communication as necessarily an engineering issue.[3]

A comparison of the attributes in information and informing systems is given in Table 1.

The following example illustrates the dynamics of the entire information process as reflected by the computerized information environment presented in Figure 8 and characterized in Table 1:

- Information environment: Let us say a global car company is looking for countries that can produce parts and components for a worldwide car model. This means that parts and components produced in any country by branches of this corporation must fit the global car model.
- The user is the CEO who decides which countries should be chosen that match the requirements of the global car corporation.
- The informed report specifies what kind of knowledge (information) should be made available to the head of the company. To define these requirements, one must specify the following:
  - The goal – e.g., this global company should be a significant global car manufacturer, which can achieve at least a 15% market share.
  - Expected usability – e.g., the company will attain global dominance in the market of low-cost cars.
  - Information mode – e.g., through negotiation-motivation, the search for information on tax credits and other benefits motivating foreign investors in Asia, Europe, America, Africa, and Oceania.
  - Quality of information – e.g., providing information to board members based on well-chosen information with an excellent GUI.
- Delivery system selected: The management panel is based on the enterprise ERP system and has been extended to external data and information sources that provide unstructured information.

The development of information systems can be characterized by the following challenges for the user environment and the IT environment:

- It is to be expected that the development of information systems will be difficult, just as the academic environment is not suitable for interdisciplinary cooperation required for the development of such systems (Cohen, 2009a).
- The IT system should be a system that increases the sensitivity of companies, corporations, and government agencies in recognizing resonant changes and applying the right strategy to its needs.
- However, the IT system - even the best - does not guarantee a solution to every documented problem because the user must decide whether he wants to follow the suggestions of this system or neglect them. The latter situation of "do nothing" and/or weak political will are now very popular with executives and politicians.
- The development of information systems must be accepted by academia and practiced by organizations that care for good leadership and governance to sustain and develop these organizations

Table 2. The trends of digitalized systems

Date	Design Method	Technology	Result
1920-1960	Mechanization of records	Punched cards machines	Information islands
1961-1971	Automation of records	Computers with punched cards, sequential memory on magnetic tapes	Information islands, cutting red tape
1972-1990	Computerization of applications through Management Information Systems (SIK)	Computers with online input, random memory on magnetic disks	Information islands, support for technocracy and leadership
1991-2000	Enterprise Comprehensive AI Design[4] (ERP)	Networked and AI computers with shared database	Reducing redundancy of data records and gradual elimination of indirect management, replaced by computerization
2001-2017	*Outsourcing* AI to countries with cheaper IT services, mainly to India	Debugging and implementing the enterprise system via the extranet	Reduced reliability and ICT services and their regression, but reduced ICT costs
2018+	Moving user ICT structure to the digital cloud	Increased network utilization and minimizing the presence of users' ICT service in an enterprise. Robotization of HELP and customer services	Reduced ICT reliability due to increased *cybercrime* vulnerability

and civilizations.

- Information and decision-making information systems are positive because they improve cognitive function and respond to changes - especially negative ones that need correction - and contribute to updated learning and a better understanding of the dynamics of civilization and the world.

Figure 13. Enterprise Systems Model (Targowski Model) (Targowski, & Rienzo, 2008). U2A = User-To-Users Application; A2A = Application-To-Application; B2B = Business-To-Business; B2K = Business-To- customer; C2C = Client-To-Client

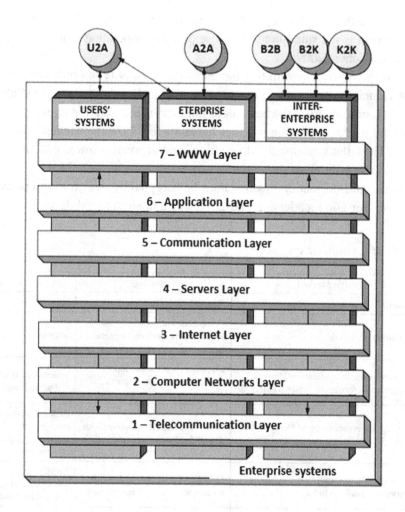

TRENDS IN THE DEVELOPMENT OF INFORMATION SYSTEMS DESIGN METHODS

Trends in the development of the organization's digital design methods are characterized in Table 2.

Apart from outsourcing IT services to India or to a digital cloud with an unknown location, the method of designing IT systems has adopted the abbreviated name "enterprise systems design". The word "enterprise" means the complexity of the systems, as illustrated by the enterprise system model given in Figure 13.

SUMMARY

In summary, the following can be stated about the development trends of computerization:

1. The development of ICT-related application systems is evolving towards an increasingly broader horizon regarding the importance of digital content (semantics) at the level of data evaluation. This evolution is taking place from information about status and change, which is enriched by inferences based on knowledge about a given business, to suggestions about what a wise decision-making solution is.
2. To enable a wise decision, data engineering, knowledge engineering, and wisdom engineering are being developed based on Big Data, Big Information, Big Knowledge, and Big Wisdom.
3. Progress in the advancement of complexity and greater usefulness in digitalization has been accompanied by a negative strategy of outsourcing and either getting rid of infrastructure abroad or moving to a digital cloud with an unknown location, vulnerable to cybercrime.

REFERENCES

Cohen, E. (2009a). A philosophy of informing science. In E. Cohen & G. Gill (Eds.), *Foundations of informing science: 1999-2008* (pp. 767–788). Informing Science Press.

Cohen, E. (2009b). Reconceptualizing information systems as a field of the discipline informing science: From ugly duck to swan. In E. Cohen & G. Gill (Eds.), *Foundations of informing science: 1999-2008* (pp. 7–20). Informing Science Press.

Gill, T. G. (2009). Informing resonance: Beyond rigor and relevance. In E. Cohen & G. Gill (Eds.), *Foundations of informing science: 1999-2008* (pp. 239–286). Informing Science Press.

Gill, T. G. (2015). *Informing science. Volume two: Design and research issues*. Informing Science Institute.

Krawczyk, H., & Targowski, A. (2019). *Wisdom in the context of globalization and civilization*. Cambridge Scholars Publishing.

Shannon, C. (1948). A mathematical theory of communication. *The Bell System Technical Journal, 27*(3), 379–423. doi:10.1002/j.1538-7305.1948.tb01338.x

Targowski, A. (1990). *The architecture and planning of enterprise-wide information management systems*. Idea Group Publishing.

Targowski, A. (2006). *Electronic enterprise, strategy and architecture*. IRM Press.

Targowski, A. (2011). *Cognitive informatics and wisdom development*. IGI Global. doi:10.4018/978-1-60960-168-3

Targowski, A. (2013). *Harnessing the power of wisdom*. NOVA Science Publishers.

Targowski, A. (2016). *Informing and civilization*. Informing Science Press.

Targowski, A. (2017). *The power of wisdom*. Gdańsk University of Technology Publishing House.

Targowski, A., & Bowman, J. (1988). The layer-based pragmatic model of the business communication process and its implications for business communication. *Journal of Business Communication*, *25*(1), 5–24. doi:10.1177/002194368802500101

Targowski, A., & Rienzo, T. (2008). *Enterprise information infrastructure*. Paradox Associates.

KEY TERMS AND DEFINITIONS

Data: The base level of the semantic ladder. Data involves the measurement of some attribute.

Data Mining: A process that involves identifying patters in large data sets.

Enterprise Resource Planning: A form of software used to integrate and organize business tasks and processes.

Information: The second level of the semantic ladder. Information involves a measurement of some change that has taken place.

Knowledge: The fourth level of the semantic ladder. Knowledge is scientific principles, rules, and laws that are used to evaluate different options.

Knowledge Management System: An informing system that models how knowledge is managed as well as how it is related to data and information.

Semantic Ladder: A model that shows distinctions and relations between different cognitive units, including information, knowledge, and wisdom.

Wisdom: The highest level of the semantic ladder. Wisdom involves right judgement based on knowledge.

ENDNOTES

[1]   The English term *science* in the context of *computer science* does not mean computer "science" per se; it only means methods and techniques for performing calculations on computers.

[2]   It is the company with the largest sales in the world, the size of which in dollars is comparable to GDP of Poland, achieved by several million employees. The company would be the 21st most productive country in the world in 2019.

[3]   We are talking here about the 1949 Shannon-Weaver model elaborated in Bell Labs in the United States. The Shannon-Weaver model was designed to reflect the functioning of radio and telephone technology. The initial model consisted of four basic parts: sender, message, channel, and receiver. The sender was the part of the phone to which the person speaks, the channel was the phone itself, and the receiver was the part of the phone through which one could hear the sender at the other

end of the line. Shannon and Weaver noticed that static sounds or backgrounds can interfere with phone calls, so they called it noise. Some types of background sounds may also indicate a lack of signal.

4   On this subject, Targowski defended his master's thesis in January 1961 at the PW entitled "Comprehensive application of computing machines in enterprise-wide data processing systems of the radiolocation RAWAR T1 company in Warsaw".

Chapter 9
Development Trends in Automation

ABSTRACT

This chapter analyzes current development trends in automation. The chapter begins by discussing the history of automation in the 21ˢᵗ century, beginning with Honda's creation of ASIMO. Next, the chapter analyzes how automation gave rise to the relocating of many Western manufacturing centers to Asia, particularly those in the United States. The chapter then analyzes trends in the development of autonomous vehicles. This section includes a detailed projection of likely developments over the next several decades, such as the impact of autonomous vehicles on private vehicle ownership. The chapter concludes with a brief summary of these trends.

INTRODUCTION

Automation in production has been occurring since the 1930s and found its apogee in the development of car assembly lines in the Detroit area after World War II. Automation was then aimed at meeting the demand for cars and cheapening their production. Over time, production began to move from Detroit and other cities to China. This ignited automation in the United States to compete with low-cost labor in Asia. It was only when President Donald Trump began to introduce a policy of re-industrialization for the country in 2017 that these factories began to be brought back to the U.S.; however, production is automated because it is cheaper. Automation processes have also begun to be enriched with artificial intelligence engineering to minimize human labor needed to operate such factories, sometimes called "dark factories" because they do not need lighting without people. The focus on human labor savings has now shifted to designing autonomous vehicles to save on hiring drivers. These types of dilemmas will be strategically analyzed in this chapter.

DOI: 10.4018/978-1-7998-8036-3.ch009

AUTOMATION IN THE 21ST CENTURY

The development of automation discovered room for growth with the development of technology in the early 2000s. After Honda's creation of ASIMO in 2000 (which is considered "the most advanced humanoid robot in the world"), the development of automation temporarily subsided. Negative reviews of business process management (for which business process automation is an invaluable tool) have shown that the number of searches for this term more than halved between 2004 and 2011. In 2011, however, the launch of Apple's Siri interrupted a period of marketing silence about breakthroughs in automation. Siri ushered in a new era of automation and AI-based assistants. It embodied the shift away from physical robots to the development of computer automation and AI software, which, although it began in the late 1980s and early 1990s, became prominent with the effectiveness of its proposed solutions only after 20 years.[1]

The automation of business processes known by the acronym BPA (business process automation)—recently recognized as robotic process automation (RPA)—is becoming more sophisticated and enhanced by the application of robots. Nowadays, automation software has become a necessity, not a luxury. Its widespread use optimizes the labor of employees and leads to considerable savings in resources such as time, labor, materials, and machines. Every day we experience the miracle of AI, whether on Twitter, in emails, in our video games, or elsewhere. We have artificial intelligence assistants in our phones, cars, and homes. It is not perfect. Siri doesn't always have an answer, and the Alexa assistant sometimes doesn't hear us. NPCs (Non-Player Characters, i.e., a player role taken over by an AI) in video games sometimes do stupid (and hilarious) things, and back in 2016, we saw the failure of a talking AI released by Microsoft called "Tay" (Tay = Talking About You). The company had to "silence" its talk, which made inflammatory remarks about specific people on Twitter; however, despite these shortcomings, AI and automation are now more comprehensive than ever before. Today, they continually developing and improving.

RELOCATING PRODUCTION TO ASIA AND AUTOMATION

At the end of the 20th century, Western developed economies were losing manufacturing jobs because companies noticed that labor costs in emerging markets were so favorable that it was more profitable to hire a large number of employees in those locations than implementing even basic automation in the U.S. or Europe. However, trends in automation and robotics technologies are rapidly changing this equation, so much so that over the next 15-20 years, there may be a significant shift in production towards the concentration of end-user resources and markets in developed countries.

Within the context of rising labor costs and inflation in the economy as well as other economic trends, automation is becoming cost-competitive with the alternative of hiring a large number of workers. This ultimately reduces the importance of labor costs as a critical factor in deciding the location for new production. As the growth of computing power, advanced sensor technology, AI control systems, and other technological advances drive the next generation of automated manufacturing, the future of manufacturing seems ready for dramatic changes in many industries. Ultimately, companies that see the intersection of technology and geography as a strategic manufacturing opportunity are likely to be in a better position as automation changes the game.

Over the past ten years, the United States has had a poor attitude towards production. Many U.S. manufacturers, as well as manufacturers from other developed countries, have sought cost reductions

Figure 1. A configuration of Robotic Process Automation (RPA) (Thakur, 2018)

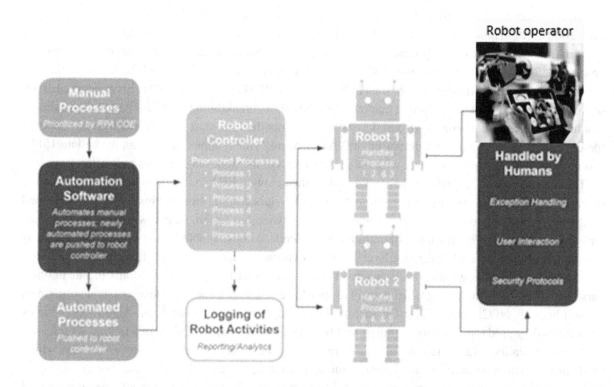

by increasing production outside of the U.S. However, since these initial attempts to shift production, U.S. companies have rethought the benefits of automation technology compared to relocation in Asia. While employment in U.S. industry as a percentage of total non-agricultural employment has declined significantly the past several decades (from 28% in 1962 to 9% in 2019), real industrial production has steadily increased (thanks to labor productivity) (Snyder, 2012).

Various factors make the current environment more conducive for the automation revolution than what we have seen in the past. New technologies appear first in an incubation environment, and then they move into full-scale manufacturing. For example, additive manufacturing, often referred to as *3D printing*, has already been effectively used to rapidly prototype aircraft parts. The technology has low entry barriers, as evidenced by the story of a Northwestern University engineering student in Chicago who created a detailed three-dimensional replica of the university campus during a three-week holiday break (Snyder, 2012).

In most cases, companies should reflect on their future impacts on the market and proactively anticipate capacity constraints by researching and piloting new technologies. In addition, countries are unlikely to regain lost capacity. Still, they have a clear opportunity to participate in the development of new products, and production can be done locally, as it used to be. To prepare for this future, companies and countries should focus on three interrelated areas and take action now: (a) research and development using new technologies, (b) talent development of leading employees, and (c) long-term strategic planning.

Figure 2. 3D printing (Photo: ISTOCK.com)

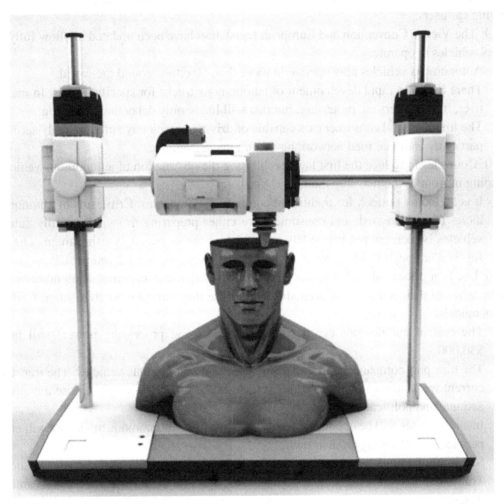

DEVELOPMENT OF AUTONOMOUS VEHICLES

According to a report by the University of Texas, if, at present, 90 percent of cars on the road in the United States were replaced by autonomous vehicles, savings in various industries, such as automakers, insurers, and the government, could reach up to $450 billion a year. This would be a considerable incentive for policymakers to pave the way for self-driving cars in the future. The complete adoption of autonomous vehicles will probably take place, but the expected improvements of safety, economy, and convenience will undoubtedly help speed up this process. In addition, air exhaust pollution will be reduced (Huang et al., 2019).

An optimistic timetable for the development of self-driving vehicles could be as follows:

- Present: Experience with autonomous vehicles shows that they are indeed much safer than the average driver. People feel comfortable in entirely autonomous cars, and there is no longer any problem with user acceptance. There is no phenomenon similar to the "fear of flying" among self-driving car users.

- 2019: The Vienna Convention and European legislation have been updated to allow fully autonomous vehicles to operate.
  - Autonomous vehicles now operate in more than 50 cities around the world.
  - There has been rapid development of autonomous trucks for specific routes. In many countries, truck drivers are protesting, but this will likely only delay their adoption.
  - The first high-end consumer cars capable of driving completely autonomously across a large part of the national road network have been made available.
- 2020: Countries introduce the first laws prohibiting the obstruction of autonomous vehicles (e.g., jumping in front of them to stop them).
  - It is a gloomy outlook for traditional automotive companies. Criticisms of autonomous vehicles have decreased, and consumers are either preparing to switch to fully autonomous vehicles (which are not yet widely available) or are increasingly using them. The fight for survival has begun: the automotive industry is having its "Kodak moment."[2]
- 2030: Used car prices will fall. Too many people will switch to conventional autonomous vehicles. Many will sell their old vehicles prematurely because they want to switch to safer, fully autonomous models.
  - The cost of autonomous car equipment (sensors and processing power) will fall below $30,000.
  - The transport companies will increasingly rely on autonomous vehicles. The transfer of the current workforce to an autonomous vehicle-based transit system will pose a major organizational and political challenge.
  - Insurance rates will be conducive for driving in a fully autonomous mode and will encourage people to stop driving on their own.
  - Small autonomous buses will increasingly be used for medium and long-distance travel. Trains will find it challenging to compete for short and medium distances with autonomous buses.
- 2040: Most companies will require business trips to be carried out in fully autonomous modes (for safety and efficiency reasons).
- 2050: Fleets of autonomous vehicles will operate in most cities in developed countries.[3]
  - Automotive companies will close more and more plants producing traditional vehicles. Major automotive countries, including Germany, Sweden, and Japan, will desperately try to support their sub-contractors, supplying subassemblies and parts.
  - The number of cars will fall sharply. Only 20% of the U.S. population will still own a vehicle (i.e., 200 vehicles per 1,000 people; in 2020, there are 439 vehicles per 1,000 people). 90% of all travel will be in a fully autonomous mode. The number of road accidents and fatalities will fall sharply.

It is uncertain whether Elon Musk's (owner of Tesla) vision of "completely autonomous vehicles" describes a vehicle that can cope with a variety of road conditions. Most existing competitors of autonomous vehicles spend their days in states with warm, clear weather, avoiding situations such as heavy rain, snow, and ice that could affect the AI's decisions. A "completely" autonomous vehicle for sunny Arizona would not be "complete" enough for snowy Michigan. The realistic capabilities of a fully autonomous vehicle accessible to the general public should be taken into account. While it is possible to create an autonomous vehicle that will be safely self-guided, there is no guarantee that local and state governments will comply with its sale and introduce appropriate traffic regulations on time. In the U.S., for example, some states such as Arizona and California are trying to be leaders in the autonomous vehicle industry by lowering regulatory standards for public testing. Other countries are more conservative, with no existing regulations for how autonomous vehicles can be tested on public roads, not to mention sales regulations for the general public. It is uncertain what regulatory or political obstacles will have to be overcome for autonomous vehicles to become publicly available. Still, it is reasonable to assume that this will extend the months, if not years.

Elon Musk (and others) have been making optimistic promises for a long time about the future of autonomous cars. Since 2016, Tesla has claimed that all of its vehicles have the hardware necessary to achieve full autonomy, with the option to "unlock" fully autonomous driving via a remote software update. In January 2017, Musk suggested that this option would be available in 3-6 months. Of course, it did not happen. In addition to the self-driving vehicle industry, Musk has a long history in giving unrealistic timeframes for his futuristic designs.

The issue of driving safety makes it possible to hold the view that such vehicles are not as safe as is sometimes optimistically believed. What is more, the prevailing view is that the programmers of self-driving cars are not able to predict all the situations that can happen on the road, which is demonstrated by following accidents:

- In May 2016, a man died in the U.S. after his Tesla vehicle hit a truck and its trailer while in autopilot mode. Tesla's sensors incorrectly identified the white truck trailer as part of the sky. There have also been cases where self-driving cars seem to be responsible for accidents; however, the human factor of not paying attention to the road (a human driver is required in the first systems for this type of car) can also be a critical factor in such accidents.
- The debate over driverless car safety intensified in 2018 after a woman in Arizona was struck and killed by an Uber vehicle that was operating in self-driving mode. The accident prompted the ride-sharing company to suspend testing of autonomous vehicles on public roads temporarily. Reports suggest that the pilot was looking down at the time of the accident, meaning the accident may have been partly the result of human error. Uber resumed testing about nine months after the fatal crash.

It seems to be more practical to develop semi-autonomous vehicles in which human participation in driving is required; otherwise, driving in such vehicles could be boring and dull. Would drinking champagne with fellow travelers in a self-driving car reduce that boredom?

SUMMARY

In summary, the following can be said about the trends of automation in the 21st century:

1. Automation is currently evolving and is attempting to meet the needs of super consumption, which will lead to a faster depletion of strategic resources such as energy and precious metals while at the same time lead to more production of waste and emissions of harmful gases that pollute the environment.

2. Autonomous vehicles, as a result of severe accidents, are not as safe as they have been emotionally believed to be. The pace of their development has decreased.

3. It seems that the production of vehicles is moving towards increased driving safety by using more cameras to avoid collisions. Development, on the other hand, is moving towards hybrid models with batteries.

REFERENCES

Huang, Y., Kockelman, K. M., & Quarles, N. (2019). How will self-driving vehicles affect U.S. megaregion traffic? The case of the Texas triangle. *98th Annual Meeting of the Transportation Research Board.* https://www.caee.utexas.edu/prof/kockelman/public_html/TRB19TXMegaregionAVs.pdf

Snyder, G. H. (2012, July 1). Automation evolution. *Deloitte.* https://www2.deloitte.com/us/en/insights/deloitte-review/issue-11/the-automation-evolution-in-manufacturing.html

Thakur, A. (October 25th, 2018). Robotic process automation (RPA): An era of operational excellence. *RPATools.* https://rpatools.com/2018/10/robotic-process-automation-rpa-an-era-of-operational-excellence/

KEY TERMS AND DEFINITIONS

3D Printing: A computer-controlled process that creates three-dimensional objects.

AI Assistants: A computer program that performs user commands and answers user questions.

Automation: A technology that reduces the need for human intervention in a process.

Autonomous Vehicles: A vehicle that uses computer technology to navigate an environment with little or no human input.

Business Process Automation: The automation of business processes through digital technologies.

Robotic Process Automation: The automation of business processes through the use of robots and artificial intelligence.

Tesla: An American electric vehicle company.

Uber: An American technology company that specializes in ride-hailing.

ENDNOTES

[1] Siri is a virtual assistant that is part of the iOS operating systems, iPad OS, Watch OS, and Apple TV. The Assistant uses voice queries and a natural language user interface to answer questions, make recommendations, and perform actions by posting requests to a set of Internet services. The software adapts to customs and the search preferences of users in each language with continued use. Siri's responses are personalized.

[2] This is a reference to the lack of Kodak's "revolution" in camera design, which never occurred because of smartphones.

[3] Provided that the development of civilization is fully sustainable.

Chapter 10
Development Trends in Robotization and Artificial Intelligence

ABSTRACT

This chapter analyzes developmental trends in robotization and artificial intelligence. The chapter begins by providing a brief history of artificial intelligence, focusing on developments during the 20th century. The chapter then examines developments of robot applications as well as their impacts on various economic sectors. Next, the ways in which AI have replaced advanced mental labor are examined, such as journalism. The chapter then focuses on the development of machine learning and deep learning. This is followed by a discussion of how AI can now be purchased and used via cloud services. The chapter concludes by considering the difficult question of whether AI can be creative and by considering security concerns related to AI.

THE HISTORY OF ARTIFICIAL INTELLIGENCE

For many centuries, there have been legends about golems in Europe. The legend holds that these strong clay beasts protect the Jews from aggression and pogroms, and that they are animated by spells, devoid of feelings and scrupulousness, and listen only to the commands of their master. This monstrosity is mainly associated with the Czech Prague. It was there that the Jews were to build this monster, where it was to take to the streets and spread destruction. However, the legend holds that Golems are not intelligent and that the command to perform a task is done literally because, by nature, they are perfectly obedient.

In the 19th century, this legend inspired the superhuman element in the novel *Frankenstein: Or, the Modern Prometheus* (1818), invented by Mary Shelley (1797–1851) with her great imagination (abusing drugs on a vacation on Lake Geneva in the company of Lord Byron "king of life" and others). In the novel, the Italian-Swiss scientist Victor Frankenstein (born in Naples, Italy) gains insight into the creation of life after dissecting living beings and studying their chemical processes. He then gives life to

DOI: 10.4018/978-1-7998-8036-3.ch010

Figure 1. The concept of a super-strong Golem, albeit without its own opinion (Photo: Wikipedia.org)

Figure 2. Frankenstein's superhuman creature that destroyed itself (Photo: TCD/VP/LMKMEDIA)

his creation, often referred to as the "Frankenstein monster", or more colloquially "Frankenstein." This superman rebels against his creator and, by his actions, leads to his destruction.

One hundred years later, the legend of creating artificial life returned in the play *The Intelligent Robot of Czech*, authored by Karela Čzapek, whose Slavic term "robot" entered permanently into English

Table 1. Essential applications of cybernetics and artificial intelligence in the years 1920-1950)

Date	Contribution/ Title of Work	Author	Country and University	Comments
1920	*R.U.R.: Rossum's Universal Robots (play)*	Karel Čzapek (1890-1938)	Austria-Hungary (Czech Republic)	This work of art introduced the term "robot." The term has its origin in Czech words meaning "forced labor" and "to work".
1938-1946	*Black Destroyer; Future Story; Runaround; I, Robot; Man from Mars*	A. E. van Vogt (1912-2000); Robert A. Heinlein (1907-1988); Isaac Asimov (1922-1992); Stanislaw Lem (1921-2006)	USA Poland	This was the Golden Age of science fiction books. Lem's books have been published in 41 countries with 45 million copies.
1943	*A Logical Calculus of the Ideas Immanent in Nervous Activity*	Warren McCulloch (1898-1969) Walter Pitts (1923-1969)	University of Illinois, USA	They developed the mathematical model "threshold logic", based on bioprocesses and artificial neural networks constructed from electrical circuits.
1945	*As We May Think*	Vannevar Bush (1890-1974); he oversaw Shannon's master's thesis-a pioneer of binary electronics and information theory	MIT, USA	During world war II, he oversaw the Manhattan Project and the development of the ENIAC computer.
1946	Automatic homeostat; ANI (Artificial Narrow Intelligence)	W. Ross Ashby (1903-1972)	United Kingdom	He explored self-learning with mice using a labyrinth.
1948	Manchester Mark I computer with a stored program	Frederic C. Williams (1911-1977) Tom Kilburn (1921-2001) Geoff Tootill (1922-2017)	United Kingdom	Their development allowed logical inference programming.
1948	*Cybernetics: Or Control and Communication in the Animal and the Machine*	Norbert Wiener (1894-1964)	MIT, USA	He developed feedback and self-controlling systems.
1950	*Computing Machinery and Intelligence*	Alan Turing (1912-1954)	United Kingdom	He famously addressed the question "can machines think?" and developed the Turing Test.

Table 2. Significant applications of cybernetics and artificial intelligence in the years (1956-1966)

Date	Contribution / Title of Work	Author	Country and University	Comments
1956	Logic Theorist- a computer program that could automatically reasoning	Allen Newell (1927-1992) Herbert Simon (1916-2001) Cliff Shaw (1922-1991)	USA	This was the first computer-based AI program.
1956	Coined the phrase *artificial intelligence* (AI)	John McCarthy (1927-2011); in 1962, he gave Paul Aries the topology of the future Internet	Dartmouth College USA	He was the first to name and define AI; he also organized the first continuous seminar on the subject
1957	*Syntactic Structures*	Noam Chomsky (1928-)	MIT, USA	He is a pioneer in mathematical linguistics
1958	Azor dog (electronic dog)	Janusz Wojciechowski	Poland	He created a cyber-intelligent dog
1963	*Man-Machine Symbiosis*	J. C. R. Licklider (1915-1990)	MIT, USA	He worked for ARPA (The United States Department of Defense Advanced Research Projects Agency) and researched AI in response to Sputnik
1958	LISP (computer language)	John McCarthy (1927-2011)	USA	This was a computer language for AI programming
1959	Artificial Intelligence Project	John McCarthy and Marvin Minsky (1927-2016)	MIT, USA	This project began systematic research on AI.
1959	*Cybernetics and Management*	Stanford Beer (1926-2002)	United Kingdom, Canada	He conducted an analysis of human cyber-management.
1960	*Steps Towards Artificial Intelligence*	Marvin Minsky (1927-2016)	MIT, USA	He is considered the father of AI.
1961	Unimate (the first industrial robot)	Joseph Engelberger (1925-2015) and George Devol (1912-2011)	General Motors, USA	The robot was able to manipulate materials.
1962	ARPA Net packet-switching topology	Paul Baran (1926-2011), born in Poland	RAND, USA	This military network was divided into Milinet and the Internet in 1983.
1962	*Whole and Parts in Light of Cybernetics*	Oskar Lange (1904-1965)	Warsaw School of Economics, Poland	This was a mathematical theory of dialectical materialism.
1966	Dendral (an expert system analyzing organic ingredients)	Ed Feigenbaum (1936-), Joshua Lederberg (1925-2008: Nobel Prize 1958), Carl Djerassi (1923-2015)	Stanford, USA	This expert system was designed to detect hostile chemical components.
1966	*Cyber-theory of Stand-alone Systems*	Marian Mazur (1909-1983)	Institute of Electrical Engineering, Poland	He also defined *qualitative information theory.*

terminology in modern science and artificial intelligence technology. Since then, this has inspired the development of science fiction literature as well as developments in cybernetics and artificial intelligence. Tables 1, 2, 3, and 4 outline the most important uses of AI as a specialization of cybernetics.

Table 3. Significant applications of cybernetics and artificial intelligence between 1968 and 1956

Date	Contribution / Title of Work	Author	Country and University	Comments
1968	General systems theory	Ludwig von Bertalanffy (1901-1972)	SUNY, USA	The theory was based on biological systems
1968	*2001: A Space Odyssey* (film)	Arthur Charles Clark (1917-2008)	United Kingdom	This was the most influential film about life in space
1971-75	National Information System (KSI) based on INFO STRADA	Andrew Targowski (1937-)	National Office of Informatics, Poland	This was a cyber-model of national IT systems supported by a national universal data transmission network
1970-1975	MYCIN (a backward chaining expert system based on 600 rules)	Edward H. Shortliffe	Stanford, USA	The system could diagnose meningitis 2% better than doctors
1973	Cybersyn	Stanford Beer (1926-2002)	Chile	This was a cyber-management system for the national economy based on the Lange model
1980	Wabot-2 (a robot for reading notes and playing music)		Waseda University, Japan	
1981	*Brain of the Firm*	Stanford Beer (1926-2002)	Canada	This Preceded the 1979 book *Heart of the Enterprise*
1982	HEARSAY (a speech-recognition program)	Lee Erman, Frederick Hayes-Roth, Victor Lesser, Raj Reddy	Carnegie- Mellon University, USA	
1982	5th generation National Computerization Development Program		Japan	The program aimed at developing AI-based support for Japanese society
1985	Aaron (a stand-alone painter)	Harold Cohen	UCSD, USA	
1985	Allen (an autonomously responsive robot)	Rod Brooks		
1986	Autonomous car	NavLab	Carnegie Mellon University., USA	
1986	*The Society of Mind*	Marvin Minsky (1927-2016)	MIT, USA	The work defines the logic of AI processes

Figure 3 shows the evolution of robots, from the cyber robot "Azor Dog", designed by Janusz Wojciechowski (author of popular-scientific books) and A. Lochiński in 1958 in Poland when artificial

Table 4. Significant applications of cybernetics and artificial intelligence between 1990 and 2019

Date	Contribution / Title of Work	Author	Country and University	Comments
1990	Human Genome Project			This was the beginning of the study of the human body by cyber-information methods
1996	IBM Deep Blue (the computer program that beat chess master Gary Kasparov)	IBM	USA	This gave rise to the idea that computers could think faster than humans—but are they smarter?
1997	Dragon System – speech-recognition software		USA	This is available to the public
2000	Kismet (a robot head that recognizes and simulates emotions	Cynthia Breazeal		
2011	IBM Watson (a question-answering 2nd generation AGI) AGI = Artificial General Intelligence	David Ferrucci, Jr.; IBM	USA	It won the $1 million prize in *Jeopardy* against quiz champions Brad Rutter and Ken Jennings
2012	IBM Watson answers the questions of specialists for a fee	IBM	USA	90% of nurses in the US use this AI system for a fee.
2019	*Wisdom in the context of globalization and civilization*	Henryk Krawczyk (1946-) and Andrew Targowski (1937-)	Gdańsk University of Technology, Poland; WMU, USA	The work offers a theory of wisdom in the context of globalization and civilization.

intelligence was in its so-called infancy (left), to the Japanese robot ASIMO (right). Azor Dog was featured in a TV show at the time, and the builders would go on to improve his super dog version, which only had conditional reflexes.

THE DEVELOPMENT OF ROBOT APPLICATIONS

In 2018, the number of robots in the world was 2,440,000. In the same year, 422,271 robots were installed worth a total value of US $16.5 billion. China installed 154,032 of them; Japan, 55,240; the United States, 40,373; South Korea, 41,373; and Germany, 26,723 (International Federation of Robotics, 2019). If the rate of installation is maintained at a level of about 400,000 per year, 12 million additional robots will be installed by 2050, bringing the total to over 14 million robots—roughly as many as the population in the Czech Republic and Slovakia.

According to statistics cited by the International Federation of Robotics, the most industrialized countries in the world dominate in the use of robotics. The high consumption of robots in China—the country with the second-largest economy after the United States, which has become the "factory of the world,"—is particularly noteworthy. Not only has China has taken the lead from the United States in consumption, it has also taken a leading role in producing all kinds of products through cheap labor. However, the competitive labor factor is gradually becoming obsolete over time, for the Chinese are

Figure 3. Cybernetic Azor Dog (1958) by Janusz Wojciechowski (photo: Waldemar Dekanski) and Japanese robot ASIMO (2000) (Photo: Wikipedia)

 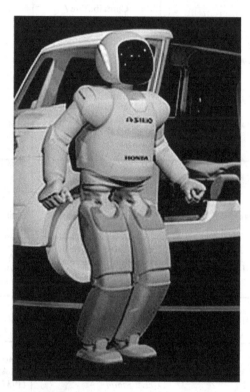

demanding higher wages for their work. To assure that Western countries do not switch production to other countries with low-paid labor, Chinese capitalists are planning to exclude workers from production altogether and replace them with robots. This is contrary to the Chinese doctrine of providing a job and a bowl of rice to every citizen of the country, which in some areas of China has led to an age barrier being established to assure younger people the opportunity to get a job (for men, this limit is sometimes set at 60 and for women, 55). It turns out that the lobbyists of Chinese manufacturers probably "make sure" that the Chinese give their work to robots, which do not receive a remuneration. The fact is that between 1992 and 2002, China lost about 10% of its GDP and 15% of its production workforce, i.e., 16 million workers (the number of all workers employed in Poland, a medium-sized country) (Baum, 2003).

Similarly, the rise of robots in Germany, a country known for its high-quality production, gives pause for thought when compared to most other industrialized countries. This is a country that is considered the "factory" of Europe. It is worth noting that the labor force in Germany is not cheap; however, it is an aging country. A similar phenomenon is happening in Japan with its aging population, which is why the country has the second most robots in the world after China.

In the already vast global robot population, the following types can be distinguished:

- **Industrial robots** can be stationary or mobile, and they tend to perform repetitive tasks. They are the least intelligent because they carry out simple tasks and because the factory environment in which they operate is isolated from unforeseen external perturbations.

- **Exploration robots** can be simple or quite complicated. A famous example is when external pilots controlled a robot moving on the surface of Mars, which performed autonomous tasks simultaneously. Their mission was to collect data about the Martian environment.

- **Household robots** include, for example, a house cleaning bot that can be connected to the Internet of Things or *Amazon Alexa* or Google *Home*. Such bots follow the instructions of the resident, such as turning the lights on and off in the apartment.

- **Medical robots** include robotic arms that help surgeons perform operations. The Da Vinci robot, for example, can perform dangerous surgeries with little risk.

- **Flying robots** include drones or specialized aircraft that perform different tasks. Some of these tasks include conducting military operations, supplying goods to a house or store, and researching at high altitudes.

- **Water robots** are used to study the world under water at great depths. Some have the ability to mimic the swimming of fish.

- Others

The use of robots in the 2020s is characterized by examples that show how far robots can go in replacing human labor as well as how they can define business strategies. A vital solution for facilitating the design and modernization of robots is the introduction of a platform for a standard operating system—ROS (Robot Operating System)—first developed in Stanford university's Artificial Intelligence Laboratory. The system was improved in 2010 by Willow Garage, Inc. from Menlo Park, California. The ROS system performs a similar role to Microsoft Windows OS[1], Macintosh OS, and Android. The system makes it easier to program and control the functioning of robots. The ROS platform is open and free, and history shows that as soon as a free and open platform becomes standard, there is an explosion in the development of applications. An example of this is the development of apps for the iPhone, iPad, and Android.

At the time when Kinect began to deliver cheap machine vision, other robotic components such as robotic hands were also developed, as the scale of robot production increased. For example, Willow Garage sells a folding robot set called TurtleBot for $1,200, and the price may even be lower ($500) if the user has a mobile computer and an *iRobot*.

When the US textile industry was decimated in the 1990s when it was moved to China, India, and Mexico, the American company Parkdale Mills in Gaffney, South Carolina, installed industrial robots to perform tasks carried out by 2,000 workers. As a result, their number has been reduced to 140. In 2009-2012, other US textile companies followed suit, leading to significant textile exports in the tens of billions per year. Although Parkdale did not create many jobs at home, thanks to the use of robots, it has created many jobs with its cooperators.

Thanks to robotics and automation, the trend *of outsourcing* factories to Asia has been slowed and, in some cases, even reversed. This trend is called *resourcing*. According to a report by Boston Consulting Group, 50% of corporations with sales of at least $10 billion per year are actively working to bring American factories to the U.S., which will reduce the high costs of transoceanic transport. Also, by placing factories close to their customers, these companies are better adapted to the consumers' needs and can shorten the production of new products. This can be seen in particular in the so-called "flexible automated output of products", especially clothing for specific sizes of buyers, which involves ordering the product directly from the manufacturer via an online system ("Coming Home", 2013).

Because of outsourcing, automation, and robotization in the 21st century, the United States has developed a mixed (industrial-service) economy. About 90% of employees work in the service industry, including administration services. Because the service industry tends to be low paying, this means the economy is not capable of growing since consumers have low purchasing power. Hence, businesses do not have good prospects for development, and, therefore, they must look for ways to reduce the cost of services through robotization and computerization.

For example, *Momentum Machine* in San Francisco automated the preparation of high-quality hamburgers, the number 1 meal in the United States. The robots shape the meat by taking raw material from a meat container. Then, the robot grills that portion of meat and even adds "sauce" to strengthen the smell. These robots also put the meat in a bun and add cheese, lettuce, tomato, onion, and pickled, which they portion beforehand. Robots can prepare about 360 burgers per hour. The head of the company states that his robots are not aimed at improving the operation of employees: their goal is to replace employees. The average fast-food restaurant spends about $135,000 a year on wages (the lowest in the economy), and the total cost of labor in American restaurants is about $9 billion per year. This is the amount that can be "saved" by American business. However, this is only if robots do not scare unemployed customers who are out of work in other companies (Roush, 2012).

In the so-called *Great Recession* of 2011, McDonald's initiated a plan of primarily political importance aimed at hiring 50,000 workers on the same day across its thousand restaurants in the US. One million unemployed people responded to this offer the next day. This means that the probability of getting a job in the lowest-paid position in the country was lower than the likelihood of gaining admission to study at Harvard University. In the past, working at McDonald's was intended for young people as their first job. Now, older employees who have lost their jobs in other companies through the development of IT are working such jobs. It turns out that half of McDonald's workers now have to rely on food stamps and social assistance, which costs taxpayers $7 billion a year (Velasco, 2013).

In Japan at *Kura Sushi*—a restaurant chain with over 450 locations—robots make sushi and conveyer belts move the food, replacing the need for waiters. To ensure the freshness of the dish, each serving has a registered duration, and when it exceeds this timestamp, it is withdrawn from the belt automatically. Consumers order meals on electronic panels, and dirty plates are taken away on another conveyor belt. The customer receives their bill on the screen and pays electronically with a credit card or smartphone. The restaurant does not employ managers; rather, it monitors its operations from a central location. Thanks to this system, Kura restaurants have reduced the cost of an average portion of food by 1 dollar, becoming unbeatable. Following the example of Kura, McDonald's introduced screen ordering at 7,000 of its restaurants in Europe.

Other fast-food restaurants need to copy the systemic solutions of these businesses. Moreover, it is significant that the food made by robots is more hygienic than those made by humans.

Until recently it was believed that the most irreplaceable job after nurses was the salesperson. Nothing could be further from the truth. The following examples support this claim:

- e-Commerce for companies such as Amazon, eBay, and Netflix has led to massive sales without the participation of traditional sellers. For example, Amazon sold 606 million different products to 300 million customers in 11 countries in 2017 (ScrapeHero, 2017). This has led to the bankruptcy of recognized chain stores such as Circuit City (home electronics), Borders (books), and Blockbuster (movie rental). Amazon and eBay can deliver some of their products on the same day in large cities, and Amazon's food services can do so within 2 hours, thereby undermining the advantages of local shops. This is especially the case in big cities, where parking can be a big problem and discourages people from visiting the shops. Companies of this type, including

Walmart (the world's largest company in terms of sales), rely on regional wholesalers that are entirely automated and robotic with product bar codes. Kroger, the largest US grocery chain, has automated grocery distributions within their stores by building a system that can automatically break down pallets containing the same product and turn them into mixed pallets that reflect how the products will be shelved in the stores.

- The self-service kiosk sector sells more than $1 trillion per year. Now, with the help of artificial intelligence, kiosks sell Apple iPods and iPads at airports as well as in high-class hotels, probably counting on customers in computer science. Kiosks of this type minimize the costs of labor, building property, and theft. They also collect email addresses for sending invoices and marketing information. On the other hand, e-kiosks generate employment in the field of repair, maintenance, and replenishment. However, e-kiosks are connected to headquarters that can automatically monitor their activities and collects data, which is then used to implement machine-learning trends. The headquarters can even remotely repair them, similar to the centralized repair system of Tesla cars in California. For example, Redbox has 42,000 kiosks in the US and Canada and rents approximately 2 million videos per day. In the vast Chicago region, 7 employees keep all kiosks in the area on the move. At the same time, the bankrupt Blockbuster company (movie rental) had 60,000 employees in 9,000 movie rental locations. In other words, on average, 7 employees served each rental company.

- As a result of Walmart's experience, robots will be able to walk through the hallways of storage cabinets at night and calculate the condition of products on the shelves (thanks to barcodes and shelf counters) to know exactly how many restorations should be ordered in warehouses (where robots also work). This thus eliminates the need for human labor to replenish goods on the shelves.

- It has become almost common place to use self-checkouts when paying for groceries, and even smartphones. Walmart is now testing a process in which customers are charged and receive invoices without having to stop at checkouts or self-service points and use their debit or credit cards. Instead, customers use their smartphones to scan items, and the money is directly debited from their account. At stake here is the integrity of customers and indirect control of their behavior.

Another issue in the design of robot intelligence and wise decision-making is access to Big Data, which is located in a centralized "cloud," that is, in the service system of those who sell these robots. This will, of course, make it possible to produce less complicated and cheaper robots. For example, Google has already designed an interface for Google services on the Android platform in 2011. The impact of access to Big Data by remote robots is particularly crucial for *machine vision* and *image recognition* robots. For example, a robot cleaning a messy house must have countless examples of patterns of what to clean. Google introduced "Goggles" in 2010 with a mobile camera. The image recognition software is continuously being improved to expand the possible patterns that can be recognized. Without such "information clouds" containing Big Data, it would be too expensive for different competing companies to provide information technology for each robot of this type. Of course, this type of Big Data will be a permanent target for hackers, who will also want to hack robots, for example, those involved in transportation. An example of such a disorienting attack was *the Stuxnet Worm*, which was designed by the United States and Israel in 2010 to attack Iranian installations possibly involved in the production of a nuclear weapon.

Agriculture in the United States has undergone the most significant of transformations. In the 19th century, about 50% of workers were employed in agriculture. In 2000, the number of farmers as a proportion of workers had decreased to 2%. This is the result of the mechanization of farms. Not only are planting and plowing being mechanized comprehensively, but animal husbandry is also at a similar level of technological development, including the automation of killing chickens. The human hand is only needed for the collection of high-quality fruits and vegetables as well as decorative flowers. However, even collecting oranges is now carried out by robots from the company *Vision Robotics* from San Diego. First, such a robot creates a 3D model of the tree and locates individual orange fruits. This "GPS" information for a given tree is transmitted to the robot arm, which precisely collects the fruit. Similar robots are available for seeding and harvesting in greenhouses. It is estimated that robots will replace 40% of manual tasks in agriculture. In France, robots with machine vision and advanced algorithms can assess which grapes are suitable for breaking and which still need to mature. In Japan, robots can distinguish the color of strawberries that are suitable for harvesting. They can work continuously by harvesting a berry every 8 seconds. Fruit robots are particularly needed in countries where low-paying labor is not available, such as Australia and Japan. In such countries as well as the USA, fertilizer distributing tractors are controlled by data on the soil quality of a given section of the farmland. This data is used to make adjustments to a fertilizer-filling device at the front of the tractor to distribute the optimal amount of fertilizer.

In California, the number 1 agricultural state in the United States (it produces 2,400 different agrarian products), agricultural employment fell by 11% in the first decade of the 21st century. Farmers, on the other hand, are reducing the production of delicate fruits and vegetables because it is difficult to collect them by machine without damage. They thus switch to the production of products such as peanuts since they are easy to manage with the help of robots. This is why tomato imports from Mexico are growing, where agricultural labor still dominates.

When the human population reaches 9 billion around 2050, each piece of land will have to be used for food production. In countries with minimal water (e.g., Africa and perhaps Poland), a system that optimizes the use of resources will be critical for the survival of the people living there. The robotization of agriculture in these less advanced countries will lead to an even faster migration of people from villages to cities, where the markets will be filled with products from automated factories. The problem will be what to do with people who no longer work and find themselves bored, falling into alcoholism and other addictions. These people will be the victims of the "advances" of technology and the "genius" of computer scientists who are fascinated with building a world that is labor free—one which will be controlled by a small elite who own the robots and a few thousand "brilliant" but naive itinerants. This will occur because politicians have allowed the pursuit "technological progress", which they deem as the most important force for human development; however, should it be allowed to develop so freely?

In the field of aerial robotics, Amazon's super e-store is developing the capability to deliver goods via drones (Figure 4). The first such delivery took place on December 7, 2016, in the UK, when an Amazon Prime Air drone soared to a height of 122 meters and delivered goods to the door of a customer's home in a surrounding farm. If this system continues to develop, the e-shop will reduce the cost of delivery since drones avoid traffic jams and there are no personnel costs. Amazon claims that this system (Figure 5) could deliver goods as quickly as 3 minutes on average for up to 90% of orders.

This system would also have platforms that would receive ready-made packages from wholesalers for loading goods on drones. As a result, Amazon plans to opt-out of other delivery systems, such as USPS and other third-party delivery companies. Amazon's drone has a 6 horizontal propeller system similar to that of a helicopter for vertical climbing and landing, and it can fly up to 24 kilometers. The company is working on drones that will have a jet system for high-speed flights up to 80 km per hour.

Figure 4. Drone delivering shopping to customers home (photo: Amazon's public domain)

They will also be able to fly at higher altitudes in order to fly over skyscrapers. However, to operate in cities, the drones will need to be equipped with visual, thermal, and ultrasonic sensors to provide accident-free navigation.

These drones will be able to communicate with each other within their communication network. Perhaps this network will become a universal network, available to third parties for a fee. This network will collect Big Data to ensure secure deliveries to known customers. Amazon will pay to install drone charging sites on the roofs of tall buildings, church towers, telephone poles, and building trusses. Also, drones will have anti-theft procedures. For example, they will place packages in places where strangers do not have access, if the customer agrees. At stake is whether neighbors need to give permission to fly drones over their area. At any rate, the drones' cameras and microphones will record obstacles in public areas, and they will have the "right" to do so on the basis that photos of houses are allowed in the current map apps, such as Google's so-called "Street View".

The system is not only intended to deliver goods but also to collect marketing data about the customer's environment. For example, the drones will take pictures of trees and assess whether the customer needs the services of a tree company. This could be accomplished, for instance, on the basis of whether the tree branches are withered and whether they are the appropriate color.

Amazon drone cameras could also record crimes. So far, the resident has a right to privacy, and, therefore, any evidence collected unlawfully would be illegal. However, it is not known whether Amazon lobbyists will press to change this law. There is no doubt that Amazon plans to emulate Google (which profiles and collects data about us to sell at high prices to those who can pay for it) and collect data about the space we live in. Such is the wealth of the richest man in the world, Jeff Bezos, owner of Amazon.

It is not only Amazon that is working to improve the delivery of goods to consumer homes: Global companies such as UPS, FedEx, Uber, and Google are working on such systems as well. It can be expected that these companies and others will follow in their footsteps and release millions of drones that will "cloud" the sky and make it a platform for accidents, spying, and a new type of crime—and all in the name of what? So the story goes, it will be for "technical progress" and the "invisible hand of the market," guaranteeing a rush of innovations that will supposedly "humanize" us.

Figure 5. The system of drone delivery of ordered goods at the customer's door, according to Amazon Prime Air (Bittle, 2020, p. 58-59)

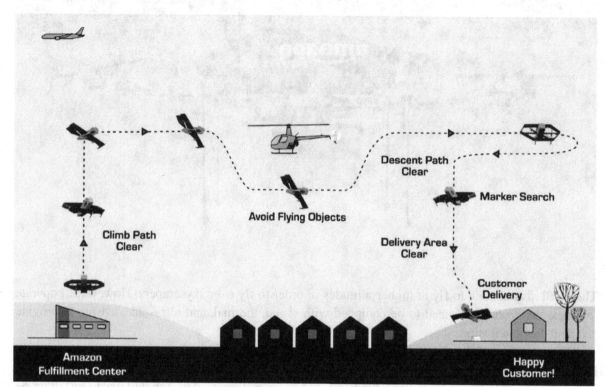

AI REPLACES ADVANCED MENTAL LABOR

Computerization has long impacted fields that require mental labor, such as simple office-related work related to recording transactions and updating files. This type of work, somewhat repetitive and routine, was computerized in the US in the 1960s in data processing systems. In the 1970s, however, organizational information processing systems were developed, which introduced question-answering systems for users (so-called "Management Information Systems"). In the following decades, subsystems developed from the bottom up were integrated into enterprise resources planning (ERP); however, the processes of complex mental labor have not yet been computerized.

Consider, however, that some authors would advise a company's administrators to purchase written speeches from trained specialists in India because they are cheaper. These very same authors sometimes naively assume that they are isolated from the situation in the USA; however, when big data and AI become sufficiently powerful, they will perhaps write speeches better than humans. This is already being explored by software systems such as Quill.

Robo-Journalism

Already, based on the DRY (don't repeat yourself) principle in software development, an AI can write a full-fledged report about a basketball match, as if it were done by a sports journalist. This can be seen in the example below, in which the DRY principle has been applied (marked in rectangles):

Short headline: UNC beats Louisville 72-71 on late Paige basket

Long headline: Led by a Paige game-winner, North Carolina defeats Louisville 72-71

The DRY principle works by identifying frames, which can be supplemented by words generated by the AI. In more extended reports, the AI will add more words, such as in the example below, which is a typical AI style implemented by deep learning.

CHAPEL HILL, N.C. Marcus Paige scored with nine seconds remaining in the game to give North Carolina a 72-71 lead over Louisville. The Heels held on to win by that same score following a missed 3-pointer by Wayne Blackshear and an unsuccessful second-chance attempt by Terry Rozier.

The AI supplements the statistics with full sentences, the sources of which are statistics about the match as well as Big Data on the teams, which was collected from various unstructured sources, such as emails, the past characteristics of the team and the players, etc. For example, the AI replaced the abbreviation "UNC" with the colloquial name "North Carolina". The words in the longer frames come from game statistics. In contrast, the terms between frames are generated by the AI.

This type of robot-journalism is made possible by the "StatsMonkey" software, which was developed by the Intelligent Information Laboratory of Northwestern University in Chicago. The software creates sentences about the statistics using natural human language. It can also employ a narrative method characteristic of a particular journalist who has been employed to write such reports. The data about such a writing style can be collected and stored in Big Data.

Most US media companies now use narrative science technology. For example, Forbes financial magazine uses this technology to "write" financial reports based on stock market indicators and data from public reports of companies whose shares are on the stock market. It is estimated that AI may write around 90% of such newspaper articles. If it is possible to automate this process, then it will occur. Thus, the number of journalists has been decreasing. Other types of Quill software are universal and can supplement the DRY principle applied to data with narration on any topic. This process begins by collecting Big Data and then unpacking it and complementing the narrative. The narrative technique has its source in the In-Q-Tel system, developed by the CIA to describe data collected by foreign intelligence while eavesdropping on phone calls. The technique involves catching keywords during the conversation, such as a word referring to a terrorist war. Then, based on the Big Data, a narrative script is generated that a human can understand. The system also correlates keywords to highlight the meaning of a phone call.

The Quill software seems to eliminate the need for human work based on university knowledge; however, good writing seems to be more of an art than a technique that can be learned from some accelerated course. It should also be mentioned that it is now known that the modern generation of university graduates is losing the art of writing because they rely on using symbols in short texts on their smartphones. This is the bane not only of lecturers at universities but also of the employers of these graduates. This is why AI is a rescue for employers and a threat to the "masters" of smartphone communication, who may find there is no work in the specializations they thought they had learned in universities.

MACHINE LEARNING (ML) AND BIG DATA

Over the last 50 years, information systems have been based on databases consisting of well-defined and well-structured data so that the data can be quickly recorded, searched, and correlated and then retrieved as information to inform decision-making processes. IT focuses on data for transaction descriptions and resources management (human, material, and financial) in a company. However, due to the development of computer memory technology, memory capacity is now virtually unlimited. Hence, unstructured data can be cheaply recorded and stored (unstructured both in terms of the information circulating inside and outside of the company in the so-called "world"). It would help if internal data could add context from external data (except such data is not structured).

Thanks to the electrification of information technology, currently in the 2020s there are thousands of exabytes (EB) of data (1 exabyte has one billion gigabytes, and 1 GB has 1000 MB). These are numbers not ungraspable by the human imagination. Meanwhile, the number of bytes of data doubles every three years, according to so-called "Moore's law".[2]. Access to this data is often free, although recently, the prices of e-information have increased, and buying them has become profitable. Today, Google processes many bytes of data every day. This data comes from websites, emails, advertisements, e-books, e-commerce, Googly queries, etc. Soon Google will scan all the books of the world (about 128 million different titles).

People are able to gain access to this mass of Big Data through computerization. This has caused considerable changes in the way things are in almost all aspects of human life. Trading, for example, uses Big Data, which, through knowledge of the customer's information profile, targets products and services that may be of interest to him/her, thereby increasing sales and revenues. Police around the world are using Big Data to predict where, when, and what crime can be expected and to find remedial strategies.

Similarly, citizens of major American cities such as New York, Chicago, and Los Angeles have access to current events. Thanks to Big Data, Target's retail network is collecting data on the purchases of cosmetics and medicaments typical for women in the first phase of pregnancy. Because of this data, a company can know whether one of their female employees is pregnant. It can be predicted that if this trend of collecting "good" information continues, then people will lose their sense of privacy and freedom because their lives will be—and in a sense, it de facto already is—controlled by the notorious Orwellian *Big Brother.*

Access to countless different sources of Big Data enables one to develop statistically based new knowledge of a situation since software that previously was only capable of storing and retrieving data can now be used to explore the structures and relationships of Big Data, e.g., on Instagram, Twitter, or Snapchat. This involves automatically creating specific algorithms that can define principles or laws of new knowledge for the case in question. These automatically self-created algorithms are then used to analyze Big Data.

Google, for example, used machine learning to automatically translate languages. Translation algorithms from language to language were developed by analyzing and comparing translations of millions of documents in two specific languages to produce the final translation algorithm. In this way, mathematical experts broke with accurate linguistic specialists, who simply did not accept the practice because of its artificiality and inadequate verification procedures. Translation algorithms were first used on official UN digital documents, and they were then improved on other digital works. In this way, a universal algorithm for translating languages has been developed that has never been seen before.[3]

DEEP LEARNING

Deep learning is learning via artificial neural networks, where network neurons are analogous to human nerve cells a person has in their brain, which help them think and make decisions (humans have about 100 billion neurons). Deep learning is a specific machine learning method that uses neural networks in subsequent layers to learn from data iteratively, and it is especially useful when trying to learn patterns from unstructured data. Deep learning from complex multi-level neural networks (the more levels of the network, the deeper the learning is—see Figure 6) is intended to mimic the action of the human brain (Figure 7) so that computers can be trained to deal with poorly defined abstractions and problems. The average five-year-old child easily recognizes the difference between the teacher's face and the janitor's face. In contrast, the computer needs to do a lot of work to find out who is who. Neural networks and deep learning are often used in applications for image recognition, speech, and computer vision.

Deep learning through multi-level learning in an artificial neural network attempts to model human learning. Suppose, for example, someone discovers that Paul Baran is the inventor of the Internet (level 1), so he "goes" (level 2) to Wikipedia and learns that Paul Baran was born in Poland in Grodno. He is then interested in this city and further learns that Grodno was a city (level 3) that belonged to Poland, Lithuania, and Belarus. Then, he is interested in investigating when Baran's parents emigrated with him (level 4). He learns that it was 1928. It further examines what happened in Poland this year (level 5). It is revealed that this was the period of the Great Depression in Europe, during which time people emigrated *en masse* to the United States (which John Steinbeck writes about in his famous book *The Grapes of Wrath*). Therefore, the researcher wants to know (level 5) what the young Paul Baran did during this crisis in the United States, and it turns out that he was a salesperson in the grocery store of his parents with Polish wickers in Philadelphia. Then the researcher wants to find out what is characteristic of polish wickers (level 6). He learns that it involves polish sausage. Thus, this hypothetical researcher went through 6 levels in a network of neurons (nerve cells, or information and communication). As a result, the researcher learned that Paul Baran not only invented the Internet but also sold Polish sausage in Philadelphia in his youth. This process can also be achieved in an artificial digital network of neurons, which can artificially computerize human thinking.

The advantage of machine learning, including deep learning, is that it is possible to use algorithms and models to predict results. The trick is to make sure that the scientists doing this work use the right algorithms, adopt the most relevant data (accurate and clean), and use models with the highest performance record. If all these elements combine, it is possible to continuously train the model and learn from the results. Automating this modeling, model training, and testing leads to accurate forecasts that can support business decisions and changes. For example, Facebook specialists used deep learning to

Figure 6. Urban data neural network topology (a raster is a pixel image of an object) where individual "neurons" are personal data

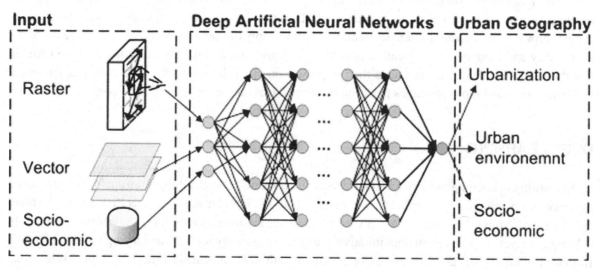

develop an algorithm for recognizing a specific person in a photograph. Thanks to this algorithm, they are able to achieve correct results in 97.53% of cases.

Unfortunately, enthusiastic companies with naive employees are recording every keystroke on their computer, every conversation and interaction in the office space, and every document and letter or memorandum of a specific employee. This helps management to manage more effectively and to accurately assess the performance and quality of the work of employees; however, the employees do not realize that such data collected about them can and probably will be used to replace them by robots, which will copy their qualifications. For example, Google has a patent for a system that responds well to customer inquiries on a so-called "blacklist." Of course, the answers are automated, and the customer does not realize that they are talking with a robot.

Work Fusion offers software for an almost completely automated project management system. In the beginning, the software automatically announces offers for specific professional specialties on popular websites such as Elance and Craigslist. It then carries out computerized and automated recruitment and employment, and it assigns tasks and controls the progress of their execution. If a person cannot complete a job, the software assigns the task to another person. The system learns and collects data that characterizes about 100,000 people and 400,000 situations, which are stored in its the records. Using more traditional methods, updating one record would cost the company $4, while in an automated system, after a year, it would only cost 50 cents and, after two years, 25 cents.

ARTIFICIAL INTELLIGENCE BOUGHT IN THE "CLOUD"

Previously, we kept our data on a computer's hard drive. Cloud services have replaced hard drive technology. A cloud service is nothing more than providing services such as memory, databases, servers, networking, and software over the Internet.

Figure 7. Comparison of a living neuron (nerve cell) with an artificial neuron, that is, a digital neuron. The sum character Σ is the aggregated input data (EC), and the function character f is the algorithm leading to the aggregated output (WY)

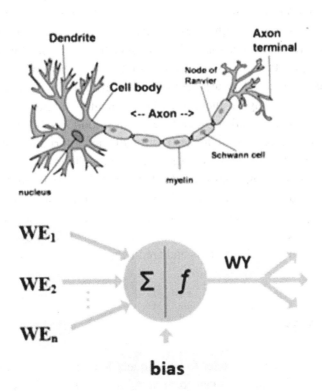

The companies that offer such computer services are called "cloud service providers". They charge clients for the use of such services, and the fees depend on the scope of the use of such services. In our daily routines, we often use cloud services without being aware of it, such as when we check our email, watch videos, edit documents, and store photos.

The most advanced cloud computing software is offered by IBM. IBM Watson, for example, is used for paid services by thousands of users. By contrast, the small company Cycle Computing offers to do complete calculations in the cloud on super-computers, which allows the average company access to super-computer calculations from their home locations. For example, an Amazon e-shop employee boasted he completed his computing task within 18 hours in the Amazon cloud (on thousands of servers), while if he had had one computer with a typical clock speed, it would have taken 260 years to accomplish this task.

IBM Watson allows users to conduct deep learning. It will also enable users to load their intelligence into behind-the-scenes robots that other manufacturers have been unable to replicate because only a giant company like IBM has able to undertake such a task.

Facebook, the largest social media network and a company with a high market value (worth over $600 billion in 2020 and generating $70 billion in revenue in 2019), can afford to employ a significant number of IT professionals. However, they decided to automate the repair of its 30,000 servers using their cyborg system. Amazon, on the other hand, has decided to sell the use of some of its 2 million servers to third parties as cloud services since most of its servers (as of 2020) are under-used. Finally, Microsoft, which has about 2 million servers as of 2020, keeps a few thousand of them underwater to secure them against hacking and to save on energy.[4]

Such a massive concentration of servers on the networks of individual service companies is good for business, but it is also suicidal since in times of active cybercrime and cyberwars, networks are easy to destroy. It does not matter that Facebook, Amazon, and Microsoft, for example, distribute their web servers all over the world, for the servers are still centralized and, therefore, vulnerable to destruction. They probably have high-end digital security services; however, following the American adage, 'what is going to go wrong will go wrong'. If these giant IT companies want to have extensive IT networks, then so be it; yet, why do companies that "outsource" to the cloud have to suffer as a result and be exposed to the risks that would follow from the destruction of such information systems? For this reason, there is a need for a strategy to deal with the possibility that the cloud is destroyed. In other words, for some time, the management of companies should still be done "by hand." Additionally, it is not known who has access to the cloud. As practice shows, service companies save on personnel costs and hire IT professionals on temporary contracts in developing countries where the laws and practices of data security are very loose. Hence, we continually hear about hackers taking over customer databases and stealing information about their bank accounts and credit cards. This happened with a large department store named Target in 2013.

CAN AI BE CREATIVE?

Creativity is a skill that we usually consider to be uniquely human. Throughout history, we have been the most creative beings on Earth. Birds can form nests, ants can form hills, but no other species on Earth is as innovative as humans. However, in the 2010s, we acquired the ability to do amazing things with computers, and robots began to imitate us. Thanks to the AI boom of 2010, computers can now recognize faces, translate between languages, answer calls, and beat players in the most complex games in the world, just to name a few. Suddenly, we must face the possibility that our ability to be creative is not unrivaled in the universe. So, is creativity no longer a purely human trait? Can AI also have originality?

It is believed that the fastest modern super-computer is still not able to learn all the processes and functions of a complex object or event (e.g., a situation involving a car driving on a road), even if it starts by working backwards on the problem (so-called "reverse engineering"). However, assuming the hypothesis of vague innovation features, which states that any innovative solution is based on at least one new or overlooked element of a problem, it can be expected that AI will develop towards creativity; however, will AI be able to come up with a whole new concept of a situation or a solution?

In the art of painting, there are examples of the successful portraits painted by creative software. Perhaps the most famous AI artist was designed by Harold Cohen, who developed a rule-based computer program, AARON, that could create original artistic images. AARON's works were sold for tens of thousands of pounds and exhibited at the Tate Gallery. Compare this success with Picasso's paintings, which adorn galleries around the world, and with the art created by a child who will never find a buyer: Whose work is most creative? Google engineer Kenric McDowell is a fan of AARON's works and has said:

The irony is that Harold wanted his system to be able to create images after his death, and he recently passed, but from my understanding, no one can really understand how to use it. So there's a kind of beauty in the embeddedness of Harold Cohens in that machine (Freedom and Safety, 2018).

Using AI as a tool to create music or support musicians has been in practice for a long time. In the 1990s, David Bowie helped develop an app called *Verbasizer*, which downloaded literary source material and randomly changed words, creating new combinations that could be used as lyrics. In 2016, Sony researchers used Flow Machines software to create a Beatles-style melody. This material was then donated to the human composer Benoît Carré and transformed into an entirely produced pop song called "Daddy's Car." Flow Machines was also used to create the entire album SKYGGE, which in Danish reads "shadow". At the consumer level, the technology is already integrated with popular music creation programs, such as Logic, a software used by musicians around the world. The software can automatically create unique patterns of drum sounds using artificial intelligence.

Can AI replace business executives? The short answer is probably not. The long answer lies in failed recruitment attempts by AI, which was ultimately abandoned by Amazon. Designed as a state-of-the-art tool to accelerate employment while eliminating prejudice, AI was given ten years to learn the patterns, content, and skills that lead to successful work. However, the male-dominated industry was reflected in the collected data, leading the AI to give priority to hiring male candidates rather than female. At the end of this project in 2018, the AI began to punish CVs and resumes that included the word "woman" as well as a list of exclusively female schools. Screening algorithms like this can help identify the best applicants at the superficial assessment level, but they are far from a comprehensive solution. Social, cultural, and, most importantly, ethical factors that are involved in employment and business are not far from the reach of AI at all.

Over the past few years, large investment banks such as Goldman Sachs and JP Morgan have hired AI professionals from academia. They have given them control over possible AI applications. Start-ups in financial technology, following investment banks, have started to use machine learning algorithms to model credit rankings and detect fraud. Hedge funds and high-frequency investors use AI to make investment decisions. If the data used for financial forecasts are out of date, economic chaos may occur.

Most importantly, we are not sure how AI algorithms will interact in the jungles of Wall Street and other exchanges. In capital markets, share prices depend to a large extent on the decisions of other market participants. If most participants rely on AI and generally adopt similar machine learning strategies, they can create echo effects in which everyone buys in unison or simultaneously sells. As a result, collapses may become more frequent.

For example, a collapse of the New York Stock Exchange took place on October 19, 1987, on so-called "Black Monday", when pre-programmed funds triggered a sudden sell-off by one of the companies, resulting in an automatic sell-off by other companies. After a long race, the crash started in Asia, gained momentum in London, and eventually ended with the Dow Jones Industrial Average falling as much as 22.6%. It was, and remains, the worst day in the history of the Dow index, in percentage terms. In fact, Hong Kong closed trading for a few days until the panic subsided.

Black Monday is considered the first disaster of the modern financial system since the innovative computer trade mechanisms exacerbated it. So-called "programming trading" meant that computers were configured to trade shares quickly when certain conditions were met. On Black Monday, this led to an automatic sale when the stock market fell. This was a shock not only because of the price meltdown but also because the market itself was significantly weakened due to the volume of sales orders overwhelming the systems. Unlike the market meltdown of 1929, Black Monday did not lead to an economic recession—or even depression—in the United States and the United Kingdom. The disaster quickly began to look like a lightning strike. Between Black Monday and the present (2020), the Dow index has risen nearly 10-fold, or 1,000 percent.

As a result, automatic programming in stock trading was prohibited; however, after 23 years, this regulation has been forgotten, and improved programming in stock trading is being conducted by most listed companies. Currently, the New York Stock Exchange uses AI in the following ways:

1. AI discover stock trading patterns. Incredibly powerful PCs can analyze almost countless data points in minutes. This means that they can detect historical and duplicate patterns of profitable stock trading, which are often hidden from human investors. People simply cannot process such a large amount of data or see these patterns at such a pace. It must be kept in mind that AI can instantly assess thousands of stocks. When it comes to high-frequency transactions, some hedge funds use artificial intelligence to analyze up to 300 million data points on the New York Stock Exchange in the first hour of daily stock trading alone.[5]
2. AI trade-in predictive shares based on sentiment. By analyzing news headlines, social media comments, blogs, and more, artificial intelligence can predict the direction of shares and movements of other brokers by analyzing sentiments that characterize opinions (or attitudes). Sometimes, this involves analyzing texts or letters brokers share with investors.
3. AI can rapidly trade shares. IT technology has greatly accelerated the ability to trade stocks on the stock exchange. Today, every millisecond counts. AI means automating stock trading without having to call a broker or use an app.

The development of AI can be categorized in terms of three generations that drive each other (Figure 8):

- Generation 1.0 (from 1946): This generation is defined by Artificial-Narrow Intelligence (ANI), which began with Ross Ashby's projects of self-learning mechanized mice that overcame complicated labyrinths. ANI robotizes well-performed tasks in production, services, home, etc.
- Generation 2.0 (since 2011): Generation 2.0 is defined by Artificial General Intelligence (AGI), which is embodied in IBM Watson's ability to answer complex questions in various areas of life. AGI can carry out advanced mental work.
- Generation 3.0 (future): Artificial Universal Intelligence (AUI) does not yet exist, but it will be better than human intelligence with advanced knowledge and qualifications.

It should be noted that the AI generations are not exclusive but additive. As a result, the general trend has been the development of the autonomous functioning of things and devices. Independent things are physical devices that use AI to automate functions previously performed by humans. They vary in size and sophistication from small drones to autonomous ships and operate in a wide variety of environments (i.e., land, sea, and air.) Increasingly, independent things work in enclosed spaces, such as mines or warehouses, but they will eventually evolve into more open areas. Autonomous things operate on a spectrum from semi-autonomous devices to fully autonomous cars.

Furthermore, as the number of autonomous things increases, there will be a shift to using things that work independently. For example, a group of robots in a production facility can communicate with each other without having to be mediated by humans. Another example is Honda's AI security system. The

Figure 8. AI Development Generations

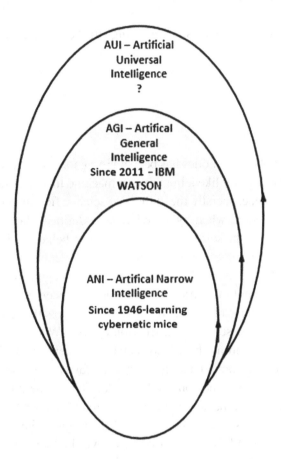

system enables communication between nearby vehicles about incidents such as accidents down the road, allowing them to act cooperatively and intelligently to avoid this and reduce traffic congestion.

AI SECURITY

The increase in AI solutions and potential attack points via IoT (Internet of Things) devices and highly connected IT services (e.g., the digital cloud) is a real security challenge. For example, consider the following: "Hi Irmina, I wanted to share some of the photos I took in Masuria. – with kisses, Mom." This may seem like a legitimate email, but it is actually a phishing scam. In phishing attacks, machine learning (ML) can be used to learn patterns of regular communication between people on social media. These patterns can then be used to defraud others by mimicking the communication style of a real person.

AI security has three critical perspectives:

1. **AI-based protection**: securing data for AI testing, training programs, and ML models (machine learning).

2. **AI-enhanced security**: using ML to understand patterns, uncover attacks, and automate parts of cybersecurity processes.
3. **The improper use of AI by attackers**: recognizing attacker patterns and defending against them.

SUMMARY

1. The development of robots and robotics has been ongoing for over 100 years because the construction of a machine that can think like a human or a machine that can copy the actions of a human has long fascinated people, especially the authors of science fiction books. The conditions of this development became possible when cybernetics were defined, the science of control utilizing feedback, which determines the self-regulation of machine behavior. The second condition is that machines can think for themselves, or at least make simple decisions.

2. Since these early developments, artificial intelligence has begun to grow as a specialization in cybernetics. The development of artificial intelligence has been going on for several decades. It has gained momentum because of the desire to construct robots that can perform dangerous tasks for humans, led by the Japanese. The construction of IBM Watson's "thinking system" and the development of autonomous drones have also been key moments in artificial intelligence research.

3. There are some who believe computers will soon think faster than humans, and, therefore, robots will displace the human species and control the world. This moment was named "the singularity" by Ray Kurzweil (2005), or perhaps it is more fitting to call it the "Big Bang" since it entails the collapse of the human species and the beginning of the reign of the robot. However, would these robots be in metal and plastic form? Or perhaps they will be like a biological organism, but with an AI-powered brain. In other words, an "electron brain" would come into being.

4. Even if computers think faster than humans through electronics and quantum technology, does that mean they will be smarter than us? This is questionable, unless they undergo education and training like people.

5. Even if robots do not become as advanced in thinking and deciding as humans, they will, unfortunately, be able to think and decide in more than 75% of everyday situations, which are rather predictable and relatively simple. The only question is why people would be so unwise to design robots that would eliminate us.

REFERENCES

Baum, C. (2003, October 4). So who's stealing china's manufacturing jobs? *Bloomberg News*. http://www.sddt.com/News/article.cfm?SourceCode=20031014fw#.Xj3c82hKjVg

Bittle, J. (2020, February). The birds: Amazon dreams of a drone-filled sky. *Harper's Magazine*. https://harpers.org/archive/2020/02/the-birds-amazon-delivery-drones/

Coming home. (2013, January 17). *The Economist*. https://www.economist.com/special-report/2013/01/17/coming-home

Freedom and Safety. (2018, May 13). *If computers can be creative, what does that mean for humanity?* https://freedomandsafety.com/en/content/blog/if-computers-can-be-creative-what-does-mean-humanity

International Federation of Robotics. (2019). *Executive summary: World robotics 2019 industrial robots*. https://ifr.org/downloads/press2018/Executive%20Summary%20WR%202019%20Industrial%20Robots.pdf

Kurzweil, R. (2005). *The singularity is near us*. Pinguin Books.

Levy, S. (2011). *In the plex: How Google thinks, works, and shapes our lives*. Simon and Schuster.

Roush, W. (2012, June 12). Hamburgers, coffee, guitars, and cars: Report from Lemnos Labs. *Xeconomy*. https://xconomy.com/san-francisco/2012/06/12/hamburgers-coffee-guitars-and-cars-a-report-from-lemnos-labs/

ScrapeHero. (2017, October 27). *How many products does Amazon sell worldwide – October 2017*. https://www.scrapehero.com/how-many-products-does-amazon-sell-worldwide-october-2017/

Velasco, S. (2013, October 24). McDonalds' help line to employee: Go on food stamps. *Christian Science Monitor*. https://www.csmonitor.com/Business/2013/1024/McDonald-s-helpline-to-employee-Go-on-food-stamps

KEY TERMS AND DEFINITIONS

Artificial Intelligence: The use of computer algorithms to performs tasks associated with human intelligence.

Deep Learning: A type of machine learning based on the use of neural networks.

IMB Watson: An artificial intelligence system designed by IBM that is capable of answering questions asked in natural languages.

Machine Learning: The design and application of computer algorithms that automatically improve when using data.

Machine Vision: A technology that provides automatic imaging analysis.

Neural Network: A network loosely modeled on biological neurons that is used in deep learning to automatically improve computer algorithms and processes.

Resourcing: The process by which a country that had previously outsourced manufacturing brings it back due to automation and robotization.

Robo-Journalism: The application of artificial intelligence to the field of journalism.

ENDNOTES

[1]   Work on this version was started by Scott Hassan when he collaborated with Larry Page and Sergey Brin on the Google search engine.

[2]   Moore's Law states that the number of transistors in computers will double every 2 years while at the same time the price of computers will continue to be halved. The law was defined by Gordon Moor in 1965.

[3]   The head of this Google project, Franz Och, is quoted by Levy (2011, p. 64).

[4]   This figure corresponds to the Polish PSC in 2020.

[5]   A hedge fund can generally invest in everything - land, real estate, stocks, derivatives, and currencies. On the other hand, mutual funds, as described to investors in terms of objectives and strategies, must essentially stick to shares or bonds and are usually only long-term. Hedge funds often use "leverage" in the form of borrowed money to increase their profits through sudden purchases of shares of companies that are at a bargain price for various reasons.

Chapter 11
Trends in Terminology:
From Punched Cards to Digital Informing

abstract

The purpose of this chapter is to analyze and review trends in digital terminology. The chapter begins by examining the origins of computerization in the United States during the 19th and 20th centuries. Next, the chapter examines the key concepts punch cards and computer science. The chapter then discusses how the term computer science is misleading. This is followed by a discussion of how information technology became the most popular term in the US. The chapter then switches focus to Europe and discusses France's promotion of informatique as well as Europe's switch from informatics to ICT. Next, the chapter considers how the internet has given rise to terms like e-commerce. The chapter concludes by considering the transition from ICT to digital informing and informing technology.

US BUSINESS STARTS COMPUTERIZATION

The development of counting machines began during the Industrial Revolution in the 19th century. After this, at the beginning of the 20th century, machine calculations developed along two distinct paths.

- Handheld arithmometers and bookkeeping machines,

- Punched cards machines for mass census mechanization (used first in 1890 in the US) and for large volumes of business data, a market which, since 1924, has been dominated by IBM.

    As a result of the Great Depression (1929-39), the *Social Security Act* was signed by President Franklin D. Roosevelt on August 14th, 1935, to create a social insurance. Social security numbers were created and provided for each resident in the US. This act triggered the broad application of IBM punch-card machines.

DOI: 10.4018/978-1-7998-8036-3.ch011

Figure 1. The 19ᵗʰ century Odhner arithmometer was in use almost up into the present, as was the book-keeping machine (Photos: public domain)

During this period, the term *punched card systems* was the dominate terminology. This technique introduced the term *programming,* which was initially done on external boards where cables connected the instructions. However, this programming system was also used on an electronic computer, ENIAC (1946). Soon, punched card machines were replaced by computers, such as IBM 1400 (where the data was still on punched cards). The Americans called this EDP (*Electronic Data Processing*) or ADP (*Automatic Data Processing*). From this point on in the United States began the popular term *data processing.*

THE UNITED STATE SWITCHES FROM PUNCH CARDS TO COMPUTER SCIENCE

The term "computer science" appears in a 1959 article in the journal *Communications of the ACM*, in which Louis Fein (1959) argues for the creation of a *Graduate School in Computer Sciences* analogous to the Harvard Business School (established in 1908). He defended the name by saying that, like *management science*, the subject is applied and interdisciplinary, while having the characteristics typical of an academic discipline. Perhaps mainly due to the broad application of computers in data processing for businesses and government in the 1960s, *computer science* came into its own as a discipline. The first *computer science* department in the US was formed at Purdue University in 1962.[1] The first person to receive a Ph. D. from a *computer science department* was Richard Wexelblat at the University of Pennsylvania in December 1965.

Computer science deals with the theory of computation, algorithms, computational problems, and the design of hardware, software, and applications for computer systems. A complete definition of computer science is provided Peter J. Denning in the article "Computer Science: The Discipline" (in the *Encyclopedia of Computer Science*).

In Poland, the term *data processing* was used for the first time in A. Targowski' s thesis "the use of computing machines in comprehensive enterprise data processing," defended on January 23, 1961, at

Figure 2. IBM tabulator, which was reading punched cards, calculating transactions, and printing reports (Photo: public domain)

the Warsaw University of Technology. The author later published the first books on this subject under the meaningful titles of "Data Processing Automation" (PWE 1970 and 1973) and "Data Processing Organization" (PWE 1975). The title of the latter book was adopted for the names of new education programs in the field of electronic digital machine applications.

THE MISLEADING TERM COMPUTER SCIENCE

Very quickly, term *computer science* showed widespread use. If someone was a professional in information technology, he/she was called a *computer scientist*. Furthermore, it did not matter whether their background was in scientific or professional calculations, electronic data processing, or machine software or computer hardware. Moreover, the term suggested that IT specialists were "scientists" because of the term *science* in *computer science*. In contrast, computer science involves a set of scientific and professional methods and techniques to complete programming tasks of a mathematical nature, which corresponds to sciences such as mathematics, physics, chemistry, biology, etc. The term was gladly adopted in the countries of the former Soviet Bloc, where business data processing was marginalized, and praise was given to those "scientists" who dealt with computations in the exact sciences.

For these reasons, the term *computer science* was replaced with the term *computing* by the Association for Computing Machinery (ACM), inspired by Peter Denning. Denning once promoted the term *computer science* but felt guilty for the ambiguity of the term. The ACM *Computing Curricula 2005* defined "computing" as follows:

Figure 3. These cables are an external program that controlled computing in the first electronic computer ENIAC (1946); this is the same way that IBM punched-card machines were programmed. (Photo: public domain)

In a general way, we can define computing to mean any goal-oriented activity requiring, benefiting from, or creating computers. Thus, computing includes designing and building hardware and software systems for a wide range of purposes; processing, structuring, and managing various kinds of information; doing scientific studies using computers; making computer systems behave intelligently; creating and using communications and entertainment media; finding and gathering information relevant to any particular purpose, and so on. The list is virtually endless, and the possibilities are vast (Joint Task Force for Computing Curricula, 2005).

INFORMATION TECHNOLOGY (IT) BECOMES THE MOST POPULAR TERM IN THE US

Most professionals in EDP use the term *information technology* (IT) as an almost universal term, embracing all kinds of data processing and computing applications. It can be defined in the following way:

Information technology (IT) is the application of computers and telecommunications equipment to store, retrieve, transmit, and manipulate data, often in the context of a business or other enterprise (Daintith,

Figure 4. Beginning in the 1960s, the IBM 1400 computer series intensified the application of the terms EDP and ADP. (Photo: IBM brochure)

2009). The term is commonly used as a synonym for computers and computer networks, but it also encompasses other information distribution technologies such as television and telephones.

However, IT is too general to specify some academic programs regarding business applications. Therefore, the following term is commonly used:

- *Information systems* (IS) degree programs are common in business schools; however, they may have different names, such as:

  ○ *management information system* (MIS) (Targowski & Tarn, 2007),
  ○ *computer information systems* (CIS)
  ○ *business information systems* (BIS)

All IS degrees combine business and computing topics, but the emphasis on technical and organizational issues varies among programs. For example, programs differ substantially in the amount of programming required (Association for Computing Machinery, 2018).

In communications between IT professionals engaged in business data processing, the term *information management* (IM) is also applied (Targowski, 1998). This term is close to the French term *informatics* (*l'informatique*). In the US, digital medical apparatus applications are called *medical informatics*.

FRANCE PROMOTES INFORMATIQUE IN EUROPE

In the 1930s, France had a very well-developed punched card culture led by Compagnie Des Machines BULL (founded in 1931). In early the 1960s, this company developed the super-computer Gamma 60, which "should" have covered all the computing needs of Europe. Furthermore, France is known for its *petit bourgeoise*, which runs an endless number of small stores and hotels. This made it a good market for data processing machines, which was fed by the BULL Serie MCT 300 and Gamma 10, which were sold by the thousands. However, France could not develop midsize mainframe computers and only produced them on American licenses, like, for example, Gamma 30, which was the American computer GE 400. Eventually, the French Government established *Plan Calcul* and *Compagnie International Informatique* (CII), which were aimed at having France manufacture French computers. In this way, the term *informatique* was found in France and spread throughout Europe.

The term *informatique* was coined in 1962 by Philippe Dreyfus (1925-2018), an employee of BULL. It is a neologism of the French language composed of shortening the words *information* and *automatique*. The term informatics became popular in many European nations. It emphasized the purpose of applying computers to automate information processing for organizations.

Figure 5. The French Serie 300 MCT (BULL) was a unique machine that mechanically combined features of punch-card devices with electronic, internally programmed Memoir Central Transit (MCT) processing cards in input/output devices twice as fast as punch-cards machines in a cycle of 300 cards per minute. (Photo: BULL brochure)

The Serie 300 MCT provided the bridge between the vast applied card-punched machines and future computers involved in business and administrative data processing, now called *l'informatique*.

EUROPE SWITCHES FROM INFORMATICS TO ICT

When the Internet became extremely popular at the beginning of the 21st century, Europeans (with exception of France) switched from using the term *informatics* to the term abbreviation *ICT* (*Information and Communication Technology*) for two reasons: first, it emphasized e-communication; second, short acronym *ICT* was easy to use.

Nowadays, almost every business in the world must apply ICT in their business operations to take advantage of the increased effectiveness and competitiveness. In Western civilization, Small and Medium Enterprises (SMEs) account for the bulk of computer users. However, the term *ICT* has spread beyond business environments and has quickly moved into areas such as education. Basically, the term *ICT* is the American term *IT* expanded by "C" for e-communication.

THE RISE OF THE INTERNET TRIGGERS TERMS LIKE E-COMMERCE

The rapid development of applications for the Internet at the beginning of the 21st century triggered the use of the letter "e" to be added as a prefix to these names, e.g., *e-commerce*, *e-book*, *e-press*, *e-conference*, and so forth.

E-commerce (electronic commerce) is the pursuit of buying or selling goods electronically on online services or over the Internet. Electronic commerce is based on technologies such as mobile commerce, electronic funds transfer, supply chain management, Internet marketing, online transaction processing, electronic data interchange (EDI), inventory management systems, and automated data collection systems. E-commerce is, in turn, driven by the technological advances of ICT technology.

Also, the term *information superhighway* became the paradigm for the new economy triggered by e-commerce. Vice-president Al Gore translated this term from the Polish project INFOSTRADA conceptualized by Targowski in 1972 (Heilemann, 1995; Targowski, 2016).

FROM ICT TO DIGITAL INFORMING AND INFORMING TECHNOLOGY

Once the term *ICT* took off in Europe, the American term *IT* was being displaced by the term *digital*. It is a synonym of the "e" (electronic) prefix, which dominated at the beginning of the 21st century. In the 2020s, almost everything computerized is called *digital*. For example, there is *digital commerce*, *digital books*, *digital networks*, and so forth. This term is easy to use and is universal in how it is applied. To a certain degree, it has replaced *IT* in daily communications.

However, the term *ICT* triggered the rise of the term *informing*. *Informing* emphasizes the advancement of information systems to the stage of becoming informing systems (see the chapter *Development Trends of Information Systems*), which means from passive to more interactive systems. This is evident in the switch from a noun to a verb.

Figure 6. The Internet triggered terms with the prefix "e," such as "e-commerce", "e-book", and others

If information systems are advancing to digital informing systems, then the information technology of the 1970s should, after 50 years of intensive development, advance to informing technology in the 2020s.

A development tree for the terminology of computational techniques is presented in Figure 7.

SUMMARY

1. The strong role of business in the United States and Western Europe in the development of information technology has led to its success in a broad range of applications.

2. The pioneering role of computer science needed "adjustments" to make its mission congruous with information technology. This took place in 2005 when computing curriculum was offered.

3. The field of information technology has greatly evolved in the last 130 years (since 1890). Still, with respect to computer-oriented development (since 1946), IT is only about 75 years old, which is a short time for such a ubiquitous technology to be consolidated under one name accepted by all involved. In consequence, as the developmental tree in Figure 7 shows, there many different terms applied in this field.

4. It is important to emphasize that early fascination with the word *computer* has been replaced by the term *information*. After all, the *bullet* is more important than the *rifle* since it makes the mark; however, both are necessary for completing the job.

5. The acronym *IT* as the top colloquial term for the field is widely applicable. However, to a certain degree, it is understood only by specialists. Hence, the new synonym *digital* is gaining worldwide recognition.

Figure 7. A development tree of the terminology of informing technology taking place in the United States and Europe. The shaded areas (computer science and computing) are self-contained areas of specializations among the wide scope of mainstream applications of computerization

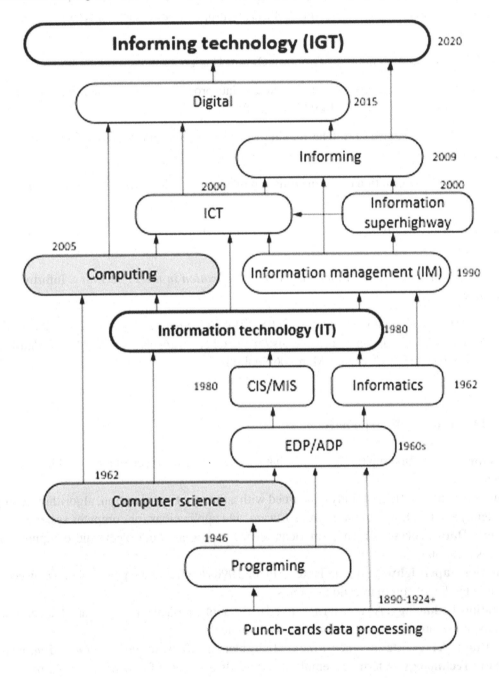

6. Network-oriented information processing, empowered particularly by the Internetization, makes information more interactive (i.e., *informing*).

7. Perhaps it is time to replace the term *information technology* by the term *informing technology*.

REFERENCES

Association for Computing Machinery. (2018, July 6). *Computing degrees & careers: Information systems.* https://web.archive.org/web/20180706021730/http:/computingcareers.acm.org/index.html@page_id=9.html

Daintith, J. (2009). IT. In *A dictionary of physics.* Oxford University Press.

Fein, L. (1959). The role of the university in computers, data processing, and related fields. *Communications of the ACM, 2*(9), 7–14. doi:10.1145/368424.368427

Heilemann, J. (1995, December 1st). The making of the President 2000. *Wired.* https://www.wired.com/1995/12/gorenewt/

Targowski, A. (1998). A definition of the information management discipline. *Journal of Education for MIS, 3*(1), 79–91.

Targowski, A. (2016). *The history, present state, and future of information technology.* Informing Science Press.

Targowski, A., & Tarn, M. (2007). *Enterprise systems education in the 21st century.* Information Science Publishing.

The Joint Task Force for Computing Curricula. 2005. (2005). *Computing Curricula 2005: The Overview Report.* ACM and IEEE Computer Society. https://web.archive.org/web/20141021153204/http:/www.acm.org/education/curric_vols/CC2005-March06Final.pdf

KEY TERMS AND DEFINITIONS

Arithmometer: The first digital calculator that was sufficiently powerful and reliable to use in office settings.

Computer Science: A field of study concerned with a theory of computation, algorithms, computational problems, and the design of hardware, software, and applications for computer systems.

Electronic Data Processing: The American term for programming electronic computers at the advent of this technology.

Information Superhighway: A popular term in the 1990s to refer to the potential of a new economy made possible by digital communication systems.

Information Technology: A broad term applied to the application of computers and telecommunications equipment to store, retrieve, transmit, and manipulate data.

Informatique: A French term coined in the 1960s by blending the words *information* and *automatique.*

Informing Technology: A term that emphasizes the advancement of information systems from having a passive to a more interactive role.

Punch Cards: A paper card that holds digital data and that is processed by machines.

ENDNOTE

[1]   In United Kingdom, the first computer science department was organized by Tom Kilburn at the University of Manchester in 1964.

Section 3
Applications of Digital Informing Strategies

Chapter 12
Digital Business Strategies

ABSTRACT

This chapter discusses digital strategies that can be used in business contexts. The chapter begins by discussing different enterprise configurations that can be used with computerization. The chapter then provides an overview of enterprise IT services. Next, key indicators of sustainable performance for IT services are analyzed using the balanced score card perspective. The chapter then puts forth a four-part IT management planning model. Next, a strategic model is put forth for integrating business systems, applications, and infrastructure. The chapter then discusses how to align digital and business strategies, and it analyzes the structure of the digital aims and strategies of business. The chapter concludes by applying these concepts to examples.

INTRODUCTION

The purpose of this chapter is to develop an approach that aligns digital strategies with the business strategies of a company or enterprise. Different types of enterprise configuration models resulting from computerization will be shown below. Based to these models, strategies for IT services can be developed. In addition, the chapter will characterize the modern organization of these services as well as methods of strategic and tactical computer planning. The basic elements of such planning, including intentions, objectives, strategies, policies, etc., will be defined. A number of examples will be provided to demonstrate the essence of this approach.

ENTERPRISE COMPUTERIZATION CONFIGURATIONS

Regarding the IT configuration of an enterprise, the following types can be distinguished, which are supported to varying degrees depending on the larger configuration of the enterprise. The hybrid configuration presented below (Figure 14) is most fitting for the modern period (Targowski, 2003).

DOI: 10.4018/978-1-7998-8036-3.ch012

- An **offline enterprise** is a system where IT applications are unintegrated data processing routines. These routines support individual workplaces that are unconnected with one another, and data is usually entered periodically. Such enterprises are usually individual shops, craft workshops, etc. (i.e., those run by families) (Figure 1).

Figure 1. Offline enterprise model with application islands (darkened fields are key systems)

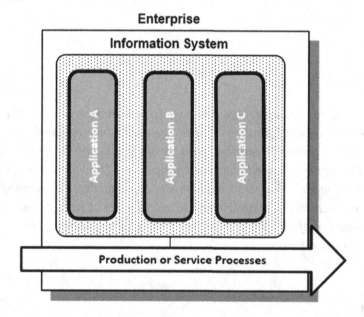

- **Online enterprise information systems** are networks of data and results that are managed in real time (Figure 2).

- **Integrated enterprise IT systems** use a common database, minimizing data redundancy, and are supported by software such as SAP, Oracle, Baan, and others (Figure 3).

- In **Agile companies**, the production of goods and provision of services are adapted to the needs of the customer (Figure 4). Agility in producing goods tailored to the demands of customers consists in integrating information systems (e.g., *computer aided engineering* [CAE], *computer aided design* [CAD], *computer aided planning* [CAP], *computer aided manufacturing* [CAM], *computer aided storage and retrieval* [CAS&R], robotics, *computer aided quality control* [CAQ], and others) into one *computer integrated manufacturing* (CIM) system. Table 1 shows the evolution of the factory system from the point of view of production flexibility.

Figure 2. An online model of an enterprise, which, based on cooperative supply chains, constitutes an extended enterprise (the darkened field is a key network system)

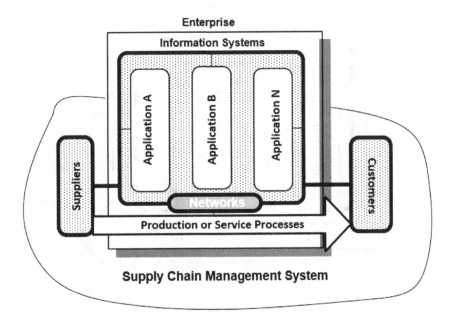

- **Informed companies** use Knowledge Management Systems (KMS) and Wisdom Management Systems (WMS) as well as AI-assisted procedures (Figure 5).

- **Communicative enterprises** use highly developed ICT and Internet networks, Intranets, Extranets, e-mail, e-commerce, teleconferences, telecommuting, telegroup work, and others (Figure 6).

- **Electronic enterprises**, recently called *digital enterprises,* are those in which most documents are stored online in digital form (Figure 7), including scanned copies and online information accessed via the website (Figure 8).

In this model, the key applications coordinate online access to websites with the *Digital Document System* (Figure 10), which allows for the organization of the *Workflow System* (Figure 9). If an active user of a personal computer can have hundreds of thousands of digital files, then a company with hundreds, thousands, and even millions of employees (e.g., Walmart has 2.2 million employees) can have thousands, millions, and even billions of documents, which must be organized along the lines of a library, with cataloged numbers and guaranteed access. The Workflow System, on the other hand, coordinates the implementation of tasks, such as quickly settling a bank loan or buying a car. In such cases, the application process would automatically flow between the computers of the bank employees involved in the process. As can be seen from the online website model, access between the systems of

Figure 3. An integrated enterprise model based on a common database (the darkened field is a key system)

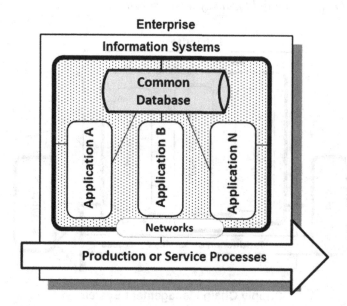

Table 1. Evolution of the factory system from the point of view of production flexibility

Factory Orientation	Mass Production	Flexible Production	Mass Specialization - According to a Customer's Needs
Period	1900-1970	1971-2000	2001+
Number of machine tools	150	50-30	25-20
Number of products made	10-15	100-1000	Unlimited
Percentage of production shortages	25%	0.02%	<0.0005%

different companies and their branches must be designed and programmed in accordance with numerous international standards in order to be collision-free.

- **Mobile enterprises** use remote user access to centralized IT systems (Figure 11).

- **Cloud-based enterprises** are those which use IT systems via a digital cloud outside the enterprise to provide services (Figure 12).

- **Virtual enterprises** do not have physical premises (buildings), except for small work areas for select employees. Most employees work from home, hotels, or the customer's location (Figure 13).

Figure 4. Agile enterprise model via the CIM system (Computer Integrated Manufacturing) (darkened fields are key systems; EIS-Executive Information System, EPM-Enterprise Performance Management)

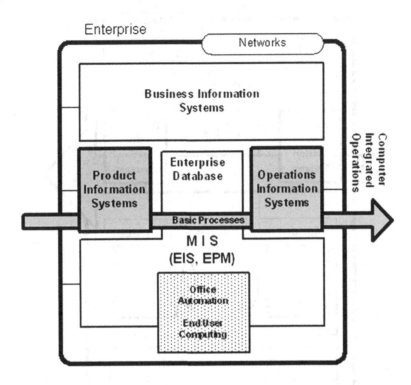

An example of a typical virtual enterprise is a virtual clothing store, which can virtually agree to contracts with various design and production companies.

- **Hybrid enterprises** are organizations that practice multiple IT configurations and use artificial intelligence (AI) in different degrees of intensity (Figure 14). This type of enterprise can be called a *learning organization* because of its complexity and because the ability to use it occurs gradually, with no one in this organization being an expert on how it functions (at least, not at present).

To the diversity of IT configurations of enterprises, one must add the End User Application System (EUA), as illustrated by the model in Figure 15. Today's end-user must be well qualified in the use of enterprise systems as well as personal systems.

To summarize this review of various digital configurations of enterprises, the following strategic conclusions and recommendations can be made:

a. The offline enterprise configuration dominates small businesses and craft workshops, as it is based on individual professionals from the so-called "old generation". However, when such an enterprise involves a family in which the younger generation participates, then it is possible for it to evolve into an online enterprise or even into an integrated enterprise, perhaps with elements of a connected enterprise.

Figure 5. Informed enterprise model (darkened fields are key systems)

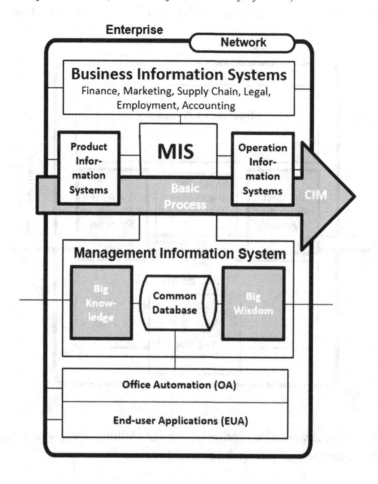

b. Mid-sized enterprises generally have the configuration of an integrated or communicative enterprise and should develop towards an electronic enterprise configuration.

c. Specialized companies in fashion or tourism and similar seasonal businesses often implement elements of a virtual enterprise in their configuration.

d. Large enterprises should develop the informed enterprise configuration, with the use of Big Data, Big Information, Big Concepts, Big Knowledge, and Big Wisdom.

e. As a result of pressure from ambitious IT professionals who are passionate about new IT technologies, a number of enterprises operate in hybrid enterprise configurations, that is, they develop elements from other configurations, although they do not necessarily fully develop any single configuration. Such a company is in permanent development and creative chaos. This is an enticing state for ambitious IT professionals, while for end users it is a big problem.

f. The issue of developing such IT configurations in public administration and non-governmental organizations—called "agencies", for short—looks better than for business enterprises, because the information processes of the former are inherently slower than in business. In addition, the path towards modernization for agencies looks promising, funds for financing projects are more easily obtained through various grants and loans.

Figure 6. Model of a communicative enterprise (darkened fields are key systems for this enterprise's configuration)

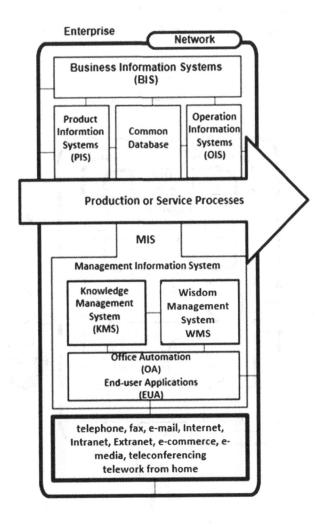

ENTERPRISE IT SERVICES

IT is the fastest growing service in most companies. Different IT orientations are given in Table 2, defined by their methods, projects, and results.

Figure 16 provides an overview of how IT specialists are organized in an IT division to manage the IT services of a global company. Depending on the company's IT strategy, this powerful management engine can be adapted accordingly.

KEY INDICATORS OF SUSTAINABLE PERFORMANCE FOR IT SERVICES

The *Balanced Scorecard* (BSC) is a management system that explains an organization's strategy and vision, translating it into tracking activities. Put simply, it is a way to understand how well a depart-

Figure 7. A model of a digital enterprise with online access through a website. Abbreviations are explained in Figure 6. The darkened fields point to key systems of this enterprise's configuration. e-SIB = electronic Business Information System (like Amazon); DDM = Digital Document Management System; Big Cognition contains Big Data, Big Information, Big Concepts, Big Knowledge and Big Wisdom

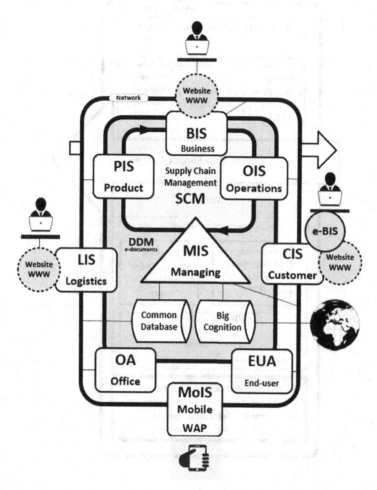

ment or an organization is doing—an alternative and sometimes preferred way to measure a successful strategy that goes beyond finance.

Initially, the BSC turns the strategy into something tangible so that it can be measured; however, BSC's real success lies in prioritizing the measurements that are most significant to the organization. When organizations adopted the balanced scorecard approach in the 1990s, there was one universal issue: how to measure the contribution of the IT department in the BSC with respect to the final results of the company's activities.

The BSC includes four perspectives that help managers plan and implement a business strategy:

- **Financial perspective**: Track financial and performance requirements,

Figure 8. Model for integrating information systems through a website

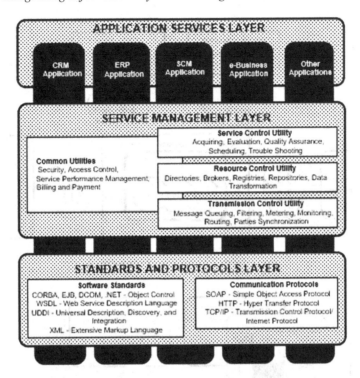

- **Customer perspective**: Measure customer satisfaction and performance requirements as they apply to both the organization and what it delivers (products or services),
- **Internal operation process perspective**: Measure internal organizational processes, such as manufacturing and design,
- **Innovation perspective** (knowledge, education, training): measure how an organization educates, acquires, and captures knowledge and uses this information to grow and remain competitive.

An important part of maintaining a balanced scorecard is the consistent evaluation of all four areas. Delaying a study or completely ignoring a key metric will lead to an unsustainable business situation with an inevitable and significant negative impact. Table 3 characterizes the BSC with Key Performance Indicators (KPI) typical of the 21st century.

With changing business processes and organizational structures, business improvements have been dramatic. It is important to realize that the benefits of IT technology are not only increased employee productivity, but also improvements in customer service, product quality, and others. In particular, productivity has been increased via the Internet, intranet, and data mining. This latest use of IT helps banks, for instance, gather more and deeper customer information. Network communication has also helped speed up the transfer of marketing information to customers, and fast and accurate customer information is a company's strongest weapon, especially in retail.

Figure 9. Workflow System

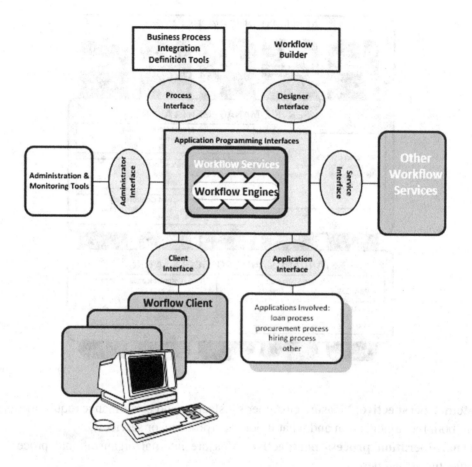

IT MANAGEMENT LEVELS

Figure 17 shows a four-step IT management planning model at the strategic level, which has the following characteristics (Targowski, 2003):

1. The strategic profile analysis phase develops an IT creed, mission, and intentions that will shape further planning activities.
2. The system planning pre-planning phase provides an overview of available applications, infrastructure technologies, and possible R&D directions.
3. The strategy planning phase formulates an informatization strategy as a derivative of a business strategy.
4. The strategic stage of system planning re-examines and refines the concepts and directions of the system pre-planning phase. This fourth step defines all the necessary architectures and solutions.

Figure 18 illustrates the management of the IT service at the tactical level, which consists of the following three-stage model:

Figure 10. Digital Document System, IBM software

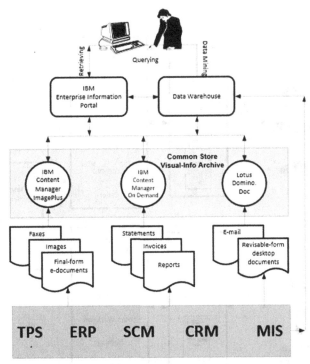

- **Stage 1**: Formulating IT intentions and policies;
- **Stage 2**: Implementing organizational structures of the IT service;
- **Stage 3**: Supporting Management via a computerization strategy and policy covering the most critical aspects of computer science management. This also involves taking care of leadership and the drive to be productive (a high-performance culture) by participating in the power dynamics of the organization, developing knowledge and skills among IT professionals, and, most importantly, establishing a culture that supports computerization for both business system technology developers and end users.

Let us look at some aspects of tactical computerization management in the enterprise:

The *Information policy* is a general guide to computerization operations. It is a set of instructions that give direction to IT professionals and users. The following are examples of such a policy:

- **General IT principles of digitalization**: plan and build the architecture of systems, data, and infrastructure for supporting e-entrepreneurship.
- **Application policy**: integrate MIS, PIS, OIS, SCM, and others via the information portal (Web).
- **Software policy**: use multi-vendor solutions that comply with open system standards and Internet-oriented solutions.
- **Digitalization financial policy**: apply a full buy-out system, assuming end-users make appropriate trade-offs in terms of calculations with other alternatives.

Figure 11. Mobile enterprise configuration

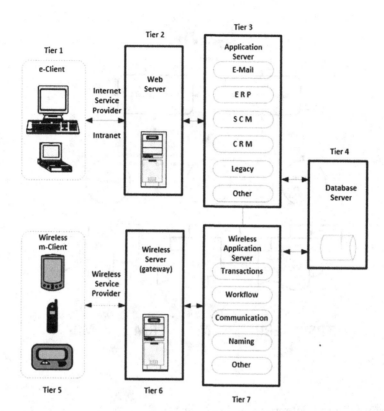

The *policy of organizing an IT service* may plan the following phases:

- **Digitalization initiation**: select application masters in the departments of users who will promote IT solutions among peers.
- **Application dissemination**: create an inter-departmental steering committee to promote the dissemination of IT applications.
- **Enterprise application integration**: build a strong IT service organization, capable of professional supervision and which can create an advanced Enterprise Digital Infrastructure.

Tactical information intentions may be planned for the entire IT service or for its main projects. Tactical information intentions should be quantitative derivatives of strategic intentions and computerization strategies. They should guide, set, and control IT projects. For example, if the strategic intention of computerization is to implement an e-enterprise, one of the tactical intentions will be the development of an intranet and extranet.

IT management is based on the budgeting process, which involves creating a plan that includes estimated expenses related to application development and computer operations. The following elements should be included in the budget:

Figure 12. Cloud enterprise

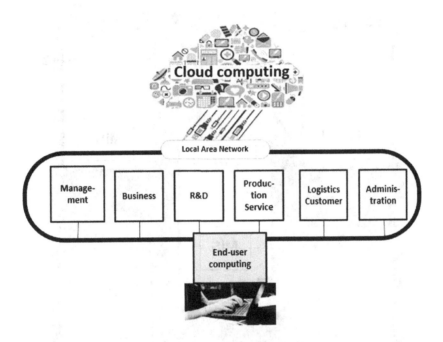

- **Costs of assets**: hardware and software, realized costs and benefits, and profits from the previous year;
- **Costs of liabilities**: depreciation provisions, unrealized costs and benefits, and the net loss from the previous year;
- **Costs**: equipment, personnel, and overheads;
- **Revenue**: external services, annual realized costs and benefits, and revenue growth attributed to applications in business;
- Others

The criteria for whether to initiate IT programs should be carried out through feasibility studies. If a cost-benefit analysis cannot be applied, it is recommended that a business impact analysis be conducted to explore possible projects.

Server and network bandwidth and service level planning include user service marketing planning, user service level planning, system recovery planning in the event of a disaster, information security planning, system audit planning, and other types of planning. Judgements that determine the value of service planning should focus on the use of IT resources, costs, and service-related workloads.

Establishing leadership and motivation: after defining the architecture of the strategy-based IT infrastructure, money, people, technology, suppliers, facilities, and communication channels should be gathered and developed. An effective IT service organization needs dynamic leadership that will lead IT professionals and business users towards computer science strategies. More attention should be paid to reward and satisfaction systems, at least if the company wants to maximize organizational engagement and minimize employee turnover. IT should be visible, imaginative, and supportive of a culture that

Figure 13. A virtual enterprise model without its own premises (buildings)

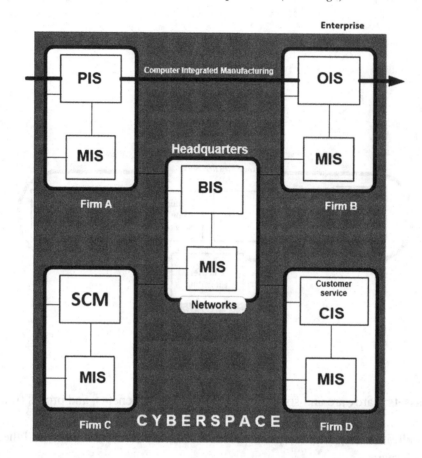

embraces strategies that allow IT professionals to react and innovate. A technique used by some of the best IT leaders is to emphasize results and to foster a high-performance culture.

Development of the knowledge and qualifications of IT professionals: Often a new computerization strategy requires new knowledge and new qualifications. At one time, when computer skills involved the ability to program in "COBOL", it was easy to replace such specialists. Today, however, the complexity of electronic infrastructure development is so great that IT professionals are a critical human resource (capital) for companies. Training a computer scientist who knows more than just a programming language can span years. In addition, the employer must maintain a reasonably large IT service sector in order to implement an advanced computerization strategy. One can distinguish the following categories of IT professionals:

- **Craftsmen** know routine work, but due to a lack of education or motivation, they have poor work efficiency and potential. Companies should minimize this kind of employment for positions that require problem-solving skills; however, they can be cost-effective in user consultation centers (i.e., help centers), data centers, etc.
- **Specialists** have very good skills in a specific field and are very motivated. Due to their highly specialized knowledge, their potential for performing multiple tasks is rather low. They are the

best type of employee to perform major recurring tasks in planning, development, maintenance, servers, and network centers. However, this kind of professional is not usually qualified for strong leadership positions in pilot projects.

- **Experts** are well-educated, highly motivated, and technically proficient. They have the best job opportunities and the highest professional potential. They are much needed in planning and development centers. They are essential, and it is better to have one of them than two craftsmen or professionals. Without experts, the company will pay dearly for expensive external consultants.

- **Advisors** are most likely former experts in computer science or business, so they can still provide useful advice (i.e., they have high professional potential), but their work efficiency is limited. They act as creators of strategy and information culture. To this end, they are important members of the IT service. In corporations like IBM and Apple, their position is known as "fellow". Most often they are needed in planning centers.

Developing a culture that supports IT professionals and users is required for new computerization strategies that introduce new technological and even civilizational solutions. Culture is a value-based system of human behavior. Values define the cultural need for rationality, meaning, emotional experience, richness of imagination, and depth of faith in solutions. Organizational culture creates a communicative

Figure 14. Hybrid enterprise model

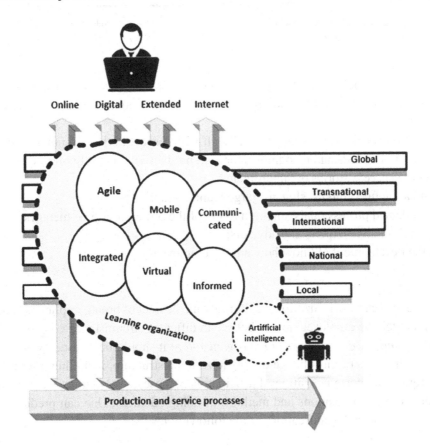

Figure 15. End-User Applications (EUA)

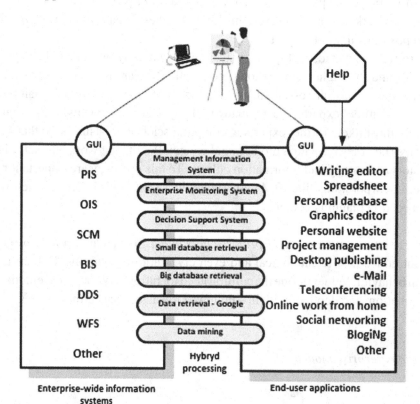

climate that affects how employees implement the intentions behind the strategies of computerization. The leader who develops a healthy IT and organizational culture should take care of the following:

- Ensuring a strong positive response from IT staff with respect to the computerization strategy;
- Providing a set of awards and recognition for high productivity and reliability of work;
- Disseminating success stories of subordinates;
- Creating meaningful symbols, slogans, jargon, and metaphors;
- Promoting talented professionals among masters of the profession to be mentors;
- Providing authoritative experts and advisors;
- Securing the development of know-how among employees;
- Others.

A consequence of such an organizational culture should be a set of broad, implicitly understood rules and procedures that tell the employee how to behave in different circumstances.

Participation in the power dynamics of the organization: it should be foreseen when implementing an IT strategy that it will certainly change the organizational structure, including power dynamics and qualifications required for certain positions. Participation in these new dynamics should aim to mitigate negative impacts on new applications and methods of doing business. One can predict changes in the power dynamics and required qualifications at the following levels:

Table 2. IT specializations in companies

Group Oriented Towards	Methods	Projects	Results
Planning	Information engineering; System engineering	Enterprise configurations	Objectives and strategies for computerization; Platform architecture; Application system architecture; IT infrastructure architecture
Design	Information engineering; System engineering; Software engineering	System analysis; Business process; Designing systems; Reengineering; System integration; Programming systems	Data architecture; Data objects; Databases; Big Cognition; Components; Procedures; Subsystems; Systems
Maintenance	Software engineering	Code updates; Modernization of old programs	List of instructions; Subprograms; Data objects
Informing	Troubleshooting problems	Online consulting	Problems solved
Servers	Operational digital infrastructure management	Computer services	Security; Reliability; Productivity; Results of processing and calculation
Networks	Topology update; Network administration	Network Services; Mobility integration	LAN; MA; WAN; GAN; VAN; Internet

- **Staff level**: Emphasis should be placed on educating users in developing new knowledge and skills in order to effectively adapt to new IT tools; however, not all users will be ready to take on the challenge of new knowledge and skills, even after carefully planned training.
- **Formal organization level**: some departments will have to reconfigure their activities and will not be willing to do so, finding rational and irrational obstacles.
- **Informal organization level**: new IT solutions can jeopardize established groups (including cliques) by restructuring their impact.

Tips for how to successfully navigate such power dynamics and politically succeed in a company include the following:

1. Allow poorly supported ideas to die from inaction and minimize political encounters with them.
2. Propose additional tests for reasonable solutions that are not supported by superiors; in other words, do not openly oppose executives.
3. Let negative decisions result from group consensus.
4. Engage in conversations and informal debates to keep up with progress and to know when to intervene.
5. Direct the IT strategy, but do not dictate it.
6. Reward high performance both Abundantly and conspicuously.
7. Assign pilot tasks to "masters" whose advancement is related to the success of the task.

Figure 16. Example of the organization of an IT division with full IT services. Server, network, and help centers are housed in a single geographic region; similarly, design sections are given for a single project

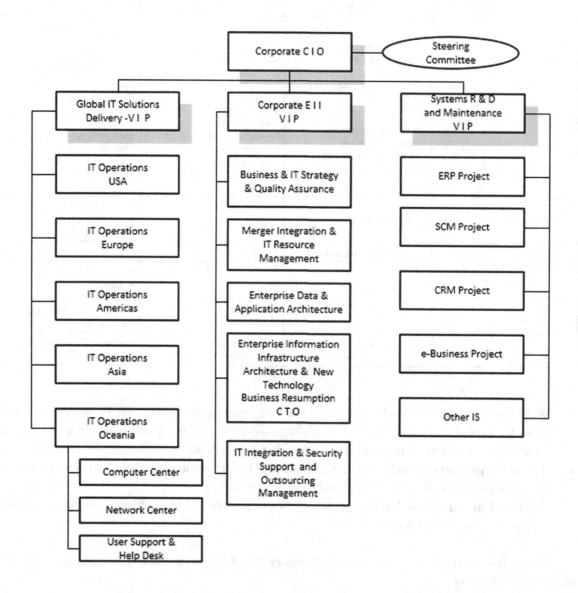

Digitalization solutions can be positive or negative factors in social transformation. Policy action should create a social background for controlled applications. With the right feedback, IT can have a positive impact on the implementation of organizational and social transformations. Since, in practice, such changes are not always compatible with the theoretical planning framework for strategic-tactical systems, a rather eclectic set of solutions should be identified.

Due to the very high specialization of IT professionals and their high salaries (the largest among other specializations in most countries today), companies for financial reasons are not able to fully develop IT services. Hence, different specialized groups can be sub-contracted to service companies (including an infrastructure group), and their services can be delivered via digital clouds. However, there remain

Table 3. The IT Balanced Score Card in the United States in the 21st century

Key Performance Indicators	Perspectives			
	Financial	**Client**	**Operations**	**Innovation and Knowledge**
IT budget	4% of the company's revenue			
IT costs per user station	$15,000			
Profit from e-business	45%			
Revenue from IT services outside the company	15%			
Outsourcing expenditures in the IT budget	15%			
Personnel costs	34%			
Service costs of e-Business		21%		
Customer participation in supply chain management (SCM)		34%		
Supplier participation in SCM			28%	
IT leadership time dedicated to business users			38%	
Budget for Research & Computer Development				5%
Investment in new technologies				19%
Workers using AI				29%

many problems. The following strategies can be implemented to address these issues (the strategies are distinguished based on the types of service provided):

- The strategy of outsourcing a complete IT service leads to a significant reduction in costs, increased profits, and shareholder satisfaction, which in turn leads to high bonuses for executives. However, this also exposes a company to *cybercrime,* the unreliability of services, and the loss of competitiveness since service providers can learn IT solutions and sell them to competitors (of course, without informing the owners).

- Design and programming outsourcing are popular, although they entail higher maintenance costs, as contractors will program systems so that only they can update them.

- Software maintenance outsourcing should be implemented by software developers, and if it is a bundled software purchase, then the company should employ its own developers so that the update is well made and not branded or poorly executed by developers from far away who are not familiar with the software.

- The strategy of outsourcing servers and networks to digital cloud service providers is popular, although it requires very good contracts and security in the event of crashes and cyberattacks. In

Figure 17. Strategic level of management of an enterprise's IT services

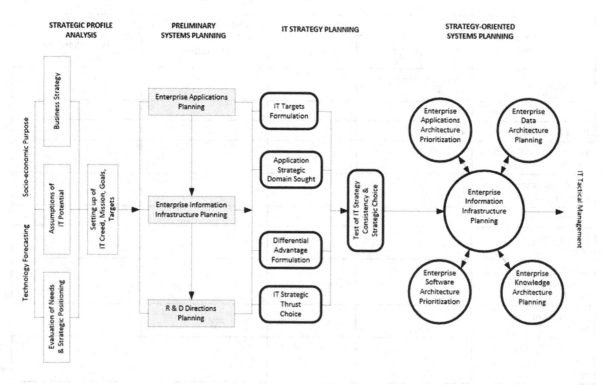

Figure 18. Tactical level of IT management

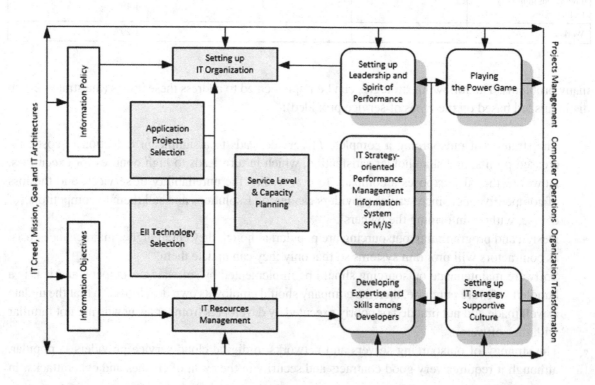

Figure 19. Integration model of the digital enterprise strategy

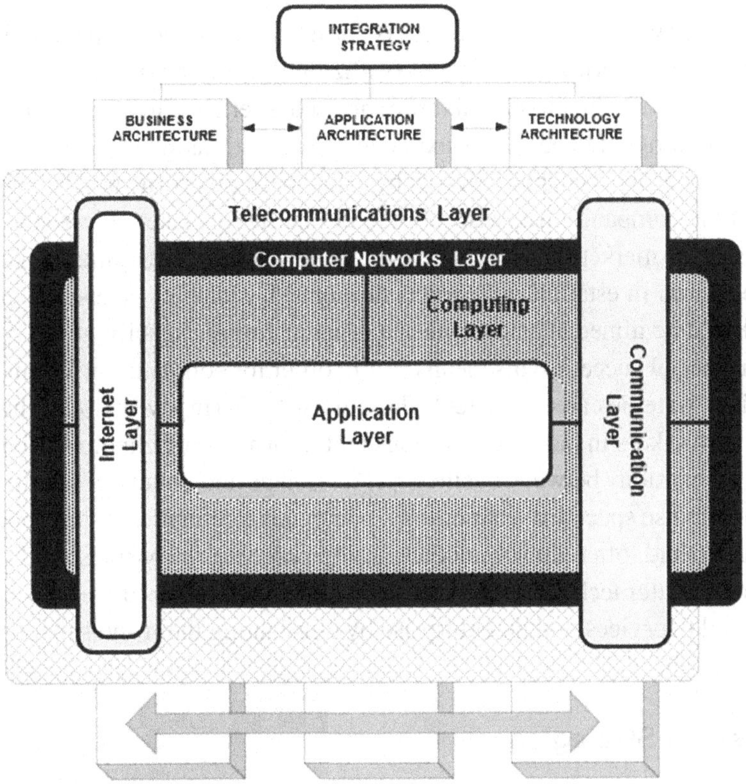

other words, services should be outsourced to two independent digital clouds; however, this raises costs and perhaps lowers the desirability of such outsourcing.

- The strategy of outsourcing the planning group means putting the company's business and IT strategy into "someone else's hands". This is a wrong strategy.
- Any outsourcing strategy requires the company to have a contact group that ensures conflict-free cooperation with service providers and the conflict-free flow of information between the parties that control the company.

STRATEGY FOR INTEGRATING BUSINESS SYSTEMS, APPLICATIONS, AND THE INFRASTRUCTURE OF THE ENTERPRISE

The infrastructure of the integration model of the digital enterprise strategy is illustrated in Figure 19. The aim of this strategy is to minimize the redundancy of system elements and the time of business processes.

ALIGNING DIGITAL STRATEGIES WITH BUSINESS STRATEGIES

Aligning digital strategies with business strategies is defined as dynamically updating the organizational (business) objectives of an enterprise and operationalizing the computerization strategy in accordance with these objectives. Typically, business goals are expressed in terms of improving financial performance and sustaining market competitiveness. For example, organizations may hope that, by using IT, they increase sales and revenues by 20%, reduce costs by 10%, increase profits by 15%, and achieve sustainable profits. In addition, companies may also want to define their market objectives, such as how much they want to increase their market share by, where they hope to enter emerging markets, and where they hope to expand their reach in established markets through IT strategies. Thus, the goals and strategies of the IT service should be aimed at improving the organizational capacity of the company to achieve lasting economic and social success. This means that in order for companies to claim that their business objectives and digital strategies are consistent, there must be harmony between them and little to no friction between policymakers in business divisions and information technology divisions.

Unfortunately, this harmony between business professionals and computer scientists is often lacking because IT professionals use specialist terminology, which management does not understand. Computer scientists, on the other hand, often do not understand the processes of business and prefer to delve into the arcane world of computer technology. For this reason, company executives often endorse solutions that reduce the role of IT services in their enterprise by eliminating them and subcontracting to external service companies.

Business Goals and Strategies

The following types of business goals and strategies can be identified:

- Business intentions defined by specific time intervals:
  - **Business goals**: long-term (2-5 years) plans to accomplish new projects, enter new markets, achieve a top-ranked position in a market, etc.
  - **Business objectives**: short-term (1 year) plans aimed at accomplishing elements of a business goal.
  - **Business targets**: short-term aims to accomplish elements of business objectives, e.g., the quarterly accomplishment of a specific objective.
  - **Business tasks**: short-term aims to accomplish elements of business targets, e.g., the monthly accomplishment of a specific target.
  - **Business activity**: a process aimed at accomplishing elements of a business task, e.g., in the course of one week.
- Business intentions not defined by specific time intervals:
  - **Business mission**: a short declaration of what the company is doing. For example, 3M's mission (known for inventing and selling sticky notes) is to "solve problems innovatively". Walt Disney's entertainment company's mission is "Making People Happy." Merck's mission is to "preserve and improve life."
  - **Business industrial strategy**: the plans typical of the business industry, as illustrated by Figure 20.

- Business strategy: a plan for achieving the goals/objectives of the business. Napoleon said that "strategy is a simple act of execution."
- Business policy: a set of rules for carrying out business tasks. For example, when travelling from the USA to China, an employee may be entitled to sit business class on the plane. The policy of the luxury department store Nordstrom is for employees to "apply good judgement in all situations, and there are no other additional recommendations."
- Company culture: values-oriented patterns of behavior of employees and management. For example, Walmart's culture is characterized by a "financial orientation towards its customers", expressed in business policy "pay less". IBM culture, on the other hand, declares "*IBM Way*".
- Business creed and the key value of the business: this is similar to a slogan, and it reflects the approach of the company's management. For example, Ford proclaims "Quality is job number 1." IBM's key business values are:
    - Give full consideration to the employee's situation.
    - Spend as much time as it takes to meet the customer's needs.
    - Take a mile to complete the task properly.
- In contrast, the key company values of Procter & Gamble are as follows:
    - product excellence,
    - uninterrupted self-improvement,
    - fairness and justice,
    - respect and interest expressed to the employee.

Figure 20. Classification of business industrial strategy

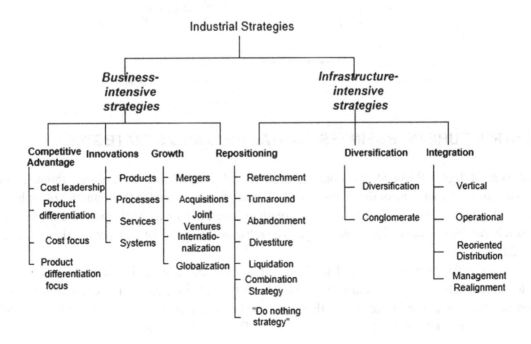

Among styles of management stand out those who engage in *clock building* versus those whose engage in *time telling* (Collins, 2001). Others want to transform a company from good to exceptional and still others want to develop a company that will stand the tests of time.

Figure 21 provides an example of the intentions and business strategies of the Singtel telecommunications company in Singapore (Targowski, 2003).

Figure 21. Singtel's Singapore business strategy (Targowski, 2003, p. 338)

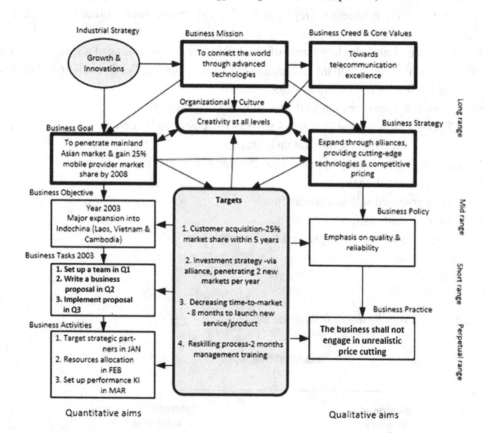

THE STRUCTURE OF BUSINESS' DIGITAL AIMS AND STRATEGIES

The network of digital aims and intentions is presented in Figure 22. It is the immeasurable and qualitative aspects of IT that control the efficiency of IT functions and situates them among other business functions. In practice, broad IT objectives are usually reduced to a measurable goal and strategy, i.e., a plan to achieve the objective. There are 16 types of relations between the elements in the network (see Figure 22).

Returning to the network displayed in Figure 21, on the left side of the network are quantitative intentions, and on the right, qualitative intentions. Each type of aim treats computerization differently. Companies that seek to become leaders in their field use IT as an accelerator for change (*clock-building*), not as a way of *time-telling*. First-class companies use IT in the following ways:

Figure 22. Network of digital aims and strategies

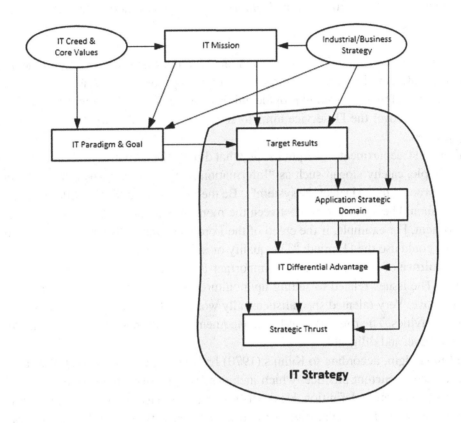

- To carefully choose applications,
- To pioneer new solutions if an IT solution fits well into a company's business philosophy,
- To accelerate change and not to measure the momentum of the entire company,
- To respond prudently and creatively to new challenges with new IT techniques, guided by the compulsion to transform and actualize the unrealized potential of the company.

Average companies respond to IT challenges with fear and end up lagging behind.

The **digital mission** of a company should explain the reason for the implementation of computerization *(raison d'etre)* in the company. It should reflect the direction and goals of a company's business strategy. A company's mission has the following structure:

- **Part I**: Basic digital mission, which is accomplished via the following:
  - *Supportive digitalization* of the company's core operations, e.g., PIS (CAD) and OIS (CAM);
  - *Fulfilment digitalization* of the company's recurring operations (e.g., the creation of automatically generated statements and account statuses by banks, which are often printed and sent by mail to customers);
  - *Strategic digitalization* of the core functions of the enterprise (e.g., the creation of an online application for customers who order on Amazon).

- **Part II**: Supporting digital mission, which may include the following objective:
  - ○ Automate employee routines and inform management about the evaluation of their performance.

The basic digital mission should be concise and clear, emphasizing how it shapes the activities of the company. This influential role in the company can be supportive, goal-oriented, or strategic. The second part of the digital mission should provide guidance at levels below critical business operations. In the bank example above, the IT service aims to solve the problem of what information should be automatically printed.

The creed of an IT department is the philosophy that directs the activities of its computer scientists. It should be a simple, catchy slogan such as "Information is power", "Information is without restrictions", "Friendly processing", "Defeat the system", "Be there", "Data quality" or "Information culture". Of course, there should be a relationship between the more over-arching business creed and the creed of the IT department. For example, if the creed of the Ford Corporation is "quality is job No. 1", then Ford's IT service could use the IT creed: "The quality of information is job No. 1".

The digital culture of a company is very important for the process of implementing the aims of computerization. The issues related to setting up a culture that supports the computerization strategy were discussed above. Very talented specialists usually work in IT services and cannot be managed by "policing" their activities. The right style of IT management is a culture that motivates employees to be productive, innovative, and diligent.

The digital paradigm, according to Kuhn's (1970) framework, can be thought of as a "model," or an accepted example of current practice, which includes laws, theory, application, and methodology. Barker (1985) gives a different definition. He describes a paradigm as a set of rules and regulations that (1) describe boundaries and (2) suggest what to do to succeed within those limits. A paradigm shift occurs when the "rules" change and, therefore, the means of success. In IT development, a paradigm shift introduces new principles (i.e., a new "era") of development. However, in some cases, two or more paradigms exist simultaneously because IT is developing at a very rapid pace. Over the past 50 years, one can recognize the following computerization paradigms (Kuhn, 1970; Barker, 1993):

- Offline internal enterprise paradigm (1950s): punch cards and automated routine processing;[1]
- Online internal enterprise paradigm (1960s and 1970s): online processing on the web;
- Internally integrated enterprise paradigm (1980s): enterprise resource planning with a common database;
- Agile enterprise paradigm (early 1990s): integrated product and operations systems (PIS and OIS);
- Informed enterprises paradigm (late 1990s): portals and the use of Big Data and other large collections of information, concepts, knowledge, and wisdom;
- Communicative enterprise paradigm (2000+): internet communication;
- Electronic enterprise paradigm (2000s): integration of all information processes through digital documents and online access;
- Mobile enterprise paradigm (2005+): wireless access of personal devices (e.g., smartphones) to a company's main IT system;
- Cloud computing enterprise paradigm (2015+): the outsourcing of IT systems and IT infrastructure either partially or completely to digital clouds;

- Virtual enterprise paradigm (2000+): an enterprise in cyberspace without physical premises (buildings);
- Hybrid enterprise paradigm (2020s): a hybrid solution that incorporates existing paradigms of computerization, including the use of artificial intelligence.

The next level of digital development will build upon solutions from the previous levels that are either still intact or have been improved or overwritten. Each level of development of the company requires new knowledge and IT skills. In addition, it requires a new approach to digital strategies. Companies that believe that their IT professionals are not ready for a new paradigm of computerization often look to outsource services. The relationship between paradigms and the missions of computerization is shown in Table 4.

Table 4. Relations between enterprise digital paradigms and missions

Paradigm Enterprise	Mission		
	Supportive	Fulfillment	Strategic
Offline	X	X	
Online	X		
Integrated		X	
Agile		X	X
Informed		X	X
Communicative	X	X	
Electronic	X	X	
Mobile	X	X	
Cloud	X	X	
Virtual			X
Hybrid	X	X	X

Table 4 shows how business strategies and paradigms translate into digital missions. For example, if a business sees computerization as only having a supportive function, then the Chief Information Officer (CIO) has seven paradigms to choose from. For a strategic mission, however, the choice is narrowed to four paradigms. Depending on the type of industrial sector, some paradigms can easily be eliminated. For example, in the banking sector, agile and virtual paradigms will not work. Thus, the choice will be between the two other paradigms and will depend on the existing priorities of the culture and governance as well as the available budget.

EXAMPLES OF IT GOALS DRIVEN BY DIGITAL BUSINESS STRATEGIES

IT goals are long-term objectives that usually take 2-5-years to accomplish. They should serve as markers for evaluating the results of the stabilized operation of a company. Goals are very often confused with "objectives," which are usually accomplished in no more than 1 year. To be technology-driven is a long-term "goal" that distinguishes digitalized companies from those with chaotic IT. IT goals should be in line with the chosen IT paradigm. Examples are shown in Table 5.

Table 5. Examples of IT-oriented goals driven by different digital paradigms

Enterprise Paradigm	Examples of IT Goals
Offline enterprise	Introduce the CATIA engineering design system within 16 months.
Online enterprise	Equip production workers with tablets within 20 months.
Integrated enterprise	Implement IBM Db2 database for the entire company within 24 months.
Agile enterprise	Introduce IBM CIM (Computer Integrated Manufacturing) within 30 months.
Informed company	Implement Big Data in 2 years.
Connected enterprise	Introduce extranet for all company partners within 3 years.
Electronic company	Implement DDS (Digital Document System) and WFS (Work Flow System) within 30 months.
Mobile enterprise	Equip field workers with smartphones that use WAP (Wireless Application Protocol) within 2 years.
Cloud enterprise	Subcontract data processing to enterprise IT systems with two independent digital clouds within 18 months.
Virtual enterprise	Negotiate a contract with Dior to design a summer collection of clothes and then with STYL, a sewing company in Bialystok; integrate the services of these companies and form a business headquarters in Gdańsk with IT systems.
Hybrid enterprise	Switch to hybrid IT systems within 5 years.

An **IT strategy** is a plan for implementing digital goals. To better define the components of an IT strategy, see the model in Figure 22. An IT strategy consists of the following:

- A list of expected computerization results and digital targets;
- A strategic domain for the application, which sets direction for the development of IT systems;
- A competitive advantage for computerization, which puts the company in a better position against competing companies in the market;
- A strategic orientation, which defines how to transition from the previous to the next stage of IT development.

Let's examine examples of defining these elements in an information strategy.

Digital targets.

The strategy should be explained in the language of measurable Key Performance Indicators (KPIs), which could be defined, for example, via a Balanced Score Card (BSC). This card translates a company's mission, goals, objectives, and strategies into four different perspectives: financial, customer, operations, and innovation. Based on existing industrial practice (Table 3), an example is presented in Table 6.

The Strategic Application Domain

Table 6. Example of an IT Balanced Score Card

Key Performance Indicators	Perspective			
	Financial	Client	Operations	Innovation
F1. IT budget, % from company revenue	4%			
F2. IT expenditure per employee	30,000			
F3. Profit from e-BIS	45%			
F4. Profit from internal IT services	45%			
F5. % of IT outsourcing budget	25%			
F6. % of IT budget for salaries and bonuses	40%			
B1. % of user queries answered without intervention				50%
B2. % of customers in the supply chain		50%		
C1. % of Suppliers in e-BIS			25%	
C2. Number of workdays in which IT managers meet with users			2	
D1. % of IT budget for research & development				10%
D2. % of IT budget for new devices and software				10%
D3. % of employees using AI				5%

The choice of the strategic application domain should be coordinated with the paradigm and business strategy. Tables 7 and 8 show a matrix of 11 IT configurations and four major business strategies. Table sections show recommended strategic application domains. Of course, these domains are just a few examples of theoretical directions, which could differ in specific cases.

It is clear that, in specific situations, the choice of the strategic domain of an application should be the result of a well-defined need for one domain rather than another and the company's ability to implement it.

Competitive Advantage of an IT Solution

If the IT solution is to effectively digitalize the business units of the company and management, it must perform well-defined functions within the practices of the industry. Factors such as fast application deployment, sophisticated application matrices, low cost information processing, user-friendly software,

Table 7. Examples of strategic application domain selection (Part A)

		Enterprise					
		Offline	**Online**	**Integr-ated**	**Agile**	**Informed**	**Comunicat-ed**
Competitive Advantage	**Diversification**	MCS	CAM	SCM	CAD CAM	Big Cognition	Extranet
	Concentration						
Innovations		CAD	CAD	CAD	CAD CAM	Big Cognition	WAP
Growth		TPS	TPS	SCM	CAD CAM	Big Cognition	SCM
Alliance	**Repositioning**	Smart phone email	Extra-Net	SCM	CAD CAM EXTRA-NET	Big Cognition	WAP
	Diversification						
	Integration						

WAP = Wireless Application Protocol

Table 8. Examples of strategic application domain selection (Part B)

		Strategy				
		Electronic	**Mobile**	**Cloud**	**Virtual**	**Hybrid**
Competitive Advantage	**Diversification**	e-BIS	Smartphone WAP	Tablet WAP	Tablet Smartphone WAP	Tablet Smartphone WAP
	Concentration					
Innovations			Smartphone WAP	Tablet WAP	CADCAM	CADCAM
Growth			Smartphone WAP	Tablet WAP	SCM	SCM
Alliance	**Repositioning**	Extranet	Extranet Smartphone WAP	Tablet WAP	Extranet	Extranet
	Diversification					
	Integration					

and more effective information quality can be used to distinguish a specific IT service contribution from a commercial software package that many companies use. IT executives may gain a competitive advantage for their company by emphasizing either internal performance or outsourcing, which can include planning, development, maintenance, data management, network services, and server centers. By focusing on all or some of these, it is possible to implement IT solutions that will meet the expected results of the company and its shareholders.

Strategic orientation modulates the course between strategic movements that are either too aggressive or too passive. Examples of strategic orientations that strongly support a company are the following:

- Application-oriented task strings:
  a) Legacy systems integration
  b) *Middleware* integration
  c) Integration of enterprise-wide applications

Figure 23. The digital strategy of Singtel Telecommunications Company in Singapore (Targowski, 2003, p. 351)

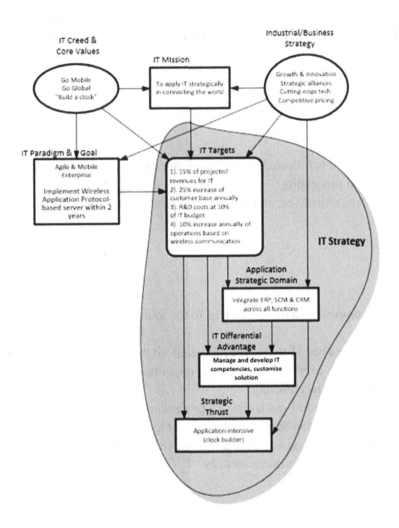

    d)   *Workflow systems*

    e)   Mobile integration

    f)   Others

- Intensive business support for the company:

    a)   Business Process Re-engineering (BPR)

    b)   Business Process Integration (BPI)

    c)   B2B

    d)   e-Market development

    e)   Cost leadership in IT tool delivery centers

    f)   Others

The determination of a strategic orientation should focus on the overall direction rather than small steps. The selected orientation can be seen in the company as offensive or defensive, with all the consequences associated with each. Leaders must select the orientation they wish to use.

Once strategic IT objectives have been defined, one can move on to the tactical planning stage and define the following (Figure 18):

- The IT Policy,
- The implementation of the computerization strategy,
- The IT strategy and policy management.

The tactical planning phase is followed by IT operations for computerization development projects and operational information processing.

An example of the goals, objectives, and strategy of an enterprise's network of aims and strategies is given in Figure 23.

SUMMARY

The digital strategies of companies in the 2020s lead to the following observations:

1. The development of advanced IT technology has enabled the implementation of 11 or more enterprise configurations, each of which requires rigorous implementation to assure computerization of organizational chaos in the company.
2. The head of the IT service must not isolate IT professionals from end-users, as this will usually result in the minimization of the service and outsourcing to digital cloud services.
3. The main aim of the IT service is to develop and improve the implementation of the digital strategy, which supports the company's business strategy.

REFERENCES

Barker, J. (1993). *Discovering the future*. Infinity Limited.

Collins, J. (2001). *Good to great: Why some companies make the leap...and others don't*. HarperCollins.

Kuhn, T. S. (1970). *The structure of scientific revolutions*. University of Chicago Press.

Targowski, A. (2003). *Electronic enterprise, strategy, and architecture*. IRM Press.

KEY TERMS AND DEFINITIONS

Balanced Score Card Approach: An approach used to measure and evaluate key performance indicators of a business.

Chief Information Officer: A company executive whose duties include managing and overseeing processes related to information processing and computer technology.

Cloud Enterprise: An enterprise computerization configuration that makes use of cloud services, such as cloud computing.

Enterprise Computerization Configuration: The way in which an enterprise uses and integrates IT technologies into their business.

Key Performance Indicator: Quantifiable measurements used to evaluate how a company is performing.

Mobile Enterprise: An enterprise computerization configuration that makes use of remote user access to centralized IT systems via devices such as smart phones.

Virtual Enterprise: An enterprise computerization configuration in which most employees work from home.

ENDNOTE

[1]   Years are approximations.

Chapter 13
Digital Healthcare Strategy

ABSTRACT

This goal of this chapter is to introduce digital strategies for healthcare. The chapter begins with an analysis of key indicators of public health and the healthcare sector. Next, the chapter presents key principles for healthcare, focusing on the constitution of the national health system. A case study focusing on Poland is then presented. After this, the chapter puts forth a digital strategy for the national health system. This is followed by an analysis of several health systems: the patient information system, the clinic information system, the pharmacy information, and the hospital information system. Next, the use of big data for healthcare is considered. The chapter concludes by putting forth a model for the national health information system and by discussing important trends in the development of digital health.

INTRODUCTION

At one time, 1000 years ago, human life expectancy was a surprisingly short 24 years. At the threshold of the Industrial Revolution in 1820, it rose to 36 years; it then reached 66 years after World War II and rose to 78 years for developed countries in 1999. This incredible extension of life expectancy—a more than three-fold increase—has been achieved thanks to the development of an economy that can develop medicine. Knowledge, including medical knowledge, has proved to be a great driver behind the development of civilization. It is worth noting that the developmental gap between the world's leader, the United States, and Africa is now as much as 20 to 1. What is more, in 1000 CE, the currently developed states (belonging to Western civilization) were more impoverished than those in Asia and Africa (Maddison, 2003).

Nowadays, citizens not only dream but demand healthcare services that effectively take care of them so that they can achieve their ambitious goal of increasing their lifespan. The foremost precondition for long life is, of course, good health, without which other dreams are hard to realize. 2350 years ago, Aristotle claimed that people are stupid because they do not know the purpose of their lives; thus, they cannot make wise decisions in everyday life. Well, at that time, the average human lived less than 24 years, and their goals were to survive until tomorrow, not be killed, not die of hunger, and not fall into captivity. Now many people live up to 100 years, but they are "worried" about what to do with such a long life.

DOI: 10.4018/978-1-7998-8036-3.ch013

The computerization of health care may help humans realize their dreams of longevity; however, before such a strategy is developed, it is necessary to consider what it should be so as to assure the strategy makes sense and that the expenditures incurred have positive results. Therefore, in this chapter, we will first reflect on the idea of what health services are worth computerizing. Then, we will deal with strategic solutions for its computerization.

A model of the goals of human life (MGL) is presented in Figure 1.

Figure 1. A model of goals of life in the 21st century (The Targowski Model) (Targowski, 2013, p. 56)

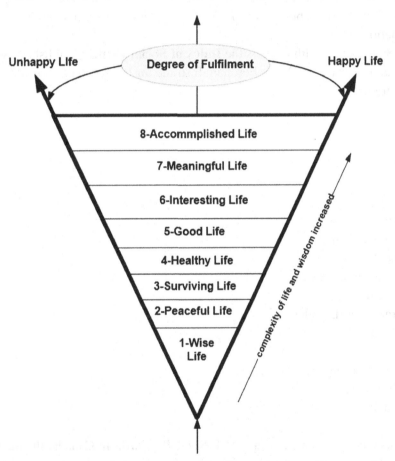

As the hierarchy of goals in the MGL model shows, living a healthy life, after securing peace, is the basis for achieving several advanced goals in life; however, one must be wise to accomplish these goals, and there are questions surrounding our conventional wisdom of life:

- Do people set appropriate operational and developmental priorities for their communities?
- Where do health services fit in among these priorities?

Patient health and prevention should be at the top of every list for the state and society.

INDICATORS OF HEALTH FOR THE PUBLIC

Economic indicators such as GDP, the Consumer Confidence Index, and more than a dozen others dominate the assessment of the quality of life. These indicators are calculated and published daily, weekly, monthly, quarterly, or yearly. There are also several health indicators, which are updated and posted in cycles every a couple of months (e.g., child abuse), annually (e.g., life expectancy), or even every 2-3 years (e.g., infant mortality and number of youth suicides). Only some countries calculate and publish health assessments for their societies. Without this type of comprehensive public health assessment, the evaluations of the state of the economy are misleading. Today, unfortunately, there are countries where the economy is growing steadily, but where society is collapsing. Can politicians be proud of their policies in such a situation?

In the United States, one health index is the **Index of Social Health**[1], published by the Institute for Innovation in Social Policy (formerly the Fordham Institute for Innovation of Social Policy). The index is based on 16 factors:

1. Infant mortality
2. Child abuse
3. Child poverty
4. Teen suicide
5. Drug abuse
6. School dropouts
7. Average weekly earnings
8. Unemployment
9. Coverage of health insurance
10. The poverty of the elderly
11. Health insurance for the elderly
12. Traffic deaths due to alcohol
13. Homicides
14. Distribution of food stamps
15. Affordable housing
16. Income inequality

Since 1973, this index has fallen, even with U.S. GDP growth. In Canada, the index has remained stable since 1985. This suggests that economic success is achieved at the expense of human health. Is it worth it?

The United States also uses another social health index, **the Genuine Progress Indicator** (GPI), which aims to change the dominant definition of progress from economic growth to quality of life (Hayes, 2021). The GPI places value on households, communities, and the environment so that their destruction and replacement is not viewed as growth and profit. GPI indicators include:

1. Unpaid work (homework, parenting, and care)
2. Crime
3. Family breakdown
4. Working from home

5. Volunteer work
6. Distribution of revenue
7. Resource exhaustion
8. Contamination
9. Defense expenditures
10. Long-term environmental damage (wetlands, ozone, farmland)
11. Changes in leisure time
12. Life of durable goods and public infrastructure
13. Dependence on foreign assets
14. Services (highways and streets)
15. Loss of leisure time (for dedication to the community, yourself, hobbies, relaxation, spending time with family)
16. Costs of car accidents
17. Underemployment costs
18. Costs of noise pollution and household pollution (disease syndrome)

Quality of life has deteriorated at a rapid pace since 1970. In the US, GPI has declined while GDP has grown. In Canada, while GDP has risen, GPI has remained steady. However, while the GPI index emphasizes economic factors which supposedly define "genuine progress", it does not include health-oriented criteria. Therefore, other indexes need to be considered.

The **United Nations Human Development Index** (UNHDI)[2], developed by the United Nations Development Programme, includes both health-driven factors as well as economic ones. The UNHDI is based on the assumption that economic growth does not necessarily mean human development or an increase in prosperity. This indicator measures the impact of growth (or lack thereof) on society and its people, not the economy. The ratings range from 1.000 (highest rating) to 0.000 (lowest rating). Norway ranked 1st (.954) in 2019, followed by Iceland in 6th (.938), Canada in 13th (.922), the US in 16th (.920), and France in 26th (.891). Poland ranked 32nd in the world with a score of 0.872 and is down 0.082 points or 9% in comparison to Norway (0.954).

HDI measures health, education, and income by the following indicators:

1. Life expectancy
2. Adult access to education and literacy
3. Years of study
4. Fair distribution of revenue
5. Control of resources indicators adjusted to reflect the purchasing power parity (PPP)
6. Health achievements
7. Gender equality
   1. 6. Quality of the environment, people, and resources and the development and impact of their changes on national income and wealth
8. Impact of global issues on the economy
9. Prosperity, quality of life, and economic development of future generations
   2. 9 Expenditures on pollution, health, floods, car accidents, etc.
10. Resources and production capacity of exploited people and ecosystems
11. Impact of economic growth on biodiversity

12. Impact of social costs and health costs on future generations and national income

Table 1. The UN Human Development Index (United Nations Development Programme, 2019)

Rank and Country	Index Value	Life Expectancy	Expected Years of Schooling	Mean Years of Schooling	Gross National Income Per Capita
1 Norway	0.954	82.3	18.1	12.6	68,059
2 Switzerland	0.946	83.6	16.2	13.4	59,375
3 Ireland	0.942	82.1	18.8	12.5	55,660
4 Germany	0.939	81.2	17.1	14.1	46,946
4 Hong Kong, China (SAR)	0.939	84.7	16.5	12.0	60,221
6 Australia	0.938	83.3	22.1	12.7	44,097
6 Iceland	0.938	82.9	19.2	12.5	47,566
8 Sweden	0.937	82.7	18.8	12.4	47,955
9 Singapore	0.935	83.5	16.3	11.5	83,793
10 Netherlands	0.933	82.1	18.0	12.2	50,013
11 Denmark	0.930	80.8	19.1	12.6	48,836
12 Finland	0.925	81.7	19.3	12.4	41,779
13 Canada	0.922	82.3	16.1	13.3	43,602
14 New Zealand	0.921	82.1	18.8	12.7	35,108
15 United Kingdom	0.920	81.2	17.4	13.0	39,507
15 United States	0.920	78.9	16.3	13.4	56,140
17 Belgium	0.919	81.5	19.7	11.8	43,821
18 Liechtenstein	0.917	80.5	14.7	12.5	99,732
19 Japan	0.915	84.5	15.2	12.8	40,799
20 Austria	0.914	81.4	16.3	12.6	46,231
21 Luxembourg	0.909	82.1	14.2	12.2	65,543
22 Israel	0.906	82.8	16.0	13.0	33,650
22 Korea (Republic of)	0.906	82.8	16.4	12.2	36,757
24 Slovenia	0.902	81.2	17.4	12.3	32,143
25 Spain	0.893	83.4	17.9	9.8	35,041
26 Czechia	0.891	79.2	16.8	12.7	31,597
26 France	0.891	82.5	15.5	11.4	40,511
28 Malta	0.885	82.4	15.9	11.3	34,795
29 Italy	0.883	83.4	16.2	10.2	36,141
30 Estonia	0.882	78.6	16.1	13.0	30,379
31 Cyprus	0.873	80.8	14.7	12.1	33,100
32 Greece	0.872	82.1	17.3	10.5	24,909
32 Poland	0.872	78.5	16.4	12.3	27,626
34 Lithuania	0.869	75.7	16.5	13.0	29,775
35 United Arab Emirates	0.866	77.8	13.6	11.0	66,912
36 Andorra	0.857	81.8	13.3	10.2	48,641
36 Saudi Arabia	0.857	75.0	17.0	9.7	49,338
36 Slovakia	0.857	77.4	14.5	12.6	30,672
39 Latvia	0.854	75.2	16.0	12.8	26,301
40 Portugal	0.850	81.9	16.3	9.2	27,935
41 Qatar	0.848	80.1	12.2	9.7	110,489
42 Chile	0.847	80.0	16.5	10.4	21,972
43 Brunei Darussalam	0.845	75.7	14.4	9.1	76,389
43 Hungary	0.845	76.7	15.1	11.9	27,144
45 Bahrain	0.838	77.2	15.3	9.4	40,399
46 Croatia	0.837	78.3	15.0	11.4	23,061
47 Oman	0.834	77.6	14.7	9.7	37,039
48 Argentina	0.830	76.5	17.6	10.6	17,611
49 Russian Federation	0.824	72.4	15.5	12.0	25,036
50 Belarus	0.817	74.6	15.4	12.3	17,039

The Bloomberg Global Health Index, published by Bloomberg media, measures a country's health (Miller & Lu, 2019). It should be remembered, however, that the state of health care is not measured in this calculation. For various reasons, the health care system is more often aimed at treating diseases than ensuring health and a healthy life. The Bloomberg index analyzes health in terms of factors such as life expectancy, primary mortality risk, high blood pressure, obesity, smoking rates, alcohol consumption, childhood malnutrition, sanitation, clean water, the number of smokers, physical movement, child malnutrition, mental health, and vaccinations.

Spain, with its Mediterranean diet and high life expectancy, is the healthiest country in the world, according to the Bloomberg 2019 Index. This year, five European countries were included in the top 10. Meanwhile, the United States ranked 35th.

What makes Spain the healthiest country? One of the likely factors is its universal health care system. Primary care is mostly provided by public institutions, specialized family doctors, and nurses who offer preventive services to children, women, and elderly patients and care for acute and chronic diseases.

Another reason may be the Mediterranean diet, which includes olive oil, vegetables, nuts, and fruits; moderate quantities of fish, wine, and dairy products; and low amounts of meat other than fish. Sticking to this heart-healthy diet is associated with longer lifespans and fewer cardiovascular diseases. However, to be sure, some say that it's not just about ingredients: it's also about a healthy lifestyle.

Figure 2. Typical ingredients in a healthy Mediterranean diet for Spain (Photo: public domain)

In terms of life expectancy at birth, Spain ranks first in the European Union and third in the world, behind Japan and Switzerland. According to forecasts by the Institute of Health Metrics and Evaluation of the University of Washington, life expectancy in Spain will reach almost 86 years by 2040, the highest in the world.

Other nations on this list include Iceland, Japan, Switzerland, and Italy, which fell from the top position in 2019. It is worth noting, however, that it is difficult to assess the health of nations accurately, and the results of indices differ because they use distinct methodologies. For example, the Legatum Prosperity Index of 2018 found that Spain ranked 22nd among the healthiest countries in the world (Singapore was number one).

Interestingly, both the Legatum Prosperity Index and the Institute of Health Metrics and Evaluations agreed that the United States is not a particularly healthy country - both ranked it 35th in health. Why is the United States lagging behind? One of the apparent factors is diet. Nearly half of Americans suffer from some chronic illness because of poor diet, including heart disease. What is more, two-thirds of American adults and almost a third of children are overweight or obese. This obesity epidemic is partly related to the prevalence of cheap and unhealthy processed foods; however, perhaps the worst American eating habit is the consumption of huge portions of food, something that can be seen in the increased size of tableware since the 1960s. Americans are also more likely to die from suicides and drug overdoses, the latter being more deadly than car accidents.

Poland in 2019 was ranked in 40th place in the Bloomberg Global Health Index with 70.2 points, losing to number one ranked Spain by 22.8 points, which means Poland has approximately 25% worse health. What puts Poland only 5 places behind the United States?—the same reasons as before: poor diet, drugs, smoking, and alcoholism (Figure 3).

Figure 3. The healthiest countries in the world according to the Bloomberg Global Health Index

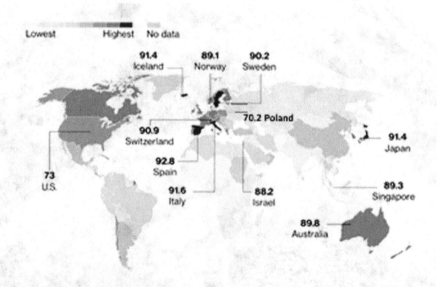

HEALTH CARE SERVICE INDICATORS

Healthcare is the maintenance or improvement of health through the prevention, diagnosis, and treatment of diseases, injuries, and other physical or mental disorders. Health care includes dentistry, psychology, nursing, medicine, physical therapy, occupational therapy, and many others. Access to healthcare varies depending on the country, municipality, and person, and it is primarily influenced by economic and social factors.

According to the World Health Organization (WHO), a well-functioning health care system requires permanent funding, an adequately trained and adequately paid workforce, well-maintained facilities, and access to reliable information upon which decisions are made.

Many people see access to healthcare as a fundamental human right. The lack of high-quality healthcare can result in a poorer quality of life and a shorter life expectancy than in countries with a stable and accessible health care system.

How is the quality of healthcare determined? Several factors determine the level of quality in each country. These include the following:

- The care process (preventive measures, safe care, coordinated care, and patient engagement and preferences),
- Access (accessibility and timeliness),
- Administrative efficiency,
- Equality of access
- Health outcomes (population health, mortality, and disease)
- Specific health outcomes of patients.

Health outcomes are health changes resulting from specific measures or investments. Healthcare outcomes include mortality, readmission, and patient experience. **Healthcare Access & Quality** (HAQ) estimates healthcare outcomes on a scale of 0 to 100, with 100 being the best result. Countries with the best healthcare systems in the world have scores between 90 and 96.1. In 2020, France is in first place, while Poland is in 50th.

In Europe, the most popular healthcare index is **the Euro Health Consumer Index** (EHCI), which compares European healthcare systems based on the following indicators (Björnberg & Phang, 2019):

- Patients' rights and information
- Waiting time for medical services,
- Results of treatments,
- The scope and extent of medical services,
- Preventing illnesses.

The index measures the "consumer friendliness" of health care systems. However, it does not attempt to measure which European country has the best health care system; rather, it creates specialized indices on diabetes, cardiac care, HIV, headaches, and hepatitis. The index shows significant improvements in healthcare standards over the last several years: In 2006, France was ranked 1ˢᵗ, with 768 points out of 1,000; however, in 2018, the same score would have received a ranking of 13ᵗʰ.

Switzerland. In 2018, Switzerland had the most highly ranked European health care system. Their system provides universal coverage and is subject to the Swiss Federal Health Insurance Act. There are, however, no free health benefits provided by the state. Still, private health insurance is mandatory for all people residing in Switzerland (within three months of residence or birth in the country). Health insurance covers the costs of treatment and hospitalization; however, insured persons must cover part of the cost of treatment.

Table 2. Euro Health Consumer Index 2018 (Björnberg & Phang, 2019)

Country	Rank	Country	Rank
Switzerland	1	Spain	19
Netherlands	2	Italy	20
Norway	3	Slovenia	21
Denmark	4	Ireland	22
Belgium	5	Montenegro	23
Finland	6	Croatia	24
Luxembourg	7	North Macedonia	25
Sweden	8	Cyprus	26
Austria	9	Malta	27
Iceland	10	Lithuania	28
France	11	Greece	29
Germany	12	Latvia	30
Portugal	13	Bulgaria	31
Czech Republic	14	Poland	32
Estonia	15	Hungary	33
United Kingdom	16	Romania	34
Slovakia	17	Albania	35
Serbia	18		

The Netherlands has universal health care, but the Government requires that all adults living or working in the Netherlands have basic insurance. The basic plan costs 100-120 €. If someone is employed, their employer will also pay a small percentage of the insurance costs. Children under the age of 18 do not pay for health insurance.

The basic healthcare plan includes a basic standard of care, such as visits to a general practitioner and a hospital. Some treatments, however, may cost a surplus, which would have to be paid for out of pocket. Many people also choose to get a higher level of insurance coverage for an additional fee, which covers treatments not included in the basic insurance package. To give an overview of some of the costs one may encounter, here are some typical healthcare expenses in the Netherlands:

- Basic insurance plan - 100 €
- One-day hospital stay -146 €
- Visit to the emergency room - 256 €
- Doctor's visit during regular business hours - 47 €
- Doctor's visit outside regular business hours - 92 €

Denmark. Healthcare in Denmark is mostly provided for by the local authorities of its five regions, with coordination and regulation by the Central Government. At the same time, 98 municipalities are responsible for nursing homes, home care, and school health services. Some specialist hospital services are centrally managed. The Danish Government's expenditures on healthcare amount to around 10.4%

of its GDP, of which approximately 84% is financed by regional and municipal taxes redistributed by the central Government. Because taxpayers fund essential healthcare services, personal expenditures are minimal and usually involve co-financing for certain services. Such expenditures are generally covered by private health insurance. It is also notable that the use of electronic medical records is widespread, and efforts are ongoing to integrate this data at the regional level.

Sweden. The Swedish health care system is mainly funded by the Government. It is universal for all citizens and is decentralized, although there are also private healthcare options. The health care system in Sweden is financed primarily by taxes levied by district and municipal councils. In the country, 21 councils oversee primary and hospital care. Private healthcare is rare in Sweden, and the private institutions that do exist operate under the mandate of city councils. City councils regulate the rules and establish potential private practices. Although in most countries the care of the elderly or those in need of psychiatric assistance is carried out privately, in Sweden local, publicly funded authorities are responsible for such care. The Swedish Government is trying to restrict private healthcare companies, and it is also taking precautions to eliminate profit-seeking in social work and public health sectors.

Austria has one of the best health systems in the world, and access to medical services can be considered internationally exemplary. The modernization program has a clear objective: the well-being of patients. The principle of statutory health insurance combined with co-insurance for children and non-working partners ensures that 99% of the total population is covered by health insurance. With the introduction of the minimum income system, its beneficiaries are also covered by compulsory social security. In the case of temporary incapacity for work, workers are entitled to disability benefits that occur in connection with a continuous payment of wages by the employer (employers are obliged to continue to pay salaries for six to twelve weeks). If the disease persists, depending on the employee's insurance history, the sickness allowance can range from six months to one year. The minimum level of monthly sickness benefits is 50% of the previous gross wage. Eight weeks before and eight weeks after the birth of a child, mothers usually receive maternity allowance corresponding to their current income from work.

France. Insurance for all residents of France is mandatory. The social security system covers 70% of the cost of treatment. All citizens pay to the state health insurance system, which is managed by 3 central funds. Rates are regulated by law and are charged based on a set percentage of the patient's or employer's income. One of the reasons why the French system is widely cited is that long-term medical problems are 100% covered by the state. With respect to other issues, patients initially pay a fee to the doctor or dentist, but they later receive a refund for this part. Subsequent refunds occur when a person pays for health insurance. All employees are entitled to plans subsidized by the company. This means that healthcare in France is one of the most subsidized and cheapest in the world. The government's insurance program is managed through the French social security office, where 70% of services cover all everyday healthcare needs, including general practitioners, hospitals, dentists, and pharmacy costs. Services for the elderly over the age of 65 or chronically ill are fully covered. To pay for additional services, such as chiropractors or long-term care in private hospitals, or to cover the remaining 30% of primary care, individuals can take out private insurance. They can either pay for it out of pocket or, in some cases, the employer covers the additional amount. Residents of France can sign up for a *mutuelle*, a non-profit insurance plan, or a private plan to get extra protection. Often, this private care can fill the gaps where people would normally have copays or where they would need to pay extra to receive scheduled treatments. If an employee is hired, they will automatically be covered by a plan in which their company spends at least half of the additional costs.

The Czech Republic has a health care system based on a compulsory insurance model, which has required employment insurance plans to fund healthcare services since 1992. The Czech health system is characterized by a high degree of decentralization and relies more on the market compared to other universal European systems.

The quality of healthcare also depends to a large extent on the expenditures it imposes. Figure 4 illustrates these expenditures in Europe.

Figure 4. Per capita health care expenditures in USD by PPP basket prices in 2014

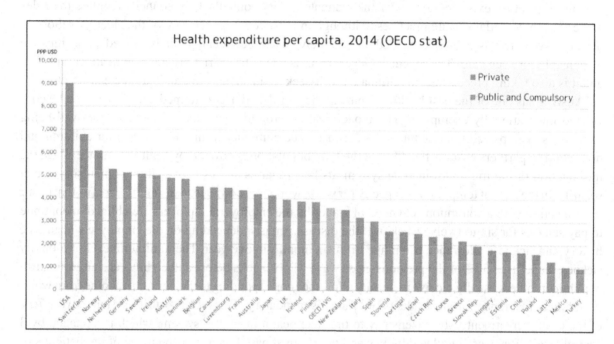

Table 3, in contrast, characterizes the profiles of selected countries in the EU and the US.

It is striking that the healthiest countries in the world, such as Spain and Italy, spend 5 times less on healthcare services per capita than the world's most developed country, the United States, whose population is struggling with health. The average health of Americans is close to that of post-Soviet countries such as the Czech Republic and Poland, where healthcare spending per capita is about 10 times less than in the US. This indicates that a healthy lifestyle is a critical part of the solution for improving the overall health of citizens.

Based on the characteristics in Table 3, the following observations can be made:

1. The health of society depends mostly on lifestyle and climate. When both factors are in their optimal condition, there are fewer sick people, and the result is less of a burden on healthcare services. This is shown by the following examples:

    a. Spain has the healthiest population in Europe (92.8), yet it is 19th place in healthcare services, which was evident in its problems during the 2020 pandemic.

Table 3. Health characteristics of selected countries in 2016-2019

Country	Health of Society Bloomberg Index	Life Expectancy	Health Care	CapEx %	Inputs w PPP euro per capita
Spain	92.8	83.4	19	6.4	1,535
Italy	91.6	83.6	20	6.6	1,847
Switzerland	90.9	83.4	1	12.2	6,917
Sweden	90.2	82.7	8	9.2	4,272
Norway	89.1	82.3	3	10.4	5,485
France	86.9	82.5	11	9.5	3,193
Austria	86.3	81.4	4	7.7	3,136
Netherlands	85.9	82.1	2	8.4	3,478
United Kingdom	84.9	81.2	16	7.7	3,874
Portugal	83.6	82.11	13	9	1,684
Germany	83	81	12	11.4	4,714
Dania	82.7	80.8	4	8.6	4,217
Czech Republic	77.6	79.2	14	5.9	978
USA	73	78.9	Not in Europe	16.9	8,643
Poland	70.2	78.5	32	4.6	510

Source: the author

    b.   Italy, like Spain, has a healthy population (91.6), but is 20th place in health care, which was also evident in its problems during the 2020 pandemic.

2.   Countries with non-ideal climates maintain their citizens' health with advanced healthcare services, as is clear from the following examples:

    a.   Switzerland has a healthy society (90.9), but due to its high-mountain climate, it must maintain high-functioning healthcare services (1st place in Europe). Moreover, these services operate at a very high cost—a whopping 12.2% of its GDP.

    b.   Norway also has a healthy population (89.1), but due to its northern climate, it also must maintain high-functioning healthcare services (3rd place in Europe). Like with Switzerland, this comes at a cost: 10.4% of its GDP.

    c.   Similar trends can be seen in between France, which has a pleasant climate and a light diet, and Germany and the Netherlands, which have a northern climate and a strict diet.

    d.   Likewise, similar trends can be seen between Portugal (a pleasant climate and a light diet) and Denmark (a northern climate and a heavy diet).

3.   Poland, on the other hand, must at least double its health expenditures from 510 € to 978 € /capita to reach the level of health in Czech society. This means spending 9.2% of the GDP on healthcare. Because of the unhealthy lifestyle of the Polish people and the country's northern climate, the morbidity of Poles is high and requires a significant and efficient intervention on the part of healthcare service. However, even if there is such an increase in expenditures, Poland will still lag far behind the countries of western Europe in terms of the health of its inhabitants and their life expectancy.

4. The current health of Americans (which is worse than the Czechs and similar to Poles) and the quality of healthcare services in the United States shows how, despite having high quality private healthcare, the health of society can suffer due to unhealthy lifestyles, such as those characterized by eating greasy foods for a significant portion of meals and by being immobilized for long parts of the day, continuously sitting in cars and offices. Also, 30% of citizens or more do not have health insurance. This is why the US healthcare system needs lifestyle flaws: to compensate for intensive treatments and expensive medications. This all costs money, but what is worse is that it does not bring progress, as is clear from the dramas caused by the 2020 pandemic.

PRINCIPLES OF HEALTH CARE: THE CONSTITUTION OF THE NATIONAL HEALTH SYSTEM (CNHS)

Health problems in some countries are due to misguided and hasty staff edits by politicians and staffers as well as quickly approved parliamentary laws. For example, so-called "Obama Care" (*The Patient Protection and Affordable Care Act* of 2010)—which contains 2,400 pages of text—was not understood even by its own authors. At the time, the Speaker of the US House of Representatives, Nancy Pelosi of the Democratic party, argued "let's approve first, and then we'll read the bill." And so it happened, and there were then and still are now many operational problems with this law.

Therefore, to avoid similar problems, it is necessary to first vote on the principles on which the health service is to operate in a concise law and then, based on such a law, proceed to the development, approval, and implementation of detailed solutions. Examples of such policies will be given below.

The principles of any health care system should include the following:

1. Human well-being means equal access to sustainable economic opportunities with minimized inequalities. It must be based on a sustainable environment that provides healthy food, freshwater, and air and activities aimed at a nurturing a culture that humanizes people's lives.
2. The well-being of citizens is achievable through human and social wisdom, which means prudent choices made in political, economic, cultural, and technological processes at all levels of society.
    a. In particular, political wisdom is essential because it affects entire regions and states.
    b. Human and social wisdom requires mentally healthy people.
    c. Human and social wisdom requires well-educated citizens.
    d. Data and knowledge are not wisdom but a prelude to wisdom, which consists of knowledge directed at proper judgment and options for solving problems. Wisdom should be taught in schools and colleges to make society healthy (Targowski, 2013).
3. Good health is possible if the lifestyles of citizens are wise and wholesome. This means that citizens must have smart and healthy lifestyles.
4. People will never achieve good health if they attempt to cure a lousy lifestyle through healthcare and negate preventive measures, including a healthy lifestyle.
5. The good health of citizens is a component of their well-being. In other words, well-being is usually an indicator of good health. Without prosperity, citizens cannot have good health.
6. Good healthcare should be a constitutional opportunity for citizens. Today, healthcare is expensive. If it made free, it will certainly not meet the high expectations of citizens. The choice is between the right and the privilege of having healthcare.

7. Seeing healthcare as a privilege can lead to a lack of social peace that state constitutions expect, so primary healthcare should be controlled by law. This means that essential medical assistance should be secured; however, its use should be monitored. If someone abuses it with a foolish lifestyle, it should be possible to suspend it.

8. The principles regulating the healthcare services should be approved by parliament and by a Universal Medical Services Basket (UMSB). How the system is controlled at the patient level should be decided by a national, apolitical expert medical committee operating at a National Institute of Health (NIH) appointed and dismissed by a Minister of Health.

9. The healthcare services should be funded through a universal health insurance (UHI) plan. On the other hand, medical services going beyond this comprehensive plan should be financed by private insurance companies. The idea is that patients should have a choice between medical services, the quality of which will result from professional competition between socialized and private health services.

10. The organization of healthcare funding should be decentralized because, as of now—being centralized in the form of a National Health Fund (NHF)—it is bureaucratic, crisis-genic, and resists innovation. Therefore, the NHF should be defined as follows:
    a. The National Health Fund (NHF) shall be nationally responsible for all funding and its normal uses.
    b. Provincial Health Funds (PHF) shall be responsible for the operational disposal of funds and constant improvement of the organization.

11. Within the UMSB, the financing of medical services should come from a National Universal Health Fund (NUHF), Provincial Universal Health Funds (PUHF), and the fees of employers and patients, as shown below (the volumes of expenditure are exemplary):
    a. For all health expenditures, the NHF should range from 8% to 10% of the GDP.
    b. UHI (Universal Health Insurance) should be 80% of the NHF.
        i. The National Universal Health Fund (NUHF) should be 75% of the UHI.
        ii. Provincial Universal Health Funds (PUHF) should be 25% of the UHI.
        iii. Expenses of employers and patients should be 20% of the NHF.

12. All legal residents of the country should be covered by Universal Health Insurance, while illegal residents should be entitled to emergency health care for a fixed basket of services.

13. The health service should be a mixed-ownership system. In addition to public health facilities, there should be private facilities of this type to assure that healthcare consumers have a choice and that there is competition in the services, which will lead to innovation and provide better quality services at reduced costs.

14. The healthcare system should have IT infrastructure and services that ensure (a) the security of personal data and healthcare facilities and (b) the correct, authentic, and accurate processing of information, with equal access to and responsibility for data, algorithms, and results. This is essential because it will be the most extensive IT system of the country and is too large to be developed by private companies, which the government would select based upon a request for tender without adequate knowledge and experience. The result of such a process would be frequent corruption, unreliability, and poor quality of information.

HEALTHCARE SOLUTIONS: THE CASE OF POLAND[3]

The health sector is enormous. In the United States, for example, it is the largest sector of the economy, five times larger than the national defense sector. The characteristics of this sector are given in Table 4.

Table 4. Characteristics of healthcare in selected countries in 2018

Types	United States	Poland	Comments
Number of patients	320 million	38 million	
Health of society	73	70.2	According to Bloomberg Global Index
Total health spending	3.6 billion USD	PLN 92 billion.	
Percent GDP	17.5%	6.3%	Poland-4.3% public spending
Number of employees	16.2 million	600,000	Poland-public sector 360,000
Number of doctors	950,000	140,000	
Number of doctors per 1000 patients	2.95	3.6	
Number of dentists and pharmacists	450,000	70,000	
Number of nurses and midwives	2.86 million	333,000	
Number of hospitals	6,146	957	

Source: Research by Author

Some attention should be drawn to the small number of doctors per 1,000 inhabitants in the United States. It would make sense that the *American Medical Association* (AMA) would try to limit the number of doctors to keep incomes high; however, the shortage can be explained in particular by the fact that medical students choose the highest-paid specialties, like dermatology and cardiology, or become surgeons.

Health Service Organizations

Health systems that are inefficient and prone to crises cannot be improved through gradual changes because of the so-called 'old bureaucracy apparatus', which effectively suppresses even the best solutions. New healthcare organizations will need to have a combination of old and new institutions, as characterized below (key institutions are given in Figure 5):

A.   The sphere of legal and normative coordination:
    a.   Old institutions:
       i.   the Ministry of Health and constitutional apparatuses of typical government administrations
    b.   New institutions:
       i.   The National Institute of Health (NHI), which will conduct research and development in the interdisciplinary fields of biomedicine and public health and will address challenges with respect to the functioning of health services. The NHI will also develop programs for training, education, and the improvement of medical staff in the field of a

smart, sustainable lifestyles. It will develop and modify the Universal Basket of Medical Services (UBMS) through the Commission of Medical Experts (CME), appointed by the Minister of Health.[4]

 ii. The National Commission for Health Quality Monitoring (NHQM), which will issue licenses and certificates and accredit national health education programs of a universal nature.

 iii. The Provincial Commission for Health Quality Monitoring (PHQM), which will issue licenses and certificates and accredit provincial health education programs in its territory.

 iv. Provincial Boards of Health Care (PBHC), which will coordinate the functioning of health services in its territory, especially the aforementioned services, as well as institutions providing medical services.

B. The realm of health care funding:

 a. New institutions:

  i. National Health Fund (NHF)

  ii. Provincial Health Funds (PHF)

 b. Old institutions:

  i. Private healthcare insurance companies

C. The realm of providing medical services:

 a. Old institutions:

  i. National specialized medical centers, such as oncology, maternal and child health, and others.

  ii. Private doctors, outpatients, laboratories, hospitals, radiology, pharmacies, rehab centers, and others.

D. The sphere of supporting IT systems

 a. New institutions:

  i. National Centre for Medical Digital Infrastructure (NCMDI):

   1. This will provide IT services to central health institutions through its servers and a national telecommunications network.

   2. It will create indexes for patients (e-addresses in the provinces), specialists, and specialized health care units.

   3. It will oversee the development of computerization at the architectural level of the NHIS (National Health Information System).

   4. It will provide standardization and certification for the components of the information systems.

   5. It will organize computerization trainings.

  ii. Provincial Centers for Medical Digital Infrastructure (PCMDI):

   1. It will provide IT services for provincial health institutions through its servers and a national telecommunications network.

   2. It will create indexes for patients (e-addresses in the provinces), specialists, and specialized health care units.

   3. It will oversee the development of computerization at the provincial architectural level of the PHIS (Provincial Health Information System).

   4. It will provide standardization and certification for the elements of the provincial

IT systems following solutions at the national level.
5. It will organize computerization trainings.

For Poland, the National Health Information System (NHIS) would need to be many times larger than the Social Security system, as it would affect 38 million Polish patients and 2 million foreign residents. A system of this size cannot be implemented via cloud computing by service companies that process contracts based on tenders. This system must have its own IT equipment and its own individual IT staff, otherwise it will be an unreliable and costly collection of "information islands" that do not serve users.

Figure 5. Structure of key health institutions in a nation like Poland

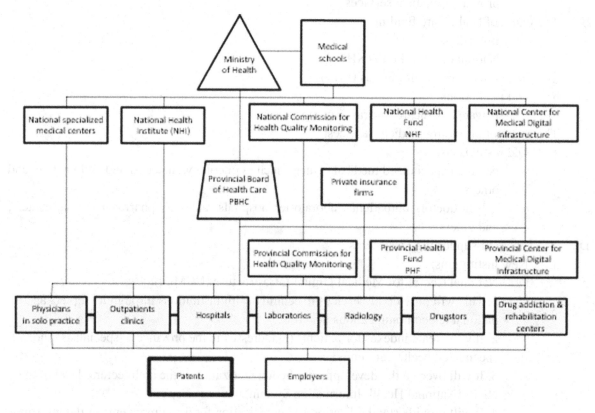

If healthcare spending in Poland were to rises to 10% of the GDP (public and private expenditures), then healthcare services should increase by 50% compared to 2020 (increasing to over 1 million employed). The new coordination apparatus, the PFZ, and the medical IT infrastructure centers should benefit from such an increase. In total, the new institutions should result in about an additional 3,000 employed professionals.

Universal Medical Services Basket (UMSB)

The general scope of the UMSB includes the following services:

- Preventive services, including screening, immunization, and vaccination programs;
- Hospital and outpatient care; medical services; hospital and outpatient medicines;
- Clinically necessary dental care;
- Some eyecare;
- Psychiatric care, including some disabilities;
- Palliative care;
- Some long-term care;
- Rehabilitation, including physiotherapy (e.g., stroke care);
- Home visits from environmental health nurses.

The size and scope of these services will generally be subject to local administration. Still, the Constitution of the National Health System (CNHS) should assure that patients are entitled to medicine and/or treatment approved in assessments by the National Institute of Health, if recommended by their doctor. In the case of medications or therapies that have not been evaluated by the NHI, medical education and rules state that doctors should make rational, evidence-based decisions.

Sharing Costs and Expenses for Healthcare

There are limited cost-sharing arrangements for services covered by a public guarantee. Payments out of pocket for general practices should be limited to certain services, such as employment or insurance exams and issuing travel or insurance certificates.

- For outpatient prescription drugs, the patient should pay a certain percentage of the prescription drugs (roughly 10%);
- Medicines prescribed in accredited hospitals should be free of charge.
- Dental services within the NHF/PHF should be subject to a fee of a certain amount, e.g., up to 1,000 PLN per treatment. These fees should be set at the national level by the NHI.

Direct expenditures on health in households should account for around 10% of the total amount of the overall health expenditures in the state. The most significant part of the out-of-pocket expenditures (about 40%) should be for medical supplies (including pharmaceuticals) as well as long-term care services, including residential care (roughly another 40%).

Human Health Safety Net

Persons exempt from prescription drug charges include the following:

- Children aged 15 years and under and aged 16 to 18 years who are full-time students;
- Persons 65 years of age or older;
- People on low income;
- Pregnant women and those who have given birth in the last 12 months;
- People with cancer, long-term conditions, or specific disabilities.
- Patients who need large amounts of prescription drugs: they should be able to buy prepayment certificates for 200 PLN for three months and 600 PLN for 12 months. Users should not incur

any additional fees for the validity period of the license, regardless of the number of prescriptions needed.

- Young people, students, pregnant women, prisoners, and those with low-income should not be responsible for dental payments. Eye tests should be free for people over 60, and for low-income and young people, financial support should be provided to cover the cost of corrective lenses.
- Transport costs to and from medical delivery points should also be covered for people with low incomes.

Restrictions and Exclusions From Universal Healthcare

- In cases of patients having bad lifestyles, such as smoking, poor diet, drug addiction, or alcoholism, the patient should receive three warnings and a set time to rectify their behavior, e.g., two years for radical improvement. Unless such corrections are made, the patient should lose a certain percentage of reimbursement for the costs of treatment.
- The UHI should not cover the costs of prolonging death in the last 6 weeks of life on medical machines.
- The costs of some operations, such as hip or knee replacement after 80 years of age, should not be covered with UHI.

Mental Health Protection

Mental health care is an integral part of Universal Health Insurance (UHI); therefore, UHI should cover the full range of mental health services. Less serious mental health diseases, for example, mild depression and anxiety disorders, should usually be treated by family doctors; however, people requiring more advanced treatments, including hospital care, should be managed by mental health companies or hospitals. Non-profit organization employees should provide some of these services. Policies in this area should aim at improving care for the more challenging conditions in the community and focus on assistance and early intervention. The overarching objective is to ensure there is "equal respect" between mental health and other types of health services. Usually, mental health treatment is underfunded compared to the treatment of physical diseases.

Long-Term Care and Social Support

The NHF/PHF should pay for certain long-term benefits, such as caring for people requiring continued medical care or qualified care. Local authorities and the private sector should provide most of the long-term care. Local authorities are legally obliged to assess the needs of all those who request it. However, unlike services funded by the NHF/PHF, state-funded social care in this area should not be universal. Except for time-limited "restoration" services as well as some modifications to equipment and homes (in some areas) and information services, housing and home care should be assessed for needs and resources. For example, full state aid for in-house care should only be available to people with assets totaling less than £100,000. A national needs assessment framework should be defined, but local authorities should be free to set eligibility thresholds for access to funds, which should gradually become limited in practice. Eligible persons are obliged to contribute, with some persons bringing almost all of the 'estimated income' (including those with pensions). Beneficiaries may receive personal budgets for the purchase of their care or may choose to have it organized by local authorities. Some additional benefits paid to users and caregivers should be exempt from testing measures, such as a 'participation allowance' with a fixed weekly value. The NHF/PHF should provide end-of-life palliative care for patients' homes, hospices (usually run by charities), nursing homes, and hospitals. Separate government funds should be made available to people with disabilities who are of working age.

How are Costs Taken Into Account?

Costs in the NHF/PHF should be limited by direct supply constraints and by a global budget that cannot be exceeded other than by cost-sharing with patients. NHF budgets should be set at the national level, usually on three-year cycles. The PHF should receive funds from local authorities and the NHF, which will closely monitor their financial performance to prevent excessive spending. They will be expected to achieve a balanced budget each year.

Existing cost-cutting strategies include freezing staff pay increases, supporting the increased use of generic medicines, reducing hospital payments, managing demand, and reducing administrative costs. In 2016, several tools enabled local buyers to maximize value by eliminating unjustified differences in use and clinical practice. Domestic buyers should competitively bid for certain services.

The cost of prescription (branded) drugs should be covered by a pharmaceutical price regulation program, including profits that pharmaceutical companies can make money from selling drugs.

DIGITAL STRATEGY FOR THE NATIONAL HEALTH SYSTEM

- **The aim of the digital strategy for the National Health System (NHS)** is to create an efficient and well-ordered system in which every year the health of the population increases by 1% according to the Bloomberg Global Health Index until the average rate for countries in Western civilization is reached. After this success and many years of effort, new goals will need to be set. Bloomberg's Global Health Index measures a country's health; however, it should be remembered that the index does not specify how healthcare is regulated and managed. For various reasons, regulations are often aimed at treating diseases rather than promoting health and healthy lifestyles.
- **The digital strategy's plan** for creating patient-friendly healthcare is supported by the following IT solutions:
  1. The introduction of electronic medical records (EMR) to the daily practice of physicians treating patients: In the Anglo-Saxon tradition, EMRs are made available to insurance companies and health organizations, including pharmacies which can use them for digital prescriptions.
  2. The gradual development of Electronic Health Documentation (EHD), also known as *Electronic Health Records* (EHR), and a Patient Portal.
  3. The introduction of the practice of everyday digital prescription.
  4. The establishment of a private Wide Area Networks (WAN) for the transfer of medical information about patients and companies, which should be common practice for authorized organizations that are members of the NHS.
  5. The assurance of common standards for recording and communicating e-information for all member institutions and companies of the NHS, based on the solutions recommended by the European Union.

6.   The creation of a common Medical Information Infrastructure for the NHS based on its national network, its metropolitan and local networks, and its own IT services to ensure the security of personal data and healthcare facilities.

7.   The assurance of the benevolent use of e-NHS by consumers of medical services and physicians providing these services, following the criteria of the *European Health Consumer Index*: This means that e-NHS should be particularly sensitive to the following criteria (each of which is measured by several indicators):

   ▪   Patient rights,
   ▪   Wait time for medical service,
   ▪   Results of treatment,
   ▪   The scope and extent of medical services,
   ▪   Prevention of diseases.

●   **The fight against inconsistent data:** The digital healthcare landscape is changing rapidly. A few years ago, when "digitization in healthcare" was equivalent to the implementation of IT solutions in hospitals, "interoperability" was mainly discussed in terms of electronic medical records. Today's healthcare has become more complex: thousands of mobile apps collect patient data, AI needs a common IT language to analyze information, and clinicians are no longer affiliated with a single facility and instead switch between different IT systems. The lack of interoperable systems leads to absurdities, such as having fully computerized hospitals send laboratory results by fax, post, or CD. To check all patient data, doctors need to switch between different systems and spend time clicking instead of taking care of patients. Imagine the American healthcare market with 600 different EMR systems produced by 600 software vendors. Similarly, imagine a world where each bank sets its standard for data exchange so that customers can only withdraw money from a specific ATM. We are all tired of data chaos. It would take years to replace or update all these incompatible systems, yet in some cases, this is the only way to improve. Meanwhile, governments should ensure that new tools such as mobile health apps meet technical interoperability requirements. However, technical, financial, administrative, and legislative barriers are only the tip of the iceberg. Social interoperability is a challenge that we must face with a strategic approach, which we can do by (a) establishing bottom-up initiatives, alliances, and regional networks, (b) changing the path to the patient as a data owner, and (c) enabling the reuse of scientific data. The General Data Protection Regulation (GDPR) has already had an impact on data sharing and portability, changing the long-term approach to data privacy in the EU. Connecting people is the best way to open data silos. While standards help, people need to lead the process of ensuring the interoperability of healthcare data.

PATIENT INFORMATION SYSTEM (PIS)

1.   **PIS's goal** is to quickly provide complete medical and health information to patients and authorized medical personnel so that they can provide biomedical and preventive services to patients and insurance companies online. Initially, the aim will be to increase the health of society 1% per year according to the Bloomberg Global Health Index until the average rate for countries in Western civilization is reached. At that point, a new goal will be set.

2.   **PIS** will be implemented via the following strategy:

a.   Gradually develop electronic medical records (EMR) first in Electronic Health Records (EHR) and then in the Patient Portal following EU standards in this area.

b.   Ensure the online exchange of patient information between healthcare organizations, which should take place on a private National Health Tele-Network (NHN) to ensure information security.

c.   Promote the use of the internet as the means for exchanging of information and sending emails between the patient and healthcare facilities as well as for accessing the PIS.

d.   Keep the PIS in one place in the province.

The architecture of the PIS is given in Figure 7. The PIS should consist of 3 subsystems:

- **Electronic Medical Records** (EMR), which are digital versions of paper cards in the doctor's office: EMRs contain a patient's medical history and their treatment history in a given medical practice. EMRs have advantages over paper records. For example, EMRs allows clinicians to do the following:
  ○   Track the dynamics of the patient's medical data over time;
  ○   Determine which patients are included in preventive or control reviews;
  ○   Check how patients are doing with specific parameters, such as blood pressure readings or vaccinations;
  ○   Monitor and improve the overall quality of care as part of a practice.
     Sometimes an EMR may need to be printed and delivered by mail to professionals and other healthcare team members. In this respect, EMRs are not much better than paper documentation.

- **Electronic Health Records** (EHR), which include EMRs but also focus on the patient's overall health: EHRs go beyond the standard clinical data collected at the medical service provider's office and includes broader insights into patient care. EHRs aim to go beyond the health organization that initially collects and compiles information. EHRs need to be developed to help foster the exchange of information between healthcare professionals, such as laboratories and specialists; thus, they must contain information from all clinicians involved in patient care. EHR data should be created, managed, and consulted by authorized clinicians and staff in more than one healthcare organization.

- **The Patient Portal**, which is a secure website that provides patients with convenient, 24-hour access to their personal health information. The Patient Portal will use a variety of IT solutions, e.g., it may remind patients of upcoming visits, the protocols required between visits, and recommendations for the treatment of diseases. The Patient Portal will make it easy for patients to send emails, search for information, schedule meetings online, and even secure information via text (the preferred method of communication for many younger users). The portal can also be used to organize and summarize user data from multiple EMRs and consumer devices, such as a fitness device. This will all be done in a way that is understandable to the average person, yet it will also provide detailed information, including the patient's medical data. For example, the portal will provide action plans for patients from their doctors as well as links to make calls and receive help getting treatment. The Patient Portal will also be used for management and self-diagnosis using artificial intelligence. In this respect, it is possible that the healthcare that would normally be provided in the doctor's office can take place in the patient's home.

Free Market Standards

While some governments struggle with the interoperability of medical data, the free market is able to find solutions to meet the expectations of patients. In 2018, Apple introduced a new feature for its iOS system: patients can download their EHR directly to their mobile phones. "Patients can collect their medical data from multiple institutions alongside their patient-generated data, creating a more holistic picture of their health," Apple announced. The connection between the patient's EHR and the Apple Health app is established via the FHIR (*Fast Healthcare Interoperability Resources*) standard. This solution helps to consolidate critical data, such as information about allergies, health conditions, vaccinations, laboratory results, medications, procedures, and other relevant statistics.

Standards such as FHIR, open APIs, blockchain, and cloud computing mean that the situation is improving in terms of technical interoperability. However, it is still necessary to pay for old sins and fix the consequences of the disorderly digitalization of healthcare from times when the fascination of new technologies outweighed strategies and standards.

EU Standards

Work in the EU on technical specifications for the exchange of health data has been carried out within the framework of the eHealth Digital Services Infrastructure (eHDSI), which has been implemented by the European Commission and the Member States through the Connecting Europe Programme (CEP). eHDSI connects the national eHealth contact points, enabling them to exchange two sets of health data: patient health summaries and e-prescriptions. The first exchanges took place between Estonia and Finland in January 2019.

The Smart Open Services for *European Patients* (epSOS) project, a large-scale pilot project funded by the European Commission between 2008 and 2014, carried out important preparatory work on the interoperability of EMRs. epSOS tested the cross-border provision of patient health summaries and e-prescription, which paved the way for the introduction of eHDSI. Several other projects supported by the Commission, such as Antilope and HITCH, have also contributed to the development of an improved European eHealth Interoperability Framework (ReEIF).

Health information about specific cases can now be exchanged abroad through one of the 24 thematic European Reference Networks (ERN). These networks enable virtual panels of clinicians to diagnose and treat patients suffering from rare, complex, and low incidence diseases. The ERN (European Reference Network) is home to around 900 highly specialized healthcare units located in about 300 hospitals in 25 Member States (as well as Norway). Individuals, however, do not have direct access to these networks: Healthcare professionals must direct patients to the appropriate network with their consent, following national health care system regulations.

A Handheld System for the Patient's Health

The elderly population is increasing significantly. According to the United Nations Population Fund (UNFPA), the global number of people aged 60 or over will increase to 2 billion by 2050 (United Nations Population Fund, 2012). Today, a significant proportion of older people suffer from age-related health problems such as Alzheimer's, dementia, diabetes, cardiovascular disease, osteoarthritis, or other chronic diseases. These common diseases, combined with the naturally occurring progressive decline in physical and cognitive skills of the elderly, prevent many from living independent lives in their own homes. Recent advances in communication and ICT, along with advances in intelligent sensor technologies, have led to the rapid emergence of smart environments. One such example is the so-called Health Smart Home (HSH) (Global Health Workforce Alliance, 2014), which has become a promising solution to the problem of aging populations. Such homes have the potential to provide eHealth services to meet the needs of this growing population. In particular, HSH systems monitor and evaluate the different health conditions that an older patient may have, and they monitor how well they perform their daily activities. These systems not only allow older people to live longer, but they also have the potential to make health care services more sustainable by reducing pressure on the public health system for the elderly as well as dependents and individuals.

Health Monitoring Systems (HMS) in smart environments are fast becoming a viable alternative to traditional healthcare solutions. HMSs aim is not only to reduce costs but also to provide eHealth services on time for those who want to maintain their independence. In this way, older people can avoid interacting with healthcare institutions (e.g., nursing homes and hospitals) for as long as possible, which in turn reduces pressure on the healthcare system.

Figure 6. Handheld Health Monitoring System (Photo:mpo-mag.com)

Wearable Health Devices (WHD) are increasingly helping people to better monitor their health, fitness level, and medical standards, providing more data to clinicians who can potentially carry out preliminary diagnoses and treatments. The technological revolution in miniaturizing electronic devices enables the design of more reliable and flexible WHDs, contributing to a global change in the approach to monitoring health.

Figure 7. The architecture of the Patient Information System (PIS) (HMS = hand-based Health Monitoring System)

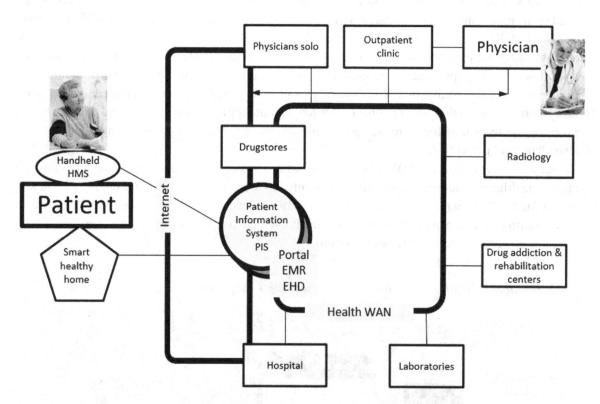

CLINIC INFORMATION SYSTEM (CIS)

- **CIS goal**: The goal of the CIS is to quickly provide complete medical and health information to patients and authorized medical personnel. This includes providing biomedical and preventive services to patients and insurance companies in a patient-friendly manner. The end goal is that the health of the population should increase 1% per year according to the Bloomberg Global Health Index until the average rate for countries in Western civilization is reached. At that point, a new goal will be set.
- **CIS Strategy**:
  - Develop a patient-friendly system for registering and scheduling outpatient visits so that the waiting time is as short as possible.
  - Increase the ease of information access regarding the results of laboratory tests and clinical recommendations to improve the effectiveness of treatments.
  - Develop treatment and preventive information about wise and balanced lifestyles to reduce the need for outpatient and hospital treatment.
  - Develop physician information panels (PIL) to strengthen communication with patients and increase the effectiveness of treatment and prevention.
  - Develop access to Big Health Data to improve the quality of treatment.

Info-Communication Processes in Clinics

In clinic visits, patients are first registered by telephone. When the patient arrives for their appointment, they are checked in, and they then wait in the waiting room until the nurse or the appropriate support staff calls them to the examination room. Here, primary information about vital parameters and nursing notes are introduced into the system. The doctor then enters the examination room, reviews the case and their history, and conducts a physical examination. The doctor might then order laboratory tests or other specialist examinations and may prescribe medication. The patient would then go to the laboratory to take tests, such as blood or urine samples. Next, the patient would go to the pharmacy, pick up their prescriptions, and after paying the bill, check whether they received everything they needed. There may be slight differences in this workflow. For example, a patient might undergo a small procedure in an exam room; however, by and large, the overall workflow will reflect the aforementioned stages.

In addition to replacing the paper medical records with digital records, EHRs will also replace paper lab forms and paper prescriptions. Ordering tests and medications will now be performed electronically by EHRs. Therefore, from the perspective of doctors, nurses, and healthcare professionals, outpatient EHRs should perform the following functions to create a viable electronic health care system in outpatient clinics:

- Clinical records, such as treatment and progress notes, nursing notes, and clinical notes, should now be recorded via EHRs.
- The creation of laboratory orders and orders for medication should be done electronically on the computer. This feature should include processes that check for drug interactions, duplicate requests, and so on. EHRs should be combined with a subsystem to introduce instructions from doctors and authorized persons into the system (i.e., Computerized Provider Order Entries or CPOEs). This will ensure that laboratory test commands are executed and that the results are delivered to the doctor. Ideally, it would also be connected to the pharmacy information system of the clinic (although until this interface is configured, printed prescriptions should still be issued).
- A messaging or email system should be created for sending and receiving messages, such as information about incorrect test results and communications between service team members to monitor patient care.
- EHRs should be well integrated into the practice management system to automate many back-office processes, such as running a clinic visit fee in the invoicing system after the doctor finishes an appointment.
- At a later stage, when dispensary staff become accustomed to EHRs and changes in their workflow as well as the electronic culture more broadly, EHRs will be ready for further improvements, and more complex features can be enabled, such as:
  - Clinical protocols and templates and be configured, such as a pneumonia protocol. This will help standardize interventions and treatments using evidence-based medicine (EBM) to achieve best practices.
  - Alerts and Decision Support Systems (DSS) can be configured to check for errors and improve patient safety. For example, a penicillin sensitivity test can be performed before prescribing penicillin injections.
  - Overviews of charts and results can be created. This feature will provide an overview of previous patient visits, laboratory results, and previous as well as current drugs a patient takes.

Some of the central clinic IT subsystems are as follows:

- Recording and scheduling patient visits,
- Electronic Medical Records (EMR) of patients,
- Computer entries of orders by doctors and other authorized personnel (CPOEs),
- Sending digital prescriptions to pharmacies,
- Decision Support Systems (DSS), which assist medical decisions such as testing or administering cures,
- Invoicing and billing patients,
- Invoicing and charging insurance companies,
- Managing accounting in dispensaries,
- Outpatient management,
- Hardware management,
- Medical materials management,
- Pharmacy management,
- Medical Information Panels,
- Management Information Panels,
- Email,
- Others

The architecture of the operation of the CIS is given in Figure 8.

Figure 8. The architecture of the Clinic Information System (CIS) (HMS = hand-based Health Monitoring System; CPOE = Computerized Provider Order Entry)

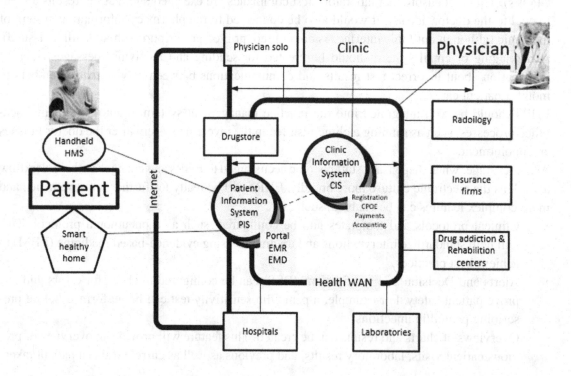

264

Pharmacy Information System (PhIS)

In the 19th century and even during the first half of the 20th century, the profession of apothecary mainly involved combining ingredients to form medicines. In the 21st century, the actual mixing of ingredients was practically eliminated from this occupation, and the modern pharmacist basically portions ready-made drugs according to the doctor's prescription. However, portioning alone does not meet current needs, and, therefore, a new role for pharmacists should be developed. The purpose of today's pharmacist must be expanded to include the concepts of pharmaceutical therapy, making the pharmacist a healthcare professional, not a seller of medicines in a "shop."

- **The pharmacy's mission** should be to provide medicines and other healthcare products and services (such as vaccinations) and to help people and society make the best use of them.
- **The main functions of the modern pharmacy should** include identifying, preventing, and solving problems related to the pharmacological properties of drugs as well as encouraging the proper use of medicines and promoting health and education. They should also aim to achieve better therapeutic outcomes through patient-centered interventions.
- **Models of pharmacists.** Pharmacists should reassess their workflow and delegation models in the light of new roles and responsibilities. Different models of current practice are (Toklu & Hussain, 2013):
  - The drug information practice model,
  - The model of self-care practice,
  - The model of clinical pharmacy practice,
  - The pharmaceutical practice model,
  - The distribution practice model.

These models have been practiced in the US and Europe either alone or in combination with one another based on an understanding of local pharmaceutical needs and pharmaceutical knowledge.

In California, new laws have created opportunities for pharmacists to take on advanced roles: they can now order and interpret tests related to drug treatments, conduct outpatient evaluations, and co-manage diseases. Today, the role of the pharmacist is evolving towards that of a clinical health service specializing in interventions and drug treatments.[5]

It can be expected that over the next 25 years, pharmacists will not only issue drugs but also provide individualized patient-oriented pharmaceutical services. As they find more time on their hands, pharmacists will have to prove their worth in the healthcare system in addition to portioning medicines. Pharmacists will need to provide drug management services (i.e., Medication Therapy Management or MTM) and operate clinics such as anticoagulant clinics and diabetes clinics. It is hoped that, in this way, pharmacists will help improve the quality of treatment, reduce healthcare costs, and improve patient safety.

- **The goal:** Provide quickly and friendly support for patients and doctors by supplying assigned medicines with a reduction in administrative costs of 1% per year.
- **Strategy:**
  - Use digital prescriptions and digital doctor orders,
  - Create a pharmacy site for patients so they can e-communicate with pharmacies to order medicines.

    ◦   Integrate the patient's pharmacy site into the Patient Information System (PIS), which is outside the pharmacy's IT infrastructure.

    ◦   Use the Pharmaceutical Decision Support System (DDS), which involves utilizing pharmacists in the drug therapies of a patient.

    ◦   Use Big Health Data.

- A model of a pharmacy's processes is illustrated in Figure 9.

Figure 9. A model of a pharmacy's processes

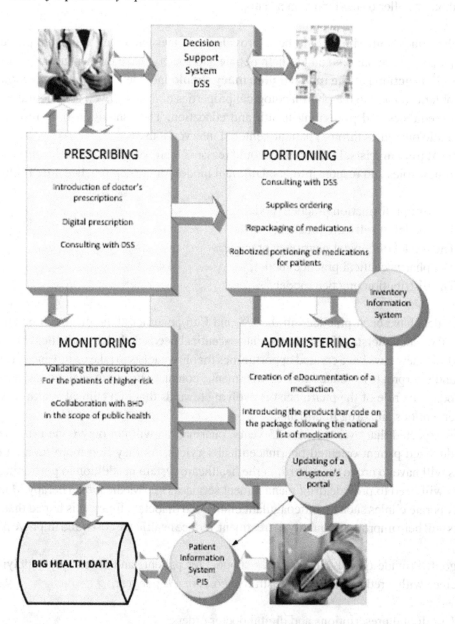

HOSPITAL INFORMATION SYSTEM (HIS)

Managing a hospital or university is one of the most difficult for all standard organizations due to the enormous complexity, specialization, and interdependence of hospital treatment processes by highly specialized and educated and, to some extent, independent medical staff. Perhaps for this reason, unusually large hospitals with several hundred beds and many treatment wards are not regarded favorably by patients. More specifically, there are three reasons for this:

• In American hospitals, the quality of treatment is only around 50%, that is, only every other patient is adequately treated in the hospital. There are, however, differences in the quality of treatment depending on the type of disease (Warner, n.d.).
• Workers sometimes have unfriendly attitudes and treat patients as if they were on a car assembly line,
• Hospital visits are costly, e.g., in American hospitals 1day (stay) costs approximately $2,500-$4,000, and with treatment about $16,000. This is because more than 30% of Americans do not have health insurance. In case of illness, they go to the hospital emergency room, which has a legal obligation to take care of every sick patient, including those who cannot pay for this assistance. The cost of this is borne by the hospital, which raises costs, accounting for insured patients.

For these reasons, hospitals are, to some extent, a problem for patients and healthcare officials due to endless questions and internal perturbations. Can an IT system improve hospital operations? Moreover, can a well-designed IT system fix a corrupt hospital system? Of course, there are many hospitals that have great reviews as well as those that are well-managed. Usually, these are academic hospitals, where the number of patients is smaller compared to others and where the medical staff is of the highest caliber.

An additional challenge is the independence of hospitals operating within the national health system. Every hospital wants to be an independent "fortress" with its own solutions, which it considers the best. There are also hospitals that, being on the verge of bankruptcy, are not capable of improving their organization, including their information systems.

In general, the hospital's IT systems facilitate the functioning of two kinds of activities:

1. The primary activity of providing healthcare to patients.
2. The secondary activity of assisting with the management of the hospital, including economic administration, hotel and restaurant services, and building maintenance and construction.

In practice, hospitals are composed of an outpatient system (in the form of specialized surgery, cardiology, oncology, and others), a pharmaceutical and pharmacy system, laboratory systems, a hospitality system (hotel and restaurant services), and a hospital-wide management system.

The IT system is intended to facilitate the implementation of the medical and hospitality processes and operations of the hospital. It is also expected that a set of IT systems and smaller applications will make optimal use of computerization to achieve the desired objectives in the following core areas:

1. Quality of treatment
2. Productivity
3. Effectiveness of treatment and handling

4. Appropriateness of treatment and services
5. Safety of treatment and stay
6. Privacy and confidentiality of information
   ○ **The goal of the HIS** is to quickly provide complete medical and health information online to patients. Authorized physicians should provide biomedical and preventive services to sick patients in a user-friendly manner so that the health of the public increases by 1% per year according to the Bloomberg Global Health Index until the average rate for countries in Western civilization is reached. At that point, a new goal will be set. The sub-purpose of the HIS is to reduce administrative costs by 2% annually.
   ○ **Strategy:**
     ▪ Develop a patient-friendly system for registering and scheduling hospital stays so that patients know what to expect and how to proceed during and after hospital stays. To do this, the Patient Information Panel (PIC) is needed, which should be integrated into the Patient Information System, which is outside the hospital system.
     ▪ Inform patients of laboratory test results and clinical recommendations through the PIC to improve the effectiveness of treatment.
     ▪ Develop treatment and preventive information about wise and balanced lifestyles to reduce the need for outpatient and hospital treatment.
     ▪ Develop physician information panels (PIL) to strengthen communication with patients and increase the effectiveness of treatment and prevention.
     ▪ Develop the scope of and access to the Medical Decision Support System (SDM).
     ▪ Develop access to Big Health Data to improve the quality of treatment, which should include the use of IBM Watson.
     ▪ Ensure the smooth online integration of hospital IT systems with other healthcare companies at the regional and national level as well as with Europe and selected countries based on national, EU, and international standards.

The HIS federation architecture is given in Figure 10, which contains the central systems. This model distinguishes between the patient and his public PIS and the patient in the hospital and his Patient Information Panel (PIC), which is only available to authorized users during his/her hospital stay.

Hospital system software packages are numerous. However, as a result of limited standardization, they differ in scope with respect to their functions as well as how they integrate with other systems. Many of these packages serve hospitals well; however, their main drawback is poor internal integration and, in particular, external integration with regional and national healthcare organizations. They are also often designed by experts in computer science for users with advanced computer skills, being unfriendly to the average computer user.

To achieve the stated objective and strategies, hospitals should develop the following critical IT systems and subsystems.

● Patient Management System (PMS)
  ○ Patient Information Panel (PIC)
    ▪ Registrations of sick persons
    ▪ Registrations of visits
  ○ Allocation of resources for the patient

Figure 10. The architecture of the Federation of Hospital Information Systems (HIS) with both PIC and PIL systems that help doctors and patients make decisions

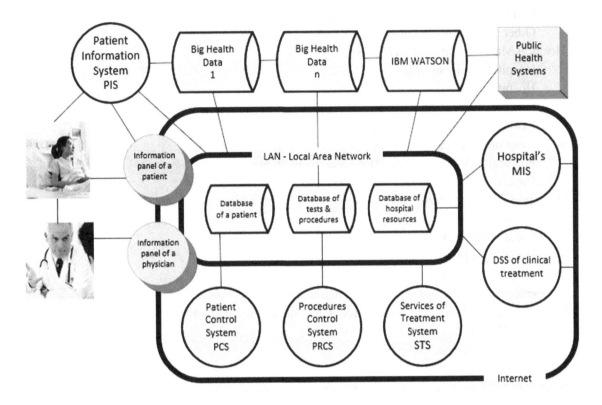

- ▪ Medical visits and scheduling
- ▪ Bed and equipment allocation
- ▪ Patient monitoring
- ◦ Charges, invoices, and charge control
- • Treatment Management System (TMS)
  - ◦ Medical Information Panel (MIP)
  - ◦ Treatment plans for patients
  - ◦ Commands and executions
  - ◦ Quality control
  - ◦ Clinical Decision Support System
  - ◦ Patient data
    - ▪ Medical records of sick persons
    - ▪ Test results
    - ▪ Mechanisms for sharing patient data with authorized users.
- • Treatment Services System (TSS)
  - ◦ Laboratory tests
  - ◦ Radiological research
  - ◦ Pharmaceuticals
  - ◦ Blood banks

- ○ Sterile products
- ○ Medical equipment
- ○ Food and beverages
- ○ Other subsystems
- Hospital Management System (HMS)
  - ○ Hospital administration
  - ○ Hospital staff
  - ○ Hospital accounting
  - ○ Hospital finances and budget
  - ○ Hospital supplies
  - ○ Physical facilities and operations and maintenance
  - ○ Others
- Hospital IT infrastructure
  - ○ Servers
  - ○ Local Area Network
  - ○ High-speed Internet access
  - ○ Hospital IT services
- Cooperation with external regional and national health systems
  - ○ Big Health Data at regional, national, and international levels
  - ○ IBM Watson[6]
  - ○ Public health systems

The most critical challenges for the hospital's digital strategy are:

- Applying national, EU, and international IT standards to ensure seamless cooperation with external IT systems at the regional and national level as well as internationally with Europe and non-European countries.
- Raising the health of society in line with the Bloomberg Global Index and close cooperation with public health systems.
- Developing friendly applications for patients, doctors, and other key HIS users following the European Health Consumer Index.

BIG HEALTH DATA (BHD) ANALYTICS

Big data in healthcare refers to the large amount of health data collected from several sources, including electronic medical records, outpatient clinics, hospitals, laboratories, medical imaging, genomic sequencing, payment records, pharmaceutical research, wearables and medical devices, scientific and statistical publications, news sources, and others. Three characteristics distinguish this type of data from traditional electronic medical data and public health data used for decision-making: (a) the data is available in enormous quantities; (b) the data can be searched for at high computer processing speeds and can cover the vast digital universe of the medical industry; and (c) the data can have quite variable data structures because it comes from many sources. This data is known by the abbreviation 4V Big Data – Volume, Variety, Velocity, and Value. Figure 11 provides a model comparing small data and big data.

Figure 11. Comparison of small and big data (Tan, 2021)

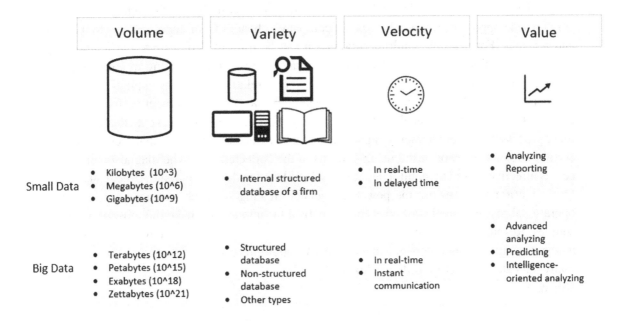

The use of BHD is applicable in the following areas of healthcare:

- **Diagnostics**: *data mining* and identifying the causes of diseases.
- **Preventive medicine**: analyzing lifestyles and social conditions that can prevent infection.
- **Precision medicine**: aggregating personalized data in a specific context for the treatment of a particular patient.
- **Medical research**: improving and planning new medical and pharmacological treatments based on extensive accounting data.
- **Reducing health risks**: using big data to detect treatment errors, including medicines and situations that commonly result in errors.
- **Reduction of treatment costs**: identifying values that result in better treatment outcomes for patients in long and short-term cycles.
- **Improving the social environment**: identifying disease trends, such as epidemics and pandemics, based on the following criteria: demographic, geographical, and social-economic factors.
- Others.

Methods for analyzing big data are evolving rapidly in the new-born discipline of data science and can, in general, be classified in the following way:

- **Descriptive analysis**: This is a simple statistical technique (e.g., a chart) that describes the contents of a dataset or database. Descriptive statistics include central trend measures (mean, median, mode), dispersion measures (range, standard deviation), graphs, sorting methods, frequency distributions, probability distributions, and sampling methods. The result of this process can be used to find opportunities for specific directions of treatment.

- **Predictive analytics** is an application of advanced statistical, IT, or operational research methods to identify predictive variables and build predictive models in descriptive analysis. The results here provide opportunities for a healthcare company to benefit from improvements to its products and services. For example, multiple regression can be used to demonstrate the relationship (or lack of association) between ease of use, cost, and security for accepting mobile payments by pharmacy customers. Awareness of the existence of a relationship helps explain why one set of independent variables affects dependent variables, such as patient treatment performance.
- **Diagnostic analytics** uses health data to determine the cause of certain events that occur in treatment processes or in epidemics. Diagnostic analytics extends descriptive analytics by asking why certain circumstances occurred using patterns in the collected data. The diagnostic analysis process is effectively used to monitor and forecast health and to detect and remove medical conditions.
- **Optimization analyses** use the power of decision-making sciences, management sciences, and operational research methodologies (mathematical techniques) to make the most of available resources. Resources are allocated to take advantage of the opportunities envisaged. For example, a hospital with a limited budget can use linear programming and decision theory models to optimally allocate a budget for different hospital wards.
- Others.

Examples: According to a market intelligence report by *BIS Research* titled "Global Big Data in Healthcare Market Analysis and Forecasts 2017-2025," it is estimated that big data in the healthcare sector was $14.25 billion in 2017. With an unprecedented increase in healthcare data, companies are using analytics, artificial intelligence, and machine learning techniques to reduce healthcare costs, increase revenue streams, develop personalized medicine, and manage proactive patient care (BIS Research, 2018).

Healthcare data is growing at a dizzying pace and, due to the falling costs of storing data, is projected to exceed 2,314 exabytes as early as 2020. Also, the emergence of cloud-based services and subscription models has reduced the initial investment and infrastructure development required to manage big data. The increase in adoption rates of wearables, health services (mobile), and eHealth services has further increased the amount of patient data available for research. A rapidly growing supply of medical information from a variety of sources can transform the healthcare system, reduce costs, improve patient outcomes, and help deliver value-based care. Examples of initiatives leading to the development of the BHD analytics are as follows:

- The European Medical Information Infrastructure (EMIF) aims to improve access to (a) the health data of around 50 million Europeans via electronic health records as well as (b) datasets of participating research communities.
- *Open PHACTS* is a platform for scientists and others who need access to pharmacological data. It was built in collaboration with academic and commercial organizations and allows users to extract information and make decisions on complex pharmacological issues.
- A division of the Dutch international company N.V. Philips has collected more than 15 petabytes of data collected from 390 million medical records, patient inputs, and imaging tests. Healthcare professionals can access this considerable dataset to inform their clinical decision-making process.
- In the United States, the National Institutes of Health has established the Big Data to Knowledge (BD2K) program, which aims to provide big biomedical data to researchers, clinicians, and others. Such initiatives will increasingly enable healthcare providers to improve patient care while

tackling the trajectory of unsustainable costs. The program will also provide scientists with a rich world of available data and information to prevent and treat diseases.

- IT businesses have made sure that health data is monitored. Consumer products, such as the Fitbit activity tracker and Apple Watch, monitor individuals' physical activity levels and can report specific health trends. The received data is already transferred to cloud servers, providing information to physicians who use it as part of their general health and wellness programs.
- Fitbit works with United Healthcare (USA), which rewards its insured persons up to $1,500 per year for regular exercise. Informed Data Systems' One Drop app for Android and Apple is making dramatic changes to people with diabetes. Meanwhile, HealthKit, CareKit, and Apple's ResearchKit use technology built into Apple's mobile devices to help patients manage their statuses and enable researchers to collect data from hundreds of millions of users worldwide.

Expected Benefits of Using BHD

BHD is pushing the scope of human knowledge almost to its limits in terms of what can be documented and computerized. This data is available online and can be rapidly accessed without having to leave one's home, office, laboratory, or dispensary. Below are statistics on the subjects investigated by scientific articles currently in press (Tan, 2021):

- Oncology – 53%
- Diabetes – 13%
- Pharmacology – 11%
- Cardiology – 9%
- Gynecology – 4%
- Alzheimer – 4%
- Personal medicine – 4%
- Ophthalmology – 2%

According to these statistics, the research is focused on the most dangerous diseases, the cures of which will significantly shape the health of individuals and society. The application of big data to these studies should have a significant impact on the development of the best therapies and prevention methods.

In a universal sense, the following values play an integral role in determining the health of individuals and society:

- **Wise living**: information and instructions about healthy lifestyles should involve healthcare consumers in self-diagnosis and self-treatment, relieving healthcare systems from having to provide services that consumers can provide themselves.
- **Smart healthcare**: a personalized case record and trends in prevention and treatment should lead to an increase in life expectancy and in life quality and satisfaction.
- **Wise preventions and treatments**: detailed records based on BHD should give patients and healthcare providers the best options to choose from.
- **Wise values**: broad knowledge of how to live, prevent, and treat health conditions should lead to sustainable lifestyles and reduce the cost of healthcare while increasing its quality.

- **Smart innovation**: broad knowledge and being able to draw connections in data should lead to the development of intelligent innovations in prevention and treatment.

Data Aggregation Issues.

Patient data and financial data are often spread across multiple payers, hospitals, administrative offices, government agencies, servers, and physical file systems. Putting this together and determining whether all data producers will work together in the future when new big data is created requires a lot of planning and harmonious cooperation. In addition, each participating organization must understand and agree on the types and formats of the big data they intend to analyze. In addition to the format in which the data is stored (paper, film, traditional databases, EHR, and EMR, etc.), the accuracy and quality of such data should be determined. This requires not only data cleaning (usually a mostly manual process), but also a review of data management: has the data been appropriately recorded, or did errors occur, perhaps for many years?

As for the formats of big data, their statistics are as follows (Tan, 2021):

- Radiological film – 16%
- Genetic spanking – 10%
- EHR and EMR – 4%
- Pharmacological data – 3%
- Behavioral data 3%
- Others

Intellectual Property in BHD

Traditional intellectual property safeguards for healthcare data may not work for big data innovations, and recent developments are causing licensing problems for these technologies. In the same way that source codes are critical for software innovation, the training data on which predictive models are based can also be fundamental to the development of machine learning techniques. The databases containing such data, therefore, have significant value in themselves.

One of the most appropriate types of protection for intellectual property is the concept of database rights introduced by the EU Databases Directive. This directive provides database owners with the power to prevent unauthorized copying or extraction of data from their databases in the European Economic Area (EEA). Any intellectual property license that includes database rights licensing must adhere to this agreement. One option, if circumstances permit, is to use related rights, such as copyrights and confidential information rights. Correctly formulating licenses and controlling the information exchanged under the licenses may be necessary to safeguard against a loss of control of this valuable intellectual property (Leach, 2020).

Problems With the Development of BHD

The development of BHD is a challenge for biomedical, health, and business organizations. Typically, in terms of general data, businesses like Google, Facebook, and Microsoft are faster and more efficient than organizations dealing with public data and professional knowledge. In the case of the former, "everything about everything" is poured into one digital bag; however, in the case of the BHD, it is different because, in order for biomedical data to be reliable, the knowledge of biomedical specialists must be taken into account, especially since health issues are often specific to geographical regions and ethnic groups. However, much of this issue is universal. Nothing good will come to be if BHD relies solely on mathematicians to analyze biomedical data. Of course, the involvement of mathematicians in this process is necessary; however, they should not have the leading role for this project.

Therefore, state health authorities must play a role in organizing the architecture of national BHD repositories, which should include access to international BHD repositories with translation interfaces. Otherwise, even ambitious bottom-up initiatives will lead to the development of incomplete and isolated solutions both nationally and globally.

NATIONAL HEALTH INFORMATION SYSTEM (NHIS)

- **The goal of the NHIS**: quickly provide complete biomedical and health information to citizens, patients, and authorized medical personnel running biomedical and preventive services as well as healthcare facilities and insurance companies in a patient-friendly and user-friendly manner so that the health of the public increases 1% per year according to the Bloomberg Global Health Index until the average rate for countries of Western civilization is reached. At that point, there a new goal will be set. A secondary purpose of the NHIS is to reduce administrative costs by 2% annually.
- **Strategy**:
  - Develop a health information system that provides top-down assurance regarding the integrity and coherence of all healthcare facilities following common IT technology standards and taking into account EU and international standards.
  - Design and operate IT systems for biomedical services in a consumer-friendly manner, following the European Health Consumer Index.
  - Design the NHIS to operate in both national and provincial infrastructures to ensure:
    - security of personal and organizational data,
    - reliability of operations,
    - the authenticity of data and reports,
    - equal access to authorized users,
    - proper functioning of the network and systems,
    - legal responsibility for the operation of networks and systems.
  - Develop and operate national coverage networks (wide area networks or WAN) and, where justified, metropolitan area networks (MAN).
  - Develop national and provincial IT services to ensure the development of information systems and to promote best practices.
  - Ensure that national and provincial IT services provide training and professional development for users and IT professionals in healthcare.

The NHIS architecture (Figure 12) is composed of the following IT systems:

- Level of service provision:

- ○ Patient IS, Clinic IS, Laboratory IS, Drugstores IS, Hospital IS, and others
- Level of provincial health management:
  - ○ Provincial Health Fund IS, Provincial Complex of Patient IS(s), Provincial Locator of Patients, Biomedical Specialists, Medical Centers, and Regional BHD
- Level of national health management:
  - ○ National Health Fund IS, Provincial Locator of Patients, Biomedical Specialists, Health Centers, and National BHD
  - ○ Public health systems
  - ○ Entries to international BHD and IBM Watson

Figure 12. The architecture of the National Health Information System (NHIS) with key systems

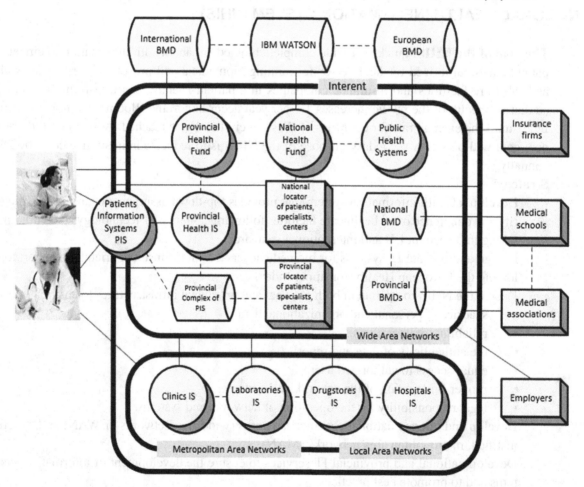

The practice of digital health services in most countries has been lively and bottom-up. Thus, it does not consist of a coherent whole that has been systematically computerized. For this reason, it is expensive, unreliable, and does not support strategies aimed at raising the health of individuals and society.

An attempt to comprehensively develop an integrated NHIS took place in the United States between 2008 and 2016 and was related to the implementation of so-called "Obama Care". This approach aimed to reduce the bureaucracy of health services and reduce operating costs. On the assumption that the "market" would introduce the best solutions, each of the 50 states was divided into 10 sections, and in each section, individual IT systems of the NHIS were launched. It contained no master plan nor established requirements and systematic patterns. The initiative was met with active interest from thousands of IT service companies that believed it to be a good opportunity. Service companies won bids and began to spontaneously design and start NHIS systems and subsystems from the bottom up. The release for this project is about 10 years ago; however, such a system was not built. The project failed.

Therefore, the most extensive system of the state, where every resident is a user, must be developed from the top with bottom-up implementation, just as a country's highway system is designed: there are intersections in the right places, and it cover the most important transportation routes.

TRENDS IN THE DEVELOPMENT OF DIGITAL HEALTH[7]

1. Gradually, there should be increases in corporate social responsibility through citizenship programs that combat homelessness, suicide, the opioid crisis, and other social problems that affect health.

2. Increases in consolidating private (competing) health facilities into large organizations should entail a larger accumulation of funds as well as more effective uses in projects, leading to better quality healthcare services.

3. Personalized medicine and population health, two seemingly opposed approaches to healthcare, will begin working together to improve outcomes in some countries of Western civilization.

4. The path to a healthier nation will be accelerated by addressing both the unique needs of the individual as well as problems common to people with similar demographics. For example, health systems should use genomics to determine a person's biological age to tailor medical intervention for a specific person. At the same time, large healthcare providers should coordinate care and resources across a wide range of people through stages such as cancer screenings and improved access to housing and nutrition. The combination of the strength of these two disciplines will dramatically help improve the health of the nation.

5. There should be increased relations with ICT technology companies to use digital "gatekeepers" to monitor the health of users via handheld health sensors.

6. Machine learning and artificial intelligence will increase the potential for breakthroughs in medicine and care, and data will be vital for such innovations; however, whether technology companies prioritize the well-being of patients remains an unresolved question for the global public. Patients will try to ensure that their service providers speak out and advocate for the protection of their health information. We should expect suppliers to defend privacy and data security and to lead the way in responsible uses of data for the common good. At the same time, big technology companies will be committed to selling patient health data to marketing companies.

7. The race for voice-activated technology in healthcare will continue to grow and will be a central feature of the hospital and clinic in the future. Just as Alexa and Siri are changing the way we live in our home, voice processing and natural language are the future of healthcare. Innovation around smart clinics and hospitals is expected to accelerate, making it easier for clinicians to treat and care for patients. Voice commands that process and analyze information will help patients make

clinical decisions at their bedside and in the exam room. Microsoft is currently working with select healthcare facilities to create a "care center of the future", where clinical communication and voice activation technology will play central roles.

8. Simplifying electronic medical records will become a cry of despair for doctors. As burnout increases among doctors, nurses, and other caregivers, reducing the time needed to record electronic medical records will be crucial to improving the working environment for doctors. Moving the national discussion from EHR *interoperability* to *usability* will require more urgent action. Simplified, more intuitive EHRs mean that clinicians can spend less time on the computer and more time directly with patients, providing a better experience for the patients they serve.

9. Healthcare professionals will continue to develop their digital skills and adopt new skill sets. At the same time, biomedical talent shortages will become more pronounced. Clinicians will also have to manage social determinants more fluently and take care of the whole person, not only physically, but also mentally and emotionally. Private health systems will strive to remain competitive in a difficult labor market by offering attractive pay and benefits packages. Commitment to investing in education and career development as well as creating engaging work environments will also be vital in maintaining and recruiting the best talent and keeping them in the country where they have been educated.

10. The current model of health care is undeniably unsustainable for many essential reasons. The burden of an aging population is at the top of the list. The proportion of older people (aged 60 and over) will grow. In contrast, the working adult population, which will support this older population, is predicted to remain constant or even shrink after 2020 due to uncontrolled automation and the robotization of the economy. Dr. Eric Topol (2015) gives concrete examples of how this is happening now and how it will proceed in the future in treatment. His examples include wearables, portable smartphone-based X-rays, and "Uber.doc," a concept that, like a car service, provides on-demand medication with doctor visits. Topol promotes technology to improve healthcare, where "[t]he patient will see you now: the future of medicine is in your hands." That is, diagnostics and monitoring of health are in the hands of the patient. The doctor only consults, although he or she will still have a decisive voice in treatment. Such consultations may occur via telemedicine (Figure 13). While such solutions are possible, it is doubtful that they will be applied relatively soon on a society-wide scale (except, perhaps, for small countries such as Luxembourg or Liechtenstein). Currently, this type of treatment solution in larger countries will lead to the medical exclusion of a significant proportion of the population.

SUMMARY

1. Because of the economic progress of the 21st century as well as the development of e-informing and the pandemic of 2020, the media and society are starting to pay close attention to their health and the health of society. This is leading to critical analyses of healthcare in the study of national health policies (especially insurance) and healthcare efficiency. Individual health challenges are becoming significant issues addressed in national politics in many countries, especially in the United States and Poland. This is why there is a need to develop optimal models of human and public health. There are many solutions in this regard, especially in Western civilization, but few

Figure 13. Model of self-treatment in the future (Topol, 2015, p. 179)

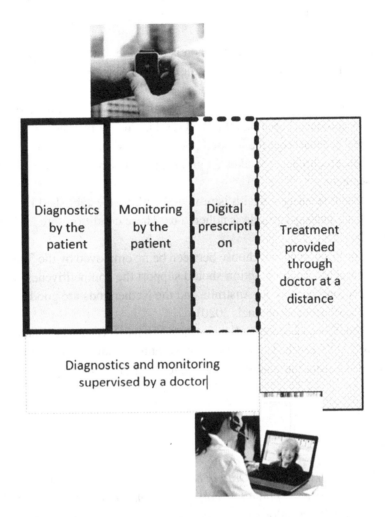

are content with those that have been thus far proposed and developed. This is because such health systems have not been designed holistically; rather, they are a patchwork of partial solutions that address problems only in certain countries or localized areas. However, they are not solutions that can be uncritically adopted by other countries.

2. The strategy for computerizing the National Health System should include support to assure that the systems are well designed and positively evaluated by consumers of biomedical services. This is because (a) computerization can perpetuate inadequate systems of healthcare, (b) unique aspects of personal healthcare are expensive, and (c) various negative factors may make solutions difficult if not impossible.

3. History thus far has shown that one's health is very much determined by having a wise, sustainable lifestyle and living in good climates (e.g., Spain and Italy). In addition, health depends on the wisdom and efforts of preventive methods. If these efforts fail, then the onus of curing society falls on the healthcare system, which will be costly and can only be afforded by the wealthiest countries and individuals. This will lead the less affluent to fall into a cycle of sickness.

4. Developing a NHIS in countries that aim for holistic solutions should be done in two steps. First, the rules of this system should be legally approved. Then, and only then, should the solutions be designed and implemented.

5. It seems that the one universal NHS in Canada is the pride of this country, but it is known for its inefficiency. Therefore, it can be proposed the following assumptions for improvements to the existing NHS:

   a. In a country, the NHS should consist of universal and private insurance systems, which should complement and ensure that healthcare should including the choice of doctor, hospital, and other medical services that the insured person wishes and can afford.

   b. The Universal Health Service takes for granted that state health care is based on citizens' right to social security.

   c. Universal social security – health is provided within an established basket of basic services provided that a healthy lifestyle is adhered to. These conditions are laid down by the parliamentary act.

   d. Healthcare professionals can choose between being employed by the State and being an independent contractor. Such an option should support the competitiveness of medical services.

   e. Systems operating in the UK, Australia and the Netherlands are good examples for adapting foreign NHS solutions (Emanuel, 2020).

6. Since the digital NHIS of a country will be its most extensive system, it should be based on its own IT infrastructure and IT services to ensure the continuity of solutions and the security of personal data. This will also ensure the quality of data, algorithms, and information.

REFERENCES

BIS Research. (2018, March). *Global Big Data in healthcare market: Analysis and forecast, 2017-2025 (focus on components and services, applications, competitive landscape and country analysis)*. https://www.reportbuyer.com/product/5370183/global-big-data-in-healthcare-market-analysis-and-forecast-2017-2025-focus-on-components-and-services-applications-competitive-landscape-and-country-analysis.html

Björnberg, A., & Phang, A. Y. (2019). *Euro Health Consumer Index: 2018 report*. Health Consumer Powerhouse. https://healthpowerhouse.com/media/EHCI-2018/EHCI-2018-report.pdf

Emanuel, E. J. (2020). *Which country has the world's best health care?* Public Affairs.

Global Health Workforce Alliance. (2014). *A universal truth: No health without a workforce*. World Health Organization. https://www.who.int/workforcealliance/knowledge/resources/GHWA-a_universal_truth_report.pdf?ua=1

Hayes, A. (2021, April 5). Genuine Progress Indicator (GPI). *Investopedia*. https://www.investopedia.com/terms/g/gpi.asp

Hochman, R. (2019, December 17). 10 health care trends to watch in 2020. *Providence*. https://blog.providence.org/blog-2/10-health-care-trends-to-watch-in-2020

Leach, S. (2020, February 17). From big data to database rights: The role of technology in the future of healthcare. *Open Access Government*. https://www.openaccessgovernment.org/database-rights-healthcare/82580/

Maddison, A. (2003). *The world economy*. OECD. doi:10.1787/9789264104143-en

Miller, L. J., & Wei, L. (2019, February 24). These are the world's healthiest nations. *Bloomberg*. https://www.bloomberg.com/news/articles/2019-02-24/spain-tops-italy-as-world-s-healthiest-nation-while-u-s-slips

Tan, J. (2021). *Adaptive health management information systems: Concepts, cases, and practical applications*. Jones & Bartlett Learning.

Targowski, A. (2013). *Harnessing the power of wisdom*. NOVA Science Publishers.

Toklu, H. Z., & Hussain, A. (2013). The changing face of pharmacy practice and the need for a new model of pharmacy education. *Journal of Young Pharmacists*, *5*(2), 38–40. doi:10.1016/j.jyp.2012.09.001 PMID:24023452

Topol, E. J. (2015). *The patient will see you now: The future of medicine is in your hands*. Basic Books.

United Nations Development Programme. (2019). *Human development report 2019*. AGS. http://hdr.undp.org/sites/default/files/hdr2019.pdf

United Nations Population Fund. (2012). *Aging in the twenty-first century: A celebration and a challenge*. HelpAge International. https://www.unfpa.org/sites/default/files/pub-pdf/Ageing%20report.pdf

Warner, J. (n.d.). Hospital care: Does your state rate? *WebMD*. https://www.webmd.com/a-to-z-guides/features/state-hospital-care-rated

KEY TERMS AND DEFINITIONS

Electronic Health Records: Health records that, in addition to containing a patient's electronic medical record, also contain information about the patient's overall health.

Electronic Medical Records: A digital version of a patient's medical and treatment history.

Euro Health Consumer Index: An index that compares European health care systems based upon factors such as waiting times and results.

Genuine Progress Indicator: An index that attempts to measure the well-being of a nation by considering social and environmental factors in addition to economic factors.

Health Monitoring System: A health system based around digital technologies that monitor a patient's health.

Human Development Index: An index that measures human development based upon factors such as life expectancy, education, and per capita income.

Patient Information System: A digital information system that quickly provides patients with medical and health information.

Wearable Health Devices: Electronic devices worn by a user that measure and record health-related data.

ENDNOTES

[1]   For details about the index, visit the following website: http://iisp.vassar.edu/ish.html

[2]   The latest index rankings can be found at the following link: http://hdr.undp.org/en/content/latest-human-development-index-ranking

[3]   This is a project being considered for implementation in a country the size of Poland (38 million people).

[4]   This institute is modeled after the *National Health Institute*.

[5]   CA Bus & Prof Code § 4113 (through 2012 Leg Sess). https://law.justia.com/codes/california/2011/bpc/division-2/4110-4126.5/4113

[6]   IMB Watson is a unique expert system that provides query services. An IBM Watson Studio subscription costs $120 for 1,000 users per month. For professors and lecturers, it is free.

[7]   This section was developed drawing on the ideas of Dr. Rod Hochman (2019), CEO of Providence St. Joseph Health.

Chapter 14
Digital Agriculture Strategy

ABSTRACT

The aim of this chapter is to examine strategies for digitalizing agriculture. The first part of the chapter examines strategies for digitalizing agriculture in Africa. This part begins with an analysis of the role of agriculture in Africa, and it attempts to answer the question of whether African can feed itself and the world through its own agriculture. The first part will also consider strategies for innovating and computerizing Africa's agriculture. The second part of the chapter will examine agricultural trends and strategies in the European Union. This part will focus specifically on the trends of digital-oriented and smart farm developments. The final part of the chapter will consider strategies for digitalizing agriculture in Latin America and Asia.

INTRODUCTION

In this chapter, we will address strategies for digitalizing agriculture. In the beginning of the chapter, we will deal with agricultural farms in Africa because African agriculture is highly fragmented and, to some extent, resembles agriculture in other countries.[1] This is in contrast to American agriculture, which is based on large farms (around 169 hectares) that are maximally automated and computerized. Despite this, they pollute the environment and produce unhealthy food. Smaller farms, on the other hand, usually produce healthy organic food. After discussing strategies for Africa, digital and automation strategies for European, Latino, and Asian countries will be discussed. Defining such a strategy is beneficial if it is seen in the context of other countries and their practices.

It should be noted that most countries with small farms, including Poland, could benefit from adopting the strategy discussed below in regard to Africa, tailoring this approach to their needs. Farming in Poland, for example, is highly fragmented. In 2013 there were 1,428,400 farms. Individual farms employ about 100,000 people and comprise 91% of the total agricultural area, including livestock farms. The average area of a farm in Poland is 11.54 hectares. There is also a territorial diversity of holdings. More robust fragmentation can be observed in the south and east of the country, while a higher concentration of land occurs in the northern regions.

DOI: 10.4018/978-1-7998-8036-3.ch014

As is shown in Table 1, the level of development of Polish farms is comparable to Greece, the lowest in Europe (although the table does not list all EU countries). In other words, Polish agriculture still has a lot to learn to match countries with higher levels of agriculture.

Table 1. Level of agriculture in selected countries of the European Union (2006) (Ziętara, n.d.)

Economy Level	Level of Agriculture (Size of Farm in ESU)			
	High		Low	
High	Belgium Denmark Holland France Germany U. Kingdom	97.9 101.0 137.6 74.7 90.8 111.3	Austria Finland Italy Ireland Sweden	29.4 40.4 28.9 20.7 50.7
Low	Czech Rep. Slovakia	107.7 127.0	Greece Lithuania Poland Hungary	9.4 64.7 10.2 18.2

Note: ESU = European Size Unit

The European Size Unit (ESU) is a measure of the economic size of a farm. One ESU is equivalent to 1,200 EUR of surplus of economic value, taking into account the cost of living of the farm owners. Ziętara (n.d.) writes:

The level of GDP per capita was used as a criterion for the distribution of countries with a strong economy. In countries with a strong economy, GDP per capita was between 35,000 and 71,000 USD, while in countries with a low economy GDP per capita was in the range of 10-25 thousand USD. The data provided refer to 2005 and 2006. The level of agriculture is determined by the economic size of the holdings expressed in the ESU. Examples of countries with strong economies and high levels of agriculture are Belgium, Denmark, the Netherlands, France, Germany, and the United Kingdom. The size of the holdings in these countries was between 75 and 140 ESU. In countries with strong economies and low levels of agriculture, the size of farms was between 20 and 50 ESU. Examples of such countries are Austria, Finland, Italy, Ireland, and Sweden. The Czech Republic and Slovakia are examples of countries with low economic levels and high levels of agriculture. The last group is countries with low economic levels and low levels of agriculture. Examples are Greece, Lithuania, Poland, and Hungary. Lithuania stands out from this group, where the holdings represented in the FADN system were characterized by a slightly larger economic size of holdings, which entails maintaining a significant share of large-scale farms established based on former production cooperatives and state-owned enterprises in agriculture.

THE ROLE OF AGRICULTURE IN AFRICA

For the last 6,000 years of civilization's development, agriculture has been humanity's primary activity in the pursuit of poverty reduction and sustainable development. In the 21st century, agriculture remains fundamental, and its prevalence is still highly visible, as three out of four people in developing countries live in rural areas.

The prevalence of agriculture in developing countries is connected with the persistence of poverty, evident in the statistics that show that in 2018, 1 billion of the world's 7.88 billion people lived on less than $1 a day (Rosling, 2018). They are mainly dependent on rural households with non-standard farming methods. Agriculture is a driver of modernization in many of these countries, and while agriculture alone is not sufficient for effectively reducing poverty, it is an indispensable element in the implementation of effective development strategies, which most developing countries aim to achieve. A productive agricultural policy is particularly essential for Africa, as two-thirds of the workforce is dependent on agriculture. Agriculture accounts for 65 percent of Africa's workforce. More than 34 percent of Africa's GDP comes from agriculture, and more than 20 percent of economic activity is agricultural (United Nations Environment Programme, 2008).

African agriculture is currently at a crossroads. The looming disasters of climate change have exacerbated water shortages, which have persisted as a source of food shortages. The prospects for the development of production and tourism are remote, as the institutional capacity and legal and political infrastructure in most African countries are weak and border on lawlessness. Where lawful and civic opportunities are lacking, African agriculture cannot offer much hope and healing for Africa. Africa is naturally equipped with adequate soil, rivers, and waterways that are capable of feeding Africa many times over. Agriculture in the 21st century could transform sub-Saharan Africa into a force for economic growth. The task of feeding Africa's vibrant population can only be achieved through the use of structured and tailored scientific knowledge complemented by formal regional markets and supported by a new generation of business leaders dedicated to Africa's economic progress (Juma, 2015).

CAN AFRICA FEED ITSELF AND THE WORLD?

In sub-Saharan Africa, agriculture can underpin economic growth, but only if the productivity of small farms increases. According to World Bank estimates, African food markets were worth USD 323 billion in 2010. By 2030, it is estimated that the agricultural population and growth opportunities will be $1 trillion. Since only 4 to 6 percent of farmland is irrigated, the growth opportunities are enormous. Even if agricultural production were to increase just 50%, the likelihood of poverty eradication through agricultural industrialization and sustainable growth would be more promising than through any other economic activity (Figure 1).

In sub-Saharan African countries, 70 percent of the rural population in 2017 was living on agricultural income (Alliance for a Green Revolution in Africa, 2017). Effective land-use policies, careful zoning, and the targeting of communities and distribution of livestock in a way that balances the efficient use of sterile land, semi-aerated land, and wetlands can make agricultural activity in Africa the basis for the flourishing of African civilization. Agriculture has been very successful in meeting the world's food demands; however, the future is uncertain. Some models predict that food prices in global markets could reverse their long-term downward trend, creating increasing uncertainty about global food security.

The global challenges in agriculture and food production are enormous and are caused by impending climate change, environmental degradation, increasing competition for land and water, and higher energy prices. Furthermore, there is skepticism that investment costs can be sufficiently kept down to encourage the adoption and effective use of new technologies. As far as sub-Saharan Africa is concerned, if current issues remain as neglected as anticipated, food imports will need to double by 2030 (Rosegrant et al., 2009).

To expand its prospects for agricultural development, the entire African continent will need to consider the current strategies and applications of production used by countries such as India and China. Fragmented and directionless applications in Africa as well as their inability to plan, implement, and evaluate policy programs make the challenge daunting and dismal. For example, the yield of grains per hectare in developed countries is 5 tons. In sub-Saharan Africa, it is only 1 ton, five times less. In China and India, investment in agricultural research and development tripled between 1986 and 2006. In sub-Saharan Africa, investment in research and development increased by only 20 percent and is declining in 24 out of 54 African countries (World Bank, 2007). These African countries are additionally disadvantaged due to their small size and inland location.

There is still optimism about the likelihood of labor being used in Africa. Adequate training and maintenance can push Africa towards sustainable modernization, where cultural heritage and civilizational pride can be re-energized. Moving in this direction, Africa could be an exporter of manufactured goods in a similar way to China by offering a location for industrialized countries to outsource manufacturing. A large amount of labor in Africa is under-utilized capital, which is waiting to be employed as a productive force. The moral and pragmatic option is to coordinate efforts to target agricultural activities to maximize production (Figure 1). This can be accomplished through supportive policies in the fields of water, energy, and fertilizers as well as through prudent and people-centered public administration policies.

Figure 1. African agriculture has great potential (Photo: Landmatrix.org)

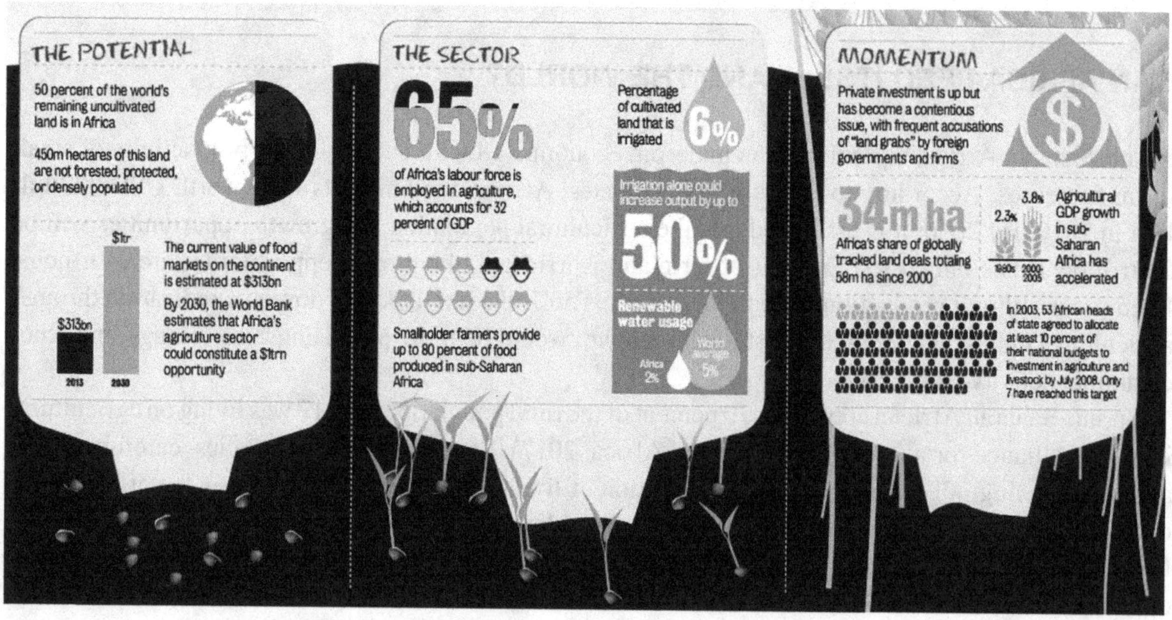

Water is most important in Africa

Not everything is lost for Africa. Of course, it is difficult to understand how such a rich continent with such vast wealth and abundant natural resources has found itself at the forefront of poverty. Be that as it may, recent evidence suggests that sub-Saharan Africa can make rapid developmental progress. There are, for example, many local successes in food production. Kenyan farmers have effectively used fertilizers and technological innovations to increase corn yields (Figure 2). Every year, the average Kenyan eats 70 kilograms of corn, which is typically ground into flour before consumption and is an essential part of their diet (Mutua, 2019). However, to meet the demand for corn consumption, Kenya still has an ambitious task ahead of them. On one hand, Kenya typically has a corn shortage, which is complicated by informal cross-border transactions with Uganda and Tanzania. On the other, the current deficit is so large that imports from the international market are often required. This has only exacerbated the problem. Corn prices in Kenya are among the highest in sub-Saharan Africa. The poorest parts of the population spend 28 percent of their income on corn. Despite progress, inefficiencies in the production and marketing of corn have resulted in a failure to meet the needs of the population. Increased productivity and efficient markets, combined with a rational government policy, could radically change the economic contribution of the corn subsector. Once appropriate reforms are carried out, the corn industry will become a crucial element in accelerating growth and reducing poverty (Kamau et al., 2011).

Figure 2. Corn is the primary food in Kenya (Photo: Kenyaweeklypost.com)

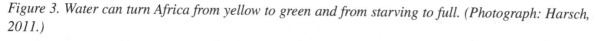

Figure 3. Water can turn Africa from yellow to green and from starving to full. (Photograph: Harsch, 2011.)

Many farmers in Kenya call genetically modified (GM) U.S.-supplied corn a Trojan horse. GM corn is currently illegal in Kenya, although the US continues to send GM corn to Kenya as a form of aid (Hand, 2008). Some activists argue that the United States deliberately sends GM crops as aid to undercut the organic export market and cause Europe to buy more from the US (Black, 2004).

Africa is known for its inability to maintain sustainable development, and this inadequacy is at its lowest in sub-Saharan Africa (SSA), which is known for being unable to feed its population due to corrupt political practices. Irrigation is relatively limited, and the use of irrigation as well as land management are inefficient (Figure 3). There is a certain irony in this since there are considerable water resources in the region. For example, the Republic of Congo has 142 times more renewable water available per capita than India and 23 times more than the United States. Even drier countries have enough water. Water users in SSA consume, on average, only 3% of available resources (Globalwaters, 2021). However, the availability of water in SSA is exceptionally seasonal and, in changing climates, variable and unpredictable. The problem in SSA is, therefore, not a lack of water, but the lack of the ability to manage it.

Households and their assets are at the heart of the agricultural system in Africa and are the main factors determining livelihood. The number of children in the household and its composition and group membership determine the availability of labor for work on the farm. Education, skills, and employment outside the agricultural sector increase household value. For example, tractor owners can increase their

Figure 4. Three agricultural technologies in SSA. (Photo: africaag.org)

income by renting agrarian tools as well as by using them to grow their farms. The farms of tractor own-ers are usually larger and better positioned to increase yields (Figure 4). They typically have access to non-agricultural income or remittances from family members abroad, and most have at least a secondary education supplemented by formal work experience outside the local community.

According to the United Nation's Food and Agriculture Organization (FAO), households using technol-ogy in farm management gain significant benefits in terms of the cultivated area, crop diversity, yields, hydration levels, family work opportunities, and household food security. For example, households that rely solely on hand tools such as hoes can only grow 1-2 hectares per year; those that with livestock farms can grow 3-4 hectares; and, those that hire tractor services can develop about 8 hectares. On the other hand, a household that owns a tractor can produce more than 20 hectares. Households relying on family work to meet all their agricultural needs live on the margin of subsistence. Women-led households are usually over-represented in this group, partly as a result of the loss of assets commonly associated with widowhood (Food and Agriculture Organization of the United Nations, 2009).

HOW TO INNOVATIVE AGRICULTURE IN AFRICA

Cooperation between universities and industry: Universities are at the forefront of agricultural de-velopment in most modernized economies in the West as well as countries such as Japan and South Korea. The US agricultural subsidy system has facilitated US industrialization by increasing agricultural production, based on the mechanization of farming. Sub-Saharan Africa, with its universities, can do the same. There are more than 100 universities in sub-Saharan Africa that are capable of setting up research parks. They could then provide innovative solutions for local farmers. Some food companies that buy agricultural products and provide agricultural services could support research and development that meet the needs of local agriculture. Such R&D projects are practiced in Nigeria, where Nestlé promotes soybean cultivation with the help of the University of Agriculture Abeokuta (Juma, 2015).

Broader institutional links: When the Nigerian government wanted to revive cocoa cultivation, it established the Cocoa Research Institute in Nigeria (CRIN) and the National Cocoa Development Committee. As a result, both institutions were able to develop genetically improved seeds that could produce 1.8 tons per hectare per year. In the end, Nigeria's national central bank was authorized to lend money to farmers who could innovate cocoa production (Juma, 2015).

Local innovation alliances: Life sciences professionals with knowledge, experience, skills, and business acumen in relevant areas should form an alliance to share successful results and experiences with other members of the community. To help these members communicate with each other, newsletters and electronic communications should be established. Periodic personal meetings should also be held to intensify the exchange of knowledge and experience at the local level and to raise awareness of what is happening in the field of agriculture in other parts of the country, SSA, and the world.

Local tacit knowledge and skills: Agricultural activity has been known in Africa for several millennia, and the memory of this knowledge is stored in the practices of local farmers. This is the so-called "hidden knowledge" passed down from generation to generation. This knowledge is the basis for determining whether a family or community survives or disappears. Therefore, people who possess such knowledge should be supported by the local government and the local community. This support can take various forms, such as helping to provide edible seeds, tools, credits, machinery, workforce assistance, printed instructions, and appropriate forms of communication.

In order to effectively innovate agriculture in SSA and provide advice about agricultural knowledge to local farmers, innovative clusters of information, knowledge, wisdom, and skills should be set up and maintained via four cluster links (Figure 5). The ability to integrate all these clusters and provide sound advice to local farmers will be ensured through the use of the Internet and mobile phones (and related applications such as websites, newsletters, email, blogs, etc.).

Needless to say, the strength of the advice lies in the complexity of the innovative clusters of local agriculture (ICLA), which will provide farmers with up-to-date information, knowledge, wisdom, and skills that can be applied to their local circumstances. Leadership in the organization and management of such clusters should promote university-industry cooperation with local governments.

INTEGRATED AGRICULTURAL INFRASTRUCTURE IN SSA

To make small SSA farms more productive and innovative, Integrated Agricultural Infrastructure (IAI) should be created, as shown in Figure 6. Its potential lies in its comprehensiveness and integration. So far, many elements in the model have been recognized as necessary by scholars, politicians, governments, and NGOs; however, the problem lies in their random and disjointed applications. Therefore, a small local farmer rarely receives sufficient help and services needed to manage their farm innovatively and rationally.

There are several levels of functioning of IAI elements, which can be divided into the following categories:

1.   Elementary level:

Figure 5. Innovative clusters for local agriculture (ICLA) in Sub-Saharan Africa (SSA)

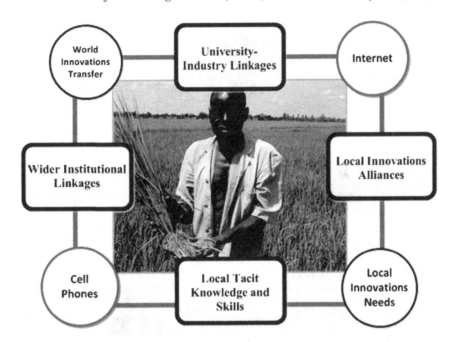

a. Microcredit for local farmers, which will finance farm improvements. This will consist of making minimal loans available to impoverished borrowers, who typically lack collateral, permanent employment, and good credit history. Its aim is not only to promote entrepreneurship and alleviate poverty but also in many cases to empower women and improve entire communities through growth. This is important because in many communities, women lack the stable employment histories that traditional lenders usually require. Furthermore, many are uneducated and, therefore, unable to complete the necessary formalities to obtain conventional loans. Microcredit is part of microfinance, which provides the poor with a broad range of financial services, especially savings accounts. Modern microcredit is believed to have been established at Grameen Bank, founded in Bangladesh in 1983.

b. Electricity, which allows for the use of energy-controlled devices and machines as well as lighting in schools and homes.

c. Water, without which agriculture is impossible.

2. Basic level:

a. Education of the farmer and his family for prudent life decisions and management of the farm.

b. Agricultural services that can install (sell or rent) and maintain irrigation systems and power equipment.

c. Delivery of fertilizers by agricultural other services.

d. Installation of telecommunication services (including the internet and mobile phones)

3. Intermediate level:

a. An organized cluster with advisors for local agriculture who provide up-to-date, innovative solutions for local farmers.

b. The skillful use of mechanized systems in agriculture.

Figure 6. Integrated Agricultural Infrastructure (IAI) in SSA

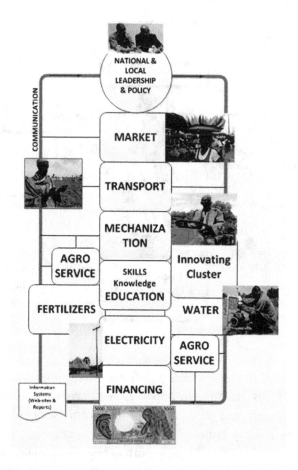

c. Others.
4. Complete level
   a. The introduction of farmers to local markets (and ultimately to national and international markets). This includes places of trade, the storage of goods, assistance in handling products, management of operations, wholesale and retail charges, evaluation and liberalization of prices and profits, market information systems, compliance with sanitary conditions, etc.
   b. Improved local transport to local markets, secured by local authorities.
   c. Others.

There are many good examples of such agricultural infrastructure elements used in SSA business practices. For instance, *TradeNet* in Ghana allows farmers and other users to use SMS alerts for selected goods and markets to buy or sell as soon as someone on the network makes an offer via their mobile phone. Users can also request and receive real-time prices for more than 80 goods from 400 markets in West Africa. Individuals can advertise their products and offers on a free website with their own web address, and farmers and trade groups can create websites to manage services for their members. Ghana is the primary beneficiary of this network. *TradeNet* has concluded agreements with trade organizations not only in Ghana but also in Burkina Faso, Mali, and Nigeria. These contracts have included the purchase of tomatoes, onions, and potatoes without intermediaries, which has significantly reduced transaction costs (DeMaagd & Moore, 2006).

The successful implementation of such an inter-institutional agreement should be established first by the demonstration of a prototype version, which, if successful, can serve as so-called 'proof' to others that they can learn and adapt such practices to their local farms. Leadership in the establishment of such pilot projects should be ensured by local, university, and industry partnerships, as such partnerships will unite powerful, world-class knowledge with local politics.

The agricultural infrastructure in question supports small farming, i.e., small farms run by a single household with a limited workforce. The use of this model of agriculture around the world is striking. Many countries have tried to promote large-scale farming, believing that small-scale farming is inefficient, backward, and fragile. The results of such large-scale farming initiatives, however, have often been disastrous. For example, state efforts to increase agricultural production in the SSA, particularly during the colonial period, focused on large-scale agriculture; however, these efforts were not sustainable.

Asian countries, on the other hand, which ultimately decided to promote small-scale agriculture, could start a Green Revolution. This refers to a series of research and development transfer initiatives that took place between the 1940s and late 1960s. The Green Revolution increased agricultural production worldwide, particularly in developing countries starting in the late 1960s. The initiatives, led by Norman Borlaug, the "Father of the Green Revolution," were designed to save more than a billion people from starvation, and they included the development of high-yielding varieties of cereal grains, the expansion of irrigation infrastructure, the modernization of management techniques, and the distribution of hybrid seeds, fertilizers, and pesticides for farmers (Gaud, 1968).

CONTINUING THE GREEN REVOLUTION IN AFRICA

Successful applications of the Green Revolution that were developed in Mexico and India have been repeatedly attempted in Africa. However, these programs have not been effective (Groniger, 2009). The reasons cited are widespread corruption, insecurity, lack of infrastructure, and a general lack of resolution on the part of governments. However, environmental factors, such as the availability of water for irrigation and the wide variety of slopes and soil types in a given area, are also part of the reason why the Green Revolution has not been successful in Africa (Gaud, 1968).

The overall objective of SSA agriculture is to ensure sustainable agricultural growth, reduce poverty, and improve food security. This objective is reflected in the *Comprehensive Africa Agriculture Development Programme* (CAADP), also known as the New Partnership for African Development. Overall, the CAADP aims to eradicate hunger and reduce poverty through agriculture. This program was approved at the African Union (AU) Assembly in 2003. The only African country that is not a member is Morocco. The AU was established on 26 May 2001 in Addis Ababa and launched on 9 July 2002 in South Africa, replacing the Organization for African Unity (OAU). The most important decisions of the AU are made by the African Union Assembly, which gathers every six months for a meeting that includes the heads of state and other government officials of member states. The AU headquarters is based in Addis Ababa, Ethiopia.

Some of the aims of the CAADP are to increase public investments in agriculture by at least 10 percent of the national budget (compared to the traditional 4 percent) and to increase agricultural productivity by at least 6 percent per year. The pillars of the CAADP are reflected in four key areas aimed at improving agriculture and investment. A different pillar leader is put in charge of each component. The four key pillars are…

- Sustainable land and water management
- Market access
- Food supply and the fight against hunger
- Agricultural research

Each pillar oversees different programs that aim to help achieve the objectives of the CAADP. However, the approach to creating integrated farm infrastructure (IFI) for small farms is more detailed and comprehensive than the four pillars, as IFI deals with small-scale farm-level issues, such as credit, electricity, education and access to innovation, technology-oriented services, mechanization, transport to and from markets, market management, and local, national, and international leadership.

ELEMENTS OF THE STRATEGY TO COMPUTERIZE AGRICULTURE IN AFRICA

A. In sub-Saharan Africa, many people do not currently have access to clean water, electricity, and financial credit due to structural poverty, which makes living in such an environment extremely difficult. Hence, to reduce poverty and turn agriculture into an economic engine for more than 65 percent of a given country's employees, it is first necessary to build an elementary level of well-being in the SSA, consisting of access to financial credit, electricity, and clean water. Once such a foundation of civilization has been reached, further layers of agricultural development should be built, which should include a basic level, an intermediate level, and a complete or wholistic level. Together, these levels would form an integrated agricultural infrastructure for small farms.

B. Regional politicians and university researchers should provide leadership in organizing innovative local agricultural clusters (ILAC), first as a demonstration of a prototype and later as models for development.

C. The success of agricultural renewal in SSA depends on the level of education of small farmers and their families. They would benefit from electrical equipment and machinery and from innovative farming techniques. Therefore, money and technology are not the only conditions for building a thriving agriculture in SSA. In a long-term sustainable way, a well-organized education aimed at developing the management skills of innovative farmers should set out a strategy for the renewal and development of agriculture.

D. To coordinate all agricultural development efforts in the 54 sub-Saharan African countries, an African Institute for Agricultural Development (AIAD) should be set up throughout the SSA as well as an African Food and Agriculture Organization (AFAO). Admittedly, the FAO regional office (the UN Agency based in Rome, Italy) is already established in Accra (Ghana), and there is a sub-regional office for Central Africa in Libreville, Gabon. However, such policies should be planned and implemented from the African Union level to influence ministries and organizations in individual SSA countries as well as global organizations, such as the UN, WB, IMF, TWO, G20, FAO, WHO, and others.

A lot of effort has been put into activating international donors, who provide some solutions, staff, and funds to improve the lives of people living in SSA. However, these efforts are dispersed, poorly coordinated, and good intentions and ideas are very often lost. Nevertheless, the working Global Donor Platform for Rural Development (GDPRD) is the right organization to take on the task of improving agriculture in the SSA. It supports the objectives of the CAADP, as its overarching priority platform shares knowledge and raises awareness of the need to strengthen aid and the effectiveness of agricultural and rural development and to promote the role of agricultural and rural development in poverty reduction.

International donors may be well organized, but their assistance is sometimes too dispersed. It would be better focused on pragmatic and short-term objectives within long-term objectives and tasks, such as the proposed computerization of small farms.

INTENSIFICATION OF DIGITAL-ORIENTED AGRICULTURE IN THE EUROPEAN UNION

The use of computer science in agriculture is set out in Table 2.

Table 2. The use of IT in select EU countries and Switzerland (Teye et al., 2012)

State	PC	Internet	Informa-tion systems	Smart-phone	LPIS	Geo fertilizing	Animals Registra-tion	Farm data
Bulgaria	Low	Low	Low	-	Average	-	-	Lack
Czech Rep	High	High	High	Low	Average	Average	-	Average
Denmark	High	High	-	High	High	High	High	Good
Iceland	High	High	Average	-	Average	Low	Average	Weak
The UK.	High	High	High	High	High	Average	High	Good
Germany	High	Average	Average	High	High	Average	High	Good
Hungary	Average	Average	Low	Low	Average	Low	Average	Weak
Italy	Average	Low	Average	Average	Average	Average	High	Average
Latvia	Low	High	Low	-	Average	Low	High	Average
Holland	High	High	High	High	High	Average	High	Good
Poland	Average	Average	Average	-	Average	Low	Low	Lack
Romania	Low	Low	Low	Low	Average	-	Average	Lack
Slovakia	High	Average	Low	Low	Average	Low	Average	Weak
Spain	High	-	Average	Low	High	Low	High	Average
Sweden	High	-	-	High	High	Low	High	-
Switzerland	High	Average	Average	High	High	Low	High	Average

Note: LPIS = Land Parcel Identification System.

The data from the Table 2 shows countries such as Holland, Denmark, and France, which have high agricultural productivity, make good use of computerization for their farms. Polish agriculture, on the other hand, only has an average level of computerization and, therefore, has low agricultural productivity.

The potential contribution of computerization to agriculture can be seen in the reduction of costs, increases in efficiency, and improvements in the productive capabilities of farms. To accomplish this, first of all, the information that farmers require should be analyzed and documented. Next, appropriate information systems (IS) should be developed. When developing such systems, the challenges arising from the deregulation and globalization of Europe's agricultural sector should be taken into account.

The scope of computerization for agriculture is broad and has excellent growth potential. Using information technology, agriculture can seek to solve problems in the supply chain and improve the management of agricultural data. Robotics and sensors can be used to optimize crop yields, effectively manage water, and improve animal health. Agribusiness managers can use computers to track data and do business using word processors, spreadsheets, online applications, precision farming software, financial services software, and databases to keep animal registries and agricultural land.

Modern farms and agricultural operations operate much differently than they did a few decades ago, mainly due to technological advances, including sensors, equipment, machinery, and information technologies. Today's agriculture routinely uses advanced technologies such as robots, temperature and humidity sensors, aerial imagery, and GPS technology. Such advanced equipment and precision farming systems have enabled farms to be more cost-effective, efficient, safer, and more environmentally friendly.

Farmers no longer have to apply water, fertilizers, and pesticides evenly throughout the field. Instead, they can use the minimum required quantities and target particular areas and even treat individual plants differently. Benefits include...

- Higher harvesting efficiency,
- Reduced consumption of water, fertilizers, and pesticides, which in turn reduces food prices,
- Limited impact on natural ecosystems,
- Reduced outflow of chemicals into rivers and groundwater,
- Increased employee safety.

In addition, robotics enables more reliable monitoring and management of natural resources such as air and water. It also gives producers more control over the production, processing, distribution, and storage of plants and animals, resulting in...

- More efficiency and lower prices
- Safer growing conditions and safer food
- Less impact on the environment and ecology

However, in addition to the farms themselves, the state should promote the efficient operation of research centers to ensure...

a. Basic research and development in physical sciences, engineering, and computer science,
b. Research into the development of agricultural equipment, sensors, and systems,
c. Applied research that assesses how to apply information technology in an economical way and with minimal disruption to existing practices,

d.   Aid and instruction for farmers on the use of new technologies.

THE TREND OF DIGITAL-ORIENTED FARM DEVELOPMENT

Farm automation, often associated with "smart farming," is a technology that increases farm productivity and automates the production cycle of plants or livestock. More and more companies are working on innovations in robotics, developing drones, autonomous tractors, harvest robots, automatic irrigation, and sowing robots. Although these technologies are entirely new, an increasing number of traditional agricultural companies are using farm automation techniques.

New advances in technology, from robotics and drones to computer software, have entirely changed modern agriculture. The primary goal of farm automation technology is to make tasks more tractable. Some of the leading technologies most commonly used by farms include harvest automation, autonomous tractors, sowing and weeding, and drones. Agricultural automation technology helps to solve significant problems, such as the growing global population, agricultural labor shortages, and changing consumer preferences.

New technology companies are emerging to develop precision farming technologies that will allow farmers to maximize yields by controlling every crop variable, such as humidity, pest stress, soil conditions, and microclimate. With more precise planting techniques, precision farming is enabling farmers to increase productivity and manage costs.

Precision farming companies have an excellent opportunity for growth. A recent report by Grand View Research, Inc. predicts that the precision farming market will reach $43.4 billion by 2025. A new generation of farmers is attracting faster, more flexible startups that systematically maximize yields.

The development of digital agriculture and related AI technologies has opened up many new opportunities for data collection for day-to-day decision-making as well as long-term planning of farm development. Remote sensors, satellites, and drones can collect information 24 hours a day across the field. They can monitor the condition of plants, soil quality, temperature, humidity, etc. The amount of data generated by these sensors is overwhelming, and the meaning of the numbers is hidden in the avalanche of the data.

The idea behind smart farming is to enable farmers to better understand environmental conditions through advanced technology (such as remote sensing), which can provide them with more information than they would be able to collect with the naked eye. Not only does smart farming do this more accurately, but it also does it faster than one's ability to walk or drive through the fields.

THE TREND OF SMART FARM DEVELOPMENT

Smart farms and smart agriculture mean applying modern information and communication technologies (ICT) to agriculture, leading to what could be called the third Green Revolution. After the revolution in plant breeding and genetics, this third revolution would involve remodeling the agricultural world based on the combined use of ICT solutions (such as precision equipment), the Internet of things (IoT), sensors and actuating devices, geo-positioning systems, Big Data, unmanned autonomous aircrafts (UAVs or drones), robotics, etc.

Smart agriculture has the real potential to ensure more productive and sustainable agricultural, as it is based on a more precise and resource-efficient approach. However, while up to 80% of farmers in the US use securities financing transactions, in Europe, this number is no more than 24%. From the farmer's point of view, smart farming should provide the farmer with added value in terms of better decision-making and/or more efficient exploitation and management of operations. In this sense, smart agriculture is closely linked to six interconnected technology platforms (Figure 7):

1. Farm Management Information Systems (MIS), which is based on a common database and the digitization of finance, accounting, marketing and sales, procurement, taxes, and other necessary reports.
2. Precision farming in regard to the following:
   a. Optimizing crop sowing and field performance
   b. Reducing water consumption, waste, and labor needs
   c. Optimizing fertilization with Global Positional Systems (GPS) and Geographical Information Systems (GIS), which control precise fertilization and sowing and other processes using Wi-Fi equipment to communication with satellites.
   d. Reducing waste in grain containers
   e. Others
3. Automated field irrigation
4. Monitoring the health of farm animals
5. Autonomous harvesting and robots (Figure 8)
6. The Internet of Things (IoT) – This involves many sensors being installed in fields that measure variables such as air temperature, wind speed, rainfall, and even the amount of solar energy we get

Figure 7. Functions of a smart farm

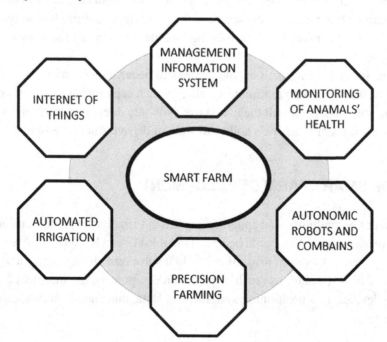

from the sun (for the sun is the driving force behind photosynthesis, and in this way, the photo-synthesis occurring in individual plants can be recorded). This data is used to grow plants that are very efficient at capturing solar energy and turning it into features that farmers are interested in.

THE EUROPEAN UNION'S DIGITAL STRATEGY FOR AGRICULTURE

Figure 8. A robot distributes pesticides (Photo: Dreamsteam.com)

The EU's agricultural sector is one of the world's leading food producers, a guarantor of food safety and quality, and a supplier of millions of jobs for Europeans; however, this sector faces many challenges. Digital technologies such as artificial intelligence (AI), robotics, blockchain, High-Performance Computing (HPC), the Internet of Things (IoT), and 5G could potentially increase farm productivity and at the same time improve economic and environmental sustainability. The increased use of digital technologies could also have a positive impact on the quality of life in rural areas, and it could help attract the younger generation to agriculture and encourage them to start businesses in rural areas.

The Declaration of Cooperation on a Smart and Sustainable Digital Future for European Agriculture and Rural Areas was issued on the EU's "Digital Day" in 2019 and signed by the following EU countries: Austria, Belgium, Czech Republic, Germany, Estonia, Ireland, Greece, Spain, France, Italy, Cyprus, Latvia, Lithuania, Luxembourg, Hungary, Netherlands, Poland, Portugal, Romania, Slovenia, Finland,

Figure 9. An autonomous vehicle takes care of weed removal (Photo: twitter.com)

Sweden, and United Kingdom. Bulgaria soon joined as well. The declaration is part of ongoing efforts to facilitate and accelerate the digital transformation of the EU's agricultural sector and rural areas.

EU-funded digital projects for agriculture include the following:

- **Sweeper**: a robot for harvesting sweet peppers (AI and robotics),
- **4D4F** (Data Driven Dairy Decisions for Farmers): a network focused on the role that animal and environmental sensors can play in collecting real-time information to help farmers make more informed decisions in dairy farming (IoT),
- **IoF2020**: Internet of Food and Farm (IoT),
- **Biodata**: Big Data on the bioeconomy,
- **SmartAgriHubs**: organizations that support the innovation of ecosystems in agriculture,
- **Humane AI**: the creation of AI systems that empower people and expand their intelligence (AI and robotics),
- **Pantheon**: robots that help hazelnut growers,
- **Flourish**: robots for more productive and sustainable agriculture.

In its communication on the Future of Food and Farming, the EU Commission recognized that the Common Agricultural Policy (CAP) should enable the EU agricultural sector to address environmental protection, biodiversity, and the development of the bioeconomy. The crucial role of the CAP in fully linking farmers and rural areas to the digital economy has become widely recognized. The Commission has also identified agriculture as one of the critical areas of application where targeted investment is needed to achieve these objectives in its Communication on Artificial Intelligence for Europe. Finally, the EU's coordinated AI plan foresees investments in platforms and large pilot programs aimed at integrating AI and robotics into agriculture.

The EU's *Digital Agriculture Platform* (Agriculture 4.0) was organized in 2018 to exchange ideas about technological and other projects (De Clercq et al., 2018).

FARM MANAGEMENT INFORMATION SYSTEM (FMIS) ARCHITECTURE

The Farm Management Information System (FMIS) should support farm production processes. A model of such processes is given in Figure 10. The number and intensity of these processes depend on the size of the farm and its production program. The model presented has 27 elements, that work together. This results in 327 e-process relationships (R).[2] If each of the process relationships can only have two states (good or bad), then the number of possible states (s) and the correlations between them is $s=2^e$, or in this case, $s=2^{27}=134,217,728$. Typically, these process relationships are in 5 states (very good, good, sufficient, bad, and very bad); thus, the number of possible correlations between these subprocesses is 5^{27}. It is a dizzying number of states and decision-making situations for farm management (7.4505806E18). Even assuming that many relationships (and, thus, states) do not need to be recorded, the number of relevant decision-making states is still astonishing.

For the people in charge to control the incoming flood of information about the state of the farm, an information system (IS) must be used, which takes into account all states at lightning-fast speeds and presents essential information needed for decision-making to management and administration employees. ISs are specialized, and a collection can be referred to as a "federation of ISs", as shown in Figure 11. Their purposes include following:

- **BIS** – Business Information Systems:
  - Finance IS
  - Marketing IS
  - Sales IS
  - Budget IS
  - Accounting IS
- **eBIS** – e-Business Information System, for online sales,
- **PIS** – Production Information System, for the production of agricultural goods,
- **MIS** – Management Information System, which assists management teams in running agricultural production operations,
- **SCM** – Supply Chain Management system, for processing purchases and sales transactions,
- **SIS** – Sales Information System,
- **MCS** – Management Control System, for daily monitoring of farm production (it is a subsystem of the farm's MIS),
- **RIS** – Resources Information System, for controlling the use of equipment and installations,
- **Management Panel** – graphical monitoring of the company's key performance indicators (KPI),
- **Common Internal Database** – A database needed for most application systems,
- **Big Database** – for external data,
- **GUI** – Graphic User Interface, for end-users,
- **E-communication systems** – e.g., Email, eConferences, and others,

Figure 10. Elements and process relationships of a smart agricultural farm

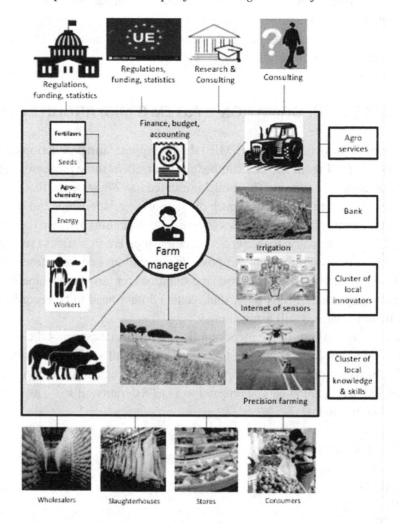

- **Networks** – e.g., Local Area Network, the Internet of People, the Internet of Things (sensors), and others.

The presented Federation of FMIS covers the tasks of a large farm. For small farms, this federation will be smaller and less complicated. This is usually expressed as so-called "customization" in software packages, which addresses the size of the farm and the number of agricultural production processes. Many ready-made software packages such as SAP or Baan are referred to as "Enterprise Resource Planning" (ERP). A more specialized version of ERP is the Supply Chain Management (SCM) software, which is presented in the model in Figure 12.

ERP or SCM packages usually have modules specialized for farm processes, which are selected according to the needs of specific companies. It is assumed that farms should spend between 2.5% and 5% of company revenue on developing digitalization. This means that small Polish farms producing 100,000 tons per year with incomes of about $12,000 per year after deducting the cost of living can invest between $300 and $600 on ICT (see Table 3: 10 ESU x $1,200). All that is needed is a smartphone. For farmers

Figure 11. Federation of Farm Management Information Systems (critical systems shown) (Targowski, 2003, p. 123)

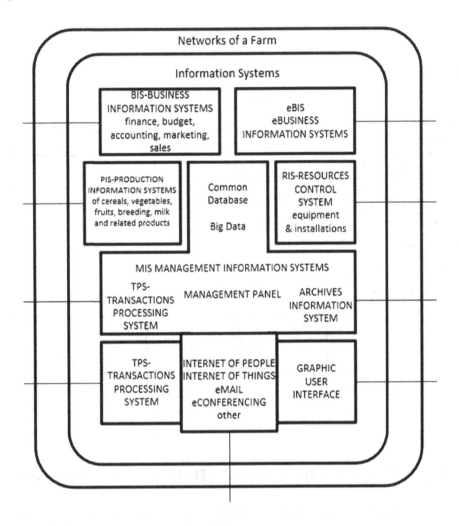

to take full advantage of digitization, they should initially invest around $5,000-$10,000. Farmers can also use the services of so-called "cloud computing," which provides software and hardware. However, the manager should make sure the cloud service will not disappear from the market, lose farm data as a result of cybercrime, or sell data to competitors. To get out of the so-called "poverty loop", farmers must receive help from local governments, the state, or the EU, as states usually subsidize agriculture in Europe and America. France is at the forefront in this respect. Moreover, the EU subsidizes Polish farms. For example, between 2004 and 2006, Polish farmers received $47,868/year on average from the EU. Currently, however, only 44% of farmers apply for subsidies (Horabik, 2004).

Figure 13 shows the IT infrastructure of the farm. Of course, the entire infrastructure will not be built immediately, but only gradually as needed.

Figure 12. The architecture of integrated Farm Resource Planning software; SCM = Supply Chain Management (also commonly referred to as Enterprise Resources Planning or ERP); FPM = Farm Production Management) (Targowski, 2003, p. 167)

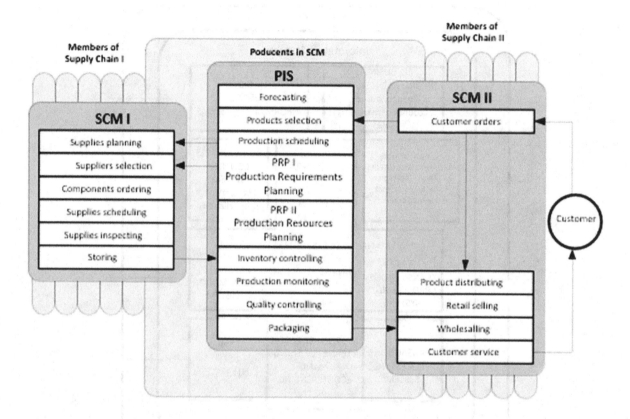

STRATEGIES FOR DIGITALIZING AGRICULTURE IN THE EUROPEAN UNION

The diversity of European farms in terms of farm type, size, geographical location, and cultural practices characterizes European agriculture as a whole. This diversity has a significant impact on farmers' decision-making. Thanks to typologies based on farm size and farm productivity, guidance on digitalization strategies in the EU can be offered.

Based on the following analysis, one can extrapolate the computerization solutions to the world at large. The total agricultural area of the EU is around 183 million hectares. About 85% of farms own plots fewer than 20 hectares. The structure of holding areas ranges from an average of about 5 hectares per holding in Greece to an average of 79 hectares in the Czech Republic (Table 3). With the accession of Romania and Bulgaria to the European Union, the number of farms has increased significantly due to the numerous small farms located in Romania. Around 32% of agricultural land in the EU is cultivated for cereals, for which wheat is most commonly grown. About 40% of cereals are produced in France and Germany.

Agriculture is less intensive in many eastern European countries (a legacy of an economy run by state capitalism), which, consequently, has resulted in decreased yields. This can be seen in two neighboring countries, Germany and Poland, where Poland has half the potato yield as Germany (21 t/ha in Poland

Figure 13. Intelligent farm IT infrastructure. (The firewall is a cybersecurity system)

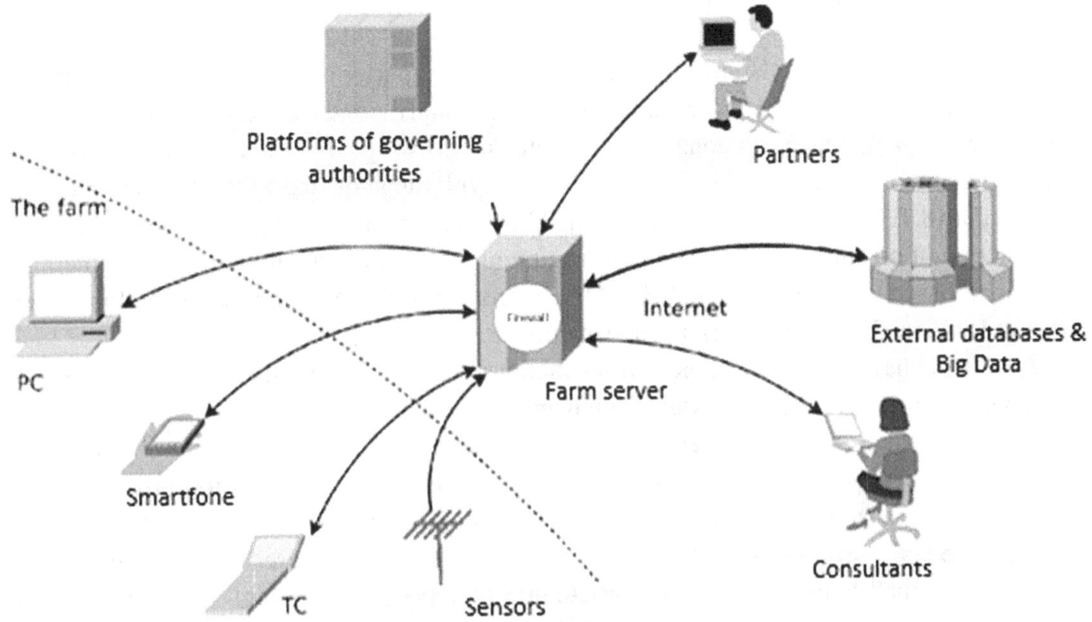

and 42 t/ha in Germany) (Food and Agriculture Organization of the United Nations, 2008). However, it is this noticeable difference in agricultural productivity—caused by the difference between the economic policies of real socialism and capitalism—that may now, after the collapse of the Soviet Bloc, prove to be of benefit for former states of the Soviet Bloc. For example, because small Polish farms produce organic food sought after in world markets, these technologically backward farms are able to help meet this demand. This is also the result of the fact that, in the Polish People's Republic, as much as 80% of farms were in private hands. In Czechoslovakia, on the other hand, 100% of farms were nationalized, with a large plot of land used for growing crops. Today, Czechoslovakia has the potential to develop smart farms to almost their fullest extent.

In addition to plant production, countries such as Denmark have focused on intensive livestock production, with a particular focus on pigs, dairy products, and related agricultural sectors, such as enzyme production for biofuels. Geographical and climatic differences in Europe determine the harvest season and the amount of solar radiation and precipitation, which vary from north to south. Crops such as olives, cotton, and citrus, which are common in Mediterranean countries, cannot be grown in the north, whereas in some areas, crops can have several growing seasons in the same year. Based on the differences presented, it is clear that it is necessary to design different computerization strategies to take account of geographical and cultural differences between European regions.

According to Table 3, most European farms have similar amount of productivity (1 ha), which is ESU 1.5, or EUR 1800 (after taking into account the cost of living). These farms, with relatively small plots of land for growing crops, are too weak financially to invest in the full range of smart farm technologies. Instead, they should develop FMIS and digital technologies that reduce production costs, such as digital technologies that assist in the development of precision agriculture and sensors integrated with the Internet of Things. On the other hand, farms with low productivity but large areas for growing crops should be able to finance the full development of smart farm technology.

Computerization strategies for select European countries are presented below:

1. The Netherlands (12.5 ESU/ha) is the 2nd largest food exporter in the world, thanks to low water consumption, chemicals, fertilizers, antibiotics, energy, and the extensive use of greenhouses (shared by several farms), which can control the climate and growing environment. The Netherlands has already applied computerization, implementing the full range of smart farm technologies.
2. Lithuania (8 ESU/ha) – Food accounts for 20% of the country's exports. It specializes in the production of organic food. The computerization of small farms should aim to make them highly efficient, based on SIZF, and there should be a broader use of greenhouses with climate sensors due to Lithuania's cold Northern European climate.
3. Italy (6 ESU/ha) – With only 5 percent of the land under cultivation, Italy is not self-sufficient when it comes to agricultural products, but it enjoys a wealth of agricultural resources and a pleasant climate. Italy is a world leader in olive oil production and a major exporter of rice, tomatoes, wine, and cheese. Because of the small amount of land being used for crop production, Italy's computerization strategy should rely on SIZF and Internet sensors.
4. Belgium (5 ESU/ha) – There are two main trends in Belgian agriculture. The first is the disappearance of the small family farm. Large agricultural enterprises increasingly dominate agriculture. Over the past three decades, the number of small farms has decreased by 80 percent. The second major trend is the growing production of the agricultural sector. New technologies and scientific research on crops have merged to achieve higher yields. Therefore, even if the total area of land being used for agriculture decreases, farmers are still able to produce more. Between 1995 and 1999, crop production increased by 9 percent. Meat production dominates. The strategy for the computerization of small farms should be based on SIZF, and large farms should model themselves after those in the Netherlands due to their geographical and cultural similarities.
5. Slovakia (5 ESU/ha) is self-sufficient in the production of milk, beef, poultry, eggs, and sugar, but lags behind in the production of pork, fruit, and vegetables. A big problem is the reluctance of the younger generation to work in agriculture, which has low social status in this country. In this situation, advanced computerization has little chance of being implemented.

The strategies for computerizing agriculture for select EU countries are given in Table 3. The common goal behind computerization should be the sustainable development of agriculture. Objectives, on the other hand, should be specific to each country. Of course, each farm faces a unique situation, which requires a tailored computerization strategy. Examples of computerization strategies are intended as guides for other European countries with similar conditions.

STRATEGIES FOR DIGITALIZING AGRICULTURE IN LATIN AMERICA

Latin America is a substantial net exporter of food and agricultural products, accounting for 16% of total global exports of food and farming products and 4% of total imports of food and farming products. The region is one of the few parts of the world with significant areas of unused agricultural land (concentrated

Table 3. Digital strategies for select EU countries in 2020

State	Farm Size in ESU	Farm Area in ha	Productivity in ESU/ha	Digitalization Goal	Strategic Technology
Austria	29	19	1.5	Optimal resource consumption	Digitization of animal agriculture
Belgium	98	19	5	Optimal resource consumption	SIZF, smart greenhouses
Denmark	101	49	2	Increased efficiency	SIZF, precision agriculture
Finland	40	31	1.3	Optimal resource consumption	Precision agriculture and Greenhouses
France	74	48	1.5	Increased efficiency	SIZF, precision agriculture
Netherlands	138	11	12.5	Optimal resource consumption	Smart farms
Germany	71	48	1.5	Increased efficiency	Smart farms
Italy	40	7	6	Increased efficiency	SIZF, precision agriculture
Greece	9	5	1.8	Increased efficiency	SIZF, precision agriculture
Czech Republic	108	79	1.4	Optimal resource consumption	Smart farms
Slovakia	127	26	5	Increased efficiency	SIZF
Lithuania	65	9	8	Organic food	SIZF, greenhouses
Poland	10	7	1.4	Organic food	SIZF, greenhouses

Source: Author's research. The *European Size Unit* (ESU) is a measure of the economic size of a farm. One ESU is equivalent to 1,200 EUR of surplus of economic value, taking into account the cost of living of the farm owners.

in Brazil and Argentina), suggesting that Latin America will continue to play a vital role in global food production and future exports.

Many countries in the region have recently achieved significant increases in agricultural productivity despite the high percentage of manual labor workers. Increasing productivity still further will be essential to meet national food needs and to maintain or increase the competitiveness of exports.

It will be equally crucial for the region to increase large-scale agricultural and small farm productivity in sustainable ways as well as export production for countries such as Brazil and Argentina. Latin America has long been associated with the production and export of a variety of agricultural goods, be it coffee from Brazil and Colombia, beef from Argentina, or bananas from Ecuador.

As regards the structure of agricultural production, most Latin American countries for which data is available (Table 4) show significant concentrations of land in the hands of large private owners, which is a legacy of the colonial period in the history of many countries.

In addition to technology, other general strategies for increasing the contribution of agriculture to the economic development of Latin America include investing in infrastructure (to reduce both costs and losses/waste) and maintaining and improving access to markets through trade agreements at regional and international levels. In particular, for small farmers, building more influential collective institutions, such as cooperatives and producer associations, has already proved useful in helping them gain better access to information, credit, and markets (Duff & Padilla, 2015).

Figure 14. The percentage of manual labor workers on Latino farms is high, but is this perhaps okay because they have excess hands for work? (Photo: http://continentalseeds.com/celery)

Table 4. The diversity of agricultural farms in Latin America (Food and Agriculture Organization of the United Nations, 2014)

State	% of National Area < 1 hectare	% of National Area > 50 hectares
Brazil	< 0.5%	88%
Argentina	< 0.5%	98%
Chile	< 0.5%	90%
Ecuador	1%	61%
Peru	< 0.5%	78%
Colombia	< 0.5%	72%
Uruguay	< 0.5%	97%
Paraguay	< 0.5%	90%
Guatemala	12%	21%
Honduras	< 0.5%	< 0.5%
Nicaragua	< 0.5%	66%
Panama	1%	67%

Large Latin American farms can use smart farm computerization strategies, including the selective use of autonomous harvesters and robots, as there is a large number of low-skilled workers in those countries who emigrate for work to the United States and other countries. Such large farms should also take care of sustainable development.

Small Latin American farms should become computerized to increase the efficiency of agricultural production based on SIZF, and food crops should be grown in compliance with organic standards.

STRATEGIES FOR DIGITALIZING AGRICULTURE IN ASIA

In Asia, the State of agricultural development is characterized by the following trends:

1. More than 2.2 billion people in the region rely on agriculture for a source of income or for securing the necessities of life (Asian Development Bank, 2009).
2. Rice is by far the most important crop in Asia: 90% of the world's production and consumption of rice takes place in the region (Jha et al., 2010).
3. Because trends show that rice consumption decreases as income increase, many economists have argued that rice is a second-rate good.
4. Despite forecasts of famine, most Asian countries became self-sufficient in the 1970s thanks to the Green Revolution (International Water Management Institute, 2009).
5. The stagnation and declining yields of crops such as rice and wheat may ultimately be linked to declining agricultural investment. For example, public investment in agriculture in India has been broadly the same since 2004 (Carrasco & Mukhopadhyay, 2012).
6. Biotech crops were estimated to have been grown on 160 million hectares of land in 2011, making it the fastest-growing crop technology (International Service for the Acquisition of Agri-Biotech Applications, 2011).
7. In most Asian countries, agriculture is the largest user of water, reaching up to 90% of total water consumption (Bird et al., 2009).

Asian agriculture should develop following the principles of sustainable food security. The production of genetically modified food should be eliminated, and emphasis should be placed on the integration of information systems with the supply chain (including suppliers, farms, wholesalers, shops, and consumers). In this way, small farms could be given a level playing field for selling their products. Small farms should develop their digital capabilities in similar fashion to African farms, discussed in the first part of this chapter.

Large farms, on the other hand, should develop smart farm technologies, focusing on the use of precision agriculture and IoT sensors to save water consumption and prevent environmental pollution. Such developments are quite possible because these countries have capable IT professionals who can develop and maintain such technologies.

Figure 15. The percentage of manual labor workers in Asian agriculture is high. Is this good because they also have excess hands for work? (Photo: developmentaid.org)

SUMMARY

1.   Considering the diversity of agricultural computerization strategies in the world, the example of the Netherlands stands out. It is a small state with a population of 17.5 million. Furthermore, 26% of the land is below sea level, where 21% of the population lives. The total area represents only 13% of the total landmass of Poland, but Poland has just 2.17 times more people. Despite such geographical disadvantages, the Netherlands is the second-largest exporter of food in the world (vegetables, cheese, dairy products, meat, processed fruit, cocoa, wildflowers, seeds, tubers, drinks, etc.). The productivity of small Dutch farms per hectare of crops is three times higher than the European average. Why is this happening? The answer is that Dutch farms benefit from an advanced agricultural science and the widespread use of technologically advanced computers and automation systems. Most important, however, are Dutch farmers, who make up 4% of the country's workforce—2.5 times greater than the percentage of farmers in the American workforce, which is also automated. In other words, the Dutch do not seek to minimize hiring in agriculture through automation.

2.   Moreover, since the 16th century, the Dutch, have traveled from their country to America and Indonesia (about 30% of the population in total), and those who decided to master the adverse geographical and climatic conditions have developed first-rate universities (13 Dutch universities are in the first 400 of the world and three are in the top 100) (Quacquarelli Symonds, 2019) and a first-class economy (5th in the world per capita in purchasing power parity[3]) with the result that their society is well educated and professional and also very talented and wise, as evidenced by the great Dutch painters.[4] More than 33% of people aged 25-64 have a higher education compared to 24% for OECD countries. This puts them at 3rd place among the best-educated countries in the world, after Finland (#2) and Singapore (#1) (Colson, 2016). The result is the highest level of agriculture in the world. Also, the production of vegetables, cheeses, processed fruit, and flowers (including seeds and bulbs) is specialized and more complicated than the monolithic cultivation of cereals, rice, or olives.

3. The example of the agricultural success of Dutch farms indicates that the mere use of advanced computerization and automation does not guarantee success in agricultural production. The manufacturing factor is also crucial, including education, qualifications, theoretical and practical knowledge, wisdom, diligence, innovation, and political and organizational culture. An example of this is Italy, which has the best climate in the world, a long history of civilization (often dated to more than 2770+ years ago), access to advanced technologies, and yet they are not self-sufficient in food, despite the famous Italian cuisine. This is due to the fact that in Italy, there is a clear division between the rich North and the impoverished South, caused by a deliberate policy of the upper class aimed at inhibiting the development of the South, which has primarily been and still is controlled by criminal groups. Yet until 200 years ago, Naples was thought to be the center of Europe, and Sicily was highly productive because it was at the center of world trade, controlled by the then "Wall Street" in Venice, which lay at the crossroads of trade routes from Europe to Asia, especially to China and the *Silk Road*. However, the exclusion of the South has impacted the current organizational and social situation of agriculture in Italy.

4. Except for large farms in the United States, Canada, Australia, and Latin America, as well as state farms in China and North Korea, we have been dealing with medium-sized (e.g., Czech, French, German, and Danish) and small-sized farms. The latter, which are many in number, should first take care of the organizational preparation that has been discussed for African farms if they plan to computerize and automate their agriculture.

REFERENCES

Alliance for a Green Revolution in Africa. (2017). *Africa agriculture status report: The business of smallholder agriculture in Sub-Saharan Africa*. https://agra.org/wp-content/uploads/2017/09/Final-AASR-2017-Aug-28.pdf

Asian Development Bank. (2009). *Building resilience to climate change in the Asia-Pacific agricultural sector*. https://www.adb.org/publications/building-climate-resilience-agriculture-sector-asia-and-pacific

Bird, J., Arriens, W. L., & Custodio, D. V. (2009). *Water rights and allocation: problems and challenges for Asia*. Asian Development Bank. https://www.adb.org/publications/water-rights-and-water-allocation-issues-and-challenges-asia

Black, R. (2004, September 16). Struggling to find GM's middle ground. *BBC*. http://news.bbc.co.uk/2/hi/science/nature/3662616.stm

Carrasco, B., & Mukhopadhyay, B. (2012). *Food price escalation in South Asia: A serious and growing concern*. Asian Development Bank. https://www.adb.org/publications/food-price-escalation-south-asia-serious-and-growing-concern

Colson, T. (2016, October 3). The 11 best-educated countries in the world. *Business Insider*. https://www.businessinsider.com/wef-global-competitiveness-report-most-educated-countries-in-the-world-2016-10

De Clercq, M., Vats, A., & Biel, A. (2018). *Agriculture 4.0: The future of farming technology*. Oliver Wyman. https://www.oliverwyman.com/our-expertise/insights/2018/feb/agriculture-4-0--the-future-of-farming-technology.html

DeMaagd, K., & Moore, S. (2006). Using IT to open previously unprofitable markets. *Proceedings of the 39th Annual Hawaii International Conference on System Sciences (HICSS 06')*, 166c-166c. 10.1109/HICSS.2006.524

Duff, A., & Padilla, A. (2015). *Latin America: Agricultural perspectives*. Rabobank. https://economics.rabobank.com/publications/2015/september/latin-america-agricultural-perspectives/

Food and Agriculture Organization of the United Nations. (2008). *International year of the potato*. http://www.fao.org/potato-2008/en/world/europe.html

Food and Agriculture Organization of the United Nations. (2009). *Contribution of farm power to smallholder livelihoods in sub-Saharan Africa*. http://www.fao.org/family-farming/detail/en/c/273614/

Food and Agriculture Organization of the United Nations. (2014). *The state of agriculture: Innovation in family farming*. http://www.fao.org/publications/sofa/2014/en/

Gaud, W. S. (1968, March 8). The green revolution: Accomplishments and apprehensions. *AgBioWorld*. http://www.agbioworld.org/biotech-info/topics/borlaug/borlaug-green.html

Globalwaters. (2021). *Democratic Republic of Congo*. https://www.globalwaters.org/WhereWeWork/Africa/DRC

Groniger, W. (2009). *Debating development: A historical analysis of the Sasakawa Global 2000 project in Ghana and indigenous knowledge as an alternative approach to agricultural development* [Unpublished master's thesis]. Utrecht University.

Hand, E. (2008). *Biotech debate divides Africa*. Knight Ridder Tribune Business News.

Harsch, E. (2011, April). Investing in Africa's farms—and its future. *Africa Renewal*. https://www.un.org/africarenewal/magazine/april-2011/investing-africas-farms-%E2%80%94-and-its-future

Horabik, W. (2004, June 9). Polish farmers at odds with subsidies. *Politico*. https://www.politico.eu/article/polish-farmers-at-odds-with-subsidies/

International Service for the Acquisition of Agri-Biotech Applications. (2011). Global status of commercialised biotech. *GM Crops, 2011*. https://www.isaaa.org/resources/publications/briefs/43/executivesummary/default.asp

International Water Management Institute. (2009). *Revitalizing Asia's Irrigation: To sustainably meet future food needs*. Asian Development Bank https://www.adb.org/publications/revitalizing-asias-irrigation-sustainably-meet-tomorrows-food-needs

Jha, S., Roland-Holst, D., & Sriboonchitta, S. (2010). *Regional trade opportunities for agriculture. Asian Development Bank*. https://www.adb.org/publications/regional-trade-opportunities-asian-agriculture

Juma, C. (2015). *The new harvest: agricultural innovation in Africa*. Oxford University Press. doi:10.1093/acprof:oso/9780190237233.001.0001

Kamau, M., Olwande, J., & Githuku, J. (2011). *Consumption and expenditures on key food commodities in urban households: The case of Nairobi*. Tegemeo Institute of Agricultural Policy and Development. https://ageconsearch.umn.edu/record/202602?ln=en

Mutua, J. (2019, May 9). Foods that Kenyans eat the most. *Business Daily*. https://www.businessdaily-africa.com/bd/data-hub/foods-that-kenyans-eat-the-most-2249422

Quacquarelli Symonds. (2019). *QS world university rankings 2019*. https://www.topuniversities.com/university-rankings/world-university-rankings/2019

Rosegrant, M. W., Fernández, M., & Sinha, A. (2009). *Looking into the future for agriculture and AKST*. IAASTD. https://cgspace.cgiar.org/bitstream/handle/10568/37336/GlobalReport.pdf?sequence=1&isAllowed=y

Rosling, H. (2018, March 19). *How many are rich and how many are poor by Professor Hans Rosling* [video]. YouTube. https://www.youtube.com/watch?v=Ihe0VdKh2e0

Targowski, A. (2003). *Electronic enterprise, strategy, and architecture*. IRM Press. doi:10.4018/978-1-931777-77-3

Targowski, A. (2014). The impact of agriculture on African civilization in the 21st century. *International Journal of African Development*, 2(1), 26–39.

Teye, F., Holster, H. P. L., & Horakova, S. (2012). Current situation on data exchange in agriculture in EU27 and Switzerland. In T. Mildorf & C. Charvat Jr., (Eds.), *ICT for Agriculture, rural development, and environment* (pp. 37–47). Czech Centre for Science and Society.

United Nations Environment Programme. (2008). *Organic agriculture and food security in Africa*. United Nations. https://unctad.org/system/files/official-document/ditcted200715_en.pdf

World Bank. (2007). *World development report 2008: Agriculture for development*. https://openknowledge.worldbank.org/handle/10986/5990

Ziętara, W. (n.d.). *The model of Polish agriculture: The current challenges* [Unpublished manuscript]. Department of Economics and Organization of Enterprises, Warsaw University of Life Sciences. http://sj.wne.sggw.pl/pdf/EIOGZ_2009_n73_s5.pdf

KEY TERMS AND DEFINITIONS

Bioeconomy: Economic activity that involves the use of biotechnology to produce goods and services.

Biotech Crops: Crops derived from the use of biotechnologies.

Enterprise Resource Planning: Software that helps to integrate and manage central business processes.

Green Revolution: The development and use of agricultural technologies in the 1950s and 1960s that led to a large increase in agricultural production.

Organization for African Unity: An intergovernmental organization established on May 25th, 1963 that included 32 African countries.

Precision Farming: The use of computer technologies to observe, measure, and create optimal crop conditions.

Smart Farms: The management of farms using computer technologies.

Supply Chain Management: The management of the flow of goods and services.

ENDNOTES

[1]   This section was developed on the basis of Targowski (2014).

[2]   R=[(e-1)e]:2, where R=number of relationships and e=number of elements.

[3]   After being excluded from the leading small states on the list, such as Brunei or Kuwait.

[4]   For example, Rembrandt, Vermeer, van Gogh, Mondrian, and others.

Chapter 15
Digital Education Strategy

ABSTRACT

This chapter analyzes and discusses key strategies for digital education. The chapter begins by examining and defining several key concepts, including global citizenship, digital citizenship, computational thinking, informational thinking, and systemic thinking. Next, the chapter analyzes the role of leadership in the age of digitalization and advocates for panoramic leadership. The chapter then discusses strategies and tools for teaching the digital humanities and compares STEM-based education with STEAM-based education. The virtual classroom is then analyzed, followed by a discussion of why Finnish schools excel in digital education. The chapter concludes by analyzing and discussing the architecture for digital schools and universities.

INTRODUCTION

The transformation of the world after the fall of communism in 1992 took place relatively recently and in a short time. China's economic liberalization since the 1980s, the development of democracy in South Korea since the 1980s, and the development of free trade treaties in the early 1990s introduced half of the population of 3.4 billion people previously locked in their national economies to the global economy. Harvard economist Richard Freeman calls it a "big doubling" of the global workforce because outsourcing has been a product of Asia, especially China. In the late 1990s, Internetization accelerated these global integration processes. The results are staggering. In the 1970s, bicycles were the primary method of transport in China, while now, in the 2020s, China is the largest vehicle manufacturer in the world. Who at that time imagined the use of the Internet would grow exponentially around the world?

The challenge of globalization in the 21st century has reached education, which has the task of preparing graduates for the smooth functioning of the global economy. The concept of training young people has begun to focus on developing global citizens based on *digital citizenship*. However, this trend has led to a mismatch, since "the world is flat" (Friedman, 2005). Because globalization is leveling the borders and privileges of developed countries, production, and services (*online*) should be invested where the labor force is cheapest. This has led to a radical reduction in the middle class in Western civilization (Targowski, 2014b) and an increase in the anti-globalization movement, especially during Donald

DOI: 10.4018/978-1-7998-8036-3.ch015

Trump's presidency (2017-2020) in the United States. The 2020 pandemic has reinforced the trend of anti-globalization because the virus has limited international connections. In addition, the blame for the virus's spread is attributed to China, which has caused a rapid reduction in the globalist strategy and has resulted in restricted trade with this World Factory.

The globalization and Internetization of the countries, societies, and organizations of the world have strongly influenced the paradigms of teaching, for graduates need to be prepared in terms of knowledge and wisdom as well as qualifications for the challenges of this kind of world—one in which Western civilization has evolved into a Global Civilization (Targowski, 2014a), which in turn is transforming into Virtual civilization (Targowski, 2015). The repercussions of these civilization processes have impacted the mode of teaching both at primary and secondary schools and at universities. Certain professions are abandoned, new ones are born (see the chapter *Strategic Digital Informing and Its Challenges in the 21st Century*), and most professions require a new way of thinking and new knowledge, wisdom, and qualifications, which will be discussed in this chapter.

GLOBAL CITIZENSHIP

Global Citizenship Education (GCED) is UNESCO's response to these challenges. It works by empowering students of all ages to understand that these are global rather than local problems and by pushing students to become active promoters of more peaceful, tolerant, inclusive, safe, and sustainable societies. GCED is based on three areas of learning – cognitive, socio-emotional, and behavioral:

- **Cognitive**: knowledge and thinking skills necessary to better understand the world and its complexity.
- **Socio-emotional**: values, attitudes, and social skills that enable students to develop affective, psychosocial, and physical traits that enable them to live with others with respect and peace.
- **Behavior**: behavior and performance needed for practical application and commitment.

The key learning outcomes, student attributes, topics, and learning goals suggested in GCED are based on the three learning domains mentioned above. They are linked and integrated into a learning process. UNESCO's work in this field is guided by the Education Agenda 2030 and the framework for action, in particular Objective 4.7 of the Sustainable Development Goals (SDG 4 on Education), which calls on countries to…

provide all learners with knowledge and skills to promote sustainable development, including, inter alia, through education for sustainable development and sustainable lifestyle, human rights, gender equality, the promotion of a culture of peace and non-violence, global citizenship and recognition of cultural diversity and cultural contribution to sustainable development.

The concept of GCED pedagogy is given in Figure 1.

This pedagogical model of global citizenship should permeate most all school subjects.

Figure 1. Pedagogy model of global citizenship (United Nations Educational, Scientific, and Cultural Organization, 2014)

DIGITAL CITIZENSHIP

The world's first computer science program, the Cambridge Diploma in Computer Science, began at the University of Cambridge Computer Laboratory in 1953. The first department of Computer Science in the United States was founded at Purdue University in 1962. In Poland, the first Management Information Systems (MIS) program was established in 1959 at the Warsaw University of Technology, which was launched by Professor Seweryn Chajtman from the Department of Engineering and Economic Engineering (Industrial Engineering). The first graduates of this program defended their master's theses in 1961. The Department of Numerical Methods (a branch of the department of mathematics) was established at the University of Wrocław in 1961 and at the Warsaw University in 1964.

In the United States, the education of non-digital students (those untrained with the use of computer technologies) was limited by the extent to which the university had computing equipment, which at that time was limited to expensive mainframes. However, the university did begin to teach programming and the use of computers for engineering calculations in FORTRAN. To expand the digital education of all students, the timesharing system was developed, that is, the use of a computer by hundreds or even thousands of students at the "same time" with remote online terminals. One of the first timesharing systems was the GE 225 (1961), for which John Kemeny designed an interactive and very easy BASIC programming language for online computing, with the immediate compilation of external instructions into machine language. Over the next 26 years, all students were educated in BASIC programming. As the quiet, creeping revolution of IBM PC/MAC microcomputers began, this type of digital training became based on this new emerging type of equipment.

In the early 2000s, when the use of the Internet became widespread in Western civilization, the concept of digital citizenship was created, which can be used to determine the proper and responsible use of technology among users. Mike Ribble (2020) has developed three principles to teach digital users how to responsibly use technology to become digital citizens: respect, educate, and protect. Each rule contains three of the nine elements of digital citizenship (Digital Citizenship, n.d.):

- **Respect**: ethical elements, access, and the rights of other digital users are promoted.
- **Education**: elements of e-literacy, e-communication and e-trade are used to explore the proper use of the digital world.
- **Protection**: elements of rights and obligations, safety, and health and well-being are used to maintain security in the digital and non-digital worlds

Within these three basic principles, nine elements should be considered regarding digital citizenship (Digital Citizenship, n.d.):

1. **Digital access**: this is perhaps one of the most basic ways of being a digital citizen. However, due to socio-economic status, location, and other disabilities, some people may lack digital access. Recently, schools have become increasingly connected to the Internet, often offering computers and other forms of access. This can be offered in kiosks, cultural centers, and open laboratories. This is most associated with digital exclusion and related factors. Digital access is available in many remote countries via cyber-cafés and small cafes.
2. **Digital trade**: users can recognize that a significant part of the economy is regulated online. It also deals with understanding the risks and benefits of online shopping, using credit cards online, and so on. As with the benefits and legal actions, there are also dangerous activities such as illegal downloading, gambling, drug contracts, pornography, plagiarism, and so on.
3. **Digital communication**: this element concerns understanding various means of online communication, such as email, instant messaging, Facebook messenger, application diversity, and so on. Each substrate is bound by a standard of etiquette.
4. **Digital literacy**: this concerns understanding how different digital devices are used, for example, how to search correctly for something in a search engine compared to a database and how to use different logs online. Often, educational institutions shape a person's digital skills.
5. **Digital etiquette**: this is the expectation that different media require a variety of labels. Some media require more appropriate behavior and language than others.
6. **Digital law**: This refers to the enforcement of laws regulating illegal downloads, plagiarism, hacking, virus creation, spam, identity theft, and cyberbullying, among others.
7. **Digital rights and responsibilities**: Just as in the American Constitution where there is a Bill of Rights, there is a basic set of rights extended to every digital citizen. Digital citizens have the right to privacy, free speech, etc. Basic digital rights must be addressed, discussed, and understood in the digital world. With these rights also come responsibilities as well. Users must know how the technology should be used in an appropriate manner. In a digital society these two areas must work together for everyone to be productive.
8. **Digital health and wellness**: digital citizens must be aware of the physical stress that using the Internet has on their bodies. They need to be aware that they cannot become too addicted to the Internet, causing problems such as eye strain, headaches, and stress.
9. **Digital security**: this simply means that citizens must take security measures, practicing the use of secure passwords, virus protection, data backup, etc.

In addition, in a study by Common Sense Media, it was found about six out of 10 American K-12 teachers used digital citizenship curriculum and seven out of ten taught competence skills using digital citizenship. Many of the sections on which these teachers focused included hate speech, cyberbullying, and digital drama. The problem with digital technology, which still exists, is that more than 35% of students do not have the appropriate skills to critically assess information online, and these problems increase as the grade level increases. Online videos such as those found on YouTube and Netflix were used by about 60% of K-12 teachers in classrooms, and educational tools like Microsoft Office and Google G Suite were used by about half of teachers. Social media was used the least (13%) compared to other digital tools of education. Looking at the differences in social classes between schools, the study found that public schools were more likely to use digital citizenship curricula than teachers in more affluent schools (Vega & Robb, 2019).

Over the past two years, there has been a major shift from digital citizenship to digital leadership having a greater impact on online interactions. While digital citizens take a responsible approach by acting ethically, digital leadership is more proactive and includes "using the Internet and social media to improve the lives, well-being, and situations of others" as part of everyday life (TeachThought, 2019).

COMPUTATIONAL THINKING

In education, *computational thinking* involves expressing problems and solving them in ways that can be assisted by computers. This involves mental skills and practices in:

1. Designing calculations that force computers to perform tasks for us,
2. Explaining and interpreting the world as a complex of information processes, including computational processes (Denning & Tedre, 2019).

Computational thinking includes ideas such as abstraction, data representation, and logical data ordering, which are also prevalent in other types of thinking, such as scientific thinking, engineering thinking, systemic thinking, design thinking, model thinking, and the like. This new term was preceded by others, such as "scientific thinking", "algorithmic thinking", "procedural thinking", and "computational skills". After all, scientific thinking was defined by René Descartes 385+ years ago in the book *Discourse on the Method* (1637), where scientific problem solving was divided into: 1) denial, 2) the division of the problem into smaller ones, 3) the solution to smaller problems and 4) the integration of partial solutions into a holistic solution.

Computational thinking is designed to develop analytical thinking based on methods of computer science. It was defined by the International Society for Technology in Education (ISTE) and the Computer Science Teachers Association (CSTA) in 2011 as a recommended approach for most subjects taught in schools and was characterized in the following way (ISTE & CSTA, 2011):

1. Formulating problems in a way that they can be solved using computers and other techniques,
2. The logical organization and analysis of data,
3. Representing data by abstraction in models and simulations,
4. Automating solutions by algorithmizing thinking into a series of orderly procedures,

5. Identifying, analyzing, and implementing possible solutions with a view to applying the most efficient combination of procedures and resources,
6. Generalizing received solutions to various other problems.

Computational thinking should not be equated with the simple use of computers or mathematical calculations. It should not be limited to inputting data into mathematical formulas to compute them in a mechanical way. For example, the use of a "whiteboard" on a computer screen may involve students in interactive problem solving, especially with the graphical modeling of the problem and its elements. For example, graphically modeling the relationship between plants and animals should lead to generalizations and algorithmic thinking and abstractions. Eventually, students will learn to formulate problems for the computer to solve them, which will require planning a program flowchart and then coding it in a programming language. The resulting software can then be used for other computational tasks. Consequently, the student can learn to use a spreadsheet to computerize his / her budget. Thanks to this, the barrier of mathematics, which is the bane of many students and sometimes an insurmountable impediment to progress in their educational careers, can be broken. Therefore, computational thinking should be learned and applied by every student in school.

Computational thinking can be taught in the classroom and through various interest groups, such as:

- The interest-oriented circles of robotics, computer games, and simulating processes in nature and economy,
- Creative writing for newspaper articles or imaginary stories that are analyzed down into elements and then put together,
- Simulating the chorography of a planned dance performance at a school event by planning the figures and then harmonizing them,
- Others.

Teachers with limited digital practice are the critical link in implementing computational thinking among pupils.

INFORMATIONAL THINKING

With respect to computational thinking as proposed by American (and copied in other countries) computer scientists in 2011, it is surprising that the development of mass MIS systems in business and administration (since the 1960s) and the rapid development of Internetization since the 2000s (including e-mail, e-commerce, e-press or e-books, as well as digital libraries and communication platforms, including social networks such as Facebook and Twitter) have left no trace in what is supposedly modern thinking recommended to every pupil/student. The reason for this is that the so-called computer scientists are machine-oriented computer introverts, while IT professionals are "extroverts" oriented towards what is "outside" the computer.

The limited amount of computational thinking is due to the roots of computer science, which is oriented towards programming syntaxes (although the 2011 recommendation suggested expanding beyond the limits of computer coding). This extension, however, completely ignores the rapid development of the Digital Revolution (discussed in the chapter *Waves of Civilization Development and the Digital Revolu-*

tion) in the 2020s. While numbers are information, not every piece of information is a number. Hence, computational thinking cannot be the only way of thinking required to computerize modern civilization.

It is worth recalling that communication strongly impacts the success of our civilization. Communication has proceeded and developed on three levels through the ages:

1. **Syntactic level** – determining how to communicate, as exemplified in the grammar of human and programming languages.
2. **Semantic level** – determining what the subject of our communication is (e.g., spoken or written).
3. **Pragmatic level** – determining why we communicate. At this level of communication, the wisdom of action is essential. This means that the "data" itself and the current fashionable data science will not lead to this level of knowledge and wisdom in the form of a wisdom-based science. After all, not only are experts wise, but children can also be wise if they know what wisdom is (Figure 2).

Figure 2. The role of wisdom in human cognizing, thinking, and deciding (Krawczyk & Targowski, 2019, p. 264)

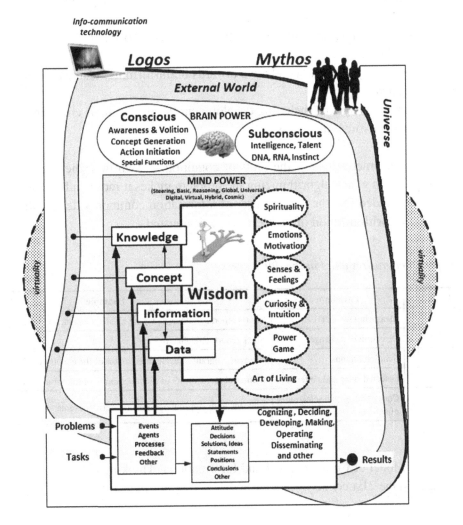

In the age of the digitization of data and knowledge, the first goal is to understand what we are curious about and what we want to convey in speech or writing to others. Therefore, informed people must be able to use a full cycle of cognizing, which consists of the following areas of semantics (Figure 2):

- Cognitive units (Table 1) (Targowski, 1990, 2017):
  - **Data**: recording and measuring events such as the Dow Jones index of the New York Stock Exchange measuring at 20,000 points.
  - **Information**: the amount of change, e.g., the index fell 2,000 points, or 20 percent, the next day. This information generates options.
  - **Concept**:
    - Option 1 to buy more shares as they fall.
    - Option 2 to sell shares as they could drop even more.
    - Option 3 to hold stocks and ride out the stock market fluctuations.
  - **Knowledge**: having knowledge about the rules of conduct for these options in the context of the state of the national and global economy.
  - **Wisdom**: a choice of options supported by your knowledge of a given decision-making situation in the context of the art of living of the decision-maker.
- Critical thinking, including analysis, interpretation, openness to different views, and solving socio-economic problems,
- Presenting ideas in ways that are conducive towards brainstorming, teamwork, discussing, arguing, and communicating,
- The ethics of computerization, including development trends and their challenges as well as the attitudes of IT professionals and users.

Understanding the characteristics of the units of cognition (shown in Table 1) is as important as computational thinking, in which algorithmizing the problem makes it more understandable and easier to solve. It can be concluded that the modern user of information commonly deals with these units of cognition, while the algorithmization of problems is more unusual.

Table 1. Example of cognition units in the daily press

Cognition Units	Paradigm	Example
Data	Measuring the fact	Sports reports, obituaries, voting results, cinema, and theatre programs
Information	Detection of a change	Stock report; epidemic reports
Concept	Solution options	Election programs; development plans of the country or companies
Knowledge	Detected rules and patterns	Statistical assessments of the functioning of the economy or companies
Wisdom	Correct rating and selection of options	Editorial with editorial opinions for current events

Figure 3 lists the Model of Computational and Informational Thinking (MCIT) as one of the types of modern thinking in the 21st century.

Figure 3. The Model of Computational and Informational Thinking (MCIT)

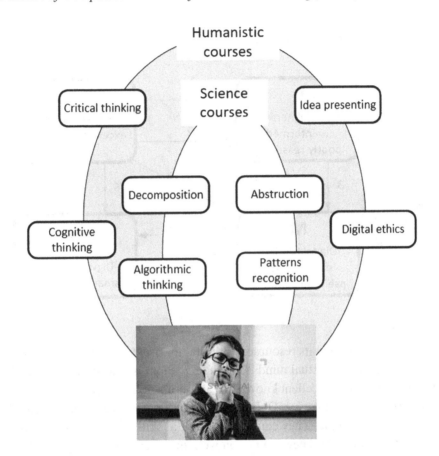

The degree of possibility for informational thinking in the 21st century determines the possible exclusion of information from society and determines entry into the information elite, as illustrated by the model in Figure 4.

The categories of membership in society regarding the use of information (according to the model in Figure 4) can be characterized as follows:

- **M – Digital tourists** are good "internet users" (mainly the younger generation) who spend hours using the Internet; however, their knowledge and ability to use and understand cognitive units are shallow, as is their reading level. They collect large amounts of data and become "datamaniacs", but their reasoning is pseudo-reasoning—sometimes it is effective, but for the most part it is questionable. If they improve their knowledge and information skills, they can become "digital natives" (path 8). Thus far, their knowledge can even be characterized as negative, and their wisdom is questionable.

- **B – Digital illiterates** use traditional (old) information and communication technologies. They are misinformed and have only their own non-digital reasoning capacities; however, if they raise their knowledge and skills, they can move on to become digital immigrants (path 1), which involves working to adapt to the new conditions for processing information. They can improve the

Figure 4. Categories of information users

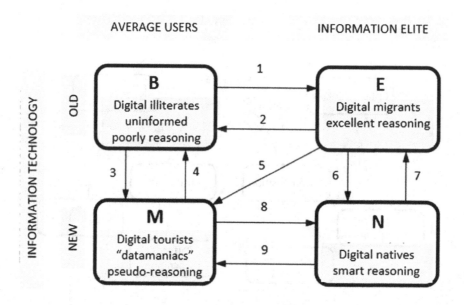

ability to use the Internet and its resources as digital tourists (path 2). Their knowledge is limited due to a lack of digital and virtual minds, and their wisdom is at a commonsense level.

- **E - Digital migrants** have excellent knowledge and skills in information handling, but they main-ly use old information technologies. Only from time to time do they use new technologies, usually with the help of other people. They can improve digital skills by becoming digital tourists (track 5) or digital natives (track 6). They can reason well; however, they struggle with the use of digital and virtual minds. Their wisdom is mainly based on traditional criteria.
- **N - Digital natives** are part of the information elite and use new ICT technologies. They under-stand and reason very well. They have good digital and virtual minds, so their knowledge is con-stantly updated, and their wisdom is based on global criteria.

If specialists do not use their knowledge and skills, they may lose them (paths 2, 4, 7 and 9). Fur-thermore, it is wrong to say that, since the information elite can understand best, we should only educate these kinds of graduates. It must not be forgotten that, not only are these individuals good at digital thinking, but they also belong to those well-educated more broadly in information. This kind of elite has a comprehensive education in the humanities as well as good professions, and their knowledge and skills in information and communication technologies are the second layer of their education. It is wrong to think that only great digital skills and qualifications make a human being a member of the information elite, for such a master of digitization lacks the ability to correctly interpret information, which can lead to one becoming a data maniac and to developing misconceptions of situations and the world.

SYSTEMIC THINKING

Thinking for modern humans cannot be based merely on computational and informational thinking because this would narrow one's perception of a situation and the world, and it would limit one's ability to function in modern Global-Virtual civilization. Because this civilization is a system of systems and subsystems that entangles all of humankind, whatever a person touches is, in some way, connected with the "system". For example, e-mail belongs to the super-internet system, as does Facebook as well as MS Word editor, in which one can write, say, an appeal against the decision of a tax office or write a letter to one's bride. If you want to fly from Warsaw to Nice for a holiday, then you need to purchase a ticket in the great booking system of the airline. Modern cars have large mechanical and electronic systems that cannot simply be repaired with a screwdriver. Similarly, a modern residential building is a large physical structure with an electronic system. Working online, in a virtual school, or in an online store like Amazon involves being a part of a great system in which one must be able to function. Furthermore, what are robots and drones? These are complex systems used for "simple" operations.

Therefore, systemic thinking is a necessary complement to computational and informational thinking. The definition of this type of thinking is as follows:

Systemic thinking is a holistic approach to analysis and design that focuses on how system components work interconnectedly, how systems evolve overtime, and how systems work in the context of larger systems.

About 2400 years ago, Aristotle (384-322 BCE) stated that "the whole is greater than the sum of its parts". Many centuries later, Frederick G. W. Hegel (1770-1831) added the following properties to describe a system:

- The whole determines the nature of the parts.
- Parts cannot be understood in isolation from their entirety.
- Parts of the whole are in mutual relations.

At the beginning of the 20th century, the concept of a living organism began to be discussed, the complexity of which cannot be determined based on the characteristics of its isolated elements. In the 1920s, German biologist Ludwig von Bertalanffy proposed a theory of systems for analyzing organisms. In a refined form, he defined the General Theory of Systems in 1951. This theory was supported by cybernetics research, with feedback proposed by Norbert Wiener (1894-1964) in 1948:

The system is a purpose-controlled structure of interconnected elements in pursuit of benefits outside the system despite adversity.

For example, a car is a transport system to drive from Warsaw to Krakow, that is, to overcome the 300 km that lay between the vehicle and its destination, despite the snowfall and icing.

The literature on systemic thinking is enormous. Here we will recall the principles of systemic engineering, which indicate the method of systemic thinking, formulated by Targowski (1990):

1. **Cybernetization**: the feedback and self-organization of the complexity of elements to return to the basic state of the system, based on homeostasis,
2. **Systematization**: the clearly and deliberately organized structure of elements,
3. **Consistency**: the harmonious relationships of elements to effectively achieve goals,

4. **Categorization**: the complete organization of elements without redundancy,
5. **Primitiveness**: the hierarchy of complexity of elements in a structure, based on the simplest elements at its base.
6. **Completeness**: the system containing all necessary elements,
7. **Value engineering**: the system containing only necessary elements and interconnections for a deliberate result.
8. **Open structure**: the structure of the system making it possible to supplement it as the system develops.

The ability to use system engineering principles is an effective way of preparing graduates to work in the fields of computer science, engineering, sociology, and others, fields where he/she will be a user of information systems.

Figure 5. Model of complexity for business and administrative type organizational system (V = view)

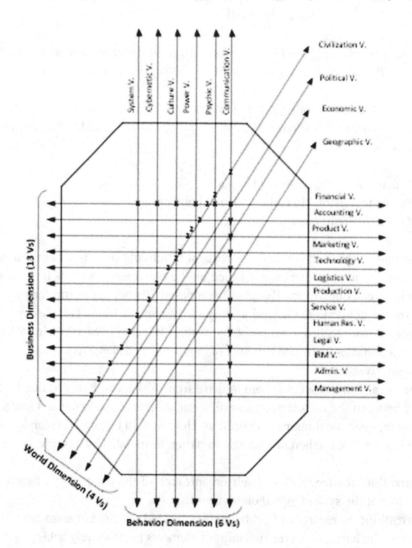

In systemic thinking, it is very important to understand the complexity of systems. It is known that most graduates of schools and universities will not work in the government but in companies and organizations that require public administration. The complexity of such systems is illustrated in the model in Figure 5.

For example, business and administrative organizational systems can be designed based on 13 business perspectives, 6 behavioral perspectives, and 4 context perspectives of the world (Figure 5), that is, 23 perspectives in total. Of course, the number of perspectives one chooses depends on the analyst or system designer. For the given example, the average system has 7 elements, shown in Table 2.

Table 2. The complexity of an organizational business system

System Level	Number of Elements	Number of Relations	Number of States	Number of Views	Number of Elemenets	Number of Relations	Number of States
Intra-view	7	21	128	23	161	483	2,944
Inter-view	23	2,553	8,388,608	1	23	2,553	8,388,608
Total				24	184	3,036	8,391,552

In the Table 2:

- Number of relations [r] among elements € of a system r = (e-1) e:2
- Minimum number of states (s) (active and not active) s =2^e

This 23-elements-based system model shows that the company's chief executive officer (CEO) should assess and make decisions about the state of his/her organization's 8,391,552 situations, which, of course, is not possible; however, thanks to IT systems, one's attention can be focused on several elements and their critical states, assuming the remaining components function under established boundary conditions monitored by the computer.

The concept of systemic thinking based on the number of elements considered leads to the methodology of student training and student education. Table 3 shows the expected ability to think system-wise depends on the number of system elements.

It is necessary to plan the pedagogical methodology of a school, university, and professional training activities based on the given number of elements that a person needs to use effectively in his/her problem-solving profession.

PANORAMIC LEADERSHIP IN THE AGE OF DIGITALIZATION

Computerization at a time of widespread use of the Internet, social networks, and various digital platforms as well as the fascination and dependence of young people on smartphones has limited real, F2F (Face-to-Face) communication and has made it possible to live through virtual communication. Of course, this is a disadvantage for people, both in terms of health and socialization. That is why digital citizenship and global citizenship as well as computational, informational, and systemic thinking cannot

Table 3. The ability to think system-wise according to the number of elements concerned

Level of Analysts	Ability to Analyze the Number of Elements	Examples
Graduate of elementary school	1	Knows the health effects of smoking cigarettes
Graduate of high school	2	Knows the health effects of smoking cigarettes and drinking sweetened "refreshing" drinks
Graduate 3-4 year-based studies	3-4	Knows the effects of coal imports on the national coal industry
Graduate 5-6 year-based studies	5-6	Knows the effects of a pandemic on the national economy
Ph.D holder	6-7	Knows the effects of a pandemic on the global economy
Professor	7-10	Knows the effects of his/her specialization on the development of civilization
CEO	7-11	Knows the effects of a pandemic on the development of the company
Secretary, prime minister, president	11-12	Knows the effects of global warming on a targeted area/country
Designer of info-decision based systems	12-13	Knows how to design a climate warming IT system
Analyst of intelligence	13-15	Knows the reasons for the 2020 pandemic

be focused on merely observing and getting to know what is happening in the world. A person with this type of thinking and skills should be active and, as far as possible, should lead in situations in which he/she finds himself/herself and which require intervention, thanks to the social resonance possible through computerization.

For years, people were raised in steep social hierarchies, as was the case, for instance, for those in the military, where the soldier was a small "cog" in a great military machine. Today, however, soldiers do not fight in the trenches as in World War I. In the wars in Iraq and Afghanistan, for example, soldiers faught in small units of several people, were mobile, and had to cope with unexpected situations and the adversaries themselves. The most help one could get in critical situations was to call a helicopter for support. In addition, in the hierarchical military tradition of the 19th century, children were raised to be "polite and sit quietly." They behaved in a similarly passive way in adulthood.

Today, civilization is facing many crises, and this requires a timely response aimed at securing the common good from every section. Therefore, the aforementioned "citizenships" and ways of thinking should be integrated and activated to ensure that the individual user is able to conduct themselves, as illustrated by the model of panoramic leadership in Figure 6.

After all, it should be recalled that one of the most dangerous crisis-producing factors of our time is the lack of conflict-free communication between people, between cultures, and between civilizations. Even in families, a significant crisis, divorce, is caused by a lack of good, friendly communication.

Hence, pupils and students as well as participants in professional development courses need, above all, to learn to communicate and distinguish the following qualities of this process (further explained in section 2.2. of this book):

- Transinformation
- Pseudoinformation
- Missed information
- Parainformation
- Misinformation
- Information about data
- Metainformation
- Debating
- Argumentation
- Conflict resolution
- Conducting meetings
- Others

Figure 6. Panoramic (all-inclusive communicating) leadership in the 2020s

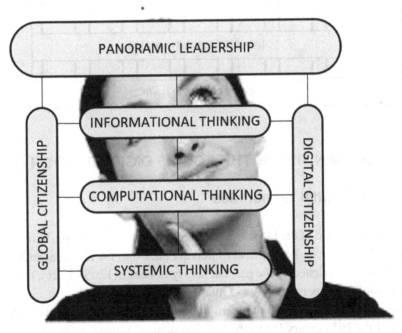

It is not being proposed that the teaching of panoramic (all-inclusive and communicating) leadership should occur in a single lecture from a silo of the school and university; rather, as illustrated by Table 3, this depends on the level of teaching and the number of elements of the system being considered. This kind of leadership is illustrated in Figure 7.

Figure 7. Infiltration of inclusive leadership into education programs

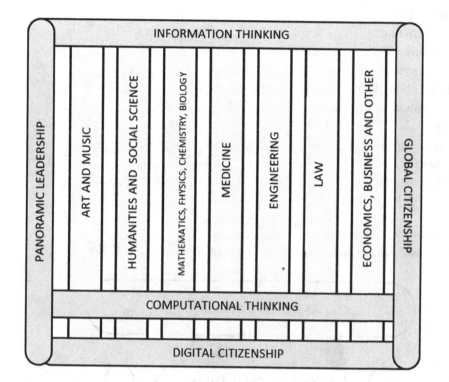

TEACHING THE HUMANITIES IN THE AGE OF DIGITALIZATION

From Humanism to Digital Humanities

Humanism developed at the end of the Dark Ages, when, after the fall of Rome, barbarism reigned. After a few hundred years the intellectual movement of delving back into the classical antiquity of Greece and Rome began to come alive, enriched by the nascent poetry of Dante (1265–1321), Petrarch (1304-1374), and Chaucer (1343-1400) and perpetuated by Gutenberg's print (1453).

The Italian Renaissance developed humanism in art and architecture, and the Industrial Revolution of the second half of the 19th century led to the development of humanism in literature and philosophy, and then also in sociology and even political science and history, which was reflected in university programs developed in modern times. This development intensified after World War II, whose genocide provoked a sharp cry from free intellectuals. Studying the so-called "Great Books" was mainly done in terms of humanism. In American universities, the humanities departments and professional sciences (medicine, law, business, and engineering) were highly separated, organizationally. With the digitization of cognition, however, the digital humanities were born, which sees opportunities for humanistic knowledge to develop through the digital penetration of existing knowledge. The movement also sees the development of humanistic knowledge as addressing challenges of civilization which, at present, are mainly addressed within the context of maximizing financial profit. What is the goal of Big Tech in the digitalization of knowledge? To the digital humanities, technology can be counted as websites, digital libraries, social networks, multimedia techniques, communication platforms, and in-depth statistics on problem solving, digital screen culture, etc.

Scientific researchers draw their knowledge from data of the physical world, while humanists draw their knowledge from the human world and from human activities that have been recorded in documents stored in libraries, archives, and museums. Currently, the digital humanities deal with "data" that can be processed on computers. This type of data includes texts, statistics, videos, images, etc., which are of two basic kinds: source data (e.g., wills, contracts for the transfer of farms or buildings, etc.) and processed data constituting published descriptions of the source data. The best data are authoritative documents that can be digitally analyzed and whose results depend on the rich digital context that can be derived from multiple digital libraries. As a result of the digital humanities, a student or researcher can develop their knowledge based on the following approaches to a research topic:

- Holistically, analytically, graphically, verbally, aurally (or visually via video), graphically, quantitatively (computationally),
- Increasing knowledge via in-depth analyses not accessible by traditional methods (Figure 8),
- Presenting knowledge logically, practically, and creatively with attractive visualizations of solutions (Figure 9).

Figure 8. Digital linguistic analysis of the use of certain words in terms of genres (Devopedia, 2019)

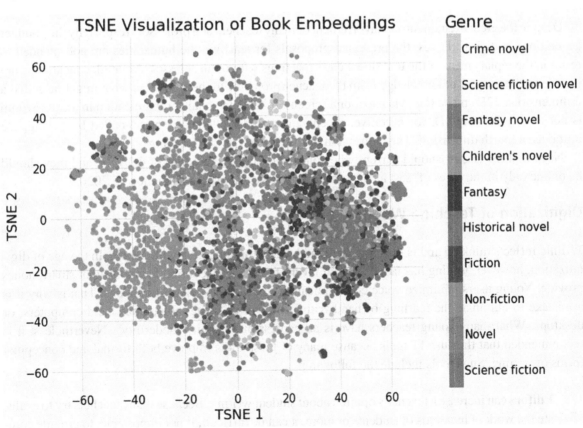

Figure 9. An example of a digital visualization of the history of life on Earth (Ramos et al., 2013)

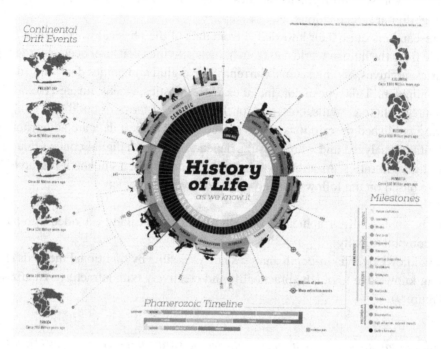

Despite the great excitement and involvement of many teachers and professors (especially the younger generation) in digital classes, the presented proposals for teaching the humanities are not intended to result in the replacement of the traditional class meetings with online classes. After all, education is not just about the transfer of knowledge from the teacher/professor to the student in what might be called a 2-dimensional (2D) mode (i.e., via paper or a screen). In fact, personal communication in the classroom is not merely 3D, but 4D, for narrative, accentuation, understatement, and so-called body language introduce a fourth dimension. This dimension is absent from online teaching.

Nevertheless, classes should currently be conducted via mixed modes of delivery, and they should be online only in the cases of, say, a pandemic, such as we are experiencing now in 2020.

Digitization of Teaching Writing

Writing reflects thinking and is the basis for thoughtful communication with people. In the age of digitalization, however, writing has faded away in favor of the use of icons and symbols that smartphones provide. Young users minimize voice communication in favor of symbols and icons. That is why it is a mistake to eliminate the learning of handwriting in favor of using tablets, handheld computers, or desktops. What many young teachers have is an expression of their "modernity". Nevertheless, it is recommended that they use IT tools because many of these tools improve both formal and conceptual forms of writing. Such tools include the following:

1. **Editors** can increase a teacher's opinion about student writing. Because many teachers try to evaluate the work of hundreds of students or more, it can be difficult, if not impossible, to provide comments and insights for each student. Although budgets do not allow teachers to take fewer classes,

there are some high-tech solutions to this problem that can ensure students receive the help they need and that teachers are not burdened with grading. Increasingly complex and comprehensive programs are available to help students fix writing errors and can provide feedback during the writing process when it matters most. Students can use feedback to make changes before they submit an article and divide it into more manageable parts so that it does not seem overwhelming. While such programs are still evolving, they will undoubtedly become a tool that will help instructors teach students to write in the decades to come.

2. **Grammar tutorials** can complement a teacher's instructions. Many students find it difficult to understand grammar rules, even if they have been taught in the classroom. They simply cannot bridge the gap between the conceptual idea and its implementation in practice. Direct interactions with teachers can help, but technology can offer a different path for overloaded teachers. There are hundreds of sites that contain grammar tutorials, and some of them even include exercises that engage students and help fill gaps in their knowledge. There is software available that can help students as they type by solving grammatical problems as they arise. With these kinds of support and guidance, students can learn how to become better writers from both teachers and technology.

3. **Digital monitoring of student learning progress**: This type of software helps teachers observe students' progress as they write or complete a task. One such product is called Essay Punch. It helps students write a step-by-step essay, from preparation to publication, and even offers contextual help and feedback throughout the text. It also allows teachers to monitor progress or lack of progress as students develop their essays. This is not the only product of its kind, and such tools allow students to get help from start to finish while writing every word of the assignment.

4. **Multimedia experiences**: Today, there are hundreds of free multimedia tools that teachers can use in the classroom, many of which combine perfectly with writing tasks that challenge and engage students. For example, some teachers ask students to combine their recorded videos with written poetry or write scripts for short films. Others allow students to turn their stories into animations. While a small investment in technology may be necessary to run these kinds of programs, many teachers report that students who are creative and use advanced technologies to improve their writing work harder, are more likely to change, and want to create something that is really great, not just please the teacher.

5. **Digitizing teams in writing projects**: This technology makes it easy for students to collaborate on anything, including writing projects. There are even free products, like Google Drive, which allow students to collaborate on a project or provide useful feedback in the writing process. Teachers can also comment if documents are shared. While there are many platforms that allow collaboration, Google has actually created a tutorial and useful materials in collaboration with Writing for Teens, which teachers and students can use to make collaborative writing easy and productive.

6. **Blogs** force students to write for wider audiences, which can result a completely different outcome than asking students to prepare an essay that will only be read by the teacher. There are many education-oriented blog sites that address problems related to student safety and protection yet still allow students to prepare writing online. On these sites, students can collaborate in the classroom or work independently to create blogs on various topics. Since most writing in a student's future work can be done digitally, learning to write in the digital sphere is a key skill to develop. What is more, most children love to be able to share their writing via blogs, so this could be a great motivator for reluctant writers.

7. **Tablets** have become a standard tool in today's classes, and, for good reason, writing is not exempt from their influence. Tablets offer students an easy way to share and view their ideas. They can also load apps that help them practice grammar, translate their writing into other media, and collaborate with classmates on different projects.

8. **Common internal tools of the school**: As national standards begin to be applied in schools in most countries (e.g., the EU), many teachers are looking for ways to help students develop new writing guidelines set out by these standards, many of which focus on writing the literature of fact (i.e., expository writing). While national standards may not yet be available worldwide, there are already useful technical tools that teachers can use to teach writing under the new guidelines. One such site is StudySync, which provides access to hundreds of digital books, offers weekly writing practices, has online writing and review options, and even includes multimedia writing lessons. It offers a wide range of tools that can be useful in helping teachers adapt to new standards and encourage students at every level to learn to love writing.

9. **Applications around the world**: Unfortunately, many students hate writing because they find it boring and unhelpful. Many students simply do not learn practical ways to apply what they learn and create. Experts suggest that teachers can facilitate greater student engagement by emphasizing the purposes and applications of student writing. Online networks can be a valuable tool for this, as most students are currently communicating through online forums. Students can compare products, write short essays describing their position on a given topic, and even create research-based websites that can inform and teach readers.

10. **Publishing student works**: When students are proud of their work, they love to publish it. In addition, knowing that something will be published so others can see it can motivate students to do a better job from the start. There are many online publishing options that teachers can use to promote student works. Student works can be presented on a school website or blog, and other sites offer different options. Google Drive and Zoho Writer allow students to turn their writing into a website, and Yudu and Issuu help turn writing into a newsletter or e-book. These are just a few of the many options available that can help student writing.

The Digital Revolution has significantly changed our views on what can be considered minimal literacy skills. Computers provide new support to writers when generating and organizing written texts and, via email and the Internet, introduce what Freedman and Daiute (2001) call "a new text component of human relationships". Amid widespread assumptions about the long-term consequences of these new technologies, researchers continue to explore the experiences of students and teachers using such tools. The consequences are numerous in terms of broadening our definitions of the writing process as well as our concepts of the relationships between writers, readers, and the texts they create.

Digitization of Teaching History

Digital history is the use of digital media for further historical analysis, presentation, and research. It consists in expanding and applying quantitative history (i.e., cliometrics, the application of methods developed in other fields, such as economics, statistics, and data processing in computer science) to the study of history. Digital history is a common digital story that primarily involves engaging online audiences with historical content or digital research methods for further research. The results of digital history include digital archives, online presentations, data visualizations, interactive maps, timelines, audio files, and virtual worlds that make stories more accessible to audiences. Recent digital history projects focus on creativity, collaboration, technical innovation, text exploration, networking, 3D modeling, and the analysis of big data. By using these resources, a historian can quickly develop new insights that can combine, expand, and revive existing stories and give them practical meanings and implications for the present. It has become possible for historians to use enormous resources of historical knowledge contained in digital libraries. Thanks to this, historians can develop the greater context of historical events and give them new interpretations.

Among interesting digital projects, one can mention the Geography of Slavery and Slavery in Texas. In each of these projects, archives containing many types of sources were combined with digital tools for analysis (statistical) and interactive presentations. This integration of content and tools into analysis is one of the hallmarks of digital history: projects go beyond archives and collections and move into the realm of scientific analysis. The differences between the way projects take these integrations into account are a measure of the development of this area, and they point to ongoing debates about what digital history can and should be.

Digital history is now a common type of course in graduate and undergraduate programs. For example, students in digital history courses at the University of Hertfordshire (UK) have acquired digital mapping and Python programming skills, making it easier to analyze large amounts of source data. One of the projects the class worked on included an analysis of trends, patterns, and data relationships related to weather, crime, and poverty. This enabled students to use their traditional historical skills to assess the importance of their discoveries. Another project, based on British History Online, used digital mapping to compare the differences between different groups of students studying at Oxford.

Digital historians can use Content System Management to store their digital collection, which includes audio, video, images, and text that can be viewed via the Internet. Examples of such systems are *Drupal, WordPress*, and *Omeka*. In addition, systems such as the Geographical Information System (GIS) can be used to analyze the movement of people and their organization in social structures.

As part of semantic interoperability of metadata and information in different environments, MIT has developed reliable open-source tools that enable access, management, and anticipation of digital asset development. Among the many tools built by SIMILE, the Timeline tool uses the AJAXu widget (graphical user interface) based on DHTML, which allows digital historians to create dynamic, configurable timelines to visualize time-based events. The SIMILE Timeline page says their tool "resembles Google Maps for time-based information." In addition, the SIMILE tool allows users to sort and present data. The visualization, written in JavaScript, creates interactive, data-rich websites without the need-to-know programming or create databases.

The faculty members of digital history programs themselves teach computer science, as illustrated by the syllabus below for a course at George Manson University, offered by a faculty member of History and Art History in 2017 (Figure 10):

Digitization of Sociology Teaching

Sociology has been used for decades in computational thinking and even systemic thinking, as it intensively uses various computational techniques for statistics. In the 2020s, however, digital sociology is moving into new territories, as it now is beginning to examine not only the impacts of the Internet or cyberculture, but also the influence of other digital media and devices that have emerged since the first decade of the 21st century. As the Internet has become more ubiquitous and associated with everyday

Figure 10. Example of a digital history course at George Mason University

Data and Visualization in Digital History

HIST697-001: Creating History in New Media. Spring 2017. Department of History and Art History, George Mason University. 3 credits. Meets Mondays, 7:20 p.m. to 10:00 p.m., at RRCHNM, Research Hall fourth floor.

Instructor: Lincoln Mullen <lmullen@gmu.edu>. Office: Research Hall 457. Office hours on Tuesdays, 1:30 p.m to 2:30 p.m.; Thursdays, 2:00 p.m. to 3:00 p.m.; and by appointment.

Course description

In this methods course you will be introduced to data analysis and visualization for historians. You will learn to work with historical data, including finding, gathering, manipulating, analyzing, visualizing, and arguing from data, with special attention to geospatial, textual, and network data. These methods will be taught primarily through scripting in the R programming language, using other command line tools as appropriate. You will also learn how to present history on the web with HTML and CSS. While historical methods can be applied to many topics and time periods, they cannot be understood separate from how the discipline forms meaningful questions and interpretations, nor divorced from the particularities of the sources and histories of some specific topic. Therefore, in this course we will examine the historiographical tradition to see how historians have used data and visualization to understand the past. And we will work together to apply these methods to a series of datasets in the history of the nineteenth-century United States, with a focus on religion.

After taking this course, you will be able to:

- perform exploratory data analysis; clean, tidy, and manipulate data; gather historical data from print and manuscript sources; use existing historical data sets provided by government or other research groups; create common visualizations; work with geospatial, textual, and network data.

- write scripts using the R programming language and its extensive set of packages, as well as use command line programs.

- understand the place of data analysis and visualization within humanities computing, digital history, and the discipline of history.

- conceive of and execute a research project in computational history suitable for treatment in a dissertation chapter or journal article.

- take the course "Programming in History/New Media," a.k.a. Clio 3, should you choose.

life, references to "cyber" in social sciences have been replaced by "digital". "Digital sociology" is associated with other specializations, such as *digital humanities* and *digital anthropology*. It is beginning to incorporate the latest digital technologies, like Web 2.0, and examines areas such as "improved" reality, man-made technology, smart objects, the Internet of Things, and big data.

Digitization of Teaching Art

As a result of pressure from authorities and education leaders, computational thinking for students of so-called STEM education (Science, Technology, Engineering, and Mathematics) was developed in the US in 2010. This strategy has mobilized art and music teachers to develop so-called STEAM education (Science, Technology, Engineering, Art, and Mathematics). This approach aims to apply computational thinking to the development of creativity, i.e., it uses computers to develop a variety of digital tools for art and music. In particular, students should be able to use different graphic editors to develop computer graphics, and students should learn to program computers that either "produce" new art in the form of images or video transmissions or assist artists in the performance of their profession. Examples of moving from STEM to STEAM are as follows (Jolly, 2014):

- **Design**: Art can perform a practical function. Students can apply design and decoration to products (Figure 11) that were created during a design challenge. They can use computer graphics to create logos or stylized designs that are included in communications or presentations. Thanks to industrial design, students can improve the appearance and usability of a product created during STEM design.

Figure 11. The STEM project enhancing the STEAM project (Orkin, 2019)

- **Stage plays such as drama and speech**: What about technical or persuasive writing? These naturally fit into the "communication" stage of the engineering design process. They would work well as part of a STEM project. If an instructor wants their students to become truly ambitious and creative, watch the video of the Paraguayan students who made instruments from discarded materials.
- **Creative planning**: As students sum up their brainstorming to solve an engineering problem, instructors can encourage them to take a fun, imaginative, and artistic approach (Figure 12). Summoning their artistic right brain can help them generate more creative and innovative thinking.

Figure 12. Brainstorming leading to the planning and implementation of new ideas and solutions

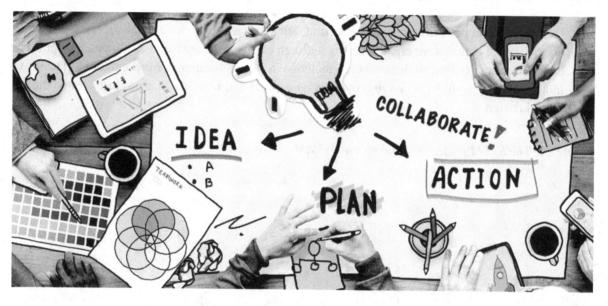

One might notice that art is often advertised as a method of adding creativity to STEM because engineers often are involved with businesses motivated for quick profits but lacking creativity and ingenuity. A look at the world around us is proof of how beauty has disappeared from the environment. STEAM's goal should not be to teach art, but to use art in real-world situations so that the knowledge used leads to deeper learning and return to what is important and beautiful in life. It is the art of life that the Greeks began teaching us 2,500 years ago.

Digitizing Music Teaching

Over the course of 2010, innovation in digital technologies significantly changed the nature of music creation and music distribution. As a result, the perception of what music is has also changed. To stay in line with these changes in music culture, music teachers need to look at the use of technology in their classrooms. Most formal music programs require students to learn to read music notation, recognize sound patterns, and master a set of physical skills, such as fingering, technical fitness, or scratching an instrument. In the 21st century, music education has gone from formal teaching to a teaching model based on the assimilation of musical knowledge and qualifications. These trends separate music creation from music notation with various types of digital editors and sound synthesizers, such as Garageband, Guitar Hero, Sibelius, and others.

EXAMPLES OF DIGITAL TOOLS USED IN DIGITAL HUMANITIES

With each passing day, the number of tools that can be used in the digital humanities is growing with new and improved solutions. Some examples of such tools being used in the 2020s are the following Gardiner & Musto, 2015):

- **3d Modeling and Printing**: After Effects is a digital application for creating visual effects, animation, and composition developed by Adobe Systems. It is used in the post-production process of creating movies, video games, and TV production. After Effects can be used, among other things, to create keys, tracks, compositions, and animations. It also acts as a quite simple nonlinear editor, audio editor, and media transcoder. In 2019, the Program won the Academy of Sciences Award for scientific and technical achievements.
- **Blogging**: Blogger is a free blog publishing software developed by Google.
- **Brainstorming**: Coogle is free software for online structuring of information.
- **Text Recognition**: OmniPage is used to scan and organize documents.
- **Team Collaboration**: Conference Maker is a tool for international conferences.
- **Communication**: Doodle is free software for scheduling conference via the Internet.
- **Data Analysis**: ATLAS software can be used for analyzing events in texts and multimedia documents. Dataverse (developed by Harvard U.) is free software for publishing, sharing results and testimonials, and analyzing data.
- **Database**: MDID (Madison Digital Image Database) is a free database (developed in James Madison U.) for storing, searching, and presenting multimedia data.
- **Data Collection**: Almetric is free software that collects data about texts published on the Internet.
- GOOGLE SCHOLAR CITATION: This is free software for tracking author citations and their statistical-graphic analysis.
- **Data Visualization**: Gephi is free software for interactive and graphic visualization of cases.
- **Manual Typing Recognition**: Evernote is free software that recognizes handwritten notes and handheld digital information stored on your computer.
- **Image Generation**: Adobe Illustrator is software used for digital drawing.
- **Image Processing**: Apertur is used for organizing, editing, and sharing photos and adding text to them.
- **Mapping**: Crowdmap is free software to build GIS applications with a universal interface. It is also used for digital cloud services.
- **Music Recognition**: Aruspis is a program that scans music from recordings and is used for informational development.
- **Organizing**: Mendeley is used for generating biographies, finding important documents, and importing them for online access.
- **Public Dissemination and Site Development**: Annotum is free software for the dissemination of scientific research based on WordPress.

- **Peer Rating**: Digress.it is a free, WordPress-based program for commenting paragraph by paragraph. It can be used to comment together on a blog.
- **Search**: Gnod is free software for searching for scientific publications and characterizing them in a bibliography.
- **Sound Recognition**: Dragon Dictate recognizes and digitizes different sounds.
- **Speech Conversion into Text**: Soundscriber is free software to convert audio into text.
- **Text Compression and Encoding**: Markdown is free text-to-XHTML or text-to-HTML conversion software.
- **Text Editing and Processing**: Classical Text Editor is free software for annotating a text being studied and for using parallel texts (placing a text next to a translation or corrected version).
- **Text Mining**: Corcordance is software for analyzing texts and their internal compatibility.
- **Text Conversion into Text**: Crowdcrafting is a platform for classifying, summarizing, geocoding, etc.
- **Text Visualization**: Lexipedia is free software for visualizing semantic and audio maps.

In this list of 27 categories of software that can be used in the digital humanities, there are at least 20 different software packages in each category. While there is almost always an example of free software, most cost money. Regardless, researchers in the humanities trained in computer science has at their disposal in total about 580 different software packages. This number will grow and over time they will be consolidated, with the best platforms becoming popularized.

With these considerations in mind, one can ask about such researchers whether they are computer scientists who study the humanities or digitalized humanists. According to this author, the latter name is correct because not all people who use computers will become IT professionals. There will be, for example, digitalized physicians since IT knowledge and skills are secondary to medical knowledge and qualifications.

TEACHING SCIENCE FROM STEM/STEAM TO WISDOM IN THE AGE OF DIGITALIZATION

What does STEM mean? In the United States, STEM is an acronym for science, technology, engineering, and mathematics. Coined in 2001 by Dr. Judith Ramaley, the term has gained widespread acceptance as a convenient way to refer to these academic disciplines. Traditionally, the four STEM elements have been taught separately. STEM education, on the other hand, emphasizes an integrated approach that highlights the interconnectedness of science (physics, chemistry, biology), technology, engineering, and mathematics. STEM education focuses on exploring new student cognition and problem solving. In schools, STEM education emphasizes stimulating students' interest in STEM subjects. In STEM education, primary school students learn the basic concepts of science, technology, engineering, and mathematics. Students also become familiar with the scope of STEM-related professions. However, over time, a trend developed aimed at humanizing STEM education, called from STEM to STEAM (science, technology, engineering, arts, and mathematics). However, it may be a mistake to insist on the omnipotence of knowledge, for even people with vast knowledge can make stupid decisions. For example, in the 1980s, large American businesses began moving factories from the US to Asia because low labor costs allowed them to make huge profits. From a business perspective, these decisions seemed logical because they were based on accurate calculations. However, these were only so-called "accurate calculations". In fact, they were shallow calculations, as they did not take into account the liquidation of the American middle class. As a result, they actually limited the number of consumers who could buy these "cheap" products since more people now had less money. For this reason, decision-makers showed a lack of wisdom in this situation.

A STEM/STEAM/WISDOM model of education for the youngest preschoolers may take the following forms:

- Go for a walk in nature, a park, or a forest.
  - STEAM: Walking in nature can be great fun for kids and frees them from boredom. Take a reusable bag and encourage children to collect interesting items they see, such as small round stones, leaves, seed pods, or flowers.
  - STEM: When arriving home, help the children organize their treasures into categories by color, texture, size, and shape. Skills used: mathematics and science.
  - WISDOM: Let the children choose which harvests are suitable for recycling and have them explain why.
- Perform cooking activities together.
  - STEAM: Cooking with children is another way to involve children in learning about life. Together, prepare an interesting online recipe.
  - STEM: Follow the recipe, allowing the children to measure and mix. Used skills: physics and mathematics.
  - WISDOM: Let the children judge whether this recipe is healthy and have them explain why.
- Set up constructions using paper or plastic cups.
  - STEAM: Let the configuration of the constructions be useful for people.
  - STEM: Challenge the children. For example, "how high can you make a tower with cups?" Measure each tower and record their height. Skills used: engineering and mathematics.
  - WISDOM: Let the children give an example from their surroundings of buildings especially useful for people
- Organize a grocery store.
  - STEAM: Let groups of children organize a shop with imitated groceries.
  - STEM: Let the children count the calories of these products, using computational skills
  - WISDOM: Let the children sort products into healthy and unhealthy ones.
- Playing with water.
  - STEAM: From a bucket of water, have children pour the water into bottles and then mark them, for example: "for sink cleaning", "for watering plants", etc.
  - STEM: Let the children put stickers on these bottles, indicating the prices, and then calculate the family's monthly budget for purchasing them.
  - WISDOM: Assuming that the budget needs to be reduced by 20%, which products should be purchased?

STEM/STEAM/WISDOM education opportunities are endless. Children love to experiment, combine new substances, build, knock down, collect, sort, and have fun while learning. Most parents have probably told their children to do activities that fit the STEM/STEAM/WISDOM model of education at home, although they may not have recognized it as such. Parents and teachers can look for additional opportunities to develop activities of this type in the daily routine of children.

STEM/STEAM/WISDOM classes for older students at school may take the following forms:

- Create rain clouds:

  ○ STEAM: Brainstorming, let the children explore the role of water for life and civilization.
  ○ STEM: Prepare a jar with a nut, and then take boiling water, ice, and matches. Pour the boiling water into the jar (about half the height). On the nut, put the ice, and then put the nut on top of the jar (the ice stays on top). Explain how the rain is made. Next, in the lid of the jar, throw in the lit match, and then cover the jar. Inside, a cloud gathers, which after a while is let out of the jar.
  ○ WISDOM: Let students explain when the cloud is useful and when it is harmful.

STEM/STEAM/WISDOM classes require joint lectures from faculty members in departments of physics/chemistry, humanities, computer science, business, and engineering in order to develop an integrated approach to the development of knowledge and qualifications. So far, these departments usually have training programs focused on their own knowledge and qualifications. The issues of wisdom are not covered.

STEM/STEAM/WISDOM classes for university students may take the following forms:

- Build a solar car or a battery:
  ○ STEAM: Students estimate the impact of pollution in their environment because of the culture of gas cars and its impact on healthcare costs.
  ○ STEM: Students calculate the average gasoline consumption for the city where the university is located and compare this with the consumption of gasoline by traditional cars to calculate the savings that would result from the use of non-gasoline cars.
  ○ WISDOM: Students develop a marketing program for selling solar and electric cars. They also assess the lifestyle and its impact on healthcare costs.
- Compare lifestyles of different countries and their respective impacts on health:
  ○ STEAM: Get acquainted with the lifestyles of Spain and Italy via Google and compare these with the lifestyles of people in the home countries of students. Among other things, have them use the Blumberg Health Index.
  ○ STEM: Students calculate how much health spending there would need to be in their country to achieve the health of Spaniards or Italians.
  ○ WISDOM: Students develop a plan of conduct to improve the health of people in the country where they live.
- Robotization assessment:
  ○ STEAM: Brainstorming, students determine how drones can be better used in service to the population.
  ○ STEM: Students prepare drones and use them.
  ○ WIZDOM: Students choose drone applications that are safe and needed.

VIRTUAL CLASS

Virtual classrooms, or online learning, is a challenge for all education. Because it is cheap to administer, it is a highly attractive solution for university administrations. This is one of three forms of training today, characterized in Table 4.

Table 4. Characteristics of forms of learning in the 2020s (Christopher, 2015, p. 5)

Element	Traditional F2F Teaching	E-Learning	Virtual Class
Information flow	Two-way flow of information between lecturer and listeners	One-way flow of information between the technology system and the learner	Two-way online information flow between lecturer and listeners
Lecturer	Physically present among the listeners	Not applicable	Lecturer separated from listeners
Place	Physical class	Access via computer or smartphone	Access via computer or smartphone
Training materials	Handed out during classes	Downloaded online from the course site	Downloaded online from the course site or uploaded via e-mail
Typical exercises	Lecturer-led discussion	Online simulations and e-copying tasks	Discussions led by assistants in small groups in separate rooms
Duration	About 1 hour	Modules divided into 30-minute sessions	60-90 minutes

For years, the university administration has been pushing for the broader use of virtual classes, which has been met with passive reactions from a profession that feels threatened in employment and is of the opinion that teaching cannot be reduced merely to the transmission of knowledge. The role of the lecturer in high-quality teaching is not replaceable.

However, in cases such as the Coronavirus pandemic in 2020, it is necessary to introduce virtual teaching to avoid infection, illness, and even death. Some of the responses of the United States to the pandemic in the area of education will be characterized and evaluated below to show ongoing issues that need to be addressed. Overall, the remote learning experiment has not gone well. In June 2020, the University of Washington's Center for Public Education Improvement released a report describing how 477 school districts across the country responded to the Covid-19 crisis. The findings reveal widespread neglect of students. The report found that only 27% of districts required teachers to register whether students were participating in remote classrooms, while remote attendance was disastrous. During the first two weeks of the break, about 15,000 students from Los Angeles did not show up for classes nor did any schoolwork ("Failure in the Virtual Classroom", 2020).

The Philadelphia Enquirer reported that, on average, the Philadelphia school district saw only 61% of students attend on an average day. In the same week, the Boston Globe reported that only "half of students log in to online classes or submit assignments online on a typical day." Students are motivated to drop out of the digital lesson because their work contributes very little to their final grade. The report shows that only 57.9% of school districts monitor progress. The rest do not even set minimum expectations that teachers evaluate or track their students' work. Homework counts towards final student grades

Figure 13. A remotely learning student at home (GETTI IMAGES)

in only 42% of districts, and some schools offer students credits or incompletes ("Failure in the Virtual Classroom", 2020).

Teachers' unions have never wanted teachers' performance to be judged on the performance of students, so they have lobbied to ensure a lack of accountability and assessment during their downtime. They have expressed this demand in the language of social justice: since the pandemic has not caused the same difficulties in all families, the only fair solution is to deprive all students of class credit or to pass them automatically.

The president of the Chicago Teachers' Union, Jesse Sharkey, said that "customary forms of judging are inadequate in the global health crisis" and asked, "how can such unequal playing conditions ensure fairness and fairness for minority students?" The Los Angeles Teachers' Union lobbied for no student to receive a negative or worse rating than before the closure. The union declared that "we are pressing [the school district] not to authorize a summer school for students who have received a D grade," which they said was "simply a matter of justice" ("Failure in the Virtual Classroom", 2020).

In fact, such "fair" treatment condemns poor and minority students to permanent disadvantages in education. In April 2020, according to the National Assessment of Educational Progress, only 24% of eighth-grade students achieved proficiency or higher in civic knowledge, and only 15% showed proficiency in U.S. history. This was before school districts decided to write off the spring semester as a loss ("Failure in the Virtual Classroom", 2020).

Wealthy parents can afford to tutor or move their children to expensive private schools where learning is still ongoing and homework still counts. The least privileged children get stuck. Without grades or tests identifying those who have been left behind, children will be moved to the next class, regardless of whether they are ready. Many will never keep up. Where is the outrage over this injustice?

Due to the pandemic, American universities have massively introduced virtual classes, which has resulted in students leaving campuses. The result has been a suspension of services such as offering dormitories and cleaning. Students are also refusing to pay 100% tuition fees. It is not known how many of them will return in person in the fall. Because of this situation, universities are faced with huge budget deficits, which has motivated them to make lecturers and administrators voluntarily give up their jobs, in some cases for the price of their annual salary. How this will impact the U.S. education system, time will tell. It is highly probable that American education will not return to its high standard before the 2020 pandemic, when young people from every other country in the world rushed there to study.

Covid-19 is also a catalyst for innovation. The Big Ten Academic Alliance, a group of US midwestern universities, offers many of its 600,000 students the opportunity to take online courses at other universities in the group. There are great opportunities to use digitization to improve education. Poor one-lessons can be replaced with online lectures from the best in the world, making time to teach in small groups that students value the most ("The Absent Student", 2020).

Universities are rightly proud of their centuries-old traditions, but their ancient lineages have too often been used as an excuse to resist change. If covid-19 pulls them out of their complacency, something good could still come out of this disaster ("The Absent Student", 2020).

Due to the pandemic, American universities introduced virtual classrooms *en masse*, which resulted in students leaving campuses. This resulted in the suspension of services such as canteens and dormitories, and cleaning. Students also refuse to pay 100% of tuition fees ("The Absent Student", 2020). It is not known how many of them will return to physical presence studies in the fall. In this situation, universities have huge budget deficits, which make lecturers and administrators motivate to resign from work voluntarily, e.g., at the price of an annual salary. Time will show how much havoc this will cause in the American education system. With some degree of high probability, American education will not return to the high standard it had before the 2020 pandemic, when young people from every country in the world were eager to study in that country ("The Absent Student", 2020).

THE BEST FINNISH SCHOOL IN WESTERN CIVILIZATION

Schools in Western civilization are struggling with curricula and computerization, and they are lagging behind the results of school training in Finland. The success of Finish schools lies in the following solutions:

- There is a more relaxed atmosphere: There is a general trend in what Finland is doing with its schools. There is less stress, less unnecessary recommendations, and more care for the students. Students usually only have a few classes a day. Everyone eats the same thing several times throughout the day, enjoys recreation, and, generally, has a chance to rest. During the day, there are 15 to 20 minutes breaks, during which children can get up and stretch, catch fresh air, and unwind.

Figure 14. The cover of The Economist for the week of August 8, 2020 ("The Absent Student", 2020)

- A relaxed atmosphere is also needed for teachers: Many Finnish schools have teacher rooms where they can relax, prepare for their day, or simply socialize. Teachers are also human and must be equanimous to do their best. Teachers work several hours a day, spending the rest of their time learning and improving their classes with their students, and they are recruited from the top 10% of the students. Their status is equal to doctors and lawyers.

- Less homework and outdoor work are required: According to the Organization for Economic Cooperation and Development (OECD), students in Finland have the least amount of homework of all other students in the world. On average, they spend only half an hour in the evening working on things from school. Finnish students also do not have tutors. Overall, they outrank other cultures that have a toxic balance between school and life without unnecessary stress.

- Finnish students receive everything they need to do at school without the additional pressure to improve in the subjects: Without worrying about their grades and improving their work outside of the class, they are able to concentrate on the learning tasks at hand and their development as universal humans.

- Finnish teachers and students use educational technologies much less frequently than those from other European countries: In eighth grade, Finnish students use computers the least amount of time in the European Union, with only 27 percent saying they used computers at least once a week. In the EU, the average proportion of teachers using educational technology for at least 25 percent of their lessons is higher than in Finland for fourth and eighth grade. In fourth grade, the overall use of these technologies is 29 percent in the EU, while in Finland it is down to 20 percent. In eighth grade, the use in the EU is 32 percent, while in Finland it is 29 percent. For teachers using educational technology, Finland ranks lowest in eighth grade in more than 25 percent of the lessons, at 29 percent.

- 90% of pupils graduate high school and 66% get into institutions of higher education: This is one of the best teaching results in the world. By comparison, 84.6% of students graduated high school in the United States in 2018, and 67% of students enrolled in higher education in 2018 (Bustamante, 2019).

Figure 15. In Finland, students learn computational thinking without touching a computer (Photo: Thomas Peter / Reuters)

According to the OECD (2015) ranking for 15-year-old students who have learned to use writing, reading, and mathematics, Finland is well ahead of the United States and Poland, but lags behind Singapore, which has the best education in the world (see Table 5 and Figure 16). The good results in Singapore

Table 5. Comparison of training results in selected states (OECD, 2015; World Bank, 2019)

State	Writing	Reading	Mathematics	Total	GDP/Capita PPP 2019 World Bank in Dollars
Singapore	564	535	556	1655	121,103
Finland	511	526	531	1568	51,324
Poland	504	506	501	1511	34,218
USA	470	497	496	1463	65,281

may be due in part to their GDP per capita PPP (purchasing power parity), which is twice as high as Finland (and 3.5 times higher compared to Poland). The results speak for themselves.

Figure 16. Learning results by PISA[1] (OECD, 2015)

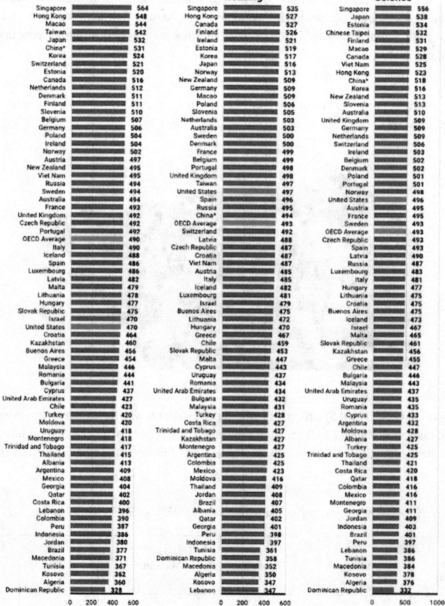

THE ARCHITECTURE OF DIGITAL SCHOOL

The architecture of the computerized school is given in Figure 17. It contains the most important technological systems, which include:

- A catalogue of compulsory courses and electives to choose from,
- Classes with IT equipment,
- Virtual classes,
- A digital library,
- Laboratories for physics, chemistry, biology, and information technology,
- Communication systems with parents,
- A Management Information System (SIK) for the school principal, substitutes, the head of special education, and heads of administrative sections,
- School Information Systems: Employment, Facilities, Materials, Finance, Marketing, e-Teacher Systems for attendance and assessment records, and syllabi, emails, and others,
- Outdoor platforms for teachers, administrators, and students,
- A Local Internet Network,
- Others.

Each school has its own history and development process, including computerization. Therefore, individual schools may differ from the architecture as represented in the model. In this lies the beauty of democracy—that schools within a national structure and operating with national standards can diversify their solutions. There are great prospects for competitions in designing schools that actualize the potential of the school.

THE ARCHITECTURE OF DIGITAL UNIVERSITY

The architecture of the computerized university is given in Figure 18. It contains the most important technological systems. These include:

- A catalogue of compulsory courses and electives to choose from,
- Lecture halls with IT equipment,
- Virtual courses,
- A digital library,
- Laboratories:
    - Specialized, e.g., computing networks, stock exchanges, digital humanities software, etc.
    - Faculty-wide for students of different specializations
    - University-wide for students of different specializations
    - Research and development for different specialized purposes
    - Others
- A Management Information System (SIK) for the head of the university, deputies and deans, heads of institutes, and heads of administrative departments and sections,

Figure 17. The architecture of digital school (key systems)

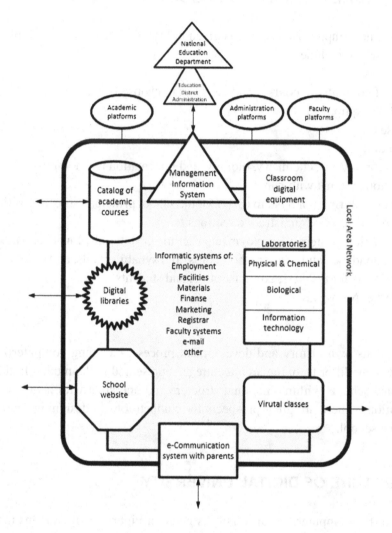

- School Information Systems: Employment, facilities, materials, finance, marketing, emails, tele-conferencing, teacher systems for recording attendance and assessment, syllabi and more,
- External digital platforms for students, faculty, and administration,
- Campus-Internet Network,
- Others.

Each university has its own history and development process, including computerization. Therefore, it may differ from the architecture as represented in the model. Once again, herein lies the beauty of democracy—that universities operating within a national framework with national standards can diversify their solutions. There are also great prospects for competitions in designing both universities that actualize the potential of the school as well as specialized laboratories.

Digital Citizenship

Figure 18. Architecture of digital university (key systems)

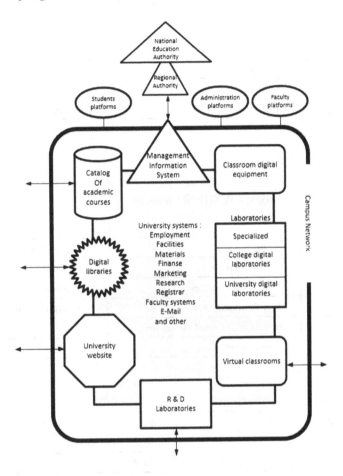

The following is an example of a syllabus for digital citizenship at Western Michigan University in the Business College, where first-year students are trained at using MS WORD, MS Spreadsheet, online databases via the university's digital library, graphical presentation, relational databases, digital cloud computing, and website use. Digital skills in these areas provide a good basis for learning in higher education in the 2020s and are also necessary for using IT systems in daily work.

CIS 1020 Introduction to Business Computing and Data Analytics

INSTRUCTOR: Thomas Rienzo
    COURSE TOPICS
    Working with Windows
    Word Processing
    Spreadsheets

Office:	3342 Schneider	Class Section:	12794; 12795
WMU E-mail:	thomas.rienzo@wmich.edu	Time:	M, W 10 AM, 11 AM
Office Hours:	M, W: 3:30 PM - 5:00 PM T: 1:30 PM - 4:30 PM	Classroom:	Schneider 2000
		Computer Lab:	Schneider 2325

Columns	Paragraph Formatting	Tables
Header and Footers	Sectioning	Table of Contents
Character Formatting	Styles	References and Citations

On-line Research - WMU databases WMU library site

Charts	Macros	Text Manipulation
Conditional Formatting	Multiple Worksheets	Validating Data / Protecting workbooks
Formatting	Multiple Data Sources	What-if Analysis
Functions	Pivot Tables and Charts	Worksheet Documentation
Lists	Relative & Absolute Cell References	
Lookup Functions	Sorting and Filtering	

Presentation Graphics

Addition of Multi-Media Effects	Multi-media sample presentation
Effective Presentations	Presentation Objectives
Embed Video	Visual Aids

Databases
Web Sites –Web Pages and the Internet

Importing and Exporting Data	Reports
Forms	Tables
Primary and Foreign Keys	Table Relationships
Queries	

Cloud Applications	Images
Document storage and web site display	Layout
Editors	Multi-media
Hyperlinks	Sharing

Education of IT Professionals

Among the challenges of a digital university is a discussion of training IT professionals in the field of information technology. From a general point of view, they are divided into:

- Designers of digital hardware and tele-computer networks,
- Computer scientists – designing and programming computers,
- Designers of software packages for application systems,
- IT executives,
- IT professionals whose underlying knowledge is in other fields of knowledge and activities, such as the medicine or the humanities.

Based on the experience of American universities, which have the greatest wealth and experience in the world in this regard, we are dealing with the following trends in IT education in the 2020s:

1. There has been an integration of conductors of IT training programs with computer software developers. Such individuals have traveled from computer science programs to engineering departments because hardware and software are inseparable, just as the car's engine is integrated into a chassis. This is why, for example, vehicle builders are trained at the Faculty of Cars and Tractors at the Warsaw University of Technology.
2. Old computer science programs are being transformed into computing programs, including super-computers.
3. The training of designers of IT system applications is taking place in many departments. For example, IT professionals in business applications are educated in business schools. On the other hand, IT specialists in automation and informatization of production are mainly trained in faculties of industrial engineering or automation or others, depending on tradition and other factors of a given college.
4. IT professionals specializing in the management of IT services in organizations are being trained in MBA programs with a concentration in IT (or MIS/CIS, depending on the tradition's terminology).
5. IT professionals in other fields are being trained in programs specific to those fields, e.g., in the field of medicine, law, and others.

SUMMARY

1. The Digital Revolution (discussed in the chapter *Waves of Civilization Development and the Digital Revolution*) has introduced radical changes into teaching, which are now being implemented by schools and universities.
   a. The biggest changes are in the digital humanities, as they allow for a deepening of the context of research and recommendations.
   b. For years, it has been argued computational thinking must be complemented by information and systemic thinking in the context of digital citizenship and global citizenship. Together, these forms of thinking should be taught to educate leaders who are inclusive in solving problems, e.g., in creating a sustainable civilization.

2. STEM training and learning should be combined with a STEAM approach that involves humanizing technology. However, for this to be possible, teaching must not be limited to merely increasing the resources of knowledge because the most important unit of knowledge is wisdom, that is, correct judgment and correct choice of options for either thinking or solutions in the context of the art of life (as mentioned in Part I and other works by the author).

3. Promoting a virtual classroom, i.e., online distance learning, is in the interest of the administration of schools and universities, which are counting on the costs of education to increase; however, this is a mode of learning that should only be used in exceptional situations, such as the ongoing pandemic of 2020.

4. Because education cannot be limited to the transmission of recorded knowledge, F2F contact between lecturers and students is a best practice for learning. There is a reason why the best and most expensive universities in the world have teacher to student ratios as low as 1 to 5-7. In master's courses, this ratio can be as low as 1 to 3. However, there is an average of 35 students per lecturer at state universities.

    a. For example, at one of the most famous U.S. universities, Caltech (California Institute of Technology), the annual cost of study and related maintenance and scientific expenses is about $80,000. In 2019, the university awarded 938 students with bachelor's degrees and 1,299 students with master's degrees on a 65-hectare campus with 300 professors and 600 research scientists. The president, deans, and department chairs are active researchers who publish their achievements in scientific journals. So far, 38 graduates and faculty have received the Nobel Prize and 71 have been awarded the United States National Medal of Science or Technology. Of course, virtual teaching at this university is sporadic.

REFERENCES

Bustamante, J. (2019, September 7). Percentage of high school graduates that go to college. *Education-data.org*. https://educationdata.org/high-school-graduates-who-go-to-college/

Christopher, D. (2015). *The successful virtual classroom: How to design and facilitate interactive and engaging live online learning*. Amacom.

Denning, P. J., & Tedre, M. (2019). *Computational thinking*. MIT Press. doi:10.7551/mitpress/11740.001.0001

Devopedia. (2019). *Word embedding*. https://devopedia.org/word-embedding

Digital Citizenship. (n.d.). *Nine elements: Nine themes of digital citizenship*. https://www.digitalcitizenship.net/nine-elements.html

Failure in the virtual classroom. (2020, June 21). *Wall Street Journal*. https://www.wsj.com/articles/failure-in-the-virtual-classroom-11592776152

Freedman, S. W., & Daiute, C. (2001). Instructional methods and learning activities in teaching writing. In J. Brophy (Ed.), *Subject-specific instructional methods and activities* (pp. 83–110). Emerald Group Publishing Limited. doi:10.1016/S1479-3687(01)80024-9

Friedman, F. (2005). *The world is flat*. Farrar, Straus, and Giroux.

Gardiner, E., & Musto, R. G. (2015). *The digital humanities: A primer for students and scholars*. Cambridge University Press. doi:10.1017/CBO9781139003865

ISTE & CSTA. (2011). *Operational definition of computational thinking for K-12 education*. https://cdn. iste.org/www-root/ct-documents/computational-thinking-operational-definition-flyer.pdf

Jolly, A. (2014, November 18). STEAM vs. STEAM: Do the Arts belong? *EducationWeek*. https://www. edweek.org/teaching-learning/opinion-stem-vs-steam-do-the-arts-belong/2014/11

Krawczyk, H., & Targowski, A. (2019). *Wisdom in the context of globalization and civilization*. Cambridge Scholars.

OECD. (2015). *Education at a glance 2015*. https://www.oecd-ilibrary.org/education/education-at-a-glance-2015_eag-2015-en

Orkin, N. (2019). *IP basics: Protecting STEAM innovators and their ideas*. NOVA Science Publishers.

Ramos, C., Saab, Z., & León, W. (2013). History of life. *Behance.com*. https://www.behance.net/gallery/10901127/History-of-Life

Ribble, M. (2020, January 28). Digital citizenship is more important than ever. *International Society for Technology and Education*. https://www.iste.org/explore/digital-citizenship-more-important-ever

Targowski, A. (1990). *The architecture and planning of enterprise-wide information management systems*. Idea Group Publishing.

Targowski, A. (2014a). *Global civilization in the 21st century*. NOVA Science Publishers.

Targowski, A. (2014b). *Western civilization in the 21st century*. NOVA Science Publishers.

Targowski, A. (2015). *Virtual civilization in the 21st century*. NOVA Science Publishers.

Targowski, A. (2017). *Moc Mądrości* [The power of wisdom]. Wydawnictwa Politechniki Gdańskiej.

TeachThought. (2019, November 26). *Moving students from digital citizenship to digital leadership*. https://www.teachthought.com/the-future-of-learning/moving-students-from-digital-citizenship-to-digital-leadership/

The Absent Student. (2020, August 8). *The Economist*. https://www.economist.com/weeklyedition/2020-08-08

United Nations Educational, Scientific, and Cultural Organization. (2014). *Global citizenship education: Preparing learners for the challenges of the 21st century*. https://unesdoc.unesco.org/ark:/48223/pf0000 227729?posInSet=1&queryId=36cccc9a-72ad-4fae-86f8-

Vega, V., & Robb, M. B. (2019). *The common sense census: Inside the 21st-century classroom*. Common Sense Media. https://www.commonsensemedia.org/sites/default/files/uploads/research/2019-educator-census-inside-the-21st-century-classroom_1.pdf

World Bank. (2019). *World development report: The changing nature of work*. https://www.worldbank.org/en/publication/wdr2019

KEY TERMS AND DEFINITIONS

Computational Thinking: A form of thinking that involves expressing problems and solving them in ways that can be assisted by computers.

Digital Citizenship: The view that persons who use digital technologies to participate in society and politics are members of a class.

Digital Humanities: An area of scholarly study concerned with the intersection of digital technologies and the humanities.

Global Citizenship: The view that people are citizens not just of individual countries and nation-states, but of the world.

Informational Thinking: A form of thinking that involves the ability to analyze cognitive units of content (data, information, knowledge, wisdom, etc.).

Internetization: The process by which business and societal relations are shaped by the Internet and digital technologies.

STEAM: An acronym standing for "science, technology, engineering, the arts, and math." STEAM aims to integrate STEM concepts with the arts.

Systemic Thinking: A form of holistic thinking that focuses on how system components work interconnectedly, how systems evolve overtime, and how systems work in the context of larger systems.

ENDNOTE

[1] The Program for International Student Assessment (PISA) is a global study by the Organization for Economic Cooperation and Development (OECD) in Member States and non-member countries, aimed at evaluating educational systems by measuring the school performance of 15-year-old students in mathematics, science, and reading.

Chapter 16
Digital Home Strategy

ABSTRACT

The goal of this chapter is to discuss and analyze strategies related to private computer users and digital homes. The chapter begins with an analysis of ICT users based on (1) age and (2) skill level in using digital technologies. Based on these two factors, four categories of users are identified: (1) young uninformed, (2) old uninformed, (3) old informed, and (4) young informed. The chapter analyzes each category in detail and discusses digital strategies for each group. Next, the chapter examines strategies that can be used to digitize houses, such as the use of temperature monitoring and light controls. The chapter concludes with an analysis of smart home trends.

INTRODUCTION

The inhabitants of small countries tend to have the best internet connections in the world. For instance, in the Falkland Islands, as many as 99% of inhabitants use the internet, ranking the country first place in the world. Looking at the map, one can see that these islands are almost at the "end" of the world. Thus far, it has been popular to classify people as either financially excluded or not excluded, that is, the "haves" and the "have nots". Among the "haves" one can distinguish "old" and "new" money; however, these groups can also be linked to the criterion of information. Doing so reveals that those with "old" money are usually less informed than those with "new" money. Furthermore, the "have nots" who are uninformed have no chance of improving their existence; however, the "have nots" who are informed have an opportunity to strengthen their presence, as their ability to access information brings new opportunities for strategic action and the possibility of breaking out of so-called "poverty cycles".

CATEGORIES OF USERS BASED ON AGE

Information technology in the 21st century is used in economic, political, and socio-cultural ways for production and communication purposes. People with better access and more technological knowledge are, therefore, better able to exploit the full potential of information and communication technologies

DOI: 10.4018/978-1-7998-8036-3.ch016

(ICT). Those with the latest technical experience benefit more, resulting in a higher socio-economic status. The skills involved in using the internet can be defined based on the number of websites visited, the time spent on the internet, proficiency in internet use, and the ability to use the internet in a variety of ways. Those who possess these skills benefit more from using ICT, resulting in a divide between information "haves" and "have nots". Furthermore, the skills used to access the internet are more complex than those used to access oneself. This indicates a paradigm shift in the commonly understood definition of digital exclusion, that is, who has access and who does not (Barupal, 2017).

The new definition of digital exclusion is now based on user skills and access quality. This division can be assessed in terms of the age, educational qualifications, and economic status of a person, which in turn are influenced by one's geographical location and government policies. According to a report by the International Telecommunications Union (ITU), people with internet access doubled worldwide in five years (2012-2017). The number of households with internet access was 16% in developing countries and 66% in developed countries. Therefore, there is an apparent digital exclusion between high-income and low-income countries. The former provides higher speeds, higher bandwidth, and better access quality, while the latter offer lower speeds, lower capacity, and worse access quality. Therefore, digital exclusion has changed from mere access to including both user skills and access quality (Barupal, 2017).

Keeping in mind the consideration of how information affects wealth, let us move on to consider the criterion of age, which plays a significant role in mastering the use of computers in the private home.

The model of user categories classified by age is given in Figure 1.

STRATEGY FOR USER Y- YOUNGER UNINFORMED USERS

This category of users includes young people and children, including those who are either out of school or are studying but have a limited budget.

- Purpose of computerization: Gain access internet and email
- Digital strategy: take possession of used equipment, such as smartphones, tablets, or PCs. If that is not possible, use digital hardware in a library or internet café.
- Adverse effects: there is a concern that fake news and data may influence the minds of users with limited training and those who have few relationships with people other than data maniacs.

Young people and children who grow up digitally excluded feel increasingly deficient and hopeless, with no chance of a better life.

The internet is becoming increasingly important in school curricula, and young people and children use home internet connections to fulfill school tasks, connect with classmates, and pursue various interests and hobbies. Young people and children who cannot access the internet risk losing the opportunity to develop their education further. This threat is even more present among communities that have faced challenges in the past.

Research shows that internet access is closely linked to socio-economic factors, such as poverty and racial demographics. In Detroit, researchers at the University of Michigan found in 2019 that up to 70% of young people and school children in economically disadvantaged neighborhoods do not have internet access at home (Rundle, 2020).

Figure 1. Model of user categories by age

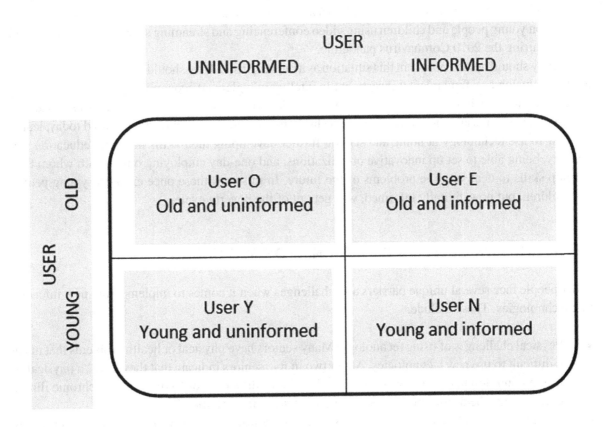

Figure 2. Smartphone rescue for digital exclusion (Photo: Toby Morris)

According to *Education Super Highway,* a nonprofit organization, last year, one in five students in the US did not have access to a reliable tele-network connection. The shift to remote learning, which depends on young people and children using video conferencing and streaming services, has exacerbated that gap during the 2020 Coronavirus pandemic.

Society should not see people in this situation as a burden; instead, we should be planning to eliminate digital exclusion as a fundamental investment in intelligently planned economic productivity.

By planning to eliminate digital exclusion, we could move closer to a genuinely optimistic view of technological change and the future. Imagine a child growing up in an excluded household today, learning how to use technology at home and school, further developing their skills in higher education and industry, being able to set up innovative organizations, and one-day employing others with whom they develop skills to deal with the problems of the future. In this way, these once excluded young people and children, but now digitally informed, will get out of the poverty cycle.

STRATEGY FOR USER O – OLDER UNINFORMED USERS

Older people face several unique barriers and challenges when it comes to implementing new information technologies. These include:

- Physical challenges of using technology: Many seniors have physical or health problems that make it difficult to use new technologies. About two in five seniors indicate that they have "a physical or health condition that makes reading difficult or 'very difficult'" or "a disability or chronic illness that prevents them from fully participating in many daily activities."
- A skeptical attitude towards the benefits of computerization: older people who do not currently use the internet are divided on whether this lack of access helps them or not. In general, the majority of these users agrees with the statement that "people without internet access are disadvantaged because of all the information they may lack,"; however, many who do not use the internet do not agree that they lack essential information.
- Learning difficulties in using new information technologies: The vast majority of older people say they need help using new digital devices. Only a few feel comfortable learning how to use a new technological device, such as a smartphone or tablet, on their own. Furthermore, among seniors who use the internet but do not currently use social media networks such as Facebook or Twitter, most would need help if they wanted to use these platforms to connect with friends or family members.

Despite these unique challenges faced by older people when it comes to information technology, most seniors who become internet users regularly visit the digital world. Among older people using the internet, 71% use the internet every day or almost every day, and an additional 11% use the internet three to five times a week (Smith, 2014).

These older internet users also have very positive attitudes toward the benefits of online information in their personal lives. Fully 79% of older adults using the internet agree with the statement that "people without internet access are disadvantaged because of all the information they may lack," and 94% agree with the idea that "the internet makes it much easier to find information today than in the past."

- The purpose of computerization: To become informed and connected to the environment.
- Computerization strategy: Use email, internet, and online shopping.
- Negatives: There is a threat of digital crime, in which contractors target older people who are not experienced in the use of computers and the internet.

An older user should apply this strategy under the guidance of an experienced IT professional, family member, or consultant.

From Table 1 (Smith, 2014), it can be seen that older users are better off, and the more they earn, the more they use the internet. In other words, it "pays off" for them.

Table 1. Characteristics of the use of the internet by older Americans (Smith, 2014)

Characteristic	Percentage
Gender	
Male	65%
Female	55%
Age	
65-69	74%
70-74	68%
75-79	47%
80+	37%
Education	
High school grad or less	40%
Some college	69%
College graduate	87%
Household Income	
<$30,000	39%
$30,000-$49,999	63%
$50,000-$74,999	86%
$75,000+	90%
Community Type	
Urban	60%
Suburban	63%
Rural	50%
Total for all 65+ (n = 1,526)	**59%**

STRATEGY FOR USER E – OLDER AND INFORMED USERS

In 33 wealthy countries, only 5% of the population have high computer skills, and only a third of people can perform tasks of medium complexity. Recent international scientific research has allowed us to estimate the difference between the broad population and the technological elite. The data was collected between 2011 and 2015 in 33 countries and was published in 2016 by the OECD (Organization for Economic Co-op and Development, a club of industrialized countries). A total of 215,942 people were tested, with at least 5,000 participants in most states. The large scale of this study explains why it took several years to publish the results.

The study was aimed at testing the skills of 16-65-year-olds, the age range described in the report as "adults." While it is true that people aged 66+ are rare in the labor market and are, therefore, of less interest to this employee-oriented project, they do nonetheless represent a large group of users for many websites.

Tasks ranged from being very simple to somewhat complicated. One of the tasks was to use the "reply all" function in an email application to send a reply to three people. This task was easy because the problem was obvious, and the solution involved just one step with a minor condition (send the email to three people).

One of the difficult tasks was to plan a conference room in a planning application, using the information contained in several emails. This was difficult because the description of the problem was implicit and included many steps and many conditions. It would have been much easier to solve a clearly defined problem, such as booking Room A on Wednesday at 3 PM; however, the participants needed to determine such needs by collecting a large amount of information from different applications, which made it a difficult task for many users.

Four Levels of Proficiency in Computing

Researchers in this study defined four levels of proficiency based on the types of tasks that users could successfully perform. For each proficiency level, the percentage of the population (averaged for the entire range of OECD countries) that achieved that level is given below as well as the report's definition of human capacity at that level (OECD, 2016).

- **Below level 1 = 14% of the adult population**. Being too polite to use the term "level zero," OECD researchers describe the lowest skill level as "below level 1". Here's what people below level 1 can do: "Tasks are based on well-defined issues involving the use of only one function in the public interface to meet one clear criterion without any categorical or inference or transformation of information. A few steps are required, and you don't need to generate a sub-goal." An example of a task at this level is "delete this email" in an email application.
- **Level 1 = 29% of the adult population**. Here is what people can do in the first level: Tasks typically require the use of widely available and well-known technology applications, such as email software or web browsers. The abilities required to access information or commands needed to resolve problems at this level are minor or do not require navigation skills. The problems can be solved regardless of the respondents' awareness and use of specific tools and functions (e.g., sorting functions). Tasks include several steps and a minimum number of operators. At the cognitive level, the respondents can easily deduce a goal from a task statement; the solution to such a problem requires respondents to apply clear criteria, and there are few monitoring requirements (e.g., respondents do not have to check whether they have followed the appropriate procedure or have made progress towards a solution). Identifying content and operators can be done by simple matching. Only simple forms of reasoning are required, such as assigning items to categories;

there is no need to contrast or integrate information. An example of a level 1 task is "find all emails from John Smith".

- **Level 2 = 26% of the adult population**. Here is what level 2 people can do: At this level, tasks typically require the use of both generic and more detailed technology applications. For example, a respondent may need to use a novel online form. To resolve the issue, some navigation between pages and apps is required. The use of tools (e.g., sorting functions) can also help solve the problem. A task can involve multiple steps and operators. The purpose of the problem may be determined by the respondent, although the criteria to be met are unambiguous. There are higher monitoring requirements. Unexpected results or deadlocks may occur. The task may require an evaluation of the suitability of the set of items to reject distractions. Integration and application may be necessary. An example of a Level 2 task is, "You want to find a sustainability document that was sent to you by John Smith last October."

- **Level 3 = 5% of the adult population**. Here is what the most skilled group of people can do, i.e., the information elite. At this level, tasks typically require the use of both general and more detailed technology applications. To resolve the issue, some navigation between pages and apps is required. The use of tools (e.g., sorting functions) is required to make progress towards a solution. A task can involve multiple steps and operators. The respondent may determine the purpose of the problem and the criteria to be met may or may not be clear. Typically, there are high monitoring requirements. Unexpected results and gridlocks may occur. The task may require an assessment of the usefulness and reliability of the information to reject distractions. Integration and application is likely needed. A level 3 task could be, "You want to know what percentage of the emails John Smith sent last month was about sustainability."

- **Cannot use computers = 26% of the adult population.** The numbers for the four skill levels do not add up to 100%, as a large proportion of respondents never completed the task because they were unable to use computers. In total, in OECD countries, 26% of adults were unable to use a computer.

The fact that a quarter of the population cannot use a computer at all is the most extreme example of digital exclusion (users of types A and B). To a large extent, this problem occurs because computers are still too complicated for many people.

Digital qualifications vary from country to country, as shown in Figure 3.

Figure 3 shows that the countries with the largest percentage of information elite are Japan (8% of the population), Singapore (8%), Scandinavia (7%), and the Netherlands (7%); the EU-average is 5% as is the USA; for Poland, it is 3%.[1] These results are corroborated by the sales of high-tech Japanese cars all over the world, well adapted to specific markets. Singapore, on the other hand, is competing with sly Hong Kong to take over financial operations in Asia. On the other hand, the result of the high level of competence of the Information Elite in the Netherlands is that the country, which has great difficulties fighting to manage flood control, has the highest level of agriculture in the world due to its advanced computerization of this sector.

People living in high-income developed countries use ICT for employment purposes as well as other applications that lead to better development opportunities. According to the latest Quantcast statistics for LinkedIn (the largest professional online service), the monthly number of users in the US is 74.9 million, the UK 14.6 million, China 2.2 million, and Jamaica 1 million. The most important countries that access LinkedIn via mobile phone are the US and the UK at 5%. This can be attributed to the importance of

Figure 3. Digital competence of adult users (16-65-years-old) among selected countries (OECD, 2016)

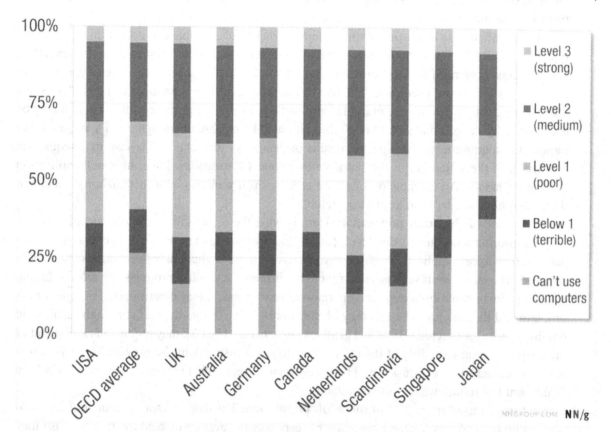

digital literacy as part of trans-literacy, i.e., the ability to interact across multiple platforms, tools, and media. These skills can also be used to find employment or entrepreneurial activities. As new information technologies are used to coordinate work-related tasks and communication between continents, in-depth knowledge of the latest internet applications and technologies will be essential for professional development and employment opportunities. The information elite understands these possibilities and, therefore, uses computerization as the art of practical living.

This means that the lack of digital knowledge makes it difficult to use mobile phones for professional development. As a result, the gap between the wealthy information elite and the poor is widening. An important factor responsible this shortcoming is exclusionary practices in regard to design and innovation processes, which favor urban consumers in high-income countries over those in low-income rural areas since digital places are seen as profitable markets. As a result, information technologies are designed for higher-status groups, and the first users of technology are usually young and wealthy. Therefore, this young and affluent population from developed countries has a high level of ICT literacy, and they are also highly cosmopolitan in their communication behaviors. This phenomenon is the result of what Gibson Burrell describes as a triad model. The triad model is based on customer-oriented design and engineering for well-known markets (Burrell & Morgan, 1997).

However, demographic data excluded from research that could be incorporated into innovative projects—causing a knowledge gap—include not only data on rural populations in the rural-urban divide, but also data on groups with low or non-existent literacy levels. According to a report by the *World Literacy Foundation*, around the world there were more than 796 million people who could not read in 2020. This leads to a new level of stratification in terms of the inability to use ICT effectively. An ethnographic analysis of the situation (see above) shows that access to ICT alone does not eliminate the digital divide. Instead, the emerging stratification, based on skill level and access quality, is visible in all demographic groups defined by age, education, and income level. For example, the age of a person partly determines his or her level of expertise in the use of ICT; however, the pervasive use of mobile phones in rural and developing parts of the world does not translate into digital equality with their counterparts in cities from developed countries. High-income people from developed countries have better access and resources to build the necessary skills and exploit the full potential offered by ICT. People from low-income developing countries are at a disadvantage due to factors such as low telecommunications network bandwidth, reduced screen space, and slow deployment of technology. Therefore, the previous understanding of the digital divide in terms of ordinary access to ICT has changed (Barupal, 2017).

It is important to note that 95% of the population in the United States (93% in Northern Europe, 92% in prosperous Asia, and 97% in Poland) does not belong to the information elite. These users have limited development and operational capabilities in the countries they live in. This is evidenced by indicators of problem-solving capacity in digital environments.

Table 2 shows that Swedes (44), the Dutch (42), and Norwegians (41) solve problems best in digital environments. Poles (19), on the other hand, have half capacity of Europe's leading countries. These European leaders are also world leaders, with Swedes occupying first place along with the people of New Zealand (44). These islanders living almost at the end of the world have developed a very prosperous country, where 3 million inhabitants are engaged in the wool and meat industry, which consists of about 5 million sheep. On the other hand, Singapore (37), the world's best-managed country with the best education, has 16% less problem-solving capacity in digital environments than European leaders. It follows that the extraordinary diligence of the people of Singapore in their highly 'caring' state still leaves them far behind the problem-solving abilities of the people of Sweden, Norway, and the Netherlands as well as others whose problem-solving horizon is not limited in 'advance.'

- The goal of the computerization for the information elite: to belong to the information elite of the village, town, country, continent, or world.
- Digital strategy: to have efficient digital equipment, provide internet access, email, digital libraries, and social networks, and have a home network if there is more than one user.
- Limitations: Digital technicians need to be present to quickly resolve any technical problems.

The architecture of the computerized home is given in Figure 4, which highlights the following five application software groups:

- Communication software: e.g., internet, email, e-media, Facebook (and others),
- Software for writing, graphic modeling, and calculations: e.g., MS Word, Visio, Excel, and PowerPoint,
- Software for online activities: e.g., workplace software, online banking, online education, online shopping, etc.,
- Organizing software, such as those that help to schedule classes, update budgets, or take notes,
- Document archiving software,

Table 2. Problem-solving ability in digital environments in the (OECD, 2016)

Country	Literacy (Mean Score)	Numeracy (Mean Score)	Problem Solving in Technology-Rich Environments (% at Level 2 or 3)
OECD countries and economies			
Australia	280	268	38
Austria	269	275	32
Canada	273	265	37
Chile	220	206	15
Czech Republic	274	276	33
Denmark	271	278	39
England (UK)	273	262	35
Estonia	276	273	28
Finland	288	282	42
Flanders (Belgium)	275	280	35
France	262	254	m
Germany	270	272	36
Greece	254	252	14
Ireland	267	256	25
Israel	255	251	27
Italy	250	247	m
Japan	296	288	35
Korea	273	263	30
Netherlands	284	280	42
New Zealand	281	271	44
Northern Ireland (UK)	269	259	29
Norway	278	278	41
Poland	267	260	19
Slovak Republic	274	276	26
Slovenia	256	258	25
Spain	252	246	m
Sweden	279	279	44
Turkey	227	219	8
United States	270	253	31
OECD average	**268**	**263**	**31**
Partners			
Cyprus	269	265	m
Jakarta (Indonesia)	200	210	m
Lithuania	267	267	18
Russian Federation	275	270	26
Singapore	258	257	37

Figure 4. The architecture of the digital home of the information elite

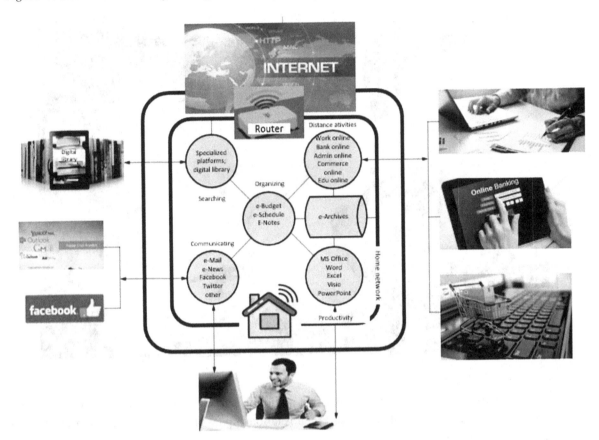

- Software for digital platforms, such as digital libraries,
- Others.

STRATEGY FOR USER T – YOUNGER AND INFORMED

Young "adults" or digital natives are fluent in video games, mobile phones, and computers because all kinds of computers and mobile devices have constantly surrounded them. While a Chinese migrant worker can use his mobile phone to take photos, the digital native can use the images to update his Facebook account. However, older users may not have the skills required to manage a Facebook account that they consider part of the youth's domain. Thus, the perception of technology by the older generation is directly related to their ability to interact with ICT. Jamaicans refer to the skills of the younger generation in using mobile phones as something "born with them; the phone is a twin." Also, the need for young Chinese women to hide their mobile phones from older family members for fear of being reprimanded implies a gap in the perception of technology between digital natives and the older generation.

It is estimated that around 55% of young people and children are addicted to the internet (Kaspersky, 2016):

Figure 5. Boys "do not see the world" outside of computer games. (Photo: <u>dailymail.co.uk</u>)

- As adolescents and children age, their internet addiction hurts their behavior at school, their ability to make friends, their intelligence, and their relationships with their parents, according to their own self-assessment.
- Young people and children addicted to the internet are more likely to argue with their parents about internet use (30% compared to just 10% of non-dependents).
- The impact of internet use is even more significant, as half (50%) of adolescents and children addicted to the internet admit that they communicate less with their parents as a result of using connected devices (compared to only a quarter of adolescents and non-internet dependent children).
- More than half (56%) of young people and children dependent on the internet hide their potentially risky online activities from their parents, compared with 28% of young people and children not dependent on the internet.
- 25% of young people and children addicted to the internet try to avoid parental control, compared with 8% of non-dependent young people and children.
- Young people and children dependent on the internet are more likely to share sensitive information on social media, such as their home address (36%) and their parents' earnings (26%) compared to 25% and 16% respectively for adolescents and children not dependent on the internet.
- Almost a third of dependents (28%) admit that they use inappropriate content for young people and children, while only one in ten non-dependent young people and children admit so.
- Young people and dependent children are more likely to face cyber threats than non-dependent young people and children (48% vs. 24%). They are also more likely to be bullied not only online but also offline (17% vs. 6%).

- One of the consequences of young people's and children's dependence on the internet is their parents' dependence on the internet: 62% of the dependent parents surveyed had dependent young people and children. This applies only to 32% of non-dependent parents surveyed.

Figure 6. Percentage of children and adolescents dependent on the Internet (Kaspersky, 2016)

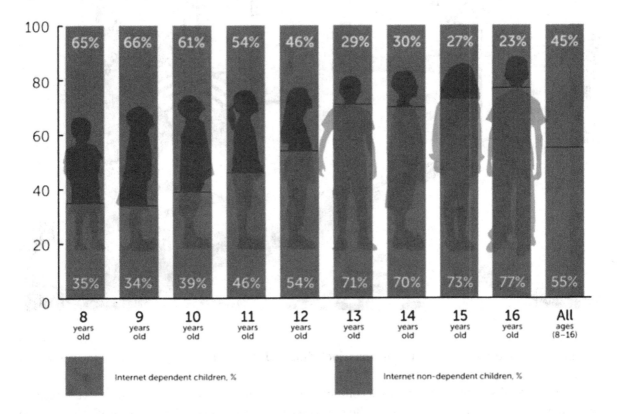

The internet provides children and young people with a world of new opportunities. Still, as the aforementioned report shows, it is crucial to be wary of the dangers of internet addiction and to effectively control children's use of the internet from an early age (Kaspersky, 2016).

As young people (12-19 years old) and adults (20-29 years old) access the internet more than any other age group and have a higher risk of internet abuse, the problem of internet addiction disorders is most important for these demographics. Internet abuse has not been recognized by the World Health Organization and its *Diagnostic and Statistical Manual of Mental Disorders* (DSM-5) as a disorder; however, a related set of computer-associated disorders has been included in the *International Classification of Diseases* (ICD-11). The controversy surrounding the diagnosis concerns whether the condition is a separate clinical unit or a manifestation of some other underlying mental disorder. Studies have approached the question from different points of view, without standardized or agreed upon definitions, leading to difficulties in developing evidence-based recommendations.

Nevertheless, mental disorders can be diagnosed when a person engages in online activities at the expense of fulfilling daily duties or pursuing other interests, regardless of the negative consequences.

Figure 7. A smart house where most of the equipment is monitored remotely and digitally

The internet can foster a variety of addictions, including addiction to playing games, auction sites, social networking sites, and surfing the web.

So-called "digital natives" develop their abilities and communication skills in virtual space at the expense of personal and social connections in real life physical spaces. This causes them to be insulated from the real world and to develop unreliable connections, including friendships in virtual spaces. Furthermore, the internet mobility of digital natives does not cover the balanced applications of the information elite.

- The goal of computerization for internet natives: to move to the information elite.
- Strategy: develop applications typical of the information elite.
- Limitations: Limit the use of IT equipment to 3-4 hours per day.

STRATEGY FOR DIGITIZING HOUSING

Intelligent people built smartphones to lead to more exciting and compelling lives. Nevertheless, they hardly realized that this digitalization would never end, for it would be used to make smart homes, where most of the equipment is digitally monitored.

The most popular smart home computerization systems include:

1. **Smart locks**, which give residents full control over home security. When an occupant leaves their home, the door will close behind them and lock and vice versa.

Figure 8. Digital control of an entrance with a smart lock

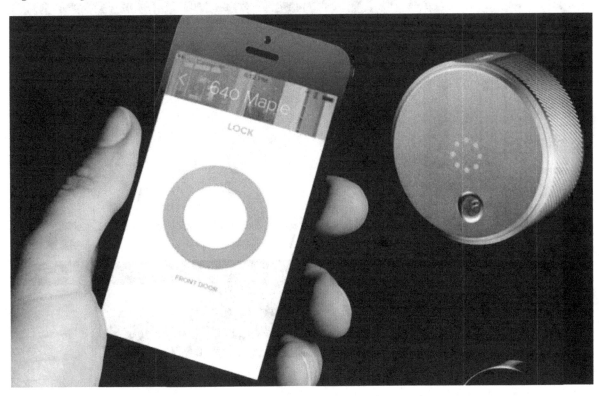

2. **Light control**, which can be accessed remotely. Many residents have already had enough of having to check around the house to make sure the appropriate lights are turned on and off.

3. **Monitoring water leaks**: a smart house notifies a homeowner if water leaks and enters a place where it should not be. However, this is often not known to be a feature of smart homes.

4. **Monitoring children and loved ones**: With digital hardware, one can monitor and protect those near and dear from potentially dangerous areas.

5. **Security cameras**, which allow one to monitor the situation at home. If necessary, security cameras can record anything at any time during day or night. Seamless camera monitoring enhances family safety.

6. **Temperature monitoring**: It often happens that we forget to adjust the thermostat before leaving the house. This can cause inconveniences, for when we get home, the temperature is either too high

Figure 9. Digital control of home lighting

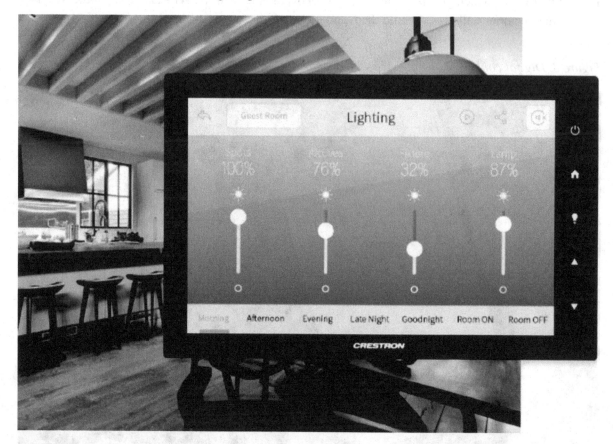

or too low. Moreover, the rise or fall in temperature takes a long time. Temperature monitoring and smart thermostats can also save energy and are, thus, profitable.

7. **Digital voice monitoring equipment**: Amazon offers its digital assistant, Alexa, who "stands" on a table or countertop in the kitchen and understands voice commands given by a resident of the house who directs Alexa to take care of matters related to the digital monitoring of the house. Amazon customers using voice-activated *Amazon Echo* speakers can also take advantage of Microsoft's artificial intelligence capabilities by saying, "Alexa, open Cortana." By doing this, they can, for example, check their Outlook calendar for upcoming meetings. At the same time, Windows 10 PC customers can say "Hi Cortana, open Alexa" to turn on the lights in their homes or add products to their shopping lists.

One of the problems with creating a smart home is the high number of competitive services offered by multiple platforms and with multiple standards. Manufacturers of these types of home devices increasingly need to ensure that their products and services run on platforms provided by Amazon, Google, Samsung, and Apple to gain the broadest possible customer base. Consumers themselves face the danger of being associated with a particular network provider, which can often limit the options available if the tool or device they need does not play well with their favorite platform. It is also tedious to use a whole set of different apps to set up and control specific devices in a smart home.

Figure 10. Security cameras monitor home situations

This will change over the next decade as more and more devices begin to use machine learning, computer vision, natural language processing, and other technologies that can think, make decisions, and learn. Some devices are already doing this: For example, Nest and Honeywell's intelligent home thermostats use machine learning to adapt their behavior to the inhabitants' routines in the house and then recreate these routines. In 2020, one can expect to see more AI-based technologies, such as facial recognition, become a feature of home security systems. We will also see more refrigerators that use computer vision to "see" what's inside, and machine learning algorithms to predict what needs to be ordered and then place the order.

Figure 11. Alexa (Amazon) can communicate with MS Cortana

 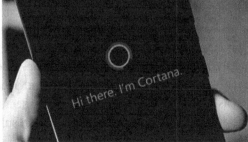

Robots at Home

This trend began with robotic vacuum cleaners and lawnmowers; however, thanks to advances in AI, we can expect them to be more intelligent and able to help us broaden our range of tasks. From cooking and cleaning to providing companionship and healthcare, all kinds of robots, such as CLOi LG and Lucy Trifo, are already available. AI advances also promise a future where machines can do everyday tasks so that we can spend valuable time on activities other than housework and routine maintenance. For the elderly and disabled, they will act as a calming pair of extra eyes that will be able to call for help if someone has fallen or help the elderly move around the house. In 2020, autonomous mobile robots will undoubtedly become more common, useful, and cheaper, as many manufacturers compete to develop the most helpful solutions.

Home Care is Getting Smarter

Smart home healthcare offers the potential to reduce the stress on traditional healthcare channels (i.e., doctors and hospitals), which has inevitably been caused by an increase in life expectancy and a growing elderly population. Some of this relief will be achieved through preventive measures, such as wearable technologies that will help us lead healthier lifestyles by monitoring our activity levels, sleep quality, and nutrition. Other devices will offer intervention services, for example, allowing us to connect remotely with doctors, alert caregivers when an older adult gets home, and even diagnose diseases. The current Apple watch, for instance, may perform an electrocardiogram (ECG) to monitor patterns or irregular heartbeats that may be early warning signs of disease. This type of technology will become more common in the following years (and beyond), reducing the need for outpatient visits. Data collected by smart home appliances at home will become increasingly useful in medicine, as they can provide round-the-clock insights into the condition of patients in their "natural environment," away from the stress experienced in clinics and hospitals.

Faster Networks Mean Smarter Homes

With the global deployment of 5G as well as improved WiFi technology, smart home devices will be connected by more rapid, more powerful networks, which means better access to data and cloud computing resources. In particular, 5G promises to revolutionize the delivery of IoT services—including smart home technology—by allowing devices to work without wires and cables while consuming minimal power. It also allows for connections to a much larger number of devices at the same time, which was not possible using older cellular standards. This will be crucial as homes in densely populated areas are filled with a growing number of devices, all of which are thirsty for data throughput. Wi-Fi 6 technology offers an advantage over previous standards when it comes to enabling devices to handle competing requests for network access (a problem many of us have experienced, even if we routinely connect only a few smartphones, tablets, and laptops to our home networks at the same time). Faster networks do not simply mean more immediate data transfer between devices or between devices and the digital cloud: it also means that applications that use larger and speedier data streams will become more advanced. Devices such as smart thermostats and automated security systems will have access to more diverse and up-to-date information to make predictions. As a result, they will become more reliable and efficient.

- The goal of home computerization: to increase the safety of the home and residents and the convenience of using digital equipment.
- Strategy: Use a single digital platform and uniform standards.
- Limitations: Users should expect failures and develop the ability to fix these problems on their own. Otherwise, the question is whether it is worth installing such a system.

SUMMARY

1. A key strategy for developing the digital skills of inhabitants in a particular area is to eliminate digital exclusion, which exacerbates poverty and keeps people in a hopeless situation in life.
2. All categories of digital users aim to enter the information elite or, in any case, to reduce their distance from it.
3. The information elite are elite not because they have outstanding computer skills, but because they understand the importance of the information they collect and because they process this information correctly.
4. Internet natives impress with their mastery of being in virtual environments, but this comes at the expense of losing their ability to thrive in real life settings. They should become aware of their own limitations and strive to enter the information elite.
5. The computerization of home appliances can be a good option for busy people as well as for the elderly and sick; however, it must be secured to quickly fix failures that often occur in complex digital hardware configurations.

REFERENCES

Barupal, S. (2017, July 1). Digital divide: A critical analysis. *Medium.com*. https://medium.com/@ShwetaBarupal/digital-divide-a-critical-analysis-7156333237f7

Burrell, G., & Morgan, G. (1997). *Sociological paradigms and organizational analysis*. Heinemann Educational Books.

Kaspersky. (2016). *Impact of Internet dependence on children*. https://kids.kaspersky.com/internet-dependence-impact/

OECD. (2016). *Skills matter: Further results from the survey of adult skills*. OECD Publishing. https://www.oecd-ilibrary.org/docserver/9789264258051-en.pdf?expires=1618177382&id=id&accname=guest&checksum=26BD4942F98104A7A537B6BCC0FBB142

Rundle, J. (2020, July 9). Chicago hopes broadband plan could help other cities address digital divide. *Wall Street Journal*. https://www.wsj.com/articles/chicago-hopes-broadband-plan-could-help-other-cities-address-digital-divide-11594287000

Smith, A. (2014, April 3). Older adults and technology use. *Pew Research Center*. https://www.pewresearch.org/internet/2014/04/03/older-adults-and-technology-use

KEY TERMS AND DEFINITIONS

Digital Divide: A division between those who have access to and benefit from digital technologies and those who do not.

Digital Literacy: The ability to access, evaluate, and utilize information from digital technologies.

Digital Natives: Individuals who grew up with close access to digital technologies.

Information Elite: Members of a population who possess the greatest skills and abilities for using digital technologies.

Internet Addiction: An addiction characterized by excessive computer and Internet use.

Smart Home: Digital automation monitors and controls for a home that are accessible through the Internet.

Smart Light Control: A smart home control that allows users to control lighting.

Smart Locks: A smart home control that allows users to control door locks.

ENDNOTE

[1]   Poland is ahead of Lithuania and Greece in the EU in 2016.

Section 4
Challenges of Strategic Informing Technology

Chapter 17
Digital Humanities Strategy

ABSTRACT

This chapter outlines a strategy for digital humanities that can address some of the challenges that have arisen due to informing technologies. The chapter begins by giving a definition of humanism and by describing the nature of the humanistic attitude. The chapter next considers the role that mythology plays in humanism. After this, a matrix model of the humanities is presented that shows the role of the humanities in a computerized society. Then, a digital humanities research strategy is discussed with specific recommendations for implementing such research. This is followed by a discussion of the role that supercomputers play in research. Strategies for creating content in the digital humanities are then explored in disciplines such as philosophy, archeology, and history. Next, strategies for publishing and distributing information are described. The chapter concludes by considering strategies for teaching digital humanities and for developing digital social resonance.

INTRODUCTION

To develop a strategy for computerizing the humanities, one must define the fields of the humanities and the values and myths surrounding them:

- Core humanities: Philosophy, literature, arts, music, theatre, dance, cinema, and media.
- Supportive humanities: Cognitive science, archaeology, history, sociology, political science, religious studies, civil studies, cultural studies, journalism, and others.

After defining these fields, strategies for computerizing disciplines in the humanities according to a development cycle will be discussed. This cycle includes phases such as research, creation, publishing, distribution, teaching, and social resonance.

Digital strategies are similar for the research and creation phases, while the remaining phases have different strategies for the core humanities. On the other hand, the supportive humanities, which are composed of sciences, have a single digital strategy, which consists in using editorial software and digital libraries to extend the context of the issues under investigation and to employ a graphical method

DOI: 10.4018/978-1-7998-8036-3.ch017

of computer science in the formulation of complex processes and systems. These systems facilitate the analysis and synthesis of critical elements and their relationships. Numerous examples of graphic modeling in the humanities will be given.

While it may seem that "the humanities are dead" (Abramson, 2020), in this chapter, it will be argued that the humanities should be a strong force that can stop IT engineering, automation, and robotics from dominating the newly evolved surveillance capitalism and the prospects of a laborless economy. These developments would almost completely destroy any prospects for humanism, and they would bring people to the brink of becoming the "living dead". For example, in Amazon e-shops, developers working from home must install software on their computer that analyzes the keys that they press and the images in their work environment (recorded from the camera above their screen). These workers must also record all bathroom breaks.

Reflections on this subject are just as chilling as the agonizing thoughts about the threat of nuclear or biological war. Compounding the problem is the fact that these informative threats are not science fiction or remote possibilities: they are current threats, although they occur in processes not visible to ordinary people. At any rate, what is at stake is the loss of privacy and intellectual enslavement.

WHAT IS HUMANISM?

Humanism developed at the beginning of the Italian Renaissance in the 15th century, when the legacy of Greece and Rome began to be creatively explored, the classical civilizations that transformed into Western civilization around 800 CE. Studying this legacy has perpetuated in Western humanism the sense of beauty brought about by Greek culture and the sense of law brought about by Roman culture. Over the past nearly 600 years, Western humanism has been evolving, and its scope is almost unlimited, as it adheres to the notion that humans are born with talents that predispose them to independent, free, creative, and happy lives. Of course, humanism acknowledges that this is not without problems, including conflicts, wars and epidemics. According to the *American Humanist Association,* humanism can be defined as follows:

Humanism is a progressive philosophy of life that, without theism and other supernatural beliefs, confirms our ability and responsibility to lead a personal ethical life of fulfillment striving for the greater good (American Humanist Association, 2021).

By contrast, according to *the Humanist,* the definition of humanism is the following:

Humanism is a rational philosophy informed by science, inspired by art, and motivated by compassion. Affirming the dignity of each human being, it supports the maximization of individual liberty and opportunity consonant with social and planetary responsibility. It advocates the extension of participatory democracy and the expansion of the open society, standing for human rights and social justice. Free of supernaturalism, it recognizes human beings as a part of nature and holds that values—be they religious, ethical, social, or political—have their source in human experience and culture. Humanism thus derives the goals of life from human need and interest rather than from theological or ideological abstractions, and asserts that humanity must take responsibility for its own destiny (American Humanist Association, 2021).

Steven Schafersman[1] characterizes it this way:

Humanists affirm that humans have the freedom to give meaning, value, and purpose to their lives by their own independent thought, free inquiry, and responsible, creative activity. Humanists stand for the building of a more humane, just, compassionate, and democratic society using a pragmatic ethics based on human reason, experience, and reliable knowledge—an ethics that judges the consequences of human actions by the well-being of all life on Earth (American Humanist Association, 2021).

The Polish Society of Rationalists believes much the same:

Humanists are people affirming humans, their creative and innovative potential. In humanity, the humanist sees the beginning and end of the world of works and values. Humanism is a system of values that calls humanity to individual fulfillment by cultivating a creative and ethical life. Humanistic rites of passage differ from the religious concentration of all attention on humanity.

It is possible to generalize from the above definitions that humanism holds that the universe is the result of an extraordinarily long and complicated evolution involving unchanging laws of nature. However, Pope John Paul II (1920-2005) argued that there is no contradiction between science and religion and that the theory of evolution should be accepted along with the fact that, in his opinion, it was controlled by God from the very beginning (Paul II, 1998). Humanists, because of their views and attitudes, consider the natural world to be outstanding and precious, offering limitless possibilities, fascination, creativity, interaction, and joy; however, there is also a certain sadness, for science cannot and will probably never be able to explain the ultimate origin and purpose of the universe. Therefore, humanism can include not only atheists and agnostics but also believers. The lack of specific answers to these definitive questions leaves rational people to hypothesize about the origin of the natural universe, and some even hope for some form of life beyond. Two great humanists, Thomas Paine[2] and Robert Ingersoll[3], hoped for an afterlife. As for whether God exists, Ingersoll was agnostic, and Paine believed in a deistic God who established laws of nature but then departed and never intervened in the world, leaving us autonomous beings. For Paine's form of Deism, it is as if God is testing our independence and wisdom in solving the problems of life. These beliefs do not deprive tolerant people of their ability to lead an eminent humanistic life. Thus, people with such views can be humanists if they believe that humanity lives in the world on its own. The absence of any evidence (beyond faith) for the existence of an afterlife means that this life should be lived as if it is the only one we have. Therefore, it must be respected and considered a boon.

Humanism is an optimistic, progressive worldview that can transform political and cultural life into one that includes justice, equality, and a better existence for all. The promotion of social justice and education by humanists and other free thinkers is an essential part of the road to a better future. Humanism, like science, evaluates itself and improves in the face of new information and new knowledge. Humanistic responses are some of the best we have at our disposal and are more effective than worldview responses, which are trapped by immutable ancient texts and subject to personal prejudices related to unexplained revelations. Thus, the progress of humanism is a critical element in achieving positive change in our world in the face of constant confrontations with crises and, in particular, depravity.

THE ART OF THE HUMANISTIC ATTITUDE

The art of humanistic attitudes includes the following tendencies:

- Humanistic predispositions
  - **A love of beauty**: This involves the love of observing nature, things, and people and distinguishing them from horror, which inspires us to have an aesthetic attitude towards life and to feel good about existence. A catalog of what is beautiful is unlimited and requires constant updating from our lived experiences and confrontations with other views of life.
  - **A passion for human and animal movements**: Movement is inextricably linked to human life, just like breathing. For example, the French painter Edgar Degas (1834-1917) painted dancers, where the focus was the beautiful movements of the dance. It gave him the pleasure of creating and us the joy of watching and admiring. Today, we also admire the beauty of figure skating and fashion, especially the designs of great French and Italian stylists and tailors as well as the beauty of architecture and bridges.
  - **A passion for language**: We gain through reading and listening, regardless of the passage of time. For example, how beautiful is the expression of William Shakespeare (1564-1616), "To be or not to be, that is the question." Or consider the prose of Adam Mickiewicz (1798-1855), "Lithuania, My Homeland! You are like health; how much you must be valued, will only discover the one who has lost you." Or the statement by the Greek philosopher Heraclitus (6th century BC), "You can't enter the same river twice." The Chinese sage Lao Tzu (6th century BC) spoke similarly: "Your journey of a thousand kilometers starts with your first step." Will Wojciech Młynarski (1941-2017) expressed the following poetic verse: "Behind the windows night. In the mountains of snow, power covers everything. Devil only knows. What threw me into this spa."
  - **A passion for ideas**: Ideas underlie a value-oriented life and inspire action. For example, people have fought and died for the idea of freedom. However, at the same time, around 95 million people died as a result of the Bolshevik Revolution in 1918, pursuing the idea of social justice (Courteous et al., 1999).
  - **Awareness of the past**: A person's current quality of life is primarily due to historically accumulated knowledge and practices. For example, beauty is more than transient notion, as is evidenced by the sculpture of the Venus de Milo from the 2nd century BCE. Furthermore, Lech Wałęsa's policy in 1980, when he led the Solidarity Revolution in Poland, involved awareness of the past so as to not repeat the mistakes of numerous bloody Polish uprisings. He was aware of Mahatma Gandhi's policy (1869-1948) of passive support, and the Polish movement ultimately led to the collapse of the Polish People's Republic in 1989 and the USSR in 1991.
- Pleasures of humanism
  - **The pleasure of emotional debate**: This can consist, for example, in debating a film that is bad and not worth recommending to friends or in delighting in a good movie, such as *the Da Vinci Code*. This film was based on Dan Brown's bestselling book, which had millions of copies published and was on the list of best-selling books for two years. Or what about the film *Corpus Christi*, about a young Polish man who was released from a juvenile deten-

tion center? Is it not pleasurable to debate issues emotionally rather than in a detached and disinterested way?

- ○ **The pleasure of creative criticism**: If a poem about love is irrational, then why not add joy and criticize it? We rely on the following elements when engaging in such criticism:
  - ▪ Defining a case,
  - ▪ Getting rid of emotional argumentation,
  - ▪ Gathering and analyzing all the necessary facts,
  - ▪ Forgetting how things affect one personally,
  - ▪ Providing an objective opinion on the problem.

Creative criticism allows the humanist to engage in fundamental social processes. These include solving problems, questioning longstanding assumptions, and identifying the contexts of the cases raised.

A humanist is an unlimited person, which means that (1) he/she does not commit any crime against humanism; (2) he/she does not knowingly take away anyone's human and civil rights; (3) he/she analyzes both sides of a conflict before giving an opinion, and the humanist does not mean for their opinion to be some kind of final say on the matter, for all opinions are subject to change based on new contexts for a situation. In other words, the humanist is not a narrow-minded person, but an honest person who approaches life's affairs with an open mind.

MYTHOLOGY AND ITS ROLE IN HUMANISM

Before modern humanism developed, growing out of the Renaissance, there was mythology in the form of cave drawings in Lascaux in France and belief in so-called "archetypes". This form of pre-humanism includes the following myths:

- The myth of distinguished heroes with super-human abilities: This can be seen in examples such as Theseus, who raised a heavy stone, discovered a golden sword, and defeated a bull-like creature with a human head known as the "Minotaur". There is also the legend of the Sphinx, a half-bird, half-female who devoured those who gave the wrong answers to riddles, and the mythical King Arthur, the legendary Celtic ruler of the British around the 5th and 6th centuries. Indeed, the latter was a hero in numerous legends, literary works, and films. King Arthur is known as a righteous ruler who introduced law into Britain. His knights searched for the Holy Grail, which could only be found by the most honest of people. Western civilization has many similar heroes, who are not considered so in life, but are revered and idolized after death, like Joan of Arc, Galileo, and John Kennedy.
- The myth of magicians: This includes examples such as wizards, witches, alchemists, fairies, and fortune-tellers.
- The myth of the power of words: Examples include "open sesame," "the Gospel according to St. John", "I give you my word", and others.
- The myth of power of numbers: For example, in the *Divine Comedy*, Dante gives mythological meaning to the number 3, which reflects the Holy Trinity. Furthermore, in the Middle Ages, the number 7 was of particular importance. It symbolized faith, mysticism, loneliness, spiritual development, intellectual development, silence, and a shift away from the world in search of the truth.

Positive vibrations of the number 7 were said to give us the strength of faith, peace of mind, and an awareness of divinity in our surroundings. In Judaism, certain combinations of numbers are held to be the secret of the world. For example, the Hebrew Kabbalah explores numerical combinations in Talmud texts.

- The myth of figures without beginnings and ends: This illustrates order in nature.
- The power of the garden: This is a symbol for something new. For example, the Polish philosopher Janusz Kuczyński (1930-2017) called gardeners 'people who sow new ideas in society'.
- The myth of the lost family: This is connected with works such as Sophocles' tragedy *Antigone*, where evil has its source in a poorly functioning family.
- The myth of human suffering: This is often held to result from excessive curiosity and punishment, as was the case, for example, in the myth surrounding the opening of Pandora's Box, which was punished by Zeus. Another example is Eve, who, against God's will, took an apple from the forbidden tree of knowledge and gave some to Adam. Both were met with punishment and banished from the garden of Eden. A similar mistake was made by Lot's wife. As the story goes, God allowed Lot's family to escape from the destruction of the city Sodom, provided no one not look behind them. Unfortunately, Lot's wife did not listen, and out of curiosity, turned around. For punishment, she was transformed into a pillar of salt.
- The myth of childhood: This occurs in the form of stories like *Harry Porter* or Disney heroes in films such as *Snow White, Cinderella, Beauty and the Beast, Aladdin*, and *the Lion King*. These stories are remembered by adults and are subconsciously recalled in life practices. This also includes fairy tales such as *Little Red Riding Hood*, a story about a young girl named after her red hooded cape, her grandmother, an evil wolf, and a lumberjack.
- The myth of the need for confirmation: This includes, for example, the *Three Little Pigs*, which indicates that diligence, not frivolity and fun, bring success in life.
- The myth of the importance of being attractive and wealthy: This indicates that good and evil stem from the physical appearance of the characters of a story. Everyone's dream is to be rich, as long as it is morally beautiful.
- The myth of the black side of power: For example, there is a haunted forest in the Wizard of Oz, which helps children learn that life is not always sunny.
- The myth of sayings: These include, for example, "All you need is love," "It must be fate," "What goes around comes from around," "Us against them," "Nice guys finish last," etc.

THE STRUGGLE FOR TRUE HUMANISM

Writers, artists, musicians, philosophers, and scholars whose works concern society have been persecuted by those who feared that they would lose power. The ancient Greeks, for example, sentenced Socrates to death. In Italy, Giordano Bruno was burned at the stake because of the proclamations involving heliocentrism. For similar reasons, Galileo Galilei was not allowed to write about such matters. In the Soviet Bloc, to be a poet, it was necessary to receive a license from the authorities. Boris Pasternak, for example, could not receive the Nobel Prize in Literature for his work *Dr. Zhivago*, for the work had passages that were regarded anti-Soviet. Artists were restricted to what is now called "Socialist realism". Similarly, Adolf Hitler did not like the paintings of impressionists and surrealists, whose works he removed from the country and referred to as "degenerate art"; instead, he only allowed art that captured "blood and soil" values. In modern China, literature is permissible if it cultivates support for the dictatorship of the party. Even in today's United States, there is self-censorship on college campuses, and only politically correct statements are permissible.

The struggle of eminent humanists for true humanism can be categorized as below:

- Late recognition of creativity, often only after death,
- Conflicts arising from the discussion of the role of religion in society,
- Conflicts arising from political attitudes,
- Conflicts arising from the subject of sexual orientation,
- Conflicts arising from the behavior of artists,
- Conflicts arising from the promotion of unknown forms of expression,
- Repression of artists for "degenerate" work,
- Repression of membership in disputed associations or interest groups in the past and present,
- Conflicts arising from various forms of explicit and covert censorship,
- Conflicts related to the mistreatment of women,
- Conflicts arising from criticism of inequalities in wealth,
- Conflicts arising from criticism about exclusion from society,
- Others.

A MODEL OF THE HUMANITIES AND ITS ROLE IN A COMPUTERIZED SOCIETY

Figure 1 depicts a matrix model of the humanities (MMH) with its disciplines and specializations.

The following disciplines and specializations of the humanities are distinguished in the matrix model:

1. Humanities disciplines:
    a. *Core humanities*: Philosophy, literature, art (painting, sculpture, and architecture), music, theatre, dance, cinema and media,
    b. *Supporting humanities*: Archaeology, history, sociology, political science, religious studies, civilization studies, cultural studies, journalism, and others.
2. Humanities specializations:
    a. *Specializations of the humanities cycle*: research, creation, publishing, distribution, teaching, social resonances,
    b. *Humanities digital specializations*: Big Data, digital libraries, social networks, graphic, visualization and interface techniques, humanities platforms and software.

In some cases, specializations of the humanities cycle have been practiced for hundreds of years, and a number of them have been practiced for many decades. Humanities computerization specializations, on the other hand, are new to humanists, who often have many problems with them. However, it is not only humanists who have issues with computerization.

So far, humanists have dominated their societies thanks to their universal education and the art of arguing and communicating. Moreover, in the past they outnumbered specialists in other fields such as engineering, medicine, biology, economics, mathematics, physics, chemistry, agriculture, and so on.

Figure 1. A matrix model of the field of humanities (MMH)

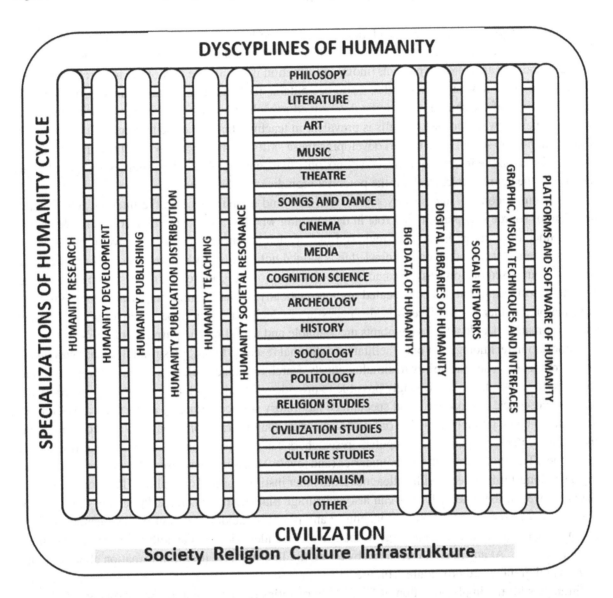

However, at present, in competing for better jobs and higher salaries, humanists have fallen behind the rest of the professionals.

The role of humanists in the computerization of the humanities lies not only in its wise application in the humanities to enrich their skills and knowledge but also in presenting humanistic requirements for specialists with engineering, medical, science, and natural sciences, who very often carry out indiscriminately computerization that threatens the humanization of civilization.

DIGITAL HUMANITIES RESEARCH STRATEGY

Gone are the days of consulting encyclopedias such as the highly regarded *Encyclopedia Britannica*. We used to be sure that the information we found was the most relevant to our study, was presented objectively, and was accurate. At present, finding information is not a large part of the research challenge. Investigators must now analyze whether a source contains fact-based, legitimate information. When it does, the origin of the source needs to be determined as well as whether the source presents information in a relevant way. This set of skills is prevalent in teaching history at the university level, but now students in middle school need to start developing these skills. Furthermore, to have the ability to assess a source found on the Internet, it is necessary not only to teach tools for finding sources, but also, before we trust in the source, to learn about the potential prejudices of the author(s).

At present, secondary and tertiary sources can be found in abundance on the Internet; thus, the assessment of source bias plays a vital role in determining whether a site is credible (Passanisi & Peters, 2013). Since the Internet is not peer-reviewed like academic journals, users will have to make an assessment themselves. Today, one's knowledge is judged not necessarily on how much information one possesses but based on how easy one can use that information. It is, therefore, necessary to analyze and evaluate information that has been scaled up very critically, which is more important than compiling information together in one place. It is also necessary to decipher different perspectives on the Internet and to ultimately decide which viewpoints are valuable and useful for the purposes of one's research.

Information technology not only facilitates traditional research tasks, it also enables what was previously impractical, such the ability to simultaneously search for and correlate information from different archives. In addition, it is increasingly possible to provide online network access to remote instruments such as telescopes, microscopes, and specialized laboratory services. Equally importantly, research results can be made publicly available online much earlier than in traditional ways. With access to email and video conferencing on their computers, researchers can now work more informally and faster with colleagues. Traditional institutional boundaries (and loyalty) are blurred as researchers are more likely to engage in long-term projects with colleagues from other institutions and disciplines (Passanisi & Peters, 2013). However, these new IT tools can also encourage plagiarism and fraud. Protecting the integrity of research will require vigilance and ingenuity and possibly the development of new technologies to enhance data security and prevent forgery, the use of false identities, and unauthorized changes to publications or data. At any rate, numerous websites on the Internet have useful information about funding sources and grant award procedures (Figure 2).

Strategies for the implementation of IT-aided humanities research include the following:

1. *Big Data collections should be expanded, and hypotheses and methods should be clarified.* Existing data collections should be used to broaden the context of the subject under examination (e.g., see Figure 3). It is necessary to subscribe (usually for a fee) to access digital libraries to get acquainted with similar research projects and their results. New software tools also allow for testing possible solutions to problems and offer advanced techniques for composing, manipulating, and evaluating alternatives.

Figure 2. Example of a European Union website on sources of research funding

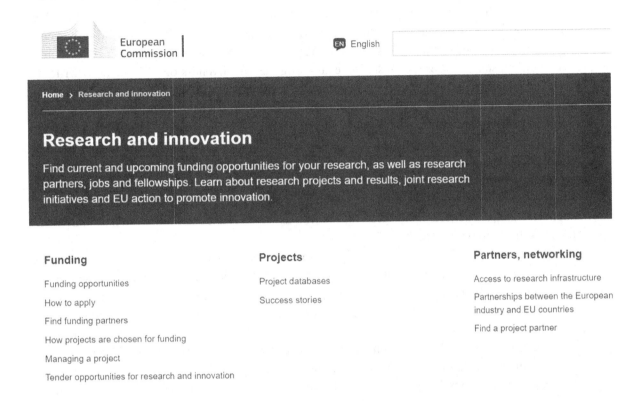

Figure 3. Example of a Big Data system used in retail marketing and supply

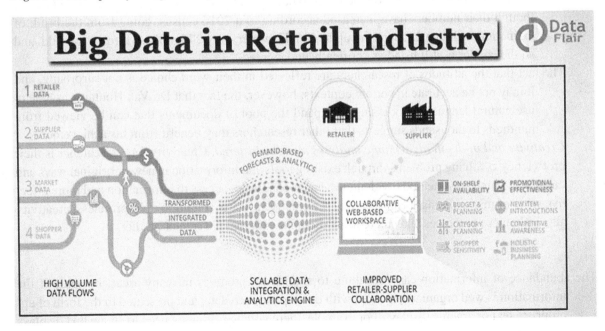

2.   *Ways of measuring progress in fields of action and knowledge must be identified.* Kyle Van Houtan, an ecologist at the Monterey Bay Aquarium in California, wondered how to accomplish this when he faced the task of investigating whether methods of increasing the population of wild endangered species have improved over the years ("A New Way to Review Scientific Literature,", 2020). Under normal circumstances, those interested in examining the effectiveness of such methods write reviews for scientific journals; however, in a thriving field, this could entail reading and extracting information from hundreds, perhaps thousands, of articles. It would thus require a large research team and cause coordination problems. In this situation, Dr. Van Houtan and his research team used a branch of machine learning known as *natural language processing* (NLP). This is a way of analyzing large amounts of text with minimal human supervision. Dr. Van Houtan used NLP to search the summaries of 434 articles on species conservation projects published over the past four decades. The software's task was to search for words related to success, such as "protection," "support," "help," "benefit", and "growth," as well as words related to failure, such as "threaten," "loss," "kill," "problem", and "risk."

Different words had different values assigned to them, depending on how positive or negative the original model makers felt they were. Based on these assumptions and five other inputs, a sentiment score was averaged and assigned to each summary. In total, the team analyzed 1,030,558 words. They found that, for articles published in the 1980s, when conservation science was in its infancy, negative list terms were much more common than positive. In contrast, success-related deadlines have become more frequent over the last decade. Average sentiment ratings increased by 140% during the study period.

This is encouraging news for environmentalists. It suggests that their methods improve with experience. However, more detailed analyses based on this procedure are also possible. For example, the giant panda, whose population was estimated at 1,864 in 2014, has since been raised from "endangered" to merely "vulnerable", and since September of this year, there has been a change of sentiment in the literature about them, going from negative to positive. California condor articles, on the other hand, are saturated with negative assessments, even though their numbers have increased according to a 2016 census, going from the brink of extinction with just 22 members up to 446. However, only 276 of these birds were wild, and so the condor is still listed as "critically endangered."

The fact that the attitudes of researchers are reflected in their word choice is not surprising, and it may not be accurate in certain contexts; however, the fact that Dr. Van Houtan was able to use natural language processing to expand the pool of documents that can be viewed from hundreds to thousands suggests that other researchers may benefit from his achievements.

3.   *Creativity and in-depth algorithmic analyses must be fostered.* Creativity for a researcher is their proficiency at solving problems through existing tools and information in new or original ways and through creating new methods, techniques, and tools. Easier access to information and more effective ways of manipulating it can speed up the creative process (Figure 4). Nevertheless, creativity also influences processes and can redirect them in ways that we cannot predict.

The abundance of information can contribute to significant progress in many areas, but only if the information is well organized, marked with descriptive metadata, and presented in the form of appropriate text or graphic displays. For example, there will be a growing need to create text displays

Figure 4. Example of Crowdicity, an application to support the development of solutions

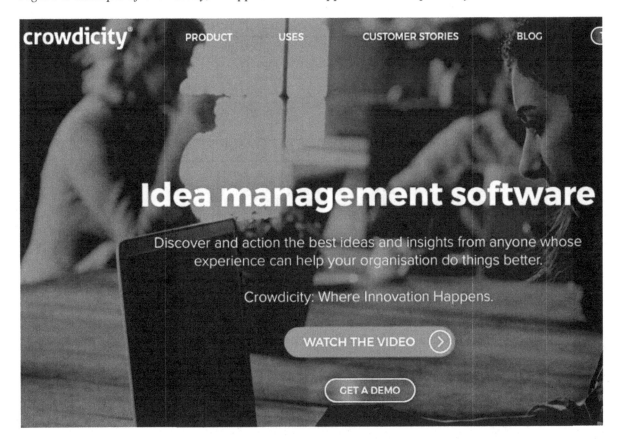

that can be controlled by users so that data can be organized chronologically, grouped by source, ranked by relevance, and identified for reliability. Compact windows for visualizing "data mining" proved that it has major advantages in "discovering" data from digital libraries. Such windows are shown on small areas of the computer screen (Figure 5). The new tools also promise to allow visualizations of the star field for multidimensional data, scale the timeline for the presentation of chronological data, and map trees or hyperbolic trees for the data hierarchy.

4. *Collaboration in research teams should be supported.* For a researcher, the steady increase in computing power offers not only access to information but also completely new ways of communicating with colleagues. High-speed networks (5G) from one gigabit up to a terabit per second and high-resolution digital displays (in the tens of megapixels) allow for increasing amounts of fidelity in reproducing human interaction at a distance, from everyday conversations to multi-screen conferences. Telepresence and virtual environments supported by high-speed networks are becoming essential tools to help scientific collaboration. Online communication with other people takes place via e-mail, websites, and mailing lists as well as software that facilitates group communication. Thanks to these measures, online communities are growing at an impressive pace. An organizer of

Figure 5. Compact visualization panes for explored data

a research project must therefore organize access to the relevant software and networks for online cooperation (Figure 6).

5. *The e-simulation of experiments should be encouraged.* Many researchers talk about simulation calculations as the "third modality" of scientific research, on a par with theory and experiments. For many years, computers have been used to simulate natural phenomena via statistical methods such as the Monte Carlo method[4] (Figure 7), which has been used to analyze neutron transport in fission chain reactions and deterministic solutions of motion equations for complex systems. Today, numerical simulations can bring modelers, theorists, and experimenters closer together, as their tools (digital sensors, simulations, networks, and databases) are increasingly interconnected. In the humanities, e-simulations are primarily used to make predictions about populations; however, their use can be expanded to predict behaviors in regard to the unsustainable use of strategic resources. One can also stimulate the development of a "future" story if the relevant Big Data is available. Currently, films can use past cinematography to create simulations of buildings and historical en-

Figure 6. GoTo and Monday.com, examples of research collaboration platforms

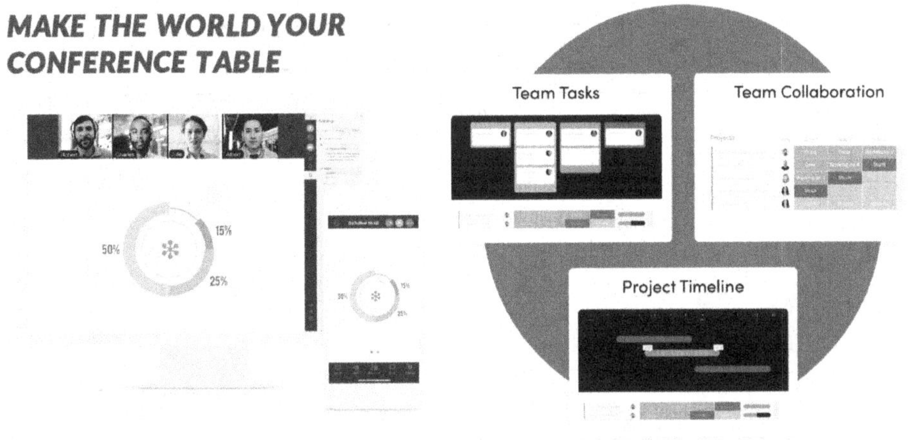

vironments (e.g., in the film the *Pianist*, one saw the ruins of Warsaw in 1944 and in the film *1917*, one witnessed the epic trenches of WWI). In political science, it is possible to simulate matters of war and peace, in particular the consequences resulting from many interacting factors. IT tools increase our understanding of natural phenomena; however, they do not diminish the importance of reliable experimental and theoretical analyses.

THE USE OF SUPERCOMPUTERS IN RESEARCH

"Supercomputers" were initially designed for highly efficient parallel processing and for calculating tasks that require detailed measures, such as the dynamics of physical objects, chemical, fluids, and gas. In the future, supercomputers will also be used as super storage systems to handle vast amounts of digital data. Some of the most extensive modern supercomputers are used with "video on demand" servers, e.g., museums use them to handle the enormous amounts of graphical data that need to be uploaded. Managing terabytes and even petabytes of geographic information or other forms of spatial information, in addition to data, text, and multimedia information, is the goal of specially designed super-memory systems with hundreds or thousands of disks and processors. An example a system used to map the earth's surface was Microsoft's Terraserver project (later named Microsoft Research Maps). Another example is the PetaPlex system for knowledge, funded initially by the US National Security Agency.

Supercomputers and super-memory systems also enable advanced, discipline-specific "search engines" for data-intensive applications that also require extensive calculations. For example, by comparing satellite-recorded images from the same area pixel by pixel at different times, one can detect ground movement caused by earthquakes. This type of calculation requires a large amount of memory and takes months on a typical computer. On the other hand, on a supercomputer, one can accomplish this in a few hours. Automated classification of large amounts of remote sensing data (such as soil type information) is also possible in high-performance systems.

Figure 7. A simulation example using the Monte Carlo method

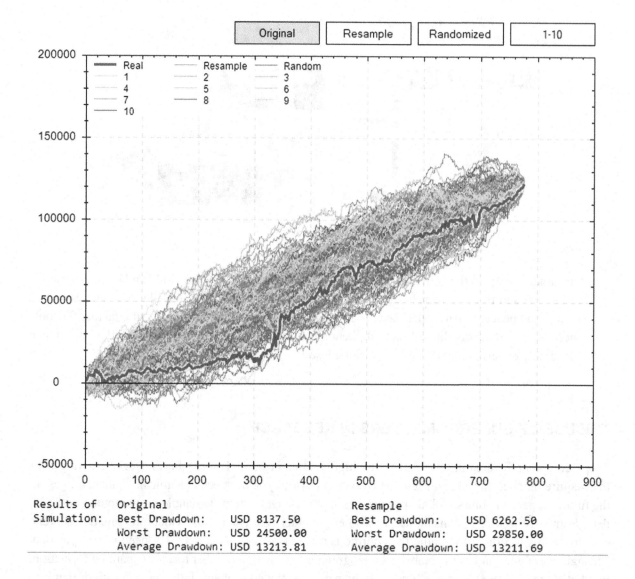

Results of | Original | | Resample |
Simulation: | Best Drawdown: | USD 8137.50 | Best Drawdown: | USD 6262.50
| Worst Drawdown: | USD 24500.00 | Worst Drawdown: | USD 29850.00
| Average Drawdown: USD 13213.81 | | Average Drawdown: USD 13211.69

COLLECTIVE INTELLIGENCE

One area of research that has enabled evolving group networks is the use of so-called "collective intelligence", which is a form of group intelligence distributed across a variety of computers, data collection engines, and connected communication networks. For instance, projects such as *Distributed.Net* rely on loosely connected groups of volunteer computer users from around the world, changing the paradigm of solving complex problems by distributing information processing activities on networks of thousands or even millions of computers.

An outline of how collective intelligence can be employed to complete projects is provided below:

1. **Storing and accessing data**: Consolidating knowledge for posterity is one of the essential functions of higher education institutions. For centuries, the intellectual goal of each university was to develop its library—a collection of written works, maps, and other important documents—to preserve knowledge of civilization. Today, both university and non-university knowledge exist in many forms scattered across different libraries and storage centers. This includes texts, graphics, videos, sound recordings, algorithms, and simulations of reality. These forms of knowledge almost literally exists in the ether and can be accessed by nearly everyone—they are certainly not limited to the powers of several privileged researchers from an academic campus. Digital libraries have thus become not only a reservoir of information but information facilitators, that is, they assist in searching for and disseminating knowledge. In a certain respect, the library and its books have combined into a "single document". For instance, hypertext links, contained in e-books, seamlessly guide readers through the web of interconnected information and concepts. The digital library network is a model for this new form of information navigation. Today's advanced search engines might lose their luster compared to the software currently being developed, which, thanks to the use of Artificial Intelligence, can collect, organize, combine, visualize, and summarize information. As they assume roles traditionally assigned to archives and museums as well as traditional libraries, digital libraries should have active plans to protect information collections. Different disciplines of knowledge should also develop standards for data formats and metadata to enable transdisciplinary syntheses of data and, more broadly, knowledge in different ways.

2. **Publishing and disseminating research findings**: Publishing is the final result of research. It involves sharing research with others, critically synthesizing and analyzing research, giving credit, and criticizing previous arguments in the studied field. Traditional publishing methods have been developed around printing technology and the economics of distributing and storing printed volumes; however, IT technology has opened up many new channels of communication for researchers, which could allow for research findings to become widely disseminated. In addition, IT technology allows researchers to publish in stages, include interactive materials, and incorporate additional information that is not made available in traditional printed publications. A significant problem, however, is archiving study descriptions. If, for example, the results of a study are presented on the Internet, it is the responsibility of the researcher and the webmaster to archive all vital information, such as source data and research notes. Using computerization, researchers can communicate more widely and directly with colleagues and the public. Many researchers set up websites and other communication channels with colleagues from the same discipline the world. Information that is openly available on the Internet is now accessible by people all over the world (Passanisi & Peters, 2013). Thus, digital publications are a significant advance over printed journals or specialized monographs, which are only available to members of organizations with well-funded research libraries.

3. **Program Evaluation and Review Technique (PERT)**: PERT is an acronym for program evaluation and review technique. It is a project management technique that helps estimate the time needed to complete a project. Of course, while having a clear timetable is crucial for the completion of a project, so is making sure the project falls within budget. The more one works on a project, the more one will have to pay. However, estimating the time needed to complete a project is not easy. Many factors need to be taken into account, many of which are complex and challenging to calculate accurately. PERT has been used by project managers to estimate this time more accurately. PERT was first developed by the U.S. Navy in the 1950s in connection with a project for develop-

ing ballistic missiles from nuclear-powered Polaris submarines (U.S., Department of Navy, 1958). This project involved an army of contractors. Due to PERT, the project was completed two years ahead of schedule. How does PERT work? PERT first divides tasks into detailed activities. It then converts a Gantt statistical schedule into an active network of interdependent activities (Figure 8).[5]

4. **Representing projects**: On a project management network, nodes represent events, and activities are represented by arrows drawn from one event to another based on their order of completion. On this basis, the earliest time (TE) and latest time (TL) for each activity as well as the slack time are determined. PERT has three estimation times, and each activity is marked with one of these estimates: An optimistic time estimate (O), which is the fastest time in which an action can be performed. The most likely estimated time (M) is the estimate that project managers provide senior management (if they are required to submit such estimates). Pessimistic estimation time (P) is the maximum time needed to complete an activity. Based on all the information collected, there is an equation to estimate the time needed for the project, known as expected time for completion, or E. E is calculated using the following equation: $E = (O+4M+P)/6$. The possible variance for the estimated completion time is represented by V. Variance is calculated using the following equation: $V = [(P - O) / 6]$ ^ 2. E and V are computed for each activity. Es are summed, which represent the total estimated time that it will take to finish the project. V-values are added to each activity, which represent the variance in completion times for the entire project. This helps project managers integrate the uncertainty associated with each project's schedule into their methodology (Landau, 2019). Over time, PERT has been simplified into the *Critical Path Method* (CPM) technique, which provides only one completion estimate. It is common for both PERT and CPM to specify in days, weeks, or months critical action paths, which are activities on the longest paths. This allows the project manager to know where to focus so as to assure the project is completed on time.

SUMMARY OF THE DIGITAL HUMANITIES STRATEGY

1. According to widespread criticism of the humanities, they involve excessive specialization, over-production, and too little teaching of crucial issues. However, others object that this is a misplaced assessment, for the humanities are not a science of economics, where such matters are studied. Justine Stover (2017), on the other hand, is of the opinion that "the humanities are not just dying… they are almost dead." The author even states that the reasons we give in defense of the humanities are hollow words and that deep down "we know it."

2. Many articles express pessimism about the humanities, saying that "the humanities are falling from grace," that "interest in the humanities is fading," or that the humanities are "under pressure all over the world" (Tworek, 2013). Commentators attribute these declines to significant financial cuts in disciplines such as history, literature, and the arts at public universities. In the U.S., Republican governors have proposed cuts to faculty in the humanities at state universities to rebalance funding for more "practical" subjects. North Carolina Governor Patrick McCrory, for example, said in January 2004 that he planned to change state legislation on higher education funding so that it is not "based on how many butts in seats but how many of those butts can get jobs." Like other critics, McCrory did not want taxpayers to subsidize items that did not lead directly to providing students with jobs.

Figure 8. A task network of a project. Rectangles show the number of weeks in which a task can be completed (earliest and latest). A thick line indicates a critical path as well as the estimated time of completion (in days, weeks, or months). Using the above data, computers calculate critical paths.

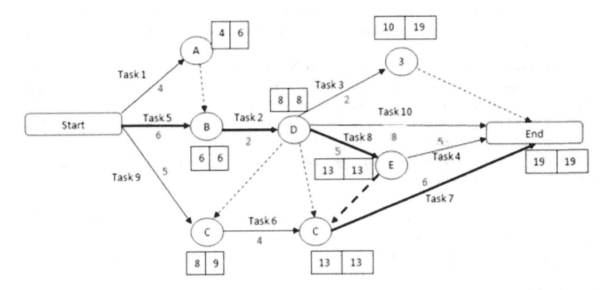

3. Rosemary G. Feal, the executive director of the Modern Language Association of America, says that the decline in funding for humanities research in the United States is related to both tax crises and the "devaluation of the humanities," particularly by lawmakers who have no experience in this field. In 2008, a task force organized by Governor Rick Scott of Florida recommended that students in humanities pay higher tuition, arguing that they are "non-strategy disciplines." In response, an online petition signed by more than 2,000 people warned that the differential tuition model would "decimate the liberated arts in Florida" (Delany, 2013).

4. In this situation, can the humanities computerize its way out of the crisis? In principle, computerizing its research could work for the following reasons:

    a. The computerization of research will foster the development of research in the humanities, not automate it. IT technology has many outstanding solutions and tools that can help scholars conduct and manage their research.

    b. The computerization of humanities research enables the interdisciplinary communication of many researchers worldwide, which can help in prioritizing research topics, implementing projects, and, most importantly, synthesizing and communicating research results in a way that is understandable to people outside the humanities.

5. The beneficial use computerized humanities research must, however, be met with a sense of duty on the part of humanists. They must be responsible for the collision-free development of social resonance, and, in particular, they must humanize not only themselves and their students, but above all non-humanities professionals. This latter group has, unfortunately, recently developed technologies that cease to support the development of culture and civilization and are, instead, detrimental to people and society.

DIGITAL HUMANITIES CONTENT CREATION STRATEGY

A famous saying by the Chinese philosopher Lao Tzu (6th century BCE) is that "a 1,000 mile journey starts with your first step". This can be translated to "your exploration of the humanities begins by writing/reading your first sentence." Accordingly, in this section, we will study the strategy of computerizing literature and writing.

The computerization of writing, including creative writing, supports authors, just as the computerization of the humanities supports humanities research. However, today's strategies for implementing computerization through computers, smartphones, and networks threatens the development of a civilization grounded in humanism. For example, *face-to-face* (F2F) communication is decreasing because email and short message services (SMS) are replacing physical meetings. Although e-communication increases the potential for human cognition, the computerization of the humanities leads to its development for the following reasons:

- Written language recorded in digital formats—particularly language sent via SMS—is subject to lexical abbreviations, random punctuations, custom spellings, and graphic symbols (such as emojis), particularly with respect to messages created by young people. These language transgressions, according to Crispin Thurlow (2006), are seen as the destruction of spelling for the English language.
- In the face of large amounts of e-information, people do not have time to read thoroughly; instead, they skim while they scroll through pages of texts. The following questions therefore arise (Targowski, 2010):
  - How should we write for those who do not read thoroughly?
  - How do we limit the amount of information we consume so as to avoid confusion?
  - What is the future of the book, regardless of its technological format?
  - What is the future of the news?
  - What is the future of professional publications?
  - Are we more likely to reason based on computerization or based on traditional intellectual tools?
  - How can journalism regain its essential role in inspiring social resonance?
  - Others.

The book is one of the most critical products of enlightened civilization and the humanities. The current trend of writing "e-books" involves creating texts that can be downloaded from online bookstores and then displayed on a screen one page at a time. JSTOR, a project developed by the Andrew W. Mellon Foundation, has made available online a wide range of scientific journals, which can be purchased at low prices by libraries, some of which could not afford the originals. The Public Library of New York provides so much information electronically to readers around the world that it reports ten million hits to its computer system every month, which can be contrasted with the 50,000 books published in the reading room at 42nd Street. It seems that everything is computerized, and each work is somehow hyperlinked to all the others. If the future brings newspapers without news, magazines without pages, and libraries without walls, what will happen to the traditional book? Will electronic publications destroy it?

Nowadays, in our "digital" era, there are computerized approaches for formatting texts, writing quickly, and publishing, which entails the degeneration of spelling and grammar and the simplification of online content. This is why employees of schools and colleges, publishing houses, and libraries—as well as in other cultural institutions—are worried about the future of literature. There was a time when, in the 19th and 20th centuries, many were able to learn about life from poetry, books, theatrical art, and literature. The outlay of money on books was high, and everyone involved in this work was able to sustain themselves. Now, however, the publishing of paper books is declining, although there are exceptions, such as bestsellers on *The New York Times*, which can only be accessed if they are released by famous publications. This can explain why in 2015 Canadian poet Rupi Kaur caused a stir among publishers by selling more than 2 million copies of her first paper-printed collection of *Milk* and *Honey* poetry, which lasted as many as 85 weeks on the Times bestseller list. How did this happen? The answer is that she has 3 million readers on Instagram and widely used social networks to spread her creativity among the generation of so-called *millennials*.

The recommended goals of computerization in regard to core areas in the humanities are proposed in Table 1.

Table 1. Recommended goals of computerization in core areas of the humanities

Core Humanities	Recommended Goal(s) of Computerization	Effects of Complete Digitization	Concerns
Composition	Help in writing content, particularly for books	Increases in content and readership	E-books enhance addiction and limits F2F communication
Theatrical art	Support script writing	Increases in content and viewership	E-art enhances the search for viewership among the young and vulgar.
Film	Support script writing	Increases in the number of unlikely scenes	E-films reduces attention and engagement.
Song and Dance	Support writing song and dance content	Increases in content and viewership	E-song and dance reduce attention and engagement.
Art (painting, sculpture, and architecture)	Support the development of a concept in a given art form	Increases digital artwork, which may be exciting but brief	This sometimes resembles the "admiration" of painting monkeys or elephants
Music	Support the development of a concept in a musical work	Increases content and viewership	E-music can reduce awareness of sounds in one's environment.
Media	Support the writing of speeches for the press, TV, and radio	Elimination of journalists via AI	E-media reduces social resonance.

When it comes to computerizing the creativity of the so-called "supporting humanities"—i.e., philosophy (which is also included in the core humanities), archaeology, history, sociology, political science, religious studies, cultural studies, civilization studies, journalism, and other disciplines—if a similar approach is applied, it should bring many positive opportunities for the development of these disciplines.

Since lengthy textual statements are typically used in these disciplines, the continuation of this traditional art of writing in the face of the increasing complexity of situations leads to muddled statements and reduced readability and understanding. Therefore, it is recommended that graphic and multimodal techniques are used, as illustrated by examples below. This is especially important since the younger generations of e-citizens do not prefer to simply read texts but instead favor graphic models of situations.

Philosophy

Philosophy is the oldest science, originating around the 8th century BCE and giving rise to the modern branches of science. Its historical developments are traced in many monographs, which, however, are more analytic than a synthetic. In any case, philosophy is not an additive science; rather, it is a collection of philosophical arguments put into conversation with one another. Philosophy teaches one how to think and value the situation. This can be seen, for example, in Władysław Tatarkiewicz's (2005) *The History of Philosophy*, which is an exciting, all-encompassing monument to the author's impressive erudition. However, the average reader could find themselves lost in this comprehensive and in-depth story. On the other hand, a graphic model of the history of philosophy (Figure 9) can help one to understand the contribution of philosophy to the quality of human thinking and decision-making over the past nearly 3,000 years.

Similarly, research on wisdom concerns complicated elements and their interdependence, which is challenging to describe adequately. The "computer" model of wisdom in Figure 10 facilitates the study and understanding of wisdom.

Cognitive science is concerned with understanding the inner mental life of humans. This has led to the development artificial intelligence, which unfortunately, could eventually lead to the replacement of humans by machines. Cognitive science is currently studying functions of the brain and mind in domains such as language learning, reading, and dialogue. It is also aiming to model mental processes such as thinking, reasoning, decision-making, emotion, problem-solving, and others. This science is inter-disciplinary and is based on contributions and influences from areas such as philosophy, linguistics, psychology, and anthropology. Thus, in a nutshell, it is the science of human cognition. One of its foremost aims has been to uncover how mental processes can carry out calculations, for it originated in the realm of computer science when Alan Turing (1912-1954) published an article entitled "Computing Machinery and Intelligence", which appeared in the Journal *Mind* in October 1950. Turing (1950) addressed the problem of artificial intelligence and proposed an experiment that became known as the "Turing test", which was an attempt to define a standard for when a machine could be called "intelligent." The idea was that it could be said that a computer "thinks" if an interrogator is not be able to distinguish it from a human in conversation. In the article, Turing suggested that instead of building a program to simulate an adult's mind, it would be better to create a simpler program that could simulate a child's mind, which could then be "educated" in other areas. The reverse form of the Turing test is widely used on the Internet under the name "CAPTCHA" (completely automated public Turing test to tell computers and humans apart), which is designed to determine whether the user of a particular site is a human or a computer.

Unfortunately, the cognitive abilities of a person are, on the one hand, more complicated and, on the other, simpler than mathematicians imagine. In the massive edited tome *the Foundations of Cognitive Science* (Posner, 1991), the terms "data" and "wisdom" do not appear in the index. Do mathematicians assume in advance that machines cannot possess wisdom?

Do such researchers not notice that the world is being flooded with data that is a "mirror" of the world, data which is leading to the development of a new kind of economy? According to a report by *The Economist*, this will require new markets, institutions, infrastructure, businesses, and even geopolitical arrangements ("The Data Economy", 2020). These are the promises and pitfalls of the new "data economy". Mirror worlds are not just mathematical representations of real situations: They also give new meaning to the saying that "knowledge is power". Increasingly, digital copies live lives of their own

Figure 9. An "Informatic" model of the development of philosophy (Targowski, 2011, p.139)

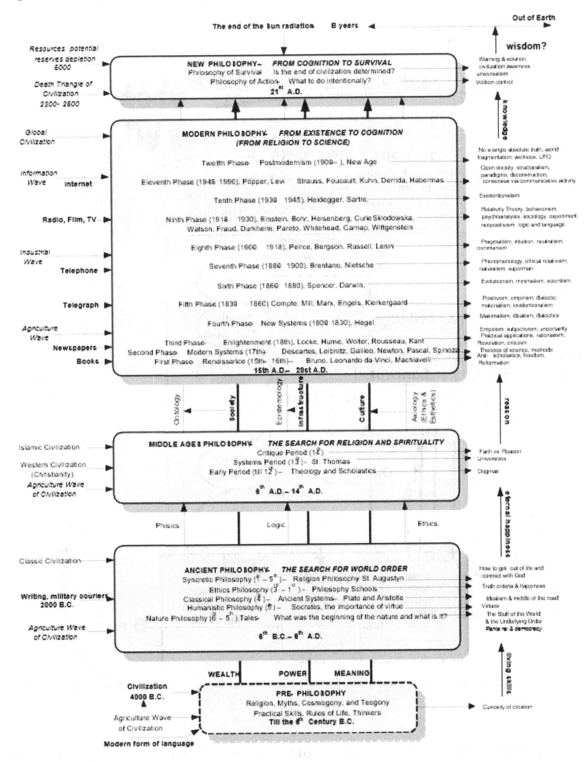

Figure 10. A computer model of wisdom (Krawczyk & Targowski, 2019, p. 264)

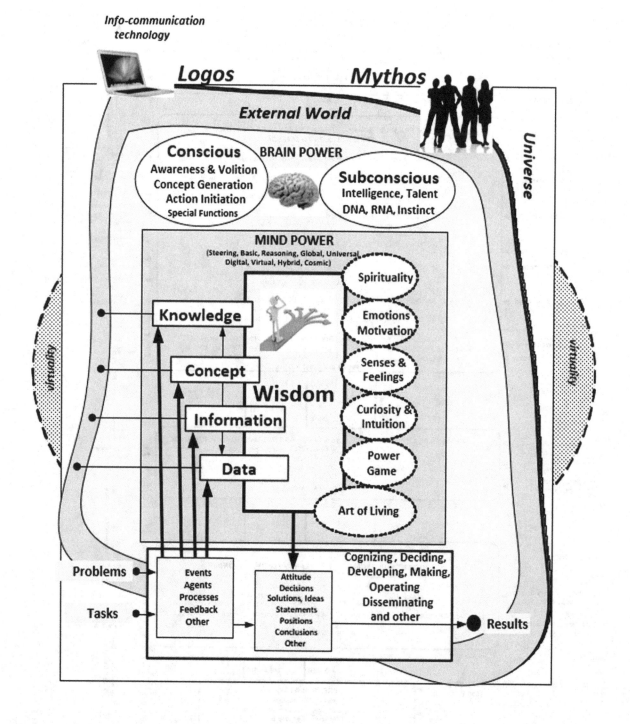

and operate in the physical world. They can be used to optimize everything from headset acoustics to the entire national rail and air networks. They enable all kinds of AI algorithms to recognize objects and faces, understand speech, and even distinguish between smells. They also allow for the creation of new business models. For example, why buy heavy equipment if its use can be accurately measured, which would allow for it to be rented for short, precise amounts of time?

An excellent way to begin to analyze this new kind of economy is to measure it. A robust methodology has not yet been developed; however, the data economy is already massive. *Statistics Canada*, a government agency, tried to estimate the value of the country's data in 2019, including the value of stored data, related software, and intellectual property among users. The result ranged from about $157 billion to about $218 billion. If this figure is a reasonable estimate—a big "if"—the value of all data in America, whose GDP is 12 times greater than Canada, could be in the range of 1.4-2.0 trillion USD, which would represent nearly 5% of U.S. private resources constituting physical capital. If the amount of data generated around the world is any indication, this new economy is increasing. The first human genome (which required about three gigabytes of data, almost filling a DVD) was sequenced 17 years ago. Now, *23andMe*, which offers genetic testing, has acquired the data of more than 10 million customers. The latest autonomous vehicles produce up to 30 terabytes of data for every eight hours of driving (or about 6,400 DVDs). The market research firm IDC estimates that the world will generate about 90 zettabytes of data (19 trillion DVDs) in 2019 and 2020—more than all the data produced since the addition of computers.

As noted by the report in *The Economist*, the infrastructure of the data economy is torn between two poles ("The Data Economy", 2020). Today, it consists mainly of massive data centers filled with servers on which data is stored and processed. However, such centralization has drawbacks, not the least of which is that it consumes enormous amounts of energy and poses a risk to privacy and data security. There is already a decentralizing movement in the opposite direction. More and more data is being processed via what is called *edge computing,* which involves moving data centers closer to where the data is collected and processed. Businesses are also facing a digital reversal. Many companies want to use data to load enterprise applications that use AI. They have built central repositories, such as *data lakes* (which probably are tributaries to "rivers", "seas", and "oceans" of data), which store all sorts of digital information about the world. Such systems, however, have limited applications if the company and its employees do not have the required skills, refuse to believe the data, and even share their opinions internally, undermining the data.

Geopolitics based on data will also not be simple. Internet giants such as Amazon, Apple, Microsoft, Facebook, and Google have assumed that the data economy will be a global issue and that digital things will flow where processing is most efficient and economical. However, governments are increasingly stressing their "digital sovereignty," demanding that data not leave their country of origin, that is, they are promoting a form of "virtual nationalism". Will this be met with resistance from computer science activists who encourage data freedom for all who want to use it? Unfortunately, there is a risk that the wealth the data economy is creating will be even more unevenly distributed than financial resources, and exclusions from data will enormously impact the have-nots, further exacerbating their already challenging living conditions. Will evil once again prevail? This is likely to happen, for liberal democracy allows a few smart and even wise billionaires to make massive amounts of wealth at the expense of the uninformed.

The data-driven economy involves profiling consumers, that is, users of FAAMG (Facebook, Amazon, Apple, Microsoft, Google) websites. Such websites collect data about sales and purchasing preferences for products and services so that they can offer users the best possible deals through personalized marketing. What should be prioritized is the use machine reasoning to learn about the outside world and the civilization in which we live. This would result in reducing chaos (entropy) thanks not only to data and knowledge, but also thanks to the remaining units of experience that are processed through computerization, illustrated in the model in Figure 11.

Figure 11. The role of computerization in exploring the world

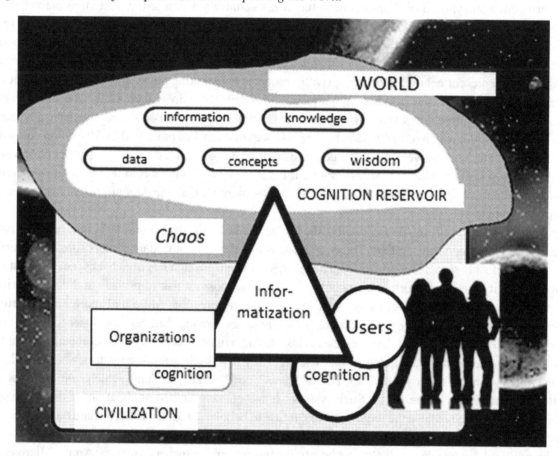

It is wrong to think that only data leads to knowledge about the world and that, the more data there is, the more our cognitive powers will grow. In fact, our disorientation is growing, which results from different types of data. Some disorientation occurs as a result of unexcepted discoveries, while some is due to mismanagement of situations, which spreads doubt. The macroecology of information is characterized in Figure 12, where three phases of the cognitive cycle are distinguished (Targowski, 1999, pp. 41-43):

- **Phase I Discovery of Knowledge**: In the first phase, the Cognition Reservoir (RC) minimizes chaos or tries to control it. Each new piece of information increases the complexity of cognition. The following relationship can be observed:

I < E

Where: I = information

E = entropy

D = darkness (net entropy E-I)

The purpose of the information (including the use of computerization) is to make $D_t \to 0$ and misinformation $I_M \to 0$.

- **Phase II Ultimate Cognition**: In this phase, there is enough information that it is possible to overcome chaos; that is, there is a balance between cognition and chaos. This situation is infrequent because it takes a very long time to achieve full cognition.
- **Phase III New chaos and knowledge**: This occurs when new cognition is confronted with chaos and misinformation. Unfortunately, this is the most common course for human life.

The full cycle of cognition consists of the Semantic Ladder, shown in Figure 13 with the example of painting. In this cycle, there are the following units of knowledge about the world, which are acquired because of manual processing as well as computerization (Targowski, 1990, p. 136):

- **Data**: Measurement of events
- **Information**: Notification of a change in a situation
- **Concept**: Solution options
- **Knowledge**: Scientific data, principles, rules, and laws
- **Wisdom**: Correct judgment and choice in the context of the art of life

Regarding analyses of cognition currently in "fashion," typically only two aspects are distinguished: Data and knowledge. This is reminiscent of the state of knowledge about the construction of the atom during the time of Niels Bohr, whose solar model distinguished only two molecules: Protons and electrons. After 100 years of research, several dozen particles and sub-particles are now included in the model of the atom. It will, therefore, also take us about 100 years before we increase our knowledge to include these other aspects of the Semantic Ladder, one of which is particularly important—wisdom. Will it be too late? With knowledge of the units of cognition, it is now possible to define human capital, as illustrated in Figure 14. The model distinguishes the following types of human capital:

- **Informed human capital**: This human capital helps us to understand data and information about changes in the environment. The more informed human capital there is, the more access there will be to Big Data and Big Information (about changes in environmental conditions).
- **Conceptual human capital**: This human capital helps us orient ourselves to the concepts of solutions. The more there is, the more we have access to Big Concepts.
- **Knowing human capital**: This human capital is based upon reasoning about sound knowledge. The more there is, the more access we have to Big Knowledge.
- **Wise human capital**: This human capital helps us correctly evaluate and select solution concept options.

As this model shows, the current trend towards the development of Big Data and Big Information will at most help people to be well-informed, especially those in charge of supply chain management. However, the key question is whether Big Data and Big Information will assure that people are good

Figure 12. Phases of the world cognition cycle

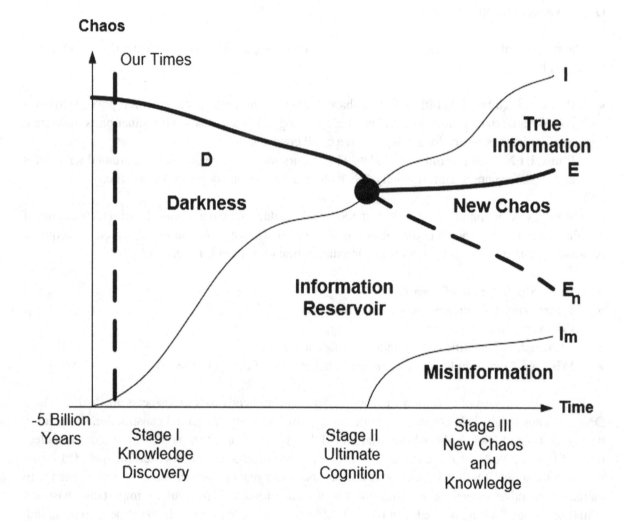

conceptualists. Another important question is whether people supported by Big Wisdom will become wise. The road to the utopia of making everyone wise is still exceptionally long and bumpy. One might wonder whether it is possible at all. In any case, this approach to achieving wise human capital is the first ever to be proposed. Some think that Big Data will solve all the problems of civilization. Perhaps someday it will help everyone know which day they will die, and even whether it will be in the morning, afternoon, or night. However, it is not known whether people will be satisfied with this information. It might also be predicted that a person will have sound knowledge (thanks to Big Knowledge) of what personality traits perfectly fit one's partner. However, without access to Great Wisdom, choosing the right personality will only be the result of intuition and good fortune, not of wisdom.

Figure 13. Semantic Ladder of units of cognition on the example of the art of painting

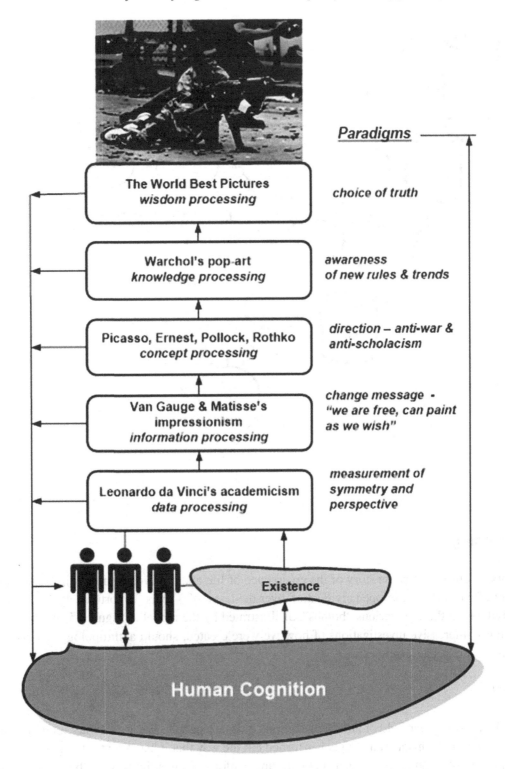

Figure 14. A model of human capital development

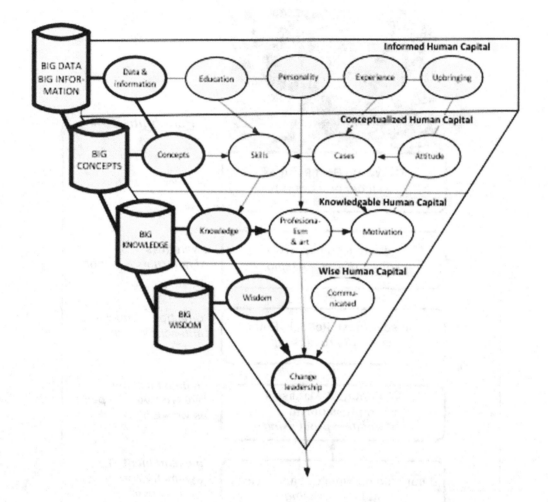

Anthropology

The story of our planet is the story of the emergence of life and the evolution of animals and humans, the latter of whom has developed civilization over the last 6,000 years. Unfortunately, humans can destroy civilization through various "bombs", as illustrated by the model in Figure 15. In addition to the increasingly impressive investigations of how we were created, should anthropology not also address the odds of our species going extinct?

History

This is the most popular field of knowledge among ordinary people. We are curious about how humans lived before us and why human society has turned out the way that it has. What is the impact of the past on our present life, and what awaits us in the future? Unfortunately, this story has been written in thousands of books and dissertations where specialization dominates. In other words, much of the study of

Figure 15. The life trajectory of humans on planet Earth and possible paths of annihilation (A-Bomb = Atomic Bomb; E-Bomb = Ecological; P-Bomb = Population Bomb; R-Bomb = Depletion Bomb Strategic Resources) what to do to prevent the operation of the Triangle of Death of Civilization as we know it.

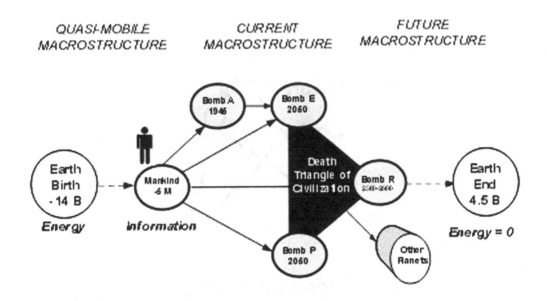

history examines only small snippets of our past. To have a view of the bigger picture is only possible when studying history in its broad strokes, which is accomplished through using extended timeframes and through using a multidisciplinary approach based on the interconnection of multiple scientific disciplines. This paradigm studies history from the Big Bang to the present day and looks for universal patterns or trends.

Similar to digital information processes in business management, in this study of history, one can focus on the critical flow of information to assure that human policy makers will benefit from it. This field of study also uses graphical modeling of information, which takes into account the sequential order and parallelism of operations and their dependencies (Targowski, 2003). This is unlike more traditional approaches, which, for the ordinary reader, looks like a sequence of episodes. This iterative approach to history also takes into account critical history and peripheral history, as illustrated in Figure 16. The model in Figure 17 presents the essential history of the 20th century.

The result of "computational thinking" (i.e., computer science) is the algorithmization of, say, history as follows:

In terms of macrostructures (*à la* Braudel), the following four levels can be distinguished:

1. Quasi-immovable structure (e.g., 1000-2000)
2. Intermediate structure (e.g., 1800-1900)
3. Current structure (e.g., 1900-2100)
4. Future structure (e.g., 2100+)

In terms of intermediate range-structures, the following two levels can be distinguished:

Figure 16. A model of critical and peripheral history

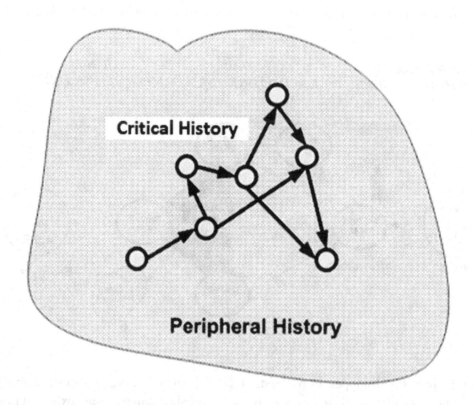

1.   **Epochs** (e.g., modernism, 1780-1990+),

  a.   **Periods** (e.g., barbarism 1914-1945).

Finally, in terms of microstructures, the following two levels can be distinguished:

1.   **Phases** (e.g., the Bolshevik Revolution, 1917-1991),

  a.   **Stages** (e.g., the Khrushchev Thaw, 1956–1964),

The term **interphase** is used to refer to interactions between phases (e.g., the Cold War, 1945-1991).

This approach enables one to demarcate and understand long-term stretches of history across different epochs in which the same values guide the dynamics of history. It also allows one to appreciate the fact that, during a certain period, the dynamics of history are subordinated to specific political goals. At the phase level, it allows one to understand a time segment in which a certain political paradigm rules the dynamics of history. Finally, at the stage level, the approach allows one to appreciate how key political players influence history.

In this classification scheme, the hierarchy of historical structures has five levels. Interactions may occur between groups in the form of epochs, inter-periods, interphases, or inter-stages. Indeed, it is pos-

Figure 17. A model of the critical history of 20th century Europe

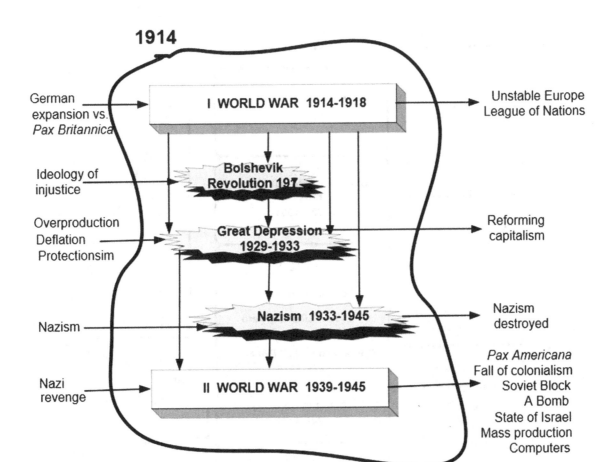

sible to "algorithmize" a critical history of Poland, as is given in the Samsonowicz-Targowski model in Figure 18 (Targowski, 2016). This model shows that Poland already had its Golden Age. Furthermore, the election of kings and the *liberum veto* led to the collapse of Poland and posed considerable difficulties for its rebirth. Hence, Poland's charismatic leaders see their success in authoritarian rule, where so-called "logical" decisions do not approval by a continuous parliamentary process.

The example of the United States further illustrates how a critical understanding of history can be achieved through the algorithmization approach. Tables 2, 3, and 4 demonstrate a framework for recognizing microstructures of American history. This framework is limited to critical structures only: It is by no means a complete table of all the structures of American history.

The above algorithmic critical history of the US allows for quick associations concerning the dynamics of history. Without commenting on the entire history of this nation and limiting the scope to only the 21st century, it can be concluded that the downward spiral of American capitalism could very well lead to protectionism and the collapse of global capitalism, reversing the process of "flattening" the world. For the first time in American history, the impact of international trade has harmed both the American

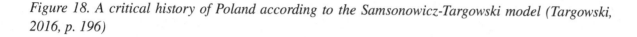

Figure 18. A critical history of Poland according to the Samsonowicz-Targowski model (Targowski, 2016, p. 196)

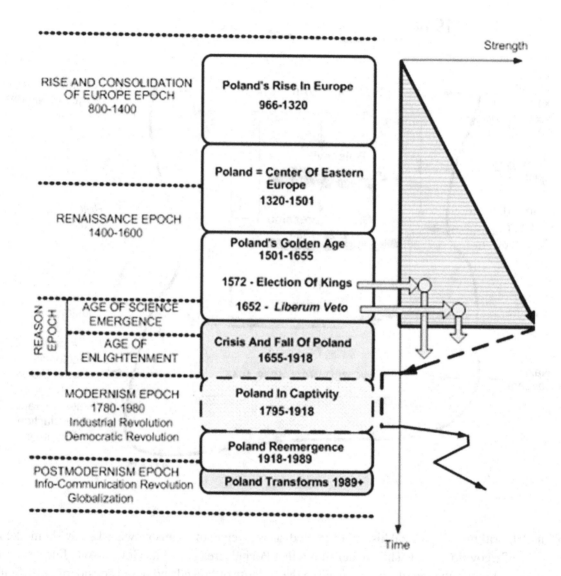

economy and the world economy in terms of workforce stability. It is reminiscent the "robber baron" period of the second half of the 19th century, when the free enterprise of the 1910s was replaced by a form of regulated capitalism (i.e., progressivism). Recently, the question has arisen of whether the US will be able to fix and return to a form of regulated capitalism (one with a human face). How much damage will be done to the national industry and workforce before business executives look for long-term optimal solutions for their citizens?

What about progressive ideas as a product of Yankee ingenuity? The specific answer offered by Christopher Hill (2007) is that Americans now live in a post-scientific society that does not need many scientists and engineers because conducting basic research abroad is "cheaper," especially since young Americans are showing a declining interest in mathematics, science, and engineering. Instead, Hill

Table 2. A critical algorithmic history of the United States from 1776 to 1900

Epoch (values)	Period (political objectives)	Phase (political paradigm)	Interphase (interaction)	Stage (political "shades")
Globalization Wave II **Forming Member States 1788-1900**	Testing the Union 1788-1865	Young Republic 1789-1861	Agricultural Wave 1607-present A wave of innovation 1830s "Yankee's Ingenuity" ------------------------ Continental Expansion 1835-1910 ------------------------ Industrialization 1840s ------------------------ Civil War 1861-1865 Preparing for Spanish-American War 1895	First President George Washington 1789-97
				Federalists 1789-1801
				Jeffersonists 1801-1829 Louisiana Purchase 1803 Lewis & Clark 1804-1806 War of 1812 1812-1815
				Jacksonian Democracy 1829-1848 Mexican-American War 1846-1848 Westward Expansion 1830s-1870s
				Slavery & southern states 1848-1861
				"Robber Barons" 1840s-1900s
				Monopolistic Capitalism 1860s
				First Gilded Age 1865-1900s

argues, Americans should focus on innovative organizational, social, artistic, and business processes, taking examples from innovators such as Google, eBay, and Amazon. Does this look like the future of progressive American ideals? It amounts to a retreat from complex thinking in exchange for offshore researchers and the idea of a "Fun Society".

Sociology

Sociology is a science that explains all kinds of puzzles, problems and issues of social life. The systems and processes it examines are complex and complicated and have endless lists of elements and dependencies. Can such processes be adequately described in the traditional language of Max Weber? The IT model of Polish society in Figure 19 (which is similar for other societies as well) is an unprecedented attempt to analyze and synthesize the dynamics of popular culture in Polish society.

Table 3. A critical history of the United States from 1901 to 1991

Epoch (values)	Period (political objectives)	Phase (political paradigm)	Interphase (interaction)	Stage (political "shades")
Globalization Wave III **Development as a superpower 1898-**	Acquisition of Strategic Resources 1898-1945	Imperial dreams 1898-1914 Spanish-American War and Philippine-American War 1898 Panama Canal 1903 Intervention in Nicaragua 1912-1925 Intervention in Mexico-1914,	World War I 1914-1918 On an equal footing with the United Kingdom, Germany, and France ------------------------ WWII 1941-1945 (Enters the war in 1941) Control of Europe & Japan ------------------------ Cold War 1945-1991 Information Wave 1980s ------------------------ The Fall of Communism 1991	Regulated capitalism taxes on income & Federal Reserve Board Central Bank 1910s-
				Ford and assembly lines 1907- Labor movements "All over the sea."
		Economic Instability 1914-1941		Jazz age 1919-1929
				Great Depression 1929-1933
				New Deal 1933-1941
				War effort 1941-1945
	World Power 1946-1991	Prosperity 1945-1960		Korean War 1950-1953
				Vietnam War 1959-1975
		"A long strange trip" 1960-1969		Civil rights The 1960s
		Energy crisis 1970-1980		The oil crisis Liberal capitalism 1970s
		"Masters of the universe" 1980-1988 (Reagan Era)		Second Gilded Age 1981-2000s

Political Science

This is an area of knowledge that has been developing intensively since the Cold War (1945-1991). One of its foremost aims has been to prevent nuclear war. In addition, since the collapse of the USSR in 1991, it has been concerned with how to organize a *new world order*. What is China's current role in all of this? The model of China's strategy in the 21st century in Figure 20 explains this better than would numerous of pages of text.

Table 4. A critical history of the United States from 1991 to 2020

Epoch (values)	Period (political objectives)	Phase (political paradigm)	Interphase (interaction)	Stage (political "shades")
Globalization Wave IV **Developing superpower 1901-** "The world is flat"	The only superpower in the world 1991 "Make America great again." Draining of the "political swamp" Donald Trump 2017-2020	A new world order 1989-2001	Information Wave 1980s	Iran-Iraq War 1990-1991
		The global economy 1990s-	War of Civilizations 9/11, 2001 Internet 1983- 1995+ Big Tech – FAAMG 2010+ Virtualization and AI Waves	
		Populism 2016+		War in Afghanistan 2001-
				Iraq War 2003-
				Managerial capitalism 1980s
				Offshore outsourcing 1980s Turbo-capitalism 2000+ Surveillance capitalism 2015

Civilization Studies

This interdisciplinary study aims at integrating knowledge from the main fields of humanities as well as engineering, medicine, and others. Civilization studies explores human development in terms of society, culture, religion, and infrastructure across large expanses of space and time. Civilization is an endless collection of different elements with various interrelations. For example, Durant and Durant's (1993) *The Story of Civilization* is 11 volumes and over 9,000 pages. It is difficult to imagine a specialist researcher reading all 11 volumes, let alone the average person. However, graphical modeling via information technology can help us achieve such a feat and understand the development of civilization. Ultimately, this will allow us to identify criteria of a civilized humanity, i.e., specific principles that should be adopted so as to harmonize human behavior with society.

Figure 21 provides an IT model of civilization in the 21st century. The model shows how civilization systems are related and the main processes behind the integration and development of our world.

Global warming is an existential threat to civilization; accordingly, political attention is being focused on this challenge. At the same time, however, the informatic model of civilizational crises below (Figure 22) identifies not one but 16 crises. This model makes it clear that modern civilization is going through a deep crisis, similar to the crisis after the fall of the Roman Empire in the 5th century A.D., which gave rise to the so-called Dark Ages, lasting about 1,000 years until the Italian Renaissance. This helps to explain the state of mind of the societies of Western civilization in the 21st century, which are struggling with information chaos, populist politics, and various negative forms of capitalism (e.g., turbo-capitalism, information capitalism, and surveillance capitalism).

Figure 19. An information technology model of culture (Targowski – Przybyszewski Model) (Targowski, 2019, p. 227)

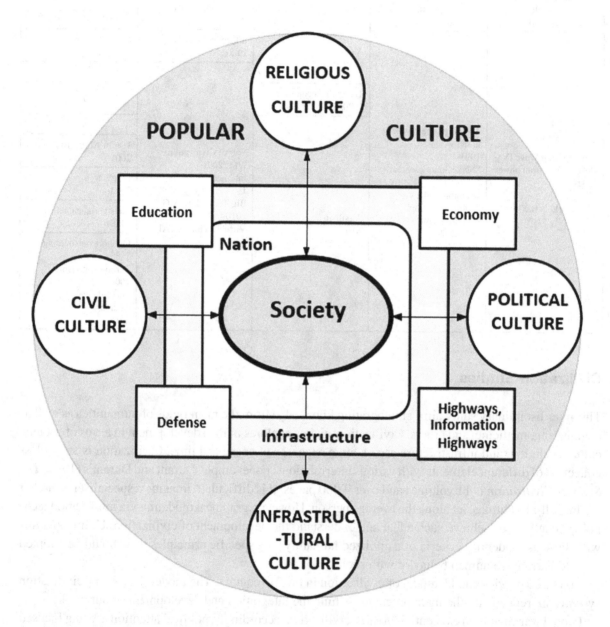

Cultural Studies

This area of study explores the development of values (religious and other types), symbols, and patterns of human behavior in social contexts. Around 100 influential cultures are simultaneously developing in the world in the 21st century. On one hand, cultures are becoming integrated into so-called "multiculturalism"; however, on the other hand, there have been reactions against the emphasis on cultural diversity. These are very complex social processes that not only take place at the state level but also at the level

Figure 20. China's digital strategy in the 21st century—the numbers set political priorities (Targowski, 2015, p. 207)

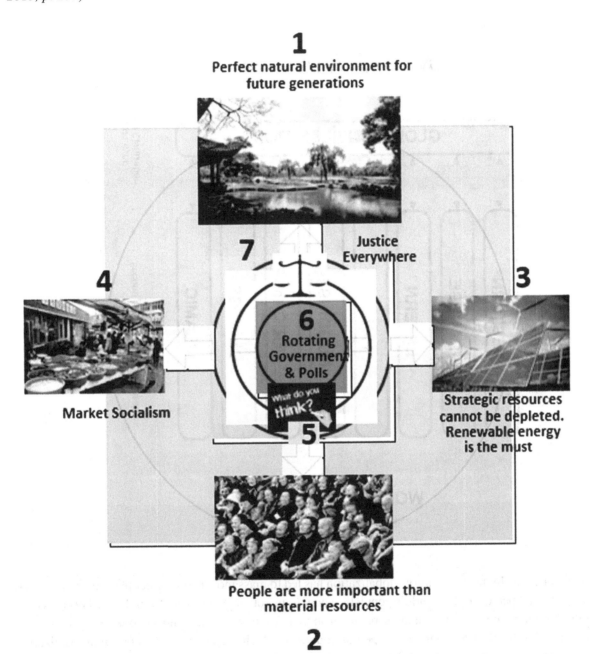

of individuals and families. For example, married people from two cultures might live in a third culture. In such cases, these individuals require exceptional tolerance to be happy.

An informatic model of culture is depicted in Figure 23, and a model of hybrid culture is shown in Figure 24. These models recognize new types of culture that need to be developed if we are to achieve

Figure 21. An IT model of civilization in the 21st century (Targowski, 2019, p. 219)

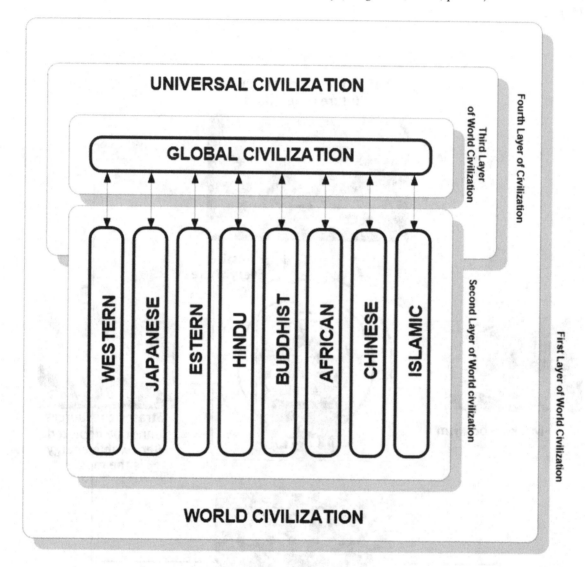

social harmony. In the 21st century, globalization has led to mass movements of people across the planet, with at least 3 percent of the world's population now living outside their country of birth. This mass migration is due to economic inequalities: people from developing countries who are looking for income for their families are attracted to more prosperous countries, which search for cheap labor. Industrialization also creates a shift from rural to urban environments, often causing mass poverty in areas surrounding the new megacities of the developing world.

This migratory trend to Western civilization, also known as the 4th wave of globalization, evokes opposing views on multiculturalism (Targowski, 2014):

- Some parties in Europe are very unhappy with multiculturalist practices, particularly in France (as evidenced by the protests in which cars are burned), the Netherlands (as evidenced by the killings

Figure 22. An informatic model of civilizational crises in the 20th century (Targowski, 2019, p. 220)

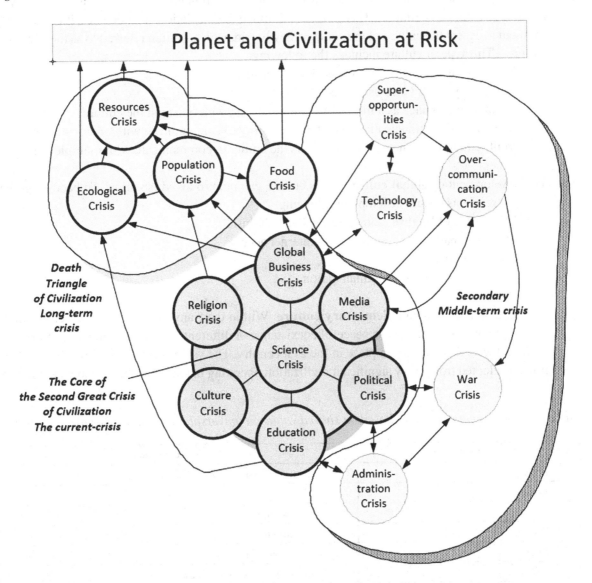

that have criticized social segmentation), the United Kingdom (as evidenced by the presence of terrorist cells), and Germany (as evidenced by the ethnic ghettos).

- The US accepts multiculturalism as a politically correct social solution, but its elites are opposed to it because it disintegrates the nation.
- If globalization and immigration are not stopped soon, a new solution must be found that can address the problems of assimilation, isolation, and national homogeneity.

The following are possible solutions to these problems:

- The development of an **intermediate culture**: The full assimilation of immigrants, especially in the first generation, is difficult. Therefore, to minimize their isolationist tendencies, it is necessary for them to accept the culture of the country they live in, which is often referred to as the "national culture". This type of culture includes the following:
  - National values (typically expressed in a Constitution),
  - National symbols (such as the national flag),
  - An official language as a means of communicating with others in the culture,
  - Intercultural communication, which is the ability to communicate with other cultures,
  - Multi-cultural communication, which is the ability to communicate with multiple cultures,
  - Others
- The development of **global culture**: This culture can help to avoid isolation. To become global citizens, residents should develop the following:
  - Knowledge of English (sometimes called "Globish"),
  - Skills in email and e-commerce via internet access,
  - A desire to travel abroad,
  - Skills in cross-culture communication,
  - Others
- The development of a **complementary culture**: Within the framework of universal civilization, this culture would allow for the peaceful coexistence of different civilizations in place of the conflicts and wars that have taken place in the 21st century. The values that would drive this civilization are adopted from every significant civilization operating in the 21st century, shown in Table 5.

Table 5. Complementary culture based on shared values in universal civilization (Targowski, 2005)

Civilization	Value Contribution
African	Spiritual communication with ancestors
Buddhist	Morality
Eastern	Self-sacrifice
Indian	Moderation
Islamic	Reward and punishment
Japanese	Cooperation and worship of nature
Chinese	Respect for elders
Western	Freedom and the worship of technology
Global	The free flow of ideas, goods, services, and people
Universal	Wisdom, kindness, access, dialogue, consent, forgiveness, human and civil rights, international law, sustainable development

- The development of **digital culture**: This is a culture in which humans are connected anytime, anywhere; where they are waiting for feedback and act in rhythm with one another; where they are fast, productive, techno-centric, informed, and seek optimization; where they are able to reason with global and local perspectives; and where they appreciate the richness of information.

However, it is also one in which they struggle with a limited attention span and dependence on smartphones and the Internet (Targowski, 2009).

Figure 23. An informatic model of culture in the multi-civilizational world of the 21st century (Targowski, 2014, p. 156)

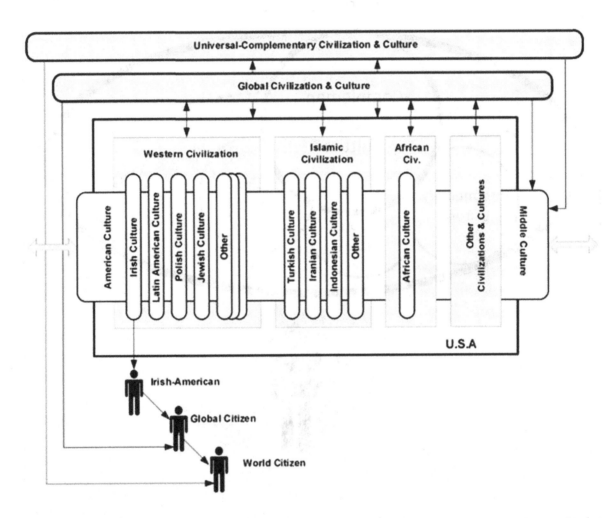

Figure 24 presents a model of **hybrid culture**, which includes all other cultural categories, such as national, intermediate, global, complementary, and IT (including digital) culture. Hybrid culture is a culture of people who want to move skillfully in an open and global world. For example, during their life in the Polish People's Republic behind the Iron Curtain, Poles only lived in a national culture. It was only in the Third Republic (after 1989) that they rapidly developed an intermediate and global culture as well as an IT culture. Complementary culture, on the other hand, awaits the world's official acceptance and recommendations for how it can be taught and applied. When will this happen? It depends on whether the humanists want to create it and whether they will be involved in its development. A possible path forward is suggested in a book about hybrid culture in Poland, which analyzes new opportunities for Poles in the 21ˢᵗ century (Olas & Targowski, 2018).

Figure 24. A model of hybrid culture (Targowski, 2014, p. 157)

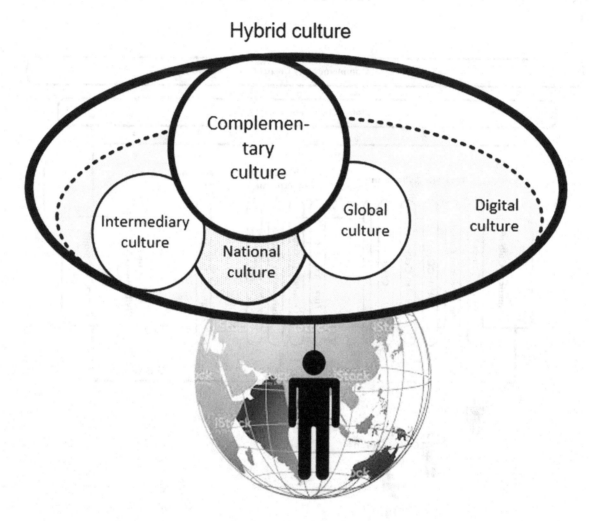

DIGITAL HUMANITIES PUBLICATION STRATEGY

The current publishing strategy has moved away from paper-printed materials in favor of digital printing, which is cheap. For scientific and professional writing, e-publishing is unstoppable. For books, however, this strategy is detrimental to the broader culture, for a book on the shelf is a knowledge resource, to which one often returns. Furthermore, physical copies of books help libraries develop, which cultivate the pleasure of reading from generation to generation. As some put it, "show me the books in your house, and I'll tell you who you are." Finally, unlike hard copies, e-books are not usually lent out and returned, for they get lost in the "sea" of e-information. This further limits the social bonds that are created between people.

It is doubtful whether publishers themselves can resist the temptation of the low costs of e-publishing. Regarding physical copies of scientific books, their prices are so high that scientists are unable to buy them for their home libraries. It is only a matter of time before they disappear. Then the university libraries will become museums of books printed on paper. Sooner rather than later, students, professors, and researchers will have e-access to Google's e-library with 128 million scanned books and to the U.S. Library of Congress with more than 100 million paper-based publications. However, what use will be made of such scientific explorations if everyone works and lives in an e-home (if jobs are still available before robots completely "eliminate" them), shops in e-shops, and gets advice from e-doctors. In other words, no one will ever need to leave the house where they were born and where they will eventually die. What dull and sad lives are promised to us thanks to computer science, robotics, and automation?

Popular books published by famous publishing houses are and will continue to be printed on paper as long as bookstores persist. Booksellers' associations, bureaus of culture, and the United Nations Educational, Scientific, and Cultural Organization (UNESCO) should develop strategies and legal solutions for sustainable publishing practices in regard to traditional and digital books. Politicians, for their part, should vote for such legislation.

Furthermore, it will be challenging to develop an acceptable strategy for regulating published content on social networks and blogs, for in this largely vulgar culture of ours, such posts tend to lead to chaos and social ferment, which can be characterized as the disagreement with anyone about anything. After all, Olga Tokarczuk stated in her Nobel speech in Stockholm on December 10th, 2019 that "the Internet is increasingly a story told by an idiot." Any attempt at regulation in this area is met with the criticism that it is an attack on people's freedom. It is forgotten that the development of civilization consists in establishing regulations that help in the attainment of the general good. It is necessary for humanists to show initiative in this regard, for we cannot expect IT professionals to stop marveling at their technological capabilities nor can we expect them to change their intention to make us happy with faster information technology and automation, which will eliminate work so that we can indulge in entertainment, travel, and food. But to what end?

Digital humanities distribution strategy

Strategies in regard to the distribution of content in the core humanities are given in Table 6. The distribution of content is currently subject to fierce competition in the free market.

DIGITAL ART PRESENTATION STRATEGY

Digital art passed the test during the 2020 pandemic. For example, Hong Kong's great contemporary art fair in March 2020 was canceled due to COVID-19. Still, anyone who planned to visit could take advantage of a practical alternative: an observation room. With a single click of the keyboard, users could enter a panoramic but private visual lounge without having to use Hong Kong's convention and exhibition center. Participating galleries were told that for a quarter of the original fee, they could participate in an online fair ("The Online of Beauty", 2020). More than 90% of the lineup—231 galleries—took advantage of the offer and digitally presented more than 2,000 works totaling $270 million. The viewing

Table 6. Development trends in the distribution of achievements in the core humanities

Core Humanities	Distribution Trend	Advantages	Disadvantages
Composition	E-books via tele-computer networks	Easy access	The disappearance of book culture
Theatrical art	Various forms; traditional and digital	Easy access and good discussion between contractors	Reduced face-to-face contacts
Film	TV channels, Netflix, Amazon, Sling, Hulu, YouTube, Amazon Prime Video, and others	Expands the comfort of the audience in homes; eliminates Hollywood's monopoly	The disappearance of cinema culture
Song and Dance	Various forms; traditional and digital	Easy access	Not applicable
Art (painting, sculpture, and architecture)	Traditional distribution	E-auctions	Not applicable
Music	Wi-Fi channels	Expands locations where music can be listened to (e.g., in the car)	The tendency to listen to limited range of music
Media	Hundreds if not thousands of specialized channels and programs	Nuanced conversions about software and distribution modes	The disappearance of objective news and opinions; information chaos

room indicated how art can be shown (and sold) in the future, whether in times affected by a pandemic or whether travel is limited.

However, not every artist, gallery, and art form has equal advantage at these alternative fairs. Not surprisingly, the best were two-dimensional works in bright colors. Sculpture and conceptual art were not included. Subtle elements, such as Lucas Arruda's impressionistic desert landscapes—which, when seen in real life, seem to include both an aspect of mood or state of mind as well as physical representations—had little effect when viewed remotely. In addition to depth and texture, there are aspects that jump out at the viewer while in the gallery, which a web page cannot easily duplicate. One such aspect is the feeling of chance, that is, an experience of wandering between works of art and encountering the unexpected. Another is sociability. Art is a communion between the artist and the viewer, but galleries and fairs are also places to exchange views and share enthusiasm. Virtual fairs cannot yet provide this.

Undoubtedly, there are ways to compensate for these inevitable shortcomings of virtual art. When exhibitions close their physical doors, some of the world's best galleries and museums offer innovative interactive visits with 360-degree films and walkthroughs for their collections, all without queues and high-ticket prices. One such outstanding virtual site is the Rijksmuseum in Amsterdam. Its virtual tour allows visitors to see the works of Vermeer and Rembrandt—including the magnificent "Night Watch"—at a distance much closer than would usually be possible.[6] Another standout offering is the Museum of Art in São Paulo, which has an even more comprehensive collection. On the virtual platform, the paintings, created over the past 700 years, seem to hang in open space, seemingly suspended on glass panels or "crystal easels" (as the museum calls them), ideal for close-up inspection. However, such capabilities in digital presentation go beyond what is possible for most galleries and artists.

Figure 25. The model of Computing and Informing Thinking (MCIT) in Teaching

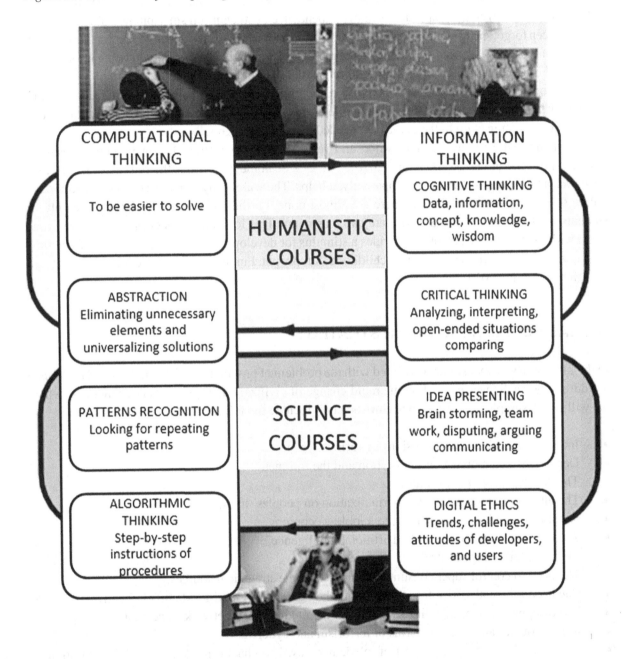

DIGITAL HUMANITIES TEACHING STRATEGY

The current strategy of learning computer science is based on so-called "computational thinking", and the most common uses of the computer are for lectures, exercises, and homework. In fact, in some schools and colleges, the use of paper has been eliminated, and all information and communication is transmitted digitally. The results of such practices include an overloading of tasks, the almost complete elimination of face-to-face (F2F) contact, and an unhealthy dependence of students on smartphones and computers.

It has been forgotten that we are dealing with the Information Wave, in which information is processed. The lives of most people are now centered on processing, manipulating, and communicating information. The model of Computing and Informing Thinking (MCIT) is shown in Figure 25.

A wisdom-based teaching strategy is to use computational and informative reasoning as well as IT equipment to support teaching rather than completely abandon manual writing in favor of digital editors and online communication in the name of so-called "technical progress".

In Finland, pupils do not do homework, and yet, 93% of Finnish students leave secondary school, compared to 75% in the US. (Couglan 2016). The lack of homework is not the only reason why they have such a high graduation rate, but apparently, it helps. There are many standardized tests in American public schools, whereas in Finland, there are almost none. Furthermore, in Finland, there are only 12 students per teacher; in the U.S., there are twice as many. This low rate gives each student more time alone with the teacher, which often provides a stimulus for development. Also, students have more time to play games and sports and enjoy their childhood. Simply put, Finnish children have time to be nurtured and grow (Couglan 2016).

DIGITAL SOCIAL RESONANCE STRATEGY

In the 21st century, humanists are presented with the problem of providing a platform for social resonance to address the challenges created by the rapid change of civilization. These current challenges (which we will call "examples of the resonance of society") include the following:

- Income inequalities and exclusions of various types,
- Dependence on mobile communication and the Internet,
- The development of hate culture,
- The effects of globalization and virtualization on peoples' lives,
- Automation and robotics, leading to a jobless economy,
- The development of uncontrolled artificial intelligence,
- The need for climate control,
- The need to control super consumerism and consume strategic resources,
- The need for equal justice for all, including the fight against hard-to-identify cybercrimes,
- The disappearance of morality and ethics in the media, social networks, and professions,
- Matters of war and peace in forms of terrorism and cyberwars,
- The rise of sentiment in support of teledemocracy, i.e., chaotic populism and the restriction of representative democracy,
- The rise of overt and covert corruption and the difficulty of combating it,
- The need for wisdom and happiness,
- Freedom and tolerance issues, the deterioration of which worries many people,
- Others

Humanists face the massive task of providing sound arguments and making sound decisions to assure social balance, which is disturbed by the uncontrolled development of IT engineering, robotization, and automation. Does computerization help humanists meet their goals? The answer to this question may lie in assessing the impact of computerization on one example taken from the humanities: Journalism in the United States in the 21st century.

Press releases decreased by 45 percent between 2008 and 2017, and by 60 percent between 1990 and 2016. (NBER WORKING PAPER SERIES REINVENTING BOSTON: 1640-2003) Despite this, newspapers, still have almost three times as many editorial staff as online news outlets. Paid newspaper circulation fell from 62.5 million in 1968 to 34.7 million in 2016, while the country's population grew by 50 percent. Between 2007 and 2016, newspaper ad revenue, which was the primary source of income for newspapers, fell from $45.4 billion to $18.3 billion. By 2016, Google generated about four times the advertising revenue of the entire U.S. press industry. Nearly 1,800 newspapers, mostly local weekly newspapers, have been closed since 2004. (NBER WORKING PAPER SERIES REINVENTING BOSTON: 1640-2003). This collapse is particularly significant because newspapers have traditionally been where most American journalists worked and where the most original reports were made.

These overall figures do not include specific stories of press organizations. The titans used to be *The Washington Post*, *Los Angeles Times*, *CBS News*, and *Time Magazine*, which seemed forty years ago like the Rock of Gibraltar. Now all four have different owners. The Washington Post sold the paper to Jeff Bezos (owner of Amazon) in 2014 at a bargain price of $250 million, after years of cuts and after selling its sister publication, *Newsweek,* to Sidney Harman in 2010 for a dollar. Newsweek's outlay—previously more than four million dollars—now stands at $100,000. By contrast, *The Baltimore Sun* reduced the number of its editors from over 400 in the late 1990s to 80 today. *The Boston Globe* has reduced the number of full-time journalists from more than 500 to less than 285. The editorial board of *The Atlanta Journal-Constitution* dropped from more than 530 to less than 150. Once major newspapers such as *Rocky Mountain News* and *The Tampa Tribune* no longer exist (Lemann, 2020).

No one imagined that a perfect search engine like Google could attract an audience much greater than any news site without creating any original content nor that the social network Facebook, whose content is mostly produced by the users themselves, could replicate the same feat. In response, the editors of well-renowned newspapers like *The Guardian* began to focus on theories about the function of newspapers. Currently, traditional newspapers deliver their content to readers via websites. Although the Internet is a democratic and informal medium, bloggers had to be hired in addition to regular reporters. This also, however, was not enough, and now armies of unpaid collaborators must continuously deliver vast amounts of new material because e-newspapers need to promote their websites. This requires newspapers send every story or message to cyberspace so that it can be found on social networks.

The following explosion of voluntary content has enabled Google and Facebook to build a much larger audience than traditional media companies thought possible. Google and Facebook provide free access to any information users want, not distinguishing between accurate and inaccurate information nor between opinions and arguments that attempt to expose users to a diversity of views instead of reinforcing what they already believed. It would be easy for these two giants to set up news departments, but why bother? Google and Facebook are protected from legal liability for the information they distribute unless they have created it themselves. They always claim that they are just enabling information to be shared, not creating content. Most of the current controversies involving Google and Facebook, especially Facebook, are almost inevitable consequences of their business strategy: They strive primarily for scale, indiscriminately allowing all possible content per page, while collecting user data (i.e., profiling) without interruption so that it can be sold to advertisers and information brokers, including political and intelligence brokers (both friendly and hostile).

According to Nicholas Lemann (2020), what happened in journalism in the 21st century is a version, perhaps extreme, of what has happened in many other areas. The blind belief that market forces and new technologies will always create a better society has led to greater inequality, the mindless dismantling of existing reasonable solutions that have had real value, and an increased gap in influence, prosperity, and happiness between dominant cities and provinces. Journalism is a case in which a whole new set of solutions and a new way of thinking must be applied to solve the current crisis. Unfortunately, thanks to the collapse of journalism, society's ability to actively resonate with the humanities is failing.

According to a published *Freedom House* report (Kelly et al., 2017), the governments of 30 countries—not only Russia but also regimes in Turkey, Venezuela, and the Philippines—"are mass producing their own content to distort the digital landscape in their favor." For instance, in Sudan, "the government maintains a virtual cyber army that has infiltrated Facebook, WhatsApp, and other services to spread the message of its leaders" (Romm, 2017). In Venezuela, government forces "regularly used manipulated footage to disseminate lies about opposition protesters on social media, creating confusion and undermining the credibility of the opposition movement ahead of elections" (Kelly et al., 2017).

The report stated that these attempts to manipulate information on the Internet—by governments or other forces—could have influenced elections in 18 countries, "damaging citizens' ability to choose their leaders based on factual news and authentic debate" (Kelly et al., 2017). This was the case for the US in 2016, when Russian-sponsored trolls fueled conflicts around controversial debates, such as immigration, gun control, and gay rights.[7]

The use of paid commentators and political bots to spread government propaganda was started by China and Russia, but it has now become a global phenomenon. The impact of these rapidly spreading techniques on democracy and civic activism is potentially disastrous.

Before the election in 2016, Kremlin-linked trolls bought ads. They created profiles on Facebook, Google, and Twitter in an attempt to cause chaos, excite protesters, and distance the media from then-candidate Donald Trump. These efforts are now under scrutiny in Congress, for lawmakers want to stop Russia or other foreign powers from interfering in future U.S. elections. The Freedom House report states that "while the online environment in the United States remained vibrant and diverse, the prevalence of disinformation and hyperpartisan content had a significant impact" (Kelly et al., 2017).

The Freedom House report estimates that at least 14 countries are trying to stop malicious bots and other malicious activities on the web by introducing laws that "actually restrict Internet freedom" (Kelly et al., 2017). This also applies to Germany, which, in June 2017, introduced a new law that requires Facebook, Google, and Twitter to remove content labeled offensive, despite being devoid of judicial oversight. The authors of the report offer the following recommendations for how to respond to this crisis:

Successfully countering content manipulation and restoring trust in social media—without undermining internet and media freedom—will take time, resources, and creativity. The first steps in this effort should include public education aimed at teaching citizens how to detect fake or misleading news and commentary (Kelly et al., 2017).

However, do the authors expect too much from Internet users?

A more recent Freedom House report—"Freedom on the Net 2019"—focused its efforts on 65 countries, examining their approaches to regulating online content and discussions (Shahbaz & Funk, 2019). Each country's internet freedom was assessed in the report. A photo from the report can be seen below in Figure 26.

Figure 26. A Student protests against e-surveillance (Photo: Shahbaz & Funk, 2019)

The following countries enjoy the greatest amount of freedom on the Internet: Iceland - 95 points (out of 100 possible); Estonia – 94; Germany – 80; Australia, the United Kingdom, and the US – 77; Hungary 72 (Shahbaz & Funk, 2019). Poland was not classified, as it probably did not participate in the study.

According to this report, more than 3.8 billion people currently have internet access. Furthermore, the report estimates that 71% reside in countries where individuals have been arrested or imprisoned for publishing content on political, social, or religious topics; 65% reside in countries where individuals have been attacked or killed for their online activities since June 2018; 59% reside in countries where officials have manipulated online discussions with the help of government e-commentators; 56% reside in countries where political, social, or religious information on the Internet has been blocked; and 46% reside in countries where officials have disconnected internet or mobile networks, commonly for political ends (Shahbaz & Funk, 2019).

As a result of surveillance capitalism—which just is the Orwellian *Big Brother*[8] put into practice—citizens are becoming fooled and mentally enslaved. Is the solution to not use smartphones and computers? Or do we need to close the market economy, which is likely to happen in a post-scarcity economy resulting from automation and promoted by non-FAAMG companies. Perhaps we are facing an economic war between big tech businesses and other technology companies.

Because politicians are not attempting to curtail and regulate surveillance capitalism, the only counter-weapon is WikiLeaks, an international nonprofit that publishes leaked information from administrations and corporations and classified media provided by anonymous sources. The website was launched in 2006 in Iceland by *Sunshine Press*, which maintains that in the first ten years, it published 10 million documents online. Julian Assange (Figure 27), an Australian online activist, is generally described as

Figure 27. The cover of Time illustrates the efforts of the American government to silence Julian Assange

its founder and director. WikiLeaks is controversial because it reveals secret government documents containing classified information. The company maintains that it does so in the name of the common good. Indeed, in many cases, transparency in regard to the activities of governments and corporations is needed; however, does this imply that public administrations, including special services and the military, are never justified in keeping certain kinds of information classified? If the company is to contribute to the common good, it should have established sources of funding (e.g., the UN) and a supervisory board (e.g., one composed of Nobel peace prize winners).

SUMMARY

1. The computerization of the humanities supports the research and creative writing phases well; however, in the rest of the humanities development cycle, computerization is a threat to culture, as it seeks to eliminate paper books and newspapers and simplify the culture of cinema and other aspects of the media, including drastically reducing the employment and role of journalism, that is, those people who continually revive the resonance of society.
2. The humanities are fighting against other disciplines to establish themselves as useful in people's lives at a time when it is believed that we "should" rely on "computational thinking", which teaching in computerized schools and colleges is geared at. While schools and colleges have the essential task of saving humanism from the invasion of capitalism, the emphasis on developing computerization has actually contributed to the development of surveillance capitalism, whose capital is data about our private lives.

Figure 28. The fate of humanity in the 2020s is e-controlled by business and politicians for the sake of money and power (Photo: Shahbaz & Funk, 2019)

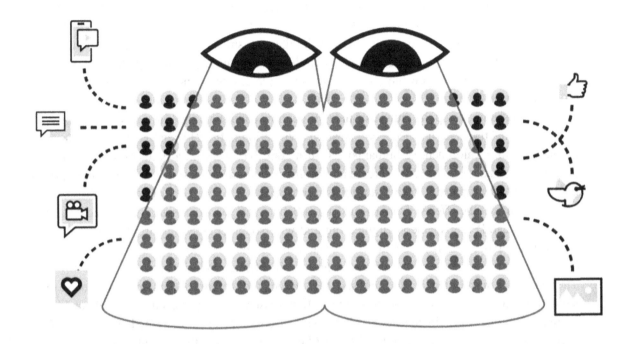

3. The Industrial Revolution, which has been ongoing for the past 200 years, has entered the phase of optimizing the "factory"; however, this economic system has largely ignored the costs ("shallow economics") of destroying nature and human labor with automation. Unfortunately, our economic system is not yet at the stage of "deep economics", in which these costs would be counted.

4. The Information, Virtual, Artificial Intelligence, and Surveillance Waves are designed to automate a person, that is, to make the person a camera that generates data and receives commands (eventually directly to their brain via online links with machine interfaces). This seems to be done in the name of technological progress, but in in practice, it is carried out for the good of a few billionaires who want to be trillionaires. Why do humanists (except for authors like Shoshana Zuboff and a handful of philosophers, psychologists, and other activists) not actively discuss the need to legally regulate Big Tech and surveillance capitalism and eliminate the threat of a fully automated economy? After all, IT professionals will not do this, nor will the heads of the FAAMG companies.

5. Considering the present fate and dignified future of humankind, it can be concluded that our fortune depends on the wisdom of those in the humanities and a sense of responsibility for preventing the destruction of humanity.

6. Humanists must answer the following questions:
    ◦   What is the future of a society without workers and with heavy surveillance?
    ◦   Can an educated society develop based on only computerization, robotics, and automation? Can it simply forget about work and give in to digital entertainment to ameliorate depression, financed by a low-security state where "technical progress" has become the indisputable "religion of life"?

◦ Does knowledge determine the success of humanity, or does wisdom, which is not taught by schools or universities? How is it that universities have operated for hundreds of years and have disseminated knowledge that guarantees success to their apprentices, yet they do not know that knowledge is not wisdom?[9]

◦ How do we function in an age of anti-intellectualism, in which information capitalism dominates and in which surveillance capitalism has taken away our private lives, resulting in a lack of need to educate ourselves about artificial intelligence services and the "great" Amazon e-shop?

◦ Is it possible to stop the culture of hate? If so, how can it be done? If not, what awaits us?

7. It turns out that the material success of Western civilization in the 21st century does not guarantee the successful development of humanism. It turns out that everything is uncertain and chaotic; however, this chaos will, perhaps, create an optimistic humanism, despite our biological push for conflict and our propensity toward stupidity in prosperity.

8. We must consider the effects of our actions, not 100, but 1000 years in advance when deciding what to do next year. Perhaps genetic engineering and wise social engineering are the keys to getting out of this impasse. Yet if we continue to insist on freedom in everything, where will this lead us in the face of the immense power of money and our insufficient political power?

9. The solution to the problems raised here and to the associated "techno-pessimism "is not to use more technology, for the complexity of these civilizational issues already exceeds the intellectual (and moral) capabilities of political leaders.[10] Yet would we dare replace these living leaders with robots who could think in optimal and ethical terms? For the time being, the United States government should break big tech monopolies because, not only are they dangerously organizing techno-states (along the lines of narco-states like Mexico and others), but they also have no brakes to allow for the development of human-friendly innovations.

REFERENCES

A new way to review scientific literature is being tested. (2020, March 21). *The Economist*. https://www.economist.com/science-and-technology/2020/03/19/a-new-way-to-review-scientific-literature-is-being-tested

Abramson, B. (2020, July 2). The humanities are dead. *Newsweek*. https://www.newsweek.com/humanities-are-dead-opinion-1514862

American Humanist Association. (2021). *Definition of humanism*. https://americanhumanist.org/what-is-humanism/definition-of-humanism/

Couglan, S. (2016). Why do Finish pupils succeed with less home work. *BBC News*. https://www.bbc.com/news/education-37716005

Courteous, S., Werth, N., Paczkowski, A., Bartosik, K., Panné, J. L., & Margolin, J. L. (1999). *The black book of communism: Crimes, terror, repression* (J. Murphy & M. Kramer, Trans.). Harvard University Press. (Original work published 1997)

Delaney, E. (2013, December 1). Humanities studies under strain around the globe. *The New York Times*. https://www.nytimes.com/2013/12/02/us/humanities-studies-under-strain-around-the-globe.html

Durant, W., & Durant, A. (1993). *The story of civilization*. MJF Books.

Hill, C. T. (2007). The post-scientific society. *Issues in Science and Technology*, *24*(1), 78–84.

Kelly, S., Truong, M., Shahbaz, A., Earp, M., & White, J. (2017). Freedom on the net 2017: Manipulating social media to undermine democracy. *Freedom House*. https://freedomhouse.org/report/freedom-net/2017/manipulating-social-media-undermine-democracy

Krawczyk, H., & Targowski, A. (2019). *Wisdom in the context of globalization and civilization*. Cambridge Scholars Publishers.

Landau, P. (2019, September 3). *5 Project management techniques every PM should know*. Project Manager. https://www.projectmanager.com/blog/project-management-techniques-for-every-pm

Lemann, N. (2020, February 27). Can journalism be saved? *The New York Review of Books*. https://www.nybooks.com/articles/2020/02/27/can-journalism-be-saved/

NBER Working Paper Series Reinventing Boston 1640-2003. (n.d.). https://www.nber.org/papers/w10166.pdf

Olas, A., & Targowski, A. (2018). *Hybrid Poles*. Oficyna Publishing Kucharski.

Passanisi, J., & Peters, S. (2013, May 2). Research in the digital age: It's more than finding information. *Scientific American*. https://blogs.scientificamerican.com/guest-blog/research-in-the-digital-age-its-more-than-finding-information/

Paul, I. I. J. (1998). *Fides et ratio*. Vatican. https://www.vatican.va/content/john-paul-ii/en/encyclicals/documents/hf_jp-ii_enc_14091998_fides-et-ratio.html

Posner, M. I. (Ed.). (1991). *Foundations of cognitive science*. MIT Press.

Romm, T. (2017, November 14). Governments in 30 countries manipulated media online to silence critics, sow unrest or influence elections. *Vox*. https://www.vox.com/2017/11/14/16640300/internet-freedom-facebook-twitter-google-us-russia-disinformation

Shahbaz, A., & Funk, A. (2019). Freedom on the net in 2019: The crisis of social media. *Freedom House*. https://freedomhouse.org/report/freedom-net/2019/crisis-social-media

Stover, J. (2017). There is no case for the humanities. *American Affairs*, *1*(4), 210–224.

Targowski, A. (1990). *The architecture and planning of enterprise-wide information management systems*. Idea Group Publishing.

Targowski, A. (1999). *Enterprise information infrastructure*. Pearson Custom Publishing.

Targowski, A. (2003). In pursuit of critical total history theory: The modeling of civilization's history. *Mazowieckie Studia Humanistyczne*, *9*(1-2), 61–83.

Targowski, A. (2005). Universal-complementary civilization as a solution to present day catastrophic international conflicts. *Dialogue and Universalism, 15*(7-8), 73–99. doi:10.5840/du2005157/883

Targowski, A. (2009). *Information technology and societal development.* Information Science Reference. doi:10.4018/978-1-60566-004-2

Targowski, A. (2010). The future of reasoning in the digital and virtual waves of civilization: How to educate and act in a new society? In A. Targowski & T. Rienzo (Eds.), *Newspapers in crisis: Can an educated society be sustained solely by digitalization?* (pp. 33–50). Civilization Press.

Targowski, A. (2011). *Cognitive informatics and wisdom development.* Information Science Reference. doi:10.4018/978-1-60960-168-3

Targowski, A. (2014). *Global civilization in the 21st century.* Nova Science Publishers.

Targowski, A. (2015). Chinese civilization versus global civilization in the 21st century. In A. Targowski & B. Hun (Eds.), *Chinese civilization in the 21st century.* Nova Science Publishers.

Targowski, A. (2016). *Informing and civilization.* Informing Science Press.

Targowski, A. (2019). *The limits of civilization.* Nova Science Publishers.

Tatarkiewicz, W. (2005). *History of philosophy.* Polish Scientific Publishers.

The data economy. (2020, February 20). *The Economist.* https://www.economist.com/special-report/2020/02/20/a-deluge-of-data-is-giving-rise-to-a-new-economy

The online of beauty: How art galleries are adapting to the lockdown. (2020, March 28). *The Economist.* https://www.economist.com/books-and-arts/2020/03/26/how-art-galleries-are-adapting-to-the-lockdown

Thurlow, C. (2006). From statistical panic to moral panic: The metadiscursive construction and popular exaggeration of new media language in the print media. *Journal of Computer-Mediated Communication, 11*(3), 667–701. doi:10.1111/j.1083-6101.2006.00031.x

Turing, A. M. (1950). I.—Computing machinery and intelligence. *Mind, 59*(236), 433–460. doi:10.1093/mind/LIX.236.433

Tworek, H. (2013, December 18). The real reason the humanities are 'in crisis'. *The Atlantic.* https://www.theatlantic.com/education/archive/2013/12/the-real-reason-the-humanities-are-in-crisis/282441/

U.S. Department of Navy. (1958). *Program evaluation research task, summary report, phase 1.* Government Printing Office. https://apps.dtic.mil/dtic/tr/fulltext/u2/735902.pdf

KEY TERMS AND DEFINITIONS

Big Data: Large collections of either structured, semi-structured, or unstructured data that is processed by computer applications.

Collective Intelligence: A form of intelligence that grows out of collaborative or collective efforts.

Metadata: A form of data that provides information about data, such as a keyword associated with a text.

Monte Carlo Method: A kind of computational algorithm that utilizes repeated random sampling to obtain results.

Natural Language Processing: An area of study that aims at discovering methods for analyzing natural language via computer programs.

Social Resonance: The degree to which environmental and social factors facilitate the ability of humans to form successful relationships with others.

Supercomputers: A class of computers that performs at extremely high levels in comparison to more general-purpose computers.

Telepresence: A form of technology that creates the sense of being present at a place other than the actual location.

Yankee Ingenuity: A colloquial stereotype for the ingenuity of "Yankees", a term that refers to early citizens of the US who lived in New England.

ENDNOTES

[1]   Steven Dale Schafersman (1948-) is an American geologist and current president of *Texas Citizens for Science*, an advocacy group that opposes the teaching of creationism as a science in public schools. He is also known for his blog BadGeology.com.

[2]   Thomas Paine (1737-1809) was an English-born American political activist, philosopher, political theorist, and revolutionary. He is the author of two of the most influential pamphlets at the beginning of the American Revolution and inspired American patriots in 1776 to declare independence from Britain. His views reflect the ideas of transnational human rights from the Enlightenment era. Historian Saul K. Padover described him as "a corsetmaker by trade, a journalist by profession, and a propagandist by inclination."

[3]   Robert "Bob" Green Ingersoll (1833 - 1899) was an American writer and speaker during the Golden Age of Free Thought (the mid-19th century in the United States, in which a socio-political movement promoting free thought developed). He was given the nickname the "Great Agnostic".

[4]   The Monte Carlo method is a simulation method formulated by Polish American mathematician (from the Lwów School of Mathematics) Stanislaw Ulam (1909-1984) in 1947 in the US. Ulam is considered the father of the American hydrogen bomb because, thanks to his calculations, he was able to prove that, in order to make an H-bomb explode, it must be fired by an atomic bomb (A-bomb).

[5]   In Poland, the PERT technique was first used in 1962 in a computerization project by Kasprzak and Zakłr in Warsaw under the direction of Andrew Targowski. Also under the direction of Targowski, between 1972 and 1974 PERT was used to control the simultaneous development of 400 particularly important investments in the country under the Vector system, enriched with the AWIZO-MOC subsystem for balancing the declared processing needs with the capacity of construction companies. It should be recalled that at that time the so-called "Iron Curtain" stood between the United States and the Polish People's Republic; thus, the flow of innovation between advanced "America" and Poland was slow and difficult. When it did take place, it was thanks to the ambitions of many pro-

fessionals involved in the modernization of the country, who had private channels of information, whether during foreign internships or private contacts.

6   Details about the virtual tour can be found at the following website: https://www.rijksmuseum.nl/en/from-home

7   Trolling is defined as causing discord on the Internet by starting an argument or annoying people by posting inflammatory or non-related messages to an online community. Basically, a social media troll is someone who deliberately says something controversial to gain popularity among other users.

8   Big Brother was a fictional character created by George Orwell in his dystopian novel *1984*. Big Brother is presumably the party leader of the fictional state "Oceania". This leader is symbolized as being middle-aged with a large head and a black mustache. Under his poster image is the inscription: "Big Brother is watching you".

9   Wisdom can be defined as knowledge aided by correct judgment and the correct choice of solution options in the context of the art of life (Krawczyk & Targowski, 2019).

10   After all, some argue that, as a result of technology, mortality in car accidents has decreased from 240 per billion miles travelled in 1920 to 12 at present, which is supposed to indicate that modern technology is a cure for techno-pessimism.

Chapter 18
Digital State Strategy

ABSTRACT

The purpose of this chapter is to characterize indicators used to advance the computerization of various countries in the European Union (EU) and across the globe. To this end, typical state computerization configurations are classified, and graphical models of critical computerization application systems are presented for each type. Smart city concepts are included in one of the configurations. The chapter begins by examining the history of the development of computerization in the state. It then discusses how, in the 21st century, computerization has changed the relationship between governments and businesses. Next, criteria for assessing computerization are discussed. This is followed by a discussion of different computerization configurations, including the state offline configuration (SOFC), state online configuration (SONC), state integrated configuration (SITC), and others. The chapter concludes by examining Poland's state configuration, which aimed at helping their economic strategy during 2016-2020.

THE HISTORY OF COMPUTERIZATION DEVELOPMENT IN THE STATE

The history of the development and use of counting machines in state governments dates back to 1890 when the United States census was calculated on punch card machines (for 80 column cards with electric readings) produced by Hollerith. At the same time, these machines were gradually being used to mechanize data processing in business, which increased after the creation of IBM in 1924. Furthermore, the creation of the Social Security Number triggered a wave of development of data processing systems in order to meet the needs of the federal, state, and local administrations. This mainly occurred in administrative areas that dealt with multiple employee records, materials, fixed assets, funds (including bank accounts), buildings and premises, inventory, and payroll accounting.

Soon, the mechanization of censuses developed in Europe thanks to IBM, which resulted in the development of the French company Bull, which began manufacturing punch card machines in 1931. These machines were sold to many European countries, where, in competition with IBM and UNIVAC-Powers machines (for 90 column cards with mechanical readings), they began to be used to mechanize data processing in keeping records and payroll accounting in administration and business. In Central and

DOI: 10.4018/978-1-7998-8036-3.ch018

Eastern Europe, cheaper Czechoslovakian Aritma machines (for 90 column cards with mechanical readings) and Soviet (Belarusian) SAM machines (for 80 column cards with electric readings) were also used.

During World War II (1939-1945), Germans, who value good organization, used mechanized censuses in several European countries (in particular France, the Netherlands, and Poland) to arrest "undesirable elements," including Jews. Unfortunately, around 4 million people died (Targowski, 2014a).

For the United States and the United Kingdom as well as in France, World War II gave rise to the development of electronic counting machines, called "computers" (USA-ENIAC 1946 and UNIVAC I 1951; United Kingdom-LEO I 1951; France-Gamma 60 1957). Beginning in the 1950s and intensifying in the 1960s, these electronic counting machines began to replace punch card machines and began to automate data processing, mainly in keeping records and storing accounting and payroll information. The spectacular development of the IBM 1400 series in the late 1950s and early 1960s with its business and administration applications came as a surprise to Western Europe.

In response to the US information technology challenge, President Charles de Gaulle developed *Plan Calcul* to encourage the production and use of computers in France. As a result of this plan, the company CII *(*Compagnie International pour Informatique*)* was established. Furthermore, the *Delegue pour l'informatique* was found in 1966, which aimed to coordinate and supervise the implementation of *Plan Calcul*. Thus, at this point, in addition to the American terms *computing, data processing, computer science,* and *software*, the French added the word *Informatique*, which means the technique of information processing. After five years, such a plan was adopted in Poland. In the wake of *Plan Calcul* (Targowski, 1971), the book *Le Défi Américain* ("the American Challenge") was published by Jean-Jacques Servan-Schreiber (1967), a politician who described the United States and Europe as engaged in a silent economic war in which Europe seemed outclassed entirely on all fronts: management techniques, technological tools, and research capabilities. At that time, 600,000 copies were sold in France, which was unprecedented for a political essay, and it was translated into 15 languages. This book contributed to the revival of French nationalism and highlighted the importance of transnational cooperation in Europe.

In Poland, even though the pro-Soviet Polish People's Republic prevailed, technical intelligence was aware of the American challenge. This resulted in the creation (even before France) of the Office of the Government Representative for Electronic Computing Technology in 1964. Thanks to this decision, a network of ZETO service computing centers (Electronic Computing Technology Plants) developed in all 49 provinces.[1] It had about 6,000 employees, including the country's best IT professionals at the time. Because this was a pioneering period in the development of computer science applications in Poland, the strategy at the time had to address the problem that there were not enough IT specialists to develop applications in dozens of ministries, including those concerned with economics, education, and health. By focusing on the ZETO network, data processing applications in these areas was developed at a reasonable level, and they were carried out on real computers, which were sorely lacking at the time. At present, service policies are rapidly evolving due to the so-called "digital cloud", which is an IT service. This confirms the validity of the creation of the ZETO network 56 years ago.[2]

In 1971, the implementation of the first Computer Science Development Programme for 1971-75 began, based on the National Information System (NIS) model shown in Figure 1. The model provides vital Information Control Systems (CIS) for the centrally planned economy. However, these systems do not arise from the Lange Model, which tied together all suppliers and customers into a single system and calculated (*apriori*) the optimal trade. This would all be accomplished thanks to a supercomputer that would ensure a stable balance in the economy.

NIS development aimed to:

1. Activate the centrally planned economy by computerizing 'top-down' management systems, based on the philosophy that 'fish rot from the head down'.
2. Reduce the growing bureaucracy by computerizing resource records and thereby allowing for hundreds of thousands of different documents and files to be processed,
3. Enable communication among citizens in an informed society (not just an information society), thanks to the INFOSTRADA (ICT) network.

The development of the INFOSTRADA network was a threat to the regime of the Polish People's Republic, as the authorities were afraid of the uncontrolled flow of real information. In 1974, because of a decision by the Political Bureau of the Polish United Worker's Party (PZPR), the implementation of the program was stopped, and the National Bureau of Informatics was dissolved. This ultimately resulted in the cessation of implementing information systems at the national level until the end of the Polish People's Republic in 1989. In the Third Republic, the prestige of ICT in the state government has risen, even resulting in the creation of the Ministry of Digitalization. Still, no official digital development program has been approved.

On the other hand, there has been an exuberant mood toward IT applications in business, secured mainly by branches of foreign software and consulting companies. The authorities of "digitalization" have primarily focused on selected online applications in public administration and schools and colleges.[3] Political parties have not concentrated on using social networks to promote political hate by anonymous trolls.

Since its liberation from the Soviet Bloc in 1989, the Third Republic has witnessed the implementation of several NIS systems (discussed in the chapter *the History and Repercussions of Strategic Informing Technology*). One such system is the Social Security (PESEL) system, which is currently used in 500 administration applications.

Today, the world is not looking for better governance through the computerization of public administration. Still, the world is fascinated by the possibilities of social networks, which, in early 2010, helped facilitate the overthrow of the four longest-serving dictators in the world in Egypt, Libya, Tunisia, and Yemen. It has been argued that in a world of unrestricted access to information and one in which the activities of citizens are strengthened by information technology, autocrats are unable to maintain their power, which is dependent on their information systems. On one hand, it is the case that these political movements led to the collapse of 10 authoritarian regimes between 2000 and 2017, or 23 percent of the 44 authoritarian regimes in place during that period. Furthermore, another 19 authoritarian regimes lost power as a result of elections, and although there were almost twice as many regimes displaced by elections as protests, many elections also took place after campaigns of mass protests (Kendall-Taylor et al., 2020).

On the other hand, computerization not only serves protesters, but it also helps dictators stiffen older methods of controlling citizens. Computerization allows dictators to increase the use of digital repression (for example, through surveillance and trolls). Of course, this is not to say that they will not increase the use of violent forms of repression in real life, especially torturing and killing political opponents. In other words, dictators do not replace traditional repression with digital repression; rather, digital powers allow them to more effectively determine on whose door they should knock and who should be in a cell. Nevertheless, this tighter IT-aided identification of opponents does reduce the need to resort to mass repression, which can provoke widespread opposition and criticism from the rest of the world.

Figure 1. The architecture of the National Information System in 1972 (the Targowski model) [4]

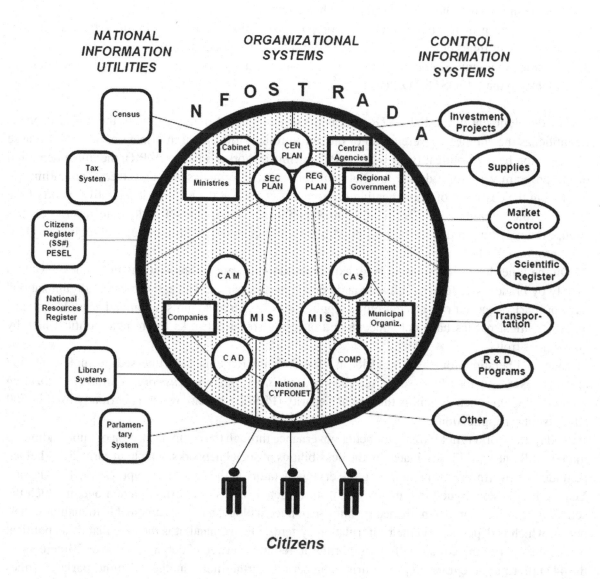

NATIONAL
INFORMATION
UTILITIES

ORGANIZATIONAL
SYSTEMS

CONTROL
INFORMATION
SYSTEMS

Citizens

Thus, over time, it does not appear that computerization necessarily favors citizens seeking to have their voices taken into account; rather, because authoritarian regimes increasingly fear societal opposition, they are using advanced computerization to stay in power.

Today's authoritarian governments, led by China, use the "power technology"—such as the Internet, social media, and artificial intelligence—to reinforce long-standing traditional authoritarian survival tactics. They now have a new arsenal of techniques to counter typical threats faced by authoritarian regimes. As a result, dictators have become much more entrenched than their non-computerized predecessors.

The Chinese Communist Party collects a large amount of data about individuals and businesses, such as tax returns, bank statements, purchase histories, and criminal and medical records. The regime then uses artificial intelligence to analyze this information and compile a "social credit index," which it uses to establish parameters of acceptable behavior and improve the control of citizens' behavior. Persons or companies deemed "unreliable" may be excluded from state-sponsored allowances, such as renting no-deposit apartments, and they may be blocked from air and rail travel. An example of the use of facial recognition technology in China is shown in Figure 2.

Figure 2. Facial recognition technology is used at Wuhan railway station (Photo: Xuong Qi / Xinhua / Eyevine / Redu x)

When the protest movement intensified in Hong Kong in the summer of 2019, the Chinese regime strengthened its firewall by immediately removing subversive content from the Internet in mainland China. Furthermore, even if censorship fails and public opposition intensifies, digital autocracies have an additional line of defense: they can block all citizens' access to the Internet (or a large part of it) to prevent opposition members from communicating, organizing, or disseminating their messages. In Iran, for example, the government effectively shut down the Internet across the country following widespread protests in November 2019 (Kendall-Taylor et al., 2020).

Computer-oriented integration between government agencies allows the Chinese regime to more accurately control access to public administration services so that it can reduce or increase the distribution (or refusal) of everything from passports to jobs and access to schools and colleges. China's emerging social credit indexing system punishes citizens critical of the regime and rewards their fidelity. Citizens with an excellent social credit rating enjoy a range of benefits, including accelerated foreign travel, reduced energy bills, and less frequent tax audits.

Over time, as autocracies have learned to computerize social processes, they have become a more dangerous threat to democracy because they are more durable. Between 1946 and 2000—the years when computer science began to spread—a typical dictatorship prevailed for about ten years. Since 2000, this number has doubled to almost 20 years (Kendall-Taylor et al., 2020).

Modern dictatorships buy surveillance technologies from countries such as China or Israel and then train a small group of officials for their use. For example, the Chinese company Huawei, a state-backed telecommunications company, has implemented digital surveillance technology in more than a dozen authoritarian regimes. In 2019, there were reports that the Ugandan government was using the system to hack the social media accounts and electronic communications of its political opponents. Israeli and Italian companies have also sold digital surveillance software to the Ugandan regime. Israeli companies have sold a Pegasus-type spyware that collects intelligence to many authoritarian regimes around the world, including Angol, Bahrain, Kazakhstan, Mozambique, and Nicaragua. U.S. companies export facial recognition technology to governments in Saudi Arabia and the United Arab Emirates (Kendall-Taylor et al., 2020).

State computerization is extremely dangerous for weak democracies, as many of these information systems have dual applications: they can increase the efficiency of public administration and provide the ability to face crime and terrorism, but they can also use these systems as a gag to limit the activity of political opponents. International civil and professional society agencies and groups (including IT professionals) should take action to minimize the harmful effects of the spread of IT surveillance systems, especially in fragile democracies. Such action should focus on strengthening the political and legal framework governing the use of IT surveillance systems and building the capacity of civil society and supervisory organizations to control abuses by governments using these systems.

COMPUTERIZATION IN THE 21ST CENTURY AND THE RELATIONSHIP BETWEEN PUBLIC ADMINISTRATION AND BUSINESS

The alleged mutual understanding and partnership between governments and companies has become impossible and increasingly threatens the very structure of democracy for the following reasons:

1. "Distance is dead." Whether it's the companies themselves, their tax headquarters, or the teams that build and run them, locations are no longer relevant, and boundaries are irrelevant, for in IT companies, resources like talent and money are fluid and can be located anywhere in the world. Not so long ago, if one wanted to sell one's software product or service in, say, India, one needed a distribution network, offices, and employees. Today one can design a thriving software as service (SaaS) product in India, London, Amsterdam, or Palo Alto, California. Furthermore, as a startup in Paris or Stockholm, one can outsource all of one's backroom or sales team to, say, India without even getting on a plane.

2. Many online companies are simply digital information platforms or digital trading platforms (for example, eBay, Uber, Airbnb, and Etsy) that combine demand and supply or buyers and sellers. While there is still a battle over whether Uber is an employer or merely an intermediary for self-employed "enterprising" drivers, there is no doubt which side the company itself is on. IBM, founded about

a century ago (in 1924), had more than 377,000 employees in 2015; that same year, Google had just over 60,000. Meanwhile, WhatsApp only had about 35 employees when Facebook acquired it for $19 billion in 2014. What a fully automated digital business will look like in 20 years will depend on what Big Tech decides.

3. The network effect enjoyed by IT companies creates a winner-take-all environment, and a constant and ever-growing flood of data enables such companies to increase productivity and accomplish more with less effort. The net result of fewer successful companies employing fewer and fewer people is, of course, a significantly reduced tax base, with the burden of healthcare and pensions falling on individuals and, ultimately, the government. Moreover, the fact that these companies are not linked to any specific location but instead can be based out of wherever is most tax-efficient (in fact, governments are trying to offer tax incentives to attract corporations) explains why corporate tax rates in the G20 and OECD countries fell from an average of 45% in 1983 to 25% in 2020.

4. The reduction in corporate tax revenues and the upcoming impact of AI/automation on the number of jobs make it difficult for governments to tax and regulate business. Consequently, this hampers the government's role as a wealth distributor. Meanwhile, according to the McKinsey Global Institute, a growing number of workers—20-30% of the US and 15% of the EU workforce—are now classified as independent (contract) workers, making the protection of workers' rights increasingly complex.

5. Governments cannot continue to protect the privacy of their citizens effectively. The explosion in the number of data brokers (there are at least 4,000 brokerage firms of this type in the world, and the industry's value is estimated at $200 billion) who collect, repackage, and resell data from publicly available data and online activities means that private corporations are increasingly expecting more and more financial and systemic assistance from the government. Areas such as security, census, and healthcare are just another market opportunity for data trading for IT companies, which in practice prioritize profit over the public good and, thanks to lobbyists, help maintain *the status quo*.

All of these factors pose a challenge to Western liberal democracy. As the power of Big Tech and other IT companies increases, the government's proper legitimacy as governor of the state ceases to be fully valid. After all, how can the government enjoy the trust of its citizens if it can no longer fulfill its essential responsibilities? Even more harshly, if it is unable to serve its citizens or adapt to the excessive speed of the digital economy, then the government itself is in danger of becoming irrelevant, and the state is in danger of having its borders disappear.

It follows that governments will become mere guardians of business as they become increasingly vulnerable to computerization and that policies will be shaped by data and IT services outsourced to private companies at market prices. In such circumstances, it is almost certain that regulatory oversight of corporations will be drastically reduced, resulting in the government's trusted contact with its citizens being severed.

To save liberal democracy from collapse, the following steps are necessary according to the *World Economic Forum* (WEF):

•   Require computerization to be able to increase government transparency by designing all business interactions of the user around the user (as is the case in the UK and Estonia): This would include publishing daily government activities and online spending, opening up all government data to boost transparency and innovation, and allowing as many administrative tasks as possible—

whether renewing a driver's license or requesting a power of attorney—to be conducted online. Perhaps the government will act proactively and predictably and will replace the traditional model (in which the responses of authorities to events—which are largely based on how popular they perceive their decisions will be—are out of date the moment they are published.[5]

- Call for computerization to improve governance by eliminating unnecessary duplications of documents indefinitely, cutting red tape, speeding up decentralization, and changing existing rules to ensure that they are in line with the objectives of liberal democracy and its computerization: This may entail enabling the development of participatory democracy, in which citizens play a much more significant role in local decision-making. Greater accountability of citizens will only strengthen democracy, giving it a new dimension of life.

- Implement reforms: It is no exaggeration to say that the traditional order is now under threat. As Western governments fight for borders (which are easily crossed by waves of migrants) and as their budgets crack under pressure, the information revolution offers an opportunity for renewal. A correctly implemented reform based on computerization can refresh democracies and regenerate forces integral to this process.

The demands made by the WEF are quite superficial, not to mention it is trivial given state of knowledge about computerization in the 21st century.[6] Based on several hundred employees, the WEF is a center of global and stateless business that centrally plans recommended proceedings each subsequent year for its members. Do these members aim to maintain liberal democracy through such "convenient" means?

MODERN OFFICIAL CRITERIA FOR ASSESSING STATE COMPUTERIZATION

The specific strategy for computerizing a given state depends on whether it is democratic, authoritarian, or totalitarian. This work is centered on the democratic state. To this end, it is necessary to look at the criteria used by the European Union (EU) in assessing the applications of state computerization.

The EU uses the Digital Economy and Society Index (DESI) for assessing state computerization. It is based on five indicators, shown in Figure 3 (European Commission, 2019):

1. **Connectivity** measures the deployment and quality of broadband infrastructure. Access to high-speed and ultra-fast broadband services is a prerequisite for business competitiveness.
2. **Human capital** measures the skills needed to take advantage of the opportunities offered by information technology (Figure 4).[7]
3. **Use of internet services** includes a variety of online activities, such as online content consumption (texts, video, music, games, etc.), video calls, as well as online shopping and banking.
4. **Integration of digital technology** measures the digitization of companies and e-commerce. By using digital technologies, businesses can increase productivity, reduce costs, and better engage customers and business partners. In addition, the Internet, as a point of sale, offers access to broader markets and growth potential.
5. **Digital public services** measure the digitization of available services, focusing on eAministration and e-health. Modernizing and digitizing public services can lead to increased efficiency for public administrations, citizens, and businesses.

Figure 3. Digital Economy and Society Index used by the European Union 2019 (European Commission, 2019)

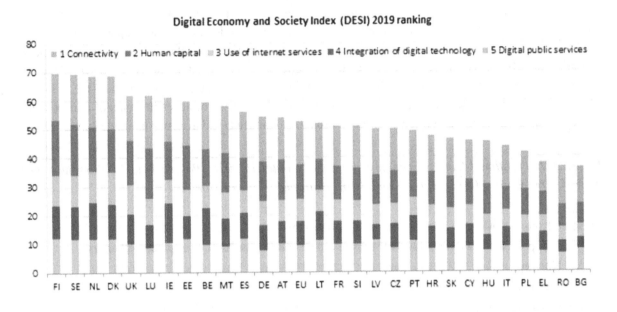

Figure 4. Human Capital Index in EU Computer Science 2018 (European Commission, 2018)

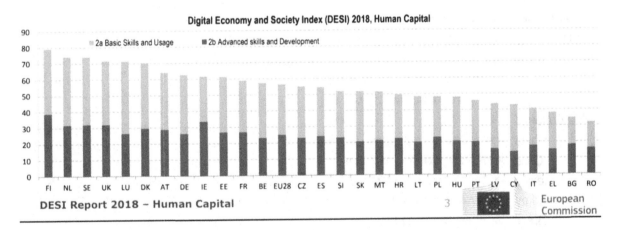

The EU also uses the International Digital Economy and Society Index (I-DESI) (Figure 5), which reflects and expands on the Digital Economy and Society Index by using 24 datasets to analyze trends and to compare the digital performance of 45 countries, including 17 non-European countries. The motivation behind this report is that the EU does not want to lag behind rapidly developing countries in Asia.

I-DESI combines 24 indicators and uses a weighting system to rank each country based on its digital performance to benchmark the development of its digital economy and society. The index measures ef-

443

ficiency in the same five dimensions or policy areas noted above: connectivity, human capital (digital skills), citizens' internet use, technology integration, and digital public services.

The 2016 analysis, shown in Figure 5, revealed that the 28 EU Member States are comparable to the 17 non-EU countries (Australia, Brazil, Canada, Chile, China, Iceland, Israel, Japan, Mexico, New Zealand, Norway, Russia, Serbia, South Korea, Switzerland, Turkey, and the United States) (European Commission, 2016). By contrast, the best of the EU countries have digital results at the same level or higher than the best global countries. Indeed, Denmark was the leading country in the I-DESI index. The 28 EU Member States performed best compared to 17 non-EU countries in terms of connectivity (deployment and absorption of fixed and mobile broadband internet) and in terms of citizens' internet use.

Figure 5. International Digital Economy and Society Index in 2016: Poland is in EU Bottom 4, just above China, Chile, Mexico, Turkey, and Brazil (European Commission, 2016)

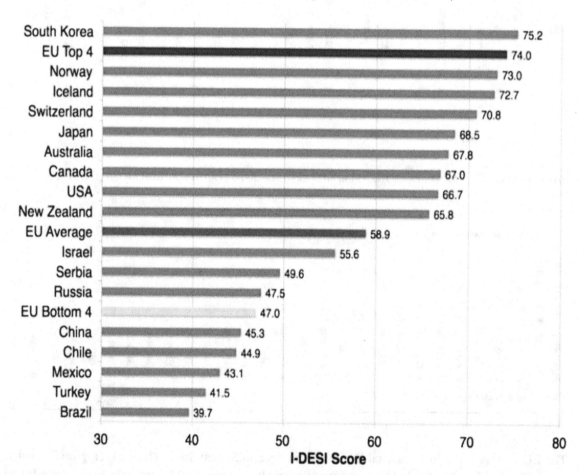

As regards human capital, this is depicted in Figure 6.

The United Nations E-Government Survey assesses the development of eAdministration at the national level. It is based on three elements: the online services index, the telecommunications infrastructure index, and the human capital index. Countries in all regions of the world continue to make efforts to improve

Figure 6. International Digital Economy and Society Index regarding human capital: Use of e-government services in 2016 (European Commission, 2016)

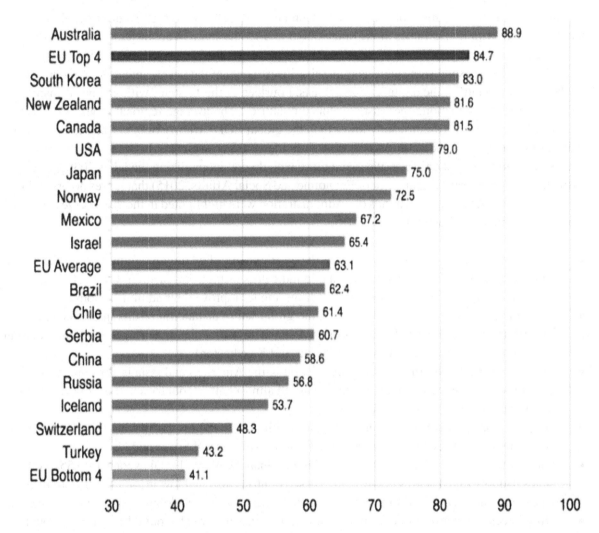

the administration and provision of public services online, according to a report published by the UN Department of Economic and Social Affairs (2018). Denmark, Australia, and the Republic of Korea topped the group of 40 countries in the 2018 e-government development index (EGDI) rankings, which measures countries' use of information and communication technologies to provide public services. The index records the scope and quality of online services, the state of the telecommunications infrastructure, and existing human capital (Department of Economic and Social Affairs, 2018).

In 2018, more countries had index values in the range of 0.75 to 1.00 than in 2016, when only 29 countries fell in this range. These same countries also excel in regional rankings in Europe, Oceania, and Asia. Mauritius is a leader in Africa with a global ranking of 66, and the United States in the Americas with a worldwide rank of 11.

For the first time, the 2018 study focused on the development of local administrations in 40 cities around the world. This included evaluating the urban portals of 7 cities in Africa, 6 in the Americas,

13 in Asia, 12 in Europe, and 2 in Oceania. There were three significant leaders among them: Moscow, Cape Town, and Tallinn.

Globally, almost two-thirds of the 193 UN Member States showed a high level of development in administration, with EGDI values in the range of 0.5 and 1. The share of countries with low eAdministration levels in the range of 0 to 0.25 decreased by 50 percent from 32 countries in 2016 to 16 countries in 2018. However, despite some gains and massive investments in the development of eAdministration made by many countries, the digital divide persists. Fourteen of the 16 states with low performance are African states that are among the least developed countries. The average regional index performance for Africa and Oceania is significantly lower than the global EGDI average of 0.55 (0.34 for Africa and 0.46 for Oceania). This indicates that the digital divide could be widening between people who have access to the Internet and online services and those who do not, jeopardizing the UN's 2030 agenda for sustainable development (Department of Economic and Social Affairs, 2015) that leaves no one behind.

Furthermore, developmental trends of eAdministration were highlighted in the 2018 survey (Department of Economic and Social Affairs, 2018):

- European countries are at the forefront in the development of eAdministrations around the world. Both Americas and Asia are almost equal in indicators of high and medium levels of administration, and many African countries are still struggling to improve their administrations.
- Eight of the 11 new countries that joined the group with outstanding results in 2018 came from Europe (Belarus, Greece, Liechtenstein, Malta, Monaco, Poland, Portugal, and the Russian Federation), and two came from Asia (Cyprus and Kazakhstan).
- Progress in the development of eAdministration in the Americas and Asia is slow but noticeable. Two-thirds of countries in Asia (31 out of 47) and almost half of countries in the Americas (15 out of 35) had an average global EGDI rating of 0.55.
- Uruguay was the only Latin American country with high EGDI results, placing this country in the company of two precursors in the Americas region—the United States and Canada.
- Only 4 out of 54 countries in Africa scored higher than the global EGDI average of 0.55, while 14 states had low EGDI scores below 0.25. These countries also had low incomes and were likely to face constraints in the allocation of resources necessary for the development of the administration.
- Differences in the level of development of eAministration were also quite large among countries in the regions of Africa and Oceania. Australia and New Zealand were the only two countries in Oceania to have EGDI scores well above the average: .9053 and .8806, respectively. The other 12 states had scores ranging from 0.2787 up to 0.5348, below the global average of 0.55.
- Generally speaking, there is a positive correlation between a country's income level and its eAdministration ranking. High-income countries tend to have very high or high EGDI scores. However, this is not universal. Twenty-two middle-income and 39 low- and middle-income countries had EGDI scores below the global EGDI average, and ten countries in the lower-middle-income group had scores above the global EGDI average. On the other hand, countries with lower incomes were still lagging due to the relatively low level of development of all components on the index.
- For the first time in 2018, the main driver of improving EDGI performance across all income groups was the development of online services, suggesting that there has been steady progress worldwide in enhancing the provision of eGovernment services and public services over the Internet.

- All 193 UN Member States had national portals and back-end systems to automate basic administrative tasks, and 140 provided at least one online transactional service. The trend of improving transactional online services was strong and consistent across all categories assessed, with the three most commonly used services being (a) payment for municipal services (140 countries), (b) income tax submission (139 countries), and (c) registration of new activities (126 countries).

- More and more countries were found to be providing online services to their most vulnerable groups. From a regional point of view, Europe continues to be at the forefront in delivering online services to all vulnerable groups, reaching almost universal coverage across the region (more than 80 percent of all European countries).

- The number of countries providing online services via email, SMS/RSS feed updates, mobile apps, and downloadable forms increased across all sectors. For example, up to 176 countries shared archived information online in 2018, compared to 154 in 2016.

The UN report on eAdministration examines how e-government can facilitate integrated policies and services in three dimensions of sustainable development. The report is produced every two years by the UN Department of Economic and Social Affairs. It is the only global report assessing the status of the administrations of the 193 UN Member States. It serves as a tool for countries to learn from each other, identify areas of strength and weakness, and shape their policies and strategies in these areas. It also aims to facilitate discussions between intergovernmental bodies—including the United Nations General Assembly and the Economic and Social Council—on issues related to eGovernment and development and the crucial role of ICT in development.

The *Portulans Institute* has created a Network Readiness Index based on four pillars: technology, people, governance, and impact. Each pillar also consists of three sub-pillars. The Network Readiness Index for 2020 ranks a total of 134 economies. The best results were achieved by Sweden, which was ahead of Denmark in 2ⁿᵈ place, Singapore in 3ʳᵈ place, and the Netherlands in 4ᵗʰ place. European countries dominated the top 10 rankings, with 8 of 10 coming from Europe. The United States was ranked in 8th place, and Poland in 33ʳᵈ, just behind Italy and Portugal.

The share of the ICT sector in the gross domestic product (GDP) of the EU in 2015 is given in Figure 7. Ireland had by far the highest percentage of ICT in GDP, with 11.6% in 2014 (latest available data), while Portugal and Greece were lagging behind with just 3.1%. After Ireland, the countries with the highest share in the ICT sector were Luxembourg (7.1%) and Sweden (6.3%). Some Eastern Member States (Romania, Hungary, and the Czech Republic) also had a high percentage (5% or more) of the ICT sector as a percentage of GDP. In most other Member States, the ICT sector remained broadly stable as a percentage of GDP over the medium term (2006-2015), except for Ireland, where the rate rose very quickly. The share of the Polish ICT sector is below 4 percent of its GDP, which is below Romania, Hungary, and the Czech Republic.

The amount of expenditure on computerization research and development in the business sector in 2016 is given in Figure 8. The six major EU countries in terms of ICT research and development spending included the four largest economies in the EU (France, Germany, the United Kingdom, and Italy), followed by Sweden and the Netherlands. Poland was in 13th place.

The amount of EU grant funds for computerization research and development in 2014-2018 is given in Figure 9. Countries such as France, Germany, the UK, Spain, Italy, and the Netherlands received the most. Poland was in 15th place, just behind Portugal and behind the Scandinavian countries.

Table 1. Countries leading in e-government development according to the UN e-government survey (Department of Economic and Social Affairs, 2018)

Country Name	Region	OSI	HCI	TII	EGDI	2016 Rank	2018 Rank	EGDI Group change
Denmark	Europe	1.0000	0.9472	0.7978	0.9150	9	1	None
Australia	Oceania	0.9722	1.0000	0.7436	0.9053	2	2	None
Republic of Korea	Asia	0.9792	0.8743	0.8496	0.9010	3	3	None
United Kingdom of Great Britain and Northern Ireland	Europe	0.9792	0.9200	0.8004	0.8999	1	4	None
Sweden	Europe	0.9444	0.9366	0.7835	0.8882	6	5	None
Finland	Europe	0.9653	0.9509	0.7284	0.8815	5	6	None
Singapore	Asia	0.9861	0.8557	0.8019	0.8812	4	7	None
New Zealand	Oceania	0.9514	0.9450	0.7455	0.8806	8	8	None
France	Europe	0.9792	0.8598	0.7979	0.8790	10	9	None
Japan	Asia	0.9514	0.8428	0.8406	0.8783	11	10	None
United States of America	Americas	0.9861	0.8883	0.7564	0.8769	12	11	None
Germany	Europe	0.9306	0.9036	0.7952	0.8765	15	12	None
Netherlands	Europe	0.9306	0.9206	0.7758	0.8757	7	13	None
Norway	Europe	0.9514	0.9025	0.7131	0.8557	18	14	None
Switzerland	Europe	0.8472	0.8660	0.8428	0.8520	28	15	None
Estonia	Europe	0.9028	0.8818	0.7613	0.8486	13	16	None
Spain	Europe	0.9375	0.8885	0.6986	0.8415	17	17	None
Luxembourg	Europe	0.9236	0.7803	0.7964	0.8334	25	18	None
Iceland	Europe	0.7292	0.9365	0.8292	0.8316	27	19	None
Austria	Europe	0.8681	0.8505	0.7716	0.8301	16	20	None
United Arab Emirates	Asia	0.9444	0.6877	0.8564	0.8295	29	21	None
Ireland	Europe	0.8264	0.9626	0.6970	0.8287	26	22	None
Canada	Americas	0.9306	0.8744	0.6724	0.8258	14	23	None
Italy	Europe	0.9514	0.8341	0.6771	0.8209	22	24	None
Liechtenstein	Europe	0.7986	0.8237	0.8389	0.8204	32	25	H to VH
Bahrain	Asia	0.7986	0.7897	0.8466	0.8116	24	26	None
Belgium	Europe	0.7569	0.9740	0.6930	0.8080	19	27	None
Monaco	Europe	0.6250	0.7901	1.0000	0.8050	31	28	H to VH
Portugal	Europe	0.9306	0.8170	0.6617	0.8031	38	29	H to VH
Malta	Europe	0.8403	0.7973	0.7657	0.8011	30	30	H to VH
Israel	Asia	0.8264	0.8635	0.7095	0.7998	20	31	None
Russian Federation	Europe	0.9167	0.8522	0.6219	0.7969	35	32	H to VH
Poland	Europe	0.9306	0.8668	0.5805	0.7926	36	33	H to VH
Uruguay	Americas	0.8889	0.7719	0.6967	0.7858	34	34	H to VH
Greece	Europe	0.8194	0.8867	0.6439	0.7833	43	35	H to VH
Cyprus	Asia	0.7847	0.8083	0.7279	0.7736	64	36	H to VH
Slovenia	Europe	0.7986	0.8923	0.6232	0.7714	21	37	None
Belarus	Europe	0.7361	0.8681	0.6881	0.7641	49	38	H to VH
Kazakhstan	Asia	0.8681	0.8388	0.5723	0.7597	33	39	H to VH
Lithuania	Europe	0.7986	0.8323	0.6293	0.7534	23	40	None

Table 2. Net Readiness Index (Dutta & Lanvin, 2020)

Rank	Country/Economy	Score	Income group	Region
1	Sweden	82.75	High-income	Europe
2	Denmark	82.19	High-income	Europe
3	Singapore	81.39	High-income	Asia & Pacific
4	Netherlands	81.37	High-income	Europe
5	Switzerland	80.41	High-income	Europe
6	Finland	80.16	High-income	Europe
7	Norway	79.39	High-income	Europe
8	United States	78.91	High-income	The Americas
9	Germany	77.48	High-income	Europe
10	United Kingdom	76.27	High-income	Europe
11	Luxembourg	75.27	High-income	Europe
12	Australia	75.09	High-income	Asia & Pacific
13	Canada	74.92	High-income	The Americas
14	Korea, Rep.	74.60	High-income	Asia & Pacific
15	Japan	73.54	High-income	Asia & Pacific
16	New Zealand	73.27	High-income	Asia & Pacific
17	France	73.18	High-income	Europe
18	Austria	72.92	High-income	Europe
19	Ireland	72.13	High-income	Europe
20	Belgium	70.67	High-income	Europe
21	Iceland	70.55	High-income	Europe
22	Hong Kong (China)	70.52	High-income	Asia & Pacific
23	Estonia	70.32	High-income	Europe
24	Israel	69.81	High-income	Europe
25	Spain	67.31	High-income	Europe
26	Malta	66.73	High-income	Europe
27	Slovenia	66.58	High-income	Europe
28	Czech Republic	66.33	High-income	Europe
29	Lithuania	64.70	High-income	Europe
30	United Arab Emirates	64.42	High-income	Arab States
31	Portugal	64.40	High-income	Europe
32	Italy	63.69	High-income	Europe
33	Poland	61.80	High-income	Europe
34	Malaysia	61.43	Upper-middle-income	Asia & Pacific
35	Slovakia	60.78	High-income	Europe
36	Cyprus	60.67	High-income	Europe
37	Latvia	60.47	High-income	Europe
38	Qatar	60.26	High-income	Arab States
39	Hungary	60.05	High-income	Europe
40	China	58.44	Upper-middle-income	Asia & Pacific
41	Saudi Arabia	57.97	High-income	Arab States
42	Bahrain	57.59	High-income	Arab States
43	Croatia	55.94	High-income	Europe
44	Oman	55.33	High-income	Arab States
45	Greece	55.20	High-income	Europe
46	Bulgaria	55.03	Upper-middle-income	Europe
47	Uruguay	54.87	High-income	The Americas
48	Russian Federation	54.23	Upper-middle-income	CIS
49	Romania	54.16	High-income	Europe
50	Chile	54.06	High-income	The Americas

Figure 7. Classification of EU countries in terms of ICT contribution to Gross Domestic Product (European Commission, 2018)

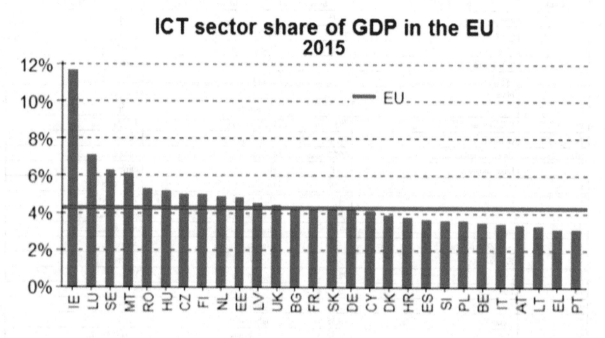

Figure 8. Amount of investment in research and development of computerization in the business sector in 2016 (European Commission, 2019)

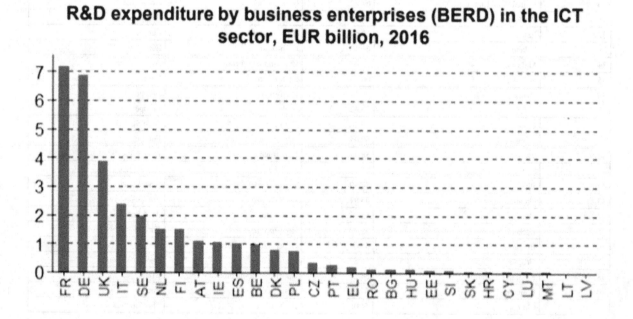

Figure 9. EU funding for computerization research and development in 2014-2018 (European Commission, 2019)

EU funding by Member State, cumulated values, 2014-2018, in EUR million

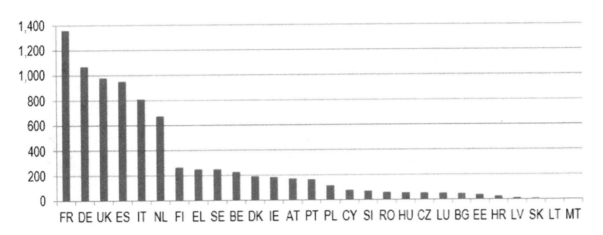

Using 42 indicators, the EU identified 34 regions that were considered advanced cities in terms of their IT, as illustrated in Figure 10.

As Figure 10 indicates, the three main centers are located in London, Paris, and Munich, while other notable centers are located in Western Europe, Sweden, and Finland. It is notable that the centers are grouped in a short distance from each other. This is reminiscent of the large number of U.S. pharmaceutical companies grouped together in the small state of New Jersey. Whether it is a group of automotive companies centered around Detroit, Michigan or ICT companies in Silicon Valley and Silicon Beach, California, in this way the best and brightest in computer science have an easy way of communicating face-to-face, which promotes rapid access to the latest knowledge (directly and indirectly) and developmental policies as well as employment opportunities. Unfortunately, the map shows that Poland does not contain any of the 34 advanced computer centers.

Three main activities were used to score the quality of advanced IT centers:

- The amount of R&D expenditure available in a given center,
- The number of innovations developed in a given center,
- The number of new business people investing in R&D ICT.

Furthermore, each of these activities were scored according to three characteristics:

- The number of researchers concentrated in a given locality,
- The number of international relations (foreign researchers, foreign companies, foreign investors),
- The quality of networked contacts (intensity and quality of communications on a global scale, foreign co-parenting, location of international collaborators).

Figure 10. Advanced IT centers in the EU (European Commission, 2014)

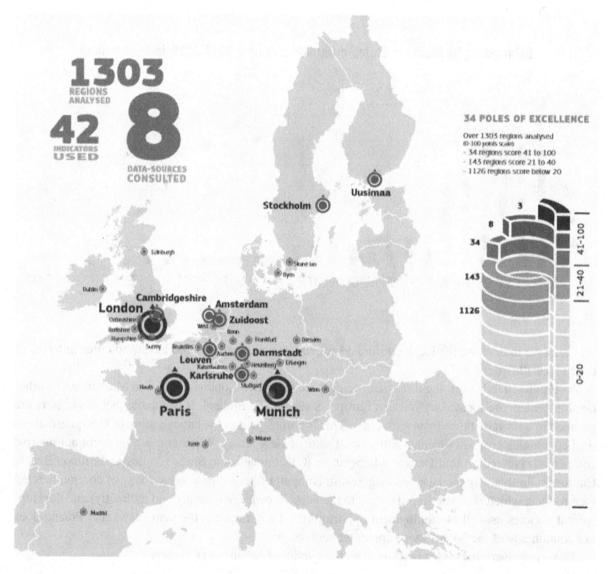

The 2015 EU assessment of what countries were prepared to apply eAdministration in a typical digital market in Europe were based on the considerations shown in Figure 11 (European Commission, 2015).

The criteria used to determine the level of computerization needed to establish a single digital market in Europe were the following:

- **Penetration** means the use of online eGovernment services.
- **Satisfaction** includes a user's overall assessment of their experience and whether their expectations were met. On one hand, this criterion was included in order to understand the ability of public administrations to meet the wants and needs of citizens in implementing attractive services, and on the other, it was used to find out the various causes of non-penetration.
- **Digitization** measures the efficiency and effectiveness of internal public administration procedures.

Figure 11. Criteria to determine the level of computerization needed to establish a single digital market in Europe (European Commission, 2015)

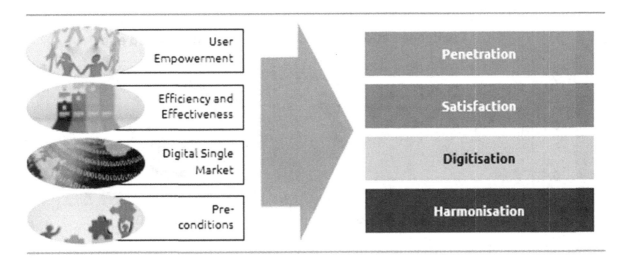

- **Harmonization** is an indicator of the ability of public administrations to coordinate innovative activities, harmonize the supply of eGovernment services to reduce barriers to use, exploit economies of scale, and support the Digital Single Market in Europe.

When comparing penetration with user satisfaction, four scenarios can be identified:

1. **Discovering eGovernment**: Low satisfaction levels and low penetration levels can be signs of an eGovernment that needs further development. Considerable efforts are required for an eGovernment to reach maturity. These typically include (a) adopting more structured innovation policies and plans that must be implemented and (b) not forgetting to take a citizen-centered approach.
2. **Challenged eGovernment**: A low level of satisfaction with a high level of penetration may indicate an eGovernment that finds it challenging to providing citizens with services that meet their needs. Future actions should include a more citizen-centered approach.
3. **Hidden eGovernment**: A high level of satisfaction with a low level of penetration indicates that, while a eGovernment is able to offer high-quality services, they may be under-utilizing those services to capitalize on their investment.
4. **Market-oriented eGovernment**: A high level of penetration and satisfaction indicates an eGovernment's ability to meet the needs of users in a market approach where citizens use and appreciate online services.

Figure 12 shows the assessment of EU countries in these four scenarios.

To understand a country's ability to use ICT to increase the efficiency of its eAdministrative processes, penetration with digitization is compared. Four scenarios are possible (Figure 13):

- **Non-consolidated eGovernment**: Low digitization and low penetration levels characterize administrations that are not yet taking advantage of ICT but intend to do so in the future.

Figure 12. Assessment of penetration and satisfaction with eAdministration in EU countries in 2015 (European Commission, 2015)

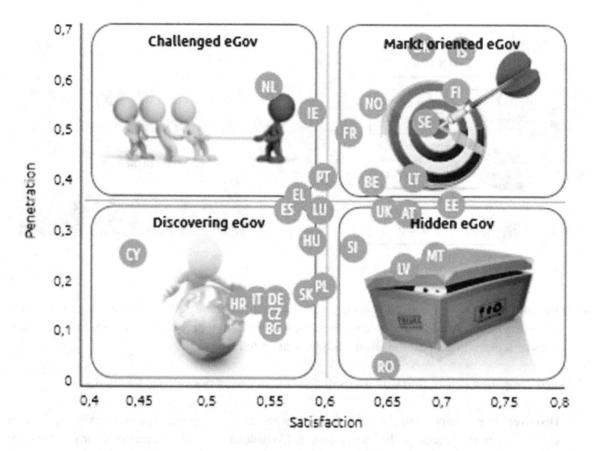

- **Unexploited eGovernment**: A low level of digitization combined with a high level of penetration may indicate an administration that has mainly digitized its interface but not its back end. For this reason, these countries have a low level of efficiency in managing their resources. Such administrations could take advantage of the high use of eGovernment services over the Internet.
- **Expendable eGovernment**: A high level of digitization with low penetration levels may suggest a scenario where, although process innovation has been carried out efficiently, it is still necessary to increase the number of online users, which currently prevents the administration from reaping potential benefits.
- **Fruitful eGovernment**: A high level of digitization and penetration points to a successful innovation process in which public organizations have achieved an efficient way of working.

Figure 13 shows the assessment of each EU country in these four scenarios.

Comparing satisfaction with digitization processes enables a country to assess their ability (a) to lead an internal innovation process without overlooking the needs of citizens and (b) to maintain an internal and external balance. Four scenarios have been identified:

Figure 13. Penetration and digitization for integrating eAdministration in EU countries in 2015. Poland is at the lowest level of development of the eAdministration (European Commission, 2015)

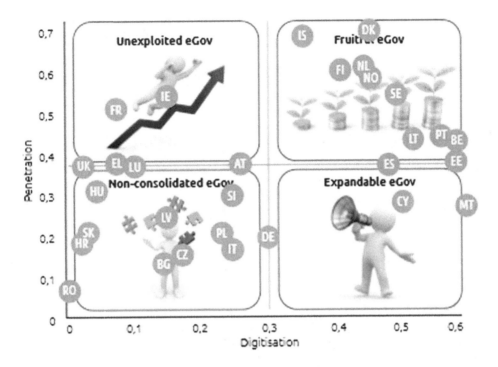

- **Early eGovernment**: A low level of digitization and satisfaction indicates that a public administration is having difficulties in developing eGovernment services that meet users' needs and in generating a high level of efficiency in digitizing internal processes. For these governments, it is vital to understand whether contributing factors are exogenous or endogenous.
- **Narrow e-Government**: Low digitization and high levels of satisfaction suggest that, while citizens may believe that the quality of online services is high, the extent to which the digitization of internal processes supports these online services is limited.
- **Growing e-Government**: A high level of digitization combined with low levels of satisfaction shows that, although an e-Government places strong emphasis on the digitization of internal processes, there is no strong correlation with user needs. Increasing user satisfaction would lead to another scenario.
- **Fulfilling e-Government**: A high level of both digitization and satisfaction indicates a well-developed administration where the digitization process serves as an example for others and where the services offered meet the needs of the user.

Figure 14 shows the assessment of each EU country in these four scenarios.

Figure 14. Penetration and digitization assessments of EU eAdministrations in 2015 (European Commission, 2015)

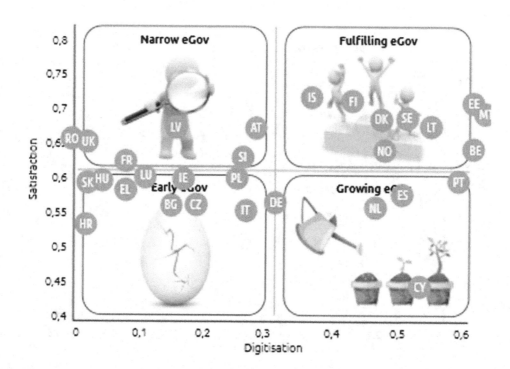

COMPUTERIZATION CONFIGURATIONS

The computerization of the state does not begin with advanced configurations; rather, it is preferably implemented in stages. Moreover, not all state entities (e.g., municipalities, cities, counties, and provinces) are simultaneously computerized: Typically, some entities become more developed than others, and the entities may differ in regard to what state configurations they implement (see Table 3).

For a democratic state, a standard strategy adopted for all state configurations is the development of a Constitution on the Application of Technology in Society (CATS), which is approved by councils of local governments as well as the parliament or congress (in the case of Poland, the Sejm). If a parliament is unable to pass some version of a CATS, then local governments may vote on their own versions; however, if a national CATS is later approved, the local versions will have to be updated.

An example of a CATS is as follows:

1. Robots can only be used for work with a high risk of danger to humans.
2. Automation may not eliminate jobs unless (a) the automating company can guarantee another job after training or (b) it can guarantee an annuity for redundant workers for the next ten years or until the employee retires (as long as the time until retirement is less than ten years).
3. Computerization may not eliminate jobs unless (a) the computerizing company can guarantee the impacted employee another form of work after training or (b) it can guarantee an annuity for

Table 3. Typology of state configurations

State	Intention	Key Technology	User Role
Offline (OFSC)	Maintain status quo.	Paper	Passive
Online (ONSC)	Reduce bureaucracy and office time for business and bring business closer to consumers	A screen with a mouse and keyboard connected to the Internet	Active
Integrated (ITSC)	Reduce lead time and multifaceted transactions; facilitate business entry into the Digital Single Market with its goods and services	Joint State Registers and National Computing Network (NCN)	Active
Informed (INSC)	Use resources effectively	Big Data, Universal interfaces	Involved
Mobile (MOSC)	Keep operations up-to-date	Smartphones	Whenever, anywhere
Knowledgeable (KNSC)	Improve situational assessments in the context of the good of humanism	Digital libraries	Aroused curiosity
Smart Cities (SMCC)	Improve infrastructure monitoring	Internet of Things, 5G	Fear of inability to repair
Wise (WISC)	Balance the development of civilization	Green apps	Belief in humanism

redundant workers for the next ten years or until the employee retires (as long as the time until retirement is less than ten years).

4. Computing centers are legally obliged to protect personal data.
5. Social networks cannot profile users and sell their data.
6. Social networks must not conduct political marketing and political discussions.
7. Media promoting hatred and discord cannot operate in certain domains.
8. Political discussions (not political marketing) may be conducted on specialized platforms whose owner is legally responsible for the quality of those discussions and for ensuring that profiling of participants is prohibited.
9. The creation and dissemination of knowledge must be based on the following rights (according to UNESCO's findings) (United Nations Educational, Scientific and Cultural Organization, 2005):
   a. Cultural diversity,
   b. Equal access to education,
   c. Universal access to information (in the public domain),
   d. Freedom of expression,
10. eNews along with local news may be available provided that paper copies are printed, which not only serve as carriers of local news but also as a "glue" connecting residents and orienting them towards the common good.
11. The Internet of Things (IoT) can be used in so-called "smart towns" and "smart villages" provided that there are regulations to ensure safety and reliability. Smart towns and villages must have a disaster or cybersecurity plan that is approved by the relevant authorities.
12. Management in a given area must have a certificate of training in the application of CATS and in its professional ethics.

13. Intelligence and counter-intelligence services can only digitally monitor citizens with a court issued warrant. The parliament must supervise this.
14. Other rules suitable for the specific state entity.

Offline State Configuration (OFSC)

- **Intention**: Maintain the *status quo* with paper-oriented information technologies.
- **Strategy**: Keep information systems in good condition with legal and technical assistance; maintain computers (without networking); maintain the use the Internet, subject to the development and approval of a CATS adapted to the area(s) concerned.

Business companies, health care, education, and infrastructure (energy, water, sewers, garbage, roads, bridges, railways, and others) as well as cinemas, theatres, museums, and media all develop their own form of computerization, which is implemented via solutions created in corporate headquarters, among other places. However, in this configuration, government administrations do not use computerization; rather, they develop and approve a CATS. Nonetheless, some localities may want to bring in business at all costs in order to provide their residents with jobs. Indeed, some even allow their land to become a landfill for other countries (e.g., in Nigeria). What will become of such localities when factories are automated?

OFSCs are useful in peripheral villages, towns, municipalities, and counties. The OFSC architecture is shown in Figure 15.

The Online State Configuration (ONSC)

- **Intention**: Reduce bureaucracy and time spent in offices by employees and bring business closer to consumers.
- **Strategy**: Develop e-services in trade, healthcare, and government administration based on the requirements of the digital common European market.

One can expand the range of online services provided by businesses to consumers in the eCommerce system. However, eAdministration and ePatient systems are developed by various private software companies on different servers using different clouds and formats, with separate systems for profiling, cybercrime, and cyberwars. Although agencies and companies use the Internet, it is a public network that can easily be hacked or destroyed by cybercrime and cyberwar. The ONSC model is illustrated in Figure 16.

The European Commission has adopted the principle that there is no uniform eAdministration solution for member states. Instead, it recommends 20 essential services, 12 for citizens, and 8 for businesses, as illustrated in Table 4.

The state of progress in the EU is measured via a four-stage process:

- Stage 1 - Publish administration information
- Stage 2 - One-way citizen/business interactions with the office
- Stage 3 - Two-way citizen/business interactions with the office

● Stage 4 - Full checkout (delivery/fee)

Figure 15. The Offline State Configuration (OSC) Architecture

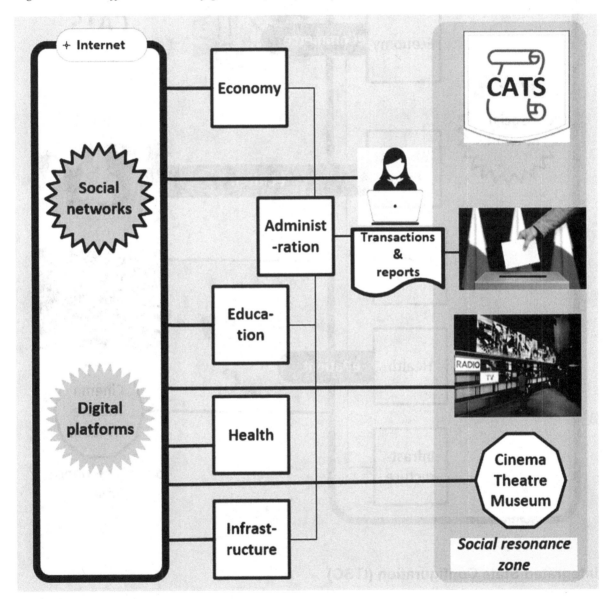

Much of this progress in eAdmininistations took place at the beginning of the 21st century when the EU had not yet adopted many countries from Central Europe. It can be assumed that the countries of the so-called "Old Europe" have advanced through these four stages while the countries of so-called "New Europe" are at stage 1 and sometimes stage 2.

Figure 16. The online state configuration architecture (ONSC)

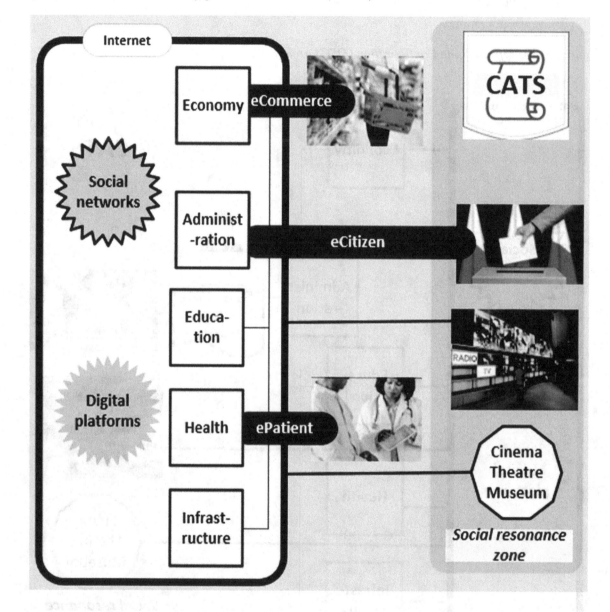

Integrated State Configuration (ITSC)

- **Intention**: Reduce lead time and multifaceted documents and facilitate business entry into the digital common European market.
- **Strategy**: Develop online services in many sectors of the country, aiming at greater penetration, user satisfaction, and harmonization with the remaining applications; develop services in line with EU requirements for the development of the Digital Single Market in Europe.

The ITSC model is shown in Figure 17.

Table 4. A standard list of online e-services in the European Union

No	Public Services for Citizens	Stage of Advancement in the 21st Century
1	Taxes on income (declarations, notifications, etc.)	4
2	Finding a job (at labor offices)	3
3	Social assistance • Unemployment benefits • Family allowances • Medical expenses (reimbursement of fees or otherwise) • Student scholarships	4
4	Personal documents (driver's licenses, passports)	3
5	Automobile registrations (new, used, imported)	4
6	Planning applications (sites, construction, etc.)	4
7	Police reports (e.g., on theft)	3
8	Book loans from public libraries	3
9	Certificates (e.g., birth certificates, marriage certificates)	3
10	Enrolling in college	4
11	Social records (e.g., changes of address)	3
12	Healthcare services (e.g., hospital registration, searching for an available specialist, e-mailing a doctor)	4
	Public services for business	
13	Social charges for employees	4
14	Business taxation (declarations, notifications)	4
15	Value added tax (VAT) (declarations and notifications)	4
16	Registration for a new enterprise	4
17	Sending data	3
18	Customs declarations	4
19	Environmental permits	4
20	Public purchases	3

The EU's requirements for the development of the Digital Single Market (DSM) consist of the following:

- Connecting Europe Facility (CEF), which includes the following EU-wide harmonized elements:
  - eSignatures allow lawyers, judges, citizens, and businesses to create and verify electronic signatures.
  - eIDs enable users to legally authenticate their identity on a platform from anywhere in the EU via the eIDAS network (identification in EU networks).
  - eDelivery provides a secure and reliable solution for the electronic exchange of information between citizens, businesses, governments, and judicial authorities.
  - eTranslation is a machine translation service for 24 official EU languages for judicial entities and users across Europe.

Figure 17. The Integrated State Configuration Architecture (ITSC) (abbreviations explained in text): The European portals deal with Europe's cultural heritage, while the eJustice portal concerns judiciary services

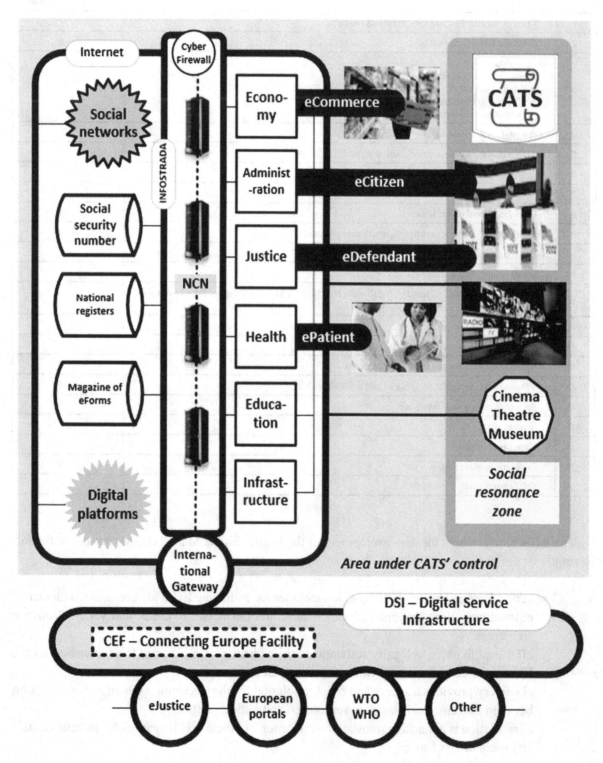

Figure 18. The European eJustice portal website within the Digital Single Market

- Digital Service Infrastructure (DSI) includes networks (5G), servers (including supercomputers), software, the Internet of Things, the digital cloud, and Big Data.

For Poland to benefit from the Digital Single Market in Europe, it must launch the following:

- A National Computing Network (NCN) in the form of nationally deployed servers on which all eAdministration, eHealth, and eCommerce services will be run, ensuring their reliable functioning and digital security with the Cyber Shield system.
- A Private National Telecommunications Network (INFOSTRADA), which is necessary because the data in the National Information System (NIS) complex cannot be carried out on a public Internet network.
- A Gateway between INFOSTRDA and the EU Digital Service Infrastructure.

Poland is behind in computerization development because it lacks a National Computing Network and it outsources processing services to various private companies on their servers, most recently via trendy digital clouds. In addition, Poland commissions software development from increasingly different and sometimes random software companies, which win bids for services. In this way, solutions are patchy, ad-hoc, and incompatible. In any case, they are not based on EU requirements.[8]

An example of European computerization is the eJustice portal, which helps citizens, businesses, lawyers, and judges find answers to legal questions. For example, suppose that an Italian traveling in Germany needs a lawyer; that a French entrepreneur wants to search the Hungarian property register; or that an Estonian judge has a question about the Spanish judicial system. All these questions can be answered in the 23 official EU languages on the European eJustice Portal (Figure 18). The portal, which

Figure 19. The Polish eJustice portal

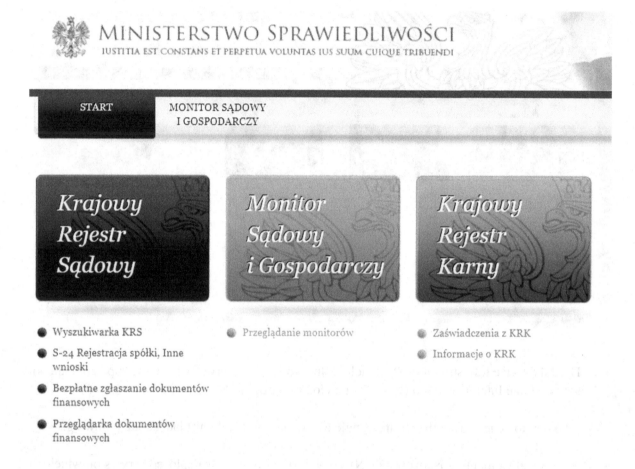

contains more than 30,000 pages of content, includes a large amount of information and links on laws and practices in all EU countries. Information on legal aid, training for judicial staff, small claims in Europe, and videoconferencing are available as well as links to traditional databases, online bankruptcies, business, and land registers. The portal also contains user-friendly forms for various court proceedings.

Comparing the European and Polish eJustice portals (Figures 18 and 19, respectively), can they not be harmonized with each other?

Configuration of the Informed State (INSC)

- **Intention**: Support the effective acquisition of resources.
- **Strategy**: Help users cope with the flood of information and chaos by establishing a universal interface for online systems that will facilitate access to essential information portals, including Big Data of various types.

Currently, only very efficient users can cope well with access to various sources of information in the world. Most people use limited sources of information, and many do not even know what information is

Figure 20. The Informed State Configuration (INSC) architecture

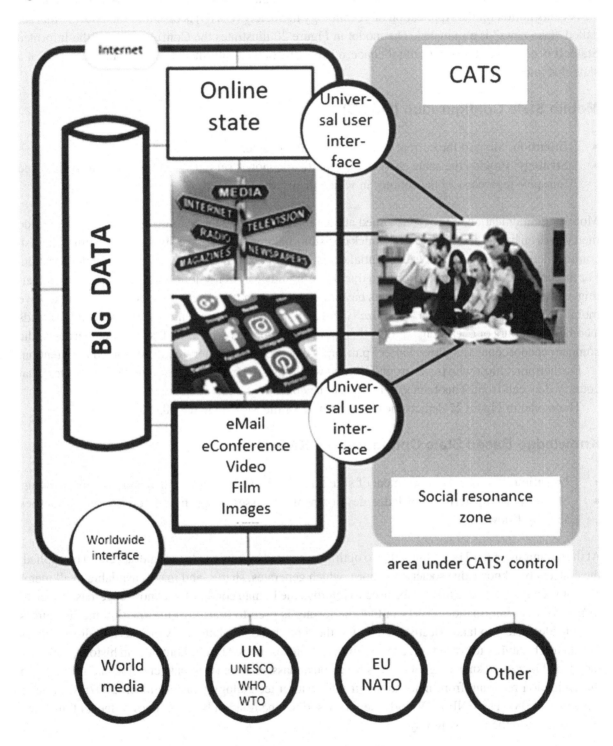

available in the world. Of course, Google can search for them, but is there any certainty that Google will give them a neutral list of sources? Furthermore, will Google instruct users on how to use the sources?

A Constitution for the Application of Technology in Society (CATS) is essential for assuring that so-called "fake news" is eliminated. The model in Figure 20 illustrates the Configuration of the Informed State. It is understood that the central concern is the creation an informed society, not the creation of a state that knows "a lot."

Mobile State Configuration (MOSC)

- **Intention**: Support the current activities of active people.
- **Strategy**: Provide the same charges for mobile telephones services—for example, in Poland and Europe—regardless of the country in which the user is located.

Mobile communication in the EU is aimed at meeting the needs of the younger generations, who pride themselves on living "fast"; however, is quick decision-making an advantage? In the 20th century, English commanders were advised to make essential decisions the next day so as to assure careful deliberation. For the same reason, some have proposed that there should be a twenty-four hour waiting period for getting a tattoo in order to assure that clients have thought through their decision. Companies want to have mobile workers because they can "mobilize" them 24/7 without interruption, which significantly extends a company's hours of operation. On the other hand, at companies such as Volkswagen in Germany, the company cannot contact employees after 5 p.m. on Friday, except for matters requiring immediate attention.

Furthermore, most who travel around Europe would like to be charged the same fees no matter what country they call from. This forces them to face the concept of a mobile Europe.

The model in Figure 21 depicts the Configuration of the Mobile State (MOSC).

Knowledge-Based State Configuration (KNSC)

- **Intention**: Improve the assessment of situations for the good of humanism and decision-making.
- **Strategy**: Computerize knowledge development processes using digital collections of libraries and Big Knowledge.

At the beginning of the 21st century, due to optimism created by how easily the Internet could be applied, the concept of a knowledge society was born, which generates, shares, and makes available to all members of society knowledge that can be used to improve the human condition. A knowledge-based society differs from an information society in that the former is used to transform information into resources that enable society to take effective action. On the other hand, the latter only creates and disseminates raw data. The ability to collect and analyze information has existed throughout human history; however, the idea of a modern knowledge society is based on a massive increase in data creation and information dissemination resulting from innovations in information technology (Castelfranchi, 2007; Vallima & Hoffman, 2008). The UNESCO World Report describes the relation between knowledge and information societies in the following way:

The rise of a global information society spawned by the new technology revolution must not overshadow the fact that it is valuable only as a means to achieve genuine knowledge societies. The growth of networks alone will not be able to lay the groundwork for the knowledge society. While information is a

Figure 21. Mobile State Configuration (MOSC) architecture

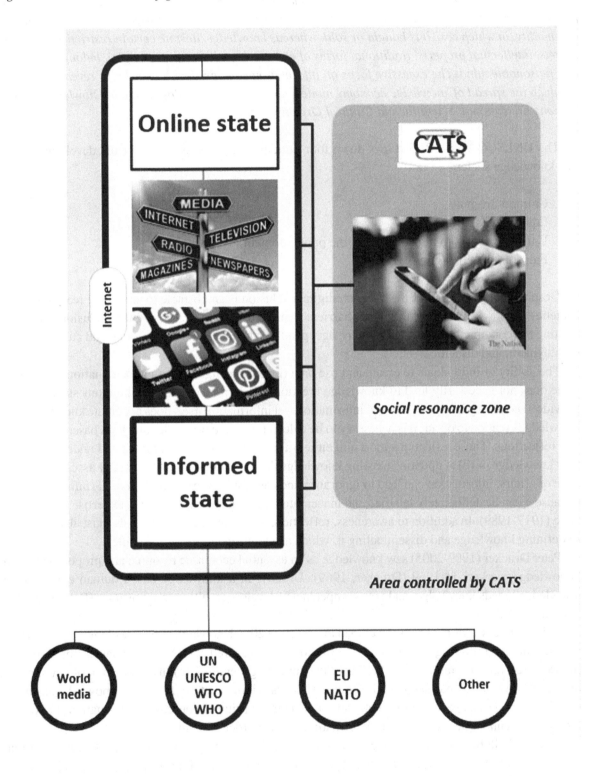

knowledge-generating tool, it is not knowledge itself. Emerging from the desire to exchange knowledge by making its transmission more efficient, information remains a fixed stabilized form of knowledge, pegged to time and to the user – news is either fresh or it is not. Thus, information is in many cases a commodity, in which case it is bought or sold, whereas knowledge, despite certain restrictions (defence secrets, intellectual property, traditional forms of esoteric knowledge, for example), belongs of right to any reasonable mind. The excessive focus on information compared with knowledge reveals the extent to which the spread of knowledge economy models has changed our relationship to knowledge (United Nations Educational, Scientific and Cultural Organization, 2005).

The UNESCO World Report lays down four principles that are essential for the development of a just knowledge society:

- Cultural diversity,
- Equal access to education,
- Universal access to information (in the public domain),
- Freedom of expression.

Despite the broad reach of the Internet, digital exclusion is an obstacle to achieving real knowledge societies worldwide. Among the many barriers that contribute to global digital exclusion are issues relating to economic resources, geography, age, gender, language, education, social and cultural origin, employment, and disability.

The ability of individuals to create and use data (including Big Data) on a local, national, or global scale does not necessarily lead to knowledge creation. Modern media and publications such as books provide a seemingly infinite amount of information, yet information itself does not create knowledge. For knowledge creation to occur, it is necessary to be able to formulate principles and laws based on substantive reflections. These reflections must aim either (a) at developing an awareness and understanding of new knowledge or (b) at updating existing knowledge. Without thinking and critically assessing a given state of affairs, information can lead to ignorance and can result in the formation of harmful knowledge because it can be deliberately falsified and inaccurate. This was the case of social expertise in the Soviet Bloc (1917-1989). In addition to awareness, reflection, and evaluation, individuals must also be skilled in defining knowledge and disseminating it, which academic centers specialize in.

Peter Drucker (1909-2005) saw knowledge as an essential economic resource and proposed the term "knowledge worker" in 1969 (Drucker, 1969). Usually, in a knowledge-based human environment, knowledge breeds knowledge, and new competencies develop, resulting in innovation (Paavola & Hakkarainen, 2005).

Being impressed by the newly developed Internet, the 2005 Knowledge Societies Index (Table 5) took into account the following: (a) the wealth of the country, measured in GDP; (b) taxpayer capital (including expected years of training and the size of the younger generation; (c) the circulation of newspapers; and (d) the use of the Internet and telephones. This is a minimal set of criteria for knowledge, as if one could rely on newspapers, the Internet, and phone calls as primary sources of information. In point of fact, these technologies contribute to information on the border of chaos.

The 2019 Global Knowledge Index (United Nations Development Programme, 2019) is better than the 2005 UN Index because it takes into account criteria such as the following:

Table 5. The United Nation's Index of Knowledge Societies for 2005 (Department of Economic and Social Affairs, 2005)

Country Name	Assets Index	Expected Schooling	Young Pop. (<15)	News-papers per 1000 Pop.	Internet users per 10,000 Pop.	Phone +Cells
1 Norway	0.801	1.000	0.192	1.000	0.876	0.935
2 Sweden	0.749	0.907	0.124	0.755	1.000	0.960
3 Finland	0.714	0.981	0.125	0.772	0.887	0.805
4 Republic of Korea	0.683	0.870	0.237	0.666	0.963	0.682
5 Denmark	0.656	0.824	0.140	0.521	0.894	0.898
6 Netherlands	0.652	0.917	0.142	0.516	0.883	0.803
7 Japan	0.648	0.759	0.012	0.983	0.782	0.706
8 Australia	0.645	0.991	0.208	0.494	0.840	0.695
9 United Kingdom	0.644	0.944	0.146	0.556	0.737	0.836
10 USA	0.618	0.852	0.231	0.357	0.962	0.687
11 Israel	0.614	0.806	0.442	0.489	0.523	0.813
12 New Zealand	0.611	0.954	0.269	0.362	0.844	0.624
13 Switzerland	0.602	0.833	0.086	0.569	0.610	0.913
14 Germany	0.590	0.852	0.039	0.525	0.717	0.817
15 Austria	0.566	0.806	0.077	0.499	0.713	0.738
16 Canada	0.551	0.824	0.154	0.264	0.894	0.621
17 France	0.529	0.861	0.151	0.367	0.545	0.719
18 Belgium	0.519	0.917	0.101	0.266	0.570	0.742
19 Ireland	0.502	0.815	0.241	0.249	0.470	0.735
20 Italy	0.482	0.815	0.000	0.170	0.613	0.814
21 Malaysia	0.466	0.556	0.636	0.262	0.555	0.320
22 Czech Republic	0.464	0.694	0.069	0.427	0.444	0.686
23 Estonia	0.460	0.769	0.097	0.293	0.569	0.573
24 Greece	0.427	0.815	0.027	0.254	0.266	0.771
25 Spain	0.419	0.870	0.025	0.163	0.268	0.770
26 Chile	0.406	0.639	0.447	0.160	0.411	0.374
26 Uruguay	0.406	0.704	0.346	0.494	0.203	0.283
28 Hungary	0.389	0.694	0.077	0.310	0.271	0.594
29 Poland	0.383	0.796	0.152	0.185	0.398	0.383
30 Slovakia	0.373	0.648	0.171	0.307	0.276	0.461
31 Latvia	0.358	0.667	0.077	0.415	0.228	0.404
32 Bolivia	0.344	0.676	0.814	0.086	0.051	0.093
33 Mexico	0.338	0.500	0.637	0.160	0.167	0.226
34 Croatia	0.335	0.537	0.085	0.187	0.311	0.557
35 Costa Rica	0.328	0.380	0.558	0.148	0.333	0.220
36 Bulgaria	0.327	0.611	0.041	0.432	0.136	0.417
37 Brazil	0.318	0.676	0.465	0.060	0.138	0.249
38 Trinidad & Tobago	0.307	0.491	0.355	0.202	0.180	0.308
39 Panama	0.294	0.583	0.548	0.098	0.067	0.175
40 Tunisia	0.283	0.704	0.485	0.045	0.085	0.099
41 Colombia	0.275	0.463	0.595	0.070	0.075	0.169
42 Egypt	0.250	0.370	0.673	0.060	0.043	0.102
43 Madagascar	0.200	0.000	1.000	0.000	0.000	0.000
44 Ukraine	0.176	0.491	0.097	0.084	0.025	0.182
45 Republic of Moldova	0.175	0.333	0.250	0.094	0.054	0.141

- Pre-school education,
- Technical training and other vocational training,
- Higher education,
- Research, development, and innovation,
- Information and communication technologies,
- Economics,
- Knowledge-friendly environment

A knowledge index based on these criteria characterizes the potential of a society to create and use knowledge; however, it is possible that countries with a high potential for knowledge use it badly. For example, the United States is in 3rd place in the 2019 aggregate index (behind Switzerland and Finland) (United Nations Development Programme, 2019). Nonetheless, despite the fact that it is the world's leading power in research, development, and innovation and is the country with the highest number of Nobel prizes every year, it is in a distant 28th place with respect to the criterion 'knowledge-friendly environment'. Does this perhaps reflect the fact that American society has been highly polarized during the past several years (2017-2020)?

The situation of Luxembourg is very significant.[9] In the overall index, it ranks very highly in 5th place, and according to the criterion of having a knowledge-friendly environment, it is in 8th place; however, according to the criterion of research, development, and innovation, it is in 20th place (United Nations Development Programme, 2019). Having a friendly environment explains why Luxembourg is in 5th place according to the overall index. In other words, citizens of this country know how to use knowledge (and are able to do so with the help of ICT, where they rank second, only behind Singapore), as evidenced by their having the highest GDP (nominal) per capita at roughly $110,000 dollars, which is higher than Switzerland's approximately $82,000 and the US's $65,000 per capita (International Monetary Fund, 2020). This means that, thanks to their level of knowledge, a Luxembourg citizen can produce almost 1.7 times more money than a resident of the United States, 2.5 times more than a German resident, and 7.5 times more than a resident of Poland. Poland's scores in this global index are low, with its lowest score in ICT use where it ranks 44th place in the world (United Nations Development Programme, 2019).

These knowledge indices refer to society as a whole and are based on a culture of knowledge. Raising the culture of knowledge in society to a higher level is a long process. The question is, to what extent can the computerization of knowledge increase this culture of knowledge? The Knowledge-based State Configuration model answers this question in Figure 22.

In our current age where all forms of knowledge are being digitized, it can be hoped that over the next few years, Google will scan all the roughly 130 million books that have ever been published. Moreover, most academic libraries are being converted into a digital format, and several business platforms are being developed to sell digitized knowledge. The U.S. Library of Congress is also digitizing their works, as are many organizations that publish scientific articles. Conservatively, it can be estimated that, by 2050, almost all recorded knowledge will be available to users in digital formats.

However, how much will consumers of digital knowledge actually benefit from this increased access? Will they merely scan more digital pages with their eyes? In some Asian countries, students are assessed based upon who can memorize the most from a textbook. This is not the right path. On one hand, there are research and development centers that produce new knowledge and update old knowledge. On the other hand, there are users who need knowledge to help them solve practical problems here and now. This latter group does not have time to read everything that google offers for "sale".

Figure 22. The Knowledge-based State Configuration (KNSC) architecture

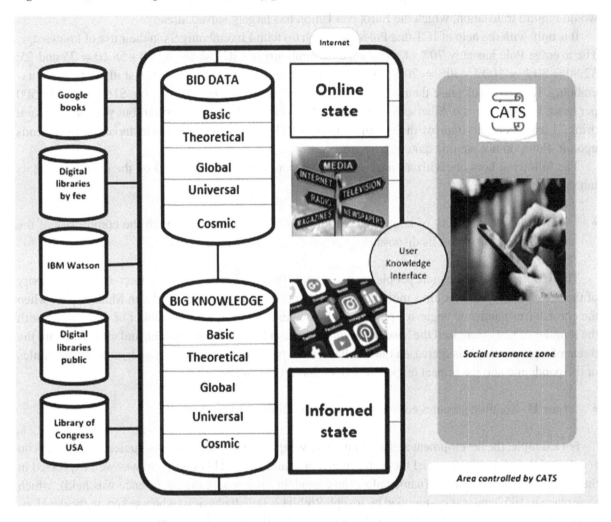

The solution is to develop Big Knowledge to aid the different kinds of *minds*, i.e., basic, theoretical, global, universal, and cosmic minds (for those interested in knowledge of the universe and travel to other planets). These minds correspond to Big Data sets and the collection of Great Wisdom. These should be developed along the lines of Wikipedia, i.e., by communities interested in knowledge. These communities would operate at local, national, and international level. Of course, these collections of knowledge are subject to factors such as the level of interest, cost, regulations, and ethics. The scope of each type of aforementioned knowledge is infinite; however, this can be managed by categorizing knowledge based upon metadata such as time, field, specialization, aspect, and domain, which would make it accessible to the average user. For example, suppose Big Theoretical Knowledge for the Polish user is developed by the Polish Academy of Sciences: Is such theoretical knowledge only useful for Poles but not for the French? Of course not.

It can be assumed, of course, that Poles have lived through events that may not interest the French and vice versa. Regardless, over time, the Big Knowledge of the French should be nearly equivalent with the Big Knowledge of the Poles, and such knowledge should complement each other. Another issue worth noting here is that the formulation of such knowledge involves different languages and, thus, would require translation, which the European Union has largely solved already.

It is only with the help of ICT that Poles can catch up with Luxembourgers in their use of knowledge. The average Pole has only 70% of an average Luxembourger's ICT skills (82.80 - 58.10 = 25 and 25: 82.80 = 30% or 100% - 30% = 70%). If Poles are able to raise their average ICT skills to that of Luxembourg, they could increase their productivity (in a big way), i.e., by 30% or from $15,000 to $19,500 per head. However, as the American saying goes, "you can lead a horse to water, but you can't make it drink." Luxembourgers improve their qualifications in ICT because their success in the economy depends upon it. Poles do not see this quite yet.

The following laws of civilization govern the development of a state based on the knowledge of its inhabitants:

- **Law I**: The complexity of knowledge about the ecosystem increases with the complexity of the knowledge reservoir at its disposal.

This law implies that the more people know, the more they become aware and reflect on the complexity of the ecosystem, which requires more knowledge to understand it. For example, in March 2020, when the coronavirus pandemic began to spread worldwide, knowledge about the number of cases along with the number of tests increased the awareness and reflection of leaders, the media, and citizens about the threat of a pandemic. This increased the emphasis on expanding tests to better understand the dynamics of the pandemic and the impact on people's lives and the economy.

- **Law II**: Cognition creates consequences that are difficult to predict.

For example, the development and use of nuclear weapons has resulted in anti-nuclear movements on account of their horrific potential for destroying people and cities. This sentiment was well expressed in the first Pugwash Conference (named after the Canadian town where the conference was held), which took place in 1957 and was co-founded by Joseph Rotblat, a Polish physicist who worked on the development of the atomic bomb. Rotblat would later be awarded the Nobel Peace Prize in 1995 for his efforts against nuclear weapons. The physicists who enthusiastically designed the A-bomb in Los Alamos did not anticipate that they would be the first to protest against its use. The same is true of the development of robotization and automation, which are impressive in design and require advanced knowledge; however, they have the frightening consequences of leading to a laborless economy and outcasting people. The world is waiting for prominent IT societies to act like the physicists. Let the voice of these computer scientists initiate the much needed dialogue on the subject.

- **Law III**: The accuracy and certainty of cognition increase according to the simplicity of the object or process it describes, and, contrariwise, decreases as the complexity of the item or process increases.

For example, systems for computerizing simple bureaucratic processes are accurate, reliable, and serve users well. Expert systems for complex decision processes, on the other hand, are sometimes too simplified.

- **Law IV**: Advances in state-of-the-art computerization, robotization, and automation are a source of ignorance among policymakers and users who rely on simplified marketing and extreme opinions of hidden lobbyists.

There has been an apparent belief among politicians and professionals that every advance in technology is positive. As a result, advances in information technology are considered positive, despite their negative impact on the state of humanism.

- **Law V**: The reservoir of knowledge has no saturation point.

For many millennia, knowledge of the world was based on superstition and predetermined dogma. This was undermined only a few hundred years ago, after the so-called Copernican Revolution in science in the 15th century. Hence, there is still a great deal to know. Furthermore, what was scientific truth in the 19th century has ceased to be so in the 20th and 21st centuries. An additional complication is the fact that each new piece of knowledge not only reduces chaos, but also creates new possibilities from the confusion that accompanies it. For example, the 2012 confirmation of the existence of the Higgs boson particle at the Large Hadron Collider near Geneva caused new chaos in views about the origin of the universe, which was well captured by one physicist who called this the "God particle."

The five laws of knowledge in civilization show that knowledge developed and used by society requires constant development, updates, training, and education so that members of society know what they are doing and why. Otherwise, they will not know if the information they access is credible or intentionally falsified. Every resident of the state should develop this art of reflection if they want to be satisfied and have success in life. To facilitate this development, the state should offer its full support.

Smart City Configuration (SMCC)

- **Intention**: Organize a city capable of monitoring and responding to traffic, telemedicine, energy, water, wastewater, garbage, and air quality.
- **Strategy**: Computerize urban processes using the Internet of Things (IoT) and 5G telecommunications.

The concept of a 360-degree smart city aims to be able to analyze every aspect of the city's infrastructure through computerization. The digital infrastructure of a smart city lays the groundwork for a network of partnerships focused on one goal: to create a smarter city. Smart cities aim not only to use technology to improve their operations but also to connect with citizens, businesses, and nonprofits in new ways.

Futurists have long imagined smart cities of the future, where satisfied residents and visitors thrive. These modern urban environments are buzzing with advanced multimodal communication systems, self-sufficient power grids, clean and safe neighborhoods, integrated services, and essential amenities. While some cities have made progress towards this bright future, cities and communities still face complex challenges, such as maintaining reliable infrastructure, controlling population growth and migration, and dealing with sustainability problems.

Smart city optimists typically note three advantages of smart cities:

- **Quality of life**: A positive quality of life includes improving every aspect of citizens' daily lives. From safe streets to green spaces and from reasonable commutes to access to art and culture, the smart city is said to create an environment that promotes the best living conditions in the city and minimizes the problems associated with city living. Smart cities are supposedly great places to live.

- **Economic competitiveness**: Cities have long been important centers of trade, using the proximity of so many diverse citizens to support an innovative economy. A smart city is supposed to be a business-friendly city, ensuring that jobs and tax revenues provide a healthy economic platform.

- **Sustainable development**: The smart city is supposed to ensure the promotion of economic growth and quality of life not only in the short term but also for future generations. Being a good environmental steward and promoting sustainable consumption of natural resources is part of the overall vision of a smart city.

Figure 23 presents a smart city configuration according to a concept developed by the European Union, which justifies the introduction of high-speed 5G telecommunications networks.

Figure 23. Smart City Configuration (SMCC) architecture (European Commission, 2020)

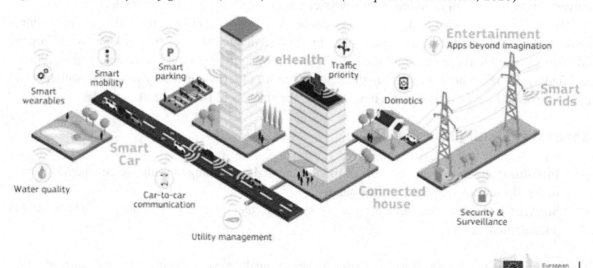

A 5G telecommunications network will provide virtually ubiquitous high bandwidth and low latency connectivity not only for individual users but also for connected facilities. Therefore, the future 5G infrastructure is expected to support a wide range of applications and sectors, including automated mobility applications, eHealth, power management, digital security applications, etc. 5G will also be the "eyes and ears" of AI systems, as it will ensure real-time data collection and analysis. At the same time, it will introduce a new dimension to the "cloud", enabling the distribution of calculations and memory throughout the infrastructure in places close to specific fixed and mobile installations (edge cloud and mobile edge processing).

A white paper by the European Commission and the 5G Public-Private Partnership (5GPPP) (2016) presents a series of 5G uses that are considered realistic for implementation in 2020. They should form the basis of a consolidated set of 5G requirements that will support a 5G standardization process.

- The automotive sector believes that 5G will be used for automated co-driving, allowing thousands of vehicles to exchange information with each other in real-time. Because of the lightning-fast data transmission time (low latency) of the 5G network, future connected cars will have a safety app that allows users to see the road far in front of vehicles ahead of them, which will help to avoid accidents. Road travel can become safer and more efficient as connected vehicles share real-time information amongst themselves. Furthermore, information about road conditions can allow drivers to change routes quickly. Ultimately, vehicles could become smart enough and react so quickly and reliably to network data that they could become autonomous and drive themselves. Traveling by train could be more productive or fun, as passengers traveling at 200 miles/hour on high-speed rails could work with 5G via cloud computing resources or receive their selection of high-definition videos.
- In the healthcare sector, 5G is intended to be useful for asset management and hospital interventions, remote monitoring robotics, and smart medicines. For example, 5G can improve the experience of surgeons using operational robots. Super high performance 5G data transmission means that a robot surgeon could immediately respond to the instructions or movements of a surgeon performing a virtual operation remotely. E-health apps can use wearable devices worn by patients at home to monitor parameters such as blood pressure, pulse, and respiratory rate. These devices can then securely and reliably transfer near real-time data to healthcare workers, who can quickly intervene (perhaps remotely) when needed. These applications can reduce healthcare costs by allowing some patients to stay outside hospitals and care facilities in their own homes.
- With respect to smart factories, 5G can be useful for critical process control, factory automation, remote control, enterprise communication, and corresponding parts and subassembly conveyor belts. This is often necessary for robot-based manufacturing processes, where detecting an incident may require an ultra-fast response from the network. Intelligent connected robots in the *Factory of the Future* can communicate with each other to increase production efficiency, reduce costs, and produce customized disposable products. Sensors in connected products can warn service centers promptly about the need for service or can be used to create new service-based businesses. It is assumed that employees equipped with augmented reality glasses (i.e., those that allow for interactions between virtual and real-world spaces) can function more efficiently.
- Regarding energy, 5G will be necessary to control access to the power grid. It can help energy companies balance supply and demand in the future when a growing share of energy will be generated from solar and wind (which are sometimes unpredictable). In addition, the ever-increasing number of electric vehicles creates diversified and unexpected energy demands.
- The media and entertainment sector will possibly use 5G to support ultra high fidelity media, live events, immersive and integrated media, collaborative media production, and cooperative games. For example, virtual reality games can be played on different continents, and football matches can be viewed in 3D using immersive lounge lenses that make it seem as if one were in a stadium. In a densely packed crowd at a sporting event, any spectator can use their device to watch or instantly view events from different points of view. Two-way interactive electronic games can be enriched with near instant high-capacity virtual reality information.

Indeed, a network dedicated to a single industry would not be economically attractive. 5G, however, offers a solution. Transforming networks into service platforms for different industries should aid the development of specialized advanced services supplied by various providers and operators.

The white paper by the EU and 5GPPP (2016) also sets out consolidated technical requirements for 5G networks that result from different use cases presented by vertical markets:

- Increase wireless capacity by a thousandfold.
- Connect 20 billion human-oriented devices.
- Connect 1 trillion objects on the Internet of Things (IoT).
- Save 90% of energy consumption.
- Protect up to ten years of battery life on IoT devices.
- Keep latency low, below 5 ms.
- Keep network reliability above 99.999% at all times.
- Allow for a connection density of up to 100/m2 devices, including strict territorial and population limits; also allow for a peak mobile terminal bandwidth of up to 1 Gbps.

These findings will be instrumental in targeting the standardization process that has just begun and is likely to be completed in the 2020s.

Several cities are undertaking plans to develop smart cities. One of them is the Italian town La Spezia, which has a population of about 95,000 and is located in northwestern Italy, in the Liguria region. Thanks to its location, in the past La Spezia Bay was chosen as a privileged place to establish military settlements and develop trade. Economically and socially, La Spezia has always been strongly characterized as an important port, which is one of Italy's most crucial economic activities (currently in third place). The bay and its surroundings (51 km^2 or 20 square miles) are a popular tourist destination and sites of unique natural landscapes.

The urban economy is also characterized by (a) vigorous shipbuilding activities, coordinated by one of Italy's most important maritime technology clusters (DLTM), (b) the presence of a university branch specializing in marine engineering, and (c) the presence of several national maritime research centers (CNR, ENEA, CSSN, INGV). The coal and gas power plants, which are some of Italy's largest, are another critical element that have shaped the city's economy, having 1,300 megawatts of installed capacity and producing more than 3% of Italy's total electricity.

The city of La Spezia developed their first strategic plan as early as 1999 and their second in 2012. They aim at developing a sustainable and intelligent smart city, which includes the following:

- An integrated mobility plan with several ongoing interventions on sustainable mobility and projects for the development of information mobility;
- An energy plan, which members of the Covenant of Mayors approved in 2012 and is considered a Sustainable Energy Action Plan (SEAP);
- A plan for implementing broadband and WiFi projects, with funding from the European Regional Development Fund (ERDF);
- Several urban regeneration plans and instruments (neighborhood agreements and projects integrated into the ERDF).

By 2020, the smart city's energy solution will be implemented:

Figure 24. The configuration of the smart city La Spezia in Italy 2020

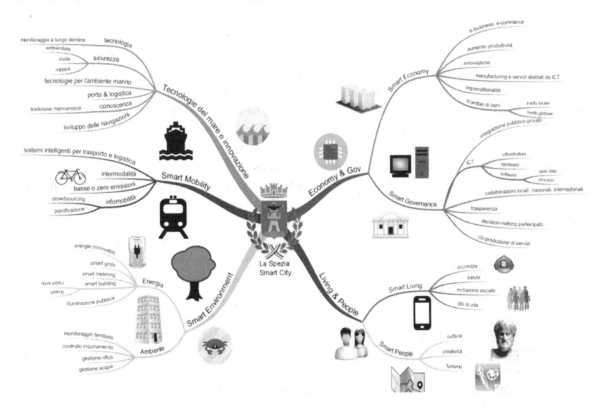

- Public lighting efficiency projects (ERDF 2007-2013);
- Photovoltaic (PV) systems on three public buildings;
- Interventions on window frames and envelopes of 7 school buildings;
- A pilot program of economic support to ensure free energy audits in private facilities, which is aimed at further interventions in energy efficiency;
- Agreements with La Spezia industry associations on the creation of an "energy ATM" for citizens (aimed at providing technical and financial guidance to facilitate private interventions in the field of energy efficiency and renewable energy sources);
- Remote management of urban heating systems (included in a more complex framework aimed at intelligently monitoring energy and emissions data);
- Regional database of private thermal installations.

As can be seen, envisioning the development of a smart city is easier than creating and implementing specific plans and solutions, despite how attractive certain visions can be, such as the one shown in Figure 24.

Rather than the concept of a smart city, the concept of a smart, post-industrial, 5G-based society was developed 50 years ago in Japan. The idea of an information society as Japan's post-industrial society was created by Yonei Masuda in 1971 (Masuda, 1981). In the second half of the 20th century, Japan was one of the most dynamic and influential countries in the world, and it looked as if the world would be operating under the rule of *Pax Niponnica* (Vogel, 1986). In the mid-1980s, Japanese high-tech exports to the United States far exceeded imports, with annual trade surpluses approaching $50 billion a year. Meanwhile, America's trade deficit had grown to $150 billion a year. By 1986, the United States had become the largest debtor nation in the world, and Japan had surpassed the United States and Saudi Arabia, becoming the world's largest creditor. In such a favorable climate for the development of Japan's industrial economy and society, Yonei Masuda saw far beyond the Industrial Revolution and founded the Information Society Institute. He would also be appointed executive director of the Japanese Institute for Computer Use Development in Tokyo. Here, in 1971, he developed the "Information Society Plan: Japan's National Goal for 2000". His plan was the result of his idealistic impression that computers would lead to a "Computopia," which he defined in his 1966 book with the same name.

In the 20th century, information technology was considered the driving force behind the entire economy in the US, France, England, and Poland, which was reflected in the creation of national plans for the development of information technology. For example, in Poland, this included the NIS (1970) and INFOSTRADA (1972), and in France, *Plan Calcul* (1966). Canada had a plan as well, *Telidon* (1981), and Sweden developed project *Terese*, which used telecommunications technology for regional development (in particular in the field of traffic control, information about local citizens, and health systems). In 1980, however, its scope was narrowed to distance learning and information systems for small businesses. Chile, at that time, had a more ambitious plan: Left-wing President Salvador Allende attempted to develop a centralized *Cybersyn* computer information system to plan the production and services of nationalized companies. This system was designed by the British-Canadian cyberneticist Stanford Beer. Allende's assassination in 1973 halted the use of the system in Chile, which returned to a market economy.

The 1971 Japanese plan aimed at the realization of a society flourishing with human intellectual creativity instead of material consumption. According to Masuda (1981), "[i]f the goal of industrial society is represented by volume consumption of durable consumer goods or realization of heavy mass consumption centering around motorization, information society may be termed as a society with highly intellectual creativity where *people may draw future designs on an invisible canvas and pursue and realize individual lives worth living*" (p. 3).

The following strategic computer communication systems were planned (terms date back to the 1970s):

1. A banking plan, in which administrative data should be made available by various government agencies, mainly the Ministry of International Trade and the Agency for Industry and Economic Planning.
2. A "computopolis" plan for a computerized city, which entailed the building of a new city with the following services:
   a. CATV: A multi-channel computer TV with two-way communication from homes,
   b. Local news,
   c. Shopping and leisure consultation,
   d. Emergency communication
   e. Medical care consultations for infants,
   f. Education,
   g. CVS (computerized vehicle system),
   h. Automated supermarkets (no maintenance staff: magnetic cards would be used, and fresh materials would be sent from manufacturers),

  i. Regional health control (disease prevention, health checks, and individual medical records of all residents, who would be checked twice a year),

  j. Regional cooling and heating systems.

3. A regional, remote control medical system with automated hospitals and emergency medical systems, which was particularly suitable for isolated islands using private health services over computer networks.

4. Computer education in experimental school districts to rationalize the work of the school office and individual educational counseling systems and to solve academic problems with the help of computers.

5. Pollution prevention systems in large regions for direct and indirect measurements, warnings, and control of gas emissions in cars, houses, factories, the atmosphere, oceans, and rivers.

6. A think-tank center containing all government institutes and centers in one large building equipped with advanced computer communication tools to facilitate the development of opinions and solutions.

7. The introduction of management information systems (MIS) in small enterprises.

8. Staff training centers, each with a capacity of around 1,000 young adults and seniors: The centers would not "retrain" these individuals, but rather help them discover and develop their potential.

9. A Computer Peace Corps to strengthen economic aid to developing countries through system engineers and programmers sent to developing countries.

Many of these strategic systems were implemented with some exceptions, such as the "Computopolis", the automated healthcare systems, and the automated supermarkets. However, all things considered, Masuda's assumptions about the potential of computer communication tools for the development of the Japanese Information Society by 1985 are debatable because even now, in 2020, Japan is still far from fulfilling his dream.

To be sure, today, in 2020, we can say that Masuda's vision of computer technology and social development is impressive. However, after 50 years of using ICT, it can be concluded that his expectations have not been met. It is not his fault, but rather super consumerism is to blame, which develops much faster with ICT than without it. Masuda was also wrong that automation would increase leisure time. To some extent, he was right; however, "leisure time" today means unemployment or low-paid part-time employment.

Moreover, ICT did not increase participatory democracy; instead, it triggered the development of direct democracy, which means chaos. In addition, ICT has led to the emergence of a virtual civilization that continually moves the younger generation from reality to both virtuality and isolation from real society. As a result, science has also not improved due to ICT tools; rather, it has tended to deteriorate due to shrinking student attention and a lack of focus on developing knowledge and wisdom in classrooms and beyond, which is a direct result of using smartphones in a way that could be considered an addiction (Targowski, 2014b).

The Japanese engineering effort, on the other hand, was directed at the development of robots for much of the work needed in an aging society. The progress made by Japanese robotics engineers was also made possible by the friendly image of the Japanese towards robots. By comparison, in Western countries, citizens seem to imagine robots as evil and dangerous creatures and fear that robots may take their jobs. Japan has created the most industrial robots, more than half a million, in an aim to reduce high labor costs and support further industrial mechanization. For its 21st century economy, Japan wants robotics to be what cars were for the 20th century.

Honda, for instance, developed the ASIMO robot in 2000 and continues to improve it every year. Its artificial intelligence is spectacular. For example, the robot can move without the operator's help and can observe human behavior and predict results. This means that if ASIMO sees someone rushing down the aisle, it may calculate that it has to get off the road. It can also capture multiple voices and faces from a crowd and identify multiple agents when everyone is talking simultaneously. Even more impressive is that the robot can even communicate in sign language, thanks in part to redesigned hands.

Robots are seen in Japan as a solution to the declining birth rate and shrinking workforce, which is a significant problem for Japanese society in the 21st century. Although the number of workers a robot can replace varies from industry to industry, a single robot can often do the work of several workers. Not only can robots respond to a dwindling workforce in the country, in addition, they will not have much of an impact on future pensions and health care programs. In this situation, should robots pay taxes?

Based on the examples of Japan in the 1970s and La Spezia, Italy in the present as well as the credibility of advertised applications of the 21st century, the following conclusions can be drawn:

1. The concept of autonomous vehicles was trendy at the beginning of the 21st century, but the pilot solutions that have taken indicate that such vehicles are still dangerous. Hence, the expectation that 5G will enable their full development with vehicle-to-vehicle communication is premature. Even if it were possible, it would be vulnerable to hacking, which is already the case with electric cars. The concept of such vehicle-to-vehicle communication is one of the most spectacular applications of a smart city, but it is not yet ready to materialize. Also, if the development of the "green" city is taken into account, then this might result in restrictions on the number of cars in city centers. Cities around the world are facing a crisis: cars are wreaking havoc, "growling" in the streets, and contributing to increased air pollution. The World Health Organization says that about three million deaths a year are associated with exposure to outdoor air pollution, much of which is emitted as exhaust from the cars we drive every day.

   a. **Oslo**: As one of the first leaders in car-free traffic, the Norwegian capital plans to permanently ban all private vehicles by 2019. Oslo will replace 35 miles of roads that were previously used by cars with bike paths and hopes to introduce a car-free zone within the city's central ring road. Drivers can also expect peak hour charges (in addition to existing congestion charges) and a parking ban until 2019. Because Oslo often has weather inversions that keep air pollution at ground level, the city has, in the past, had to ban diesel cars for set periods. This effort has reduced pollution levels by at least a quarter.

   b. **Bogota**: Colombia's capital has been working to remove cars from the streets since 1974. Every Sunday from 7 a.m. to 2 p.m., more than 76 miles of city roads are closed to vehicles—an event called Ciclovía—and now Bogota has a total of more than 200 miles of bike-only paths to serve the city.

   c. **Paris**: In recent years, Paris has been forced to restrict cars in its city center, primarily due to harmful air pollution that plagues the city. Vehicles registered before 1997 have been banned from entering the city on weekdays. Furthermore, the Champs-Élysées closes once a month to traffic, and a 1.8 mile stretch of the right bank of the Seine River has recently been shut down from traffic. Paris has also committed to banning diesel vehicles until 2025. Finally, the mayor plans to double the number of bike lanes in the city.

d. **London**: By 2020, London plans to ban diesel vehicles. London also has an Ultra-Low Carbon Zone (ULCZ) plan, which will ultimately target buses and coaches and expand coverage. London Mayor Sadiq Khan says ULCZ would be "the toughest emissions standard in any city in the world." In 2003, London also introduced congestion charges on the innermost streets, and the city plans to spend a record $1 billion on improving cycling infrastructure by 2026 (see Figure 25).

Figure 25. Londoners traveling to work by bike will not benefit from autonomous cars connected by 5G in the city center. (Photo: Shutterstock)

e. **Berlin**: In 2008, Berlin introduced the Low Emission Zone (LEZ), which banned all diesel and petrol vehicles that did not meet emission standards. The LEZ zone covers 88 square kilometers of downtown and about a third of Berlin's population. Recently, Berlin also announced a plan to install a dozen new bike highways at least 13 feet wide and completely separated from cars and pedestrians.

f. **Madrid**: Mardin is on track to remove passenger cars from 500 acres of its city by 2021. The capital's main street, Gran Via, will allow access to bicycles, buses, and taxis. Also, 23 other busy streets will be redesigned for walking instead of driving. All this is part of a broader sustainability plan that also bans all diesel cars from Madrid until 2025 and imposes higher charges for parked vehicles.

Figure 26. Copenhagen residents traveling to work by bicycle will not benefit from autonomous cars connected by 5G in the city center (Photo: Shutterstock)

g. **Athens**: The Athenians have decided to ban diesel cars by 2025. Athens has already, on some days, been restricting diesel vehicles from the city center based on registration numbers.

h. **Tokyo**: In 2000, Tokyo banned the entry of all diesel vehicles, except those which have installed exhaust gas purifiers. This reduced pollution in the city, and residents can now regularly see Mount Fuji, which is two hours away.

i. **Milan**: Since 2016, Milan has banned the most polluting kinds of cars from entering its city center, and in the past, it has denied all vehicles from entering as smog levels rise. More positive incentives include public transportation vouchers for commuters who leave their vehicles at home.

j. **Brussels**: Brussels wants to expand its pedestrian zones, including the zone along Boulevard Anspach. The city also introduced a ban on diesel cars built before 1998, and the city announced that public transportation would be free on days with abnormally high air pollution.

k. **Hamburg**: Hamburg developed a "green network" without cars, which will cover 40% of its urban area in hopes that more people will walk or ride a bike instead of driving a car. The plan includes more parks, playgrounds, and sports fields and should be completed by 2035. The city is also transforming the congested A7 motorway into parks to reconnect neighborhoods and make walking more comfortable. It has become the first city in Germany to ban older diesel cars.

l.   **Copenhagen**: the green capital, which has committed to carbon neutrality by 2025, is one of the most bike-friendly places to live in the world. More than half of the city's residents ride their bikes every day (see Figure 26). Now Copenhagen is developing a 500-kilometer cycle network called a "motorway" that will connect to the surrounding suburbs. Diesel cars are also banned in the city.

m.   **Mexico City**: More than 2 million cars are removed daily from the city's streets by a system first introduced in 2016 that restricts road use by registration number (although similar programs have been in place since the late 1980s). This move came in response to heavy smog that haunts the city, which now has about 20 million inhabitants.

n.   **Helsinki**: The capital of Finland has developed a new plan to transform densely populated suburbs cars into neighborhoods that are walker-friendly and easily accessible from the city center by public transportation. All of this is part of what is called "on-demand mobility", which the city hopes to have by 2025. Citizens will be able to use shared rides, buses, taxis, bicycles, and ferries through a single app. While this initiative is not an attack on cars as such, Helsinki leaders want to make alternative transportation available so that no one has a reason for owning a car.

2.   The concept of using 5G in manufacturing, especially robot-based manufacturing and automation, concerns factories that are not subject to city management. Often factories are located outside cities. Italy and France and parts Germany are getting rid of their factories, moving them to Asia and Eastern Europe as part of the so-called "global economy" in the early 21st century. It is worth recalling that the United States got rid of about 70,000 of its factories. The coronavirus pandemic in 2020, which started in China, has caused some of these factories to relocate back in the US. Presumably, European companies will do the same. More importantly, as early as the 1990s, *just-in-time* (JIT) production systems were introduced in Western factories, which consists in not maintaining an inventory of buffer parts and components between production operations (so as not to freeze capital). In JIT, production materials are imported from sub-suppliers "on time," which means that they are delivered to the assembly plant a few minutes before they are included in assembly. This strategy was commonly adopted for large components, such as engines or vehicle wheel drive separation systems. Will instant 5G communication in factories that import materials shorten this process of ordering parts "just in time"? As can be seen, this is not a particularly critical application of a smart city.

3.   The use of 5G communication is intended to justify the use of the Internet of Things (IoT), i.e., connecting a large number of "things" to a shared network, such as installations, equipment, valves, taps, lighting poles, cars, buses, semis, tanks, etc. That is, each of these "things" will have a chip—that is, a micro-computer—capable of logical monitoring and response. Moreover, these things with chips are called "smart" because they are capable not only of monitoring but also of self-repairing, as is the case with Tesla electric cars and others, which from a central location can update their software and correct/repair their systems and components. This is possible because the electric vehicle is designed from the very beginning so that it can be monitored and fixed remotely. In the case of cities, their "things" often have long years of use, such as bridges and houses that date back hundreds of years. While other things are "younger" (e.g., things that are decades-old), many were not designed for electronic cooperation with IoT devices. Therefore, monitoring and repairing such things online are challenging and in most cases impossible.

4. Smart cities are primarily promoted by owners of software and communication companies (such as Cisco), for in their opinion, the IoT has opened an market selling various interfaces, routers, and chips as well as design and software services, whose sales number in the billions of dollars per year. Thanks to this, IT professionals will find excellent jobs working on such projects, which for laypeople are within grasp; however, are these projects necessary, and are they even sometimes harmful? After all, they will have to be continuously repaired.

As a result of this critical analysis of the reality of these spectacular smart city applications in the 2020s, the following applications can be proposed:

- A traffic monitoring system for vehicles and people: This system is already well developed in the form of numerous cameras installed in most cities of Western civilization. Thanks to the use of Artificial Intelligence, this system can be improved, but it must be done so with ethical solutions, i.e., not via unlawful surveillance. This system may have a vehicle traffic monitoring subsystem to respond to congestion and accidents.
- A tele-medicine system: This system would allow for the treatment of patients at a distance, including remote surgical operations in cases where only a slim number of doctors are available in a given critical specialty. 5G communication is constructive here because every second counts, and delays in remote controls should be kept to a minimum.
- Monitoring systems for energy, water, waste, and air: These systems are already in use, but with 5G, they can be further improved. Can these systems be repaired remotely, for example, if there is a failure in the wastewater system or sudden air pollution coming from a distance? This depends on the specific failure and the particular solution of a given distribution of public services and factories.
- Smart home monitoring and repair systems: These systems apply to newly built homes. These houses do not need to be remotely monitored and repaired under the smart city system.

Video and conference application systems: These are currently available on 4G. Of course, 5G will make them quicker, much to the delight of young people, who love playing computer games and watching movies even while, say, riding an elevator or cycling (so as to not waste time that could be spent on entertainment). Unfortunately, 5G will make young people even more dependent on their smartphone and will reduce their real-life qualifications in favor of those related to virtual life.

Figure 27 illustrates the Smart City Configuration in the 2020s.

SUMMARY

1. The development of computerization at the state level is reminiscent of the development of computerization at the company level between 1980 and 2000, which was characterized by "information islands." At the end of the 20th century, projects were undertaken in the United States to convert these subsystems into Enterprise Resource Planning (ERP) software, which was eventually upgraded to the Computer Integrated Manufacturing (CIM) system complex. Therefore, a similar redesign is necessary for national IT systems.

Figure 27. Smart City Configuration (SMCC) architecture

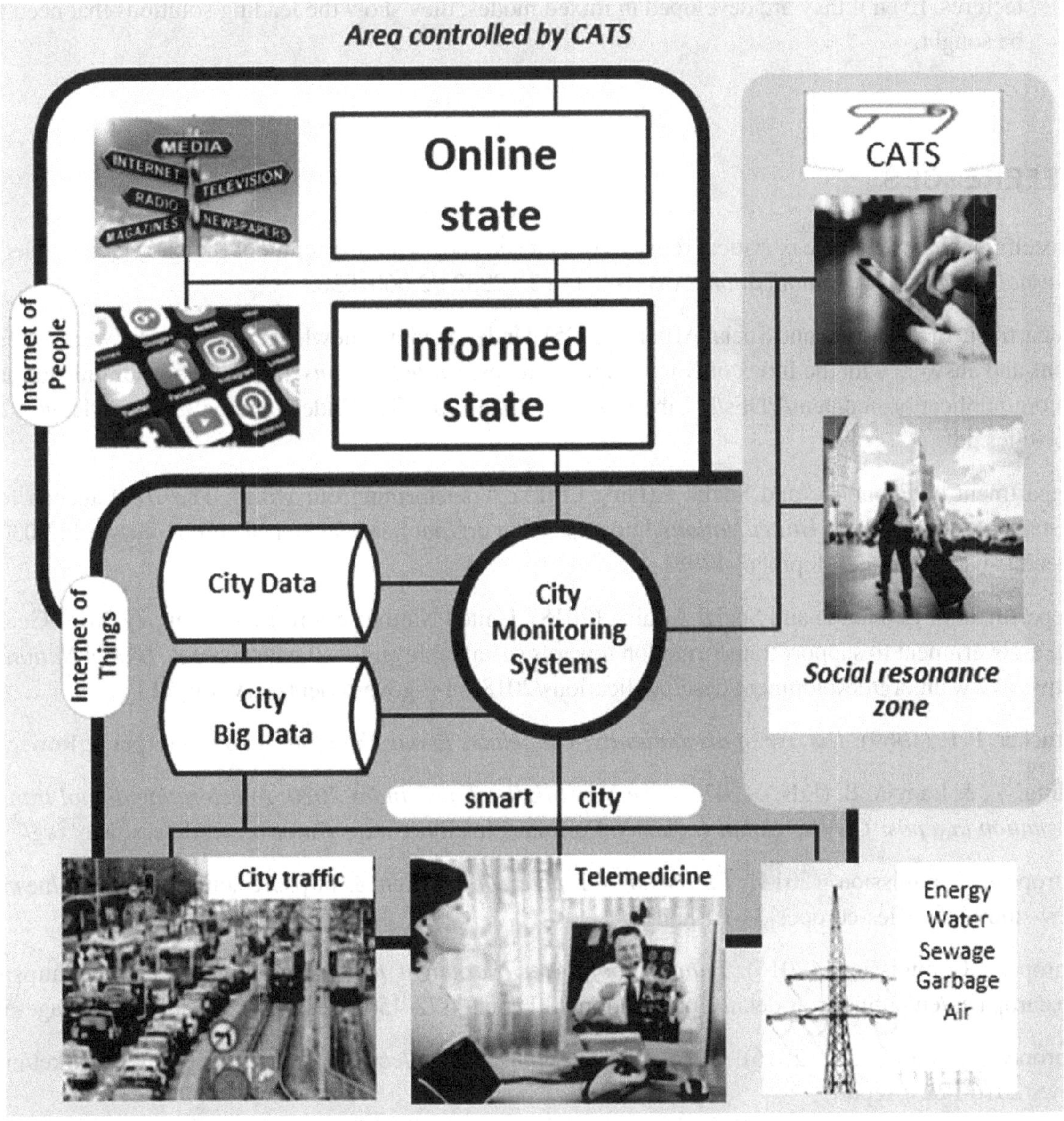

2. The employment of about 20 million IT professionals worldwide is causing a race for advanced projects that are well-paid and that promise exciting work. This results in high staff turnover and instability in the design and software of IT centers. Furthermore, business leaders disappointed with the advancements of computerization now seek out the services of consulting companies and various digital clouds. As a result, many projects are undertaken in an ad hoc way, poorly funded, and eventually abandoned. In this way, more and more information islands are being created, and national IT systems are a patchwork of different configurations (which have been classified in this chapter).

3. The characterizations of the main configurations of national systems give insight into their architectures. Even if they are developed in mixed modes, they show the leading solutions that need to be sought.

REFERENCES

Castelfranchi, C. (2007). Six critical remarks on science and the construction of the knowledge society. *Journal of Science Communication*, *6*(4), 1–3. doi:10.22323/2.06040303

Department of Economic and Social Affairs. (2005). Understanding knowledge societies: In twenty questions and answers with the Index of Knowledge Societies. *United Nations*. https://publicadministration. un.org/publications/content/PDFs/E-Library%20Archives/2005%20Understanding%20Knowledge%20 Societies.pdf

Department of Economic and Social Affairs. (2015). Transforming our world: The 2030 agenda for sustainable development. *United Nations*. https://sdgs.un.org/publications/transforming-our-world-2030- agenda-sustainable-development-17981

Department of Economic and Social Affairs. (2018). United Nations e-government survey 2018: Gearing e-government to support transformation towards sustainable and resilient societies. *United Nations*. https://www.un.org/development/desa/publications/2018-un-e-government-survey.html

Drucker, P. F. (1969). *The age of discontinuity: Guidelines to our changing society*. Harper & Row.

Dutta, S., & Lanvin, B. (Eds.). (2020). *The Network Readiness Index 2020: Accelerating digital transformation in a post-COVID global economy*. Portulans Institute. https://networkreadinessindex.org/

European Commission. (2014). *European ICT poles of excellence*. https://ec.europa.eu/jrc/en/news/ new-study-identifies-europes-34-ict-hubs

European Commission. (2015). *Future-proofing eGovernment for a digital single market*. https:// op.europa.eu/en/publication-detail/-/publication/78fbc6cd-4f72-45b2-9e3a-f8395eb2b539/language-en

European Commission. (2016). *2016 I-DESI report*. https://ec.europa.eu/digital-single-market/en/ news/2016-i-desi-report

European Commission. (2017). *Digital Economy and Society Index (DESI) 2017*. https://ec.europa.eu/ digital-single-market/en/news/digital-economy-and-society-index-desi-2017

European Commission. (2018). *Digital Economy and Society Index 2018 report*. https://ec.europa.eu/ digital-single-market/en/news/digital-economy-and-society-index-2018-report

European Commission. (2019). *Digital Economy and Society Index (DESI) 2019*. https://ec.europa.eu/ digital-single-market/en/news/digital-economy-and-society-index-desi-2019

European Commission. (2020). *Towards 5G*. https://ec.europa.eu/digital-single-market/en/towards-5g

European Commission & the 5G Public-Private Partnership. (2016). *5G empowering vertical industries*. https://ec.europa.eu/digital-single-market/en/news/more-smartphones-white-paper-shows-how-5g-will-transform-eu-manufacturing-health-energy

International Monetary Fund. (2020). *World economic outlook database*. https://www.imf.org/en/Publications/WEO/weo-database/2020/October

Kendall-Taylor, A., Frantz, E., & Wright, J. (2020). The digital dictators: How technology strengthen autocracy. *Foreign Affairs*, *99*(2). https://www.foreignaffairs.com/articles/china/2020-02-06/digital-dictators

Masuda, Y. (1981). *The information society as post-industrial society*. World Future Society.

Paavola, S., & Hakkarainen, K. (2005). The knowledge creation metaphor: An emergent epistemological approach to learning. *Science & Education*, *14*(6), 535–557. doi:10.100711191-004-5157-0

Servan-Schreiber, J. (1967). *Le défi Americain* [The American challenge]. Denoël.

Targowski, A. (1971). *Informatyka klucz do dobrobytu* [Informatics the key to prosperity]. State Publishing Institute.

Targowski, A. (2014a). *The deadly effect of informatics on the Holocaust*. Tate Publishing.

Targowski, A. (2014b). *Virtual civilization in the 21ˢᵗ century*. NOVA Science Publishers.

United Nations Development Programme. (2019). *Global Knowledge Index 2019*. https://www.knowledge4all.com/DataDownload2020.aspx?language=en&type=report

United Nations Educational, Scientific and Cultural Organization. (2005). *Toward knowledge societies*. UNESCO Publishing. https://unesdoc.unesco.org/ark:/48223/pf0000141843

Välimaa, J., & Hoffman, D. (2008). Knowledge society discourse and higher education. *Higher Education*, *56*(3), 265–285. doi:10.100710734-008-9123-7

Vogel, E. F. (1986). East Asia: Pax Nipponica? *Foreign Affairs*, *64*(4), 752–767. doi:10.2307/20042686

KEY TERMS AND DEFINITIONS

Augmented Reality: A real-world environment that is enhanced or modified by computer-generated information.

CATS: An acronym standing for "Constitution of the Application of Technology." CATs are standardized strategies adopted to regulate, prohibit, or facilitate the use of technologies in society.

eAdministration: The use of computer technologies to carry out governmental and administrative tasks, typically with the goal of increasing efficiency.

Firewall: A security system used in computer networks to monitor network traffic.

Information Society: A society in which information, including its creation, dissemination, and use, plays an essential role.

Knowledge Society: A society that generates, shares, and makes available to all members of society knowledge that can be used to improve the human condition.

Plan Calcul: A plan created by the French government and approved by President Charles de Gaulle in 1966 to encourage the production and use of computers in France.

Smart City: A city that uses computer technology and electronic information to improve and enhance city infrastructure.

ENDNOTES

[1] Andrew Targowski was director of ZETO-ZOWAR in Warsaw from 1965 to 1971.

[2] This was the result of enormous pressure from the IT community, which in the daily and specialist press expressed its outrage at the chaotic and slow development of digital technology and its application in Poland, especially in the context of its spectacular development in the West. These discussions were uncomfortable for the government, as they highlighted its bad image. Discussions and confessions of computer scientists were used by its members for personal games. On this subject, Andrew Targowski published a dozen articles in the central press, which were mostly critical.

[3] As referred to in the chapter *Strategic Digital Informing and Its Challenges in the 21st Century.*

[4] For more information, see the model in the chapter *the History and Repercussions of Strategic Informing Technology.*

[5] Perhaps excluding military and intelligence data.

[6] The World Economic Forum (WEF), based in Coligny-Geneva, Switzerland, is an NGO founded in 1971. The WEF is "committed to improving the state of the world by engaging business, policy, science and other society leaders to shape global, regional and industry programs." It is a membership-based organization, and membership is made up of the largest corporations in the world. The WEF hosts an annual meeting at the end of January in Davos, a mountain resort in Graubünden in the eastern Alps of Switzerland. The meeting brings together about 3,000 business leaders, international political leaders, economists, celebrities, and journalists for up to five days to discuss global issues in 500 public and private sessions.

[7] The human capital dimension of the Digital Economy and Social Index (DESI) includes two subdimensions: 'basic skills and use' and 'advanced skills and development'. The first includes indicators of internet use by individuals and digital skills. The second includes indicators with respect to the employment of ICT professionals and graduates in STEM fields (science, technology, engineering, and mathematics). According to 2017 data, the Netherlands, Sweden, and Luxembourg are the best in basic skills and use; Finland, Ireland, Sweden, and the UK achieved the highest scores in advanced skills and development. Romania, Bulgaria, Greece, and Italy generally rank lowest in the DESI Human. Poland is in 21st place below the EU average (European Commission, 2017).

[8] An NCN network operated in the form of a ZETO network in 1964-74, which was then deliberately destroyed for political reasons. Its remnants were privatized after 1989.

[9] Luxembourg has a population of less than 1 million. It is a manufacturer of high-end steel, chemicals, and rubber, and it is the center for many international banks. It is the second richest country in the world.

Chapter 19
Digital Strategy for a Sustainable Civilization

ABSTRACT

This chapter analyzes aspects of a digital strategy aimed at developing a sustainable civilization. The chapter begins by examining the arrangement and configuration of a green state. Specifically, core values and critical subsystems of this configuration are considered. Next, the chapter suggests a digital format for computerizing a wise civilization. The chapter then presents sustainable society indices for Norway, the US, Russia, China, and India. After this, the Geoinformatic Management System (GMS) of 8D Civilization is introduced. It is followed by a discussion of some of the existential dangers that face civilization. The chapter concludes by discussing the GMS 8D Civilization architecture for the world, continents, countries, and enterprises.

INTRODUCTION

Global warming is one of the predominant world issues in the 2020s. However, solving this problem requires that it be put in the broader context of a sustainable civilization, in which the preservation of nature is a priority. Looking at society today, it is clear that there is a strong trend toward urban settlement. Many cities have tens of millions of inhabitants (taking into account the vast metropolises). Therefore, before planning a sustainable civilization, we must consider the arrangement and configuration of a "green" (wise) city[1] as the nucleus for a sustainable civilization. Next, we must plan how to monitor this process via computerization.

GREEN (WISE) STATE CONFIGURATION (GRSC)

- **Intention**: Employ Wisdom when deciding how to manage and use resources in the context of humanism.

DOI: 10.4018/978-1-7998-8036-3.ch019

- **Strategy**: Complement the online configuration and inform applications that control the sustainable development of civilization.

The use of a knowledge-based state configuration (KNSC) is a marvelous achievement. Still, it is critical that a knowledge-oriented configuration wisely choose "green options" (in a broad sense of the word) when making decisions. These choices should occur within the context of the art of living and humanism, and they should aim at the sustainable development of the state. Figure 1 illustrates the architecture of the green (wise) state configuration.

In the KNSC model, computerization applications are essential for climate control, the "green" environment, and the fate of people in vital economic processes. For a state to be wise, however, it must support the development of a wise civilization.

A wise civilization means the adoption of the following values (Targowski, 2016):

1. Nature comes first.
2. People are more important than markets.
3. Human health is more important than money.
4. Economic sufficiency is more important than performance.
5. Businesses serve people and are effectively controlled by people.

Since capitalism and socialism are based on continuous economic growth (which leads to the depletion of strategic resources), a policy developed by a systems ecology outlook (a field of study that takes a holistic approach to ecological systems) should be developed, which would consist of the following subsystems:

- **Eco-education**: Education based on eco-knowledge and Wisdom;
- **A wise society**: A society trained and educated in the field of eco-education and qualified to make wise decisions;
- **Eco-democracy**: A system where everyone is equal and where citizens' voices are central in environmental decision-making;
- **Eco-justice**: A legal system in which environmental damages are taken into account, and one in which, under certain circumstances, perpetrators are punished;
- **Eco-infrastructure**: Infrastructure that functions in harmony with nature and protects it from destruction;
- **Deep economics**: An economic outlook that, in addition to business and administrative costs, includes environmental and social costs in cost-benefit calculations;
- **Deep media**: Media that comprehensively and objectively inform the public about the state and progress of sustainable civilization;
- **Eco-communication**: Communication-based on techniques that are friendly to nature and humankind.

The model of a balanced (green/wise) civilization is given in Figure 2.

The first prerequisite for a green (sustainable) civilization is that civilians commit to adopting a second layer of religion, called "Spirituality 2.0." This religion would not replace any of the existing religions (or "Religion 1.0"), which would be seen as heresy and an unprecedented revolution. Such a replacement

Figure 1. The configuration of the green (wise) state (GRSC)

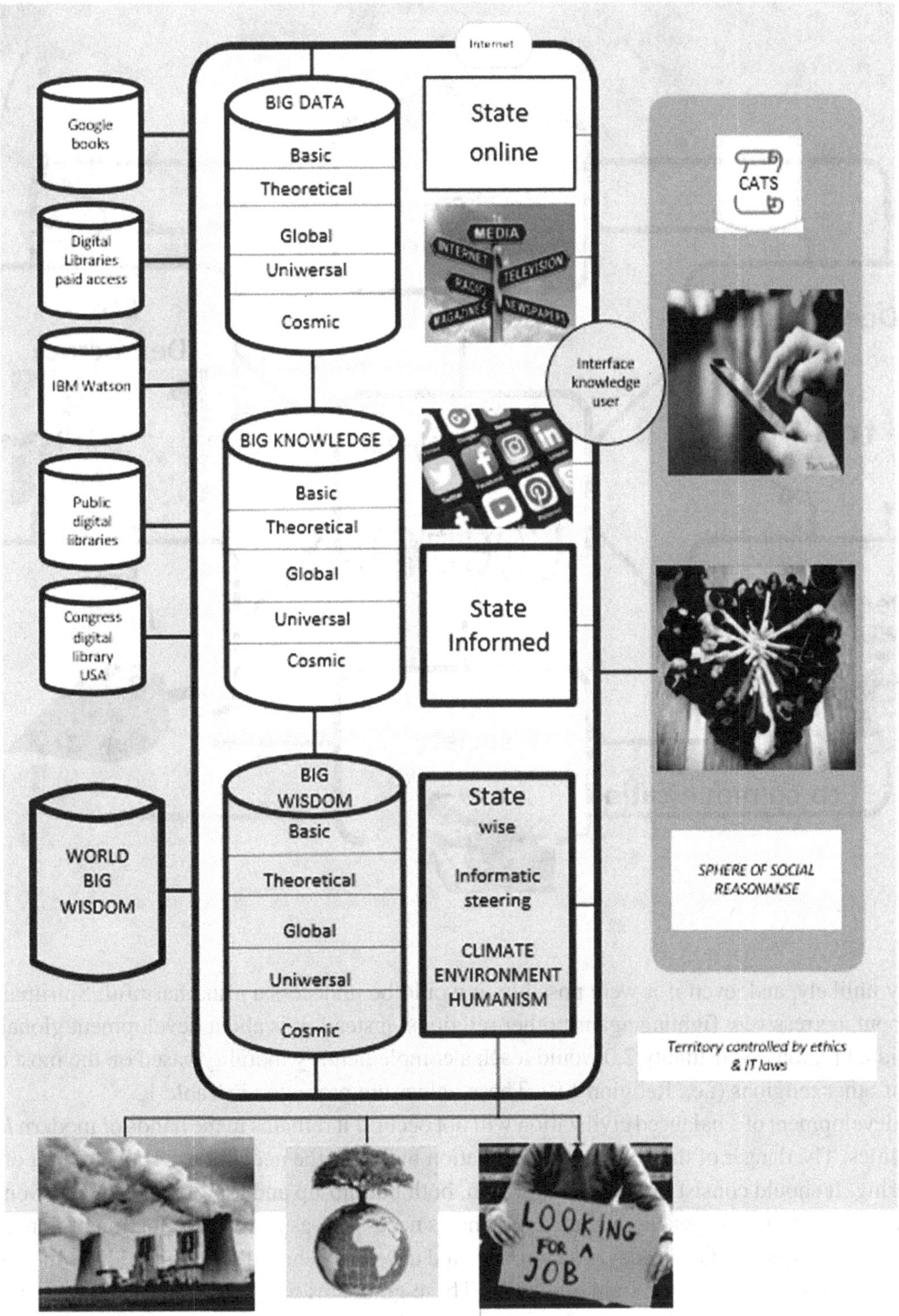

Figure 2. A model of sustainable (green) civilization (Targowski, 2016, p. 164)

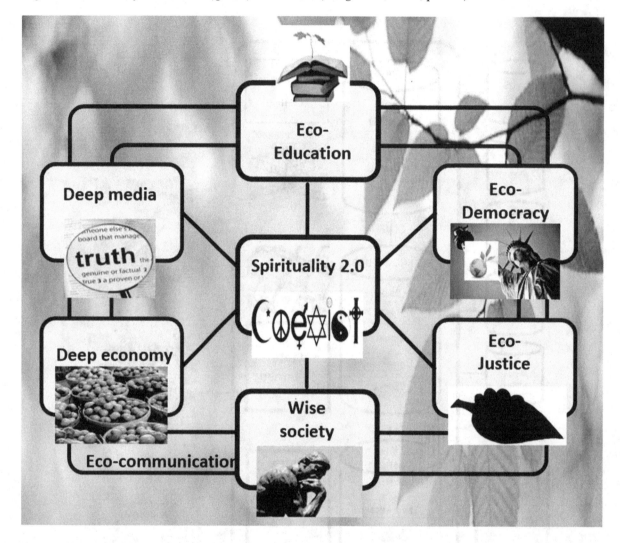

is highly unlikely, and, even if it were possible, it would be unnecessary and harmful. Spirituality 2.0 is not about aggressively fighting against other religions; instead, it is about development globally, not in individual regions. Spirituality 2.0 would teach a complementary morality based on the most critical values of other religions (i.e., Religion 1.0). These values are presented in Table 1.

The development of a balanced civilization will not occur if it remains in the hands of modern *laissez-faire* politics. The danger of the collapse of civilization indicates the need for a certain amount of social engineering. It should consist of a mixed approach, both bottom-up and top-down. The involvement of organizations such as UN agencies and governments is necessary, as is the participation of non-governmental organizations (NGOs). Today, every school and university should seriously address the development of eco-knowledge and wise train graduates. These graduates will become wise citizens, workers, and leaders who will eventually apply wise solutions to develop a wise society and wise civilization.

The proposal to transform modern civilization into a sustainable (wise-universal) civilization grows out of a structural crisis affecting Western civilization and global civilization (replacing Western civili-

Table 1. Complementary values of Spirituality 2.0 (Targowski, 2005)

Civilization	Contribution of Value
African	Spiritual communication with ancestors
Buddhist	Morality
Eastern	Self-sacrifice
Indian	Moderation
Islamic	Reward and punishment
Japanese	Cooperation and worship of nature
Chinese	Respect for elders
Western	Freedom and the cult of technology
Global	The free flow of ideas, goods, services, and people, according to *Pax Orbis*
Universal	Wisdom, kindness, access, dialogue, consent, conditional forgiveness, human and civil rights, international law, sustainable development

zation). The driving force behind these civilizations is the United States, which has entered a structural rather than cyclical crisis. Therefore, the question must be asked: "Can America be repaired?" Some believe, yes, that more money is invested in technology and that labor costs are reduced. It could be accomplished by maintaining economic growth with machines that replace the human workforce. This argument is wrong-headed. It would only exacerbate America and Western civilization's crisis even further, as evidenced by the turbulent years of Donald Trump's presidency (2016-2020).

TOWARDS COMPUTERIZING A WISE CIVILIZATION

Saving Western civilization and, more generally, the world civilization depends on whether we can break from the development of a self-destructive civilization and begin developing a wise civilization.

The GRSC model clarifies that it is necessary to digitally store cataloged examples of Wisdom concerning green (sustainable) development matters. The question is, how can this be done? The answer is that it must be accomplished by computerizing knowledge and Wisdom in this domain in the format of descriptive sentences, that is, in the format of symbols and numbers. It will not happen immediately, nor will it help if there are many different projects and studies in various formats before an international standard is agreed upon. To address the problem of standardization, one can start with an example of the descriptive format used to characterize the seed of the Wisdom in the Polish Revolution in 1980-1989, given in Table 2 (Krawczyk & Targowski, 2019). The bold row was chosen and is considered wise.

Of course, in addition to seeds of Wisdom, there are also seeds of stupidity, as illustrated by the Warsaw Uprising of 1944 in Table 3. The bolded row was chosen and is considered unwise.

The use of hypertext makes it possible to move from Big Wisdom to collections of Big Knowledge or other information collections. Examples of descriptions of Wisdom are those given in a colloquial language, which is unstructured from the point of view of a Database Management system (DBMS). This unstructured text data can be converted to structured data using standard DBMS system techniques (e.g., Oracle or IBM DB2). This process is called textual disambiguation, abbreviated as ETL from "extract/transform/load."[2]

Table 2. The seed of Wisdom in the Polish Solidarity Revolution 1980-1989

Elements	Solutions	Knowledge Used	Option Selection and Result
Problem	Revolution Strategy	Revolutions of 1789 and 1917	Bloody
Option 1	Armed confrontation	The defeat of the Home Army (PW) in 1944	200,000 killed
Option 2	**Passive resistance**	**Mahatma Gandhi's policy in opposition to the British in India**	**Peaceful victory**
Option 3	Go underground	Underground State 1939-45	Terror
The art of life	Historical memory and compromise	Defeats of Polish uprisings	Compromise
Global context	Council of Pope John Paul II	Gandhi's victory in India	Relying on a proven strategy
Sustainability context	Minimizing losses	Destroyed Warsaw in 1944, and 30% of Polish fixed assets	Avoiding a repetition of typical Polish policy mistakes

Table 3. The seed of stupidity in the Warsaw Uprising in 1944 (Zychowicz, 2013)

Elements	Solutions	Knowledge Used	Option Selection and Result
Problem	Decide the Uprising	The Polish uprisings in the 19th century	Lost
Option 1	**Armed confrontation**	**1830-31, 1848, 1863-1864**	**The disaster of 200,000 dead and the ruin of the capital**
Option 2	Passive resistance	Politics of France	Peaceful victory
Option 3	Waiting for Germany to lose to the USSR	The arrest of the leaders of the Warsaw Uprising in Vilnius in July 1944	Terror
The art of living	Symbol of heroism	Numerous uprisings and wars	Bloody
Global context	Invasion of Europe on June 6, 1944, and refusal of allies to help the Uprising	The decision in the Tehran Conference in 1943 to divide Europe led to the victims impacting the conscience of the world	Rejection of Allies' decisions
Sustainable context Development	Risk of the destruction of Polish civilization	Experience of attacking and defending Warsaw in 1939	Destruction of the capital and monuments; reconstruction for 20+ years

The purpose of unifying a text is to read the raw text and turn it into a standardized record in a standard database. This text will then look like any other analytical database. It allows users to attach one analytical database to another, thereby activating the ability to analyze all data associated with the same query. Each entry in the analytical database can be linked directly to the source document. This feature is essential. Suppose a question arises about the context of the data found in the analytical database. In that case, it can be easily and quickly verified because the source document that was disambiguated was not modified or altered in any way.

To unify a text, it must be "mapped," which involves documenting the appropriate parameters specified inside a text. Mapping is guided by textual clarity about how a document should be interpreted. Each document has its own mapped processes. The exact mapping can handle all documents of the same type. For example, one mapping for attributes of Wisdom is associated with the transportation of environmentally harmful materials; another mapping may relate to documents used in R&D management, etc.

Electronic texts contribute to the process of unifying texts. There are many forms of electronic texts. Indeed, electronic texts regarding attributes of Wisdom can come from anywhere. Electronic texts include uses of formal language, slang, comments, database entries, and others. Textually unifying the attributes of Wisdom should consist of all forms of electronic texts. Furthermore, electronic texts can occur in different languages. The result is that unifying texts can take various forms, depending on the types of users.

To help process unstructured texts, taxonomies that have already been developed for a given category of Big Wisdom should be used. Taxonomies are an essential tool in the general processing of natural language and text analysis. For example, an organism can have several classification levels, such as animal, mammal, primate, human; likewise, one can distinguish between IT, system software, operating system, Microsoft.

As can be seen, natural language processing (NLP) involves the classification of texts. IBM Watson's Natural Language Classifier (NLC) leads the way in this regard. It allows users to classify custom text categories. Developers with no machine learning (ML) experience or NLP can improve their applications by using IBM's service, which combines various advanced ML techniques to ensure the highest possible accuracy without requiring a large amount of data.

The NLC service uses several classification models and unattended and supervised learning techniques to achieve its level of accuracy. After completing the user-trained data, NLC evaluates the data against multiple Support-Vector Machines (SVM) and Convolutional Neural Networks (CNN) using IBM's Desktop as a Service (DaaS).[3]

INDICES OF A SUSTAINABLE CIVILIZATION

Gross Sustainable Development Product (green GDP or GGDP) measures growth and development with environmental consequences factored in. The index was developed by the Global Community Assessment Centre and the Society for World Sustainable Development. Specifically, the index is defined as the total value of production in a region over time. It is measured using market prices for transactions of goods and services in the economy. It is intended to replace GDP and is calculated based on the following indicators:

1. Economic effects of degradation or improvement of the environment and health,
2. Depletion of resources and depreciation, recognition, and finding of new resources (stocks)
3. Impacts of human activity on the environment,
4. Impacts of human activity on resource availability,
5. Impacts of human activity on economic development.

Figure 3. The Norwegian Sustainable Society Index 2016, where 10 is best, and 1 is worst. The red line represents the average values of the world (Sustainable Society Index, 2016).

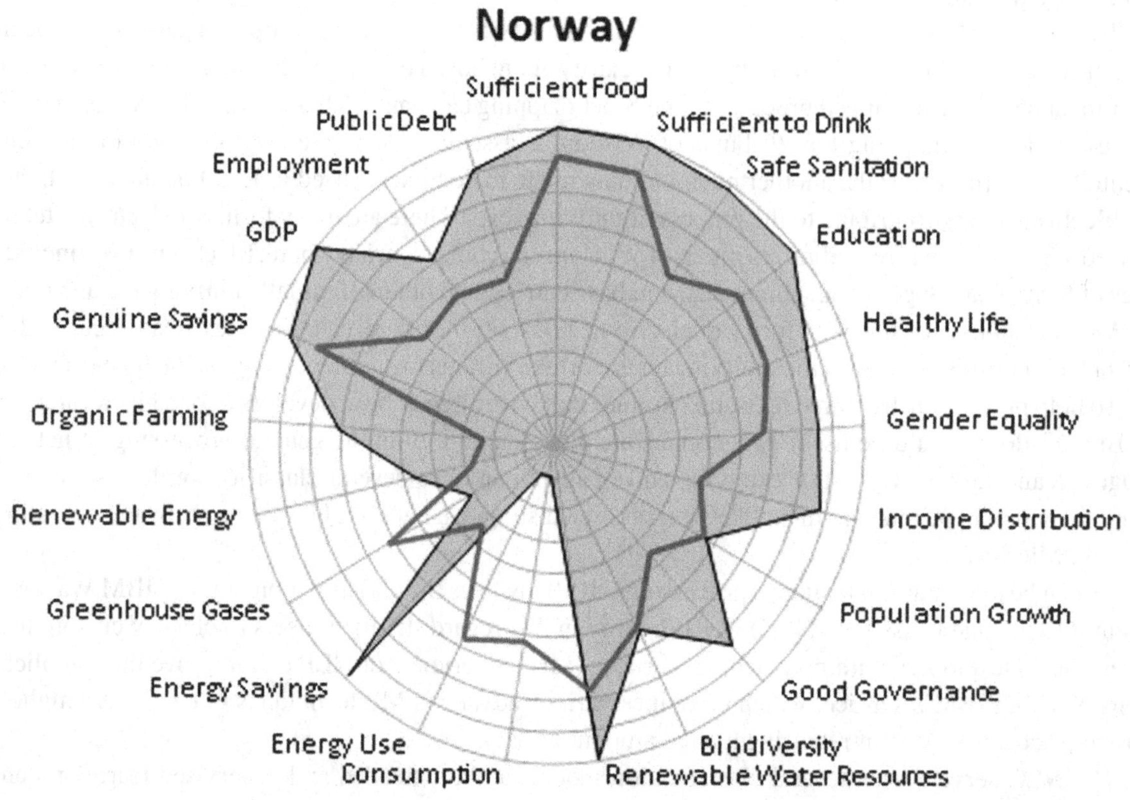

The Sustainable Society Index calculates indicators in three categories: (1) human wellbeing, (2) environmental wellbeing, and (3) economic wellbeing. In total, Norway, whose graphical model of this index is given in Figure 3, is the best performer. The index for American society is shown in Figure 4, China's in Figure 5, India's in Figure 6, and Russia's in Figure 7.

INTRODUCTION TO THE GEOINFORMATIC MANAGEMENT SYSTEM (GMS)

This section aims to develop an approach known as the Geoinformatics Management System (GMS) of 8D Civilization ("GMS 8D civilization", for short) at all necessary levels of control for a sustainable civilization, that is,,, from global to regional and local perspectives. It is essential because, in terms of protecting the climate and nature, civilization knows no borders, and its impacts are ubiquitous. Moreover, the adverse effects of technology on traditional human labor must also be considered when developing a sustainable civilization. At present, because of the business aims, technological development will lead to widespread unemployment (a labor-free economy) and perhaps even the disappearance of the human species in favor of cyborgs.

Figure 4. The American Sustainable Society Index 2016, where 10 is best, and 1 is worst. The red line represents the average values of the world (Sustainable Society Index, 2016).

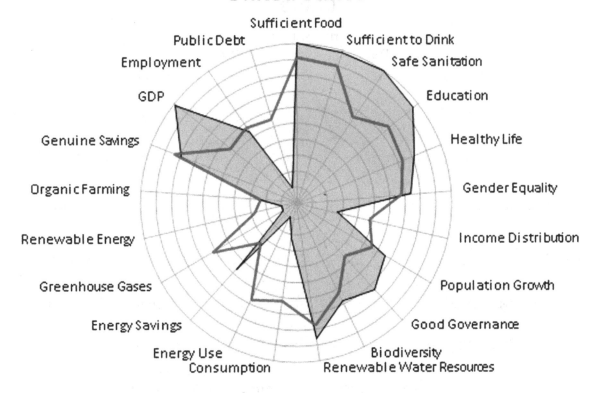

A necessary condition for the development of the hierarchical GMS 8D civilizational approach is that this system is designed holistically, for uncoordinated solutions with different levels of control will lead to information and decision-making chaos, which will only exacerbate the problem of the crisis of civilization and reinforce the feeling that we are facing the 'end of the world.'

Three strategies can be taken for designing the GMS 8D civilizational approach (and, more generally, for developing large and complex IT systems):

- **Bottom-up strategies**: These result in the formation of subsystems (so-called "information islands"), which usually concern the lowest levels of companies and organizations. This type of system solution dominates in Poland and in countries that develop computerization vigorously.

- **Top-down strategies**: These result in comprehensive and integrated systems that can affect enterprises and organizations, e.g., systems applications and productions (SAP) software. However, these systems are not hierarchical.

- **Mixed strategies**: These consist of replacing old fragmented systems with new comprehensive systems; however, such systems are gradually implemented. An example was the National Information System (NIS), implemented in 1971-74 (Targowski, 1980, 2018).

Figure 5. The Chinese Sustainable Society Index 2016, where 10 is best, and 1 is worst. The red line represents the average values of the world (Sustainable Society Index, 2016).

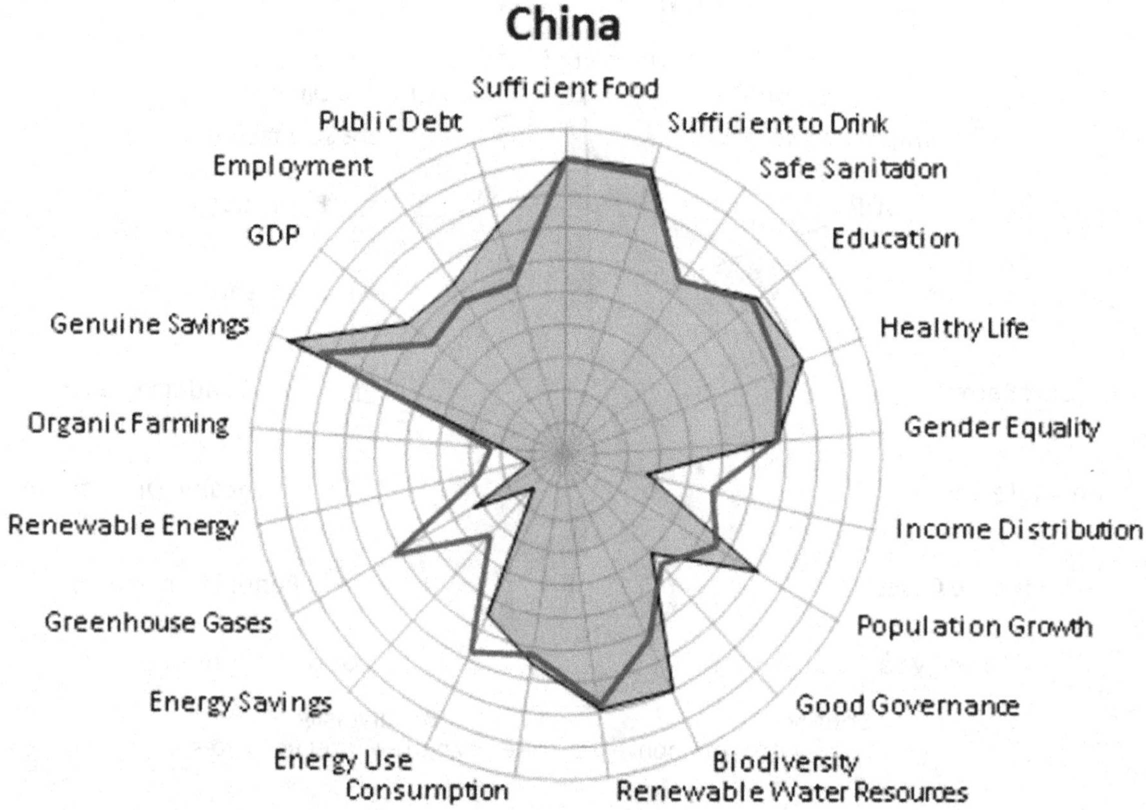

In designing a GMS 8D civilization, it is necessary to adopt a mixed strategy emphasizing top-down elements. It needs to be a hierarchical system, for not only is it concerned with local, regional, and national issues, but global issues (after all, monitoring and improving the climate and the consumption of strategic resources do not know geographical boundaries). Furthermore, the development of sustainable civilization (DSC) depends on supportive multi-area systems with information roots in the lowest forms of human organization. One can expect several well-designed enterprise and organization systems to be upgraded in a mixed approach, based on a top-down model.

The development of computer science applications has resulted from advances in computing technology, which have dictated systemic solutions. For example, IT professionals have designed systems in the health service sector, and doctors have had to adapt to them; however, it should be the other way around. The GMS 8D civilizational approach should reverse this direction, and IT professionals should aim at designing a system that can solve the crisis of civilization. It will require that they improve their qualifications. To demonstrate this, an overview of the development of IT applications will be briefly presented:

1.   Examples of computational techniques that impose a mode of application:

Figure 6. The Indian Sustainable Society Index 2016, where 10 is best, and 1 is worst. The red line represents the average values of the world (Sustainable Society Index, 2016).

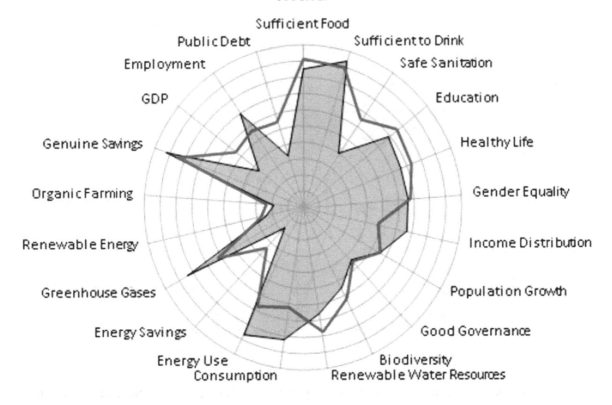

India

- ○ Weather and agricultural calculations carried out with tools such as the abacus in Mesopotamia around 2700 BCE did not impact the functioning of primitive civilization.
- ○ The mechanical calculator, starting with Blaise Pascal's serial calculator *Pascaline* in 1652 (soon followed by Gottfried Leibniz's parallel arithmometer in 1694), was initially met with fierce opposition from bankers since, if the calculator broke down, only Pascal was able to repair it. Furthermore, others worried that the machines would introduce unemployment. During the Industrial Revolution in the second half of the 19th century, parallel arithmometers began to be widely used. The best-selling arithmometer was one patented by Thomas de Colmar in 1820. Later, by 1940, one invented by Willgodt Odhner became the most popular. Since the second early half of the twentieth century, electronic calculators have dominated business and education (Targowski, 2013).
- ○ In the second half of the 19th century, censuses were conducted approximately every 10 years via Hollerith and punch-card machines by almost all countries in the world. Since the second half of the 20th century, computers have been used to complete this task (Targowski, 2013).
- ○ Mechanical cash registers, the first mass-produced and sold by the American company National Cash Register (NCR), dominated the market up until present times. While small

Figure 7. The Russian Sustainable Society Index 2016, where 10 is best, and 1 is worst. The red line represents the average values of the world (Sustainable Society Index, 2016).

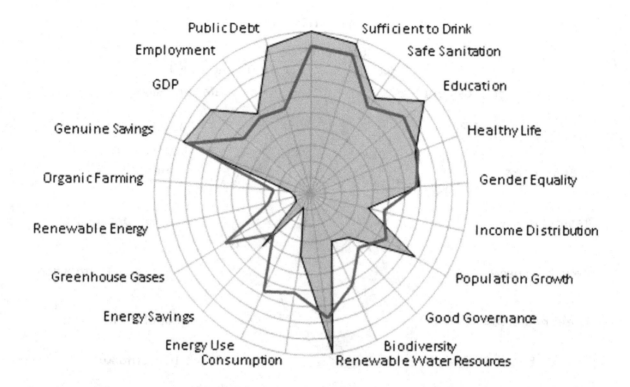

companies sometimes still use them, many large companies have transitioned to online electronic transactions.

- ○ Commercial transactions carried out on punch cards dominated in the early 20th century. Punch card machines began to be manufactured by IBM in 1924, the French company BULL in 1931, and the Czech company ARITMA and the Soviet company SAM shortly before World War II.
- ○ Beginning in the second half of the 20th century, commercial data processing on computers was dominated by IBM; however, more computer companies have since penetrated this market, both American and European.

2. Examples of computational techniques that must comply with the objectives of users:
   - ○ Today, every IT system should be designed and implemented with the future user in mind. One strategy, *joint application design* (JAD), includes approaches to improve user participation through review workshops. Urban users, however, believe they are not qualified to review IT systems, and IT professionals like to impress them.
   - ○ Artificial Intelligence (AI) systems should be designed by future users and verified by law to prevent the economy from becoming laborless.
   - ○ The Internet of Things (IoT) should have regulations developed by future users and verified by law.

Table 4. Degrees of development of civilization controlled by ICT

Degree of Civilizational Development	Resulting System	Benefits	Sponsorship	Consequences
2D (1880-1970)	Punch cards and tabs	Streamlined bureaucracy	Business and administration	Reduction in the number of officials
3D (2000-)	Holograms on screens	Improved citizen safety	Better visualization of situations, including geography	Better land management
4D (1983-)	4G Wi-Fi; Internet of People (IoP)	Global communication	Almost every company and user	A profane culture of hate; better climate monitoring
5D (2000)	Street view technologies; monitors for buildings	Improved citizen safety	The city administration, business, hospitals, colleges, etc.	Better detection of criminals
6D (2020)	5G Wi-Fi; Internet of Everything (Internet of People and Internet of things Things)	An unintelligent and unreliable machine civilization	Promoted by naïve IT youth	Widespread unemployment and communism; helplessness on the part of political leaders
7D (2030)	Cyborgs	Attack civilization from within	Promoted by greedy Big Business	A war between the "antiquated" human species and the modern e-species
8d (2040)	Humankind's victory?	Smart civilization	Strict legal regulations of applications	Will the "antiquated" human species win against the modern cyborgs?

An IT system that can "do something" technically does not mean that it is necessary to develop such a system. For example, Ilona Weiss, President of ABC DATA, says: "AI not only increasingly leads to in-depth automation of various processes but also more accurate inference and diagnosis. It will drive the dynamic development and sale of all kinds of medical devices and platforms that each of us will be able to use." Unfortunately, Weiss forgets that the first expert medical system that used AI was Mycin, based on 500 principles developed at Stanford University in the early 1970s. That was almost 50 years ago. However, the system was not used in practice because of the financial difficulties of acquiring malpractice insurance for such a device. It remains a barrier to purchasing such systems.

Furthermore, 5G can encrypt transmitted data in a 256-bit code, which is "supposedly" impossible to decipher. Hackers who would like to break such codes would have to use quantum computers, which are not yet widely available. However, for some countries (e.g., the US, China, Russia, Iran), supercomputers are a kind of cyberwar armament, and access is not a problem. If a large-scale attack were to occur, a significant issue would be the unavailability of massive IoT networks, which would break down or freeze like home computers at present. In this case, however, there would be no one to repair them to "move the stopped city."

The development of computational technology is occurring at a speed of development that at one time would have seemed imaginable only in science fiction, especially the development of e-computational technology (so-called "digitalization"). Table 4 characterizes different periods of civilization (represented by the degree of development - D) and the consequences of varying ICT systems.

Analyzing these stages of machine civilization development is not the subject of this article; instead, the goal is merely to provide classification, as was done in Table 4, to prove that the GMS 8D Civilizational approach must be designed top-down way. Moreover, the purpose of this classification is to awaken a sense of responsibility and duty. For a while, the possibilities of what artificial intelligence can do for humankind are exciting, and they are also dangerous. AI could lead to widespread unemployment (a laborless economy) and a form of communism in which everyone would receive an equal allowance from the state to pay their bills. This allowance would be created from a fund generated by the few oligarchs who own most of the world's robots as a form of taxation for their " technical progress." There is already support for people out of work in Finland as well as Stockton, California, where there is high unemployment and where select poor workers (70% of whom are ethnic minorities) get a universal basic income of $500 per month in addition to temporary state insurance for the unemployed (Treisman, 2021).

As for the development of cyborgs, many laud the predictions made by the most famous American futurologist, Ray Kurzweil (2005), who has claimed that by about 2025, computers will think faster than humans. In this way, we will create the so-called *singularity*, i.e., a point at which technological growth is uncontrollable and irreversible due to a runaway self-improving AI system. Thus, Kurzweil believes computers will lead to the Bing Bang and the creation of new intelligence. He forgets, however, that thinking fast does not mean thinking wisely. Furthermore, why would we allow fast-thinking cyborgs to destroy us? Is the situation analogous to when our early ancestor Cro-Magnons "got rid of" Neanderthals in central Europe? Isaac Asimov (1950) had already foreseen this situation concerning computer development when, in the 1940s and 1950s, he developed three laws for how to deal with robots. First and foremost, we must not design robots that will kill us.

What is worse, before *machine* civilization destroys us, we will first end up alone to promote a way of life that destroys *human* civilization, as will be mentioned in different sections of this work.

THE DEATH TRIANGLE OF CIVILIZATION

The general public is not aware that modern civilization has led to creating the *Death Triangle of Civilization*. It is a combination of population, environmental, and raw material (i.e., resources) bombs (Targowski, 2009). The concept is illustrated in the model in Figure 8. The severity of this triangle lies in the interdependence between the bombs.

- **Population bomb**: The greatest threat to civilization is that we will overcrowd this small planet Earth. In the year 2020, the population was about 7.8 billion. It has been growing annually by about 80 million people, almost double the current population of countries like Poland. Over the last 50 years (1960-2010), the world's population has more than doubled from three billion to 6.8 billion people. It is a more significant increase than any of the last two million years. Since the start of the third millennium, people have reproduced at a rate of 1.2% per year, which will lead to a doubling of the current population over the next 58 years. At that point, there would be about 14 billion people on Earth. In recent years, an additional one billion people are born nearly every 12-13 years (Population Media Center, 2021). The current population size should be considered the number one problem for modern civilization.

Figure 8. The Death Triangle of Civilization (Targowski, 2009, p. 404)

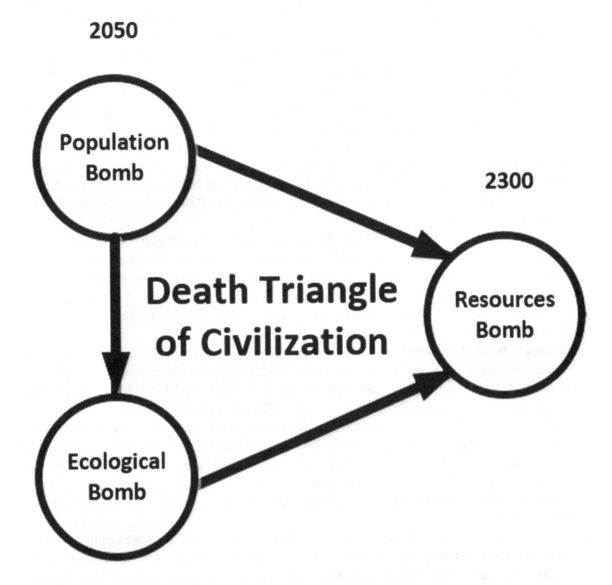

- For this reason, an agreement must be reached between organized sacred religion, business, and governments on a system for controlling population development in the world. So far, organized religions (especially the Catholic Church) have opposed birth control; however, they do not feel responsible for the fate of the born. Governments in democratic states are also passive, not wanting to repeat China's alleged mistakes, which introduced a strict birth control system. The role of business, on the other hand, is not taken into account at all. What is striking about all of this is the passivity towards the conclusions. This attitude is resulting in the sense of helplessness, exacerbating the situation.
- **Ecological bomb**: The ecological bomb comes from overcrowding the planet and from destroying the natural environment. Overcrowding and extravagant lifestyles make the environmental (or en-

vironmental) footprint of humanity too large to keep the environment intact. One's environmental footprint measures (a) how much land and water a person requires to remain alive biologically, (b) how much space a person needs for buildings and roads, and (c) how much fresh air a person needs to for breathing. The size of a person's footprint varies over time, depending on the dynamics of the civilization (its development and decline). This measure also assesses how quickly people consume resources and generate waste compared to how fast nature can absorb waste and restore resources. Considering the total environmental footprint of civilization, we currently consume the equivalent of one and a half planets in terms of the resources used and the possibility that the Earth can absorb our waste. It is analogous to taking supplies from a warehouse that we cannot replenish to their initial level. If the current trend of population growth and strategic resources continues, civilization will need two Earth-sized planets by around 2030 to support human activity. What is worse, by about 2050, it will take as many as three earth-sized planets to keep civilization functioning at its current levels.

- Regarding global warming, NASA scientists have discovered that the Thwaites Glacier in Western Antarctica, dubbed the "glacier of doom" by the media, has become even more unstable. News about the glacier intensified in early 2019 when NASA found a cavity nearly two-thirds the size of Manhattan in it. The total melting of Thwaites would raise sea levels by 50 cm, which would sink many coastal cities. Moreover, the instability of the ice giant leads to the conclusion that other glaciers face a similar fate (Jacobs, 2019).

- **Resources bomb**: For 5,800 years, or 96% of its existence, civilization functioned based on human and animal muscles and was not limited by any energy resources except food availability. Since the Industrial Revolution—that is, in the last 200 years—civilization has been operating based on the power of internal combustion engines. Thanks to this, it has become self-propelled, insanely comfortable for people, and very productive. However, by some estimates, oil reserves will run out in about 53 years at the current consumption rate (Kuo, 2019). Simultaneously, the price of oil will increase as mining techniques are increasingly advanced and costly. A similar fate awaits reserves of natural gas, uranium, and coal. The first two raw materials will be enough for the next 40-50 years of civilization, while coal reserves are more extensive and may last until 2300 (Gore, 1993).

- Similarly, stocks of rare-earth metals, many of which are located in China, are small. Rare earth metals are essential for the manufacture of electronic devices, which are the most characteristic product of modern civilization because they control complex systems. If these metals become depleted, civilization may cease to function. The answer to the depletion of these resources is the hope that human knowledge will solve the dilemma. Indeed, engineers have developed ways to obtain renewable energy based on wind power, solar radiation, and biofuels.

In conclusion, the following points are worth highlighting (Targowski, 2019).

1. The greatest threat to civilization is overcrowding the planet. It would result in the destruction of the environment and the depletion of strategic resources. Therefore, the world population should aim at having an optimal size of about five billion people by 2050.

2. A lifestyle change should reduce the world's population so that the environmental footprint of individual countries is sustainable by 2050, i.e., most states must get rid of their current footprint deficit.

3. Modern civilizations, particularly NGO think tanks, are well informed and discuss overcrowding problems, environmental destruction, and resource depletion. Nonetheless, politicians elected in cycles of two to four years do not attach importance to such issues. By and large, this is because they listen not to their constituents but to lobbyists who, in various legal forms, financially support their careers. Thus, the world should be controlled by new goals in the 21st century.

THE GMS 8D CIVILIZATION ARCHITECTURE OF THE WORLD

The approach to sustainable civilization has mainly been limited to agreements to reduce harmful greenhouse gas emissions to reduce or maintain the current temperature. For example, the Paris Agreement of 2016 aimed to ensure that, by the end of the 21st century, temperatures would not rise by 2°C. However, there has been almost no discussion of creating an information system for monitoring and directing a sustainable civilization. Until a World Civilization Organization (WCO) with regional and national branches is created, it will not be possible to develop and execute a sustainable civilization.

The creation of a WCO should not come as a surprise to anyone, as similar organizations are already in places, such as the World Trade Organization (WTO), the World Health Organization (WHO), the World Bank, the International Monetary Fund (IMF), UNESCO, the United Nations, the World Tourism Organization, the International Atomic Energy Agency, the International Labor Office, and many others.

Figure 9 depicts the architecture of the World Geoinformatics Management System (GMS) of 8D Civilization, which includes the following elements:

- **Objective**: Monitor and support activities that aid in the development and control of a sustainable civilization;
- **Mission**: Ensure the preservation of the human species in a sustainable civilization, where work is a means of enriching humanistic values;
- **Strategy**: A top-down approach;
- **Principle**: The wellbeing of humankind and nature are more important than money;
- **Credo**: Humans are more valuable than machines;
- **Areas of Knowledge**:
  - *Drinking water*: agricultural, industrial, and other areas;
  - *Climate*: temperature, greenhouse gases, changes, hazards;
  - *Nature* – ecology, animals, greenery, forests, rivers, seas, mountains, glaciers, and more
  - *Resources (Natural)*: energy, metals, minerals, and others;
  - *Energy Creation:* nuclear and renewable energy;
  - *Society*: populations, lifestyles, healthcare, education, construction, work, globalization, mechanization, automation, computerization, artificial intelligence, business relationships, and others;
  - *Land*: space development, urbanization, eco-construction, and others;
  - *Waste*: organic, wastewater, landfills, renewable, and others;
  - *Recycling*: metals, plastics, paper, and other types of materials;
  - *Leadership*: leaders and organizations;
  - Others.

- **A GMS 8D Civilization Management Dashboard**: Users of the dashboard would belong to the World Organization of Civilizations, a continental organization that monitors civilizations in the Americas, Europe, Africa, Asia, the Oceania region Polar regions.
- **A World Base in Poznań**: This base would serve as a center for exchanging units of cognition between continents. The units of cognition include the following (Targowski, 1999, 2016):
  - *Big Data*: logging processes and events;
  - *Big Information*: calculating changes in processes and events that trigger corrective or streamlined actions;
  - *Big Concepts*: collecting ideas that are functioning and innovative but waiting to be implemented;
  - *Big Knowledge*: scientific data and principles that generate awareness of a situation;
  - *Big Wisdom*: optimal choices for problem solving and decision-making.
- **A World Civilization Infostrada**: This Global Area Network (GAN) would be a private network of the world with regional and national offshoots. It is not an Internet-based network, which would not provide security for the information being transmitted.
- **Other Elements**: Numerous other elements do not need to be defined in this first conceptual architecture. Future versions will refine the assumptions made in the model.

The GMS management dashboard will process and make available all kinds of information about Key Performance Indicators (KPIs). These indicators must be calculated, updated, and communicated to users, and they must be harmonized and integrated into aggregations at all levels of the system. Although there are already several indicator systems in place at the level of companies, these systems are not well integrated because there is not yet a World Civilization Organization (WCO) that can provide geoinformatics coordination.

The WCO should operate based on the following main principles:

1. Each state is obliged to be a member of the WCO because civilization spans across every continent and is not selective. Countries that disregard the development of sustainable civilization can pose a serious threat to others regarding areas such as climate, water, and strategic raw materials.
2. Each state will contribute 1% of its GDP at the beginning of the WCO, but this will be multiplied by taking into account a global hectare limit (gha/per country). Most countries exceed their limit twice over, and some emirates exceed it by up to 10 times.
3. In the event of non-compliance of individual countries with the objectives, strategies, and rules of the WCO, different types of penalties will be imposed. The principle must be adopted that ecology has priority over democracy, disregarding its responsibilities to share the planet. The WCO should also operate according to the principles of Wise Civilization (Targowski, 2019).

THE GMS 8D CIVILIZATION ARCHITECTURE OF CONTINENTS

This architecture is similar to the GMS 8D Civilization architecture of the world (Figure 9), with the nuance that its primary users are from the countries of the continent concerned. For example, the European continent is involved with European Western Civilization, European Southern Civilization, European Central Civilization, European Eastern Civilization, and European Northern Civilization.

Figure 9. The architecture of the Geoinformatic Management System of 8D Civilization for the world

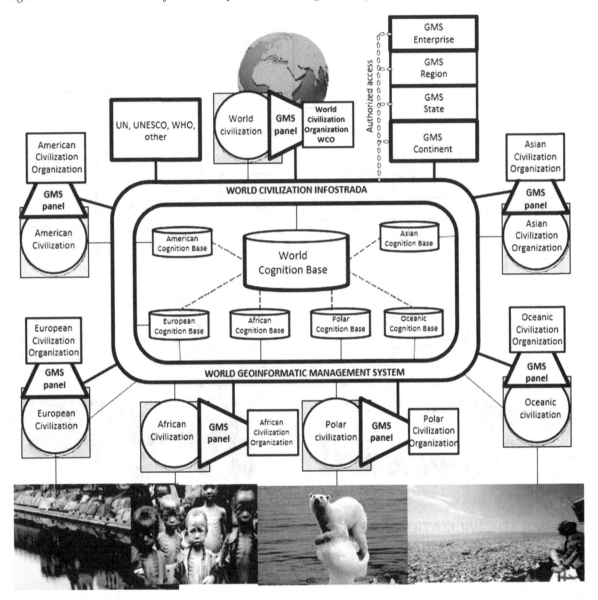

THE GMS 8D CIVILIZATION ARCHITECTURE OF COUNTRIES: THE CASE OF POLAND

The GMS 8D Civilization architecture of individual countries is shown in Figure 10. The model shows the case of Poland, which was adopted as an example of such a system.

The architecture of the GMS 8D Civilization for a region is similar to that of a country, except it will be limited to the region's specific territories, and its elements will be enterprises, described below.

Figure 10. The GMS 8D Civilization architecture at the country level (Poland)

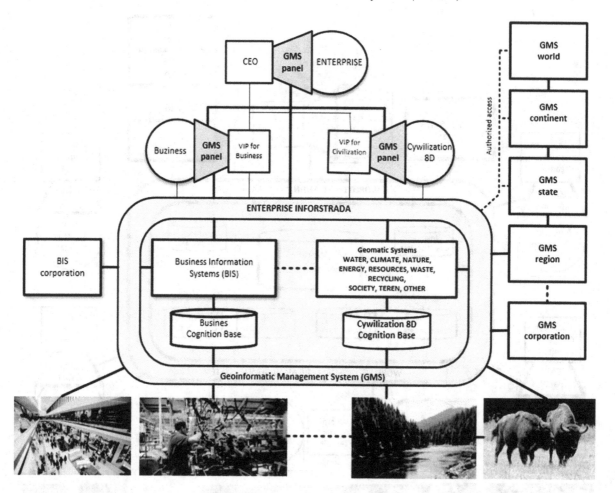

THE GMS 8D CIVILIZATION ARCHITECTURE OF ENTERPRISES

The GMS 8D Civilization architecture for enterprises is shown in Figure 11.

SUMMARY

1. The use of information systems to drive the sustainable development of Earth requires planning and designing a top-down approach, for the climate knows no borders, and a solution at the level of a single country, region, or enterprise—even if suitable at that level—may not be effective if applied at a larger scale, such as at the level of a continent or the world.

2. For such systems to be implemented, it is necessary to create a World Civilization Organization (WCO) along the lines of the World Health Organization, the World Trade Organization, and others with similar frameworks.

Figure 11. The GMS 8D Civilization architecture at the enterprise level

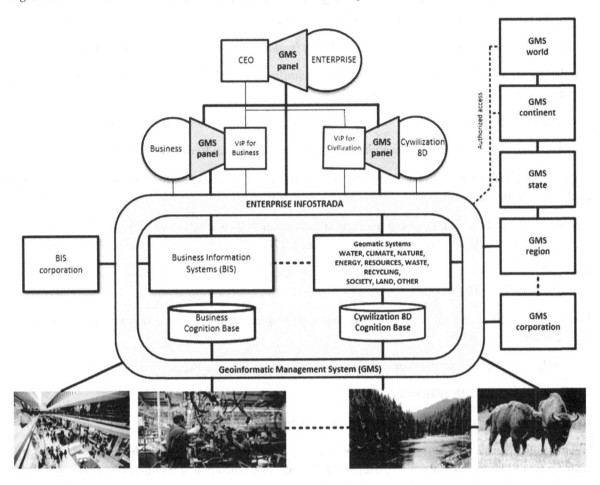

3. Poland can pioneer this approach if it establishes a National Organization for Civilization (NCO), which will support the WCO and the European Organization of Civilization (ECO) creation.

REFERENCES

Asimov, I. (1950). *I, robot*. Gnome Press.

Gore, A. (1993). *Earth in the Balance: Ecology and the human spirit*. Rodale.

Jacobs, J. (2019, February 1). A cavity in Antarctica glacier is two-thirds the size of Manhattan, scientists say. *The New York Times*. https://www.nytimes.com/2019/02/01/climate/thwaites-glacier-antarctica-cavity.html

Krawczyk, H., & Targowski, A. (2019). *Wisdom in the context of globalization and civilization*. Cambridge Scholars Publishers.

Kuo, G. (2019). When fossil fuels run out, what then? *Millennium Alliance for Humanity and the Biosphere*. https://mahb.stanford.edu/library-item/fossil-fuels-run/

Kurzweil, R. (2005). *The singularity is near: When humans transcend biology*. Penguin Books.

Population Media Center. (2021). *PMC works to stabilize the global population*. https://www.populationmedia.org/issue/population-growth/

Sustainable Society Index. (2016). *The world perspective*. https://ssi.wi.th-koeln.de/spiderwebs.php

Targowski, A. (1980). *IT, development models, and systems*. Polish Economic Society.

Targowski, A. (1990). *The architecture and planning of enterprise-wide information management systems*. Idea Group Publishing.

Targowski, A. (2005). Universal-complementary civilization as a solution to present-day catastrophic international conflicts. *Dialogue and Universalism*, *15*(7/8), 73–100. doi:10.5840/du2005157/883

Targowski, A. (2009). *Information technology and societal development*. Information Science Reference. doi:10.4018/978-1-60566-004-2

Targowski, A. (2013). *History, present, and future of computer science*. Publishing Houses of the Technical University of Lodz.

Targowski, A. (2016). *Informing and civilization*. Informing Science Press.

Targowski, A. (2018). *Development of KSI and Pesel*. Oficyna Publishing Kucharski.

Targowski, A. (2019). *The limits of civilization*. Creator Publishing House.

Treisman, R. (2021, March 4). California program giving $500 no-strings-attached stipends pays off, study finds. *NPR*. https://www.npr.org/2021/03/04/973653719/california-program-giving-500-no-strings-attached-stipends-pays-off-study-finds

Zychowicz, P. (2013). *Obłęd'44: Czyli Polacy zrobili prezent Stalinowi, wywołując powstanie Warszawskie* [Madness in 1944: The Polish gift to Stalin and the triggering of the Warsaw Uprising]. Rebis.

KEY TERMS AND DEFINITIONS

Environmental Footprint: This measure compares the rate of human consumption of resources and generation of wealth with how quickly nature can absorb waste and regenerate resources.

Joint Application Design: A process that emphasizes enhancing user participation in information systems.

Key Performance Indicators: A type of performance measurement that assesses targeted organizational activities, such as programs and projects.

Machine Learning: A type of computational algorithm that improves its ability to analyze data automatically through data input.

Natural Language Processing: The use of computers to process and analyze natural language data.

Singularity: A hypothesis that there will be a point in time at which technological development becomes uncontrollable and irreversible. One popular version holds that this will occur with a self-improving artificial intelligence.

Spirituality 2.0: An integration of complementary values promoted by different religions of the world.

Systems Ecology: An interdisciplinary branch of ecology that studies ecology through a holistic approach.

ENDNOTES

1 Terms such as "balanced", "green", and "wise civilization" are treated as synonyms and used depending on the context.

2 Readers interested in this type of information technology should refer to detailed manuals.

3 Users can try to develop a health check for their own needs within 30 days by logging in to the *Build for free IBM Cloud*: https://cloud.ibm.com/registration/trial

Chapter 20
Digital Security Strategy

ABSTRACT

This chapter analyzes digital security strategies for the 21ˢᵗ century. The chapter begins by examining different types of cyberattacks, such as identity theft, malware, and phishing. Next, the chapter reviews statistics about cyberattacks in the US and the world, focusing on the monetary costs. The typical targets of cyberattacks are then considered, followed by a discussion about how to prevent cybercrime. The chapter next reviews digital security indicators that can provide valuable information about cybercrime and cyberattacks. After this, the chapter discusses cyberwar, which involves cyberattacks not just used against individuals and companies, but against entire states. The chapter concludes by advancing a digital security strategy that can be used in the 21ˢᵗ century.

INTRODUCTION

A cyberattack is an attack carried out from one or more computers against another computer(s) or a computer network. Cyberattacks can be divided into two general types: (a) attacks designed to disable the target computer or take it offline, and (b) attacks that aim to gain access to the data of the target computer or gain administrator privileges.

Data breaches and digital security incidents are becoming increasingly costly. Desjardins Group, a Canadian lender, revealed that it spent $53 million as a result of a disclosure of 2.9 million of its members. In addition, the manufacturer Norsk Hydro reported that a recent cyberattack could cost them as much as $75 million. Finally, British Airways and Marriott, in addition to the costs of recent cyberattacks, had to pay $100 million each for failing to comply with the General Data Protection Regulation (GDPR) (Swinhoe, 2020).[1]

DOI: 10.4018/978-1-7998-8036-3.ch020

TYPES OF CYBERATTACKS

To achieve the goal of accessing or disabling computer networks, cybercriminals use several different technical methods. New methods are always being developed, and some categories overlap, but the following are some of the most popular:

- **Identity theft** is also one of the worst-case scenarios that can meet a victim of cybercrime. It starts with someone stealing another's identity by using identifiable data, such as victim's name, driver's license, and social security number. The thief then commits fraud, steals property, embezzles goods or uses services in the victim's name.
- **Cyberbullying** is when person tries to intimidate or harass others using computer systems connected to the Internet. Most cases of cyberbullying involve the use of communication systems such as email, social networks, and instant messaging, which allows the cyberbully to keep their identity anonymous.
- **Social engineering** is one of the most classic types of cyberattacks that can be carried out against individuals or organizations. It involves manipulating people to obtain valuable information that can later be used to illegally log into privately protected systems or networks. Often, the primary motivation behind social engineering is the theft of money, financial data (such as bank accounts or credit card information), and other confidential information from a company or customer.
- **Botnets** are cyberattacks that involve the use of one or more bots connected over a network (e.g., the Internet). The word "botnet" comes from blending the words "robot" and "network". These botnets are used to spread malicious files and software, infect other systems, carry out Distributed Denial-of-Service (DDoS) attacks, steal data, and send spam messages.
- **Malware** refers to any software, regardless of its structure or operation, which is designed to damage a single computer, server, or computer network. Worms, viruses, and Trojans are variations of malware that differ in the way they multiply and spread. These attacks can cause a computer or network to stop working or give an attacker root access to control the system remotely.
- **Phishing** is a technique in which cybercriminals produce emails to deceive a target and take malicious actions. The recipient may be tricked into downloading malware that is hidden in a valid document, or they may be asked to click on a link to a fake website where they will be asked to provide sensitive information, such as bank usernames and passwords. Many phishing emails cast a wide net and are sent by email to thousands of potential victims, but some are designed explicitly for valuable targets to try to convince them to share useful information.
- **Ransomware** is a variant of malware that encrypts the victim's files. The attacker then demands a ransom from the victim to restore access to the data after payment. Users are shown instructions on how to pay for obtaining a decryption key. The costs can range from a few hundred dollars to thousands and are usually paid to cybercriminals in cryptocurrencies.
- **Denial of service** is a method of brutal force, which involves preventing the proper functioning of some online services. For example, attackers can send so much traffic to a website or so many requests to a database that it overwhelms the ability of these systems to operate, making them inaccessible to anyone. Distributed Denial-of-Service (DDoS) attacks use an army of computers, usually compromised by malware and under the control of cybercriminals, to direct traffic towards targets.

- **The Man in the Middle** (MITM) attack is a method by which attackers secretly intervene between a user and internet services they are trying to access. For example, an attacker could set up a Wi-Fi network with a sign-in screen designed to mimic a hotel network; when a user logs on, the attacker can collect any information sent by the user, including bank passwords.
- **Cryptojacking** is a specialized attack, which involves forcing another user's computer to mine cryptocurrency. Attackers either install malware on the victim's computer to perform the necessary calculations or sometimes run a JavaScript code that is executed in the victim's browser.
- **Illegal content** is prohibited content on the Internet. This includes all content prohibited by international law around the world. Examples of unlawful content include child and animal pornography, online prostitution services, online drug sales, and copyrighted material (such as movies, music, books, software, etc.).
- **Online fraud** includes fraudulent companies offering fake services, goods, or rewards to unwitting victims. Examples of online fraud include charity scams, gambling scams, Ponzi schemes, online ticket fraud, counterfeit gift cards, car fraud, and more.
- **SQL injection** is one way through which an attacker can exploit a security vulnerability to take control of a victim's database. Many databases are designed to match commands written in structured query language (SQL), and many web pages that retrieve information from users send this data to SQL databases. In a SQL injection attack, a hacker saves some SQL commands to a web form asking for a name and address; if the website and database are not programmed correctly, the database may try to execute these commands.
- **Zero Day** attacks target software vulnerabilities that need to be fixed. The attack was termed "zero day" because it is carried out the same day on which a security vulnerability is discovered. Techniques for exploiting such vulnerabilities are often bought and sold on the dark web and are sometimes discovered by government agencies, which can controversially use them for hacking purposes rather than disclosing information about them for the benefit of all.

STATISTICS OF CYBERATTACKS IN THE USA

To understand the dark world of cybercrime, it is necessary to delve into the world of statistics. While we may have become insensitive due to the constant stories of personal data breaches, the total amounts are truly staggering: In just the first half of 2019, 4.1 billion records were hacked. Verizon, which publishes a detailed report on data breaches every year, helped determine who the victims and perpetrators were in 2019. According to their estimates, 34 percent of violations were inside jobs, 39 percent were committed by organized crime, and 23 percent by state entities. In regard to the victims, the largest category by far was small businesses, which suffered 43 percent of the attacks (Fruhlinger, 2020).

The costs of cyberattacks are also staggering. Ransomware alone cost $8 billion in 2018; however, only $1 billion of that amount was actually ransom payments: the rest was lost revenue and damage to the company's reputation as a result of downtime. Other types of cybercrime have also taken a toll. Radware estimated that a cyberattack on a large company could cost about $1.7 million. For small businesses, the cost is lower, just $86,000; however, this can still be disastrous for a company without large reserves (Fruhlinger, 2020).

In the past, a breach that compromised the data of several million people was a big story; however, at present, data breaches that affect hundreds of millions or even billions of people are far too familiar.

In fact, around 3.5 billion people had personal information stolen from them in just the top two of the 15 most significant breaches of this century. The smallest incident on the list involved a data breach of "only" 134 million people (Swinhoe, 2021).

CSO (the Central Statistics Office, USA) has compiled a list of the most massive violations of the 21st century, using a simple criterion: the number of people whose data has been compromised (Swinhoe, 2021). The list also distinguishes between incidents where data was stolen with bad intentions and those in which an organization inadvertently left data unsecured and exposed. For example, Twitter left the passwords of 330 million users unmasked in a log; however, there was no evidence of misuse. In Table 1, the ten most massive data breaches in recent history are listed.

Table 1. The most significant data breaches in the 21st century in the U.S. (Swinhoe, 2021)

Company	Service	Year Attack	Number of Records Captured	Effect
Heartland Payment Systems	Payment processing for small businesses	2008	134 million	Records and data of 175,000 small businesses were captured.
LinkedIn	A social network for professionals	2012 & 2016	165 million	Names and addresses were sold for five bitcoins on the black market.
Adobe	Graphics	2013	153 million	Passwords and card numbers of customers were stolen.
MySpace	Social network	2013	360 million	Stolen user data was sold for six bitcoins, worth $3,000.
eBay	Online trading market.	2014	145 million	Passwords and other personal information were stolen, prompting the company to request that customers change their passwords.
Marriot International	Hotel chain	2014-2018	500 million	Credit card information of 100 million cards was seized.
Yahoo	Search engine	2014	3 billion	The breach cost Yahoo around $350 million while being acquired by Verizon.
Adult Friend Finder	Adult content and dating services	2016	420 million	Personal-sensitive data was intercepted.
Equifax	Credit bureau	2017	163 million	User passwords and credit cards were compromised.
Dubsmash	Video messaging service	2018	162 million	Customer records were exposed.

STATISTICS OF CYBERATTACKS IN THE WORLD

The following statistics provide an overview of how cyberattacks have impacted the world ("2021 Cyber Security Statistics", 2021).

- In 2018, there were 80,000 cyberattacks per day, or more than 30 million attacks per year.
- 21% of all files are not protected in any way.

- 41% of companies have more than 1,000 confidential files, including credit card numbers and medical records, that are left unprotected.
- 69% of organizations do not believe that their antivirus software can block threats they encounter.
- 50% of the security risks to organizations are posed by having multiple suppliers and security products.
- 7 out of 10 organizations say their security risk increased significantly in 2017.
- 65% of companies have more than 500 users who are never asked to change their password.
- Ransomware attacks are increasing by more than 350% per year.
- Internet of things (IoT) attacks increased by 600% in 2017.
- In 2017, 61 percent of the victims of breaches were from companies with fewer than 1,000 employees.
- Coin mining was the largest area of cybercrime growth in 2017.
- 90% of remote code execution attacks are related to cryptocurrencies.
- More than 50 IoT devices on the market have security vulnerabilities.
- 61% of organizations experienced an IoT security incident.
- The average cost of a data breach for businesses around the world is $3.86 million.
- It takes organizations an average of 191 days to identify data breaches.
- 88% of companies spent more than $1 million preparing for the GDPR.
- 25% of organizations have an independent security department.
- 54% of companies experienced an industrial inspection system security incident.
- It is predicted that cybercriminals will steal approximately 33 billion records in 2023.

TARGETS OF CYBERCRIME

The following targets of cybercrime can be distinguished (Borges, 2019).

- **Cybercrime against Individuals:** These types of cybercrime include, but are not limited to, social engineering, phishing, email harassment, cyberstalking, and the dissemination of illegal adult material.
- **Cybercrime against Companies and Organizations:** When an online company or any of its products are hacked, it becomes a severe problem that can have many consequences for the company as well as for its employees, associates, and customers. Examples include data breaches, cyberspace enforcement, and the distribution of illegally copied software.
- **Cybercrime against Society:** Crimes against public organizations include the sale of illegal products, human trafficking, online gambling, forgery, etc.
- **Cybercrime against the Government:** This is one of the worst types of cybercrime in the world and can result in prosecutions by state cybersecurity agencies and traditional law enforcement. This area of cybercrime includes cyberterrorism, such as breaking into government systems and networks, destroying and shutting down military websites, and disseminating propaganda.

HOW TO PREVENT CYBERCRIME?

Here are popular ways to prevent cybercrime in computer systems (Borges, 2019):

- **Update Software:** This is a critical requirement for any computer system and application. It is important to always update operating systems, services, and applications to patch the latest bugs and vulnerabilities. This advice also applies to smartphones, tablets, local desktops, notebooks, online servers, and all internally run applications.

- **Enable a System Firewall:** Most operating systems include a fully configured firewall to protect against malicious packages both inside and outside. The system firewall acts as the first digital layer of defense every time someone tries to send a wrong packet to an open port.

- **Use Different and Strong Passwords:** A user should not use the same password on more than one site, and they should always make sure their password combines letters, special characters, and numbers. The best way to solve this problem is to use a password manager, such as 1Password, LastPass, or Keepass, which helps users to generate strong passwords for each website while keeping them in an encrypted database.

- **Use Antivirus and Anti-malware Software:** This is an excellent measure for both individual and corporate users. It is always recommended to update antivirus and anti-malware software and to run scans on local data. While free antivirus/anti-malware solutions can be helpful, they are often only trial software and do not provide full protection against the most common viruses/malware and other network threats. There are many options for Windows. One of the best is the Windows Malware Removal Tool. Linux and Unix also offer excellent options, such as ClamAV, LMD, Chkrootkit, and Rootkit Hunter.

- **Activate Spam Blocking in Email:** Any time a user opens unwanted emails containing suspicious links or attachments, their computer could be hacked. To prevent this, users must enable their email client's anti-spam features. In addition, and more importantly, users should never open links or attachments from unsolicited recipients. This will protect against phishing attacks and unwanted infections.

- **Use 2FA for all Online Services:**[2] Most online services and products offer two-factor authentication (via services such as Authy, Google Authenticator, etc.). These security mechanisms allow users to add a second layer of authentication with the result that, even if an attacker steals a username and password, they will not be able to log into the online account because they will not have access to the 2FA code sent, generated by, or created on the user's computer.

- **Encrypt Local Hard Drives:** Cybercrime does not just occur on the Internet. For example, a thief could break into someone's house and steal their notebook. Therefore, the best way to protect data against this kind of crime is to encrypt hard drives so that, thereby preventing criminals from reviewing the contents of the drive. When using encryption, the user is the only one with the key to unlock it. Encryption services are provided by Linux, Windows, and MacOS.

- **Make Purchases only from Secure and Well-Known Websites:** Not all websites based on secure socket layers (SSL) are safe.[3] To prevent becoming a victim of man-in-the-middle attacks and crimes against credit cards or online wallets, users should make sure that the site they are buying from is encrypted with a Hyper Text Transfer Protocol Secure (HTTPS) certificate. Users should also make sure they are shopping on a well-known website like Amazon, eBay, Walmart, etc.

- **Use a WHOIS Private Service:** To protect registered domain names, users can enable WHOIS protection. This service allows users to stay hidden without revealing their name, address, city, country, phone number, and email address. While using a private WHOIS service will not completely prevent a domain takeover, it can help protect personal and confidential data.
- **Use a Private DNS Server:**[4] DNS hijacking has become a common threat. Therefore, using a personal and secure DNS may be one of the best ways of preventing unwanted third-party attacks, while preventing the government and Internet service providers (ISPs)[5] from viewing historical data about communication records with the host.
- **Use a VPN:**[6] VPNs are becoming more and more popular every year. Using them helps to prevent third parties (especially your ISP) from spying on online activities. Another reason for using a VPN is to log into a secure network from a remote location, such as when using unreliable internet connections during travel.
- **Encrypt Email** - Using a PGP[7] key can help ensure that intended email recipients will only read emails from legitimate senders. PGP helps users sign, encrypt, and decrypt texts, emails, and files, thereby helping to make email communications more secure.
- **Monitor Online Activity of Children**: In local networks, cybercrime can happen as a result of breaches on tablets, phones, and notebooks of one's children. Therefore, it is important to teach children to not fall victim to cybercriminals by using some of the same tips mentioned above. It is also important to review their historical online activities in browsers, social networks, and emails to protect them from bad actors. Using parental control software to protect against threats is also an option.

With cyberspace comes cybercrime. While it is a harsh truth, it is part of our nature. There are many ways to become a victim of cybercrime; however, by following the above techniques, this can help reduce the chances of an attack from malicious users.

DIGITAL SECURITY INDICATORS

Here are some of the digital security indicators used by security leaders that can help assess digital security (Pratt, 2020):

- **Results of Simulated Phishing Attacks**: Simulated phishing attacks are used to help assess the effectiveness of awareness training and set improvement goals.
- **Average Time to Recovery:** This measures the percentage of users affected by a cyberattack and the speed with which the security team solved the problem. It also assesses whether the time to recovery meets, exceeds, or does not reach the target time established by the organization.
- **The Average Time to Detect a Cyberattack:** It is recommended that organizations use an indicator known as average detection time—a measure of the time that has elapsed from a successful attack to the moment of detection—because it indicates how well the security program works. This information can also be used to show security improvements and can help leaders take into account what investments are needed to make improvements. What is more, these indicators encourage continuous improvement: If, for example, the average detection time is around a few minutes, the security team can aim to reduce it to a few seconds.

- **Penetration Tests:** Like simulated phishing attacks, penetration test metrics indicate how well an organization can resist such events and can track improvements over time. This is information that management and board members understand and value.
- **Vulnerability Management:** This involves assessing a security department's ability to deal with vulnerabilities. The aim is not to entirely eliminate all risk, but to ensure that security threats that pose the most significant risks can be stopped as soon as possible.
- **Enterprise Security Audits:** Audits can be conducted using scorecards developed by organizations such as the National Institute of Standards and Technology (NIST), the Information Technology Infrastructure Library (ITIL), and the Center for Internet Security (CIS).

FROM CYBERATTACKS TO CYBERWAR

Cyberwar is the use of information technology to attack the state, causing comparable damage to actual war (Singer & Friedman, 2014). Cyberattacks carried out against states includes those that took place in Estonia in 2007, Georgia in 2008, Iran in 2010, and North Korea in 2017 (Lockie, 2017). These all occurred in international contexts, resulting only in condemnation and denial by the parties involved. An alternative definition of cyberwar is that it is a cyberattack that cause physical damage to people and objects in the real world (Green, 1981; Lucas, 2015).

The 2007 attack by Russian hackers on Estonia was a warning signal to all developed countries. Russian hackers, using a simple denial-of-service attack, were able to cripple the Baltic state for several days. The functioning of government, ministries, banks, hospitals, telecommunications companies, and the media was virtually paralyzed.

Other cyberattacks carried out around this time period were done on a smaller scale, with objectives such as extracting information and exploiting vulnerabilities by penetrating networks and computers. For example, the United States and Israel developed Operation Stuxnet to slow Iran's nuclear program. This was accomplished by remotely damaging uranium enrichment centrifuges through a complex attack involving, among other things, a computer virus.

Becoming aware of the growing potential for cyberattacks in the wake of events such as the Estonian incident, the United States and China have steadily advanced their cyberwar strategies. They have been developing organizations, procedures, and weapons to deliver them.

The cyber strategy of President Barack Obama's administration (2009-2016) was mostly defensive. Under President Donald Trump (2017-2020), the strategy became more proactive, in line with his vision of American supremacy. The shift in tone between military and cyber strategies under the Obama and Trump administrations reflects rising tensions between the US and China. This cyberwar, or Cold War 2.0, is based on the development of technical and human resources, intelligence gathering, sabotage, and influential operations (Venard, 2019).

Resources for cyberwar are growing on both sides. Being the cradle of giant digital companies and having the world's most massive military budget, the US undeniably has tremendous cyber-firepower. In 2009, the federal government set up a new military command center, the US Cyber Command, which currently employs more than 6,000 professionals (Venard, 2019).

For its part, China relies on the Third Department of the People's Army, internal cybersecurity forces, and several technology companies. In 2015, Beijing created the equivalent of the US Cyber Command

Center—the Strategic Force—which combines the resources of the People's Army in cyber, space, and electronic warfare.

The number of espionage cases between the two countries has been increasing, including the theft of plans for US F-35 military aircraft. This led to the "miraculous" creation of the Shenyang FC-31 after Chinese spies allegedly stole American plans. Cold War 2.0 is also aimed at economic interests. In 2012, former FBI Director Robert Mueller stated that there are only two types of companies: those that have been hacked and those that will be (Venard, 2019).

Since then, more than 80% of economic espionage cases against the United States have been linked to China. For example, hackers linked to china's Ministry of State Security hacked the Marriott Group over four years, stealing the personal information of about 500 million customers (Venard, 2019).

Physical sabotage is also part of cyberwar. In 2017, using its digital arsenal, the US managed to defeat a missile fire attempt by North Korea, who are loyal allies of China. According to the Cartwright doctrine (named after US General James Cartwright), for a cyber strategy to be effective, it must be backed up by an operational component, supported in some cases by messages warning opponents of the risks incurred and revealing enemy threats (Venard, 2019).

Influence and destabilization are essential objectives of the Cold War 2.0. During the Aurora cyberattack of 2009-2010, China allegedly attacked 34 U.S. companies, undermining flagship companies such as Northrop Grumman, Dow Chemical, and Google. Will the next step be a Chinese digital propaganda campaign in a US presidential election or in an allied democratic nation? China has already demonstrated its ability to hack accounts and spread disinformation in the media during the recent unrest in Hong Kong (Venard, 2019).

Cold War 2.0 is a kind of guerrilla warfare characterized by constant digital skirmishes between the United States and China as well as the proliferation of spying, sabotage, and influence. Given that both countries have nuclear weapons, the most important thing now is for the two countries to avoid a Thucydides Trap.[8]

States should organize their cyber defenses based on the following monitoring and command centers:

- United States:
  - United States Cyber Command,
  - Joint Task Force Ares,
  - Army:
    - U.S. Army Cyber Command,
    - U.S. Army Network Enterprise Technology Command,
    - 1st Information Operations Command (Land):
      - 1st Information Operations Battalion,
      - 2nd Information Operations Battalion,
    - 780th Military Intelligence Brigade (Cyber) "Pretorians":
      - 781st Military Intelligence Battalion "Vanguard",
      - 782nd Military Intelligence Battalion "Cyber Legion",
      - 915th Cyber Warfare Battalion,
      - Cyber Solutions Development Detachment,
      - Task Force Echo (Army Reserve),
  - Army Reserve:

- Cyber Protection Brigade:
  - North East Cyber Protection Center:
    - 180th Cyber Protection Team,
    - 181st Cyber Protection Team,
  - National Capital Region Cyber Protection Center:
    - 182nd Cyber Protection Team,
    - 183rd Cyber Protection Team,
  - South West Cyber Protection Center:
    - 184th Cyber Protection Team,
    - 185th Cyber Protection Team,
  - North Central Cyber Protection Center:
    - 186th Cyber Protection Team,
    - 187th Cyber Protection Team,
  - Western Cyber Protection Center:
    - 188th Cyber Protection Team,
    - 189th Cyber Protection Team,
  - Arizona Cyber Warfare Range,
  - Navy (no list of cyber command centers listed),
  - Air Force (no list of cyber command centers listed),
  - Others.
- NATO:
  - Cyber Operation Center,
  - NATO Cyber Range,
  - Cooperative Cyber Defence Centre of Excellence,
  - European Centre of Excellence for Countering Hybrid Threats.
- European Union:
  - European Union Agency for Cybersecurity (ENISA).
- Poland:
  - Cybernetic Operations Center (*Centrum Operacji Cybernetycznych*),
  - National Center for Cyberspace Security,
  - Defense Ministry Coordination Center for Computer Incident Response (Military Counterintelligence Service).

DIGITAL SECURITY STRATEGY

- **Intention**: Defend against cyberattacks and effectively protect IT infrastructure, organizations, administrations, and the state.
- **Strategy**: Make available cyber self-defense services, create a chief digital security officer position for organizations, and have a digital security service for the country.
- **Limitations**: Insufficient qualifications among digital security professionals and insufficient budgets for this type of defense.

The best digital security strategy is to have offline documentation and communications. In international relations, in particular, such as diplomatic services, access to online documentation should be maximally limited.

The strategies of individuals and organizations should be based on a national digital defense strategy. In the context of ever-changing global cyber threats, EU Member States must have flexible and dynamic cybersecurity strategies. A National Cybersecurity Strategy (NCSS) is an action plan to improve the security and resilience of national infrastructures and services. It is a top-down high-level approach to cybersecurity, which sets out several national objectives and priorities that should be achieved within a specific timeframe. Today, all countries in the European Union have an NCSS as a critical political function that helps them deal with risks that could potentially threaten the economic and social benefits of cyberspace.

In addition to combating cybersecurity threats, a cybersecurity strategy must be based on cooperation. One of the most critical means of improving collaboration among stakeholders is the exchange of information and the creation of public-private partnerships.

For example, ENISA's aim is to do the following:

- Improve the NCSS;
- Develop and implement the NCSS;
- Identify and raise awareness of acceptable practices to provide guidance and practical tools for Member States and to assess them by the NCSS;
- Update the NCSS Good Practice Guide;
- Innovate cybersecurity within the NCSS;
- Develop a deployment guide;
- Provide examples of cybersecurity strategies;
- Create a framework for assessing the situation of the NCSS;
- Create cybersecurity market incentives and barriers in Europe;
- Inform stakeholders about the latest advances, acceptable practices, and challenges in cybersecurity.

The common objective of any European national cybersecurity strategy is to work together to enhance cybersecurity at all levels, from sharing information about threats to raising awareness. Cooperation is often achieved through two formal structures: information sharing and analysis centers (ISAC) and public-private partnerships (PPPs).

SUMMARY

1. Cybersecurity involves the endless defense against hostile attacks. There is no hope that a solution to the problem will be found in the foreseeable future.
2. Systemic improvements in cybersecurity for individuals, businesses, government agencies, and states have significant value in reducing the losses and damage caused by cyberattacks.
3. Cybersecurity improvements require two different types of activities: (a) work aimed at making more effective and broader use of what is known about cybersecurity techniques, and (b) work aimed at developing new knowledge about effective cybersecurity techniques.

4. The publicly available information and policy actions are insufficient to motivate politicians to feel urgency and accountability for cybersecurity problems.
5. Knowledge, wisdom, and qualifications about cybersecurity are often divided into disciplines. This reduces trans-disciplinary knowledge, which could help adapt technical solutions to broad contexts and promote effective defenses.

REFERENCES

Borges, E. (2019, July 9). Types of cybercrime and how to protect yourself against them. *SecurityTrails*. https://securitytrails.com/blog/types-of-cyber-crime

cyber security statistics: The ultimate list of stats, data and trends. (2021). *PurpleSec*. https://purplesec.us/resources/cyber-security-statistics/#:~:text=Nearly%2060%20million%20Americans%20have,United%20States%3A%2038%25

Fruhlinger, J. (2020, February 27). What is a cyber attack? Recent examples show disturbing trends. *CSO*. https://www.csoonline.com/article/3237324/what-is-a-cyber-attack-recent-examples-show-disturbing-trends.html?page=2

Green, J. (1981). *Cyber warfare: A multidisciplinary analysis*. Routledge.

Lockie, A. (2017, April 17). North Korea's embarrassing missile failure may have been due to US cyber sabotage. *Business Insider*. https://www.businessinsider.in/North-Koreas-embarrassing-missile-failure-may-have-been-due-to-US-cyber-sabotage/articleshow/58226086.cms

Lucas, G. (2015). *Ethics and cyber warfare: The quest for responsible security in the age of digital warfare*. Oxford University Press.

Pratt, M. K. (2020, March 12). 6 security metrics that matter – and 4 that don't. *CSO*. https://www.csoonline.com/article/3530230/6-security-metrics-that-matter-and-4-that-don-t.html

Singer, P. W., & Friedman, A. (2014). *Cybersecurity: What everyone needs to know*. Oxford University Press.

Swinhoe, D. (2020, August 13). What is the cost of a data breach. *CSO*. https://www.csoonline.com/article/3434601/what-is-the-cost-of-a-data-breach.html

Swinhoe, D. (2021, January 8). The 15 biggest data breaches of the 21st century. *CSO*. https://www.csoonline.com/article/2130877/the-biggest-data-breaches-of-the-21st-century.html

Venard, B. (2019, October 16). The Cold War 2.0 between China and the U.S. is already a virtual reality. *The Conversation*. https://theconversation.com/the-cold-war-2-0-between-china-and-the-us-is-already-a-virtual-reality-125081

KEY TERMS AND DEFINITIONS

Cyberbullying: A form of bullying that occurs through electronic communications, such as messages on social media.

Cyberwar: The use of digital attacks directed at a state that cause harm comparable to that of actual war.

Distributed Denial-of-Service: A form of cyberattack that aims to make a machine or network unavailable to intended users.

General Data Protection Regulation: An EU regulation concerning data protection and privacy for individuals and organizations within the EU and the European Economic Area.

Identity Theft: The use of another person's personally identifiable information (e.g., name, social security number, credit card number) to commit a crime.

Malware: A form of cyberattack involving software designed to damage a computer or network.

Phishing: A form of cyberattack that aims at obtaining sensitive information (e.g., usernames, passwords, credit card numbers) by the impersonation of trustworthy entities.

Social Engineering: A form of cyberattack that involves psychologically manipulating people into providing sensitive information (e.g., usernames, passwords, credit card numbers).

ENDNOTES

[1] The GDRP is an EU data protection regulation aimed at all entities that collect or use the personal data of individuals located within the European Economic Area (EEA).

[2] 2FA—two-factor authentication—is an additional layer of security to make sure that people trying to access an online account are who they claim to be. First, the user enters their username and password. Then, instead of being granted access immediately, they will have to provide additional information to authenticate their identity.

[3] Secure Sockets Layer (SSL) is a standard protocol used to securely transfer documents over a network. Netscape's SSL technology creates a secure connection between a user's web server and browser to ensure private and integrated data transmission. SSL uses transport control protocol (TCP) for communication.

[4] A Domain Name System (DNS) translates domain names into IP addresses so that browsers can load Internet resources. Each internet-connected device has a unique IP address that other devices use to find the device. DNS servers eliminate the need for remembering IP addresses.

[5] An Internet service provider (ISP) is a company that provides services for accessing and using the Internet.

[6] A virtual private network (VPN) is a private network that encrypts and transmits data that is traveling from one place to another on the Internet. Using a VPN to connect to the Internet allows a user to privately and securely surf websites as well as access restricted websites and overcome censorship bans.

[7] Pretty Good Privacy (PGP) is a public key encryption program that has become the most common standard for encrypting email messages. In addition to encrypting and decrypting email messages, PGP is used to sign messages so that the recipient can verify both the sender's identity and the integrity of the content.

8   Thucydides, an ancient historian who wrote on the conflict between Athens and Sparta, hypothesized that conflict was inevitability between great powers when a rising power threatens a ruling power.

Chapter 21
Digital Ethics

ABSTRACT

The purpose of this chapter is to discuss strategies that can be applied in the domain of cyberlaw. The chapter begins by distinguishing between ethics, morality, and law. It then focuses on the relation between ethics and digital technologies. The chapter then examines proposals for what should be included in codes of ethics as well as examples of codes of ethics for IT companies. The examples include the British Computer Society, the Association for Computer Machinery, and the Data Processing Management Association. Next, ethical codes for regulating automation, computerization, and artificial intelligence are summarized. The chapter then discusses ethical issues surrounding privacy, anonymity, and personal data, including the EU's right of access by data subjects as well as issues connected with big data. The chapter then focuses on crimes caused by digitization and the protection of intellectual property. The chapter concludes by considering recent laws of ecommerce as well as social and international legal challenges of regulating cyberspace.

INTRODUCTION

Ethics is the study of proper professional action based on morals and applicable laws. In the field of information technology, some of the major ethical concerns include automation, ICT, robotization, and the Internet. The specialization that studies ICT and law—also known "cyberlaw" or "IT law"—aims to regulate the digital dissemination of information on a variety of media, such as video/film, software, e-commerce, and other forms. This field also considers issues relating to intellectual property, contract law, privacy, freedom of expression, and jurisdiction.

One of the predominant issues in IT law is net neutrality, which is the principle that Internet service providers (ISPs) must treat all Internet communications equally and not discriminate or charge different rates depending on the user, content, website, platform, application, type of hardware, source address, destination address, or method of communication (Easley et al., 2018).

Another major concern has been freedom of expression on the Internet (e.g., see Figure 1). Article 19 of the Universal Declaration of Human Rights calls for the protection of freedom of expression in all media. This includes the right to have an opinion without interference and to seek, receive, and

DOI: 10.4018/978-1-7998-8036-3.ch021

communicate information and ideas through any media, regardless of borders. Compared to traditional print media, the availability and relative anonymity of cyberspace have lifted the conventional barriers between a person and their ability to publish. Anyone with an Internet connection can potentially reach millions of people (Zittrain, 2013).

Figure 1. Freedom of expression on the Internet in Asia (Funk, 2019)

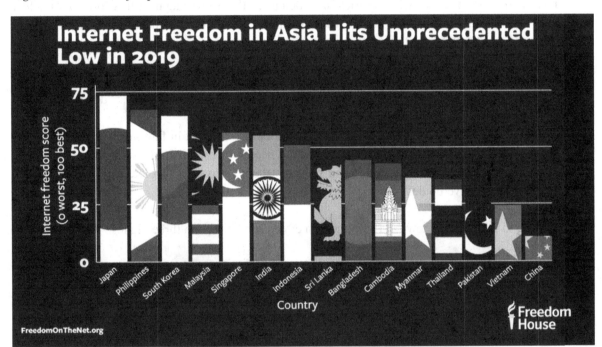

One of the more well-known laws of information technology is the Sarbanes-Oxley Act of 2002, which was a response to financial scandals in the early 2000s involving companies such as *Enron, Tyco International,* and *WorldCom.* Such high-profile frauds shook investor confidence in the credibility of company financial statements and prompted many to demand a review of multi-annual regulatory standards. The law introduced strict new rules for accountants, auditors, and corporate officials and imposed more stringent record-keeping requirements. The law also added new criminal penalties for securities violations. For example, the head of a company cannot offer as a defense the argument that he has not read a digital report on the state of the company if he has signed it.

Crime in cyberspace develops very quickly and can multiply its range at the speed of light. Hence, cyberlaw often lags behind these kinds of crime. To be successful, it requires effective international cooperation. These issues will be briefly discussed in this chapter, but in strategic terms, for the full characterization of these rights would require a book of its own.

ACCESS TO DIGITAL ETHICS

The world was once ruled through empires based on strong central powers and strong militaries. Since the Industrial Revolution, however, the world has been led by capital and its subordinate politicians. In the 21st century, money and sympathetic politicians continue to rule. Nonetheless, they are supported by computerization, which in practice controls the world through ultra-fast transcontinental communication of business and political decisions. Societies have defended themselves against this form of "nuclear capitalism" or authoritarianism by promoting the cultivation of behaviors characterized by the following three virtues of conduct (Figure 2):

- **Morality**: Morality is the foundation of behavior in matters related to life, sex, money, and power. It consists of right and proper conduct, for example, "don't kill," "don't molest," "don't cheat," and "don't persecute." Usually, moral norms define religions.
- **Ethics**: Ethics are based on historically justified codes of conduct in families or other group affiliations. It aims at the harmonious coexistence of people by establishing predictable behaviors.
- **Law**: Law perpetuates ethical codes and prevents them from being violated by legislation approved by legislative bodies.

According to Abbe Mowshowitz (1980), human ethics can be seen in three planes:

- **Autonomy**: to what extent a person free in their ability to consider what is ethically right,
- **Opportunities**: to what extent a person has the chance to make consistent choices based on ethics,
- **Correctness**: to what extent ethics are based on the ethos of a company and personal morality.

Examples of the use of these criteria for evaluating the ethics of a computer designer are given in Table 1.

When considering ethics, it is imperative to distinguish between (a) corporate and professional ethics—i.e., ethics related to business issues, professional behavior, the humane treatment of employees, and corporate and social responsibility—and (b) technological ethics. What is meant by the latter? A whitepaper by the *World Economic Forum* argues that "technologies have a clear moral dimension - that is to say, a fundamental aspect that relates to values, ethics, and norms. Technologies reflect the interests, behaviours and desires of their creators and shape how the people using them can realize their potential, identities, relationships, and goals" (Philbeck et al., 2018, p. 7).

Ethical technologies are essentially a conversation focused on the relationship between technology and human values, the decisions we make concerning technological advances, and the impact they may have. The concept of ethical technology refers to the set of values that govern an organization's approach to using technology as a whole and how employees at all levels implement these technologies to drive business strategies and operations. It is a multifaceted concept that can cover a wide range of issues, from data privacy to bias in algorithms and from turning people into machines to committing to not manipulate data and human reactions. Furthermore, just because organizations do not develop frameworks for assuring technology is used ethically, this does not mean that leaders are ignoring problems: research by the consulting firm *Deloitte* indicates that the biggest concerns of social and ethical leaders caused by digital innovation (in addition to privacy) are related to cybersecurity threats, job swapping, and the unethical use of data (Bannister et al., 2020).

Figure 2. IT professionals in control of the world should be moral, ethical, and law-abiding

According to John Naisbitt (1982) in his work *Megatrends*, "the new source of power is not money in the hands of a few, but information in the hands of many." Richard Mason (1986), on the other hand, believes that "information forms the intellectual capital from which human beings craft their lives and secure dignity" (p. 5). According to him, one must reckon with the following four categories of information ethics:

Table 1. The scope of ethics available to an ICT designer

Computerization Scope	Examples	Autonomy	Opportunities	Correctness
Collection and search of information	Management information system (MIS) organization	Activities limited by the company's strategy	Can enrich the interpretation of reports and the scope of data	Must be sensitive to the so-called 'creativity' of accounting
Communication	Facebook	Must act according to the company's strategy	Can create a graphic user interface (GUI), but not a marketing policy (e.g., to sell people's data)	If one wants to be ethically correct, one takes a risk by staying at work.
Troubleshooting	Artificial Intelligence	Can refine algorithms	Can show off advanced solutions	Some want to replace human thinking, but is it right?
Control	Production processes	Can refine system sophistication	Limit purpose(s) of the company	Limit business purpose(s)

- **Privacy**: What information about a person should be disclosed to other interested parties? Under what conditions? How secure must the information be? What information can people hold for themselves, and what information does not have to be disclosed to others?
- **Accuracy**: Who is responsible for assuring that information is authentic and accurate? Who is responsible for information errors? How can victims of incorrect information claim compensation? What forms of compensation can they claim?
- **Ownership**: Who owns information? What is a fair price for information for those who provide it? Who owns the information channels? How should access be allocated?
- **Access**: What information does a person or organization have the right and privilege to receive? Under what conditions and under what safeguards?

These four paradigms of information ethics amount to a paradigm for the ethics of computerization, which should aim to improve human dignity and create a world worth living in.

EXAMPLES OF CODES OF ETHICS FOR IT COMPANIES

According to Johnson and Snapper (1985), a code of ethics should aim at five functions:

- **Inspiration**: Inspire members to act ethically.
- **Sensitization**: Make members sensitive to moral, ethical, and legal actions.
- **Discipline**: Instill regulation in members in applying established rules of conduct.
- **Advice**: Provide guidance for how to proceed in challenging situations.
- **Awareness**: Make customers and employees aware of what behaviors and services they can and cannot expect from member of the association.

A company should also take into account the following additions to a code of ethics (Dejoie et al., 1991):

- **Certificates**: Confirmations of the possession of professional qualifications specified by the state or society concerned,
- **Licenses**: Permissions to perform certain services,
- **Accreditations**: Confirmations that an institution such as a university fulfills the conditions laid down by the state or society for training, education, or improvement,
- **Ethics**: Standards and values adhered to by a company that customers can rely on to be sure that unfair practices are not applied.

Before looking at specific examples, it is worth noting that Effy Oz (1992) argues that, because many IT organizations promote the same goals, there is reason to try to create an international code of ethics for IT professionals. A unified code would improve public perception of IT professionals as representing a real, responsible profession. It would also ensure the public that IT professionals care about the ethical development of digital systems rather than digital systems as such. Perhaps most importantly, a unified ethical code for IT professionals would allow them to ethically develop computerization, automation, and robotization for the sake of humanity and not against it. Unfortunately, many businesses aim to eliminate human work through the development of such processes.

With this in mind, let us consider codes of ethics used by IT companies.

The British Computer Society

The British Computer Society (BCS) was founded in 1957 and has 82,000 members in 151 countries. The society has set professional standards for competence, conduct, and ethical computer practices in the UK; however, their code of conduct is addressed to all members of the British Computer Society. To facilitate understanding, these principles have been grouped into the following primary responsibilities, which all members should apply in the course of their working lives:

- Public interest
- Obligation to employees
- Obligation to the profession
- Professional competence and integrity

BCS Ethical Code of Conduct[1]

- The British Computer Society Code of Conduct is addressed to all members of the British Computer Society. It consists essentially of a series of statements setting minimum standards of practice that must be respected by all members.
- The Code of Conduct concerns professional responsibility. All members have responsibilities: towards customers, users, the state, and society as a whole. These members, who are employees, also have obligations to their employers and employers' clients, and often even to trade unions. In the event of an apparent conflict of responsibilities, duties, or recommended practices, the Secretary-General of the Society should be consulted at the earliest opportunity.
- The code should be seen as a whole: the individual parts are not intended for different use to justify errors, omissions, or commissions. The Code is to be observed in spirit, not just in word. BCS

membership covers all computer-related professions, and it is not possible to define the code in terms directly related to each member. For this reason, the code was established at two levels to enable each member to make appropriate interpretations.

Public Interest

1. Members shall, in their professional practice, protect public health and safety and shall have regard to the protection of the environment.
2. Members shall take due account of the legitimate rights of third parties.
3. Members shall ensure that, within the selected fields, they have knowledge and understanding of the relevant laws, regulations, and standards and comply with such requirements.
4. Members shall take into account fundamental human rights in their professional practice and avoid any action which adversely affects those rights.

Obligation to Employees

1. Members shall carry out their work with due care and diligence, following the requirements of the employer or client and, if their professional judgment is rejected, shall indicate the likely consequences.
2. Members shall complete the work undertaken on time and to the budget and shall notify the employer or customer as soon as possible if an overrun is envisaged.
3. Members will not offer, provide, or receive in return incentives to enter a business from a customer unless the customer is fully disclosed.
4. Members shall not disclose or permit the disclosure of, or use for personal gain or to benefit a third party, confidential information obtained in the course of professional practice, except with the prior written consent of the employer or client or as required by a court.
5. Members should avoid being a party to activities or information relating to actions that would interfere with their duties in points 1 to 4 above.
6. Members may not mislead or conceal information about the capabilities of the products, systems, or services they are interested in, nor may they benefit from other people's lack of knowledge or experience.
7. Members may not, except where expressly ordered to do so, deal with the customer's money or place contracts or orders in connection with the work in which they are involved when acting as independent consultants.
8. Members should not make an independent judgment on behalf of the client on any product or service in which they knowingly have any interests, financial or other.

Obligations to the Profession

1. Members shall maintain the reputation of the profession and shall seek to improve professional standards by participating in their development, use, and enforcement and shall avoid any action which adversely affects the good standing of the profession.
2. Members in their professional practice shall seek to improve public knowledge and understanding of information systems and technologies and shall seek to counter false or misleading statements that are detrimental to the profession.
3. Members shall encourage and support other members in their professional development and, where possible, provide opportunities for the professional development of new entrants.
4. Members shall act with integrity towards colleagues and members of other professions to which they are professionally bound and shall avoid engaging in any activity incompatible with their professional status.
5. Members may not make public declarations in the course of their professional activities unless they are qualified and, where appropriate, authorized to do so, and they shall take due account of the likely consequences of any declaration for others.

Professional Competence and Integrity

1. Members shall seek to improve their professional knowledge and skills and seek to be aware of technological developments, procedures, and standards appropriate to their field; they shall also encourage their subordinates to act similarly.
2. Members shall strive to comply with recognized acceptable practices, including quality standards they consider relevant, and encourage their subordinates to do the same.
3. Members shall only offer services or the provision of services that fall within their professional competence and shall not offer services that require a level of competence which they do not have; any professional opinion requested should be objective and reliable.
4. Members shall assume professional responsibility for their work and the work of their subordinates and associates under their direction and shall not conclude any assignment without due cause and in good time.
5. Members shall avoid any situation which may give way to a conflict of interest between themselves and their client and shall disclose information to the client in full and without delay in the event of any dispute.

The Association for Computer Machinery

The Association for Computer Machinery (ACM) was founded in 1947 and has approximately 100,000 members from around the world. The association deals with standardization and recommended computing solutions that are widely respected.

ACM Ethical Code of Conduct[2]

Preamble

The actions of computing professions change the world. To act responsibly, they should reflect on the broader impacts of their work, consistently supporting the public good. The ACM Code of Ethics and Professional Conduct (the "Code") expresses the conscience of the profession.

The Code as a whole deals with how basic ethical principles apply to the conduct of computer scientists. The Code is not an algorithm for solving ethical problems; instead, it serves as a basis for ethical decision-making. When considering a specific issue, an IT specialist may find that many principles need to be taken into account and that different rules will have distinct relevance to the problem. Questions related to such issues can best be answered by carefully considering basic ethical principles, understanding that the public good is paramount. The entire IT profession benefits when the proper decision-making process is responsible and transparent to all stakeholders. Open discussions on ethical issues promote this responsibility and transparency.

1. GENERAL ETHICAL PRINCIPLES
    1.1 Contribute to the well-being of people and society by recognizing that all people are computer stakeholders.
    1.2 Avoid harm.
    1.3 Be honest and trustworthy.
    1.4 Be fair and take action not to discriminate.
    1.5 Respect the work required to develop new ideas, inventions, creative works, and computer artifacts.
    1.6 Respect privacy.
    1.7 Honor confidentiality.
2. PROFESSIONAL COMMITMENTS
    2.1 Strive to achieve high quality in both processes and products of professional work.
    2.2 Maintain high standards of professional competence, conduct, and ethical practice.
    2.3 Know and comply with applicable professional rules.
    2.4 Accept and provide a proper professional review.
    2.5 Provide comprehensive and in-depth assessments of computer systems and their effects, including an analysis of possible risks.
    2.6 Perform work only in areas of competence.
    2.7 Promote public awareness and understanding of information technology, related technologies, and their consequences.
    2.8 Access computing and communication resources only if authorized or compelled by the public good.
    2.9 Design and implement systems that are robust and safe.
3. PROFESSIONAL LEADERSHIP PRINCIPLES
    3.1 Ensure that the public good is of significant interest during all professional IT work.
    3.2 Articulate, encourage acceptance of, and evaluate the performance of social responsibilities by members of the organization or group.
    3.3 Manage staff and resources to improve the quality of working life.
    3.4 Articulate, apply, and support policies and processes reflecting the principles of the Code.

3.5 Create opportunities for members of the organization or group to grow as professionals.

3.6 Be careful when modifying or rolling back systems.

3.7 Recognize and pay particular attention to systems that will be integrated into society's infrastructure.

4. CODE COMPLIANCE.

4.1 Endorse, promote, and comply with the Code.

4.2 Treat Code violations as a violation of ACM membership.

The Data Processing Management Association

The Data Processing Management Association (DPMA) was established in 1996 after a series of transformations by the National Machine Accountants Association (NMAA) in 1949. In 2017, it was taken over by the Computing Technology Industry Association (CTIA), which operates in 120 countries, providing courses for specialized certificates to about 2.2 million professionals.

DPMA Ethical Code of Conduct

1. I have the responsibility to manage; therefore, I will promote an understanding of the methods and procedures of automatic data processing for using each resource on hand.

2. I have a duty to other members to respect the high ideals of the DPMA as set out in its international rules. Also, I will work with my other members to disseminate knowledge about the overall development of data processing. Furthermore, I will not use confidential knowledge related to the activities of the employer of the co-worker to pursue my interests.

3. I have a duty to my employer, whom I trust, so I will do my best to fulfill this obligation to the best of my ability, guarding his interests, and advising him wisely and honestly.

4. I have an additional obligation to not engage in direct sales at a regularly scheduled DPMA meeting unless specifically and officially invited. Furthermore, I will not be incriminating in any of my activities in which an association or other member participates.

5. I have a duty to my country as well as my personal, business, and social contacts. I will sustain this great nation and respect the chosen way of life of my fellow citizens.

6. I accept these responsibilities as personal responsibility, and, as a member of this association, I will actively carry out these duties and dedicate myself to this goal.

THE ETHICS OF DEVELOPING AUTOMATION, COMPUTERIZATION, AND ARTIFICIAL INTELLIGENCE IN THE 21ST CENTURY

The aforementioned ethical codes do not adequately account for the challenges of automation, computerization, and artificial intelligence. We will therefore recall here four sets of ethical codes that decision-makers and IT professionals should be guided by in policy-making and civilizational projects (some of which were mentioned in the chapter *Strategic Digital Informing and Its Challenges in the 21st Century*).

Laws of robotics – Asimov (1951):

1. A robot must not injure a person or, by lack of reaction, allow a person to be injured.

2. A robot must obey every human order, except for orders contrary to the first Law.

3. A robot should protect its existence as long as it is not contrary to the first and second Laws.

Laws of service systems – Targowski (2009):

1. Do not implement service systems that require no human presence.

2. Do not implement service systems that harm a person.

3. Do not implement service systems that harm the human race.

Laws of Production Automation - Targowski-Modràk (2011):

1. Do not develop automation unless the aim of automation cannot be achieved by other means.

2. Do not develop automation to eliminate human labor in production.

3. Do not develop automation that harms a person and the human race.

Universal Laws of Asimov-Targowski-Krawczyk (2019):

1. The most important value and the primary decision-maker in any civilization is humanity.

2. AI objects can perform vital roles in civilization, but they must obey every human order, except for orders contrary to Law 1.

3. AI objects should take care of their existence as long as this is not contrary to Laws 1 and 2.

Are these laws currently abided by now in the 21st century? Probably not. Few IT professionals know about them. State standardization committees and professional associations are too weak to force their members to adhere to these laws. Global companies, including many IT companies, do not use and do not intend to apply these laws. Politicians, on the other hand, have "more important" issues on their minds.

PRIVACY, ANONYMITY, AND DATA PROTECTION

The role and value of privacy are the subject of many controversies. The combination of the growing power of new technologies and the decline of transparency and privacy agreements is causing problems with law, policy, and ethics. Many of these conceptual debates and issues take place in the context of interpretating and analyzing the General Data Protection Regulation (GDPR), which was adopted by the EU in the spring of 2018.[3]

Personal data is defined in law as data that can be associated with a natural person. There are two ways to create this link: (1) a reference mode and (2) a non-reference mode (Van den Hoven et al., 2019). The law focuses primarily on the reference use of descriptions or attributes. This type of use takes place when a speaker's knowledge is associated with a definite object, as in the following example: "Kennedy's murderer must be crazy," so-and-so said, pointing out the murderer in court. This can be contrasted with descriptions such as "Kennedy's murderer must be crazy, whoever he is." In this latter case, the speaker is not—and may never be—familiar with the person (the object) he or she is talking about. If the legal definition of personal data only includes the referring mode, the processing of a significant part of data will not be protected nor restricted for legal reasons related to privacy since it does not "directly" refer to persons and, therefore, does not constitute "personal data" in the strict sense.

Furthermore, the processing of personal data requires that its purpose be clarified, that its use restricted, that individuals be notified, that inaccuracies be corrected, and that the data holder be held accountable to the supervisory authorities (Organisation for Economic Cooperation and Development, 1980). As it is impossible to guarantee compliance of all types of data processing in these areas and applications with these policies and regulations in traditional ways, so-called "Privacy Enhancing Technologies" (PET) and identity management systems are expected to replace human supervision in many cases.

The challenge concerning privacy in the 21st century is to ensure that technologies related to software, architecture, infrastructure, and workflows are designed to take into account privacy requirements in a way that makes privacy violations unlikely. New generations of privacy rules (e.g., GDPR) now require a standard "from the outset" approach. Data ecosystems and socio-technical systems, supply chains, and organizations—including their incentive structures, business processes, technical equipment and software, and staff training—should be designed in such a way that the likelihood of privacy breaches is as low as possible.

Anonymity involves cases of hiding one's identity while engaged in online activities. In short, others may be able to see what you are doing, but not who you are. From the earliest days of the Internet, anonymity has been very popular. It is closely related to concerns with the limits of free speech and censorship. Some argue that anonymity makes it easier to make false statements and that it creates a lack of responsibility for online activities. Others see the regulation/prohibition of anonymity as an obstacle to the freedom of expression.

Some efforts to curb this behavior include Facebook's introduction of a "real name" policy, aimed at providing safer spaces, as well as Twitter's ban on the editor and conservative political commentator Milo Yiannopoulos, which was carried out in an attempt to distinguish free speech from harassment (Russell, 2016). Forcing people to reveal their identity may seem like a move in the right direction. On the other hand, it also prevents users of social media (and other platforms) from hiding who they are to prevent online bullying and threats from people who know them.

Over the past few years, the discussion seems to have intensified, as anonymous hate speech and online teasing have become more widespread, more accessible, and harder to trace. Some argue that anonymity allows (or even encourages) actions outside of social norms and cultural expectations and that it allows the expression of harmful and dangerous ideas without social retaliation.

The Right of Access by Data Subjects

Article 15 of the GDPR lays out the right of access by data subjections (European Union, 2016):

1. The data subject shall be entitled to obtain confirmation from the controller as to whether personal data concerning him or her are being processed and, if so, shall be allowed to access the data and the following information:
    a. the purposes of the processing;
    b. categories of personal data concerned;
    c. information on recipients or categories of recipients to whom personal data have been or will be disclosed, in particular recipients in third countries or international organizations;
    d. where possible, the planned retention period for personal data and, where this is not possible, the criteria for determining that period;
    e. information on the right to request the controller to rectify, delete, or restrict the processing of personal data concerning the data subject and to object to such processing;
    f. information on the right to complain about a supervisory authority;
    g. if the personal data have not been collected from the data subject, any available information on their source;

h.   information on automated decision-making, including profiling as referred to in Article 22(1) and (4), and, at least in those cases, relevant information on the rules for taking the data, as well as on the significance and expected consequences of such processing for the data subject.

2.   Where personal data are transferred to a third country or an international organization, the data subject shall have the right to be informed of the relevant safeguards referred to in Article 46 relating to the transfer.

3.   The controller shall provide the data subject with a copy of the personal data to be processed. For any subsequent copies requested by the data subject, the controller may charge a reasonable fee resulting from the administrative costs. If the data subject asks for a copy electronically and unless otherwise indicated, the information shall be provided by commonly used electronic means.

4.   The right to obtain a copy referred to in paragraph 3 shall not adversely affect the rights and freedoms of others.

Databases (DB) and Big Data

Users generate a lot of data online. This data is not just what is entered directly by the user, but it also includes numerous statistics about the user's behavior: pages visited, links clicked, search terms entered, etc. Data mining can be used to extract patterns from such data, which can then be used to create user decisions. Not only can this affect a user's internet experience (e.g., what ads they are shown), but, depending on what websites have access to a user's information, it can also affect users in entirely different contexts (Van den Hoven et al., 2019).

Specifically, Big Data can be used to profile a user, creating patterns of typical combinations of user properties, which can then be used to predict interests and behaviors (Hildebrandt, 2008). Depending on the available data, more sensitive information, such as the likely religion of the user or their sexual orientation, can be derived. These derivatives may, in turn, lead to unequal treatment or discrimination. When a user can be assigned to a specific group, even if only probabilistically, it can affect the actions taken by others. For example, profiling can lead to a refusal of insurance or a credit card, in which case profit is the leading cause of discrimination (Taylor et al., 2017).

Big Data is not just about online transactions. Data may also be collected during purchases, via recordings captured by surveillance cameras in a public or private space, and when using smart card-based public transport payment cards. All this data can be used to profile citizens and make decisions based on such profiles. For example, purchase data can be used to send information about healthy eating habits to specific people, but it can also be used to make insurance decisions. Following EU data protection laws, authorization to process personal data is needed. Furthermore, personal data can only be processed for the purpose for which it was obtained. The specific challenges are, therefore, (a) how to get permission when the user is not explicitly involved in the transaction (as in the case of supervision), and (b) how to prevent "function creep," i.e., how to avoid the use of data for different purposes after it has been collected (which can happen, for example, in DNA databases) (Dahl & Sætnan, 2009).

The model in Figure 3 illustrates possible IT solutions that provide (relative) privacy, anonymity, and security in cyberspace.

Figure 3. Solutions for privacy, anonymity, and security in cyberspace (Pirate Bay – an information file-sharing service; VPN – virtual private network)

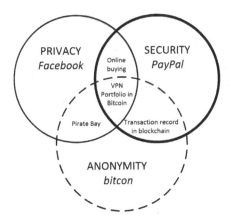

CRIME CAUSED BY DIGITIZATION

Although the Internet and the digital economy represent a significant opportunity, they are also a tool for criminal activity. These digital crimes are broadly referred to as *cybercrime*. Cybercrime law covers computer crimes, internet crimes, information crimes, communication crimes, and technological crimes.

Cybercrime can be used to refer to either of the following:

- Crimes against computers, information, and information communication technologies (ICT),
- Crimes committed by persons using computers or ICT.

Cybercrime is a global problem that requires a coordinated international response. We must help organizations comply with legal requirements under cyberlaw. This can be done with the help of international conventions on cybercrime, which include the following:

- The African Union Convention on Cybersecurity and the Protection of Personal Data,
- The Council of Europe Convention on Cybercrime (also known as the Budapest Convention on Cybercrime).

There are also model laws, which contain series of laws pertaining to cybercrime:

- Model law CW: A model law on computer and computer crimes
- SADC Model Law: The Southern African Development Community model law on Computer Crime and Cybercrime
- HIPCAR: A Harmonization of ICT policies, legislation, and regulatory procedures in the Caribbean community
- ITU: International Telecommunication Union legislative resources on cybercrime, including a toolkit for cybercrime legislation.

The following are specific provisions on cybercrime:

- Law on Cybercrime – South Africa (South Africa signed the Budapest Convention in 2001)
- Cybersecurity Information Sharing Act (CISA) – United States of America
- Directive on Network and Information Security – EU
- Penal Code 1995 – Australia
- Cybercrime Act 2001 – Australia
- Chapter 08:06 (cybercrime and computer-related crime) – Botswana
- Computer Abuse Act 2007 – Brunei Darussalam
- Criminal Code – Canada
- Penal Code – France
- Computer Crimes Act – Malaysia
- Crime Act, 1961 – New Zealand
- Cybercrime Prevention Act 2012 – Philippines
- Law on computer crimes – Thailand
- Cybercrime Act, 2015 – Tanzania
- Computer Abuse Act, 2013 – United Kingdom
- Computer Fraud and Abuse Act – United States of America

The points below show the development and modifications made to EU laws on cybercrime:

- 2011 – A directive on combating the sexual exploitation of children on the Internet and child pornography was passed, which addressed new developments in online environments, such as seduction (criminals pretending to be children to lure minors for sexual exploitation). In 2016, The Commission published two reports on the measures taken by the Member States to ensure compliance with the directive (one concerning the whole directive and the other focusing on efforts against websites containing child pornography).
- 2013 – A directive was passed to combat large-scale cyber-attacks by requiring the Member States to strengthen their national cybercrime laws and introduce tougher criminal sanctions. In 2017, the Commission published a report assessing the extent to which the Member States had taken the necessary measures to ensure compliance with the directive.
- 2018 – The Commission proposed a regulation and directive to facilitate cross-border access to electronic evidence in criminal investigations.
- 2019 – A new directive on non-cash payments was passed, which updated the legal framework, removing obstacles to operational cooperation and improving prevention and assistance to victims. The directive aimed to improve law enforcement action on fraud and counterfeit digital payments.

EU legislation on cybercrime corresponds to the principles set out in the Council of Europe Convention on Cybercrime. The convention signed a treaty obliging the Member States to develop and implement criminal law on the following offenses:

1. Acts committed using telecommunications networks, such as illegal money transactions, offerings of illegal services, and copyright infringements, as well as acts that violate human dignity and the protection of minors.

2. Important criminal law issues where a common approach may be necessary for international co-operation, such as definitions, sanctions, and liability of cyber actors, including internet service providers.

3. The use of coercive force (including the possibility of cross-border cases) in technological environments (e.g., telecommunications networks and electronic information networks), including the interception of information, the search and confiscation of information processing systems (including websites on the Internet), the prevention of access to illegal material, and the requirement that service providers comply with specific obligations, taking into account problems caused by particular information security measures (e.g., encryption);

4. The issues of jurisdiction concerning crimes, including determining the place of the crime *(locus delicti)*, determining which law should be applied, and, in multi-jurisdictional cases, determining how to resolve jurisdictional disputes.

5. International cooperation in cybercrime investigations, which should be done in close collaboration with the Committee of Experts on the Operation of European Conventions on Co-operation in Criminal Matters (PC-OC).

With respect to the case of Poland and cybercrime laws, Andrzej Janicki (2015) states the following:

Computer crime and cybercrime are not legal notions in Poland. These terms do not appear in the body of substantive criminal law at all. An auxiliary definition of 'cybercrime' is provided by the Minister of Justice regulation concerning the European arrest warrant...As opposed to the Council of Europe Convention on Cybercrime (Article 1), the Polish Penal Code does not comprise a definition of the terms "computer system" or "computer data," even though such terms are used in the description of cybercrime offenses. The said definitions are also not covered by the Act of 2008 aimed at unification of computer terminology in the Polish legal system. A more general problem, still under discussion in Poland in the context of constitutional law, concerns a direct application of definitions laid down in the ratified international conventions by the courts (Janicki, 2015, p. 2).

PROTECTION OF INTELLECTUAL PROPERTY

The emergence of information technology at the end of the 20th century triggered a whole new set of challenges for the legal system. When intellectual property rights were first developed, computer technology did not exist. At that time, it was not envisaged that information stored by digital means would need to be protected, nor was it envisaged that such information would become such a sought-after commodity. The Internet, software, business methods for e-commerce applications, and electronic databases have opened relatively new territories, in which large quantities of information are accessible to large numbers of people. However, due to the lack of specific rules, the Internet has become a hotbed of illegal activities, most of which concern intellectual property rights, namely, copyrights and trademarks (Somu, 2006).

In the United States, research from the beginning of the 21st century estimated that more than 50 percent of US exports depended on some form of intellectual property protection, while this number had been less than 10 percent five decades earlier (Field, 2006). Persons who are intellectually or artistically gifted have the right to prevent the unauthorized use or sale of their works, as well as owners of physical property such as cars, buildings, and shops. However, compared to manufacturers of chairs, refrigerators, and other tangible goods, people whose work is essentially based on intangible assets face greater challenges to their livelihood if their property rights are not respected. Artists, authors, inventors, and others cannot rely on walls and fences to protect their work. The protection of intellectual property enables innovators and artists to receive fair compensation. Without intellectual input, most progress would not exist in transportation, communication, agriculture, healthcare, and other areas of life.

Forms of intellectual property laws include patents, copyrights, trademarks, and trade secrets. Because intellectual property has many characteristics similar to immovable property, the rights associated with intellectual property are treated as an asset that can be bought, sold, licensed, and even distributed at no cost. The laws discussed below help protect the property of owners, inventors, and creators from unauthorized use (Field, 2006).

Copyright is a legal term that describes the economic rights granted to authors of literary and artistic works, including the rights to reproduce and copy works and to display them to the public. Copyright is the only form of protection for music, films, novels, poems, architecture, and other works of cultural value. Computer programs and audio recordings can now also be protected under copyright. The US Copyright Office serves as the place where copyright claims are registered and where copyright-related documents can be recorded when the requirements set out in U.S. copyright laws are met. Legal access to copyrights has spawned a considerable industry in the U.S. The main copyright industries were estimated to account for approximately 6 percent of the US GDP, or a $626.2 billion, in 2002 (Field, 2006).

Patents are agreements between society as a whole and inventors. Under the terms of this social contract, the inventor has the exclusive right to prevent others from creating, using, and selling a patented invention for a fixed period (in most countries up to 20 years) in exchange for the inventor disclosing the details of the invention to the public (Field, 2006).

Trade secrets include any information that may be used in the course of economic activity and that is valuable enough to provide an actual or potential financial advantage. Examples of trade secrets include (a) product formulas, such as the Coca-Cola formula, (b) sets of information that give companies a competitive advantage, such as a customer listing database, and (c) advertising and distribution strategies. Unlike patents, trade secrets are protected for a theoretically unlimited period without procedural formalities. Trade secrets, however, tend to be found out by others, and protection is not free. Therefore, the larger company, the more it needs legal protection for its trade secrets (Field, 2006).

Another intellectual property issue concerns IP domain names and Internet addresses. The basic form of an Internet address is "123.456.123"; however, most addresses are also alphanumeric, such as "BBC.uk," "BBC.com," or "yale.edu." The unique part of each name (e.g., "BBC" or "Yale") is registered as a domain name. Just as mail addresses indicate unique physical locations, domain names indicate particular areas in cyberspace. Different entities control the registration, renewal, and transfer of domain names, depending on the end of any alphanumeric address. Addresses ending in ".fr" or ".uk" are governed by the laws of France and the United Kingdom, respectively. If they end with ".edu," they are controlled by Educause (a US non-profit organization) under an agreement with the US Department of Commerce. There are also rules for those ending in ".com" established by the Internet Corporation for Assigned Names and Numbers (ICANN) (also under an agreement with the US Department of Commerce). In order to transfer a domain name, time and money are usually required. Furthermore, many addresses may falsely suggest sponsorship by the same person or video. Canceling these addresses is insufficient if others can then re-register; however, maintaining registrations and probably hundreds of fake addresses is a severe waste of money. These types of problems have been mitigated by imposing significant civil and criminal sanctions on cybercriminals. Still, some remain out of reach, and more resources are needed to stop actions that often mislead computer users around the world (Field, 2006).

In the European Union, intellectual property owners should know how to manage and protect their property. They should check the benefits of protecting their intellectual property, the types of protection available, and the procedures to be followed in the following areas:

- Patents
- Trademarks
- Author's rights
- Trade secrets
- Design protection
- Site domains
- Database protection
- Geographical indications

If commercializing intellectual property, property owners should read the EU guidelines on licensing and selling copyrights, trademarks, patents, and other intellectual property rights. It is also important that property owners find out how to assert their rights in cases of infringement of intellectual property rights:

According to the EU, the protection of intellectual property has several advantages:

- If an owner protects their invention, such as a new product, they become the only person who has the right to use or reproduce it. Others may not copy or replicate what the owner has done without their permission.
- When an owner protects their invention, the quality of the product is guaranteed, and its origin is evident. This can be an advantage for the owner's business because customers may prefer to purchase a product that is regulated by strict product controls.
- An owner can make money not only through the direct use of intellectual property but also indirectly through license agreements. This happens when the owner licenses a third party to use an IP-protected item for a specified period.
- In some cases, such as copyright and unregistered design, the protection of an owner's IP address is automatic and does not require any formalities.
- Owning a patent or trademark can increase market value and make it easier for an owner's business to find investors or other financing opportunities.

Laws for eCommerce

Ecommerce (sometimes spelled as "e-commerce" or "eCommerce") refers to the online industry of buying and selling products and services electronically. Ecommerce involves the combined use of internet technology, mobile commerce, electronic transfers of funds, escrow services, electronic data exchange, supply chain management, inventory management systems, internet marketing, data collection systems, and many other technologies and innovative business systems. Most, if not all, ecommerce transactions use the Internet for at least one point of the transaction.

Table 2. Comparison of digital buyers in regions of the world (United Nations Conference on Trade and Development, 2015)

	Total (millions) 2013	Total Predicted (millions) 2018	Growth 2013-2018 (%)	Share of world total of digital buyers (%) 2013	Digital buyers as a share of population % 2013	Digital buyers as a share of Internet users (%) 2013
Asia–Pacific	460.3	782.4	70	42.6	14.9	42.1
Western Europe	182.3	210.2	15	16.9	49.0	64.0
North America	172.3	203.8	18	16.0	59.7	72.0
Africa and the Middle East	93.6	170.6	82	8.7	7.1	31.3
Latin America	84.7	139.3	64	7.8	18.6	28.2
Central and Eastern Europe	86.4	117.4	36	8.0	24.1	41.6
World	1,079.6	1,623.7	50	100.0	15.2	41.3

As can be seen in Table 2, it is estimated that 1.1 billion people made at least one online purchase in 2013, accounting for just over 40 percent of all Internet users (United Nations Conference on Trade and Development, 2015). With about 460 million online shoppers, Asia-Pacific had the largest share (43 percent), which was predicted to grow further by 2018. The fastest growth between 2013-2018 was projected for the Middle East and Africa. By contrast, the highest percentage of digital buyers as a portion of the population was in North America. Surprisingly, Central Europeans, with a long history of computerization, were actively involved in ecommerce, just like digital buyers from Latin America.

Based on a report by the United Nations Conferences on Trade and Development (2015), the following generalizations were made:

- **Electronic transaction rules**: Such rules already exist and have been adopted by 143 countries, 102 of which are developing countries (United Nations Conference on Trade and Development, 2015).
- **E-consumer protection**. Despite the importance of consumer confidence in business-to-consumer (B2C) e-commerce around the world, mapping consumer protection legislation indicates that many countries developing and transforming their economies still do not have adequate regulations. Of 119 countries for which data was available, 90 (56 of which were in developing or transition countries) have adopted consumer protection rules on ecommerce. However, as many as 73 states have not been able to obtain data, suggesting that online consumer protection has not been fully addressed. As regards regional benchmarks, the scope of consumer protection legislation in Africa is remarkably low. Only 18 of the 54 African countries have adopted such legislation. It is larger in Latin America, where 16 of the region's 20 countries have existing legislation. For Oceania and most economies, data on the state of consumer protection rules was not available during the transition period (United Nations Conference on Trade and Development, 2015).
- **Data protection**: Companies must adopt policies to ensure information security and develop plans to respond to data security incidents as well as avoid fraudulent and unfair practices. To this

end, international best practices and standards are promoted (United Nations Conference on Trade and Development, 2015).

- **Cybercrime**: Cybercrime is a growing concern for countries at all levels of development and affects both buyers and sellers. The most important international instrument in this field is the Council of Europe and its Convention on Cybercrime. In developing regions, laws are based on the Commonwealth Law on Computers and Computer-Related Issues as well as the Convention and the African Union on Cybersecurity and Personal Data, adopted in June 2014 (United Nations Conference on Trade and Development, 2015).

The EU has made it easier and safer for Consumers in Europe to shop online wherever they are in the EU. To fully exploit the potential of ecommerce, the EU has done the following (European Commission, 2020):

- Revised the Payment Services Directive and created new rules on cross-border parcel delivery services that are already in force;
- Created new rules to stop unjustified geo-blocking;
- Revised consumer protection rules, which entered into force in 2020;
- Created Value Added Tax (VAT) rules for the sale of goods and services on the Internet, which will enter into force in 2021.

Regarding the new rules concerning cross-border parcel deliveries, the European Commission (2020) notes that the following changes will take place:

- Delivery prices are not limited, but companies must now clearly disclose their prices so that the consumer can easily compare. Starting next year, consumers will also be able to check package delivery prices on the European Commission's dedicated website.
- National authorities will collect information from parcel delivery companies every year. If parcel delivery is subject to universal service obligations, national regulatory authorities must assess cases in which tariffs are unreasonably high.

The European Commission (2020) has proposed a new deal for consumers that will further strengthen their online rights by:

- Online markets will have to inform consumers whether they are buying from a trader or a private individual so that consumers are aware of their rights if something goes wrong.
- When consumers search the Internet, they will be informed when a trader pays for a search result, and online markets will have to inform consumers about the main parameters determining the ranking of results.
- When consumers pay for a digital service, they will have 14 days to withdraw and will be granted certain information rights.

SOCIAL PROBLEMS IN CYBERSPACE

One of the foremost social problems in connection with cyberspace is obscenity. From a legal point of view, obscenity refers to words, images, or actions that offend the moral sensibilities of its viewers. It may include both profanity and offensive photos or videos. Under US law, the Supreme Court has ruled that, in the context of the First Amendment and freedom of speech, obscenity must relate to sexually explicit material.

In the United States, the Communication Decency Act of 1996 was amended by the PROTECT Act of 2003, which states that the known transmission of commercial information via the Internet that contains profanity and is available to minors under the age of 17 is illegal.

Another social problem concerns cyber defamation, which can be defined as insulting or otherwise causing harm through false statements about a person in cyberspace. If the defamatory case concerns the public, the fault amounts at least to negligence on the part of the publisher.

Cyber defamation is usually done over the Internet via websites, blogs, forums, emails, instant messaging, chatrooms, and now also on social networks. Defamation law generally considers a delict to be committed in cases of "issuing a false statement about another person that causes harm to that person". This covers both libel and slander. The Internet generally falls under the same purview of defamation law as print and published media since cyber defamation is often a form of libel. Other elements used for defamation include the following (Penn State, n.d.):

- An unprivileged publication of a statement to third party.
- If the defamatory case concerns the public, negligence on the part of the publisher.
- Discernible damage to the plaintiff.

Along with the essential elements of defamation, the burden of proof rests with the plaintiff, injuries are usually awarded monetarily, and in the United States, the truth is an "absolute defense."

With the approval of the Communications Decency Act (CDA) of 1996—in particular Section 230—new internet-oriented legislation was introduced and exempted from liability "interactive computer services" and their users. To be considered protected from a CDA case, courts apply a three-step test (Penn State, n.d.):

- The defendant must be a "provider or user" of an "interactive computer service."
- The plaintiff must "treat" the defendant "as the publisher or speaker" of the harmful information at issue.
- The information must be "provided by another information content provider", i.e., the defendant must not be the "information content provider" of the disputed and harmful information.

One of the first uses of section 230 of the CDA was an early internet affair involving AOL, Matt Drudge of the Drudge Report, and Bill Clinton's White House aide, Sidney Blumenthal. Matt Drudge was an early internet blogger who often created tabloids and gossip about public figures in Washington. Drudge was sued when he published false statements about Blumenthal's involvement in marital disputes and abuse. Blumenthal pursued a $30 million lawsuit against Drudge and his employer America Online (AOL), alleging that he defamed and seriously damaged his reputation. Drudge removed the story from his website, but the court did not dismiss the case. The problem was that AOL claimed that they had been granted immunity under Section 230 of the CDA. Still, the court had to take into account the fact that Drudge was their employee and that he could be considered a publisher or distributor and, therefore, not immune to being held liable. After the debate, the court finally ruled that AOL was, in fact, liability-free, and Blumenthal settled the case out of court (Penn State, n.d.).

In the European Union, there is an opinion that the abuse of defamation laws in cyberspace poses a severe threat to the freedom of the press and to the free flow of news and information (International Press Institute, 2015). This abuse often takes the form of excessive compensation claims, which can mean financial ruin even for the wealthiest media corporations. Courts do not always respect the principle of proportionality, and the financial burden on small and independent media can lead to closure. In some cases, the purpose of a lawsuit may not actually be to go to court and collect damages but to force defendants who fear financial consequences to remain silent. For these reasons, there is more work to be done.

INTERNATIONAL LEGAL CHALLENGES TO CYBERSPACE

The international community did not have a single source for intellectual property right laws until the 1994 Uruguay Round of the General Agreement on Tariffs and Trade (GATT), which led to the creation of the World Trade Organization (WTO) in 1995 and, included under its purview, the Trade-Related Aspects of Intellectual Property Rights (TRIPS).

TRIPS included and built upon the latest versions of intellectual property rights regulated by the World Intellectual Property Organization (WIPO), the Paris Convention for the Protection of Industrial Property, and the Berne Convention for the Protection of Literature and Artistic Works, agreements that go back to the 19th century.

TRIPS sets minimum standards for the availability, scope, and use of seven forms of intellectual property: copyrights, trademarks, geographical indications, industrial designs, patents, layout designs for integrated circuits, and classified information (e.g., trade secrets). TRIPS indicates acceptable restrictions and exceptions to balance intellectual property interests with interests in other areas, such as public health and economic development (United States Patent and Trademark Office, 2017).

Since the TRIPS agreement was formed, the World Intellectual Property Organization (WIPO) has been dealing with digital copyright issues in so-called "internet treaties", including the following:

- WIPO Treaty on copyrights (WCT)
- WIPO Treaty on Artistic Performances and Phonograms (WPPT).[4]

The challenge for intellectual property rights is to obtain the consent of developing countries to apply this right in their own countries.

SUMMARY

1. IT law is not a separate area of law. Nonetheless, it develops as a specialization in the discipline of law, dealing with aspects such as agreements, intellectual property, privacy, and data protection. Intellectual property is an integral part of IT law, including copyright laws, fair use rules, and special

rules on the protection of copies from digital media. Furthermore, the issue of software patents is debatable and is still evolving in Europe and beyond.

2. Software license agreements, end-user license agreements, free software licenses, and open-source licenses may include product liability, professional responsibility for individual developers, warranties, contract rights, trade secrets, and intellectual property.

3. Computer and communications industries are regulated by different government bodies in different countries. There are policies regarding unauthorized access, data privacy, and spamming. There are also restrictions on the use of encryption and hardware that can be used to defeat copy protection schemes.

4. Rules have been established that govern online commerce, taxation, consumer protection, and advertising.

5. Several countries have laws on censorship and freedom of expression, rules on public access to government information, and individual access to information held by private parties. There are legal provisions regarding what data must be stored for law enforcement and which cannot be collected or retained for privacy reasons. Some countries restrict access to the Internet, both by law and by technical means.

6. The new methods of eavesdropping and surveillance made possible by ICT have very different rules on how they can be used by law enforcement and as evidence in court.

7. Computerized voting technology, from polling machines to the Internet and voting on mobile phones, has created many legal problems.

8. The generic argument that 'the law does not apply in cyberspace' is not valid. Conflicting rules from different jurisdictions may apply to the same event at the same time. The Internet has no clear geographical and jurisdictional boundaries, but Internet users remain in physical jurisdictions and are subject to the laws of those jurisdictions. For instance, a US user who trades with another user in the UK through a server in Canada could theoretically be subject to the laws of all three countries that relate to the transaction.

9. The claim that the Internet can be self-regulated as its own "international" nation is being replaced by many external and internal regulators and forces, both governmental and private, at many different levels. The nature of Internet law is the subject of extensive legal discussions.

10. Having an IT law and applying it is a matter of professional ethics for IT professionals, end-users, politicians, and law enforcement. The lack of or selective use of applying IT law causes significant damage in society.

REFERENCES

Adamski, A. (2015). *Cybercrime legislation in Poland* [Unpublished manuscript]. Department of Law and Administration, Nicolaus Copernicus University. doi:10.13140/RG.2.1.1946.2249

Asimov, I. (1951). *I, Robot.* Gnome Press.

Bannister, C., Sniderman, B., & Buckley, N. (2020, January 28). Ethical tech: Making ethics a priority in today's digital organization. *Deloitte.* https://www2.deloitte.com/us/en/insights/topics/digital-transformation/make-ethical-technology-a-priority.html

Dahl, J. Y., & Sætnan, A. R. (2009). It all happened so slowly: On controlling function creep in forensic DNA databases. *International Journal of Law, Crime and Justice, 37*(3), 83–103. doi:10.1016/j.ijlcj.2009.04.002

Dejoie, R., Fowler, G., & Paradice, D. (1991). *Ethical issues in information systems*. Boyd & Fraser Publishing Company.

Easley, R. F., Guo, H., & Kraemer, J. (2018). Research commentary—From net neutrality to data neutrality: A techno-economic framework and research agenda. *Information Systems Research, 29*(2), 253–272. doi:10.1287/isre.2017.0740

European Commission. (2020). *New EU rules on e-commerce*. https://ec.europa.eu/digital-single-market/en/new-eu-rules-e-commerce

European Union. (2016). Regulation (EU) 2016/679 of the European Parliament and of the Council. *Official Journal of the European Union*. https://eur-lex.europa.eu/legal-content/EN/TXT/PDF/?uri=CELEX:32016R0679

Field, T. G. (2006). *Focus on intellectual property rights*. Bureau of International Information Programs. https://kr.usembassy.gov/wp-content/uploads/sites/75/2017/04/Focus-On-Intellectual-Property-Rights2.pdf

Funk, A. (2019, December 9). Internet freedom in Asia hits unprecedented low. *Freedom House*. https://freedomhouse.org/article/internet-freedom-asia-hits-unprecedented-low

Hildebrandt, M. (2008). Defining profiling: A new type of knowledge? In M. Hildebrandt and S. Gutwirth (Eds.), Profiling the European citizen: Cross-disciplinary perspectives (pp. 17-45). Springer. doi:10.1007/978-1-4020-6914-7_2

International Press Institute. (2015). *Defamation laws in Europe 2016-2017*. http://legaldb.freemedia.at/defamation-laws-in-europe/

Johnson, D. B., & Snapper, J. (1985). *Ethical issues in the use of computers*. Wadsworth Publishing Company.

Krawczyk, H., & Targowski, A. (2019). *Wisdom in the context of globalization and civilization*. Cambridge Scholar Publishers.

Mason, R. O. (1986). Four ethical issues of the information age. *Management Information Systems Quarterly, 10*(1), 5–12. doi:10.2307/248873

Mowshowitz, A. (1980). Ethics and cultural integration in a computerized world. In A. Mowshowitz (Ed.), *Human choice and computers* (pp. 251–269). North-Holland.

Naisbitt, J. (1982). *Megatrends*. Warner Books.

Organisation for Economic Cooperation and Development. (1980). *OECD guidelines on the protection of privacy and transborder flows of personal data*. https://www.oecd.org/sti/ieconomy/oecdguidelinesontheprotectionofprivacyandtransborderflowsofpersonaldata.htm

Oz, E. (1992). Ethical standards for information systems professionals: A case for a unified code. *Management Information Systems Quarterly*, *16*(4), 423–433. doi:10.2307/249729

Penn State. (n.d.). *Cyber and online defamation*. https://wikispaces.psu.edu/display/IST432TEAM4/Cyber+and+Online+Defamation?atl_token=26ae53905435229fcf2ef0cd29c5a2c77c037b98

Philbeck, T., Davis, N., & Larsen, A. M. E. (2018). Values, ethics and innovation: Rethinking technological development in the fourth Industrial Revolution. *World Economic Forum*. http://www3.weforum.org/docs/WEF_WP_Values_Ethics_Innovation_2018.pdf

Russell, J. (2016, July 19). Twitter finally bans Milo Yiannpoulos, one of its notorious trolls. *TechCrunch*. https://techcrunch.com/2016/07/19/twitter-finally-bans-milo-yiannopoulos-one-of-its-most-notorious-trolls/

Somu, C. S. (2006). Intellectual property rights in cyberspace. *Paradigm*, *10*(1), 62–68. doi:10.1177/0971890720060110

Targowski, A. (2009). *Information technology and societal development*. IGI Global. doi:10.4018/978-1-60566-004-2

Targowski, A., & Modràk, V. (2011). *Automation with human face in times of structured unemployment on the overpopulated planet*. CENTERIS.

Taylor, L., Floridians, L., & Van der Sloot, B. (Eds.). (2017). *Group privacy: New challenges of data technologies* (Vol. 126). Springer. doi:10.1007/978-3-319-46608-8

United Nations Conference on Trade and Development. (2016). *Cyberlaws and regulations for enchancing e-commerce: Case studies and lessons learned*. https://unctad.org/system/files/official-document/ciiem5d2_en.pdf

United States Patent and Trademark Office. (2017, November 6). *Trade related aspects of IP rights*. https://www.uspto.gov/ip-policy/patent-policy/trade-related-aspects-ip-rights

Van den Hoven, J., Blaauw, M., Pieters, W., & Warnier, M. (2019). Privacy and information technology. *Stanford Encyclopedia of Philosophy*. https://plato.stanford.edu/entries/it-privacy/#PerDat

Zittrain, J. (2003). *Be careful what you ask for: Reconciling a global internet and local law*. The Berkman Center for Internet & Society. https://cyber.harvard.edu/wg_home/uploads/204/2003-03.pdf

KEY TERMS AND DEFINITIONS

Anonymity: A situation in which an acting person's identity remains unknown to others.

Code of Ethics: A set of ethical values, principles and standards adopted by organizations to help members regulate their conduct ethically.

Copyrights: A form of intellectual property that grants an owner exclusive rights to make copies of the work for set period of time.

Cybercrime: Crime that either (1) is carried out through the use of computers and networks or (2) targets computers and networks.

Cyberlaws: Laws that regulate behavior with respect to the use of computer technologies.

Intellectual Property Rights: Legal rights granted to creators to protect original works, inventions, products, etc.

Internet Service Provider: An organization that provides services in connection with accessing and using the internet.

Net Neutrality: The principle that internet service providers must treat all internet communications equally and that they must not charge different rates based on factors such as the user, content, website, etc.

Patents: A form of intellectual property that gives an owner the legal right to bar others from producing, using, or selling an invention for a limited period in exchange for publicly disclosing details of the invention to the public.

Personal Data: Information that is related to an identifiable person, such as an IP address, location data, an email address, etc.

ENDNOTES

[1]   The BCS Code of Conduct can be found on the following website: http://www.bcs.org.uk/

[2]   The ACM code of conduct can be on the following website: https://www.acm.org/code-of-ethics

[3]   The GDPR is based on Regulation (EU) 2016/679, which aims to protect individuals in regard to the processing of personal data and the free movement of such data. The regulation is a necessary step to strengthen the fundamental rights of individuals in the digital age and to facilitate the conduct of business by clarifying the rules for businesses and public authorities in the Digital Single Market. Having a single regulation will also eliminate the current fragmentation of different national systems and unnecessary administrative burdens. The regulation entered into force on 24 May 2016 and has been in force since 25 May 2018.

[4]   A discussion of these treaties can be found on their website: https://www.wipo.int/.

Conclusion

As a result of the Digital Revolution, the creation by the Industrial Revolution of thousands of categories of permanent work supported by engines and machines is wasted because human work, thinking and decision-making using by artificial intelligence are being eliminated. There is a tragedy of the human species, which, in the name of supposed technical progress, self-annihilates.

To stop this unfriendly trend of IT development, informing technology should take the following actions:

1. Most scientific and professional societies need to promote the approach to wise strategic development of informing technology in its many applications, but which are human-friendly and sustainable.
2. Educational and training programs should be reviewed in the areas of a wise strategy for the development of Informing technology so that graduates should know what is moral and ethical and what is not right in their profession.
3. Authorities (governments and parliaments) should unify their wise development strategies for informing technology and implement it into practice in agencies, organizations, and companies.
4. Agencies, organizations, and companies should develop smart strategies for informing technology applications in accordance with international and national regulations. If these laws are flouted, they should be punished.
5. Users of information technology should be familiar with legal regulations and their ignorance is not a valid excuse.

About the Author

Andrew Targowski was engaged in the development of social computing in totalitarian Poland (INFOSTRADA and Social Security # for 38 million citizens-PESEL, 1972) and received political asylum in the U.S. during the crackdown on Solidarity in 1981. He has been a professor of business information systems at Western Michigan University (WMU) since 1980. He published 50 books on information technology, history, and political science (Red Fascism, 1982) in English and Polish. During the 1990s, he was a director of the TeleCITY of Kalamazoo Project, one of the first digital cities in the U.S. He investigates the role of information-communication in enterprise, economy, and civilization. He was a president of the International Society for the Comparative Study of Civilizations (2007-2013) and a former chairman of the Advisory Council of the Information Resources Management Association (1995-2005). He is Professor Emeritus of WMU.

Index

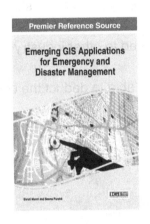

Publisher of Peer-Reviewed, Timely, and
Innovative Academic Research Since 1988

IGI Global's Transformative Open Access (OA) Model:
How to Turn Your University Library's Database Acquisitions Into a Source of OA Funding

Well in advance of Plan S, IGI Global unveiled their OA Fee Waiver (Read & Publish) Initiative. Under this initiative, librarians who invest in IGI Global's InfoSci-Books and/or InfoSci-Journals databases will be able to subsidize their patrons' OA article processing charges (APCs) when their work is submitted and accepted (after the peer review process) into an IGI Global journal.

How Does it Work?

Step 1: **Library Invests in the InfoSci-Databases:** A library perpetually purchases or subscribes to the InfoSci-Books, InfoSci-Journals, or discipline/subject databases.

Step 2: **IGI Global Matches the Library Investment with OA Subsidies Fund:** IGI Global provides a fund to go towards subsidizing the OA APCs for the library's patrons.

Step 3: **Patron of the Library is Accepted into IGI Global Journal (After Peer Review):** When a patron's paper is accepted into an IGI Global journal, they option to have their paper published under a traditional publishing model or as OA.

Step 4: **IGI Global Will Deduct APC Cost from OA Subsidies Fund:** If the author decides to publish under OA, the OA APC fee will be deducted from the OA subsidies fund.

Step 5: **Author's Work Becomes Freely Available:** The patron's work will be freely available under CC BY copyright license, enabling them to share it freely with the academic community.

Note: This fund will be offered on an annual basis and will renew as the subscription is renewed for each year thereafter. IGI Global will manage the fund and award the APC waivers unless the librarian has a preference as to how the funds should be managed.

Hear From the Experts on This Initiative:

"I'm very happy to have been able to make one of my recent research contributions *freely available* along with having access to the *valuable resources* found within IGI Global's InfoSci-Journals database."

– Prof. Stuart Palmer,
Deakin University, Australia

"Receiving the support from IGI Global's OA Fee Waiver Initiative *encourages me to continue my research work without any hesitation*."

– Prof. Wenlong Liu, College of Economics and Management at Nanjing University of Aeronautics & Astronautics, China

For More Information, Scan the QR Code or Contact:
IGI Global's Digital Resources Team at eresources@igi-global.com.

Printed in the United States
by Baker & Taylor Publisher Services